ESSENTIALS OF COMPARATIVE POLITICS

SEVENTH EDITION

PATRICK H. O'NEIL

W. W. Norton & Company
Independent Publishers Since 1923

W. W. Norton & Company has been independent since its founding in 1923, when William Warder Norton and Mary D. Herter Norton first published lectures delivered at the People's Institute, the adult education division of New York City's Cooper Union. The firm soon expanded its program beyond the Institute, publishing books by celebrated academics from America and abroad. By midcentury, the two major pillars of Norton's publishing program—trade books and college texts—were firmly established. In the 1950s, the Norton family transferred control of the company to its employees, and today—with a staff of four hundred and a comparable number of trade, college, and professional titles published each year—W. W. Norton & Company stands as the largest and oldest publishing house owned wholly by its employees.

Copyright © 2021, 2018, 2015, 2013, 2010, 2007, 2004 by W. W. Norton & Company, Inc.
All rights reserved
Printed in Canada

Editor: Laura Wilk
Project Editor: Linda Feldman
Editorial Assistant: Catherine Lillie
Managing Editor, College: Marian Johnson
Managing Editor, College Digital Media: Kim Yi
Production Manager: Elizabeth Marotta
Media Editor: Spencer Richardson-Jones
Media Associate Editor: Michael Jaoui
Media Editorial Assistant: Lena Nowak-Laird
Marketing Manager, Political Science: Ashley Sherwood
Design Director: Marisa Nakasone
Text Design: Faceout Studio
Map Design: Mapping Specialists
Photo Editor: Catherine Abelman
Permissions Manager: Megan Schindel
Composition: Six Red Marbles
Manufacturing: TC–Transcontinental Printing

Permission to use copyrighted material is included on page A-25.

Library of Congress Cataloging-in-Publication Data
Names: O'Neil, Patrick H., 1966- author. | W.W. Norton & Company.
Title: Essentials of comparative politics / Patrick H. O'Neil.
Description: Seventh Edition. | New York : W.W. Norton & Company, 2020. | Sixth edition published 2018. | Includes bibliographical references and index.
Identifiers: LCCN 2020024763 | **ISBN 9780393422948 (Paperback)** | ISBN 9780393532746 (ePub)
Subjects: LCSH: Comparative government. | State, The. | Capitalism. | Democracy. | Post-communism.
Classification: LCC JF51 .O54 2020 | DDC 320.3—dc23
LC record available at https://lccn.loc.gov/2020024763

W. W. Norton & Company, Inc., 500 Fifth Avenue, New York, NY 10110-0017
wwnorton.com
W. W. Norton & Company Ltd., Castle House, 15 Carlisle Street, London W1D 3BS
1 2 3 4 5 6 7 8 9 0

CONTENTS

LIST OF MAPS xi
ABOUT THE AUTHOR xiii
PREFACE xv

1 INTRODUCTION 2

What Is Comparative Politics? 6
  The Comparative Method 7
  Can We Make a Science of Comparative Politics? 11
A Guiding Concept: Political Institutions 18
A Guiding Ideal: Reconciling Freedom and Equality 22
  INSTITUTIONS IN ACTION: CAN WE MAKE A SCIENCE OF POLITICS? 24
In Sum: Looking Ahead and Thinking Carefully 26

2 STATES 28

Defining the State 31
The Origins of Political Organization 36
The Rise of the Modern State 38
Comparing State Power 43
  Legitimacy 44
  Centralization or Decentralization 47
  Power, Autonomy, and Capacity 48
INSTITUTIONS IN ACTION: WHY HAS PAKISTAN SUFFERED STATE FAILURE? 54
In Sum: Studying States 58
QUESTIONS AND METHODS

3 NATIONS AND SOCIETY 60

Ethnic Identity 64

National Identity 66

Citizenship and Patriotism 68

Ethnic Identity, National Identity, and Citizenship: Origins and Persistence 70

  Ethnic and National Conflict 72

Political Attitudes and Political Ideology 75

  Political Attitudes 76

  Political Ideology 80

Religion, Fundamentalism, and the Crisis of Identity 85

Political Culture 88

In Sum: Society and Politics 91

INSTITUTIONS IN ACTION: HAS NEPAL'S NEW CONSTITUTION ENDED CIVIL WAR? 92

QUESTIONS AND METHODS: CAN FEDERALISM SOLVE ETHNIC CONFLICT? 96

4 POLITICAL ECONOMY 98

The Components of Political Economy 102

  Markets and Property 102

  Public Goods 104

  Social Expenditures: Who Benefits? 105

  Taxation 106

  Money, Inflation, and Economic Growth 107

  Regulation 110

  Trade 111

Political-Economic Systems 112

  ...ism 113

  ...cracy 114

Political-Economic Systems and the State:
Comparing Outcomes 120
  Measuring Wealth 121
  Measuring Inequality and Poverty 122
  Human Development Index (HDI) 124
  Happiness 126

The Rise and Fall of Liberalism? 128

In Sum: A New Economic Era? 131

INSTITUTIONS IN ACTION: WHY HAVE POVERTY AND INEQUALITY DECLINED IN LATIN AMERICA? 132

QUESTIONS AND METHODS: ARE LIBERAL ECONOMIES REALLY THAT LIBERAL? 136

5 DEMOCRATIC REGIMES 138

Defining Democracy 141

Origins of Democracy 143

Contemporary Democratization 145
  Modernization and Democratization 145
  Elites and Democratization 147
  Society and Democratization 147
  International Relations and Democratization 148
  Culture and Democratization 149

Institutions of the Democratic State 150
  Executives: Head of State and Head of Government 150
  Legislatures: Unicameral and Bicameral 151
  Judiciaries and Judicial Review 152

Models of Democracy: Parliamentary, Presidential, and Semi-Presidential Systems 153
  Parliamentary Systems 154
  Presidential Systems 155
  Semi-Presidential Systems 156

Parliamentary, Presidential, and Semi-Presidential Systems:
Benefits and Drawbacks 158

Political Parties 160
Electoral Systems 161
Referendum and Initiative 169
INSTITUTIONS IN ACTION: WHAT EXPLAINS DEMOCRATIZATION IN ASIA? 170
Civil Rights and Civil Liberties 172
In Sum: Future Challenges to Democracy 173
QUESTIONS AND METHODS: WHAT IS UNDERMINING DEMOCRACY? 176

6 NONDEMOCRATIC REGIMES 178

Defining Nondemocratic Rule 182

Totalitarianism and Nondemocratic Rule 183

Origins and Sources of Nondemocratic Rule 185
- *Modernization and Nondemocratic Rule* 185
- *Elites and Nondemocratic Rule* 186
- *Society and Nondemocratic Rule* 187
- *International Relations and Nondemocratic Rule* 188
- *Culture and Nondemocratic Rule* 189

Nondemocratic Regimes and Political Control 190
- *Coercion and Surveillance* 190
- *Co-optation: Corporatism and Clientelism* 193
- *Personality Cults* 195

Models of Nondemocratic Rule 196
- *Personal and Monarchical Rule* 197
- *Military Rule* 198
- *One-Party Rule* 199
- *Theocracy* 201
- *Illiberal Regimes* 202

In Sum: Retreat or Retrenchment for Nondemocratic Regimes? 203

INSTITUTIONS IN ACTION: WHAT EXPLAINS THE DIFFERENT PATHS OF ZIMBABWE AND SOUTH AFRICA? 204

QUESTIONS AND METHODS: ARE RESOURCES GOOD FOR DEMOCRACY? 208

7 POLITICAL VIOLENCE 210

What Is Political Violence? 213

Why Political Violence? 214

Institutional Explanations 214

Ideational Explanations 215

Individual Explanations 215

Comparing Explanations of Political Violence 216

Forms of Political Violence 218

Revolution 218

Terrorism 223

Terrorism and Revolution: Means and Ends 228

Political Violence and Religion 229

Countering Political Violence 233

INSTITUTIONS IN ACTION: WHY DID THE ARAB SPRING OF 2011 OCCUR? 236

In Sum: Meeting the Challenge of Political Violence 238

QUESTIONS AND METHODS: WHY HAS SUICIDE TERRORISM EMERGED? 240

8 DEVELOPED DEMOCRACIES 242

Defining Developed Democracy 246

Freedom and Equality in Developed Democracies 250

Contemporary Challenges for Developed Democracies 252

Political Institutions: Sovereignty Transformed? 253

The European Union: Integration, Expansion, and Resistance 254

Devolution and Democracy 259

Societal Institutions: New Identities in Formation? 261

Postmodern Values and Organization 262

Diversity, Identity, and the Challenge to Postmodern Values 263

Economic Institutions: A New Market?   265
- *Postindustrialism*   266
- *Maintaining the Welfare State*   267

In Sum: Developed Democracies in Transition   269

INSTITUTIONS IN ACTION: WHAT EXPLAINS THE GREEK ECONOMIC CRISIS?   270

QUESTIONS AND METHODS: WHAT EXPLAINS AUTHORITARIAN VIEWS IN DEVELOPED DEMOCRACIES?   274

9   COMMUNISM AND POSTCOMMUNISM   276

Communism, Equality, and the Nature of Human Relations   281

Revolution and the "Triumph" of Communism   283

Putting Communism into Practice   285

Communist Political Economy   289

Societal Institutions under Communism   291

The Collapse of Communism   293

The Transformation of Political Institutions   296
- *Reorganizing the State and Constructing a Democratic Regime*   296
- *Evaluating Political Transitions*   297

The Transformation of Economic Institutions   301
- *Privatization and Marketization*   301
- *Evaluating Economic Transitions*   303

The Transformation of Societal Institutions   306
- *Changing Identities*   306
- *Evaluating Societal Transitions*   307

INSTITUTIONS IN ACTION: WHY DID REFORM FAIL IN THE SOVIET UNION BUT SUCCEED IN CHINA?   310

In Sum: The Legacy of Communism   313

QUESTIONS AND METHODS: WHAT EXPLAINS VARIATIONS IN THE EXIT FROM COMMUNISM?   316

10 DEVELOPING COUNTRIES 318

Freedom and Equality in the Developing World 322
Imperialism and Colonialism 324
Institutions of Imperialism 326
Exporting the State 327
Social Identities 328
Dependent Development 330

The Challenges of Post-Imperialism 332
Building State Capacity and Autonomy 333
Creating Nations and Citizens 336
Generating Economic Growth 338

Puzzles and Prospects for Democracy and Development 341
Making a More Effective State 342
Developing Political Engagement 344
Promoting Economic Prosperity 345

INSTITUTIONS IN ACTION: WHY DID ASIA INDUSTRIALIZE FASTER THAN LATIN AMERICA? 348

In Sum: The Challenges of Development 350

QUESTIONS AND METHODS: HOW CAN COUNTRIES AVOID THE MIDDLE INCOME TRAP? 352

11 GLOBALIZATION AND THE FUTURE OF COMPARATIVE POLITICS 354

What Is Globalization? 358
Institutions and Globalization 360
Political Globalization 362
Economic Globalization 365
Societal Globalization 369

Taking Stock of Globalization 372
Is Globalization New? 372
Is Globalization Exaggerated? 374
Is Globalization Inevitable? 376

INSTITUTIONS IN ACTION: IS GLOBALIZATION CAUSING CLIMATE CHANGE? 378

In Sum: The Future of Freedom and Equality 380

QUESTIONS AND METHODS: DOES GLOBALIZATION CREATE MISTRUST? 382

NOTES A-1
GLOSSARY A-15
CREDITS A-25
INDEX A-27

LIST OF MAPS

AFRICA xxi
ASIA xxii
THE MIDDLE EAST xxiii
EUROPE xxiv
CENTRAL AND SOUTH AMERICA xxv
NORTH AMERICA xxvi
ETHNOLINGUISTIC DIVERSITY IN AFRICA 74
EUROPEAN UNION MEMBERSHIP, 2020 259

ABOUT THE AUTHOR

Patrick H. O'Neil is distinguished professor of politics and government at the University of Puget Sound in Tacoma, Washington. He received his PhD in political science from Indiana University. Professor O'Neil's teaching and research interests are in the areas of authoritarianism and democratization. His publications include the books *Revolution from Within: The Hungarian Socialist Workers' Party and the Collapse of Communism* and *Communicating Democracy: The Media and Political Transitions* (editor).

PREFACE

The past four decades have seen the dramatic transformation of comparative politics: the end of the Cold War and the collapse of the Soviet Union, the spread of democracy across the globe, the rise of new economic powers in Asia, the deepening (and perhaps fragmentation) of globalization. For a time, many looked upon these changes as unmitigated progress that would bring about a decline in global conflict and produce widespread prosperity. Recently, however, there has been growing doubt, as the uncertainties of the future seem to portend more risk than reward, more inequality than prosperity, more conflict than peace. One can no longer suggest that a country and its citizens can function well without a good understanding of the billions of people who live outside of its borders. Clearly we ignore such uncertainty at our peril.

This textbook is meant to contribute to our understanding of comparative politics (the study of domestic politics around the world) by investigating the central ideas and questions that make up this field. It begins with the most basic struggle in politics—the battle between freedom and equality and the task of reconciling or balancing these ideals. How this struggle has unfolded across place and time represents the core of comparative politics. The text continues by emphasizing the importance of institutions. Human action is fundamentally guided by the institutions that people construct, such as culture, constitutions, and property rights. Once established, these institutions are both influential and persistent—not easily overcome, changed, or removed. How these institutions emerge, and how they affect politics, is central to this work.

With these ideas in place, we tackle the basic institutions of power—states, markets, societies, democracies, and nondemocratic regimes. What are states, how do they emerge, and how can we measure their capacity, autonomy, and efficacy? How do markets function, and what kinds of relationships exist between states and markets? How do societal components like nationalism, ethnicity, and ideology shape political values? And what are the main differences between democratic and nondemocratic regimes, and what explains why one or the other predominates in various parts of the world? These are a few of the questions we will attempt to answer.

Once these concepts and questions have been explored, subsequent chapters will apply them directly to various political systems—developed democracies, communist and postcommunist countries, and developing countries. In each of these, the basic institutions of the state, market, society, and democratic or nondemocratic regime all shape the relationship between freedom and equality. What basic characteristics lead us to group these countries together? How do they compare to one another, and what are their prospects for economic, social, and democratic development? Finally, we will conclude with a discussion of globalization, linking what we have studied at the domestic level to wider international forces.

The format of this text has long differed from that of traditional comparative politics textbooks. In the past, these books were built around a set of country studies, with introductory chapters for the advanced, postcommunist, and less-developed world. While such a textbook can provide a great deal of information on a wide range of cases, the trade-off is often a less thorough consideration of the basic grammar of comparative politics. We might know who the prime minister of Japan is but have less of an understanding of political culture, mercantilism, or state autonomy—all ideas that can help us make sense of politics across time and place. This text strives to fill this gap and can be used alongside traditional case studies to help draw out broader questions and issues. By grasping these concepts, arguments, and questions, students will better understand the political dynamics of the wider world.

This thematic approach to the essential tools and ideas of comparative politics is supported by a strong pedagogy that clarifies and reinforces the most important concepts. Key concepts lists and "Institutions in Action" boxes in every chapter highlight important material that students will want to review. Numerous figures and tables illustrate important concepts and provide real world data related to the topic at hand. Timelines and thematic maps show important political developments over time and around the globe. The importance of institutions is emphasized by the opening and closing discussions in each chapter. Finally, in this edition we have added a new "Questions and Methods" feature that allows students to consider puzzles in comparative politics. This feature illustrates how data can be used to find answers as well as develop new questions for further exploration.

Essentials of Comparative Politics is designed to offer instructors flexibility in creating the course that they want to teach. In addition to the core textbook, a corresponding casebook and a reader are also available. *Cases in Comparative Politics*, coauthored by Karl Fields, Donald Share, and myself, applies the concepts from *Essentials of Comparative Politics* to thirteen country studies. An integrated version of both texts, with shorter case studies, *Cases and Concepts in Comparative Politics*, is also available. In *Essential Readings in Comparative Politics*, my coeditor, Ronald Rogowski, and I have selected key readings to accompany each chapter in the textbook.

We realize resources that support teaching and learning are essential to helping students meet the goals of your course, whether you're teaching online or in person. That's why we've expanded our suite of resources with this edition. New to the Seventh Edition is InQuizitive, Norton's adaptive learning tool that reinforces students' understanding of the key concepts, helps them to better prepare on areas of weakness, and challenges them to recognize these concepts in action in diverse, real-world examples that go beyond the text. InQuizitive comes free with new copies of the text and ebook. See the back cover for more information. Norton also offers the textbook, casebook, and integrated version in ebook format. Support materials for instructors, which include a test bank, PowerPoint lecture outlines, and a supplementary image bank, are also available at https://digital.wwnorton.com/esscompol7.

Many people have contributed to this work. The text itself is inspired by Karen Mingst's *Essentials of International Relations*. When Norton released Mingst's book more than 20 years ago, I was struck by its concision and came to the conclusion that comparative politics would benefit from a similar kind of text. At Norton, Peter Lesser first encouraged me to submit a proposal for this textbook, and Roby Harrington encouraged me to develop the initial chapters, supported its publication, and provided important feedback at many stages. As editor, Ann Shin held me to a high standard of writing argumentation in the first edition. For the second, third, and fourth editions, Peter Lesser, Aaron Javsicas, and Jake Schindel took over editorial duties, helping to further improve the work. In the fifth and sixth editions, Peter, who first challenged me to write this text, returned to the helm to guide me through a number of complicated revisions and edits that have improved the content and style. My current editor, Laura Wilk, has been an exceptional guide and source of support and insight in this new edition. I am grateful to all of them for their investment in this work.

In addition to the people at Norton, many academics have helped improve this work. Most important have been my colleagues at the University of Puget Sound, in particular Don Share and Karl Fields. Over many years Don, Karl, and I have taught alongside each other, and learning from these two outstanding teachers and scholars helped generate many of the ideas in this book. Don and Karl continue to provide important feedback and numerous suggestions. I am fortunate to have such colleagues.

Many thanks as well to those numerous reviewers who have provided useful critiques and suggestions that have improved this work:

James Allan, Wittenberg University
Malasree Neepa Acharya, University of Delaware
David C. Andrus, College of the Canyons
Oana Armeanu, University of Southern Indiana
Jason Arnold, Virginia Commonwealth University
Gregory Arey, Cape Fear Community College
Alan Arwine, University of Kansas
Alex Avila, Mesa Community College
Pavel Bacovsky, University of Colorado at Boulder
Gregory Baldi, Western Illinois University
Oksan Bayulgen, University of Connecticut
Emily Beaulieu, University of Kentucky
Caroline Beer, University of Vermont
Marni Berg, Colorado State University
Prosper Bernard Jr., College of Staten Island
Guillaume Bogiaris, University of West Alabama
Sean Burns, William & Mary
Jeremy Busacca, Whittier College
Ryan Carlin, Georgia State University
Matthew Carnes, Georgetown University
Crystal Chang Cohen, University of California, Berkeley
Robert Compton, SUNY Oneonta
Isabelle Côté, Memorial University of Newfoundland
Lukas K. Danner, Florida International University
Suheir Daoud, Coastal Carolina University
Bruce Dickson, George Washington University
Sebastian Elischer, University of Florida
Kenly Fenio, Virginia Tech
Bonnie Field, Bentley University
Nathan W. Freeman, University of Georgia
John French, Depaul University/University of Illinois at Chicago
John Froitzheim, College of William & Mary
Julia George, Queens College, CUNY
Sarah Goodman, University of California at Irvine
Jonathan Hassid, Iowa State University

Amelia Hoover Green, Drexel University
Anna Gregg, Austin Peay State University
Kikue Hamayotsu, Northern Illinois University
Ivy Hamerly, Baylor University
Cole Harvey, University of North Carolina, Chapel Hill
Alexandra Hennessy, Seton Hall University
Jeffrey Hernden, State College of Florida
Yoshiko Herrera, University of Wisconsin at Madison
Robert Hinckley, SUNY Potsdam
Matthew Hoddie, Towson University
Maiah Jaskoski, Northern Arizona University
John Jaworsky, University of Waterloo
Catherine Kane, University of Maryland, College Park
Hanna Samir Kassab, East Carolina University
Joon S. Kil, Irvine Valley College
Jelle Koedam, University of North Carolina at Chapel Hill
Tamara Kotar, University of Ottawa
Brian Kupfer, Tallahassee Community College
Ahmet Kuru, San Diego State University
Rebecca Larsen, University of Utah
Lisa Laverty, Eastern Michigan University
Jeffrey Lewis, Cleveland State University
Kelley Littlepage, University of Houston
Gregory Love, University of Mississippi
Mona Lyne, University of Missouri, Kansas City
Audrey Mattoon, Washington State University
Michael Mitchell, Arizona State University
Christopher Muste, University of Montana
Daniel C. O'Neill, University of the Pacific
Kristen D. Parris, Western Washington University
Sahar Razavi, California State University, Sacramento
Sharon Rivera, Hamilton College
Paul Rousseau, University of Windsor
Jennifer Rutledge, John Jay College of Criminal Justice
Stephanie Sapiie, SUNY Nassau Community College
Hootan Shambayati, Florida Gulf Coast University
Steve Sharp, Utah State University, Logan
Shane Singh, University of Georgia

Richard Stahler-Sholk, Eastern Michigan University
Boyka Stefanova, University of Texas at San Antonio
Aaron Stuvland, George Mason University
Sandra L. Suarez, Temple University
Markus Thiel, Florida International University
Hubert Tworzecki, Emory University
Ann Wainscott, Miami University
Brian Wampler, Boise State University
Shawn H. Williams, Campbellsville University
Mark A. Wolfgram, Oklahoma State University
Stacy Philbrick Yadav, Hobart & William Smith Colleges
Jeremy Youde, University of Minnesota, Duluth
Lyubov Zhyznomirska, Saint Mary's University

Finally, I would like to thank the students of the University of Puget Sound for their questions and insights, the university administration for its support of this project, and my family for their patience.

Patrick H. O'Neil
Tacoma, Washington
May 2020

AFRICA

ASIA

THE MIDDLE EAST

EUROPE

CENTRAL AND SOUTH AMERICA

NORTH AMERICA

ESSENTIALS OF COMPARATIVE POLITICS

1

Protesters gather in Bouazizi Square in Tunisia in front of a mural commemorating Mohamed Bouazizi. In December 2010, the Tunisian street vendor set himself on fire to protest corruption in his home country, inspiring the Arab Spring that ignited the region the following year.

INTRODUCTION

What can political science tell us that we don't already know?

Who would have predicted 15 years ago that the Middle East would change so much in such a short period of time? Dramatic historical events often take scholars, politicians, and even participants by surprise. For example, in the 1980s few people expected that communism would come to a dramatic end in Eastern Europe—if anything, modest reforms in the Soviet Union were expected to give communist institutions a new lease on life. Following the collapse of communism and increased democratization in parts of Asia and Latin America, many scholars expected that regimes in the Middle East would be next. But by the turn of the century, these expectations appeared unfounded; authoritarianism in the region seemed immune to change. Scholars chalked this up to a number of things—the role of oil, Western economic and military aid, lack of civic institutions, or the supposedly undemocratic nature of Islam.

Yet again, history took us by surprise. The opening events of the Arab Spring were disarmingly simple. In December 2010, a young Tunisian man, Mohamed Bouazizi, set himself on fire to protest police corruption and government indifference. Angry protests broke out shortly thereafter, and the long-standing government was overthrown within weeks. New protests then broke out across the region in January and February 2011. In Egypt, President Hosni Mubarak was forced to resign after 30 years in office. In Libya, protests turned to widespread armed conflict and led to the killing of Mu'ammar Gaddhafi after more than 40 years of rule. In

Syria, Bashar al-Assad clung to power as peaceful protests eventually turned into a civil war that has devastated the country, killed perhaps as many as half a million people, and triggered a migration crisis that roiled European politics.

The immediate political future of these and other countries in the region is uncertain. Tunisia has transitioned into a fragile democracy, while Egypt has returned to dictatorship; Libya is in the midst of civil war, while the Syrian conflict helped catalyze a new wave of international terrorism. At the same time, an entire range of countries in the region have faced down public protests or did not face them at all. This is especially true among the monarchies of the Persian Gulf, where one might have imagined that these anachronistic forms of rule would be the first to fall.

We are thus left with a series of puzzles. Why did the Arab Spring take place? What was the source of these tumultuous changes—revolution, civil war, and one of the largest refugee crises in recent history? Why did these uprisings take different forms and differ in the level of violence from place to place? Finally, why did some countries not see significant public protest to begin with? The hopeful nature of an Arab Spring has since been replaced by a much darker sense of the future politics of the region. Democracy, even political stability, seems further away than ever, and there have been serious repercussions for the Middle East and beyond. Can political science help us answer these questions? Can it provide us with the tools to shape our own country's policies in this regard? Or are dramatic political changes, especially regional ones, simply too complex?

LEARNING OBJECTIVES

- Explain the methods political scientists use to understand politics around the world.
- Trace the development of the field of political science.
- Define key terms in the study of political institutions and behaviors.

During the past 35 years, the world has seen an astonishing number of changes: the rise of new economic powers in Asia, the collapse of communism, revolutions across the Middle East, the return of religion to politics, the spread of information technology and social media, and the shifting effects of globalization. Many of the traditional assumptions and beliefs held by scholars, policy makers, and citizens have been overturned. New centers of wealth may reduce poverty, but they may also increase inequality within and between countries. Democracy, often seen as an inexorable force, can founder on such obstacles as religious or economic conflict. Technological change may create new, shared identities and sources of cooperation, but it can destabilize and fragment communities.

One pertinent example is the role of ethnic and religious conflict, which we have seen emerge in Syria and Iraq. Why does this form of political violence occur? Is it a response to inequality or political disenfranchisement? Is it a function of cultural differences, a "clash of civilizations"? Is it fostered or tempered by globalization? Perhaps the explanation lies somewhere else entirely, beyond our purview or comprehension. How can we know what is correct? How do we scrutinize a range of explanations and evaluate their merits? Competing assumptions and explanations are at the heart of political debates and policy decisions, yet we are often asked to choose in the absence of reliable evidence or a good understanding of cause and effect. To be better citizens, we should be better students of political science and **comparative politics**—the study and comparison of domestic politics across countries. Comparative politics can be contrasted with another related field in political science, **international relations**. While comparative politics looks at the politics inside countries (such as elections, political parties, revolutions, and judicial systems), international relations concentrates on relations between countries (such as foreign policy, war, trade, and foreign aid). Of course, the two overlap in many places, such as in ethnic or religious conflict, which often spills over borders, or political change, which can be shaped by international organizations or military force. For now, however, our discussion will concentrate on political structures and actions within countries.

This chapter lays out some of the most basic vocabulary and structures of political science and comparative politics. These will fall under three basic categories: *analytical concepts* (assumptions and theories that guide our research), *methods* (ways to study and test those theories), and *ideals* (beliefs and values about preferred outcomes). Analytical concepts help us ask questions about cause and effect, methods provide tools to seek out explanations, and ideals help us compare existing politics with what we might prefer.

Our survey will consider some of the most basic questions: What is politics? How does one compare different political systems around the world? We will spend some time on the methods of comparative politics and how scholars have approached its study. Over the past century, political scientists have struggled with the challenge of analyzing politics and have asked whether such analysis can actually be considered a science. Exploring these issues will give us a better sense of the limitations and possibilities in the study of comparative politics. We will consider comparative politics through the concept of **institutions**—organizations or activities that are self-perpetuating and valued for their own sake. Institutions play an important role in defining and shaping what is possible and probable in political life by laying out the

Introduction

rules, norms, and structures in which we live. Finally, in addition to institutions, we will take up the ideals of freedom and equality. If institutions shape how the game of politics is played, then the goal of the game is the right mix of freedom and equality. Which ideal is more important? Must one come at the expense of the other? Perhaps some other ideal is preferable to both? With the knowledge gained by exploring these questions, we will be ready to take on complex politics around the world.

What Is Comparative Politics?

First, we must identify what comparative politics is. **Politics** is the struggle in any group for power that will give one or more persons the ability to make decisions for the larger group. This group may range from a small organization to the entire world. Politics occurs wherever there are people and organizations. For example, we may speak of "office politics" when we are talking about power relationships in a business. Political scientists in particular concentrate on the struggle for leadership and power in a political community—a political party, an elected office, a city, a region, or a country. It is therefore hard to separate the idea of politics from the idea of **power**, which is the ability to influence others or impose one's will on them. Politics is the competition for public power, and power is the ability to extend one's will.

In political science, comparative politics is a subfield that compares this pursuit of power across countries. The method of comparing countries can help us make arguments about cause and effect by drawing evidence from across space and time. For example, one important puzzle we will return to frequently is why some countries are democratic, while others are not. Why has politics in some countries resulted in power being dispersed among more people, while in other countries politics has concentrated power in the hands of a few? Why is South Korea democratic, while North Korea is not? Looking at North Korea alone won't necessarily help us understand why South Korea went down a different path, or vice versa. A comparison of the two, perhaps alongside similar cases in Asia, may better yield explanations. As should be clear from our discussion of the Arab Spring, these are not simply academic questions. Democratic countries and pro-democracy organizations actively support the spread of like-minded regimes around the world, and democracy has backslid in many countries over the past few years. If it is unclear how or why democracy emerges, it becomes much harder to promote or defend it. It is therefore important to separate ideals from our concepts and methods and not let the former obscure our use of the latter. Comparative politics can inform and even challenge our ideals, providing alternatives and guiding us to question our assumption that there is one right way to organize political life.

The Comparative Method

If comparison is an important way to test our assumptions and shape our ideals, how we compare cases is important. If there is no set of criteria or guide by which we gather information or draw conclusions, our studies become little more than collections of details. Researchers thus often seek out puzzles—questions about politics with no obvious answer—as a way to guide their research. From there, they rely on some **comparative method**—a way to compare cases and draw conclusions. By comparing countries or subsets within them, scholars seek out conclusions and generalizations that could be valid in other cases.

To return to our earlier question, let us say that we are interested in why democracy has failed to develop in some countries. We might approach the puzzle of democracy by looking at North Korea. Why has the North Korean government remained communist and highly repressive even as similar regimes around the world have collapsed?

A convincing answer to this puzzle could tell scholars and policy makers a great deal and even guide our tense relations with North Korea in the future. Examining one country closely may lead us to form hypotheses about why a country operates as it does. We call this approach **inductive reasoning**—the means by which we go from studying a case to generating a hypothesis. But while a study of one country can generate interesting hypotheses, it does not provide enough evidence to test them. Thus we might study North Korea and conclude that the use of nationalism by those in power has been central to the persistence of nondemocratic rule. In so concluding, we might then suggest that future studies look at the relationship between nationalism and authoritarianism in other countries. Inductive reasoning can therefore be a foundation on which we build greater theories in comparative politics.

Comparative politics can also rely on **deductive reasoning**—starting with a puzzle and from there generating some hypothesis about cause and effect to test against a number of cases. Whereas inductive reasoning starts with the evidence as a way to uncover a hypothesis, deductive reasoning starts with the hypothesis and then seeks out the evidence. In our example of inductive reasoning, we started with a case study of North Korea and ended with a testable generalization about nationalism; using deductive reasoning, we would start with our hypothesis about nationalism and then test that hypothesis by looking at a number of countries. By carrying out such studies, we may find a **correlation**, or apparent association, between certain factors or variables. If we were particularly ambitious, we might claim to have found cause and effect, or a **causal relationship**.[1] Inductive and deductive reasoning can help us better understand and explain political outcomes and, ideally, could help us predict them.

Unfortunately, inductive and deductive reasoning is not easy, nor is finding correlation and causation. Comparativists face seven major challenges in trying to examine political features across countries. Let's move through each of these challenges and show how they complicate the comparative method and comparative politics in general. First, political scientists have difficulty controlling the variables in the cases they study. In other words, in our search for correlations or causal relationships, we are unable to make true comparisons because each of our cases is different. By way of illustration, suppose a researcher wants to determine whether increased exercise by college students leads to higher grades. In studying the students who are her subjects, the researcher can control for a number of variables that might also affect grades, such as the students' diet, the amount of sleep they get, or any factor that might influence the results. By controlling for these differences and making certain that many of these variables are the same across the subjects, with the exception of exercise, the researcher can carry out her study with greater confidence.

But political science offers few opportunities to control the variables because the variables are a function of real-world politics. As will become clear, economies, cultures, geography, resources, and political structures are amazingly diverse, and it is difficult to control for these differences. Even in a single-case study, variables change over time. At best, we can control as much as possible for variables that might otherwise distort our conclusions. If, for example, we want to understand why gun ownership laws are so much less restrictive in the United States than they are in most other industrialized countries, we are well served to compare the United States with countries that have similar historical, economic, political, and social backgrounds, such as Canada and Australia, rather than Japan or South Africa. This approach allows us to control our variables more effectively, but it still leaves many variables uncontrolled and unaccounted for.

A second, related problem concerns interactions among the variables themselves. Even if we can control our variables in making our comparisons, there is the problem that many of these variables are interconnected and interact. In other words, many variables interact to produce particular outcomes, in what is known as **multicausality**. A single variable, such as a country's electoral system or the strength of its judicial system, is unlikely to explain the variation in countries' gun control laws. The problem of multicausality also reminds us that in the real world there are often no single, easy answers to political problems.

A third problem involves the limits to our information and information gathering. Although the cases we study have many uncontrolled and interconnected variables, we often have too few cases to work with. In the natural sciences, researchers often conduct studies with a huge number of cases—hundreds of stars or thousands of individuals, often studied across time. This breadth allows researchers to select their cases in such a way as to control their variables, and the large number of cases prevents any single unusual case from distorting the findings. But in comparative politics, we are typically limited by the number of countries in the world—fewer than 200 at present, most of which did not exist a few centuries ago. Even if we study some subset of comparative politics (like political parties or acts of terrorism), our total number of cases will remain relatively small. And if we attempt to control for differences by trying to find a number of similar cases (for example, wealthy democracies), our total body of cases will shrink even further.

A fourth problem in comparative politics concerns how we access the few cases we do have. Research is often further hindered by the very factors that make countries interesting to study. Much of the information that political scientists seek is not easy to acquire, necessitating work in the field—that is, conducting interviews or studying government archives abroad. International travel requires time and money, and researchers may spend months or even years in the field. Interviewees may be unwilling to speak on sensitive issues or may distort information. Libraries and archives may be incomplete, or access to them restricted. Governments may bar research on politically sensitive questions. Confronting these obstacles in more than one country is even more challenging. A researcher may be able to read Russian and travel to Russia frequently, but if he wants to compare authoritarianism in Russia and China, it would be ideal to be able to read Chinese and conduct research in China as well. Few comparativists have the language skills, time, or resources to conduct field research in many countries. There are almost no comparativists in North America or Europe who speak both Russian and Chinese. As a result, comparativists often master knowledge of a single country or language and rely on inductive reasoning. Single-case study can be extremely valuable—it gives the researcher a great deal of case depth and the ability to tease out novel observations that may come only from close observation. However, such narrow focus can also make it unclear to researchers whether the politics they see in their case study has important similarities to the politics in other cases. In the worst-case scenario, scholars come to believe that the country they study is somehow unique and fail to recognize its similarities to other cases.

Fifth, even where comparativists do widen their range of cases, their focus tends to be limited to a single geographic region. The specialist on communist Cuba is more likely to study other Latin American countries than to consider China or North Korea, and the specialist on China is more likely to study South Korea than Russia. This isn't necessarily a concern, given our earlier discussion of the need to control variables—it may make more sense to study parts of the world where similar variables are clustered rather than to compare countries from different parts of the world. This regional focus, however—often referred to as **area studies**—is distributed unevenly around the world. For decades, the largest share of research tended to focus on Western Europe, despite the increasing role of Asia in the international system.[2] Why? As mentioned earlier, some of this is a function of language; many scholars in the West are exposed to European languages in primary or secondary school, and in many European countries the use of English is widespread, thus facilitating research. But English is also widespread in southern Asia; in spite of this, scholarship has lagged behind. For example, we find that over the past 50 years one of the top journals in comparative politics published as many articles on Sweden as on India. To be fair, much of this is changing thanks to a new generation of scholars, many of whom come from or work in a much wider array of countries around the world. Yet overall, comparative politics remains slow to redirect its attention when new issues and questions arise.

Sixth, the problem of bias makes it even harder to control for variables and to select the right cases. This is a question not of political bias, although that can sometimes be a problem, but of how we select our cases. In the natural sciences, investigators randomize case selection as much as possible to avoid choosing cases that support one hypothesis or another. But for the reasons mentioned earlier, such randomization is not possible in political science. Single-case studies are already influenced by the fact that comparativists study a country because they know its language or find it interesting. Yet even if we rely instead on deductive reasoning—beginning with a hypothesis and then seeking out our cases—we can easily fall into the trap of **selection bias**.

For example, say we want to understand revolutions, and we hypothesize that their main cause is a rapid growth in inequality. Revolution is what we would call our **dependent variable**—the variable that is dependent on, or affected by, another variable. Rapid growth in inequality would be our **independent variable**—the variable that doesn't depend on changes in other variables and is the presumed cause. How should we select our cases? Most of us would respond by saying that we should find as many cases of revolution as possible and then see whether a rapid growth in inequality preceded those revolutions. But this seemingly logical approach is a mistake, as it leads to what is known as bias on the dependent variable—in other words, a bias in sampling on the effect, rather than the cause. Why is this a problem? By looking only at cases of revolution (the dependent variable, or effect), we miss all the cases with rapid growth in inequality (the independent variable, or cause) where revolution has *not* taken place. Indeed, even if every revolution is preceded by changes in inequality, there may still be many more cases without revolution than with it, undermining our hypothesis. So, we would do better to start with what we think is the cause (growth in inequality) rather than working backward from the effect (revolution). While this may seem the obvious choice, it is a frequent mistake among scholars who are naturally drawn to particular outcomes and so start there.

A seventh and final concern deals with the heart of political science—the search for cause and effect. Let us for the sake of argument assume that the half-dozen problems we have laid out can be overcome through careful case selection, information

> ## IN FOCUS: Problems in Comparative Research
>
> - Controlling a large number of variables
> - Controlling for the interaction of variables (multicausality)
> - Limited number of cases to research
> - Limited access to information from cases
> - Uneven research across cases and regions
> - Cases selected on the basis of effect and not cause (selection bias)
> - Variables may be either cause or effect (endogeneity)

gathering, and control of variables. Let us further imagine that with these problems in hand, research finds, for example, that countries with a low rate of female literacy are less likely to be democratic than countries where female literacy is high. Even if we are confident enough to claim that there is a causal relationship between female literacy and democracy—a bold statement indeed—a final and perhaps intractable problem looms. Which variable is cause and which is effect? Do low rates of female literacy limit public participation, empowering nondemocratic actors, or do authoritarian leaders (largely men) take little interest in promoting gender equality? This problem of distinguishing cause and effect, known as **endogeneity**, is a major obstacle in any comparative research. Even if we are confident that we have found cause and effect, we can't easily ascertain which is which. On reflection, this is to be expected; one political scientist has called endogeneity "the motor of history," for causes and effects tend to evolve together, each transforming the other over time. Thus early forms of democracy, literacy, and women's rights may well have gone hand in hand, each reinforcing and changing the others. In short, many things matter, and these many things affect each other. This makes an elegant claim about cause and effect problematic, to say the least.[3]

Can We Make a Science of Comparative Politics?

We have so far elaborated many of the ways in which comparative politics—and political science in general—makes for difficult study. Variables are hard to control and can be interconnected, while actual cases may be few. Getting access to information may be difficult, and comparisons may be limited by regional knowledge and interests. What questions are asked may be affected by selection bias and endogeneity. All these concerns make it difficult to generate any kind of political science **theory**, which we can define as an integrated set of hypotheses, assumptions, and facts. At this point, you may well have concluded that a science of politics is hopeless. But it is precisely these kinds of concerns that have driven political science, and comparative politics within it, toward a more scientific approach. Whether this has yielded or will yield significant benefits, and at what cost, is something we will consider next.

Political science and comparative politics have a long pedigree. In almost every major society, there have been masterworks of politics that prescribe rules or, less often, analyze political behavior. In the West, the work of the philosopher Aristotle (384–322 B.C.E.) departed from the traditional emphasis on political ideals to conduct comparative research on existing political systems (what we will call *regimes*), eventually gathering and analyzing the constitutions of 158 Greek city-states. Aristotle's objective was to delineate between what he took to be "proper" and "deviant," or despotic, political regimes. He also framed this discussion in terms of a puzzle—why were some regimes despotic and others not? With this approach, Aristotle conceived of an empirical (that is, observable and verifiable) science of politics with a practical purpose: statecraft, or how to govern. Aristotle was perhaps the first Westerner to separate the study of politics from that of philosophy.[4]

Aristotle's early approach did not immediately lead to any systematic study of politics. For the next 1,800 years, discussions of politics remained embedded in the realm of philosophy, with the emphasis placed on how politics should be rather than on how politics was actually conducted. Ideals, rather than conclusions drawn from evidence, were the norm. Only with the works of the Italian Niccolò Machiavelli (1469–1527) did a comparative approach to politics truly emerge. Like Aristotle, he sought to analyze different political systems—those that existed around him as well as those that had preceded him, such as the Roman Empire—and even tried to make generalizations about success and failure. These findings, he believed, could then be applied by statesmen to avoid their predecessors' mistakes. Machiavelli's work reflects this pragmatism, dealing with the mechanics of government, diplomacy, military strategy, and power.[5]

Because of his emphasis on statecraft and empirical knowledge, Machiavelli is often cited as the first modern political scientist, paving the way for other scholars. His writings came at a time when the medieval order was giving way to the Renaissance, with its emphasis on science, rationalism, secularism, and real-world knowledge over abstract ideals. The resulting work over the next four centuries reinforced the idea that politics, like any other area of knowledge, could be developed as a logical, rigorous, and predictable science.

During those centuries, a number of major thinkers took up the comparative approach to the study of politics, which slowly retreated from moral, philosophical, or religious foundations. In the seventeenth century, authors like Thomas

Hobbes and John Locke followed in Machiavelli's footsteps, advocating particular political systems on the basis of empirical observation and analysis. They were followed in the eighteenth century by such scholars as Jean-Jacques Rousseau and Baron de Montesquieu, whose studies of the separation of power and civil liberties would directly influence the writing of the U.S. Constitution and other constitutions to follow. The work of Karl Marx and Max Weber in the nineteenth and early

TIMELINE: Major Thinkers in Comparative Politics

Aristotle (384–322 b.c.e.)	First separated the study of politics from that of philosophy; used the comparative method to study Greek city-states; in *The Politics*, conceived of an empirical study of politics with a practical purpose.
Niccolò Machiavelli (1469–1527)	Often cited as the first modern political scientist because of his emphasis on statecraft and empirical knowledge; analyzed different political systems, believing the findings could be applied by statesmen; discussed his theories in *The Prince*.
Thomas Hobbes (1588–1679)	Developed the notion of a "social contract," whereby people surrender certain liberties in favor of order; advocated a powerful state in *Leviathan*.
John Locke (1632–1704)	Argued that private property is essential to individual freedom and prosperity; advocated a weak state in *Two Treatises of Government*.
Charles-Louis de Secondat, Baron de Montesquieu (1689–1755)	Studied government systems; advocated the separation of powers within government in *The Spirit of Laws*.
Jean-Jacques Rousseau (1712–78)	Argued that citizens' rights are inalienable and cannot be taken away by the state; influenced the development of civil rights; discussed these ideas in *The Social Contract*.
Karl Marx (1818–83)	Elaborated a theory of economic development and inequality in *Das Kapital*; predicted the eventual collapse of capitalism and democracy.
Max Weber (1864–1920)	Wrote widely on such topics as bureaucracy, forms of authority, and the impact of culture on economic and political development; developed many of these themes in *Economy and Society*.

twentieth centuries, which analyzed the nature of political and economic organization and power, would further add to political science. All these developments reflected widespread changes in scholarly inquiry and often blended political ideals with analytical concepts and some attempt at a systematic method of study.

Thus, by the turn of the twentieth century, political science formally existed as a field of study, but it still looked much different from the way it does now. The study of comparative politics, while less focused on ideals or philosophy, resembled a kind of political journalism: largely descriptive, atheoretical, and concentrated on Europe, which still dominated world politics through its empires. Little of this work was based on the comparative method.

The two world wars and the rise of the Cold War would mark a turning point in political science and comparative politics, particularly in the United States. There were several reasons for this. First, a growing movement surfaced among universities toward applying more rigorous methods to the study of human behavior, whether in sociology, economics, or politics. Second, the world wars raised serious questions about the ability of scholars to meaningfully contribute to an understanding of world affairs. The creation of new countries, the rise of fascism, and the failure of democracy throughout much of interwar Europe were vital concerns, but political scholarship did not seem to shed enough light on these issues and what they meant for international stability. Third, the Cold War with a rival Soviet Union, armed with nuclear weapons and revolutionary ideology, made understanding comparative politics seem a matter of survival. Finally, the postwar period ushered in a wave of technological innovation, such as early computers. This development generated a widespread belief that, through technological innovation, many social problems could be recast as technical concerns, finally to be resolved through science. The fear of another war was thus married with a belief that science was an unmitigated good that had the answers to almost all problems. The question was how to make the science work.

Although these changes dramatically transformed the study of politics, the field itself remained a largely conservative discipline, taking capitalism and democracy as the ideal. In comparative politics, these views were codified in what was known as **modernization theory**, which held that as societies developed, they would become capitalist democracies, converging around a set of shared values and characteristics. The United States and other Western countries were furthest ahead on this path, and the theory assumed that all countries would eventually catch up unless "diverted" by alternative systems such as communism (as fascism had done in the past).

During the 1950s and 1960s, comparativists influenced by modernization theory expanded their research to include more cases. Field research, supported by government and private grants, became the normal means by which political scientists gathered data. New computer technologies combined with statistical methods were also

> **IN FOCUS: Trends in Comparative Politics**
>
> | | |
> |---|---|
> | **TRADITIONAL APPROACH** | Emphasis on describing political systems and their various institutions. |
> | **BEHAVIORAL REVOLUTION** | The shift from a descriptive study of politics to one that emphasizes causality, explanation, and prediction; emphasizes the political behavior of individuals more than larger political structures and quantitative over qualitative methodology; modernization theory predominates. |

applied to this expanding wealth of data. Finally, the subject of investigation shifted away from political institutions (such as legislatures and constitutions) and toward individual political behavior. This trend came to be known as the **behavioral revolution**. Behavioralism hoped to generate theories and generalizations that could help explain and even predict political activity. Ideally, this work would eventually lead to a "grand theory" of political behavior and modernization that would be valid across countries.

Behavioralism and modernization theory were two different things: modernization theory was a set of hypotheses about how countries develop, and behavioralism was a set of methods with which to approach politics. However, both were attempts to study politics more scientifically to achieve certain policy outcomes.[6] Behavioralism also promoted deductive, large-scale research over the single-case study common in inductive reasoning. It seemed clear to many that political science, and comparative politics within it, would soon be a "real" science.

By the late 1970s, however, this enthusiasm began to meet with resistance. New theories and sophisticated methods of analysis increased scholars' knowledge about politics around the world, but this knowledge in itself did not lead to the expected breakthroughs. The theories that had been developed, such as modernization theory, increasingly failed to match politics on the ground; instead of becoming more capitalist and more democratic, many newly independent countries faced violent conflict, authoritarianism, and limited economic development. This did not match Western expectations or ideals. What had gone wrong?

Some critics charged that the behavioral revolution's obsession with appearing scientific had led the discipline astray by emphasizing methodology over deep knowledge of the countries under consideration. Others criticized the field for its ideological bias, arguing that comparativists were interested not in understanding the world on its own terms but in prescribing the Western model of modernization. At worst, comparativists' work could be viewed as simply serving the foreign policy interests of the United States. Since that time, comparative politics, like all of political science, has grown increasingly fragmented—or, if you prefer, more diverse. While few still believe in the old descriptive approach that dominated the earlier part of the century, there is no consensus about a direction for scholarship and what research methods or analytical concepts are most fruitful. This lack of consensus has led to several main divisions and lines of conflict.

RESEARCH METHODS

One area of conflict is over methodology—how best to gather and analyze data. We have already spoken about the problems of comparative methodology, involving selecting cases and controlling variables. Within these concerns are further questions of how one gathers and interprets the data to compare these cases and measure these variables. Some comparative political scientists rely on **qualitative methods**, evidence, and methodology, such as interviews, observations, and archival and other forms of documentary research. Qualitative approaches are often narrowly focused, deep investigations of one or a few cases drawing from scholarly expertise. However, some qualitative studies (such as work on modernization or revolution) do involve numerous cases spread out across the globe and spanning centuries. Either way, qualitative approaches are typically inductive, beginning with case studies to generate theory.

For some political scientists, a qualitative approach is of dubious value. Variables are not rigorously defined or measured, they argue, and hypotheses are not tested by using a large sample of cases. Asserting that qualitative work fails to contribute to the accumulation of knowledge and is little better than the approach that dominated the field a century ago, these critics advocate **quantitative methods** instead. They favor a wider use of cases unbound by area specialization, greater use of statistical analysis, and mathematical models often drawn from economics. This quantitative methodology is more likely to use deductive reasoning, starting with a theory that political scientists can test with an array of data. Many advocates of qualitative research question whether quantitative approaches measure and test variables that are of any particular value or simply focus on the (often mundane) things that can be expressed numerically. Overdependence on quantifiable measures can lead scholars to avoid the important questions that often cannot be addressed using such strict scientific methods.

THEORY

A second related debate concerns theoretical assumptions about human behavior. Are human beings rational, in the sense that their behavior conforms to some generally understandable behavior? Some say yes. These scholars use what is known as

> **IN FOCUS**
>
> ## Quantitative Method versus Qualitative Method
>
> | | |
> |---|---|
> | **QUANTITATIVE METHOD** | Gathering of statistical data across many countries to look for correlations and test hypotheses about cause and effect. Emphasis on breadth over depth. |
> | **QUALITATIVE METHOD** | Mastery of a few cases through the detailed study of their history, language, and culture. Emphasis on depth over breadth. |

rational choice or **game theory** to study the rules and games by which politics is played and how human beings act on their preferences (for instance, how and why people decide to vote, choose a political party, or support a revolution). Such models can, ideally, lead not only to explanation but also to prediction—a basic element of science. As you might guess, rational choice theory is closely associated with quantitative methods. And like the critics of quantitative methods in general, those who reject rational choice theory assert that the emphasis on individual rationality discounts the importance of things like historical complexity, unintended outcomes, or cultural factors. In fact, some consider rational choice theories, as they do behavioralism, to be Western (or specifically American) assumptions about self-interest, markets, and individual autonomy that do not easily describe the world.

As these debates have persisted, the world around us continues to change. Just as the wrenching political changes in the Middle East were not anticipated, neither was the end of the Cold War some twenty years earlier. Few scholars, regardless of methodology or theoretical focus, anticipated or even considered either dramatic set of events. Similarly, religion has reemerged as an important component in politics around the globe—a force that modernization theory (and research focused on Europe) told us was on the wane. New economic powers have emerged in Asia, coinciding with democracy in some cases but not in others. Terrorism, once the tactic of secular revolutionary groups in the 1970s, has also resurfaced, albeit in the hands of different actors. It seems that many political scientists, whatever their persuasion, have had little to contribute to many of these issues—time and again, scholars have been caught off guard.

Where does this leave us now? In recent years, some signs of conciliation have emerged. Scholars recognize that careful (and sloppy) scholarship and theorizing are possible with both qualitative and quantitative methods. Inductive and deductive reasoning can both generate valuable theories in comparative politics.

Rational choice and historical or cultural approaches can contribute to and be integrated into each other. One finds more mixed-method approaches that use both quantitative and qualitative research. As a result, some scholars have spoken optimistically of an integration of mathematics, "narrative" (case studies), and rational choice models, each contributing to the other. For example, large-scale quantitative studies of political activity can be further elucidated by turning to individual cases that investigate the question in greater detail.[7] At the same time, it is worth noting that the difficulties in making comparative politics and political science more rigorous and scientific are not unique. Across the social and life sciences there is what has been termed a "replication crisis," where numerous influential studies cannot be replicated. Much to the relief of parents, this includes the famous "marshmallow test," which concluded that a child's ability to delay gratification—for example, waiting to eat a marshmallow—could predict future achievement in school and work.[8]

A final observation is in order as we bring this discussion to a close. Irrespective of methodology or theory, many have observed that political science as a whole is out of touch with real-world concerns, has become inaccessible to laypersons, and has failed to speak to those who make decisions about policy—whether voters or elected leaders. Commentators and scholars often assert that political science has created "a culture that glorifies arcane unintelligibility while disdaining impact and audience."[9] This is misleading, given the growing emphasis on reconnecting political science to central policy questions.[10]

Comparative politics should not simply be about what we can study or what we want to study but also about how our research can reach people, empower them, and help them be better citizens and leaders. A call for greater relevance may represent a change for some scholars, but relevance and rigor are not at odds. They are in fact central to a meaningful political science and comparative politics.

A Guiding Concept: Political Institutions

A goal of this textbook is to provide a way to compare and analyze politics around the world. Given the long-standing debates within comparative politics, how can we organize our ideas and information? One way is through a guiding concept, a way of looking at the world that highlights some important features while deemphasizing others. There is certainly no one right way of doing this; any guide, like a lens, will sharpen some features while distorting others. With that said, our guiding concept is institutions, defined at the beginning of this chapter as organizations or activities that are self-perpetuating and valued for their own sake. In other words, an institution is something so embedded in people's lives as a norm or value that it is not easily dislodged or changed. People see an institution as central to their lives, and, as a result, the institution commands and generates legitimacy. Institutions embody the rules, norms, and values that give meaning to human activity.

Consider an example from outside politics. We often hear in the United States that baseball is an American institution. What exactly does this mean? In short, Americans view baseball not simply as a game but as something valued for its own sake, a game that helps define society. Yet few Americans would say that soccer is a national institution. The reason is probably clear: we do not perceive soccer as indispensable in the way that baseball is. Whereas soccer is simply a game, baseball is part of what defines America and Americans. Even Americans who don't like baseball would probably say that America wouldn't be the same without it. Indeed, even at the local level, teams command such legitimacy that when they merely threaten to move to another city, their fans raise a hue and cry. The Brooklyn Dodgers moved to Los Angeles in 1958, yet many in New York still consider them "their" team over half a century later. For many Canadians, while baseball is important, hockey is a national institution, thought of as "Canada's game" and an inextricable part of Canadian identity and history. In Europe and much of the world, soccer reigns as a premier social institution, and teams provoke such fervent loyalty that fan violence is quite common. Because of their legitimacy and apparent indispensability, institutions command authority and can influence human behavior; we accept and conform to institutions and support rather than challenge them. Woe betide the American, Canadian, or European who derides the national sport!

Another example connects directly to politics. In many countries, democracy is an institution: it is not merely a means to compete over political power but a vital element of people's lives, bound up in the very way they define themselves. Democracy is part and parcel of collective identity, and some democratic countries and their people would not be the same without it. Even if they are cynical about democracy in practice, citizens of democracies will defend and even die for the institution when it is under threat. In many other countries, this is not the case: democracy is absent, poorly understood, or weakly institutionalized and unstable. People in such countries do not define themselves by democracy's presence or absence, and so democracy's future there is less secure. However, these same people might owe a similar allegiance to a different set of institutions, such as their ethnic group or religion. Clearly, no single, uniform set of institutions holds power over people all around the world, and understanding the differences among institutions is central to the study of comparative politics.

What about a physical object or place? Can that, too, be an institution? Many would argue that the original World Trade Center was an American institution—not just a set of office buildings, but structures representing American values. The same can be said about the Pentagon. When terrorists attacked these buildings on September 11, 2001, they did so not simply to cause a great loss of life but also to show that their hostility was directed against America itself—its institutions, as they shape and represent the American way of life, and its relation to the outside world. Like the World Trade Center and the Pentagon, the city of Jerusalem is a powerful cultural and national institution, in this case reflecting the identity and ideals of two peoples: Israelis and Palestinians. Both groups claim it as their capital, and for both the city holds key historical, political, and religious significance.

The examples just described raise the distinction between formal and informal institutions. When we think of **formal institutions**, we assume they are based on officially sanctioned rules that are relatively clear. Yet there are also **informal institutions**—unwritten and unofficial, but no less powerful as a result. And of course, institutions can be a combination of both.

Because institutions are embedded in each of us, in how we see the world and what we think is valuable and important, it is difficult to change or eliminate them. When institutions are threatened, people will rush to their defense and even re-create them when they are shattered. This bond is the glue of society. However, one problem that institutions pose is this very "stickiness," in that people may come to resist even necessary change because they have difficulty accepting the idea that certain institutions have outlived their value or need to be reformed. Thus, while institutions can and do change, rising and falling in power, they are by nature persistent. This, however, is not to say that institutions are eternal. Such structures can decline in power in the face of alternative norms, or be swept away when people find them too constraining or outmoded. The rise and institutionalization of soccer in the United States may mirror the decline of baseball, which is viewed by many young Americans as an outdated sport. Many assert that democracy seems to be losing its legitimacy even in places where it has long been a norm.

Politics is full of institutions. The basic political structures of any country are composed of institutions: the army, the police, the legislature, and the courts, to name a few. We obey them not only because we think it is in our self-interest to do so but also because we see them as legitimate ways to conduct politics. Taxation is a good example. In many Western democracies, income taxes are an institution; we may not like them, but we pay them nonetheless. Is this because we are afraid of going to jail if we fail to do so? Perhaps. But research indicates that a major source of tax compliance is people's belief that taxation is a legitimate way to fund the programs that society needs. We pay, in other words, when we believe that it is the right thing to do, a norm. By contrast, in societies where taxes are not institutionalized, tax evasion tends to be rampant; people view taxes as illegitimate and those who pay as suckers. Similarly, where electoral politics is weakly institutionalized, people support elections only when their preferred candidate wins, and they cry foul, take to the streets, and even threaten or use violence when the opposition gains power. Institutions can thus be stronger or weaker, and rise or decline in power, over time.

Institutions are a useful way to approach the study of politics because they set the stage for political behavior. Because institutions generate norms and values (good and bad), they favor and allow certain kinds of political activity and not others, making a more likely "path" for political activity (what is known as *path dependence*). As a result, political institutions are critical because they influence politics, and how political institutions are constructed, intentionally or unintentionally, will profoundly affect how politics is conducted.

In many ways, our institutional approach takes us back to the study of comparative politics as it existed before the 1950s. Prior to the behavioral revolution, political scientists spent much of their time documenting and describing the institutions of politics, often without asking how those institutions actually shaped politics. The behavioral revolution that followed emphasized cause and effect but turned its attention toward political actors and their calculations, resources, or strategies. The actual institutions were seen as less important. The return to the study of institutions in many ways combines these two traditions. From behavioralism, institutional approaches take their emphasis on cause-and-effect relationships, something that will be prevalent throughout this book. However, institutions are not simply the product of individual political behavior; they powerfully affect how politics functions. In other words, institutions are not merely the result of politics;

IN FOCUS

Institutions

- Organizations or activities that are self-perpetuating and valued for their own sake
- Embody norms or values that are considered central to people's lives and thus are not easily dislodged or changed
- Set the stage for political behavior by influencing how politics is conducted
- Vary from country to country
- Exemplified by the army, taxation, elections, and the state

they can also be an important cause. Their emergence—and disappearance—can have a profound impact on politics.

There is a tremendous amount of institutional variation around the world that needs to be recognized and understood. This textbook will map some of the basic institutional differences between countries, acknowledging the diversity of institutions while pointing to some features that allow us to compare and evaluate them. By studying political institutions, we can hope to gain a better sense of the political landscape across countries.

A Guiding Ideal: Reconciling Freedom and Equality

We've spoken so far about analytical concepts (such as institutions), methods (such as inductive or deductive, quantitative or qualitative), and political ideals. We defined politics as the struggle to attain the power to make decisions for society. The concept of institutions gives us a way to organize our study by investigating the different ways that this struggle can be shaped. Yet this raises an important question: People may struggle for political power, but what are they fighting for? What do they seek to achieve once they have gained power? This is where ideals come in, and we will concentrate on one core debate that lies at the heart of all politics: the struggle between freedom and equality. This struggle has existed as long as human beings have lived in organized communities, and it may be that these are more than ideals—they were a part of our evolutionary history as we transitioned from small, nomadic bands to larger, settled communities.

Politics is bound up in the struggle between individual freedom and collective equality and in how these ideals can be reconciled. Since *freedom* and *equality* can mean different things to different people, it is important to define each term. When we speak of **freedom**, we are talking about an individual's ability to act independently, without fear of restriction or punishment by the state or other individuals or groups in society. At a basic level, freedom connotes autonomy; in the modern world, it encompasses such concepts as free speech, free assembly, freedom of religion, and other civil liberties. **Equality** refers to a material standard of living shared by individuals within a community, society, or country. The relation between equality and freedom is typically viewed in terms of justice or injustice—a measurement of whether our ideals have been met.

Freedom and equality are tightly interconnected, and the relation between the two shapes politics, power, and debates over justice. It is unclear, however, whether one must come at the expense of the other. Greater personal freedom, for example, may imply a smaller role for the state and limits on its powers to do such things as redistribute income through social expenditures and taxes. As a result, inequality may increase as individual freedom trumps the desire for greater collective equality. This growing inequality can in turn undermine freedom if too many people feel as though the political system no longer cares about their material needs. Even if this discontent is not a danger, there remains the question of whether society as a whole has an obligation to help the poor—an issue of justice. The United States, as we shall see, has one of the highest degrees of economic inequality among developed democracies. Is this inequality undermining democratic institutions, as some suggest?

Alternatively, a focus on equality may erode freedom. Demands for greater material equality may lead a government to take greater control of private property and personal wealth, all in the name of redistribution for the "greater good." Economic and political powers may threaten individual freedom when concentrated in one place since people control fewer private resources of their own. In the Soviet Union the state held all economic power, giving it the ability to control people's lives—where they lived, the education they received, the jobs they held, the money they earned. Levels of inequality were in turn quite low, as was freedom.

Is the balance between freedom and equality a zero-sum game, in which the gain of one represents the loss of the other? Not necessarily. Some would assert that freedom and equality can also reinforce each other: material security can help to secure certain political rights, and vice versa. In addition, while a high degree of state power may weaken individual freedom, the state also plays an important role in helping to define individual freedom and protect it from infringement by other individuals. Finally, the meaning of *freedom* and *equality* may change over time as the material world and our values change. For some, managing freedom or equality necessitates centralized political power. Others view such power as the very impediment to freedom and equality. We will look at these debates more closely when we consider political ideologies in subsequent chapters.

In short, politics is driven by the ideal of reconciling individual freedom and collective equality. This inevitably leads to questions about power and about the people's role in political life. How much should any individual or group be allowed to influence or impose their will on others? Who should be empowered to make decisions about freedom and equality? Should power be centralized or decentralized, public or private? When does power become a danger to others, and how can politicians and citizens manage this threat? Each political system must address these questions and in so doing determine where political power shall reside and how much shall be given to whom. Each political system creates a unique set of institutions to structure political power, shaping the role people play in politics.

INSTITUTIONS IN ACTION

Can We Make a Science of Politics?

In much of our discussion, there is a sense that political science remains hindered by problems of data and theory that could prevent explanation, or even prediction, of political behavior. To use a metaphor coined by the philosopher Karl Popper: Do humans function in a regular, clocklike way, such that we can find out "what makes us tick" and predict how we will act? Or are humans more like clouds, shifting and complex? Some people do believe that humans are more clocklike and that science can produce better explanations and perhaps even predictions of human behavior. In this view, the main problem has been a lack of the necessary tools. However, certain scientific advances are under way that some believe will transform the social sciences. Researchers are at work in two interesting areas, both focusing on human nature in different but complementary ways.

The first we can call a macro-level approach to human nature. In this approach, the future of the discipline lies in the integration of life sciences, such as neuroscience and related fields. Politics can be investigated by starting with psychological and biological factors as the foundation of political actions and institutions. For example, biological studies of politics increasingly suggest that many key aspects of politics, such as ideological orientation, levels of social trust, and propensity toward political participation, may be as much inherited as learned. This does not suggest that people have a gene for such things as democracy or authoritarianism, conservatism or liberalism. But the macro-level approach does argue that biology can partially shape people's view of some issues and that political orientation is not simply a function of individual preference or existing social structures.

To return to our discussion of the wave of revolutions and civil conflict across the Middle East, macro-level research might focus on demographics, such as the large population under age 30, and the intersection of particular forms of youth behavior (such as risk-taking) and institutionalized barriers to opportunity (such as corruption). It might also consider the interaction between culture and biology in levels and sources of shame and humiliation. Mohamed Bouazizi did not set himself on fire because he was crazy or because he thought it would touch off a revolution. In our understanding, his act was irrational. But if we reconsider it as an explicable psychological response based on his particular environment, we gain a different insight. This of course does not provide any prediction of why a revolution would happen in the first place, or why in Tunisia as opposed to Morocco, which escaped the Arab Spring.

This is where micro-level approaches come into play. If macro-level studies look at how biological forces can interact with the social environment, micro-level research focuses on the science of cognition—how our tools for judgment frequently lead to a range of involuntary cognitive errors, including overconfidence, misunderstandings of statistics and probability, mental "shortcuts" that lead to biases and stereotypes, and the tendency to discern cause-and-effect relationships where none exist. In this scholarship, the very notion of human rationality is deeply problematic. This understanding can help explain why political scientists were surprised by the Arab Spring and the collapse of communism. The human tendency to construct narratives that explain the past and downplay the role of chance typically leads people to mistakenly project the present into the future. This behavior discounts the possibility for dramatic political change.[a]

While this discussion has gone some way to bringing more science into political science, these explanations don't seem to give us more in terms of prediction. Yet there is hope. Political psychologist Philip Tetlock's Good Judgment Project asked several thousand volunteers to regularly make predictions about a range of world events up to one year out. Among them emerged a group of "superforecasters" whose predictions even beat those of intelligence analysts with access to classified information. What made these superforecasters so good? Tetlock noted that forecasters can be divided into two basic categories, borrowed from the late philosopher Isaiah Berlin: hedgehogs and foxes. Hedgehogs know one big thing; they tend to look for a single overarching explanation that can explain many different political events and are more likely to reject information that runs counter to their beliefs. Foxes are less confident in their views, which consist of many small ideas cobbled together and are subject to frequent revision. As you might suspect, hedgehogs are much worse predictors of world events and are more interested in trying to fit the world into their preconceptions than revising their beliefs on the basis of new information.

Which approach one uses—for instance, a particularly open-minded and self-critical mode of thinking—may simply be inherited. But Tetlock also found that good prediction can be taught, reducing biases and increasing clarity in forecasts. No one believes that superforecasters will be able to predict the next Arab Spring. In fact, the majority of forecasters incorrectly predicted that the United Kingdom's 2016 referendum to leave the European Union would fail (see Chapter 8), nor did they predict President Trump's 2016 victory in the United States. But there is clear evidence that we can approach politics more systematically and draw better conclusions about what might happen in the near future.[b]

Egyptian demonstrators face off against the army in 2011, eventually leading to the downfall of President Hosni Mubarak.

1. What are the key differences between micro- and macro-level approaches to political science? Do you think one is more effective than the other? Why?

2. Consider a world event from the news this past week. How would researchers apply micro- and macro-level approaches to explain this event? What questions would they ask?

3. What makes superforecasters better than others in predicting world events?

In Sum: Looking Ahead and Thinking Carefully

Politics is the pursuit of power in any organization, and comparative politics is the study of this struggle around the world. Over the past centuries, the study of politics has evolved from philosophy to a field that emphasizes empirical research in the quest to explain politics and even predict political change. This approach has limitations: despite the earlier desire to emulate the natural sciences, comparative politics, like political science as a whole, has been unable to generate any grand or even smaller theories of political behavior. Yet the need to study politics remains as important as ever; dramatic changes over the past 30 years have called on comparativists to shed light on these developments and concerns.

Political institutions can help us organize this task. Since institutions generate norms and values, and different configurations of institutions lead to different forms of political activity, they can help us map the political landscape. Specifically, they can show how political activity attempts to reconcile the competing values of individual freedom and collective equality. All political groups, including countries, must reconcile these two forces, determining where power should reside. In the chapters to come, we will return to this question of freedom and equality and to the way in which these values influence, and are influenced by, institutions.

A final thought before we conclude on how to use all this information. Much of our discussion in this chapter has been about the controversies over how best to study politics—What method? What concepts? What role for ideals? In all of this, it may seem that we have gained little understanding of how to "do" political science well. If scholars can't agree on the best way to analyze politics, what hope do we have of making sense of the world?

Our "Institutions in Action" feature provides some insight. We note that Philip Tetlock's study of political predictions found that participants can be divided into hedgehogs and foxes; the former look for an overarching explanation and may reject information challenging their view, while the latter are less confident of their explanations and more willing to change their views in the face of evidence to the contrary. The flexibility and even humility of foxes leads to a better track record in forecasting future events.

An important lesson we can take away from these findings is that the most fruitful approach to comparative politics is to be skeptical, not simply of others—that's the easy part—but also of what we believe and take for granted. The new "Questions and Methods" section at the end of each chapter gives you a chance to do this by exploring contemporary research. We should be ready to reconsider our beliefs in the face of new evidence and arguments and to remember that every explanation in this book is conjecture, subject to revision if we can find new or contradictory evidence. With this approach, by the end of this course you will be able to draw your own conclusions about the contours of politics and what combination of values might construct a better political order. So, drop your assumptions about how the world works, and let's begin.

Key Terms

area studies (p. 9)
behavioral revolution (p. 15)
causal relationship (p. 7)
comparative method (p. 7)
comparative politics (p. 5)
correlation (p. 7)
deductive reasoning (p. 7)
dependent variable (p. 10)
endogeneity (p. 11)
equality (p. 22)
formal institutions (p. 20)
freedom (p. 22)
game theory (p. 17)
independent variable (p. 10)

inductive reasoning (p. 7)
informal institutions (p. 20)
institution (p. 5)
international relations (p. 5)
modernization theory (p. 14)
multicausality (p. 8)
politics (p. 6)
power (p. 6)
qualitative method (p. 16)
quantitative method (p. 16)
rational choice (p. 17)
selection bias (p. 10)
theory (p. 11)

For Further Reading

Aristotle. *The Politics*. Translated by T. A. Sinclair. New York: Penguin, 1981.

Brady, Henry E., and David Collier, eds. *Rethinking Social Inquiry: Diverse Tools, Shared Standards*. 2nd ed. Lanham, MD: Rowman & Littlefield, 2010.

Goodin, Robert E., ed. *The Oxford Handbook of Political Science*. Oxford: Oxford University Press, 2011.

Kahneman, Daniel. *Thinking, Fast and Slow*. New York: Farrar, Straus and Giroux, 2011.

King, Gary, Robert O. Keohane, and Sidney Verba. *Designing Social Inquiry: Scientific Inference in Qualitative Research*. Princeton, NJ: Princeton University Press, 1994.

Machiavelli, Niccolò. *The Prince*. Translated by W. K. Marriott. New York: Knopf, 1992.

Munck, Gerardo L., and Richard Snyder. *Passion, Craft and Method in Comparative Politics*. Baltimore, MD: Johns Hopkins University Press, 2007.

Tetlock, Philip E., and Dan Gardner. *Superforecasting: The Art and Science of Prediction*. New York: Crown Publishing, 2015.

INQUIZITIVE

Earn a better grade on your test. InQuizitive personalizes your learning path to help you master the concepts from this chapter and practice applying them to examples from the text and beyond (see back cover).

2

A woman holds a lightbulb in her mouth as part of a protest against electricity shortages in Pakistan. Millions endure electricity cuts for up to 12 hours a day, calling into question the effectiveness of the Pakistani state.

STATES

How do countries create and maintain political power?

Pakistan is a country known for its troubled political institutions. Born out of a violent partition with India in 1947, the country has been subject to long periods of military rule, ethnic and religious conflict, terrorism, and war. The Legatum Institute, which ranks countries in terms of prosperity according to a series of social, economic, political, and environmental variables, places Pakistan at position 140 among 167 countries surveyed. On the positive side, since 2008 the country has been under civilian rather than direct military rule (though the military retains substantial political powers). In the 2018 elections Imran Khan came to power as prime minister, having campaigned in part on a pledge to expand social services and create what he called an "Islamic welfare state." One major part of this promise was to improve basic utilities, notably electricity.

For such a large country (at around 200 million, it is nearly two-thirds the population of the United States), Pakistan suffers from an acute shortage of energy. Many wealthier countries in Europe, such as France and Germany, consume around 7,000 kilowatts of electricity per capita per year. Pakistan consumes less than a tenth of that. We might think that this is simply a function of the fact that Pakistan is a poorer country, yet many countries with a comparable level of development have much higher levels of consumption. Moreover, while Pakistan's population has grown by more than 20 million over the past decade, electricity consumption has stagnated. This is not an issue of demand; it is a problem of supply. Although

Pakistan has been actively developing nuclear technology for military purposes, it has been much less successful in meeting the energy needs of its citizens, providing only around half of what is required (something we will turn to at the end of this chapter). Pakistan is a country that literally cannot keep the lights on. Why?

Pakistan's energy problems are an excellent example of many of the points we will cover in this chapter. Part of the problem is a function of a growing population that is outstripping supply. But the country's failure to keep up with demand has been exacerbated by bureaucratic infighting and poor management, including the inability to collect payments. In addition, power theft is widespread; by some estimates a quarter of all electricity produced is stolen. The result is a financial drain on the electrical sector, which then lacks the funds to pay for oil, coal, or gas to generate electricity in the first place. Blackouts—sometimes lasting for a day or more—have become common, especially in the hot summers. These problems are emblematic of a much bigger issue. While security in Pakistan is often viewed by outsiders in terms of terrorism or other forms of political violence, this ignores basic state institutions, like laws, roads, or education, which generate political legitimacy. Where weak states are unable to build and maintain these institutions, legitimacy erodes. And where legitimacy is low, a weakly institutionalized democracy, or even the state itself, can collapse.

Over the past decade Pakistani leaders have made a number of promises to deal with the energy crisis. A major problem is the inability of the state to simply meter and bill for electricity and collect revenues. While this might sound easier than building power plants, it is no small feat when a huge part of the public relies on illegal electrical lines, and when state institutions like the national railway, the military, and even parliament have at times failed to pay for the energy they consume. Prime Minister Khan has ordered a crackdown against power theft, and over a thousand violators were arrested in the first few months of his term. But successfully supplying power requires not just policing but also the ability to effectively manage the entire public service, from production to consumption.

LEARNING OBJECTIVES

- Differentiate between states, regimes, and governments.
- Trace the development of the modern state from its pre-medieval roots to today.
- Describe how states can vary in legitimacy, centralization, and strength.

We begin our study of the basic institutions of politics by looking at the state. This discussion is often difficult for North Americans, who are not used to thinking about politics in terms of centralized political power. Indeed, for Americans the word *state* typically conjures up the idea of local, not centralized, politics. But for most people around the world, *state* refers to centralized authority, the locus of power.[1] In this chapter, we will break down the basic institutions that make up states and discuss how states manage freedom and equality and distribute power in a way that allows them to maintain their authority. The chapter will define what states are and what they comprise, distinguishing a state from a government and a regime. We will also consider their origins. For most of human history, politics was built on organizations other than states, and myriad forms of authority existed around the world. Yet now only states remain. What caused them to come into existence?

Once we have discussed the nature and origins of the state, we will look at some different ways in which states can be compared. This discussion will analyze the different forms of legitimacy that give states their power and the varying degrees of this power. Can we speak of states as weak or strong? If so, how would we measure their strength or weakness? To answer this question, we will make a distinction between state capacity and state autonomy and examine how this might differ across cases and policy areas. Here, we consider states as a cause, a force that can shape other institutions. With these ideas more clearly in hand, we will return to our theme of individual freedom and collective equality and consider the future of the state.

Defining the State

What exactly do we mean by *state*? Political scientists, drawing on the work of the German scholar Max Weber, typically define the **state** as the organization that maintains a monopoly of force over a territory.[2] This definition of what a state is and does may seem severe, but a bit of explanation should help flesh out this concept. One of the most important elements of a state is what we call **sovereignty**, the ability to carry out actions and policies within a territory independently of external actors and internal rivals. In other words, a state needs to be able to act as the primary authority over its territory and the people who live there, passing and enforcing laws, defining and protecting rights, resolving disputes between people and organizations, and generating domestic security.

To achieve this, a state needs power, typically (but not only) physical power. If a state cannot defend its territory from outside actors such as other states, then it runs the risk that its rivals will interfere with its authority, inflicting damage, taking its territory, or destroying the state outright. Similarly, if the state faces powerful opponents within its own territory, such as organized crime or rebel movements, its rules and policies may be undermined. Thus, to secure control, a state must be armed. To protect against international rivals, states need armies. And in response to domestic rivals, states need police forces. In fact, the word *police* comes from an old French word meaning "to govern."

A state is thus a set of institutions that wields the most force within a territory, establishing order and deterring challengers from inside and out. In so doing, it provides security for its subjects by limiting the danger of external attack and internal crime and disorder—both of which threaten the state and its citizens. In some ways, a state (especially a nondemocratic one) is a kind of protection racket—demanding money in return for the maintenance of security and order, staking out turf, defending those it protects from rivals, settling internal disputes, and punishing those who do not pay.[3]

But most states are far more complex than mere entities that apply force. Unlike criminal rackets, the state is made up of a large number of institutions that are engaged in the process of turning political ideas into policy. Laws and regulations, property rights, health and labor, the environment, and transportation are but a few policy areas that typically fall under the responsibility of the state. Because of these responsibilities, the state serves as a set of institutions (ministries, offices, army, police) that society deems necessary to achieve basic goals. When there is a lack of agreement on these goals, the state must attempt to reconcile different views and seek (or impose) consensus.

The public views the state as legitimate, vital, and appropriate. States are thus strongly institutionalized and not easily changed. Leaders and policies may come and go, but the state remains, even in the face of crisis, turmoil, or revolution. Although destruction through war or civil conflict can eliminate states altogether, even this outcome is unusual and states are soon re-created. Thus, the state is defined as a monopoly of force over a given territory, but it is also the set of political institutions

---

IN FOCUS

The State Is . . .

- The organization that maintains a monopoly of force over a given territory.
- A set of political institutions that generates and carries out policy.
- Typically highly institutionalized.
- Sovereign.
- Characterized by such institutions as an army, a police force, taxation, a judiciary, and a social welfare system.

that helps create and implement policies and resolve conflict. It is, if you will, the machinery of politics, establishing order and turning politics into policy. Thus, many social scientists argue that the state, as a bundle of institutions, is an important driver of economic development, the rise of democracy, and other processes.

Beyond *state*, a few other terms need to be defined. First, we should make a distinction between a state and a **regime**, which is defined as the fundamental rules and norms of politics. More specifically, a regime embodies long-term goals that guide the state regarding individual freedom and collective equality, where power should reside, and how power should be used. At the most basic level, we can speak of a democratic regime or a nondemocratic one. In a democratic regime, the rules and norms of politics give the public a large role in governance, as well as certain individual rights and liberties. A nondemocratic regime, in contrast, limits public participation and favors those in power. Both types of regimes can vary in the extent to which power is centralized and in the relationship they create between freedom and equality. The democratic regime of the United States is not the same as that of Canada; China's nondemocratic regime is not the same as Cuba's or Syria's. Some of these regime differences can be found in basic documents such as constitutions, but often the rules and norms that distinguish one regime from another are informal, unwritten, and implicit, requiring careful study. Finally, we should also note that in some nondemocratic countries where politics is dominated by a single individual, observers may use *regime* to refer to that leader, emphasizing the view that all decisions flow from that one person. As King Louis XIV of France famously put it, *L'état, c'est moi* ("I am the state"). However, the term *regime* is not inherently negative any more than the terms *rules* or *norms* are.

In summary, if the state is a monopoly of force and a set of political institutions that secure the population and generate policy, then the regime is defined as the

IN FOCUS

A Regime Is . . .

- The norms and rules regarding individual freedom and collective equality, the locus of power, and the use of that power.
- Institutionalized, but can be changed by dramatic social events such as revolutions.
- Categorized at the most basic level as either democratic or nondemocratic.
- Often embodied in a constitution.

norms and rules that establish the proper relation between freedom and equality and the use of power toward that end. If the state is the machinery of politics, like a computer, one can think of a regime as its software, the programming that defines its capabilities. Each computer runs differently, and more or less productively, depending on the software installed. Over time, software becomes outdated and unstable, and machines become less efficient or even crash. However, states and regimes are not like consumer electronics that we can simply throw away or upgrade. In fact, as we know all too well, it can be disastrous to upgrade from one operating system to another. No matter how hard we try to erase old political institutions, many aspects of them tend to persist. This is a particularly big obstacle to reforming or transforming states and regimes—building democracy, reducing corruption, or ameliorating ethnic conflict all involve changing existing, deeply embedded institutions. We cannot simply reformat or reboot existing institutions.

Our third term related to the concepts of state and regime is the most familiar one: *government*. **Government** can be defined as the leadership that runs the state. If the state is the machinery of politics, and the regime its programming, then the government operates the machinery. The government may consist of democratically elected legislators, presidents, and prime ministers, or it may be made up of leaders who gained office through force or other nondemocratic means. Whatever their path to power, governments all hold particular ideas regarding freedom and equality, and they all attempt to use the state to realize those ideas. But few governments are able to act with complete autonomy in this regard. Democratic and nondemocratic governments alike must confront the existing regime that has built up over time. Push too hard against an existing regime, and resistance, rebellion, or collapse may occur. For example, Mikhail Gorbachev's attempt to transform the Soviet Union's regime in the 1980s contributed to that country's dissolution. Today, the Chinese government fears similar chaos if political reforms allow for greater citizen participation and political competition against the Communist

IN FOCUS
Government Is . . .

- The leadership or elite in charge of running the state.
- Weakly institutionalized.
- Limited by the existing regime.
- Often composed of elected officials, such as a president or prime minister, or unelected officials, such as a monarch.

Party. Many Americans are highly skeptical of modifying the U.S. Constitution, in part because of fears that this would open the door to polarizing debates over things like gun control or civil rights that could not be peacefully resolved.

In part because of the power of regimes, governments tend to be weakly institutionalized—that is, the public does not typically view those in power as irreplaceable or believe that the country would collapse without them (Figure 2.1). In democratic regimes, governments are replaced fairly frequently, and even in nondemocratic settings rulers are continuously threatened by rivals and by their own mortality. Governments come and go, whereas regimes and states may live on for decades or centuries.

Finally, the term **country** can be taken as shorthand for the political system that combines the entities defined so far—state, regime, government—as well as for the people who live within that system. We will often speak about various countries in this textbook, and when we do, we are referring to the entire political entity and its citizens.

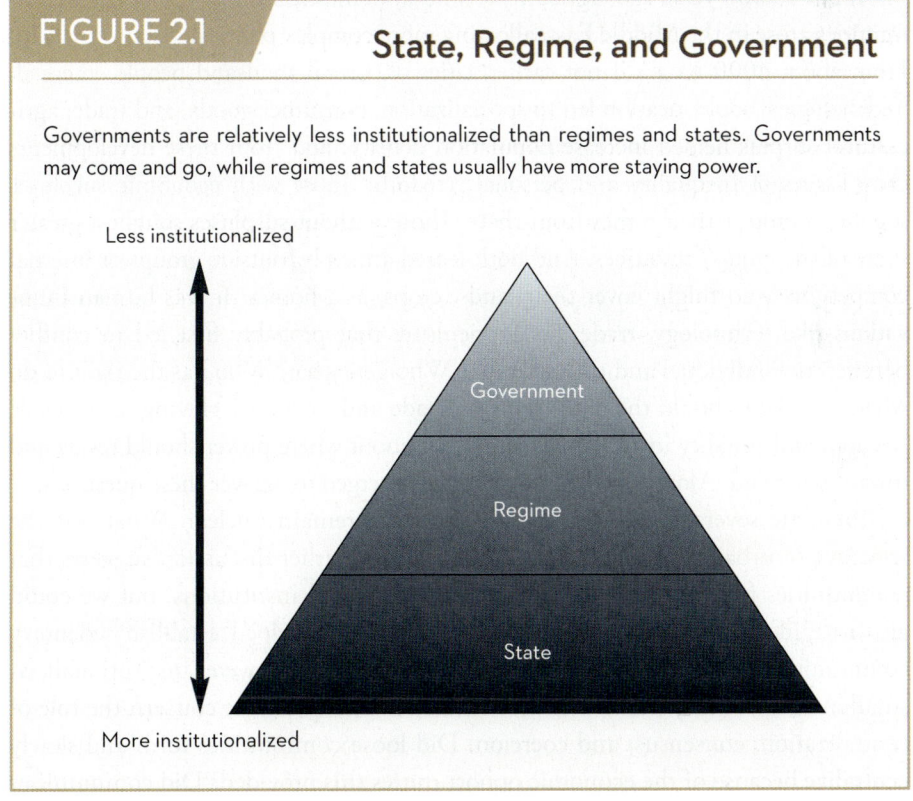

FIGURE 2.1 State, Regime, and Government

Governments are relatively less institutionalized than regimes and states. Governments may come and go, while regimes and states usually have more staying power.

The Origins of Political Organization

So far, we have noted that modern politics is defined by states, which monopolize force and generate and realize policy. This political machinery is directed by a particular regime and by the government in power. Governments generate short-term goals regarding freedom and equality, which are in part based on an existing regime that provides an institutionalized set of political norms and values. This combination, linking state, regime, and government, is relatively new in human history, though, to be clear, as long as there have been human beings (around 200,000 years), there has been some form of human organization. In our earliest stages, we were likely organized by families and tribes. Genetic research suggests that the modern human population derives largely from a group of people who originated in Africa and rapidly migrated outward less than 100,000 years ago, displacing other archaic human populations around the world as they went. Groups descended from these bands also traveled by sea (at least 60,000 years ago, and perhaps much earlier). These developments suggest organization, some technological sophistication, and the ability to pass knowledge from generation to generation.

About 10,000 years ago, agriculture, animal domestication, and sedentary communities arose in the Middle East, allowing more complex political systems to form. From about 4000 B.C.E., if not earlier, cities of several thousand people emerged. Technological sophistication led to specialization, consumer goods, and trade; agricultural surplus helped increase population density; and from these developments came issues of inequality and personal freedom. Those with economic surpluses sought to protect their riches from theft. Those without surpluses sought a greater share of the group's resources. And both feared attack by outside groups or internal competitors who might covet their lands, crops, and homes. It was human innovations like technology, trade, and agriculture that probably first led to conflict between the individual and the collective. Who gets what? Who has the right to do what? And how should these decisions be made and enforced? Having to reconcile freedom and equality in turn raises questions about where power should reside and toward what end. Alongside the city, the state emerged to answer these questions.

There are several things in this account that remain unclear. What was the sequence of urbanization and state building? Our earlier discussion suggests that communities formed, settled, and then built political institutions, but we could also imagine early forms of political leadership that helped establish sedentary communities. An endogenous explanation—that both were institutionalized simultaneously—may make the most sense. Further questions concern the role of centralization, consensus, and coercion. Did loose communities form and slowly centralize because of the economic opportunities this provided? Did communities

perhaps develop for primarily defensive reasons? Were these systems constructed through consensus or coercion?

In the absence of evidence, philosophers have long debated these questions. Some, like the philosopher Thomas Hobbes, believed that human beings voluntarily submitted to political authority to overcome anarchy, which ensures neither freedom nor equality. In return for giving up many of their rights, people gained security and a foundation on which to build a civilization. In contrast, Jean-Jacques Rousseau believed that human beings were in essence "noble savages" who were instinctively compassionate and egalitarian. It was civilization and the rise of the state that corrupted them by institutionalizing a system of inequality. These competing visions provide different interpretations of civilization and political organization, but both emphasize that sovereignty emerged through a "social contract" between rulers and ruled.

For a long time, scholars have debated whether Rousseau or Hobbes provided a more accurate view of early state development. Recent research, however, indicates that neither was correct. Many assumed that humans lived relatively solitary lives—what one scholar calls "primordial individualism"—before modern forms of political organization took hold, but we now know that family and tribal organization has a much older past. In addition, while warfare was possibly a driver of political organization, it may have broken out less between individuals, as was often assumed, than between rival groups. As human populations expanded, tribes battled one another for resources and territory. Pre-state societies were probably much more violent than states are now. By some estimates, anywhere from a quarter to over half of the male population died at the hands of others, and the expansion of pre-state societies coincided with the extermination of many large animal species around the world that were apparently hunted to extinction. The widespread taking of life appears to have begun with the emergence of modern humans, long before the rise of the state.

States, then, appear to have emerged out of this history of violence, rather than the other way around. As certain groups conquered others, political organizations brought new peoples and territories under control. Such organizations also allowed for more effective defense, especially in urbanized communities that could build city walls and stockpile weapons. In short, where the inherent conflict between people intersected with agricultural technology, population density, and urbanization, state building followed.[4]

Complex organizations began to emerge about 8,000 years ago in the Middle East, bearing the hallmarks of politics that exist to this day, such as taxation, bureaucracy, laws, military force, and leadership. Some of these political units were relatively small, such as the city-states that emerged in ancient Greece some 2,700 years ago. In other cases, large and highly sophisticated empires emerged, as in China, South America, the Middle East, and Africa. Across these political systems, economic relations were based on agricultural production, while specialized goods and trade were secondary activities. Unlike modern countries, many of these early political systems often did not have clearly defined and defended borders.

The Rise of the Modern State

The diversity of early political systems eventually gave way to the modern state, which first took shape in Europe. Why the modern state emerged in Europe and came to dominate the world is uncertain, but it may in part be due to historical chance and the curious advantage of backwardness. Two thousand years ago, Europe, like other parts of the world, was dominated by a single, large empire—in this case, the Roman Empire. Spanning thousands of miles across western Europe and North Africa, the Roman Empire developed a complex political system that tied together millions of people and generated an advanced infrastructure of cities, laws, trade, knowledge, and roads. After a thousand years, however, the Roman Empire eventually declined, succumbing to the pressures of overexpansion and increased attacks by rival forces. In the fifth century C.E., Rome itself was sacked by invaders.

As the Roman Empire collapsed, the complex political institutions and the other benefits that had extended across its territory largely disappeared, particularly in western Europe. The security generated by imperial control evaporated, replaced by roving bands of marauders. Population and urbanization declined. Roads and the other basic forms of infrastructure that people depended on eroded. Rules and regulations fragmented and lost their power. The knowledge and technology accumulated under the empire were lost or forgotten, and the advanced system of trade and travel between communities came to an end. Europe's rise to power was thus not preordained; around 1000 C.E., Europe's total wealth may have been less than half that of China or India, and it would not begin to close this gap until the nineteenth century. By some estimates, during the first millennium C.E. virtually every part of the globe experienced consistent growth and innovation—except Europe.[5]

Yet, paradoxically, this period of dramatic decline and anarchy appears to have set the stage for the creation of the modern state. As the sociologist Charles Tilly has noted, in Europe's fragmented, unstable, and violent environment, new political organizations began to develop, in constant competition with their rivals.[6] In some cases, these were formed by marauders who realized that they could earn a better living by controlling and taxing one group of people than by pillaging one place and moving on to the next. Warlords staked out small areas of land that they could easily defend and consolidated control over these regions, fighting off rival groups. In other cases, the people banded together to defend themselves. As Tilly and others have concluded, the modern state emerged from and in reaction to what was essentially organized crime: armed groups staking out turf, offering protection, and demanding payment in return. The constant warfare among these numerous rivals, which created a competitive and fluid environment, seems to have generated a kind of rapid organizational evolution. Groups that could quickly adapt in response to new challenges and challengers survived, while less successful groups were conquered and disappeared.

Not only history but also geography has played a role in the rise of the modern state. Europe's rapid political evolution probably owed something to the continent's proximity to Asia and the Middle East, which gave it access to new plants, animals, and technological innovations that were unavailable to peoples in the Americas or southern Africa. China, which also benefited from its ability to import a range of foreign goods and technologies, had by the third century B.C.E. developed one of the most sophisticated political organizations of the time, at least a thousand years before Europe. Why then did China not come to rule the world instead of Europe, and why did "Europe" come to mean a collection of rival states while "China" came to mean a single enormous country? One explanation may involve the centralization of the Chinese Empire, which was facilitated by the absence of significant internal geographic boundaries, the related ethnic and cultural homogeneity of the population, and the absence of major neighboring political rivals. This led to an early and highly developed state—though its lack of major competitors eventually limited its organizational evolution. In contrast, Europe's weaknesses—ethnic and linguistic fragmentation, numerous rival actors, and geographic boundaries—hindered the creation of a single European state and fostered competition. That said, we should not be too deterministic in explaining these outcomes. For example, the preceding discussion largely discounts the role of ideas. It may be that Europe's political development was driven by the rise of Christianity and the impact of religious values and/or the struggle between the Catholic Church and various states. And like Europe, China faced numerous upheavals, warfare, and religious challenges across its history. At various points, these struggles could have led to the permanent fragmentation of China into a collection of states similar to Europe—albeit with a thousand-year head start in technology, bureaucracy, and education.[7]

Out of the constant warfare of the European Middle Ages emerged the first modern states, which possessed three important advantages over alternative forms of political organization. First, states encouraged economic development. Before and during the Early Middle Ages, most Europeans lived under an economic system based on subsistence agriculture. Property such as land tended to be monopolized by those in power rather than owned by those who worked it. Warlords could tie the people to the land (through serfdom), extract their labor, and levy heavy taxes on those who produced nonagricultural goods. However, such economic conditions were counterproductive for society as a whole: individuals had little incentive to produce if the fruits of their labor were simply taken by others. Rulers who created laws, regulations, and infrastructure that permitted and respected private property and individual profit found that production grew, giving them more resources to tax or borrow (and with which to make war). Property rights thus became a hallmark of state development.[8]

Second, states encouraged technological innovation. Some rulers who pursued such innovation to increase their economic and military power recognized that, like private commerce and trade, new technologies would stimulate economic development by providing new goods and services. When technological innovation was harnessed to commerce, economic development grew dramatically. These rulers viewed technological change not as a threat to their power but as a means to expand it. Many of the technologies that made Europe powerful as it set off to conquer the world—gunpowder, advanced mathematics, modern mapmaking, paper, astronomy—originated in other parts of the world. But the Europeans absorbed these innovations and put them to new use. What mattered most was not who made the discoveries but how these discoveries were encouraged or used by the state. Whether this application of innovation was a function primarily of intense European competition or of cultural values is still a source of debate (see our discussion of culture in Chapter 3).[9] Whatever the reason, technological innovation, combined with state power, set the stage for modern politics.

A third advantage was domestic stability, which increased trade and commerce and permitted the development of infrastructure. People's ability to travel more freely within the territory of their country encouraged interaction and the emergence of a shared identity. The state, through printed documents, education, and legal codes, also contributed to the standardization of language. People in Europe began to see themselves as having a common identity comprising shared values. Instead of defining themselves primarily by their trade, clan, religion, or town, people began to see themselves as, for example, English, French, or German. Ethnicity proved to be a powerful asset to the state, for it in turn fostered nationalism. This will be discussed in detail in the next chapter.

Although the modern state offered all these advantages, by around 1500, modern states covered only 20 percent of the globe—the rest was ruled by alternative forms of centralized organization or none at all. But this was soon to change. Well organized and armed with advanced technologies, growing national identity, and economic resources, the states of Europe began to rapidly accrue power. As their economic power grew, so did their ability to manage ever greater numbers of people and ever more territory. Increased finances and state organization also allowed for the development of major militaries. Able to conquer and control larger pieces of land, states began to defeat and absorb their European rivals. Spiritual rivals also lost political power. The Thirty Years' War (1618–48), in part a struggle between Roman Catholicism and Protestantism, culminated in the Treaty of Westphalia in 1648. Under this treaty, the authority of the pope over Europe's people was radically curtailed. Without this rival spiritual authority, states were free to direct religion within their own territories, subordinating the spiritual to the political. State sovereignty as we understand it today is often dated from the Treaty of Westphalia.

European states now began to expand their economic, technological, and military powers beyond their own shores. During the seventeenth and eighteenth centuries, Spain and Portugal took control of large parts of the Americas, while the Dutch, French, and British expanded state power into Asia. By the nineteenth century, nearly all of Africa had similarly been divided up among European states and incorporated into their respective empires.

The organizational structure of the state was thus imposed around the world by force. Yet as European control receded in the twentieth century, the structure

TIMELINE

Political Organization

8TH–7TH CENTURIES B.C.E.	Beginning of Greek city-states; centralization of political power in Europe.
6TH–5TH CENTURIES B.C.E.	Establishment of Roman Republic; first development of democracy in Athens.
5TH–3RD CENTURIES B.C.E.	Unification of China under Qin dynasty.
2ND–1ST CENTURIES B.C.E.	Roman conquest of Greece.
1ST–2ND CENTURIES C.E.	Roman Empire expands across Europe and into the Middle East; zenith of centralized imperial power in Europe.
3RD–4TH CENTURIES C.E.	Internal decline of Roman Empire; beginning of European Middle Ages; development stagnates.
5TH–6TH CENTURIES C.E.	Rome sacked by the Visigoths; widespread strife among competing European warlords.
7TH–8TH CENTURIES C.E.	Rise of Islamic Empire from southern Europe to Central Asia.
9TH–10TH CENTURIES C.E.	Viking raids across Europe.
11TH–12TH CENTURIES C.E.	European crusades into Middle East; beginning of consolidation of Europe into distinct political units through warfare.
12TH–13TH CENTURIES C.E.	Period of rapid innovation and development in Europe: invention of mechanical clock; adoption of paper and compass from Asia and the Middle East.
13TH CENTURY C.E.	Rise of Ottoman Empire in southern Europe, North Africa, and the Middle East.
14TH–15TH CENTURIES C.E.	Voyages of exploration and early imperialism; centralization of early European states.
16TH–17TH CENTURIES C.E.	Scientific revolution; development of modern states; development of modern identities of nationalism and patriotism.

of the state remained—indeed, states grew in number as the lands and peoples subjugated by Europe gained sovereignty. Although peoples all around the world resisted and eventually threw off European domination, they viewed the state as a superior—or at least inevitable—form of political evolution, and they adopted it for their own purposes. The world thus became a world of states. States established international boundaries and rules and were the primary actors in domestic and international politics around the world. Countries like Mexico and Nigeria threw off colonial rule, but they retained and expanded the state institutions originally imposed by imperialism.

The rapid spread of states may be viewed as the triumph of a form of organization that allowed groups of people to destroy political rivals, no matter how sophisticated. But this has not come without cost. Whereas Europe took several hundred years to create the modern state, much of the world has been forced to take up this form of organization and its institutions more quickly. And the historical paths of Africa, Asia, and South America were radically different from that of Europe. Many of the new states on these continents have lacked the resources, infrastructure, shared national identities, and capital that much older states developed over a thousand years. Consequently, these newer states often face significant challenges, such as establishing sovereignty over territories where a multitude of peoples, languages, religions, and cultures may coexist—problems that most European states solved only over the course of centuries and at the cost of many lives lost in wars and revolutions.[10] For better or worse, although Europe no longer directly rules over much of the earth, it has left us with the legacy of the state.

Comparing State Power

It is clear from the preceding discussion that political evolution has been a lengthy and somewhat arbitrary process. Where conditions allowed for human beings to settle permanently, complex forms of political organization emerged, with features that reflect modern struggles over freedom, equality, and the allocation of power. But only over the past few centuries has the modern state taken shape, forging new political, economic, and social institutions that have made it so powerful. States quickly eradicated every other form of political organization and now lay claim to all corners of the earth.

Still, not all states are the same. (See "Questions and Methods" on pp. 58–59 for a discussion of how political scientists measure states.) As we have observed, some states are powerful, effective, prosperous, and stable; others are weak, disorganized, and largely incapable of effective action—even basic tasks we take for granted in countries with stronger states. Moreover, a single state can have a commanding presence in one area but be ineffectual in another. Pakistan, for example, is able to build nuclear weapons but unable to provide regular electricity. What explains this range? How do we understand differences in what we might call "stateness"—that is, in the power of states? To answer this question and make effective comparisons, we need a few more conceptual tools with which to work.

Legitimacy

The first concept, **legitimacy**, is a value whereby something or someone is recognized and accepted as right and proper. A legitimate institution or person, therefore, is widely accepted and recognized by the public. Legitimacy confers authority and power. In the case of states, we know that they wield a great deal of force. But is that the only reason that people recognize their authority? In the absence of legitimacy, states must rely largely on coercion to retain their power. However, where there is legitimacy, people obey the law even when the threat of punishment is slight. We may pay our taxes, stand at the crosswalk, or serve in the military not because we fear punishment or seek immediate reward but because we assume that the state has the authority to ask these things of us. As states provide security and other benefits, they can engender in their citizens a sense of reciprocal responsibility to the state. Legitimacy thus creates power that relies not on coercion but on consent. Without legitimacy, a state would have to use the continuous threat of force to maintain order—a difficult task—or expect that many of its rules and policies would go unheeded. As one scholar puts it, in the absence of legitimacy "the state can never be anything but a predatory imposition upon many or most citizens."[11]

Legitimacy is therefore a critical component of stateness. Legitimacy, however, does not depend on freedom or equality; a society may be largely unfree or unequal and still view its state as legitimate, no matter how difficult we might imagine that to be.

How then does a state become legitimate? Let us turn again to Max Weber, who argued that political legitimacy comes in three basic forms: traditional, charismatic, and rational-legal.[12] **Traditional legitimacy** rests on the idea that someone or something is valid because "it has always been that way." In other words, this legitimacy is built on the idea that certain aspects of politics are to be accepted because they have been built over a long period of time. They are viewed as part of the historical identity of the people themselves. Traditional legitimacy often embodies historical myths and legends as well as the continuity between past and present. Rituals and ceremonies all help to reinforce traditional legitimacy by providing actions and symbols that are ancient, unique, and dramatic. A long-standing monarchy, where one family retains power over generations, is a good example of a traditionally legitimate institution. However, *traditional* is not the same as *outdated*. Even a modern institution, like an elected office or a regime, can develop traditional legitimacy if it is in place long enough. In short, traditional legitimacy is built on history and continuity. Its legitimacy comes in part from the simple fact that it has the weight of history on its side. Change becomes difficult to imagine if an institution has existed "since time immemorial."

Charismatic legitimacy is in many ways the opposite of traditional legitimacy. When we use the word *charisma* in everyday conversation, we often mean someone who is good-looking or charming. But this is a much-reduced version of the term's original meaning, sometimes rendered as "the gift of grace," meaning the favor of God. Instead of relying on the weight of history and the continuity of certain roles or values, charismatic legitimacy is based on the power of ideas or beliefs. Charisma is typically embodied by individuals who can move and persuade the public through ideas and the manner in which they present them. Some individuals possess a certain magnetism that binds who they are to what they say. Jesus and Muhammad are perfect examples of charismatic figures who could gather huge followings through the power of their ideas, which they asserted were transmitted to them from God. Although the origins of *charisma* indicate this spiritual link, in modern politics charisma can encompass secular ideas as well. Adolf Hitler was clearly a charismatic figure who wielded ideas and language to articulate the need for war and genocide.

As you can imagine, charismatic legitimacy is not institutionalized and thus is fairly tenuous, since it commonly dies with the individual who possesses it. But charismatic legitimacy can be transformed into traditional legitimacy through the creation of rituals and values that are meant to capture the spirit and intent of the charismatic leader's power. Religions, monarchies, even constitutions and regimes can be examples of this. Weber called this kind of institutionalization "the routinization of charisma."

In contrast to the first two forms of legitimacy, **rational-legal legitimacy** is based not on history or rituals (traditional legitimacy) or on the force of ideas and those who present them (charismatic legitimacy) but rather on a system of laws and procedures that are presumed to be neutral or rational. Leaders or political officials gain legitimacy through the rules by which they come to office. People abide by the decisions of those in power because those individuals are abiding by existing institutionalized rules. In this case, it is not the individual leaders who are important, or even their values or ideas, but the offices they hold. Once they leave office, they lose much of their authority. This can be contrasted with traditional or charismatic legitimacy, where authority tends to reside with individuals rather than a set of rules.

The world of modern states is built on a rational-legal foundation. States rely on bureaucracies, paperwork, and thousands of individuals to make daily decisions on a wide range of issues. Ideally, the public accepts these decisions as the proper way to get things done, and it presumes that these decisions are reasonably fair and predictable. For example, if there are elections, the people accept the outcome even if their preferred candidate loses, and they obey those who win. What's more, legitimacy is not confined to political actors within the state; our own individual legitimacy as citizens comes from a rational-legal foundation: our driver's licenses, identification numbers, passports, and voter registration cards all confer a certain form of authority and power—from the state to the citizen.

Although modern states are built on rational-legal legitimacy, traditional and charismatic legitimacy have not disappeared. In almost any country, one can see variations in the mix of traditional, charismatic, and rational-legal legitimacy. Political leaders in many countries throughout modern history have wielded a great deal of charismatic power and have sometimes become the centers of large "cults of personality," which we will explore further in Chapter 6. These cults portray the leader as the father (or, occasionally, the mother) of the nation and imbue him or her with almost superhuman powers. Charismatic leadership, and the power that it places in the hands of one individual, can corrupt, as in the case of North Korea's Kim Jong-Il and his son, Kim Jong-Un. But some charismatic figures—political leaders like Mohandas K. Gandhi, who fought for independence from British rule

IN FOCUS

Three Types of Legitimacy

TYPE	CHARACTERISTICS	EXAMPLE
TRADITIONAL LEGITIMACY	Built by habit and custom over time, stressing history; strongly institutionalized.	Monarch (Queen Elizabeth II)
CHARISMATIC LEGITIMACY	Built on the force of ideas and the presence of the leader; weakly institutionalized.	Revolutionary hero (Vladimir Ilyich Lenin)
RATIONAL-LEGAL LEGITIMACY	Built on rules and procedures and the offices that create and enforce those rules; strongly institutionalized.	Elected executive (Donald Trump)

in India, or Nelson Mandela, who struggled to end apartheid in South Africa—have dramatically changed the course of politics for the better.

Traditional legitimacy can similarly be found in a wide variety of countries. The United Kingdom, Japan, Saudi Arabia, and more than 40 other countries still have monarchs. The powers of most, though not all, of these monarchs are now quite limited, yet even constitutional monarchs remain important symbols and attract national and sometimes even international attention. Families can have a similar legitimacy in politics. In India, Indira Gandhi (no relation to Mohandas), leader of the Congress Party, served as prime minister for 15 years in the 1960s, 1970s, and 1980s. On her death, her son Rajiv became prime minister. After his death, his wife, Sonia, became head of the Congress Party, and her uncharismatic son, Rahul, was head of the party until 2019. Not just individuals and families but also rules and regulations can gain a kind of traditional legitimacy if they function for so long that people can't imagine doing things any other way. The U.S. Constitution, for example, is not only a set of rules for conducting politics; it is also considered a sacred symbol of what makes the United States unique and powerful. Is it difficult to modify the Constitution because of the procedures involved, or because a resistance has developed over time to tinkering with this "sacred" document? If the latter is true, then it is not simply rational-legal legitimacy but also traditional legitimacy that binds American politics together.

To summarize, legitimacy is a central component of stateness. Traditional legitimacy stresses ritual and continuity; charismatic legitimacy, the force of ideas as embodied in a leader; rational-legal legitimacy, laws and rules. Whatever its form, legitimacy makes it possible for the state to carry out its basic functions. Without it, states find it very difficult to function. If the public has little faith in the state, it will frequently ignore political responsibilities, such as paying taxes, abiding by regulations, or serving in the armed forces. Under these conditions, the state has only one tool left to maintain order: the threat of force. While we might assume that violent states are somehow inherently powerful, states that use the most coercion against their citizens are often the most weakly institutionalized; without violence they cannot get the public to willingly comply with the rules and duties they have set forth.

Centralization or Decentralization

In addition to enjoying various kinds and levels of political legitimacy, states are defined by different distributions of power. Individual freedom is typically associated with the decentralization of power, whereas collective equality usually accompanies a greater centralization of power.

State power can be centralized or decentralized in a couple of different ways, the first of which is the dispersal of power within the state. Under **federalism**, powers such as taxation, lawmaking, and security are devolved to regional bodies (such as states in the United States and India, *Länder* in Germany, and provinces in Canada) and to local legislatures that control specific territories within the country. These powers are defined in the national constitution and therefore cannot be easily constricted or eliminated by any government. Here the argument is that federalism helps represent local interests as well as check the growth of central power (which may be viewed as a threat to democracy). We should note that federalism need not be uniform; some countries, like Russia and India, rely on **asymmetric federalism**, whereby power is divided unevenly between regional bodies. Some regions are given greater power over taxation or language rights than others, a more likely outcome in a country with significant ethnic divisions. In **unitary states**, by contrast, political power is concentrated at the national level, and local authority is limited. The central government is responsible for most areas of policy. Territorial divisions in unitary states like China, Japan, and France have less bearing on political power. If federalism reflects a view that overcentralization is unrepresentative or dangerous, the argument for a unitary state is that local interests can be well represented without recourse to regional political institutions. Federalism may weaken state efficiency by dispersing power among too many competing authorities and exacerbate, rather than weaken, ethnic or regional conflict.

In recent years, there has been a greater tendency toward decentralization in many states. This process, called **devolution**, has become popular for a number of reasons. In some cases, devolution has been viewed as a way to increase state legitimacy by moving political power closer to the people, a concern as states have grown larger and more complex over time. In other cases, devolution has been seen as a way to resolve problems like ethnic or religious differences by giving greater local powers to regions. This has sometimes meant the elimination of unitary government. In 2005, Iraq became a federal country for the first time in its history. Nepal abolished its monarchy in 2008 and in 2015 adopted a new federal constitution with seven provinces. Often devolution does not lead to outright federalism but nevertheless results in a significant movement of power downward from the central state. We will speak more about devolution in subsequent chapters.

Power, Autonomy, and Capacity

At the most basic level, we can make a distinction between **strong states** and **weak states**. Strong states are those that are able to fulfill basic tasks: defend their territory, make and enforce rules and rights, collect taxes, and manage the economy, to name a few. In contrast, weak states cannot execute such tasks very well. Rules are haphazardly applied, if at all; tax evasion and other forms of public noncompliance are widespread; armed rivals to the state, such as rebel movements, organized crime, or even other states, may control large chunks of territory or the economy. State officials themselves, having little faith in their offices or responsibilities, may use their jobs simply to fill their own pockets through corruption and theft. Economic development is certain to be much lower as a result of this unstable political environment. In general, weak states are not well institutionalized and lack authority and legitimacy. At an extreme, the very structures of the state may become so weak that they break down. When this occurs, a country is commonly termed a fragile or, at a more severe level, a **failed state** (see Table 2.1).[13] Before 2001, Afghanistan was typically viewed as a failed state, and it remains one today, with only limited power that must be backed up by international force. But a failed state does not necessarily mean complete anarchy. The writ of the state may run in large cities but not the countryside, in places where one ethnic group is dominant but not another, or in wealthy regions as opposed to poor ones. Indeed, in even the most wealthy countries there are areas where the state is thin on the ground, like poor neighborhoods where crime is high and public services are lacking. States can fail to different degrees, in different areas, and in different ways. (See "Institutions in Action" on pp. 54–55 for a discussion of Pakistan's slide toward state failure.)

In short, speaking of states as merely weak or strong fails to capture the complexity of state power. In fact, we get stuck in a loop of circular logic if we simply argue that if a state can do something it must be strong and if it can't it must be weak. American elected officials can wage large-scale wars around the globe but can't significantly restrict gun ownership, whereas in Canada just the opposite is true. Which one, then, is weak or strong? Comparative politics builds on the categories of weak and strong states through the use of two other terms: *capacity* and *autonomy*. **Capacity** is the ability of the state to wield power in order to carry out the basic tasks of providing security and reconciling freedom and equality. A state with high capacity is able to formulate and enact fundamental policies and ensure stability and security for both itself and its citizens. A state with low capacity is unable to do these things effectively. High capacity requires not just money but also organization, legitimacy, and effective leadership. Roads get paved, schools get built, regulations are created and followed, and those who break the law are tried and punished.

In contrast, **autonomy** is the ability of the state to wield its power independently of the public or international actors. This is closely related to the idea of sovereignty. In the case of sovereignty, we are speaking of a state's formal and legal independence. In the case of autonomy, we are speaking of the informal, practical ability to act on that independence. In other words, if an autonomous state wishes to carry out a

TABLE 2.1

FRAGILE STATES INDEX, 2019

RANK	COUNTRY	SECURITY APPARATUS	FACTIONALIZED ELITES	GROUP GRIEVANCE	ECONOMIC DECLINE AND POVERTY	UNEVEN ECONOMIC DEVELOPMENT
1	Yemen	10.0	10.0	9.6	9.7	8.1
2	Somalia	9.6	10.0	8.9	8.8	9.4
3	South Sudan	9.7	9.7	9.4	9.8	8.9
4	Syria	9.8	9.9	10.0	8.8	7.5
5	Congo (D.R.)	8.8	9.8	10.0	8.3	8.6
6	Central African Republic	8.6	9.4	8.3	8.7	9.9
7	Chad	9.5	9.8	8.2	9.0	9.0
8	Sudan	8.4	9.7	10.0	8.1	7.7
9	Afghanistan	10.0	8.6	7.8	8.6	7.5
10	Zimbabwe	8.8	10.0	6.7	8.1	7.9
11	Guinea	8.6	9.6	9.1	8.6	7.3
12	Haiti	7.2	9.3	5.9	8.4	9.2
13	Iraq	8.7	9.6	8.8	5.9	6.7
14	Nigeria	9.0	9.9	9.4	7.8	8.1
15	Burundi	8.6	7.9	7.9	8.4	7.2
16	Cameroon	8.5	9.6	8.5	6.5	7.5
17	Eritrea	6.6	8.1	7.7	7.7	8.4
18	Niger	8.7	8.9	7.7	7.1	8.0
19	Guinea-Bissau	8.3	9.6	4.9	7.7	9.2
20	Uganda	7.5	8.9	8.3	6.3	7.0

Note: Areas are ranked on a 10-point scale, where 10 represents the worst conditions. Countries may share rankings. Brief definitions for each indicator are as follows: *Security Apparatus*: Security threats from inside and outside of the state; *Factionalized Elites*: Elite fragmentation along such divisions as ethnicity, class, or religion; *Group Grievance*: Schisms between different groups in society over access to the state; *Economic Decline and Poverty*: Patterns of economic hardship; *Uneven Economic Development*: Levels of inequality; *Human Flight and Brain Drain*: Human displacement for economic or political reasons; *State Legitimacy*: Representativeness and

Source: The Fund for Peace, http://fragilestatesindex.org/data (accessed 10/3/19).

Top 20 Fragile States

HUMAN FLIGHT AND BRAIN DRAIN	STATE LEGITIMACY	PUBLIC SERVICES	HUMAN RIGHTS AND RULE OF LAW	DEMOGRAPHIC PRESSURES	REFUGEES AND INTERNALLY DISPLACED PERSONS	EXTERNAL INTERVENTION
7.3	9.8	9.8	9.9	9.7	9.6	10.0
9.2	9.0	9.4	9.3	10.0	9.4	9.2
6.5	10.0	9.8	9.3	9.7	10.0	9.4
8.4	9.9	9.4	10.0	7.9	10.0	10.0
7.0	9.4	9.2	9.6	9.8	10.0	9.7
7.1	9.1	10.0	9.5	9.1	10.0	9.2
8.5	9.6	9.1	8.8	9.5	9.5	8.0
8.3	9.8	8.6	9.4	9.4	9.6	8.9
7.8	9.0	9.8	7.9	9.3	9.6	9.1
7.3	9.4	8.6	8.2	9.0	8.2	7.3
7.1	9.8	9.2	7.1	8.6	7.6	6.8
8.4	8.8	9.2	7.2	8.7	7.4	9.6
7.1	8.9	8.7	8.1	8.4	9.1	9.1
6.9	8.0	8.9	8.3	9.2	7.2	5.9
6.0	9.0	8.2	9.0	9.1	8.4	8.4
7.5	9.2	8.2	7.7	8.3	8.3	7.2
8.9	9.4	7.8	8.7	8.4	7.7	7.0
7.6	7.3	9.3	6.8	8.8	8.3	7.8
7.5	8.9	8.9	7.2	8.5	6.7	8.0
7.3	8.6	7.8	8.0	9.0	9.1	7.5

openness of government; *Public Services*: Presence of basic state functions and public goods; *Human Rights and Rule of Law*: Respect for fundamental freedoms; *Demographic Pressures*: Impact of population or environmental pressures on state capacity; *Refugees and Internally Displaced Persons*: Impact of forced displacements of large communities; *External Intervention*: Impact of external actors in functioning of state.

policy or an action, it can do so without having to consult the public or worry about strong public or international opposition that might force it to reverse its decision. A state with a high degree of autonomy may act on behalf of the public, pursuing what it believes are the best interests of the country, irrespective of public opinion. A state with a low degree of autonomy will act largely at the behest of private individuals, groups, or other states and will be less able to act contrary to public opinion or the demands of well-organized groups. Scholars sometimes describe states with low autonomy as "captured" by certain interests that control specific issues or policies.

The concepts of capacity and autonomy help us to evaluate differences in state power. Strong states with a high degree of capacity and autonomy may be able to execute major policies relatively easily. A case in point is China's infrastructure, including new roads, rails, and dams, which it has been able to construct despite technical challenges, enormous cost, and sometimes domestic opposition. High capacity and autonomy, however, may come at the expense of individual freedom

IN FOCUS: State Autonomy and Capacity

	HIGH AUTONOMY	**LOW AUTONOMY**
HIGH CAPACITY	State is able to fulfill basic tasks with a minimum of public intervention; power highly centralized; strong state.	State is able to fulfill basic tasks, but public plays a direct role in determining policy and is able to limit state power and scope of activity.
	Danger: Too high a level of capacity and autonomy may prevent or undermine democracy.	Danger: State may be unable to develop new policies or respond to new challenges owing to the power of organized opposition.
LOW CAPACITY	State is able to function with a minimum of public interference or direct control, but its capacity to fulfill basic tasks is limited.	State lacks the ability to fulfill basic tasks and is subject to direct public control and interference; power highly decentralized among state and nonstate actors; weak state.
	Danger: State is ineffectual, limiting development, and slow development may provoke public unrest.	Danger: Too low a level of capacity and autonomy may lead to internal state failure.

(though this is not always the case). By contrast, states with high capacity but lower autonomy may have widespread powers but are more subject to public intervention. The United States and Canada are good examples of states with lower autonomy, facilitated by federalism. Individual freedom may be high, but this can constrain central authority and consequently hinder national policy making. States with high autonomy but low capacity, meanwhile, may have few limits on their decision making but lack the ability to realize policies effectively. Russia falls into this category; during the last decade the state has become more centralized and autonomous, but it still does not have the capacity to successfully promulgate and enforce regulations.

Finally, states may be weak in both autonomy and capacity. This is true of many developing countries that have been "captured" by elites or certain ethnic or religious groups and are largely unable to fulfill important national tasks, like encouraging economic development and ensuring public education.

In short, speaking of state power in terms of autonomy and capacity can help us better understand stateness: what states are and are not able to do, and why. However, we should note that the degree of a state's autonomy and capacity may vary widely depending on the issue at hand. An observer of China may conclude that this state enjoys high autonomy and capacity. However, China's corruption can also suggest that its autonomy and capacity are in some ways circumscribed. Japan's state capacity was long seen as a model for successful development, but its ongoing economic difficulties and inability to reform its economy raise questions in this regard. Brazil's Bolsa Família, a novel and ambitious social welfare program, helped dramatically reduce poverty. Yet at the same time, the country has been unable to bring to heel organized crime and rogue police forces that virtually function as a parallel state.[14] Autonomy and capacity, therefore, are useful concepts for comparing states, but the degree to which an individual state possesses them depends on the issue or task at hand.

Finally, we are left with some big questions: Why are some states more centralized or decentralized? Why do they have more or less capacity or autonomy? Some of the answers lie in history, particularly the nature of international threats and how they have affected the relation between taxation (needed to pay for wars) and representation (how much say people have in how the state conducts itself). Cultural norms regarding freedom and equality may also play a role. For more recently founded states, however, such idiosyncratic and historical explanations are not particularly useful. Can one develop policies for countries like Afghanistan or Nigeria that would lead to more viable and effective states? Is there an ideal mix of different forms of legitimacy, centralization, autonomy, and capacity? Where does one start? Scholars and policy makers are often at odds over these issues, which we will take up in subsequent chapters.

INSTITUTIONS IN ACTION

Why Has Pakistan Slid toward State Failure?

Pakistan displays many of the hallmarks of a typical failing state. It is not just a problem of electricity, as we spoke of in the chapter opener. Other public services, like education and health care, are also lacking. The level of corruption is extremely high. The judicial system is unresponsive to the public, and the military and intelligence institutions appear unaccountable to government officials. The country suffers from the world's fifth-largest number of deaths from terrorism, and large swaths of the country's border with Afghanistan are not effectively under state control. The killing of Osama bin Laden, who had been living for several years in a home in Pakistan, raised serious questions inside and outside the country: Were segments of the Pakistani military or intelligence involved in sheltering him, or were they unaware of his presence? Many of Pakistan's issues of state capacity and autonomy are not unique; however, they are of particular concern to the international community because Pakistan supports guerrilla and terrorist activity in Afghanistan and India and possesses nuclear weapons.

The broad problem, as numerous scholars have expressed, is that a failing Pakistani state may also be an "irrational" one. Many scholars assume that states are "rational" in the sense that they focus primarily on national security. However, this also assumes that governments are able to coordinate with and control their states. Without some centralized authority, rationality may give way as different segments of the state pursue contradictory and competing goals. Because central authority is weak, Pakistan lacks the ability to gain control over the violence that occurs within its borders. Terrorist attacks have been frequent, and in some regions the state has lost much of its territorial sovereignty. At the same time, the country's armed forces are fragmented and lack a clear chain of civilian or military authority. Such state fragmentation can breed risky behavior, as individual leaders or segments of the state vie for power or their own short-term interests. There is clear evidence that military and intelligence forces in Pakistan have supported terrorist attacks inside India, which have on several occasions brought the two countries to the brink of war. In addition, while the United States views Pakistan as a key ally in its war against the Taliban, it is evident that the Taliban finds support among elements inside the Pakistani state. Most worrisome, it is unclear who has effective control over Pakistan's nuclear weapons or how secure these weapons are. Although until recently Pakistan was one of the top recipients of U.S. foreign aid, there is little sign that this aid did much to stop the erosion of Pakistan's state capacity.

How did Pakistan end up this way? This is quite puzzling, especially when we compare Pakistan with its neighbor, India. In 1947, as India gained independence from British rule, Muslim leaders demanded their own independent state of Pakistan so that they would not be a perpetual minority under Hindu rule in India. On independence both countries faced similar kinds of opportunities and problems, including poverty, weak states, linguistic and regional differences, and democratic institutions inherited from the British.

If anything, Pakistan would seem to have had more potential—it was built on a common religious identity and was wealthier than India. Yet now Pakistan's per capita GDP (gross domestic product) is lower than India's, with a weaker state that has experienced military rule for most of its history. Perhaps we have constructed our puzzle in the wrong way: that Pakistan would succumb to military rule and state failure is not the mystery, as this has been the fate of many poor countries. Perhaps the puzzle is why India escaped this trap.

There are some institutional factors, though, that scholars believe help explain Pakistan's trajectory. First, while the Indian state attained independence with limited disruption, inheriting British colonial institutions, in the newly created Pakistan a state had to be constructed largely from scratch. Second, Pakistan's birth was almost immediately followed by a war with much larger India over disputed territory. This subsequently led to an emphasis on building a new state with a strong military force, which ultimately became stronger than the government. Finally, the initial ruling party, the Muslim League, had been built around the struggle for Indian independence; after this goal was accomplished, it lacked strong leadership and a set of ideological values on which to institutionalize a new regime. This combination of a weak state, regime, and government left the military a powerful but largely unaccountable force, and it became the primary institution of sovereign power and national identity. In the absence of accountability, the Pakistani military

Public support for Pakistan's Inter-Services Intelligence (ISI) agency is high, though many observers believe it is directly connected to the Taliban, Al Qaeda, and Pakistan's nuclear program.

has continued to grow and has helped sponsor conflict in Afghanistan and India in part to justify its dominance. At its core, the state is a monopoly of violence, but without nonmilitary political institutions, this monopoly can be just as destabilizing as its absence.[a]

1. In what way has Pakistan struggled to meet the definition of a state (and thus might be considered failing)?

2. What kinds of political institutions does Pakistan lack (or have weak versions of)? How has this led to continued military rule?

3. What is meant by describing Pakistan as an "irrational" state?

In Sum: Studying States

This chapter began by defining the state as a monopoly of force but also as the set of institutions charged with transforming freedom and equality from ideas into concrete action. The kinds of decisions made toward this end are shaped by regimes and governments. Regimes are the fundamental rules and norms of politics, providing long-term goals regarding individual freedom and collective equality and scaffolding where power is located and how it should be used. Governments, in contrast, are the political elites in charge of running the state. Influenced and constrained by the existing regime, they attempt to formulate policy that may then be executed by the state. These represent the most basic facets of states everywhere—and, indeed, states are everywhere. Although similar political organizations have existed for thousands of years, only within the past few centuries did modern states arise in Europe and quickly come to dominate the globe. States are the main political players in the world today.

The universal presence of states, and variations in their stateness, compel comparativists to find some way to study and evaluate them. One way is by assessing their legitimacy; different kinds of legitimacy—traditional, charismatic, and rational-legal—create their own kinds of authority and power. The other is by assessing the dispersal of power; states may be weaker or stronger, with more or less capacity and autonomy, depending on how power is distributed within each state and between the state and the public. Too much power in the hands of the state risks tyranny; too little power risks instability. Finding the right mix is not simply a technical question but one that shapes how states and societies reconcile freedom and equality. This debate over freedom and equality ranges far beyond the boundaries of the state itself. As we shall see in the chapters that follow, it is influenced by ethnic and national identity, by culture and ideology, by economic institutions and the interaction between states and markets, and by democratic and nondemocratic practices.

Since the dawn of humanity, people have relied on some form of political organization to construct a relationship between individual freedom and collective equality. For the past few centuries, modern states have been the dominant expression of that relation. We might thus conclude that states now represent an end point in human intellectual and organizational evolution. But why should this be so? It seems logical that in the future new forms of political organization will displace states, just as states displaced empires, city-states, and other institutions. Perhaps challenges to states—environmental, economic, or cultural—will overwhelm many of them, and old political forms, like empires and city-states, will reappear in response. Or perhaps technological innovation will make old forms of political centralization weak or irrelevant, changing or making irrelevant the idea of sovereignty. Perhaps the core debate over freedom and equality will be radically reconsidered, changing the very nature of politics as we understand it. These questions may seem unanswerable, more amenable to fortune-telling than to research. But as we shall see, they lie at the heart of ideas and conflicts that have transformed the world in the past and may dominate our future.

Key Terms

asymmetric federalism (p. 48)
autonomy (p. 49)
capacity (p. 49)
charismatic legitimacy (p. 45)
country (p. 35)
devolution (p. 48)
failed state (p. 49)
federalism (p. 48)
government (p. 34)

legitimacy (p. 44)
rational-legal legitimacy (p. 45)
regime (p. 33)
sovereignty (p. 31)
state (p. 31)
strong state (p. 48)
traditional legitimacy (p. 44)
unitary state (p. 48)
weak state (p. 48)

For Further Reading

Brown, Archie. *The Myth of the Strong Leader: Political Leadership in the Modern Age.* New York: Basic Books, 2014.

Fukuyama, Francis. *The Origins of Political Order: From Prehuman Times to the French Revolution.* New York: Farrar, Straus and Giroux, 2011.

Gilley, Bruce. *The Right to Rule: How States Win and Lose Legitimacy.* New York: Columbia University Press, 2009.

Landes, David S. *The Wealth and Poverty of Nations: Why Some Are So Rich and Some So Poor.* New York: W. W. Norton, 1999.

Maddison, Angus. *Contours of the World Economy, 1–2030 AD: Essays in Macro-Economic History.* New York: Oxford University Press, 2007.

Tilly, Charles. *Coercion, Capital, and European States: AD 990–1990.* Oxford: Blackwell, 1990.

Turchin, Peter. *Ultrasociety: How 10,000 Years of War Made Humans the Greatest Cooperators on Earth.* Chaplin, CT: Beresta Books, 2016.

Weber, Max. "Politics as a Vocation," in *From Max Weber: Essays in Sociology*, edited and translated by H. H. Gerth and C. Wright Mills. New York: Oxford University Press, 1946.

INQUIZITIVE

Earn a better grade on your test. InQuizitive personalizes your learning path to help you master the concepts from this chapter and practice applying them to examples from the text and beyond (see back cover).

QUESTIONS AND METHODS

How Do We Measure Stateness?

We spent a great deal of time in this chapter talking about stateness—that is to say, the relative power of the state. We also noted that scholars will often break down state power into different components, in particular autonomy and capacity, to understand the difference between the relative distance between the state and the public and the ability of states to accomplish the tasks they set before themselves. State capacity is of particular interest to policy makers worldwide because much basic human development hinges on it. The assumption is that without states to provide security and basic public services, human development is challenging if not impossible. A look at the quality of life in countries with very weak or failed states is strong evidence for this.

If policy makers are interested in studying and hopefully improving capacity, one important first step would be to measure it. But how? One obvious and commonly used way to measure capacity is to look at state outputs, like education or physical infrastructure. This would seem to be relatively straightforward, but even here making comparisons can get problematic. Does a country with an extensive commuter rail system have greater, or more effective, state capacity than one that relies on roads and private transportation? Does a country with low rates of crime exhibit a strong legal system and effective police? Or could it be the case that common drivers of criminal activity, like inequality or poverty, are low?

If the output approach to measuring states is problematic, then another way in which we can think about this is to distinguish, as Francis Fukuyama has done, between *strength* and *scope*.[a] This can be seen in the figure at left. *Strength* here captures our earlier discussion of capacity—the ability to plan and execute policy. But in addition, Fukuyama argues that it is important to consider scope. Scope

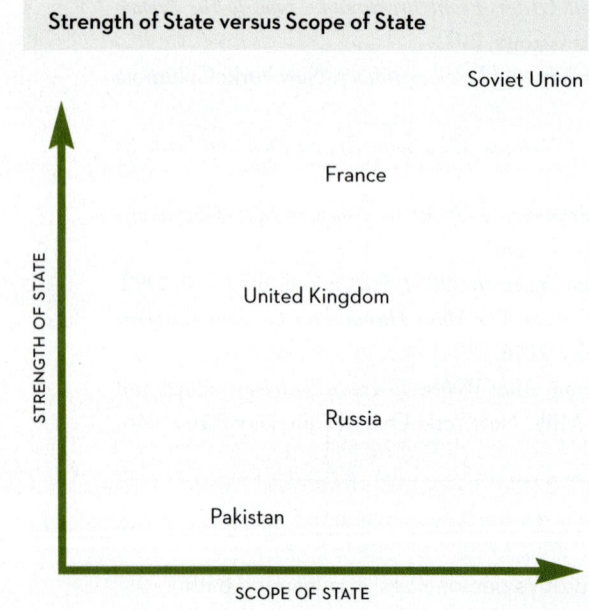

Strength of State versus Scope of State

means the goals and functions that a state takes on in the first place, such as health care or business regulation. States differ dramatically in their scope, depending on their regime. Some have a capacious sense of their mandate; others are more limited.

The Soviet Union was a powerful state with a wide scope, and it essentially eliminated most aspects of personal freedom and private property. In contrast, its successor state, Russia, is far more limited in both areas, in part by choice, and in part as a result of weakened institutions. The British state, while relatively powerful, has a more limited scope than many other European states, which is a function of its liberal regime. By thinking about stateness in terms of strength and scope, we can compare not just what states are able to do, but what their regimes and governments believe is the ideal role of the state.

1. *Articulate ways in which particular concepts can be evaluated*

What are some of the ways that a comparativist could measure state strength? What about scope?

2. *Consider the implications of variables on political institutions*

If a country had a high level of scope but low strength, what would that look like in practical terms? What impact would that have on state legitimacy?

3. *Generate new questions and assertions*

Where would you place the United States in terms of scope and strength? Has this changed over the past few decades? If so, why and how?

---

a. Francis Fukuyama, "The Imperative of State-Building," *Journal of Democracy* 15, no. 2 (April 2004): 17–31.

3

Indian police march at celebrations for India's newest federal state, Telangana, which was created in 2014. The establishment of a new state is one example of how countries manage diverse cultural identities.

NATIONS AND SOCIETY

How do people organize themselves into political communities?

In the previous chapter we addressed the question of why Pakistan has been unable to institutionalize democracy and has slid toward state failure. In that discussion, we made some comparisons with India because the two states were part of a single country under British rule until 1947. Both countries faced similar challenges, including poverty, ethnic diversity, a weak state, and linguistic and regional differences. In fact, in a number of these areas it can be argued that India was at a greater disadvantage.

On independence, India was forced to contend with several major religious divisions, including those between Hindus, Muslims, Christians, and Sikhs; at least 10 major languages; hundreds, if not thousands, of caste divisions (hereditary classes); and the sheer size of the country, the seventh largest in the world geographically and the second largest in population (then and now). In the course of partition, approximately 15 million people moved between India and Pakistan, a situation that led to hundreds of thousands of deaths from ethnic and religious violence.

Following partition, India continued to face internal threats to its stability and sovereignty. For example, jurisdiction of the Indian state of Jammu and Kashmir was contested by Pakistan because of the state's overwhelmingly Muslim population. Many Indian Kashmiris have continued to seek greater autonomy within India, unification with Pakistan, or outright independence. Adherents of the Sikh religion (established in India in the fifteenth century) similarly agitated for greater rights and complained of discrimination in the Hindu-majority country. This revolt eventually culminated in a separatist movement for an independent Sikh state and a violent conflict between government forces and Sikh separatists in the 1980s. After that uprising was crushed, India's Prime Minister Indira Gandhi was assassinated by her own Sikh bodyguards. Although Sikh separatism has abated, violent conflict, both backed by and directed toward the Muslim community, has increased. In the past two decades, riots and acts of terrorism have left several thousand dead. Hindu nationalism has also increased, led by the ruling Bharatiya Janata Party (BJP), which has been associated with anti-Muslim violence.

Yet in spite of these difficulties, India not only has been able to stay intact, it has been willing and able to devolve power to an ever greater number of federal states, often along ethnic lines. In 1956 India had only 14 full-fledged states; as of 2019, it had 29, having added the newest, Telangana, in 2014. Why has India experienced so much devolution, and to what effect?

Instead of founding India on a strong, unified national identity, on independence the country's leaders attempted to accommodate as many religious, ethnic, and cultural differences as possible. Indian identity in the new constitution was built around citizenship rather than ethnicity. English, alongside Hindi, was established as a national language of government, allowing for greater integration while not giving any single Indian language political dominance. Religious holidays for all major groups were officially recognized. To meet local demands, a system of asymmetric federalism (see Chapter 2) devolved power differently across states. Finally, central executive and legislative institutions were set up in a manner that decreased the chance that any one group could come to dominate. As a result, some scholars have concluded that India has managed to encourage multiple and complementary identities that have strengthened, not weakened, democracy. Rather than a nation-state, India can be seen as a state-nation, in which multiple nations are given varying degrees of autonomy under one central state.[1] This structure is quite the opposite of Pakistan, where the state has not succeeded in effectively drawing diverse groups into a functioning political system. These explanations are valuable in solving the puzzle of India's national and democratic success but also raise questions as to how states might craft institutions to prevent or resolve ethnic and national conflict.

However, we should not conclude that India's solution is perfect. As we noted, regional, ethnic, and national conflicts continue in India, and it can be argued that religious conflict in particular between Hindus and Muslims has intensified over time. Hindu nationalists resent the fact that Hindu identity is not the core national identity, and many Muslims feel disenfranchised from Indian democracy because of this growing Hindu nationalism and Muslims' continuing exclusion from economic and political power. In 2019 the Indian government in fact eliminated certain autonomous powers that Kashmir had enjoyed since the 1950s, leading to widespread protests and violence.

Finally, the ongoing devolution of power acts as a significant check on central state power. Though we might assume automatically that this is a positive component of democracy, it also can create barriers to implementing national policies, a task at which India falls short. Until recently, India contended with a variety of tariffs between states, requiring border checkpoints that undercut productivity and trade. What is the proper balance between devolution, autonomy, and capacity? In a country with major ambitions and significant deficiencies, this is no small concern. We will return to this issue at the end of the chapter in the "Institutions in Action" section when we look at the case of federalism in Nepal.

LEARNING OBJECTIVES

- Understand different types of identities and their social and political effects.
- Summarize the history and causes of ethnic and national conflict.
- Compare and contrast political ideologies and attitudes.

Society is a broad term that refers to complex human organization, a collection of people bound by shared institutions that define how human relations should be conducted. From country to country and place to place, societies differ in how individuals define themselves and their relationships to one another, to government, and to the state. Each relationship is unique; for all the surface similarities that may exist between societies, each country views itself and the wider world around it in a distinct way. These differences make comparative politics a rich field of study but also a frustrating one, as social scientists seek to find similarities that are often few and far between.

In this chapter, we look at the ways people identify themselves and are identified, both as individuals and as groups, and how these identifications relate to politics and the state. We will start with the concepts of ethnic and national identity, two of the most basic ways that individuals and groups define themselves. What does it mean to be part of an ethnic group? How is such a group defined? What is the difference between an ethnic group and a nation? We will also make distinctions between ethnicity, nationality, and citizenship. A related question arises in the distinction between nationalism and patriotism: What is the difference between being patriotic and being nationalist? We will answer these questions by looking at some examples and tracing their historical origins. Throughout recent history, the world has seen violent domestic and international conflicts connected to national and ethnic identities. Why do such conflicts occur? Are they a natural and inevitable part of human organization, or are such conflicts manufactured by political leaders to serve their own purposes? In this chapter, we will also look at some of the effects of conflict between different ethnic and national identities.

From there, we will move on to a discussion of political attitudes and ideologies. Whereas ethnicity, nationality, and citizenship are group identities, political attitudes and ideologies are the values individuals hold and the positions they take regarding freedom and equality. How should these values and positions be reconciled and to what end? One thing we will see is that although there are only a few basic political attitudes and ideologies, which can be broadly compared across countries or regions, their relative strength or influence differs dramatically from country to country. We'll discuss why this is the case.

Before moving ahead, we should ask whether identities like ethnicity, nationality, or ideology are a fixed part of our nature. Scholars have answered this question in different ways. At one end, many social scientists argue that identities exist independent of any biological functions and are a set of "social constructions" that have emerged largely in the modern era. At the other end, many evolutionary psychologists emphasize the role that biological functions (such as kin recognition and genetic similarity) have played in building human identities for tens of thousands of years.[2] These views appear diametrically opposed, and their supporters are often dismissive of each other. But there clearly is room for integration—a view that not only recognizes an underlying human instinct to sort groups by preference and to elevate one over another but also notes how modern politics has helped shape that instinct into particular political identities. Whatever their approach, social scientists have grown skeptical that ethnicity or nationalism will become a thing of the past or that collective identities will somehow no longer be a central part of defining who we are. Let us consider some of the most powerful societal institutions that shape comparative politics.

Ethnic Identity

People identify themselves in many ways. One way is by ethnicity, as when they speak of themselves as German or Irish, Kurdish or Zulu, Latino or Ukrainian Canadian. When we use the term **ethnic identity** or **ethnicity**, we emphasize a person's relation to other members of society. Ethnic identity is a set of institutions that bind people together through a common culture. These institutions can include language, religion, geographic location, customs, appearance, and history, among other things. As these distinct attributes are institutionalized, they become signifiers of a group's shared identity. This process is called *ascription*—the assigning of a particular quality at birth. People do not choose their ethnicities; they are born into them, and their ethnic identity remains largely stable throughout life, though the borders between ethnic groups may be more blurry than we think. Ethnicity provides social solidarity and can generate greater equality as well. Groups with a high degree of ethnic solidarity may be more willing to redistribute resources within the group and, conversely, less willing to share resources with groups that are ethnically different. Related research has focused on the relationship between trust, inequality, and ethnic diversity.[3]

Each ethnic group is characterized by a set of institutions that embody norms and standards of behavior, and a single society can be broken up into numerous ethnic groups. For example, Singaporean society is made up of ethnic Chinese, Malays, and Indians. Most countries in the world are not ethnically homogeneous; rarely are society and ethnicity one and the same. Societies are made up of various ethnic groups—in some cases only a few, in other cases tens or even hundreds—each with its own identity, as in the case of India. It is important to note that ethnicity is at its core a social, not a political, identity. People may identify with an ethnic group without drawing any particular conclusions about politics on that basis. Ethnicity and the solidarity it provides are not inherently political, though they can become so.

Although we have looked at a number of attributes that often define ethnic differences, there is no master list of differences that automatically distinguish one group as ethnically different from another. In Bosnia, for example, the main ethnic groups—Croats, Serbs, and Muslims—speak the same language and are similar in numerous other ways. What divides Bosnians is primarily religion: Croats are mostly Roman Catholic, Serbs are Eastern Orthodox Christian, and Muslims practice Islam. Yet we speak of Germans as a single ethnic group, even though many are traditionally Catholic and others Protestant. Why are ethnic groups in Bosnia divided by religion, while in Germany such divisions don't produce different ethnic groups? In an even more confusing case, that of Rwanda, the Hutu and Tutsi ethnic groups cannot be easily distinguished by any of the factors we have discussed. Both groups speak the same language, practice the same religions, live in the same geographic regions, and share the same customs. To most outside observers, there is no real ethnic difference between the two, and even Hutus and Tutsis cannot easily distinguish between one another, since they rely

> **IN FOCUS**
>
> ## Ethnic Identity Is...
>
> - A set of specific attributes and societal institutions that makes one group of people culturally different from others.
> - Often based on customs, language, religion, or other factors.
> - Ascriptive, generally assigned at birth.
> - Not inherently political.

on such vague distinctions as differences in diet. But we cannot say that ethnicity is therefore a fiction because it has no single, neat origin. Ethnicity exists when people acknowledge and are acknowledged by outsiders as belonging to a distinct group. In Rwanda, even though ethnic distinctions between Hutus and Tutsis are unclear, ethnic conflict in the 1990s led to the deaths of several hundred thousand civilians. Rwanda shows us that, though ethnic distinctions may be difficult to observe, these ascriptive identities can have powerful effects.

National Identity

In contrast to ethnicity, which may be constructed in a unique manner from group to group and is not an inherently political concept, the idea of a **nation**—a group that desires self-government, often through an independent state—is largely consistent from case to case and is inherently political. If ethnic identity is a set of institutions that bind people together through a common culture, then **national identity** is an institution that binds people together through common political aspirations. Among these, the most important are self-government and sovereignty. National identity implies a demand for greater freedom through sovereignty, as when a colony revolts against its colonial master. It also involves a demand for equality, as when a secessionist movement argues that sovereignty would eliminate unequal treatment of one group by another. Pakistan's secession from India in 1947, Kosovo's declaration of independence from Serbia in 2008, and independence movements in Xinjiang and Tibet in China each reflect one group's aspirations toward greater freedom (from another, dominant group) and for equality with others in the international system (through the creation of a sovereign state).

As you can see, national identity often—but not always—develops from ethnic identity. For example, an ethnic group may chafe against the existing political system because its members may feel that they lack certain rights or freedoms. As a result, some leaders may argue that the ethnic group should have greater political control and that the group's interests would be better served if it controlled its own political destiny. The interaction between ethnicity and national identity can be seen in past developments in Canada. There the French-speaking population of the province of Québec constitutes its own ethnic group, quite distinct from the English-speaking citizens of the rest of Canada (as well as from its French ancestors). By the 1960s, this ethnicity began to develop into a sense of national identity as some in Québec argued for separation from Canada, where they saw themselves as a minority whose unique concerns were not being considered. Such arguments actually led to national referenda on the issue of secession in 1980 and 1995. In the latter case, Québec's proposal to secede failed by little more than 1 percent of the vote. Surveys still suggest that perhaps as many as one-third of French-speaking Québécois consistently support independence, and only a third feel very proud to call themselves Canadian (the national average is closer to 60 percent).[4]

National identity can create **nationalism**, a pride in one's people and the belief that they have a unique, sovereign political destiny. In Québec, we find people uncertain about whether they are just an ethnic group or also a nation—a group that desires self-government through an independent state. This lack of clarity between ethnicity and national identity is also evident in other groups, such as the Scots in the United Kingdom, who similarly held an unsuccessful referendum for independence in September 2014. In other words, although ethnic identity often leads to a political identity built on nationalism, this is not always the case. Just as groups can vary in the strength of their ethnic identification, people may also vary in the degree of their nationalism. Peruvians and South Africans have strong ethnic identification across numerous groups and at the same time a high degree of pride in their national identity; in the more homogeneous Germany and Japan, national pride is far lower, reflecting the disastrous results of extreme nationalism in both countries in the past.

If we can have ethnicity without national identity, can we have national identity without ethnicity? Must ethnicity always be the source of nationalism? At first glance, it would seem logical that without ethnicity there would be no foundation for national identity; people would lack a common source of solidarity and a set of institutions on which to build national pride. But like ethnicity, nationality lacks a "master list" of defining attributes. In the case of the United States, it is easy to conclude that there is no single American ethnic group. But is there an American

> **IN FOCUS**
>
> ## National Identity Is...
>
> - A sense of belonging to a nation (a group that desires self-government through an independent state) and a belief in its political aspirations.
> - Often (but not always) derived from ethnic identity.
> - Inherently political.
> - The basis for nationalism: pride in one's people and the belief that they have a unique political destiny.

nation? Some might say no, because nationalism is often assumed to require an ethnicity on which political aspirations can be built. Yet Americans are bound by certain common historical symbols, such as flags, anthems, a constitution, and common cultural values (recall our discussion of baseball in Chapter 1). The same could be said about Australia. Thus it could be argued that even in the face of great ethnic diversity, the United States and Australia are indeed nations whose people are bound together by, among other things, a sense of pride in certain democratic ideals. Some attempt to explain this difference by distinguishing between "civic" and "ethnic" nationalism. Finally, we should recognize that nationalism is not inherently bad, as is often believed. Nationalism carries within it a tension with those who are outside the group. But it can also be seen as a vehicle for much of what we consider modern civilization, a vehicle to extend trust and make commitments that will serve the larger community.

Citizenship and Patriotism

Our final form of identification is citizenship. So far, we have noted that ethnicity is not inherently political, although it may develop a political aspect through nationalism. At the other end of this spectrum, citizenship is a political identity developed not out of some unique set of circumstances or ascribed by birth but, rather, developed explicitly by states and accepted or rejected by individuals. **Citizenship** can be defined as an individual's or group's relation to the state; those who are citizens swear allegiance to that state, and the state in return is obligated to provide rights to those individuals or the members of that group. Citizenship can also convey certain obligations, such as the duty to serve in the armed forces or pay taxes. Citizens are therefore defined by their particular relation to one state rather than to one another.

IN FOCUS

Citizenship Is...

- An individual's relation to the state; citizens swear allegiance to the state, and the state in turn provides certain benefits or rights.
- Purely political and thus more easily changed than ethnic identity or national identity.
- The basis for patriotism: pride in one's state and citizenship.

Although citizenship is often gained at birth, it has qualities quite separate from those of ethnic or national identity.

Citizenship is a potentially more inclusive or flexible concept than national or ethnic identity. Like those two identities, however, citizenship can vary in clarity and power. Citizenship may confer a host of benefits, such as education and health care, or relatively few, depending on the state. In addition, one state may not necessarily grant citizenship to all those born in its territory, while another may allow citizenship in more than one country. Matters can be further complicated if citizenship is founded on ethnic or national identity. In an extreme example, in the 1950s, South Africa's apartheid regime created internal "homelands" for black persons as a means of stripping them of their South African citizenship. Many Palestinians lack any citizenship, living in areas under Israeli occupation or as refugees in nearby countries. The boundaries between citizenship and ethnic identity can be murky if the former is conditional on the latter.

Citizenship, in turn, can give rise to **patriotism**, or pride in one's state. People are patriotic when they have pride in their political system and seek to defend and promote it. When we think of patriotism, some of the things that may come to mind are flags, important historical events, wars, anthems—anything that people associate with politics and the state. It can be hard to separate the definitions of patriotism and nationalism. National identity is bound up in the quest for sovereignty, as is patriotism. As a result, the two can closely overlap. However, they can also be quite distinct: there may be a high degree of national identity without patriotism. Returning to the Palestinians, we can note that they have a strong sense of national identity but, for now, no state of their own—hence, the term *patriotism* is problematic with reference to their community. An ethnic minority's sense of nationalism may be confined to the political aspirations of its own members, and as a result that group may have a low level of patriotism—that is, of pride in their state, which they do not see as their own. The United States (along with India and Canada) may be a case where there is not one clear sense of nationalism, as we argued earlier, but rather strong patriotism that emphasizes pride in the state. Since patriotism emphasizes the state, those states that are weak or illegitimate often have difficulty instilling patriotism in their citizens. This situation makes tasks like defending the state in times of war very difficult. Being a citizen does not automatically make you patriotic, nor does a strong ethnic or national identity.

To sum up, ethnicity, nationality, and citizenship are institutions that define groups in different ways and that carry different political implications. Ethnic identity is built on social attributes, such as language or culture, that are unique to a group of people, whereas national identity implies political aspirations, specifically sovereignty. Although a dominant ethnic identity often leads to a national identity and nationalism, it does not always do so, nor does the absence of a dominant ethnicity necessarily prevent nationalism from developing. Finally, citizenship is an identity built on a relation to the state. As should be clear, none of these identities is exclusive; all of us possess different combinations of ethnicity, national identity, and citizenship, and each contributes to how we see the world and our role within it.

Ethnic Identity, National Identity, and Citizenship: Origins and Persistence

Now that we have distinguished among these three identities, it is worth considering their origins: Where did they come from and why do they exist? From our earlier discussion, we might assume that before the modern era people lacked clear identities. In truth, for thousands of years communities defined themselves by culture, language, and gods, often contrasting themselves with "barbarians"—people who were different and therefore, in their view, uncivilized. Some communities in Asia and the Middle East—China, for example—similarly viewed themselves as distinct from other communities. However, the specific concepts of ethnic and national identity are relatively recent, having emerged in Europe toward the end of the eighteenth century. Citizenship, too, has relatively recent origins; although the concept can be traced back to ancient Athens and to the Roman Empire, it disappeared with the fall of Rome, only resurfacing centuries later.

The emergence (or reemergence, in the case of citizenship) of these identities had much to do with the formation of the modern state.[5] As states took form in Europe in the fifteenth and sixteenth centuries, asserting sovereign control over people and territory, people could travel greater distances, enjoying the security provided by the state. This mobility in turn increased commerce, which was often centered near the city where the state leadership was based. These fortified capitals served as centers for trade, information, and new social relations. Such interaction in turn fostered increased homogeneity. Languages and dialects began to merge into common tongues, further standardized by the state through education and documentation. Common cultural and religious practices also developed, often created or supported by the state (as was the case during the Protestant Reformation in the sixteenth century). Local identities were often forcibly eradicated. Social institutions began to take shapes that were meaningful to most of a country's population. People could now identify themselves not only by village or profession, clan or tribe, but also, more abstractly, by the institutions they shared with many thousands of other people across space and time. These institutions formed the foundation for ethnic identity. People in turn slowly began to identify with each other primarily on the basis of these broad cultural institutions—as, for instance, German or French or English.

Growing ethnic identity was thus tightly connected to state development. Moreover, state leaders saw this development as something that could serve their own interests. By encouraging the formation of a single ethnic identity, the state could in turn claim that it existed to defend and promote the unique interests and values of its people. The state came to be portrayed as the institution that embodied the people's collective identity.

In the linked development of ethnic identity and of the state, we can see the seeds of national identity, which became a potent force in the eighteenth century. National identity, when added to ethnic identity, powerfully asserts that the state is legitimate because it is the defender of national values. Further, national identity unites the people and the state in the quest to chart an independent political future. The development and fusion of ethnic and national identities radically transformed states. Based on the idea that the people and their state were bound together in common cause, states could mobilize the public in ways never before possible. Most important, countries with a strong sense of nationalism could more easily raise mass armies and generate tax revenue because people would sacrifice their resources and very lives for the glory and destiny of their nation.

The thought that individuals would fight and die for an abstract political concept marked a radical change in human history. In Europe, Napoleonic France became the first country to use such nationalist sentiment to its own advantage, raising a huge volunteer army that would conquer much of Europe. Both threatened and inspired by such nationalist fervor, other European peoples and states in turn forged their own national identities and aspired to independence and self-government. This transformation gave rise to the idea of the **nation-state**, a sovereign state encompassing one dominant nation that it claims to embody and represent. Within a hundred years, most of the multiethnic empires that dominated Europe would be destroyed, replaced by nation-states controlled by distinct ethnic groups and political identities.

Finally, the development of ethnic and national identities paved the way for the concept of citizenship. As societies viewed themselves first in ethnic and then in national terms, their relation to the state began to change. If the state was the instrument of national will, some extended this logic to conclude that the state and its people must be bound by mutual accountability and obligation in the form of a social contract, as we mentioned in Chapter 2. How far citizenship should be extended and what rights it should entail have come to be central concerns for all societies and states.

With the rise of European imperial power, the institutions of ethnic and national identity and citizenship began to spread around the world. Just as states now lay claim to almost all the earth, so too have nearly all human beings become identified by some ethnicity, some nationality, or some form of citizenship. In some cases, this has been the foundation for political stability, economic development, and democracy; at the other extreme, where identities are weakly held or come into conflict, the result can be civil strife. Why these conflicts emerge and how to prevent them from becoming violent can be a matter of life and death.

Ethnic and National Conflict

Why are some countries able to forge consensus between groups with different ethnic and national identities, whereas in other countries such differences lead to seemingly irreconcilable conflict? Why is it that different identities can coexist peacefully and then suddenly clash? Political scientists have a range of often contending explanations for such forms of conflict, and the debate has intensified rapidly over the past two decades as ethnic and national conflicts have grown in number and intensity. Before discussing these debates, we should clarify our terms.

Ethnic conflict can be defined as conflict between ethnic groups that struggle to achieve certain political or economic goals at each other's expense. Each group may hope to increase its power by gaining greater control over existing political institutions like the state or government. By contrast, groups involved in **national conflict** seek to gain (or prevent the other from gaining) sovereignty, clashing with one another over issues of autonomy, such as the quest to form an independent state. In both of these cases, violence is a common tool for using, bypassing, or destroying the coercive powers of the state.

Around the world, we can find examples of ethnic and national conflict as well as cases where both are present. Afghanistan, for example, has seen frequent ethnic conflict that is not national; most Afghan groups are seeking not independence but greater power over each other. Ethnic conflict in Nigeria has similarly pitted rival ethnic groups against one another over contested presidential elections. In contrast, the American Revolution can be seen as a national rather than an ethnic conflict. The American colonies broke away from Great Britain to form a separate country, but this separation was based more on conflicts over political rights and the desire for sovereignty than on a strong "American" identity, which did not yet exist. And finally, conflicts can be both ethnic and national, such as those in Yugoslavia and the Soviet Union in the 1990s, where various ethnic groups seceded to create their own nation-states.

Why do such conflicts break out in the first place? Scholars emphasize different factors, which we can group by where they place the primary cause: society, the economy, or politics. Societal explanations tend to emphasize such issues as ethnic heterogeneity—the number of ethnic groups and their degree of integration or polarization. Economic explanations concentrate on the struggle for resources (natural or otherwise) between groups, as well as the general level of poverty across a country as a whole. Political explanations emphasize the state and regime, considering such factors as the relative capacity or autonomy of the state and the degree and form of democratic or nondemocratic regimes.

Of course, these three categories bleed into one another, and in the case of actual conflicts it can be hard to distinguish cause from effect. Still, we can see how each explanation can give us a way to think about ethnic and national conflict. For example, in Africa we see a great deal of ethnic heterogeneity, particularly across the central part of the continent, and these divisions correspond to several

---

IN FOCUS — Views of Ethnic and National Conflict

- Societal explanations emphasize such issues as ethnic heterogeneity.
- Economic explanations emphasize poverty and the struggle for natural or other resources.
- Political explanations emphasize state capacity or autonomy and the type of regime.

major conflicts, such as those in Nigeria, Kenya, and Sudan (see Figure 3.1). In a number of these cases, ethnic clashes are influenced by the presence of natural resources. The Congo is a horrific example. Although ethnic divisions were less pronounced there than in other countries, when ethnic conflict spilled over from Rwanda in the 1990s it sparked battles over gold and diamonds in a war that left between 2 and 5 million people dead—the worst conflict since World War II. Finally, political difficulties abound in much of Africa: borders drawn by

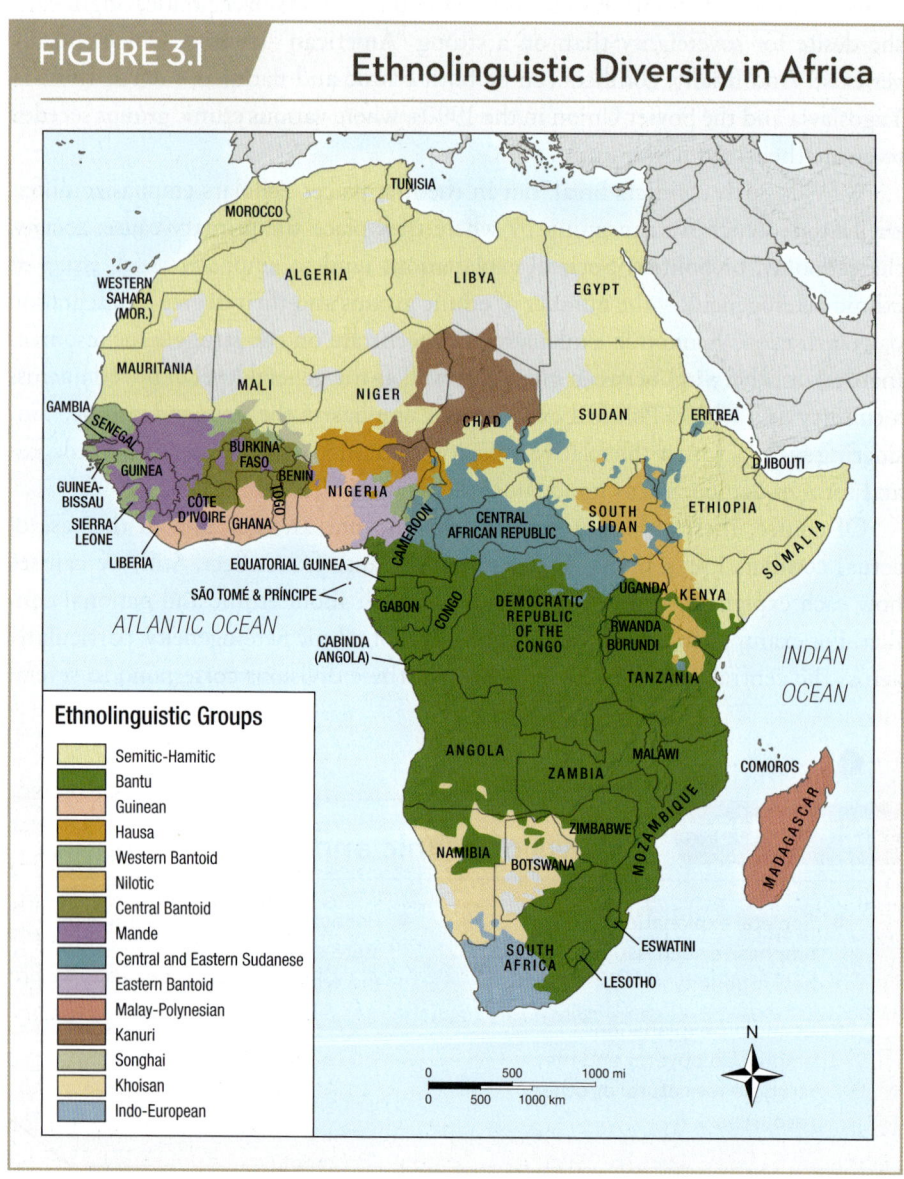

FIGURE 3.1 Ethnolinguistic Diversity in Africa

colonial powers that do not conform to major ethnic divisions; weak states that are often "captured" by one ruling ethnic group that benefits disproportionately from that control and dominates the military; and authoritarian systems that prevent effective participation or conciliation. Any one of these three factors can contribute to ethnic conflict, and when all are present they can create a dangerous dynamic.[6]

How do we prevent ethnic and national conflicts or bring them to an end? In part, this effort depends on the nature of the conflict, and whether the struggle is based on demands for greater equality or on some territorial demand, like autonomy or secession. It may be possible to create institutions that make most of the players feel that the political system is fair and serves their needs. One example of power sharing can be devolution; federal structures, asymmetric or otherwise, can provide groups with greater rights and autonomy. (See "Questions and Methods" on pp. 96–97 for a discussion of how political scientists measure the success of federalism in solving these conflicts.) Representative structures (such as presidencies or legislatures) and electoral systems could make a difference as well, something we will address in detail in Chapter 5.

However, not all scholars are convinced that power-sharing institutions, even when carefully crafted, necessarily resolve these problems. One concern is that such structures may "freeze," or institutionalize, group divisions and conflicts. The challenge, then, is to build institutions that can meet existing group demands while remaining flexible enough to foster cooperation and integration across these divides.[7]

Political Attitudes and Political Ideology

We have spent some time discussing ways that people's identities are shaped by their membership in larger ethnic or national groups. But such groups do not completely define our political identity. We also hold individual views regarding the ideal relation between freedom and equality. In the rest of this chapter, we will divide these views into two categories: political attitudes and political ideology. Political attitudes are concerned with the speed of political change and the methods used to achieve it. Political ideology comprises the basic values an individual holds about the fundamental goals of politics with respect to freedom and equality. Political attitudes are particularistic: they focus on the specific context of political change in a given country. By contrast, political ideologies are more universal, since they assume there is one ideal way to balance freedom and equality.

Where do political attitudes and ideologies come from? These views are not defined by birth or by the state, although they may be influenced by either. Nor are the boundaries between such views as clear or evident as are those that define ethnicity, national identity, or citizenship. At the same time, these views do not simply materialize out of thin air. Ideologies are built over time out of a set of ideas, and attitudes are articulated in response to the institutional conditions around us. More fundamentally, it may be that attitudes and ideologies—our individual or group preferences regarding freedom, equality, and the degree of change needed to achieve them—stem from basic human traits that balance our need to establish order and our need to embrace change. While our own political views may not be inherited, having such views in the first place is central to what makes us human.

Political Attitudes

Political attitudes describe views regarding the necessary pace and scope of change in the balance between freedom and equality. Attitudes are typically broken up into the categories of radical, liberal, conservative, and reactionary and are often arrayed on a spectrum from left to right.

Radicals are placed on the extreme left. **Radicals** believe in dramatic, often revolutionary change of the existing political, social, or economic order. Radicals believe that the current system is broken and cannot simply be improved or repaired; it must be scrapped in favor of a new order. As a result, most radicals do not believe in slow, evolutionary change. Politics will be improved, they believe, only when the entire political structure has been fundamentally transformed, remaking the political institutions of government, regime, and state. As a result, some radicals may be more inclined to favor violence as a necessary or unavoidable part of politics. The institutions of the old order, in some radicals' view, will not change willingly; they will have to be destroyed. Not all or even most radicals hold these views, however. Many argue that radical change can be achieved through peaceful means, by raising public consciousness and mobilizing mass support for wide-ranging change.

IN FOCUS

Political Attitudes Are . . .

- Concerned with the speed and methods of political change.
- Generally classified as radical, liberal, conservative, or reactionary.
- Particularistic: relative to the specific context of a given country. "Radical" in one country may be "conservative" in another.
- Distinct from political ideologies.

Liberals, like radicals, believe that much can be improved in the current political, social, and economic institutions, and liberals, too, support widespread change. However, instead of revolutionary transformation, **liberals** favor evolutionary change. In the liberal view, progressive change can happen through changes within the system; it does not require an overthrow of the system itself. Moreover, liberals part from radicals in their belief that existing institutions can be instruments of positive change. Liberals also believe that change can and sometimes must occur over a long period of time. They are skeptical that institutions can be replaced or transformed quickly and believe that only constant effort can create fundamental change.

Conservatives break with both radicals and liberals in their view of the necessity for change. Whereas radicals and liberals both advocate change, though disagree on the degree of change and the tactics needed to achieve it, **conservatives** question whether any significant or profound change in existing institutions is necessary. Conservatives are skeptical of the view that change is good in itself and instead view it as disruptive and leading to unforeseen outcomes. They see existing institutions as key to providing basic order and continuity; should too much change take place, conservatives argue, it might undermine the very legitimacy of the system. Conservatives also question whether the problems that radicals and liberals point to can ever really be solved. At best, they believe, change will simply replace one set of problems with another, and, at worst, it will create more problems than it solves.

Reactionaries are similar to conservatives in their opposition to further evolutionary or revolutionary change. Yet, unlike conservatives and like radicals, they view the current order as fundamentally unacceptable. Rather than transforming the system into something new, however, **reactionaries** seek to restore political, social, and economic institutions. Reactionaries advocate restoring values, reverting to a previous regime or state that they believe was superior to the current order. Some reactionaries do not even look back to a specific period in history but instead seek to return to an envisioned past ideal that may never have existed. Reactionaries, like radicals, may in some cases be willing to use violence to advance their cause.

This left–right continuum of political attitudes gives the impression that the farther one travels from the center, the more polarized politics becomes. By this logic, then, radicals and reactionaries are miles apart from one another and have nothing in common (Figure 3.2, top). But our preceding discussion indicates that in many ways this impression is incorrect. Viewing left and right as extending along a single continuum is misleading, for the closer one moves toward the extremes, the closer the attitudes become. In other words, the continuum of left and right is more aptly portrayed as a circle, bringing the two ends, radical and reactionary, close together (Figure 3.2, bottom). And in fact, radicals and

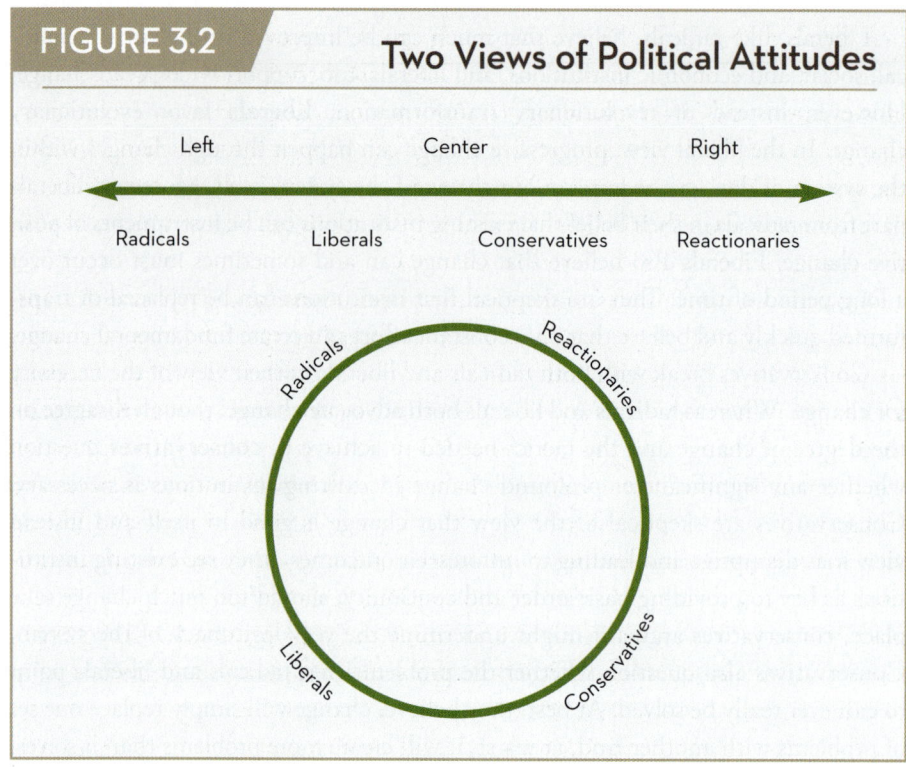

FIGURE 3.2 Two Views of Political Attitudes

reactionaries have much in common. Both believe in dramatic change, though in different directions, and both contemplate the use of violence to achieve this change. Although their ends may be quite different, the means of both groups can often be similar. Just as liberals sometimes become conservatives and vice versa, radicals and reactionaries often cross over into each other's camps. For example, many reactionary fascists in Europe became supporters of radical communism after World War II. More recently, voters who may have gravitated in the past to more radical parties have embraced reactionary politics that include xenophobia (the fear of foreigners). Psychologically, studies indicate that individuals with radical and reactionary political attitudes share in common a strong resistance to recognizing and updating their personal views when they are shown to be wrong.[8] This may explain why those resistant to updating their viewpoints would be more likely to jump from one extreme to another, given the similarities between the two.

You may have noticed that our discussion of the spectrum of political attitudes has not provided any specific examples of political issues, such as welfare, civil liberties, immigration, or national defense—common sources of political division that separate right from left in most industrialized democracies. But these policy areas are the concern of political ideology, the basic beliefs that people hold about how politics should be constructed. It is important to emphasize again that ideology and political attitudes are not interchangeable. The attitudes of radicals, liberals, conservatives, and reactionaries often take on different ideological content in different societies, depending on the context. What might be considered radical in one country could be conservative in another.

Consider some examples. In the United States, Canada, and Western Europe, radicals are viewed as those who seek to fundamentally transform or overthrow the current capitalist democratic order, replacing it with a system of greater economic and social equality. Liberals in these countries are sympathetic to some of these ideas but believe in pursuing gradual changes within the current system, engaging democratic institutions. Conservatives believe that the current economic and social structures are as good as they are likely to be and that change is unlikely to improve the state of humanity and might make it worse. Reactionaries, meanwhile, would likely reject the radical and liberal critique of the status quo and favor a restoration of greater inequality or hierarchy between people. The foregoing is a simplified but accurate description of how political attitudes are manifested in North America and much of the West.

These same political attitudes would manifest themselves quite differently in a country such as China, however. Despite dramatic economic reforms, China still has a nondemocratic regime dominated by a communist party. A Chinese radical, defined as someone who seeks the destruction of the current system, would advocate the overthrow of communist rule, perhaps replaced by a democracy like those found in the West. Students who were active in the Tiananmen Square protests for democracy in 1989 were frequently described or condemned by observers and the Chinese government as "radicals" because of their demands for sweeping political changes. Chinese liberals are also likely to support increased democracy, although they would favor a process of gradual change within the existing political system. Chinese conservatives, skeptical of institutional change, resist calls for democratic reform. They may support market reforms, but they do not view these steps as leading down an inevitable path to democracy. This might best describe those currently in power. Finally, Chinese reactionaries strongly oppose any reforms that might jeopardize communist rule. These neo-Maoists, as they are sometimes called, favor a return to earlier, "purer" communist values and policies, rolling back changes and restoring their communist ideal.

Clearly, American or Western European radicals would have little to say to Chinese radicals; they are united by their attitudes toward the scope and speed of political change, but their political values and goals—their ideologies—are dramatically different. Indeed, Chinese radicals might have more in common with American or European conservatives in terms of their ideological values, which we will discuss next. Chinese reactionaries, on the other hand, might have more in common with American or Western European radicals. Context matters.

Political Ideology

The importance of context in understanding political attitudes might lead to the conclusion that comparing political attitudes across countries is impossible: what is radical in one country might be conservative in another. To move past these particularistic differences between countries, political scientists also speak about political ideologies.

Like much of modern politics, the concept of ideology is relatively recent: the term was first used during the French Revolution to speak of a "science of ideas."[9] This meaning reflects the fact that ideologies emerged with the construction of modern secular states as a means to guide politics. Ideologies were thus viewed as alternatives to traditional sets of values such as religion; they were seen as based on rational thought rather than spiritual notions of good and evil. For our purposes, **political ideologies** are defined as sets of political values held by individuals regarding the fundamental goals of politics. Instead of being concerned with the pace and scope of change in a given context, as political attitudes are, ideologies are concerned with the ideal relation between freedom and equality for all individuals and the proper role of political institutions in achieving or maintaining this relation.

IN FOCUS

Political Ideologies Are . . .

- Sets of political values regarding the fundamental goals of politics.
- Exemplified by five dominant modern ideologies: liberalism, communism, social democracy, fascism, and anarchism.
- Universalistic: not specific to one country or time.
- Distinct from political attitudes.

Supporters of each ideology work to ensure that their values become institutionalized as the basic regime. In the modern world, there are five primary ideologies.

Liberalism as an ideology (rather than as a political attitude) places a high priority on individual political and economic freedom. Adherents of a liberal ideology believe that politics should seek to create the maximum degree of liberty for all people, including free speech, the right of association, and other basic political rights. This goal requires a state with a limited degree of autonomy so that the state can be easily controlled or checked by the public should it begin encroaching on individual rights. For liberals, the lower the ability of the state to intervene in the public's affairs, the greater are the scope and promise of human activity and prosperity. As Thomas Jefferson said, "The legitimate powers of government extend to such acts only as are injurious to others. But it does me no injury for my neighbour to say there are twenty gods, or no god. It neither picks my pocket nor breaks my leg."[10]

From these ideas of liberalism, we take our current definition of democracy, which is often called **liberal democracy**—a system of political, social, and economic liberties, supported by competition, participation, and contestation (such as voting). To be sure, liberals do recognize that if everyone is left to their own devices not all individuals will succeed, and great economic inequality inevitably will exist between the wealthiest and the poorest. Liberals argue that despite this shortcoming, a high degree of freedom will produce the greatest amount of general prosperity for the majority. As a final point, we should note that liberalism as an ideology and liberalism as a political attitude are very different things.

IN FOCUS

Different Meanings of the Term *Liberalism*

- As a political attitude: favoring slow, evolutionary change.

- As a political ideology outside North America: favoring free markets and individualism, accepting greater inequality.

- As a political ideology in North America: favoring a greater state role in limiting inequality; many outside the region would call this ideology "social democracy."

- As a political-economic system: favoring a limited state role in the economy.

Communism differs greatly from liberalism in its view of freedom and equality. Whereas liberalism enshrines individual freedom over equality, communism rejects the idea that personal freedom will ensure prosperity for the majority. Rather, it holds that in the inevitable struggle over economic resources in a liberal society, a small group will eventually come to dominate both the market and the state, using its wealth to control and exploit society as a whole. Prosperity will not be spread throughout society but will be monopolized by a few for their own benefit. The gap between rich and poor will widen, and poverty will increase. For communists, liberal democracy is "bourgeois democracy"—of the rich, by the rich, and for the rich. Such institutions as free speech and voting are meaningless when a few control the wealth of society.

To eliminate exploitation, communism advocates that the state control all economic resources and thus produce true economic equality for the community as a whole. This goal requires a powerful state in terms of both autonomy and capacity—a state able to restrict those individual rights (such as the freedom to own property or oppose the current regime) that would hinder the pursuit of economic equality. Individual liberties must give way to the needs of society as a whole, creating what communists would see as a true democracy. In the Soviet Union, from 1917 to 1991, this communist ideology was the political regime, as it has been in China since 1949 (though much less so since the 1980s).

Social democracy (sometimes called **socialism**) draws from ideas connected to both communism and liberalism to form its own distinct ideology. Social democracy accepts a strong role for private ownership and market forces while maintaining an emphasis on economic equality. A state with strong capacity and autonomy is considered important to social democrats to ensure greater economic equality through specific policies like job protection or social benefits like medical care, retirement, and higher education. This commitment to equality means that social democracy may limit freedom more than liberalism does, through such mechanisms as regulation or taxation. However, social democracy recognizes the importance of individual liberty as complementary to equality. In much of Europe, social democracy, rather than liberalism, is the guiding political regime. Many environmental parties, which seek to balance human and environmental needs, also have social-democratic influences.

Fascism is hostile to the idea of individual freedom and also rejects the notion of equality. Instead, fascism rests on the idea that people and groups can be classified in terms of inferiority and superiority, justifying a hierarchy among them. Whereas liberals, social democrats, and communists all see inherent potential in every person (although they disagree on the best means to unleash this potential), fascists do not. Fascism conceives of society as an organic whole, a single living body, and the state as a vital instrument to express national will. State autonomy and capacity must therefore be high, and democracy, no matter how it is defined, is rejected as anathema, just as freedom and equality are rejected. No fascist regimes currently exist in the world, although fascism is well remembered from the Nazi regime that ruled Germany from 1933 to 1945. More recently, parties and movements with a fascist orientation have resurfaced in Europe and America. This includes some strains of a philosophy tellingly known as *neo-reaction*, which expresses a hostility to liberal democracy and a belief in a hierarchy of racial differences.[11]

Anarchism departs from these other ideologies quite drastically. If liberalism, communism, and fascism differ over how powerful the state should be, anarchism rejects the notion of the state altogether. Anarchists share with communists the belief that private property leads to inequality, but they are opposed to the idea that the state can solve this problem. As the Russian anarchist Mikhail Bakunin (1814–76) once stated, "I am not a communist, because communism unites all the forces of society in the state and becomes absorbed in it . . . while I seek the complete elimination of the principles of authority and governmental guardianship, which under the pretense of making men moral and civilizing them, has up to now always enslaved, oppressed, exploited, and ruined them."[12]

Thus, like liberals, anarchists view the state as a threat to freedom and equality rather than as their champion, but they believe that both individual freedom and equality can be achieved only by eliminating the state entirely. Without a state to reinforce inequality or limit personal freedom, argue anarchists, people would be able to cooperate freely as true equals. Given that we live in a world of states, anarchism is the only one of the five primary ideologies that has never been realized. However, anarchist ideas played a role in the Russian Revolution (1917) and in the Spanish Civil War (1936–39). In North America, some versions of libertarianism come close to an anarchist view in their hostility to the state, though libertarians differ from anarchists in their emphasis on private property. Digital currencies are a good example of where libertarian and anarchist views overlap.

Political ideologies differ according to what they consider the proper balance between freedom and equality to be as well as what role they believe the state should have in achieving that balance. Building on the preceding chapters' discussion of freedom and equality and state strength, Figure 3.3 shows how liberalism, social democracy, communism, fascism, and anarchism try to reconcile freedom

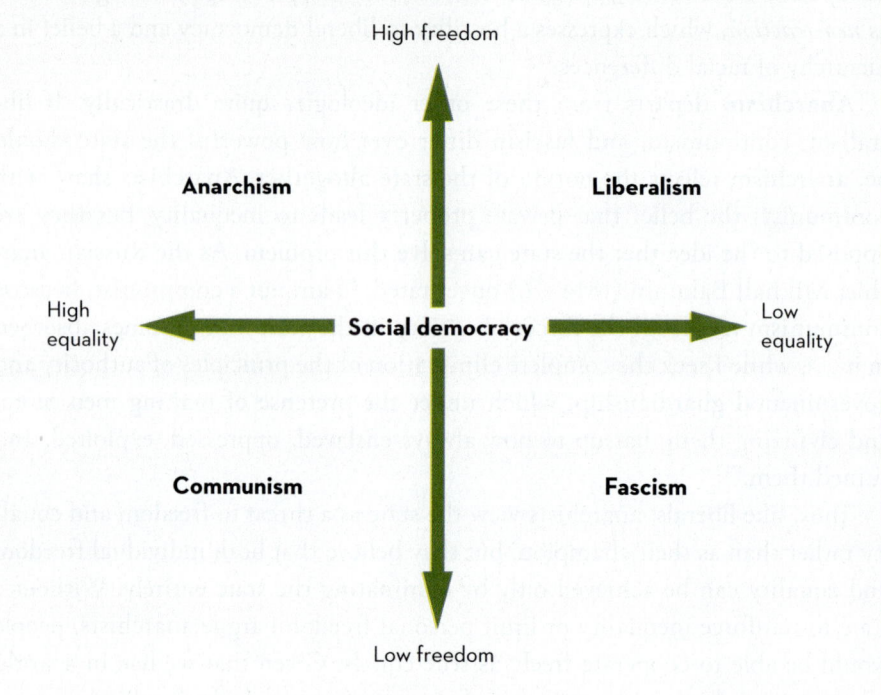

FIGURE 3.3 — Political Ideologies: Balancing Freedom and Equality

Liberals and anarchists favor decentralized power and weaker (or nonexistent) states as well as high levels of individual freedom; communists and fascists favor the concentration of state power at the expense of individual freedom; social democrats prefer a balance between state power and individual freedom.

and equality with state power. These ideologies are not particularistic, like political attitudes, but are universal in their outlook. And although ethnic and national identities and citizenship may draw the lines of conflict between groups, ideologies and attitudes shape the arena of political conflict within groups. How much change should there be? How fast should it occur? Should it be achieved through peaceful or violent means? What end should it serve? This is the essence of political life, as ideologies rise and fall in prominence, compete peacefully or violently, and pass from the scene as new ones take their place. In 200 years, such ideologies as liberalism and social democracy may make no more sense than monarchism does for most today.

IN FOCUS: Ideology and Political Attitudes

IDEOLOGY	TENETS	CORRESPONDING POLITICAL ATTITUDE IN NORTH AMERICA
LIBERALISM	Favors a limited state role in society and economic activity; emphasizes a high degree of personal freedom over social equality.	Conservative
COMMUNISM	Emphasizes limited personal freedom and a strong state in order to achieve social equality; property is wholly owned by the state and market forces are eliminated; state takes on task of production and other economic decisions.	Radical
SOCIAL DEMOCRACY	Supports private property and markets but believes the state has a strong role to play in regulating the economy and providing benefits to the public; seeks to balance freedom and equality.	Liberal
FASCISM	Stresses a low degree of both personal freedom and equality in order to achieve a powerful state.	Reactionary
ANARCHISM	Stresses the elimination of the state and private property as the only way to achieve both a high degree of personal freedom and social equality for all.	Radical

Religion, Fundamentalism, and the Crisis of Identity

Political identities like nationalism and ideology emerged alongside the modern secular state in many ways as an alternative or a rival to religion. If religion helped describe the world and prescribe people's behavior in relation to freedom, equality, and power, then political identities were nonspiritual guides to those same ends. Accordingly, political identities and religions are similar in many ways: both make assertions about the fundamental nature of humans and society and about the keys to a good life and an ideal community, and both provide their adherents with core texts, prophets, and a promise of salvation.

For more than a century, secular political identities have increasingly replaced religion in public life. Whereas in the premodern world religion was central to public affairs, including politics, the rise of political identities such as citizenship, nationalism, and ideology led to "the privatization of religion," which entailed removing faith from the public sphere and relegating it to private life. This change was never complete or uniform from country to country, but the emergence of ideology and modern states was central to the development of secularism and the retreat of religion. Max Weber described the process as "the disenchantment of the world"—that is, the replacement of faith in the mystical and spiritual by faith in the material world, in human institutions, and in the notion of progress. But in the past few decades, the claims and power of secular politics have themselves come under attack.

Among many of the most developed countries, ideological values such as liberalism and social democracy have been weakened by their inability to grapple with economic challenges and demographic and social changes. This has intensified disagreements about national identity and citizenship: Who are we? What are the core values of our political community, and who gets to belong to it? In other parts of the world where the political identities are much more weakly institutionalized, the challenge can be greater. The utopian claims associated with modernization theory—that economic growth, science, and rationalism would usher in a golden age—have been discredited. As a result, many people have sought to make religion a powerful force in their lives again. This can affect politics in a number of ways. When religions become intensely political, fundamentalist ideas and organizations emerge within them.

We should be clear about the meaning of fundamentalism. As with many politically charged words like *fascism* or *terrorism*, we speak indiscriminately of fundamentalism, often using it to describe any strong view that repels us. Some scholars even think the term should be restricted to its original use—a description of a particular movement among Protestant Christians in the nineteenth century. But despite these concerns, the term is useful and can describe a similar pattern across many religions.

The scholar Bruce Lawrence has defined *fundamentalism* as "the affirmation of religious authority as holistic and absolute, admitting of neither criticism nor reduction; it is expressed through the collective demand that specific creedal and ethical dictates derived from scripture be publicly recognized and legally enforced."[13] Following from this, we can view **fundamentalism** as an ideology that seeks to unite religion with the state or, rather, to make faith the sovereign authority—that is, to create a theocracy. This definition implies several things. First, fundamentalism is not the same as religiosity, puritanism, or religious conservatism. For example, Orthodox Jews or the Amish are by definition not fundamentalists; any group that retreats from public life and is suspicious of politics hardly fits our definition. The belief that there should be an increased role for spirituality in politics or society, such as religious parties or a state-established church, is also not fundamentalism. Second, fundamentalism is not a premodern view. As mentioned earlier, in the premodern world religion played a central role in public life. The rise of the modern state pushed faith into the private realm, replacing it in part with ideology. However, fundamentalism seeks not to return faith to a premodern role but rather to restructure religion as the central political identity—to make faith the sole foundation for a modern regime, a concrete and inerrant guide for politics in the contemporary world.

To that end, fundamentalists base their beliefs on the failures of ideology and the modern state. Through secular political identities, people sought to create heaven on earth, believing they could deny the authority of God and seize control of their own destinies. The result has been, in the fundamentalists' view, greater human misery as well as spiritual malaise. Fundamentalists would point to ongoing injustice and conflict within all societies. Even those who have benefited materially are still truly lost, spiritually empty, and morally adrift, forced to fill their lives with mindless distractions—consumption, entertainment, sex—to avoid confronting this terrible truth. Fundamentalism is thus a critique of modernity itself.[14]

As a political attitude, fundamentalism can appear reactionary, radical, or as a combination of the two. Fundamentalists will often claim they want to return to a golden age of faith, but they also seek to solve the problems of the modern world, not simply turn back the clock. This mixture of reactionary and radical attitudes also explains why fundamentalism is often associated with violence. However, we should be clear that only a small number of fundamentalists embrace such an approach. We will delve into this issue in depth in Chapter 7 when we consider political violence. To reiterate, we should not confuse religiosity or piety with fundamentalism, or fundamentalism with violence.

How does fundamentalism approach the relation between freedom and equality? Even within fundamentalist trends in a single religion, there may be a great diversity of ideas. Some fundamentalist views emphasize collective equality and reject individual freedom in favor of submission to God; others posit an expression of individual freedom made possible through a political system based on faith and are less concerned with specific economic or social inequalities between people. Other views reject both freedom and equality in favor of hierarchy and the domination of believers over nonbelievers, men over women, or the more faithful over the less so. Some forms of fundamentalism see the possibility of a religiously correct state; for others, the very notion of the state is incompatible with faith. It is thus a mistake to think of fundamentalism as a single bundle of common values; rather, it is a recurring pattern across many religions and has produced various ideological forms. In some cases, these forms remain nebulous and attract few adherents. In other cases, they are well defined and exercise significant political power. As the politics of fundamentalism continues to develop, this aspect of the "return of God" may prove to be one of the most important developments in comparative politics.[15]

Political Culture

Our final area of consideration in this chapter is political culture. First, we need to understand what is meant by *culture* in general. If a society is a group of people bound by shared institutions, as it was defined at the start of this chapter, then **culture** is the content of the institutions that help define a society. Culture acts as a kind of social road map, providing norms and priorities that guide people as they organize their lives. While ethnicity, nationality, and citizenship define which group an individual belongs to, culture is the repository for the activities and ideas that the group considers proper and normal. **Political culture**, in turn, refers to a society's norms for political activity.

The study of culture in political science has changed over time. In the past, the economic and political development of countries was often explained as a function of cultural or religious factors. For example, Weber famously argued that a "Protestant work ethic" linked to religious values fostered the accumulation and investment of wealth that was critical in sparking the Industrial Revolution. A related argument has stressed that the emphasis by Protestantism on private property and individualism also contributed to the emergence of democracy in Europe—in contrast to Catholicism, whose religious values were more authoritarian and anticapitalist. However, over time these kinds of arguments lost favor for several reasons. First, as we noted in the previous section, from the beginning of the twentieth century religion lost much of its authority in the developed world as ideologies and secular regimes grew in power. Second, modernization theory argued that culture in general was undergoing a process of transformation, such

> **IN FOCUS**
>
> ## Political Culture Is . . .
>
> - The basic norms for political activity in a society.
> - A determining factor in what ideologies will dominate a country's political regime.
> - Unique to a given country or group.
> - Distinct from political attitudes and ideologies.

that as states modernized they would develop shared secular values. Inasmuch as there were different cultures, they were, like faith in God in general, remnants of a premodern era that would be swept away by material and technological progress. Given enough time and money, every society would eventually wind up looking like Western Europe. Third, even for those who advocated cultural explanations for politics, there was the problem of how to measure and compare cultures.

But if God has returned as a subject of study, so has culture. As in the past, culture and religion are often interlinked—political scientists and social psychologists who define major cultural differences still do so largely on the basis of religion and region. As you can imagine, this resurgent interest is not without controversy—the idea that culture strongly influences politics goes against decades of scholarship that emphasized modernization and secularization. The best example of this debate has been the work of political scientist Samuel P. Huntington, who caused a firestorm with his 1996 book, *The Clash of Civilizations and the Remaking of World Order*.[16] In it, he argued that with the end of the Cold War cultural differences were now the main fault lines defining international relations. Huntington has been both praised and pilloried—for example, he wrote that Islam has "bloody borders," drawing scorn for the implication that there is something inherently violent about the faith. At the same time, his observations about Ukraine as a "cleft country," prone to violence due to cultural divides, seem prescient. If we can get past the controversy, there are important puzzles to explore. Why are some countries richer than others? Why are some more unequal? Why are some more democratic? Why are some more prone to political violence? Can culture explain these differences?

In short, the study of political culture has resurfaced in political science, but there is disagreement about what conclusions we can draw from it. Some of the best research we have in this regard is the work of political scientist Ronald Inglehart, who for three decades has been conducting public-opinion research in nearly 80 countries around the world. His data, known as the World Values Survey, allow us to track differences in beliefs across countries, cultures, and time. In particular, Inglehart distinguishes differences between societies along two dimensions. The first distinguishes between traditional and secular-rational values. Traditional values emphasize religion, family, deference to authority, and national pride. Secular-rational values place much less emphasis on these same principles. The second distinguishes between survival and self-expression values. Survival values emphasize economic and physical security and are associated with low levels of trust in government. Self-expression values are focused on higher levels of tolerance and demands for individual participation in politics.

As we see in Figure 3.4, very poor countries are associated with traditional and survival values, much as we would expect. However, once societies develop, they do not all move in a neat diagonal line toward higher degrees of secular-rational and self-expression values. Moreover, even as they move, they tend to move along a common path that reflects their shared cultural heritage. In other

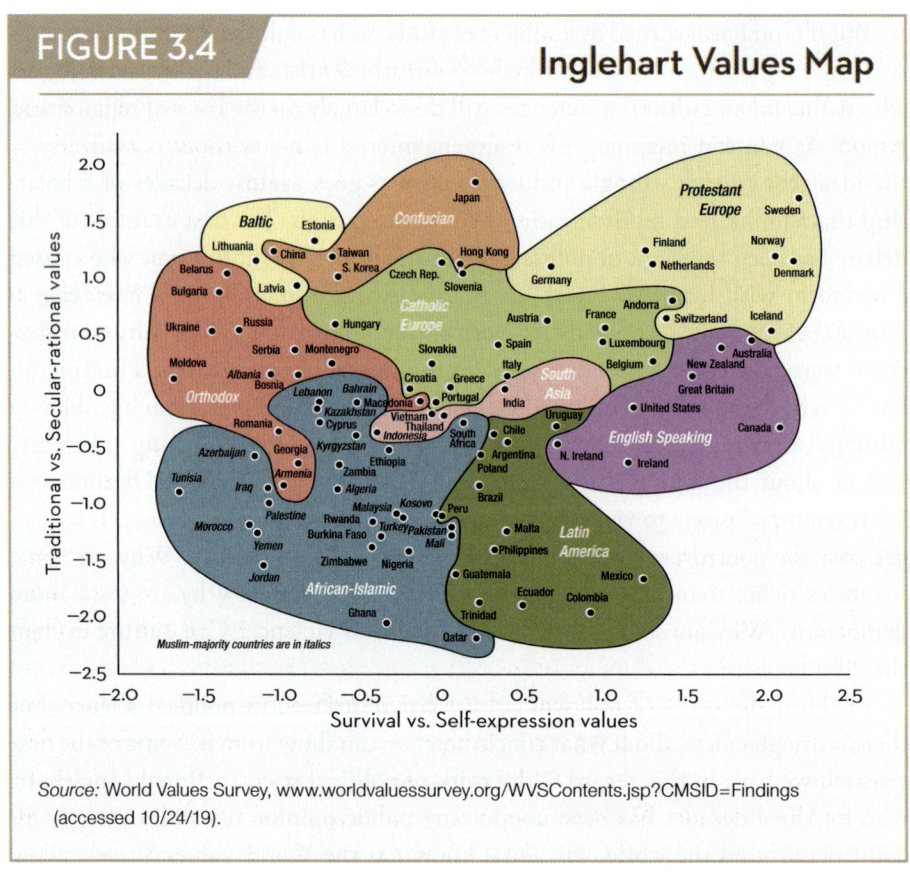

FIGURE 3.4   **Inglehart Values Map**

Source: World Values Survey, www.worldvaluessurvey.org/WVSContents.jsp?CMSID=Findings (accessed 10/24/19).

words, Scandinavian countries do not score highly in terms of secular-rational and self-expression values because they are wealthy but rather because of their Protestant heritage. Equally rich countries, such as the United States and Canada, show a lower level of secular-rational values for specific cultural reasons. Accordingly, as Islamic or Orthodox countries develop, they will move along their own particular historical path. This in turn could have an impact on the extent to which countries accept such things as same-sex marriage or gender equality. As Inglehart and his coauthor Christian Welzel assert, "a society's heritage—whether shaped by Protestantism, Catholicism, Islam, Confucianism, or communism—leaves a lasting imprint on a society's worldview."[17] That said, post-materialist theories argue that, given economic and physical security, new generations inexorably embrace values more consistent with secularism and self-expression. This is an argument not far removed from modernization theory. It also implies that fundamentalism in the long run is a waning force. Assuming that this is true, what happens if economic and physical security declines? What if societies become richer but also more unequal—does that undermine post-materialist values? This is an important question and something we will consider in the coming chapters.

It is easy to fall into stereotypes and determinism when speaking about culture. But recall our discussion of multicausality and endogeneity in Chapter 1, where we noted that it is often very difficult to identify cause and effect. Is it political culture that explains the weakness of social democracy in the United States? Moreover, in such important areas as democratization, culture has not been a barrier to change—successful democracies have emerged across the map of political culture. We will speak more about this in Chapter 5. It is more helpful to observe that even as countries develop, their cultural heritage remains a distinct and powerful institution that shapes politics.

In Sum: Society and Politics

Societies are complex and often difficult to unravel. In looking at how societal organization shapes politics, we have found that people everywhere have a number of identities: ethnicity, national identity, citizenship, political attitude, ideology, and political culture. Ethnicity provides a group identity, binding individuals to a group, engendering solidarity, and separating them from others. National identity provides a political aspiration for that group, a desire for freedom through self-government, and citizenship establishes a relation between that group and a state. Although each of these identities can be clearly defined, they are often strongly connected and in some cases blend into each other. Such identities may bind people

Has Nepal's New Constitution Ended Civil War?

Our chapter has noted the persistence of ethnic and national conflict across the globe and how these can overlap with ideological or theocratic values. For example, at the start of the chapter we spoke of India. In spite of its robust democratic institutions and practices, it has faced a rise in a reactionary Hindu fundamentalism that views India as a Hindu, rather than secular, state. This has increased tensions between different ethnic and religious groups and challenged the country's political culture of state-nations. Some worry that Indian democracy may be eroding.

At the same time, however, one of India's neighbors—Nepal—has moved in a somewhat different direction. A country known largely by outsiders for Mount Everest, in recent years Nepal has made a dramatic transition from monarchical rule to democracy, and from centralization to federalism. Yet the path has been bloody and it is by no means certain that recent changes have put an end to ethnic conflict.

Nepal is exceptionally diverse. No one ethnic group makes up more than 20 percent of the population; over 100 languages are spoken, and less than half the population speaks Nepali as their mother tongue. While 80 percent are Hindu, there are significant Buddhist and Muslim communities as well. The country also has a strong caste system, that is, hereditary social classes that have their origins in Hinduism. In many ways, then, the country resembles India. Yet a major difference is that, as opposed to India's history of British colonial rule, from 1769 until 2008 Nepal retained an independent monarchical regime. During most of that time Nepal was largely closed off from the outside world. Economic and political power was monopolized by upper caste elites within the royal court, and discussions of ethnic difference or inequality were suppressed. Attempts at democratization were unsuccessful until 1990, when, in the face of mass protests, the king accepted a new constitution with multiparty democratic elections and limitations on his power.

During the following period of constitutional reforms and democratic elections, various ethnic, religious, and ideological conflicts came to the fore. For example, a number of minority ethnic groups began to organize, challenging the existing notions of what made up Nepali identity—in essence, who was a "true" Nepali. However, one of the greatest rifts that emerged was within the Hindu majority itself. The Madhesi, a marginalized Hindu population in the lowlands, began to adopt arguments that they were a separate ethnic group relative to upper caste Hindu elites who had traditionally monopolized power. And yet even as ethnic identity sharpened, it remained illegal to form parties based on religion, ethnicity, region, or caste. The proliferation of politicized identities, fueled by the sense that democratic change had not led to a more just redistribution of power, contributed to government instability.

Civil war eventually did come in 1996, though on the surface it did not appear to be a manifestation of these ethnic, national, or religious divisions. Rather, it began when a faction of radical communists launched an uprising against the government, modeling themselves after Mao Zedong's struggle to power in China. Why did ideology, rather than ethnicity, become the engine of conflict in Nepal? While poverty was certainly a major factor in mobilizing support, many who joined the communist insurgency were motivated by group differences, supporting the communists' desire to end the political domination of upper caste Hindus. Over the course of the next decade over 15,000 individuals would die in the conflict. Peace talks, the abolition of the monarchy, and elections helped eventually bring an end to the Maoist insurgency.

A peace agreement and the creation of a republican regime was a dramatic transformation of Nepali political institutions. But a major sticking point remained: How should power be distributed in such a diverse country, where political divisions had only intensified over time? After years of negotiation, in 2015 Nepal passed a new constitution that enshrined federalism—though not, as in India, in an asymmetric form. Seven new provinces were created, each with its own legislature, and local elections were held in 2017. Importantly, the new federal provinces and lower municipalities were not drawn on the basis of a dominant identity (as many Madhesis demanded), for fear that this could exacerbate conflict by increasing divisions between groups. Indeed, violent protests broke out among Madhesis in 2015 and 2017 over their perceived marginalization in the new system. As of late 2019 four of the seven provinces still lacked names, in part because of the tension inherent in any particular choice that might reflect the preference of one identity over another. Would borders drawn more clearly around specific identities have helped create a more inclusive regime, or would they have further exacerbated existing tensions and weakened the state? When is federalism a solution to conflict—and when does it worsen it?

A Nepali woman in Birguni Parsa district examines the ballot before casting her vote in the third phase of the 2017 Nepalese local elections—the first local elections held in Nepal in almost 20 years.

1. How do India and Nepal's political institutions differ? How effective are these institutions in accommodating each country's profound ethnic diversity?

2. What is an example of ethnic conflict in Nepal? How has the proliferation of politicized identities contributed to government instability?

3. How do the Madhesi's violent protests demonstrate why Nepal's implementation of federalism was not successful, while India's implementation of federalism was successful?

together, but they can be the source of conflict when different groups see each other as threats to their own freedom and equality.

Whereas group identities establish differences between groups as a whole, an individual is positioned within a group by political attitudes, ideologies, and culture. These three identities shape an individual's view of the ideal relation between freedom and equality in society and the appropriate scope and pace of political change.

Society's role in politics is clearly complicated, shaped by an array of factors that affect the ongoing debate over freedom and equality. Not long ago, many social scientists dismissed social identities such as nationalism and religion as outdated forms of identification that were giving way in the face of modernization and individualism. However, most now believe that collective identities are more resilient than was once thought and that they may in fact sharpen in the face of new societal challenges. Politics is not simply a sum of individual actions but the product of a rich array of institutions that overlap one another, giving our lives meaning and informing our ideas, viewpoints, and values. We will consider this idea further in the next chapter as we turn to a new set of institutions and ideas that shape the struggle over freedom and equality: those concerned with economic life.

Key Terms

anarchism (p. 83)
citizenship (p. 68)
communism (p. 82)
conservatives (p. 77)
culture (p. 88)
ethnic conflict (p. 72)
ethnic identity/ethnicity (p. 64)
fascism (p. 82)
fundamentalism (p. 87)
liberal democracy (p. 81)
liberalism (p. 81)
liberals (p. 77)
nation (p. 66)

nation-state (p. 71)
national conflict (p. 72)
national identity (p. 66)
nationalism (p. 67)
patriotism (p. 69)
political attitude (p. 76)
political culture (p. 88)
political ideology (p. 80)
radicals (p. 76)
reactionaries (p. 77)
social democracy/socialism (p. 82)
society (p. 63)

For Further Reading

Alesina, Alberto, Stelios Michalopoulos, and Elias Papaioannou. "Ethnic Inequality," *Journal of Political Economy* 124, no. 2 (April 2016): 428–88.

Dalton, Russell J., and Christian Welzel, eds. *The Civic Culture Transformed: From Allegiant to Assertive Citizens.* Cambridge: Cambridge University Press, 2014.

Fearon, James D., and David D. Laitin. "Ethnicity, Insurgency, and Civil War," *American Political Science Review* 97, no. 1 (February 2003): 75–90.

Harrison, Lawrence, and Evgeny Yasin, eds. *Culture Matters in Russia—and Everywhere: Backdrop for the Russia–Ukraine Conflict.* Lanham, MD: Lexington Books, 2015.

Huntington, Samuel P. *The Clash of Civilizations and the Remaking of World Order.* New York: Simon & Schuster, 1996.

Lawrence, Bruce B. *Defenders of God: The Fundamentalist Revolt against the Modern Age.* New York: Harper and Row, 1989.

Lipset, Seymour Martin, and Gary Marks. *It Didn't Happen Here: Why Socialism Failed in the United States.* New York: W. W. Norton, 2000.

Norris, Pippa, and Ronald Inglehart. *Sacred and Secular: Religion and Politics Worldwide.* New York: Cambridge University Press, 2004.

Stepan, Alfred, Juan J. Linz, and Yogendra Yadav. *Crafting State-Nations: India and Other Multinational Democracies.* Baltimore, MD: Johns Hopkins University Press, 2011.

Welzel, Christian. *Freedom Rising: Human Empowerment and the Quest for Emancipation.* Cambridge: Cambridge University Press, 2013.

INQUIZITIVE

Earn a better grade on your test. InQuizitive personalizes your learning path to help you master the concepts from this chapter and practice applying them to examples from the text and beyond (see back cover).

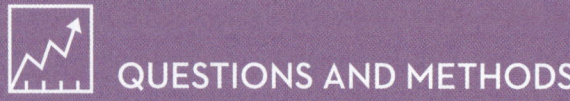

QUESTIONS AND METHODS

Can Federalism Solve Ethnic Conflict?

In this and the previous chapter we have discussed different identities that may make claims to political power, and also the way in which that power can be centralized or decentralized within a state. Often ethnic groups will over time develop a national identity within an existing state, such as the Basque and Catalan peoples in Spain. This national identity will carry within it notions of sovereignty—the desire to create a state for their own people, under their own rule. Such demands for independence inevitably clash with the goals of the existing sovereign state, and the result is often violent conflict, even civil war. With this knowledge in mind, some countries have attempted to reconcile this problem with devolution, creating a federal system where different groups have significant power in their own regions.

But does devolution work? Look at the data in the table below. We have noted India as a success story, and Canada can be viewed as one as well. However, there are counterexamples. For example, Ethiopia's 1994 federal constitution appears to have mobilized, rather than placated, various ethnic groups, with smaller ones agitating for more rights while the largest have battled for control over the central government. Scholars are so divided on whether devolution mitigates or exacerbates ethnic conflict and secession that they commonly speak of "the paradox of federalism."

Rather than relying on individual cases, a consistent review of devolution might give

MAJOR EXAMPLES OF FEDERALISM THAT ENDED IN SECESSION	MAJOR EXAMPLES OF FEDERALISM THAT DID NOT END IN SECESSION
Yugoslavia Soviet Union Czechoslovakia	South Africa India Nigeria Canada

us a better scholarly understanding and even guide policy makers considering such institutional change. One important observation takes us back to our discussion in Chapter 1 of independent and dependent variables. If, for example, we simply look at unitary states, there are few examples of secession since 1945, suggesting that this is the better option for political stability. However, if we widen our focus, scholars note a large number of cases where unitary states adopted federal institutions in order to prevent secession, often after a period of ethnic or national conflict. In those situations, the vast majority subsequently avoided secession. Federalism may often be the last resort to avoid or end conflict, but as a last resort its track record is relatively good.[a]

One subject our discussion has not addressed is exactly *what* elements of federalism may be critical to stability. All three of the failed cases in the table were preceded by a long history of communist authoritarianism; was ideology, or regime type, a factor in their dissolution? What important differences might there be among forms of federalism that could contribute to its success—or failure?

1. ***Consider the implications of variables on political institutions***

   What would be the strongest arguments for how federal or unitary states could limit or exacerbate ethnic and national conflict?

2. ***Evaluate contending hypotheses***

   Which of the arguments in Question 1 do you find the most convincing? Explain why.

3. ***Generate new hypotheses related to the discussion***

   Imagine that you were tasked with creating a new federal system in a country with several ethnic groups with varying degrees of national identity. What kinds of power would you devolve? What is your reasoning for why those powers would help reduce conflict?

---

a. Liam Anderson, "Ethnofederalism and the Management of Ethnic Conflict: Assessing the Alternatives," *Publius: The Journal of Federalism* 46, no. 1 (Winter 2016): 1–24.

4

Though Venezuela has massive oil reserves, a combination of extreme hyperinflation, mismanagement, and sanctions from the U.S. government led to fuel shortages across the country in May 2019. Here, uniformed military members can be seen directing traffic for civilians who are lined up to fill their gas tanks.

POLITICAL ECONOMY

How do people use politics to create and distribute wealth?

In March 2013, Venezuela lost its president, Hugo Chávez, who had been the country's leader since 1999. A highly charismatic and polarizing figure, Chávez had an enormous impact on the country and left behind a questionable legacy. Originally a military officer, Chávez embraced Marxist views early in his career. He concluded then that only radical change could solve the country's economic problems: Venezuela was blessed by natural resources such as oil and gas, but it was marked by extreme inequality and a high degree of poverty. In 1992, Chávez led an unsuccessful coup against the existing democratically elected government and was sentenced to two years in jail. His justification for the coup—to improve his country's social conditions—resonated with many Venezuelans, especially as the country underwent a period of wrenching economic reform. In the 1998 presidential elections, Chávez won over 50 percent of the vote and entered office with a call to transform the country.

Over the next 15 years, the country was indeed transformed, but not in ways that created greater democracy or economic stability. During his presidency, Chávez implemented a set of changes in the political-economic system. The new system, called "Bolivarian socialism," was meant both to improve the standard of living and increase Venezuela's sovereignty (which Chávez and his supporters viewed as compromised by American imperialism). One major piece of Bolivarian socialism was Venezuela's oil reserves—the largest in the world. Although much of this industry was already under state control, the Chávez government carried out further nationalization, forcing out a number of international firms. The government also nationalized parts of the agricultural, industrial, telecommunications, and financial sectors.

Alongside these nationalizations, the government dramatically expanded its social welfare system. Medical clinics were built, staffed in part by over 30,000 Cuban medical personnel; primary and secondary education were extended to the population, with a particular focus on eliminating illiteracy; food and fuel prices were subsidized; and public housing was constructed. Venezuela enjoyed high rates of economic growth during the 2000s and an improved standard of living for many people. Inequality decreased, and poverty rates fell from 50 percent to 30 percent by 2012.

So was Bolivarian socialism a success? Current problems call this into question. First, nationalizations aside, Chávez's policies were financed by a nearly 10-fold increase in the world price of oil, giving Chávez the means to implement his socialist policies. Despite his calls for greater independence from global capitalism, the country became even more dependent on oil exports to the United States and elsewhere. Second, while improvements in the standard of living were evident, when placed in comparison with the rest of Latin America they were less impressive. During Chávez's rule, most other countries in Latin America had higher rates of economic growth, lower inflation, and better improvement in infant mortality rates. This was despite the unprecedented amount of oil revenue Venezuela was dedicating to these goals. Finally, despite the economic improvements, homicide rates rose and are now the third highest in the world (after those of El Salvador and Honduras).

Venezuela entered the post-Chávez era in a politically unstable condition. Chávez's successor, Nicolás Maduro, further hobbled the weak political institutions that could act as a check on his power, increasingly relying instead on the military. This has in turn deepened the polarization between the poor and the middle and upper classes.

Protests, at times deadly, rally against shortages of basic goods like milk and flour; crime; and what is now the world's highest inflation rate, at over 1 million percent. Meanwhile, weak investment in the oil industry, a result of nationalization and the diversion of revenues toward other state expenditures, has led to a steady decline in output since Chávez first came to power. This, combined with the precipitous decline in world oil prices, has led to less state revenue overall and more national debt, making it difficult for Maduro to maintain Bolivarian socialism. Venezuela teeters on the edge of economic collapse, with as much as 90 percent of the population pushed into poverty. It is difficult to see how this situation will be easily, or peacefully, resolved in the immediate future. In April 2019 there was an attempted overthrow of Maduro by Juan Guaidó, head of the National Assembly, but while Guaidó enjoyed much international support, he failed to rally the military to his cause. The case of Venezuela shows that economics is not separate from politics, and that wealth may aggravate, rather than solve, issues of poverty and inequality.

LEARNING OBJECTIVES

- Explain how and why states are involved in the management of markets and property.
- Differentiate between political-economic systems.
- Explain how economic outcomes are measured.

Like political systems, economies are made up of many different institutions—rules, norms, and values—that strongly influence how the economic system is constructed. People often think about economic systems as somehow "natural," with functions akin to the law of gravity. In reality, an economy relies on an array of institutions that enable individuals to exchange goods and resources with one another. Moreover, economic institutions, like political ones, are not easy to replace or change once they have been constructed. They become self-perpetuating, and people have a hard time imagining life without them.

Economic institutions directly influence politics, and vice versa. The economy is one of the major arenas of the struggle over freedom and equality. Some view the economy as the central means by which people can achieve individual freedom, whereas others view the economy as the central means by which people can achieve collective equality. Inevitably, this struggle involves the government, the state, and the regime. How the balance between freedom and equality is struck directly influences such things as the distribution of wealth, the kinds of economic activity and trade that citizens may conduct, and the overall degree of security and prosperity that people enjoy. In short, the interactions between political and economic institutions in any country will profoundly affect the prosperity of every citizen. The study of how politics and economics are related and how their relationship shapes the balance between freedom and equality is commonly known as **political economy**.

In this chapter, we address these issues by investigating the relationship between freedom and equality. We will start by asking what role states play in managing an economy. States commonly involve themselves in economic life in several different areas; depending on such things as the dominant ideology and regime, the scope and impact of these actions can vary dramatically. Just as there are different ideologies concerning the ideal relationship between the state and society, as we saw in Chapter 3, there are different ideological views regarding the ideal relationship between the state and the market. And each ideology leads to a different political-economic system. Once we compare these differing views, we will consider how we might measure and compare their relative outcomes. In the process, we will look at some of the most common standards of measuring wealth and its distribution. Finally, we will consider the future of the relationship between state and market and how their interaction shapes the balance between freedom and equality.

The Components of Political Economy

Before we compare the different types of relationships between states and economies around the world, we need to familiarize ourselves with the basic components of political economy. All modern states are strongly involved in the day-to-day affairs of their economies, at both the domestic level and the global level. In shaping the economy to achieve their stated ideological goals, states and regimes use a variety of economic institutions.

Markets and Property

The most fundamental components of political economy are markets and property. When people speak of markets, the first thing that may come to mind is a physical place where individuals buy and sell goods. For as long as human beings have lived in settled communities that were able to produce a surplus of goods, there have been markets. Markets are closely connected to the rise of cities and political institutions; people would settle around markets, and markets would often spring up around fortifications, where residents could engage in commerce with some sense of security provided by the state. Such markets are still common in much of the world.

When social scientists speak of markets, they mean the interaction of supply and demand, though without a specific location. **Markets** are the interactions between the forces of supply and demand, and they allocate resources through the process of those interactions. As these two forces interact, they create values for goods and services by arriving at specific prices. An amazing feature of markets is that they can be so decentralized. Who decides how many cars should be built this year? Or what colors they should be? Or the price of this textbook? These decisions are made not by any one person or government but by millions of individuals making decisions about what they will buy and sell. If a seller produces a good and sets its price higher than people are willing to pay, the seller will not be able to sell it and turn a profit. This result will force me to either lower my price or go out of business. Similarly, if I have a good that no one wants, I must change it or face economic ruin. Sellers seek to create products that people will desire or need, and buyers seek to buy the best or the most goods at the lowest price. Because more than one seller or producer typically exists for a product, this environment tends to generate competition and innovation. Sellers seek to dominate a market by offering their goods at the cheapest price or by offering a good that is innovative and therefore superior to any alternative.

In short, markets are communities of buyers and sellers who are constantly interacting through the economic choices they make. At the same time, market forces typically require the state to enforce contracts, sanction activity, and regulate supply and demand where necessary. For example, by setting a minimum wage, a state is controlling to some extent the price of labor. By making certain drugs or prostitution illegal, the state is attempting to stamp out a part of the market altogether. Yet these goals are not always easily achieved. Minimum wages can be subverted by relying on undocumented immigrants, and "black" or underground markets appear where drugs and prostitution are illegal. While markets typically rely on states, they also have a life of their own, and each state must decide in what way and to what extent it will sustain and control the market.

IN FOCUS: Markets

- Markets are the medium through which buyers and sellers exchange goods.
- Sellers seek to create products that will be in demand.
- Buyers seek to buy the best or most goods at the lowest price.
- Markets emerge spontaneously and are not easily controlled by the state.

Property is a second element critical to any economy. **Property** refers to the ownership of the goods and services exchanged through markets. Property can refer to land, buildings, businesses, or personal items, to name some of its most common forms. In addition, a certain set of property rights can accompany ownership, such as the right to buy and sell property or the right not to have it taken away by the state or other citizens without a good reason (what is known as "just cause") and compensation. As with market forces, property rights must be regulated by the state. Without state power functioning in a fair manner, property is insecure.

In many people's minds, property has a physical presence. They can see a car, buy it, own it, and sell it when they want a new one. However, property is not always tangible. *Intellectual property*, for example, refers to ownership of a specific type of knowledge or content—a song, a piece of software code, or a treatment for diabetes. As economic developments center more and more on such intangible forms of information and knowledge, the concept of property and property rights becomes as invisible as that of markets. We have no physical entity to make transactions clearer. Anyone who has downloaded a song or software from the Internet knows exactly what we mean.

Like the role states play in regulating markets, the role they play in constructing and enforcing property rights, both between people and between the state and society, varies from state to state. States may fail to enforce the rights of individuals to protect their own property from other individuals by neglecting to enact or uphold laws against counterfeiting or theft. States may also assume certain property rights for themselves, claiming ownership over property such as airwaves, oil, land, or businesses. It is important to understand that property rights do not automatically come into being. In fact, many less-developed countries enjoy a wealth of property but have a poverty of property rights, for these states are unable or unwilling to establish and enforce such rules. We will speak about this more in Chapter 10.

Public Goods

We have so far described property as goods that individuals acquire or use through the market for their own benefit. But there are limits to what property and the markets can achieve. In some cases, their interaction does not produce benefits that society desires. Take, for example, transportation. Forms of transportation infrastructure do exist in the private realm, such as toll roads or passenger ferries, and these private forms have a long history that predates the state. But most modern societies question the moral and practical implications of allowing these goods to belong only to a few. The privatization of such goods may limit economic development. For instance, a network of privately held roads might impede trade or fail to reach certain parts of the population. Because of such concerns, all states provide some level of public goods; indeed, the core definition of a state itself—a monopoly of violence—is the underlying public good on which all markets and property rest.

Public goods can be defined as those goods provided or secured by the state that are available for society and indivisible, meaning that no one private person or organization can own them. Unlike private goods, with their inherent link to individual freedom, public goods can generate greater equality because the public is able to share broadly in their benefits.[1]

In many countries, roads, national defense, health care, and primary education are public goods, and everyone in the country may use them or benefit from their existence. But states do differ greatly in the extent of public goods they provide, largely because of the role of ideology in the relationship between states and markets. In the United States, health care is not a public good; it remains in private hands, and not everyone has equal access to it. In Canada, however, health care is a public good, provided by the state in the form of publicly owned hospitals and universal benefits for all citizens. In Cuba, the state owns most businesses, making them public goods as well. The goods and profits of these firms belong not to private owners but to the state, to be distributed as the government sees fit.

Social Expenditures: Who Benefits?

This discussion of public goods leads us to the broader subject of **social expenditures**—the state's provision of public benefits, such as education, health care, and transportation, or what is commonly called *welfare* or the *welfare state*. For many the very word *welfare*, like *taxes*, has an inherently negative connotation; it calls up images of free riders living off the hard work of others. In many countries, redistribution of wealth in this manner can be controversial; its critics assert that social expenditures lead to counterproductive behavior. High unemployment benefits, they argue, may discourage people from seeking work. Moreover, alternative forms of social security that people have relied on in the past, such as family, the community, or churches, could be weakened by too broad a welfare system. Issues of welfare are further complicated by immigration, given claims that immigrants rely on social expenditures more than the rest of the population. None of these arguments is necessarily true, or true for all countries. We'll talk more about this in a moment.

However valid these arguments may or may not be, one problem for many countries is that social expenditures can be very costly, especially where unemployment is high or the population is aging. In recent years, many countries have sought to control the growth of social expenditures, but this is often is easier said than done. We will explore this issue further in Chapter 8 as we consider problems in developed democracies.

Who benefits from social expenditures? Strictly defined, social expenditures are provided by the state to those who find themselves in circumstances where they require greater care: the unemployed or underemployed, children, the elderly, the poor, and the disabled. Such expenditures can include health care, job training, income replacement, and housing. However, many forms of social expenditures are public goods that are more widely used. For example, a national health care system treats employed and unemployed, wealthy and poor alike. Highways, public higher education, and cultural institutions such as museums may primarily benefit the middle and upper classes. In fact, if we look at social expenditures more broadly, we find that in many countries they mostly benefit the middle class, not the poor. In this sense, the modern welfare state is less a structure that taxes the middle class and the rich to benefit the poor than one that taxes the middle class and the rich for services that they benefit from themselves.

Taxation

Over time, states have become increasingly responsible for providing public goods and social expenditures. How do states pay for these expenses? One major source of funds is taxation. As with social expenditures, taxation generates passionate opinions: some view it as the means by which a greedy state takes the hard-earned revenues of its citizens, stunting economic growth, whereas others see it as a critical tool for generating a basic level of equality. Regardless of one's opinion of taxation, societies expect states to provide a number of public goods and services, and for most countries, taxation is the key source of revenue. The other option is to borrow money from domestic and international lenders.

How much tax is collected varies from country to country. Figure 4.1 illustrates this variation, showing that in some countries taxes consume a large portion of the **gross domestic product (GDP)**, defined as the total market value of goods and services produced by one country in a year. Many European countries with large social expenditures tend to have high overall tax rates to fund those expenses. In addition, countries differ in where their tax revenue comes from. Some countries

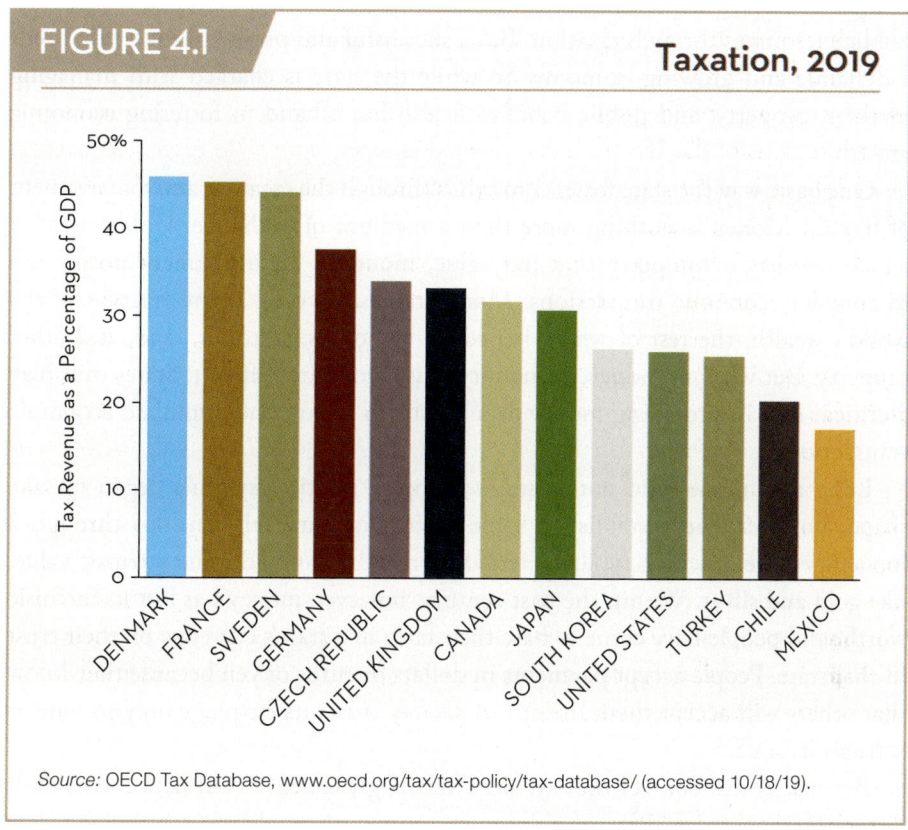

FIGURE 4.1 Taxation, 2019

Source: OECD Tax Database, www.oecd.org/tax/tax-policy/tax-database/ (accessed 10/18/19).

rely on high personal taxation, while others rely on taxes on businesses or goods and services. All countries struggle with finding the right mix and level of taxation, aiming to extract needed funds and reinvest them in a way that will generate development and prosperity.

Money, Inflation, and Economic Growth

It should be getting clearer that many political-economic processes are tightly interlinked. States must form a relationship with markets and property, deciding what goods and property should remain in private hands, what should be public, and what kinds of rights exist for each. They must also determine the level and forms of social expenditures needed to ensure a basic standard of living and security for all citizens. This distribution requires funds, and states must typically draw on the public's resources through taxation. But a successful and productive tax base needs a dynamic and growing economy. So while the state is charged with managing markets, property, and public benefits, it also has a hand in fostering economic growth.

One basic way the state fosters growth is through the creation and management of money. Money is nothing more than a medium of exchange. Unlike wealth, which consists of property that has value, money is an instrument people use to conduct economic transactions. Money represents only a tiny fraction of the world's wealth, the rest of which is tied up in houses, factories, land, and other property. But without money, economic transactions are difficult. States thus play a critical role in providing money as a means to secure and stimulate economic transactions.

Long ago, money did not exist. As complex political systems began to take shape, however, they established some basic monetary relationships through a monetary system, which typically rested on metals that held some intrinsic value, like gold and silver. Within the past century, however, money has lost its intrinsic worth, and people have come to base their faith in a state's currency on their trust in that state. People accept payments in dollars or euros or yen because they know that others will accept them in turn. A society trusts its currency only so long as it trusts its state.

Because states control money, they have a great deal of influence over their domestic economies. Part of this power comes through what is known as a **central bank**, an institution that controls how much money is flowing through the economy as well as how much it costs to borrow money in that economy. One of the main ways a central bank influences these two areas is by changing a national interest rate—the rate charged to private banks when they need to borrow funds from the central bank or one another. When the central bank lowers the interest rate charged to banks, those banks in turn typically lower their own interest rates for businesses and individuals. Loans become less expensive and saving becomes less lucrative, which can prompt people to borrow more and spend more. This activity in turn increases the amount of money active in the economy and stimulates economic growth. If the central bank raises interest rates, on the other hand, people are likely to borrow less and save more to take advantage of the higher interest their savings can earn. The money supply in the economy contracts as a result, and economic growth is likely to slow. Thus, during the first half of 2008, the U.S. Federal Reserve (the U.S. central bank) cut interest rates six times in an effort to stave off an economic downturn. As of 2020, the interest rate sat at just below two percent. In 1980, by contrast, it was 17 percent.

> **IN FOCUS**
>
> **A Central Bank . . .**
>
> - Controls the amount of money in the economy.
> - Controls the cost of borrowing money.
> - Lowers interest rates to stimulate the economy.
> - Raises interest rates to check inflation.

The actions the central bank takes are closely tied to two other important factors in any economy: inflation and deflation. **Inflation** is an increase in the general price level of goods and services in the economy when demand outstrips supply. Although small levels of inflation are not a problem, inflation can become problematic when it is too high. Wages and savings lose their value, and workers and those on fixed incomes, such as retired people, find that their money buys less and less. People press for higher wages or benefits to offset higher prices, further feeding inflation. Central banks can try to control inflation by raising interest rates, making credit more expensive, and thereby reducing spending and lowering prices. However, the prices of many things, like oil or other imports, are beyond a state's control. States can also be the cause of inflation if the government, unable to cover its expenses, is forced to borrow money at ever-higher interest rates to attract lenders. This situation can lead to very high inflation.

In extreme cases, countries can experience **hyperinflation**: inflation that is higher than 50 percent a month for more than two months in a row. (The inflation rate in North America and Europe over the past decade ranged between 1 percent and 4 percent per year.) When governments find themselves lacking the tax revenues to cover basic expenditures and are unable to borrow from lenders, they may decide to print money to cover their debts, thus expanding the money supply. At the same time, such circumstances are often accompanied by a public belief that there is no longer a strong state to support the currency—a collapse of legitimacy. Under such conditions, normal economic processes fail. Venezuela, which we discussed at the start of this chapter, has become an extreme example. As the government has lost oil revenue to support itself, it has relied on expanding the money supply, leading to an inflation rate of around 200,000 percent in 2019. Hyperinflation typically leads to currency collapse because people increasingly refuse to accept the devalued currency as payment and switch to other means of transaction, from foreign currency to barter.

The dangers of inflation might lead us to conclude that tight control over the money supply should be a government's first economic priority. But there are problems at the other end of the spectrum as well. Under some conditions, especially recently, states face the danger of **deflation**, when too many goods are chasing too little money. Dropping prices might sound like a good thing, but they can be devastating if businesses are unable to make a profit. Lowering prices leads to unemployment, less spending, and even more deflation. This has been a serious problem in Japan, which has suffered deflation almost every year since 1998. Heavy levels of debt by banks, consumers, and states, as well as related unemployment, have led to an overall tightening in spending. Central banks have set their lending rates extremely low in the hope of stimulating borrowing, spending, and growth. However, they have had limited effect.[2] States can certainly harm or hurt economies, but, as previously noted, markets also have a life of their own.

Regulation

So far, our discussion has dealt with the state's role in markets and property—what is to be provided, by whom, and at what cost. Yet states must concern themselves not only with economic output but also with the means by which that output is created. As with public goods, moral and technical issues often affect a state's approach in this area. Are some economic processes inherently counterproductive to creating goods and services? What about economic processes that can result in a detrimental impact on society, such as pollution? Whose rights are primary in these circumstances, those of citizens or businesses? These concerns draw states into the realm of economic regulation.

Regulations—rules or orders that set the boundaries of a given procedure—may take different forms. First, regulations may be fundamentally economic in nature. These regulations may control prices for certain goods or services, such as food or energy. Economic regulations may also control what firms may operate in what markets. National rail systems, for example, have functioned in many countries as either a private or state **monopoly**—in other words, a market controlled by a single producer. A second set of regulations can be described as essentially social in nature. In contrast to economic regulations that focus on how businesses function in the market, social regulations deal more with managing risk, such as safety and environmental standards. Naturally, these kinds of regulations overlap—for example, environmental regulations can strongly affect what firms may enter the market and how they can operate.

Trade

States must grapple with the challenge of regulating economic interactions not just within their country but also between their citizens and the outside world. In most economies, markets are not only local—goods and services come from all over the world. States can influence the degree of competition and access to goods within their own country by determining what foreign goods and services may enter the domestic market.

The way that a state structures its trade can profoundly affect its own economic development. States can use a number of tools to influence trade: **tariffs**, which are basically taxes on imported goods; **quotas**, which limit the quantity of certain goods coming into the country; and other **nontariff regulatory barriers**, which may create health, packaging, or other restrictions and whose purpose is to protect a state's citizens and make it difficult or expensive for foreign goods to be sold in the local market. For example, in Canada 35 percent of all music on AM and FM radio and between 50 and 60 percent of all television programs played during prime hours must be of Canadian origin. Airlines that fly only within the United States must be American owned.

Why regulate trade? States may favor tariffs as a way to generate revenue, and they and local manufacturers may see such barriers as a way to stimulate or protect local industries and firms. Those who oppose trade barriers argue that trade leads to more competition, innovation, and **comparative advantage**—the ability to produce a particular good or service relatively more efficiently than other countries.

We've covered a great deal in this section, so let's quickly review what we have discussed. The most basic building blocks of political economy are markets

IN FOCUS: Arguments over the Regulation of Trade

WHY REGULATE TRADE?	WHY NOT?
■ To generate state revenue	■ To promote competition
■ To foster local industry	■ To keep the costs of goods low
■ To protect local jobs	■ To stimulate domestic innovation in areas of comparative advantage
■ To keep wealth in the country	

and property, and states are involved in creating and enforcing rules that govern both. States help fashion markets and define property, and they use taxation in part to provide public goods and services. States can influence the growth of an economy by manipulating interest rates and, through regulation and trade, determining what is produced and where. All these responsibilities are part of a complex web of cause and effect that can shape freedom, equality, and the generation of wealth. Which mixture of policies across these areas will result in economic prosperity and state power? States have taken radically different approaches to the ideal relationship between state and market, leading to a variety of distinct political-economic systems around the world—all of which are currently under challenge.

Political-Economic Systems

A **political-economic system** can be defined as the actual relationship between political and economic institutions in a particular country, as well as the policies and outcomes they create. Various types of political-economic systems view the ideal relationship between state and market, and between freedom and equality, in different ways. Political-economic systems are often classified as liberal, social-democratic, communist, or mercantilist. Three of these political-economic systems match the political ideologies we discussed in Chapter 3. This should not be too surprising: political-economic systems can be seen as the attempt to realize an abstract ideology in the form of real economic institutions and policies.

There is always a disjuncture, however, between theory and practice. For example, some subscribers to a liberal ideology would say that existing "liberal" political-economic systems around the world do not live up to liberal ideals. Many communists similarly condemned the communist political-economic system that was practiced in the Soviet Union as a betrayal of "true" communist thought. In addition, the ideologies of fascism and anarchism do not have a political-economic counterpart to speak of. The fascist political-economic systems that arose in the 1930s were destroyed by World War II, and anarchism has never been effectively realized.

These basic classifications simplify the complexity of political economy. In reality, of course, many different variations are found within these categories. Each of these categories strikes a different balance between state power and the economy, thereby shaping markets and property, public goods and social expenditures, taxation, regulation, and trade.

Liberalism

Recall from Chapter 3 that, as a political ideology, liberalism places a high priority on individual political and economic freedom and advocates limiting state power in order to foster and protect this freedom. Liberalism assumes that individuals are best suited to take responsibility for their own behavior and well-being. Liberal scholars such as Adam Smith put their faith in the market and in private property. If people are allowed to harness their own energies, sense of entrepreneurialism, and, yes, greed, liberals believe that they will generate more prosperity than any government could produce through "top-down" policy making and legislation.

For liberals, then, the best state is a weak one, constrained in its autonomy and capacity. Other than securing property rights, the state should have limited involvement in the economy. Public goods should be located only in critical areas such as defense and education to prevent free riding (that is to say, benefiting from a good without paying for it) and to encourage individual responsibility. Unemployment should be accepted as an inevitable, even desirable part of market flexibility. Taxation should be kept to a minimum so that wealth remains in the hands of the public. Regulation should be light, and trade should be encouraged to stimulate competition and innovation. Overall, the state should act as a sort of night watchman, intervening to defend the public only when crises arise. These conditions describe the liberal tenet of **laissez-faire** (French for "let do"), which holds that the economy should be allowed to do what it wishes. This is what we typically think of as **capitalism**—a system of production based on private property and free markets.

When the government's role is minimal, liberals believe, economic growth will be maximized. Moreover, under such conditions, people will enjoy the greatest possible amount of personal and political freedom. Liberals would in fact maintain that democracy requires a free market. If too much economic and political power is concentrated in the hands of the state, they believe, this monopoly would endanger democracy. Thus, weak states are best; as Smith, one of the fathers of liberal ideology, argued in 1755, "Little else is requisite to carry a state to the highest degree of opulence from the lowest barbarism but peace, easy taxes, and a tolerable administration of justice: all the rest being brought about by the natural course of things."[3]

Liberalism as a political-economic system, then, is defined by its emphasis on individual freedoms over collective equality and on the power of markets over the state. As you might imagine, the United States is typically touted as a paragon of liberal values. Regulations are often weaker and social expenditures and taxation lower than in other industrialized democracies, and the American public is largely skeptical of state power and embraces capitalism. But the United States is not the only country in the liberal camp. The United Kingdom, the intellectual source of much of liberal thought, is also viewed as a liberal country, as are Canada, Australia, and New Zealand (all, like the United States, former British colonies). Many other countries around the world have over the past 40 years embraced the "neoliberal" economic model and are noted for their relatively low levels of government regulation, taxation, and social expenditures.

However, even though these countries can all be classified as liberal, they vary in a number of ways, such as the range of public goods they provide, like higher education and unemployment or retirement benefits. In addition, even though liberal ideology would argue that a free market and democracy are inseparable, we find countries with liberal political-economic systems that nevertheless restrict democratic rights. (See "Questions and Methods" on pp. 136–37 for a discussion of how political scientists assess liberal economics.) Singapore, Bahrain, and the United Arab Emirates are regularly noted for having some of the freest economic systems in the world, and yet they all restrict individual political and civil rights. In the 1980s, Chile, while suffering under a military dictatorship, became a model of economic liberalism. Critics of liberalism often highlight this contradiction, pointing out that the free market can sit easily with political repression. We will discuss this contradiction further when we turn to nondemocratic regimes in Chapter 6.

Social Democracy

In Chapter 3, we noted that social democracy draws from liberalism and communism in an attempt to temper the extremes of too much freedom and too much equality. Like liberalism, social democracy functions on a foundation of capitalism—private property and open markets—rejecting communists' call for revolution and the state appropriation of private property and wealth. Most notable among early social-democratic thinkers was Eduard Bernstein (1850–1932). In his 1899 work *Evolutionary Socialism,* Bernstein rejected Karl Marx's belief in inevitable revolution, concluding instead that democracy could evolve into socialism through the ballot box rather than through the gun.[4]

Rejecting revolution and embracing democracy, social democracy accepts a role for private property and market forces, but it remains more cautious than liberalism about their ultimate benefits to society. Unchecked economic development produces great inequality, social democrats argue, by concentrating wealth in the hands of a very few. This in turn can polarize society, pitting owners against laborers, rich against poor, city against countryside. Proponents of this way of thinking see the state not as a threat to society or the economy but as a creator of social rights that are otherwise lost in the vicissitudes of the market.

State power can thus manifest itself in a number of ways. According to social democracy, the state should make available a wide array of public goods, such as health care, pensions, and higher education. The need for competition should not stand in the way of strong state regulation or even ownership of certain sectors of the economy, and trade should similarly be managed in such a way that it does not endanger domestic businesses and jobs. Finally, the goal of equality requires a higher level of social expenditures to ensure basic benefits for all. Taxes make these social expenditures possible while also redistributing wealth from the rich to the poor. Thus, taxes tend to be higher and capitalism more constrained in social-democratic systems.

As with liberalism, social democracies are not all of one type. For example, social-democratic systems can vary in labor flexibility. Jobs may be highly regulated in terms of hours worked and conditions of termination, or firms may be able to fire workers more easily and hire at full- or part-time. Unemployment benefits may be generous, or more limited and contingent on retraining or government work schemes. Tax rates and the redistribution of income can also be quite varied; taxes as a percentage of GDP are not significantly different in the liberal United Kingdom and social-democratic Germany, though in general social-democratic systems rely on higher taxes.[5]

Finally, social-democratic systems may involve themselves in the economic system through partial or total state ownership of firms. The French state owns around 15 percent of the auto manufacturer Renault. Norway owns two-thirds of the firm Statoil, which controls oil and gas production in that country. Worldwide, state ownership has declined in recent decades, but it has not disappeared. Social-democratic systems are most common in Europe (particularly Scandinavia), where states have more autonomy and capacity to actively manage the economy.[6] Liberals

IN FOCUS

How Do Social Democracies Seek to Achieve Greater Equality?

- Through taxes, which make high levels of social expenditure possible while redistributing wealth from rich to poor
- Through trade, which is promoted but balanced with preserving domestic industry and jobs
- Through government regulation and even ownership of important sectors of the economy

criticize such systems as costly and a drag on innovation and competition. Social democrats respond that their system avoids the inequalities of liberalism while still encouraging entrepreneurial activity. Interestingly, the strongest social democracies have also been the most ethnically homogeneous; it may well be that people are more willing to let the state transfer wealth when it goes to other people who are like them. Whether one can build (or keep) social-democratic systems that redistribute wealth across a more diverse population is an open question.

Communism

Whereas social democracy departs from liberalism in its attempt to balance individual freedom and collective equality, the political-economic system of communism chooses effectively to eliminate individual freedom to achieve equality. We will discuss communism in detail in Chapter 9, when we look at communist and postcommunist countries; for now, we will focus on its basic political-economic institutions. Communist thinkers such as Karl Marx began with the premise that capitalism, with its private property and free markets, cannot truly serve the needs of society as a whole. Communists view private property and markets as a form of power that inevitably leads to one person or group gaining control over others. Economic competition between people creates exploitation and the development of social classes in which a small group of the wealthy dominates and benefits from the labor of the poor majority. Both domestically and internationally, this exploitation opens an ever-wider gap between those who control the economy and those who merely labor in it. Such inequalities, Marx argued, will inevitably lead to a revolution, through which a single communist party will take control of the state on behalf of all people.

Communist systems use the state to transform markets and property. Private property is fully nationalized; it is placed in the hands of the state on behalf of the people. In other words, the entire economy becomes a public good, existing for the benefit of all. In addition, market forces are eliminated by the state; almost all private transactions take place illegally, on the black market. Under communism, economic decision making is entrusted entirely to the state, which is assumed to be the only institution that can rationally and fairly allocate resources. This system requires a large bureaucracy to determine what needs to be made and how it should be distributed.

Because communist states centralize all economic decision making and ownership, many of the essential tasks of states in other political-economic systems are fundamentally different under communism. Taxation takes an indirect form through fixed prices and wages; any profit produced by a worker or a firm goes to the state for public expenditures. Labor is allocated by the state—in other

IN FOCUS: Contributors to the Theories of Political Economy

SYSTEM	THINKER	CONTRIBUTION
LIBERALISM	Adam Smith	*The Wealth of Nations* (1776), considered one of the first texts on modern economics. Articulated the idea that economic development requires limited government interference.
SOCIAL DEMOCRACY	Eduard Bernstein	*Evolutionary Socialism* (1899). Rejected Marx's belief in the inevitability of revolution, arguing that economic equality can be achieved through democratic participation.
COMMUNISM	Karl Marx	*Das Kapital* (1867). Asserted that human history is driven by economic relations and inequality and that revolution will eventually replace capitalism with a system of total equality among people.
MERCANTILISM	Friedrich List	*The National System of Political Economy* (1841). Rejected free-trade theories of liberalism, arguing that states must play a strong role in protecting and developing the national economy against foreign competitors.

words, the state decides who will work and where. Competition is eliminated, and regulations, although present, may be much weaker since the state winds up regulating itself. Social expenditures are extensive: all basic services, including health care, education, retirement, and even leisure activities, are owned and provided by the state. Finally, trade is highly restricted; the only imports are those the state deems necessary because they cannot be produced domestically. State capacity and autonomy are extremely high; the state can operate without interference from either the public or private economic actors.[7]

As you would expect, supporters of private property and market forces argue that states with communist political-economic systems lack the ability to effectively centralize all the economic decisions that are the normal product of a decentralized market. Moreover, placing all economic power in the hands of the state would essentially make democracy impossible. If the people have no property rights and if the state makes all economic decisions, there is no separation between public and

IN FOCUS: Political-Economic Systems

	LIBERALISM	SOCIAL DEMOCRACY	COMMUNISM	MERCANTILISM
ROLE OF THE STATE IN THE ECONOMY	Little; minimal welfare state	Some state ownership, regulation; large welfare state	Total state ownership; extensive welfare state	Much state ownership or direction; small welfare state
ROLE OF THE MARKET	Paramount	Important but not sacrosanct	None	Limited
STATE CAPACITY AND AUTONOMY	Low	Moderate	Very high	High
IMPORTANCE OF EQUALITY	Low	High	High	Low
POSSIBLE FLAWS	Inequality	Expense	Authoritarianism	Inefficiency
EXAMPLES	United States, United Kingdom, former British colonies	Europe (Germany, Sweden)	Cuba, Soviet Union, North Korea	Japan, South Korea

private. States wind up controlling people's fates—where they live and work, what they earn, what they may buy. In response, communists would say that what they offer is total equality for all; their system emphasizes equality over individual freedom, while liberalism does the opposite. And even if such a system is inefficient, its supporters might argue, better that economic resources are wasted in the attempt to provide for all than squandered on luxuries for a wealthy few, as seen in market economies.

Mercantilism

The final political-economic system, **mercantilism**, stands apart in the debate over freedom and equality that separates liberalism, social democracy, and communism. Whereas all three systems we have studied so far emphasize some mix of freedom and equality, mercantilism focuses on the needs of the state. National economic power is paramount, and the domestic economy is an instrument used to generate that power. Mercantilist states focus in particular on their position in the international system, for they believe that economic weakness undermines national sovereignty.[8]

Although this system may seem a strange outlier in the debate over the proper balance between freedom and equality, since it seems to emphasize neither, mercantilism is the oldest of the four political-economic systems we have covered. Historically, most states engaged in mercantilist practices. The building of empires, in particular, was an outgrowth of mercantilism, a way that a state could use its political power to gain control over resources and markets and shut out its rivals. The British Empire's policy that constrained its colonies to trade only with the home country is a good example of mercantilist practices at work. In fact, Britain only embraced liberalism well after mercantilism had helped enrich the country. More recently, mercantilism has been used to great effect in Asia.

One way that mercantilist states attempt to achieve state economic power is through an active industrial policy. Economic ministries seek to direct the economy toward certain industries and away from others through such policies as taxation and subsidies. In some cases, they may rely on partial or full state ownership of specific industries (sometimes called **parastatals**), attempting to create or control businesses that are viewed as critical for international competitiveness.

Another complementary method is the use of tariffs, nontariff barriers, and other trade regulations. Here the rationale is that foreign goods drain away wealth and promote an increased dependence on foreign economies. High tariff barriers are a common way to shield and promote domestic industry. For example, after World War II, the Japanese government relied on its Ministry of International Trade and Industry to steer the economy toward exports such as electronics and automobiles. High tariff barriers kept foreign competition at bay, and subsidies were provided to certain industrial sectors, such as producers of semiconductors. South Korea and Brazil followed a similar set of policies.

In its emphasis on state power, mercantilism does not typically focus on social expenditures in the way that social democracy does. Welfare benefits tend to be lower. Indeed, there is logic to this policy: a low level of benefits can encourage higher public savings, which can in turn be borrowed by the state or businesses. Lower levels of expenditure are also likely to translate into lower taxes. State capacity and autonomy tend to be higher in mercantilist political-economic systems, though markets and private property remain. This explains why many now use the somewhat vague term "state capitalism" to describe mercantilist systems.

Supporters of mercantilism cite its ability to direct an economy toward areas of industrial development and international competitiveness that the market, left on its own, might not pursue. For developing countries, such direction is particularly

> ### IN FOCUS: How Do Mercantilist States Seek to Achieve Economic Power?
>
> - By directing the economy toward certain industries and away from others through the use of subsidies and taxation
> - Through partial or full state ownership of industries that are considered critical (parastatals)
> - With the strong use of tariffs, nontariff barriers, and other regulations
> - By limiting social expenditures and thereby keeping taxation to a minimum
> - With low interest rates set by the central bank to encourage borrowing and investment

attractive, and Japan and South Korea are cited as exemplars of mercantilism's strengths. Critics of mercantilism observe that, as with communism, states are ill-suited to decide a country's industrial path, and the result is often inefficient industries that survive only because they are protected from outside competition. In addition, the tight relationship between private property and the state is a recipe for corruption, which may drag down development. In the past, mercantilism was often associated with nondemocratic and even fascist regimes. However, South Korea and postwar Japan are countries whose mercantilism did not preclude democracy. Recent global difficulties have made mercantilism more attractive. Many view President Donald Trump's economic policies, which emphasize higher tariff barriers and other trade restrictions, as a shift from America's long-standing liberal policies toward more mercantilist approaches. China is also a country that has come to look less communist and more mercantilist over time.[9]

Political-Economic Systems and the State: Comparing Outcomes

Having gained an understanding of the different political-economic systems used around the world and the different ways they approach their tasks, we should next consider how to compare these systems. We can use various indicators; they are by no means the only way to make comparisons and draw conclusions, but they are useful tools for thinking about the real and ideal differences between economic outcomes.

Measuring Wealth

One basic criterion for comparison is a country's level of economic development. The most common tool that economists use to measure economic development is gross domestic product, or GDP, which we earlier defined as the total market value of all goods and services produced in a country over a period of one year. GDP provides a basic benchmark for the average per capita income in a country. However, GDP statistics can be quite misleading. For one, GDP is not the same as personal income, as it includes things like government expenditures, such as for cleaning up natural disasters. Moreover, it does not assign a value to such things as leisure or innovation.

Another problem is how we compare this wealth across space and time. As we all know, a given amount of money will buy more in certain parts of a country than in others. A salary of $50,000 a year will go a lot further in Boise, Idaho, than it will in New York City, where by some estimates the cost of living is more than twice as much. The same problem arises when we compare countries: people may earn far more in some countries than they do in others, but those raw figures do not take into account the relative costs of living in those countries. Moreover, as exchange rates between national currencies rise or fall, countries can look richer or poorer than they are.

To address these difficulties, economists often calculate national GDP data on the basis of what is known as purchasing power parity. **Purchasing power parity (PPP)** attempts to estimate the buying power of income in each country by comparing similar costs, such as food and housing expenses, by using prices in the United States as a benchmark. When these data are factored in, comparative incomes change dramatically, as shown in Table 4.1. For example, without PPP, Sweden's national income is much higher than Germany's, but when the cost of living in each country is factored in through PPP, their economies are revealed to be of similar size. Incomes in poorer countries such as China and India rise quite dramatically when PPP is taken into account.

Although GDP can be a useful way to measure wealth, it has limitations. One major problem is that it fails to capture much about the quality of life in a country, such as crime levels, mortality rates, and the health of the environment. Other elements of GDP provided by the state, such as health care or education, are hard to measure—meaning that social-democratic countries, whose economies are greatly devalued using PPP, would appear to be much richer if these public goods were factored in. Many economists thus call for a revision if not the outright scrapping of GDP and its replacement with some other form of measurement.[10] Until that happens, we have other ways to determine the outcome of different political-economic systems.

Measuring Inequality and Poverty

Perhaps the most problematic aspect of GDP is that these data do not tell us how wealth is distributed among a population. One approach to this problem is the **Gini index**, a mathematical formula that measures the amount of economic inequality in a society. Complete equality is given a Gini ranking of zero, and complete inequality gets a ranking of 100. Thus the greater the Gini index number, or Gini coefficient, the greater the inequality in a given economy. Some recent Gini coefficients are given in Table 4.1. If we look at these few cases, we note that the relationship between wealth and inequality is not automatic—more wealth does not make a country more or less equal. Second, political-economic systems do matter. Social-democratic countries tend to have lower Gini ratings, which is not surprising given their emphasis on equality. Liberal political-economic systems are more unequal, but levels of income disparity vary widely among them, from Canada at the low end of the spectrum to the United States at the high end. Mercantilist and postcommunist countries show a similar range.

The most unequal countries in the world are very poor. However, inequality is not the same thing as poverty. Poverty tends to be measured in terms of absolute wealth. Organizations like the World Bank establish benchmarks for world poverty rates—typically less than $2 per person per day. In contrast, inequality is a measure of relative wealth. Thus, an entire society can become more materially wealthy and grow more unequal at the same time. Australia has become wealthier and more equal since the 1990s; South Africa has grown wealthier and more unequal.

What are the trends for poverty and inequality worldwide? First, people have grown wealthier overall. Perhaps contrary to expectations, extreme poverty has fallen dramatically. In 1981, over 40 percent of the world's population lived on less than $2 a day; in 2015, that number was 10 percent. This improvement has been driven largely by economic growth in Asia. This growth has in turn led to decreased inequality between countries like China and the United States, as the former grows wealthier. (See "Institutions in Action" on pp. 132–33 for a discussion of the decline in poverty and inequality in Latin America.) Second, economic development has been associated with increased inequality within many of these same countries, such as China and India. This result is not contradictory; a country often experiences rising standards of living across the board, while at the same time the wealthier increase their wealth faster than those who are poorer. This leads us to our third point regarding worldwide inequality between all people. It has been estimated that the Gini coefficient for the world—between all people, rather than just between individuals within a given country—is extremely high, at about 70. However, this may now be declining as economic growth expands

TABLE 4.1 Economic Size and the Distribution of Wealth

COUNTRY	GDP PER CAPITA (IN U.S. $)	GDP PER CAPITA (PPP, IN U.S. $)	GINI INDEX AND YEAR (100 = COMPLETE INEQUALITY)
United States	59,800	59,800	42 (2016)
Australia	57,300	53,400	30 (2008)
Sweden	53,200	51,200	29 (2015)
Canada	45,000	48,400	34 (2013)
Germany	44,600	50,800	32 (2015)
United Kingdom	39,900	44,300	33 (2015)
France	38,600	44,100	29 (2016)
Japan	38,300	42,900	38 (2011)
South Korea	29,700	39,500	36 (2016)
Russia	10,700	27,900	42 (2014)
Brazil	9,800	15,600	53 (2017)
Mexico	9,200	19,900	48 (2016)
China	8,700	16,700	47 (2014)
South Africa	6,100	13,600	63 (2014)
Iran	5,600	20,100	40 (2016)
India	1,900	7,200	35 (2011)
Nigeria	1,900	5,900	49 (2013)

Sources: World Bank, United Nations Development Programme, CIA World Factbook, Branko Milanovic.

around the world. In short, the conclusions we draw about inequality depend on how we compare the data: do we focus on inequalities within nations, which have been growing, or inequality among all people, which has been decreasing?[11] We'll return to this in a moment when we examine shifts in global wealth and the implications for political-economic systems everywhere.

Human Development Index (HDI)

Poverty, inequality—how can we make sense of any of this if we simply want to know whether people are better off? Another kind of measurement might help. The **Human Development Index (HDI)**, created by the United Nations Development Programme, not only looks at the total amount of wealth in a society and its distribution but also gives equal weight to income, health (life expectancy), and average years of schooling. By looking at such data, we can consider whether the wealth generated in a country is actually used in a way that provides a basic standard of living for all through public or private means. Nearly all countries in the world are ranked on the HDI. In 2018, Norway was ranked at number one and the Niger came in at the very bottom.

The HDI does show a strong correlation between standard of living and a country's GDP, as shown in Table 4.2. The countries with the highest national incomes also show the highest levels of education and life expectancy in the world. Interestingly, among the top 20 ranked on the index, we find social-democratic systems such as Sweden right alongside more liberal countries such as the United States and Canada and more mercantilist ones such as Japan and South Korea. But these findings are not quite as clear if we unpack their components of income, education, and health.

In Table 4.2, each of these indicators has been evaluated separately, showing very different sets of rankings. The United States does well in education and income, but its life expectancy lags far behind that of other wealthy countries. France's life expectancy ranks highly, but it does far less well in education

IN FOCUS: Measuring Wealth

GROSS DOMESTIC PRODUCT (GDP)	Measures total production within a country, regardless of who owns the products
PURCHASING POWER PARITY (PPP)	A way to calculate gross domestic product that takes the cost of living and buying power into account
GINI INDEX	Assesses inequality
HUMAN DEVELOPMENT INDEX (HDI)	Assesses health, education, and wealth of population

TABLE 4.2 — Measuring Wealth, Equality, and Prosperity

COUNTRY	UN HUMAN DEVELOPMENT RANKING	UN LIFE EXPECTANCY RANKING	UN EDUCATION RANKING	UN INCOME RANKING	UN GENDER EQUALITY RANKING
Germany	4	27	1	19	19
Sweden	8	11	10	17	8
Canada	13	14	17	23	18
United States	15*	40	12	11	42
United Kingdom	15*	26	8	30	27
Japan	19	2	29	25	23
South Korea	22	8	24	32	10
France	26	12	42	26	8
Russia	49	115	35	53	54
Iran	65	66	66	65	118
Mexico	76	85	97	67	74
Brazil	79	75	95	90	89
China	85	62	115	74	39
South Africa	113	173	75	101	97
India	129	145	143	133	122
Nigeria	158	203	164	150	N/A

*Countries with identical HDI values to three decimal places are ranked as ties.
Note: N/A: data not available.
Source: United Nations Development Programme, http://hdr.undp.org/en/data (accessed 1/31/20).

given its overall HDI. Finally, we can add another important variable calculated by the United Nations but not included in the HDI: gender equality. If we look at all the relevant indicators (reproductive health, proportion of legislative seats occupied by women, rates of secondary education, and labor market participation), our rankings are again quite different. The United Kingdom,

Canada, and especially the United States show a large gap between their HDI and gender equality rankings. In contrast, social democracies show a stronger commitment to gender equality. China's historical communist commitment to equality is also reflected in its high gender equality ranking relative to its HDI.[12]

Happiness

Given the rather technical nature of our discussion so far, it may seem strange to speak of happiness as an indicator that we can use to compare political-economic systems. But when we think about it, though it may be difficult to define, happiness is at the core of human activity. It is the result of the interaction between freedom and equality. From philosophers to evolutionary psychologists, a common argument holds that the pursuit of personal happiness is among the central motivations driving human behavior. If that is the case, happiness can be a useful indicator of political-economic development, and social scientists have recently paid more attention to it.

At the most basic level, we can observe that richer countries generally are happier than poorer ones. This assumption is logical; people in extreme poverty have little security and few resources to advance their lives. Past that level of poverty, however, a long-standing debate continues over the sources and levels of happiness around the world. This debate can be seen in terms of absolute versus relative happiness. For example, in the case of extreme poverty, we can view happiness as an absolute good and little different from the idea of security—having enough money to eat regularly is quite likely to increase happiness. However, many psychologists have argued that beyond basic human needs, much happiness is neither sustained nor absolute. Similarly, according to the "Easterlin paradox," developed by the social scientist Richard A. Easterlin, when standards of living rise past a certain level (perhaps $10,000–$15,000 per capita GDP), happiness stagnates. After that level, it is argued, people's relative income—our wealth relative to that of those around us—is a stronger predictor of happiness than our overall standard of living.[13]

However, not all scholars agree that people's level of happiness is a function of their relative wealth. While economic growth may generate greater "happiness returns" in poor countries, some studies indicate that richer countries, too, continue to see a modest growth in happiness. But is a country's happiness shaped only by its overall level of development?

TABLE 4.3 Measuring Happiness, 2016–2018

COUNTRY/REGION	HAPPINESS (SCALE 0–10)	COUNTRY/REGION	HAPPINESS (SCALE 0–10)
United Kingdom	7.1	China	5.2
Germany	7.0	Bulgaria	5.0
United States	6.9	Congo	4.8
Mexico	6.6	Palestinian Territories	4.7
Brazil	6.3	Iran	4.5
Japan	5.9	Togo	4.1
Pakistan	5.7	India	4.0
Russia	5.6	Tanzania	3.2
Nigeria	5.3		

Source: United Nations World Happiness Report, https://worldhappiness.report/ed/2019 (accessed 1/13/20).

If we look at Table 4.3, which calculates happiness on the basis of positive emotions and life satisfaction, we see some interesting variations. First, wealth is not necessary to happiness. It is true that the unhappiest countries in the world are the most desperately poor and that most of the happiest countries in the world are wealthy states. But there are important exceptions. Mexico, along with Costa Rica, Chile, and Guatemala all rank within the top 30 happiest countries. These are all countries with modest levels of development and high levels of economic inequality. If they have anything in common, it is culture. In contrast, postcommunist countries have much lower levels of happiness, and some individual countries fall much further down the list than very poor countries—Russians are no happier than Pakistanis, even though their GDP per capita at PPP is five times as high. East Asian countries such as Japan and South Korea are less happy than we might expect if we assumed that GDP or HDI was the most important predictor of happiness. Other factors, such as corruption, social support, or individual freedom, go some way to explain these differences but still do not fully solve this puzzle. This imperfect fit between wealth, inequality, and happiness is important to consider alongside the Easterlin paradox. Extreme poverty produces misery, and many rich countries are happy. However, levels of wealth, inequality, and development do not correlate with happiness as neatly as we would expect.[14]

The Rise and Fall of Liberalism?

We've covered a lot of ground in this chapter, laying out variations in the relationships among property, markets, the state, and political-economic systems. From there, we laid out some different tools for making comparisons, such as GDP, the Gini index, the HDI, and measurements of happiness. In this discussion, we've had glimpses of change in the international system but have not addressed this directly. Where do we seem to be heading?

For at least a century, our four major models of political economy have rivaled one another as they have sought to strike the ideal relationship between freedom and equality. At the dawn of modern capitalism, mercantilism was a dominant force, central to the establishment of empires and industries. At the same time, liberalism began to emerge as a challenge to mercantilism, particularly in the United Kingdom and its former colonies. But by the early twentieth century, liberalism was in turn threatened by fascist and communist regimes. Many believed that these regimes, coupled to powerful states, were superior to a liberalism faltering under global depression. Even when fascism was defeated, communism continued to spread worldwide, social democracy came to define much of Europe, and mercantilism drew adherents in many less-developed countries.

Yet as we stand at the beginning of the twenty-first century, the world is a quite different place. Communism has effectively vanished, even in places like China, where market forces now drive the economy, something we will discuss in Chapter 9. During the past 20 years, mercantilism, too, has been scaled back or dismantled in many developing countries, a trend we will consider in Chapter 10. For the past two decades, social democracy and liberalism have appeared to be the only viable political-economic systems, but even the countries using these systems have been undergoing further **economic liberalization**—cutting taxes, reducing regulation, privatizing state-owned businesses and public goods, and expanding property rights.

Table 4.4 compares the levels of economic change around the world consistent with liberalism, taking into account such factors as government expenditures, price controls, taxes, individual property rights, and trade. Changes in these areas that limit the state's power over private property and market forces are what we view as economic liberalization. The ratings in the table are given on a 10-point scale, where 10 is the most liberal and one is the least. Since 1980 economic liberalization has grown, in some cases dramatically, around the world.[15]

Yet when we look at the more recent data, we see that the most dramatic liberalization occurred between 1980 and 2005. Since then liberalization has slowed, and in a number of important cases regulations and restrictions on trade have

TABLE 4.4 Levels of Economic Liberalization, 2000–2017

COUNTRY	2000	2017
United States	8.7	8.2
New Zealand	8.6	8.5
United Kingdom	8.6	8.1
Canada	8.3	8.1
Japan	8.1	7.9
Germany	8.0	7.8
Sweden	7.9	7.6
France	7.6	7.4
Chile	7.5	7.9
South Africa	7.0	6.6
South Korea	6.9	7.6
World	6.7	6.8
Mexico	6.6	6.9
India	6.5	6.9
Brazil	6.0	6.2
China	5.8	6.4
Venezuela	5.8	2.6
Iran	5.5	5.7
Russia	5.4	6.8
Nigeria	5.1	6.9

Note: 10 = most liberal.
Source: Fraser Institute, https://fraserinstitute.org/economic-freedom (accessed 1/13/20).

increased. In fact, across many countries we have seen a growing resistance to liberalism perhaps unmatched since the 1930s. One immediate cause was the economic recession of the last decade. But broader forces are also at work—notably, changes in global wealth, driven by globalization and technological change. As Figure 4.2 shows, economic development around the world has changed dramatically, affected by the rise of globalization. New economic opportunities in Asia have led to astounding economic growth, reducing poverty and creating a huge middle class in that part of the world. A much smaller global elite has

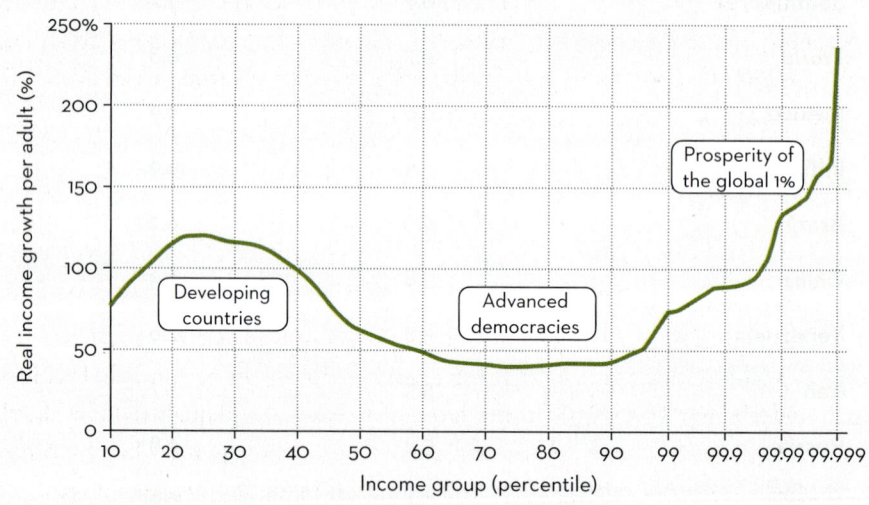

FIGURE 4.2 — Winners and Losers in the Global Economy

This data from 1980 to 2016 show that the poorest half of the global population has seen a dramatic growth in income, notable in China and India. However, because of high and rising levels of inequality within countries, the top 1 percent—that is, the wealthiest individuals in the world—enjoyed twice as much growth as the bottom 50 percent. Meanwhile, among advanced democracies, growth has been much lower or even nonexistent for both middle and lower income groups.

Source: World Inequality Report, https://wir2018.wid.world/files/download/wir2018-full-report-english.pdf (accessed 11/22/19).

equally benefited from economic globalization, such that now over 40 percent of the world's wealth is held by 1 percent of the world's population. Both of these developments have undermined the middle class in many richer countries, while the very poorest have seen little benefit overall. This continued, seemingly inexorable rise in inequality within many countries is extremely worrying. Many social scientists believe that high levels of inequality and stagnant economic growth can erode the legitimacy of state, societal, and economic institutions. Political instability can increase if people no longer believe that their future is one of greater security and prosperity. This represents a very real challenge to liberalism: the traditional prescription of a small state, low regulations and taxes, and free trade is for many no longer convincing. As a result, in many countries we have seen parties and politicians who oppose free trade or a smaller state in favor of social-democratic or mercantilist ideas. We have also seen the rise of illiberal and nondemocratic movements and leaders who see economic challenges in zero-sum terms, often with foreigners—either within or without—viewed as a threat to jobs.

Critiques of liberalism may struggle to provide alternatives; many countries simply cannot afford the social expenditures they have enjoyed or any limitation of free trade without harming their own economies. At the same time, it is not possible to roll back technological changes, like computers, the Internet, and automated production, that have eliminated many jobs altogether. Even if critiques of liberalism fail to articulate a viable alternative, we could still see the continued weakening of this ideology and related political-economic institutions, with huge repercussions for capitalism, and maybe even democracy, around the globe. We will consider this at length in chapters to come.

In Sum: A New Economic Era?

As we have seen, states play a large role in both domestic and international economies. They must manage markets and property with an eye toward generating societal wealth and revenue so that basic political tasks can be funded. This is no small undertaking, for it goes to the heart of freedom and equality: How should freedom and equality be reconciled through economic policy, and what mixture of the two will create the most wealth? Different political-economic systems give very different answers to those questions. Economic liberalism has weathered various challenges to emerge as the dominant system in much of the world. As we shall see in upcoming chapters, this "triumph" of liberalism has occurred alongside political

INSTITUTIONS IN ACTION

Why Have Poverty and Inequality Declined in Latin America?

At the start of this chapter, we discussed the economic and political fortunes of Venezuela and Hugo Chávez's attempt to use the state and natural resource revenues toward particular political-economic ends. As we noted, part of Chávez's public appeal was his call to address Venezuela's economic problems. Since the 1980s, the country's GDP per capita in PPP had been in steady decline, having lost a third of its value by the time Chávez came to power in 1999. But Venezuela is not unique in its problems.

For generations, Latin America has been marked by a high degree of poverty, inequality, and economic and political instability. Why? Some say this situation is a result of the particular forms of colonialism practiced by Spain and Portugal, which created a feudal agricultural system that stunted development and the rise of a middle class. Others, especially Marxists, point to more recent developments, laying the blame on unequal economic relations between Latin America and the United States and Europe during the twentieth century (see Chapter 10). Liberals have responded by critiquing Marxist and mercantilist political-economic ideas. Whatever the cause, the resulting economic difficulties seemed resistant to change, even as much poorer Asia surged ahead.

Yet, starting in the 1990s, poverty began to rapidly decline across the region, from over 40 percent in 1993 to around 29 percent in 2014. Equally surprising, during this same period inequality also declined from an average Gini index of 53 to 49—the lowest since industrialization and the opposite of what has occurred in much of the rest of the world. Why this dramatic change?

Some have pointed to economic liberalization, which increased dramatically across the region (Venezuela is a notable exception) and created new opportunities for economic development by removing barriers to trade and job creation. Another factor has been an increase in economic globalization, in particular a growing global (particularly Chinese) demand for Latin American commodities such as copper and iron. However, these two explanations, while important, don't account for why growth has been coupled with a decrease in inequality. As the United Nations Development Programme has noted, development indicators in Latin America have performed better than the levels of economic growth would predict.

An additional factor we might overlook is one that is central to comparative politics: the state. Marxists viewed Latin American states as under the control of capitalism and American imperialism, favoring revolution along the lines of the conflict in Cuba as a way to gain economic and political sovereignty. Mercantilists believed that only by developing domestic industries, shielded from international pressure, could the region develop (see Chapter 10). Meanwhile, liberals argued that Latin American states, bloated and inefficient, were the primary obstacle to economic growth. The argument turned into more of a discussion over whether the state was "good" or "bad" than a question of what *kind* of state might alleviate economic misery.

In this regard, Latin America has been an innovator in the provision of public goods.

Latin America has long suffered from a weak social safety net—a condition that exacerbates poverty and inequality. At the same time, weak capacity meant that developing new state institutions to improve social welfare was a challenge. As a result, a number of Latin American countries embraced what are known as conditional cash transfers. These are essentially direct cash payments to the poor, contingent on the recipients meeting particular requirements. One of the most common conditions for cash transfers is that families keep their children in school, as opposed to using them for labor to supplement family income. Amounts are often relatively small but widespread. In Brazil and Mexico, around a quarter of the population benefits from such transfers. The success of these programs has in turn improved the level of education in Latin America, because more children stay in school, and resulted in a better-educated workforce. These kinds of social-democratic policies, enacted alongside economic liberalization, are now viewed as a model for other parts of the world. Systems that rely overwhelmingly on state power, as in Venezuela, or largely on the free market with little redistribution, as in liberal Chile, have been less successful in narrowing the gap between rich and poor.

It is easy to get carried away with these findings and assume that cash transfers are the silver bullet that can solve problems of inequality and poverty. Social welfare institutions are still very weak in Latin America. Keeping children in school is a major accomplishment, but educational systems across the region, from primary to higher education, are poor. Improving schools will be particularly important as the region requires more skilled labor for continued economic growth. Basic services, such as access to drinking

Brazilian Maria Nilza shows her "Bolsa Família" conditional cash transfer plan card.

water, electricity, and sanitation, are uneven, contributing to public health problems. Continued progress will require building state capacity, which, as we noted in Chapter 2, is no easy feat. The region may already be coming up against these barriers, as continued reduction in inequality has slowed and extreme poverty has begun to rise again. This may well be a function of the same kinds of economic challenges that richer countries are facing in the areas of employment and social expenditures as their populations age. Nevertheless, we have found an important piece of this puzzle: issues like poverty and inequality are not simply economic problems that require economic solutions. The state is a critical institution in creating and redistributing wealth and prosperity.[a]

1. How has the state influenced Venezuela's economic growth, and why has it lagged behind that of other Latin American countries?

2. Do you think that direct cash transfers, which are effective in some countries, would work to alleviate poverty in all situations? Why or why not?

liberalization as many nondemocratic regimes around the globe have given way to democracy.

At the same time, in the past few years serious questions about the limits of liberalism have been raised as various countries face sustained economic difficulties. A great deal of change is on the horizon, and we will spend much of our time in the upcoming chapters trying to get a better glimpse of what may lie ahead.

Key Terms

capitalism (p. 113)
central bank (p. 108)
comparative advantage (p. 111)
deflation (p. 110)
economic liberalization (p. 128)
Gini index (p. 122)
gross domestic product (GDP) (p. 106)
Human Development Index (HDI) (p. 124)
hyperinflation (p. 109)
inflation (p. 109)
laissez-faire (p. 113)
market (p. 102)
mercantilism (p. 118)
monopoly (p. 110)
nontariff regulatory barriers (p. 111)
parastatal (p. 119)
political-economic system (p. 112)
political economy (p. 101)
property (p. 104)
public goods (p. 105)
purchasing power parity (PPP) (p. 121)
quota (p. 111)
regulation (p. 110)
social expenditures (p. 105)
tariff (p. 111)

For Further Reading

Bernstein, Eduard. *Evolutionary Socialism: A Criticism and Affirmation.* 1899. New York: Schocken, 1961.

Collier, Paul. *The Future of Capitalism: Facing the New Anxieties.* London: Penguin Random House UK, 2018.

Easterlin, Richard A. *Happiness, Growth, and the Life Cycle.* New York: Oxford University Press, 2010.

List, Friedrich. *The National System of Political Economy.* 1841. New York: Kelley, 1966.

Milanovic, Branko. *Global Inequality: A New Approach for the Age of Globalization.* Cambridge, MA: Harvard University Press, 2016.

Milanovic, Branko. *The Haves and the Have-Nots: A Brief and Idiosyncratic History of Global Inequality.* New York: Basic Books, 2011.

Olson, Mancur. *The Logic of Collective Action: Public Goods and the Theory of Groups.* Cambridge, MA: Harvard University Press, 1965.

Piketty, Thomas. *Capital in the Twenty-First Century.* Cambridge, MA: Belknap Press, 2014.

Smith, Adam. *An Inquiry into the Nature and Causes of the Wealth of Nations.* Edwin Cannan, ed. 1776. Chicago: University of Chicago Press, 1976.

INQUIZITIVE

Earn a better grade on your test. InQuizitive personalizes your learning path to help you master the concepts from this chapter and practice applying them to examples from the text and beyond (see back cover).

QUESTIONS AND METHODS

Are Liberal Economies Really That Liberal?

In this and the previous chapter we have noted the ideological and policy differences between liberalism and social democracy. Liberal political-economic systems proceed from the assumption that a weak state is necessary to encourage individual freedom. In practical terms this means lower levels of regulation, an emphasis on private property as a way to generate wealth, and a lower level of social expenditures. Redistribution of wealth is discouraged, meaning that inequality tends to be higher. In contrast, social democracy, with its emphasis on redistribution, is typically associated with what we call the welfare state. The state is viewed as a key institution to generate greater economic equality through a wide array of public goods and services funded by higher taxes. Social-democratic states therefore not only tend toward greater capacity, but also greater scope (recall our Questions and Methods box in Chapter 2). The scope of the state is more likely to stretch

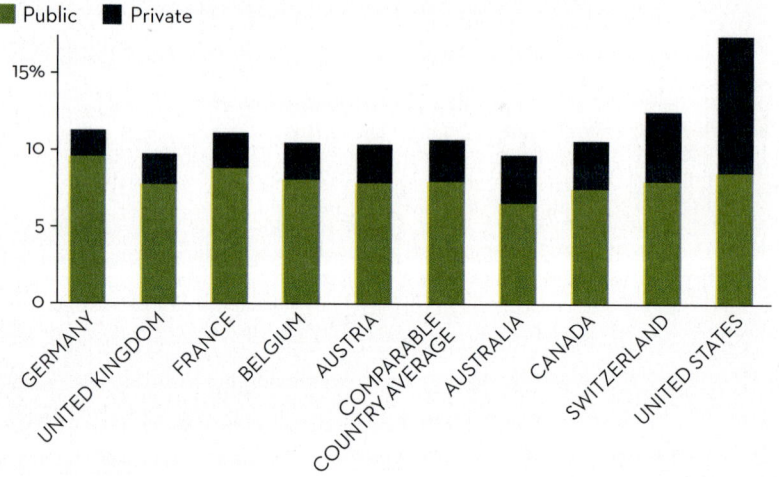

Total Health Expenditures as a Percentage of GDP by Public versus Private Spending, 2016

Source: Peterson-Kaiser Health System Tracker, www.healthsystemtracker.org/chart-collection/health-spending-u-s-compare-countries (accessed 1/13/20).

into such areas as health care, retirement, and higher education.

These arguments are clear and, when we look at things like tax rates and the Gini index, uncontroversial. But are the differences between liberal and social-democratic states so clear? For example, the U.S. government (state, local, and federal combined) employs nearly 15 percent of the workforce, compared with just 10 percent in Germany. The United States also owns entities that are in private hands in other parts of the world. Half of commercial airports in Europe have some form of partial or full private ownership. In the United States there is one private commercial airport: Branson Airport in Branson, Missouri.

Another interesting area is that of health care. Again, in a liberal political-economic system, the state provision of health care would be much more limited than we would find in a social-democratic system, relying on the market to provide these goods. But here again, we find that the United States spends as much or more than social-democratic systems—not just in private spending, which we would expect, but in public spending as well.[a] You can see this in the graph on the opposite page. What to make of this? At a minimum, it means that the ideological dividing lines between political-economic systems are not as clear as we imagine, and that there is often a large gap between the ideology behind a regime and the reality of its economic institutions.

1. **Consider the differences between alternative political institutions**

   What would be an "ideal" liberal or social-democratic political-economic system, at least in terms of its objectives? What would be the necessary social expenditures, regulations, and taxes?

2. **Evaluate possible institutional changes**

   What are some of the reasons why a liberal-democratic system might become more social democratic over time, or vice versa? What would that change look like?

3. **Generate new ideas related to the discussion**

   Imagine that you were tasked with recrafting a new political-economic system for your country to reduce inequality or to increase economic growth. What are the biggest changes you would make? What would the potential financial or social costs be to make those changes? Think not just about social expenditures and other public goods, but also taxes and regulation.

---

a. Bradley Sawyer and Cynthia Cox, "How Does Health Spending in the U.S. Compare to Other Countries?" Peterson-Kaiser Health System Tracker, December 7, 2018, www.healthsystemtracker.org/chart-collection/health-spending-u-s-compare-countries (accessed 10/21/19).

5

Former prime minister Mahathir Mohamed raises the hand of Anwar Ibrahim during an election campaign event in 2018. Do electoral institutions necessarily imply strong democracies?

DEMOCRATIC REGIMES

What makes democracy rise and prosper?

National elections in Malaysia in May 2018, like those the year before in Nepal (see Chapter 3), have been widely regarded as a sea change in that country's politics. The ruling United Malays National Organisation (UMNO), which had controlled the country since independence in 1957, lost badly to a coalition of opposition parties known as Pakatan Harapan, or the Alliance of Hope. On the surface this transition seems to have been driven by the power of individual elites and charismatic legitimacy, as the Alliance is led by two important figures. Former deputy prime minister Anwar Ibrahim had been jailed twice for nearly 10 years after opposing government corruption and favoring economic reform. In contrast, the other leader was 93-year-old former prime minister Mahathir Mohamad, who came out of retirement to lead the Alliance alongside Anwar. Remembered fondly by many for his 20 years in power, Mahathir capitalized on his legacy by fashioning himself as the savior of the people. Ironically, it was Mahathir who had had Anwar first arrested in 1998 when the two clashed over their rival visions for the country.

But while the Alliance's leadership was important, existing institutions mattered as well. Most importantly, in contrast to many other authoritarian regimes, a number of the basic democratic institutions had long been in place. The UMNO itself was not the only party in power, but rather part of a coalition that included parties representing the Chinese and Indian minorities. A number of opposition parties also existed, representing a spectrum of religious and ideological values. The country also regularly held elections, which the UMNO and its two allied parties (collectively known as the National Front) consistently won, relying on a variety of tactics.

One element of control was the electoral system, which we will discuss in detail in this chapter. The UMNO relied on a single-member-district system for elections, like that of the United States, which meant there would be only one winner from each district: whoever had gained the plurality (the largest share) of votes. This helped marginalize smaller parties, since even a second-place showing would not result in getting a seat in a district. To further make certain that the UMNO would win the most seats, the government also manipulated electoral boundaries in a way that would weaken the opposition's bases of support. One method was malapportionment. This meant that there were fewer legislative seats in states (Malaysia is a federal system) where there was strong opposition to the National Front, while states where there was greater support would send more representatives to the legislature. Thus in the 2013 elections Sarawak and Sabah, strongholds of the UMNO, comprised around 16 percent of the population, but elected 26 percent of the legislative seats. Another method was to draw electoral districts in a way that would ensure that National Front supporters would contribute the largest share of the vote (what is commonly known as gerrymandering). Prior to the 2018 elections, one electoral district in the capital, Kuala Lumpur, seemed likely to go for the Alliance. In response, the government redrew the district to include the nearby national police headquarters, who would be a bloc of loyal voters. These tactics helped ensure that the UMNO consistently won elections even as their share of the popular vote fell from over 60 percent in 1995 to less than half in 2013.

Eventually, however, these electoral mechanisms could no longer sustain the UMNO and its National Front allies. The UMNO and the head of government, Najib Razak, became embroiled in a scandal involving billions of dollars stolen from state coffers. What made the opposition effective was its ability to mobilize around the very institutions that had marginalized them for decades. Rather than needing to call for radical regime change, which might have alienated many Malaysians, opposition forces instead were able to rally the public around the idea of *Reformasi*—that the existing electoral system be reformed to function fairly and transparently. Thus, while Anwar and Mahathir are no doubt key to understanding the election outcomes, one lesson is that we should not underestimate the role that existing participatory institutions can play in providing a goal for a successful challenge to those in power.

A second lesson applies to existing democracies. Malapportionment and gerrymandering are common practices in institutionalized democracies—the latter term, in fact, comes from early American electoral history. Democratic institutions can be used to incorporate or disenfranchise people. Even the presence of elections and opposition parties does not indicate a robust democracy if those practices significantly limit public participation and the turnover of power.

> **LEARNING OBJECTIVES**
>
> - Describe the components and development of democracy.
> - Explain how executive, legislative, and judicial institutions vary in their construction and degree of power.
> - Distinguish among parliamentary, presidential, and semi-presidential democracies.
> - Summarize the differences between plurality, majority, and proportional representation systems.

For most of human history, societies have not been organized in a way that we would consider democratic. But in the last two centuries, revolution, war, and the destruction of rival ideologies have paved the way for democracy around the globe. From the perspective of those already living in a democratic society, the spread of this political system may appear natural or inevitable (though perhaps less so of late). But why would democracy be an attractive or effective form of government? How does democracy actually work? Does democracy by definition reconcile freedom and equality in a single way, or does it allow for different mixtures of the two?

This chapter will speak to these questions as we consider the origins, structures, strengths, and weaknesses of democracy. We will begin by defining democracy and then trace democracy's origins. Next we will consider the various institutions that represent the core "goods" of democracy: participation, competition, and liberty. As we shall see, there is no one relationship among these three. Various democracies construct them differently, shaping freedom, equality, and the locus of power. Finally, we will consider some of the challenges to democracy around the world as we move into the next set of chapters.

Defining Democracy

Before proceeding, we must nail down our terminology. The word *democracy* has an inherently positive connotation for many people: things that are "democratic" are good; things that are "undemocratic" are bad. Of course, in reality, this is far from the truth: businesses and nonprofits are not democratic institutions, but that does not necessarily mean they are deficient. Because of the word's symbolism, however, many individuals and organizations describe themselves as democratic but define the term in very different ways. For example, in Chapter 3 we noted that for communists democracy means collective equality and not individual freedom. Countries such as China thus see themselves as "true" democracies, which they define as featuring, among other things, full employment, universal education, and the elimination of economic classes. These societies see democracy in the United States and Europe as little more than the struggle among members of a small elite group. Naturally, capitalist countries view communist systems, with their single-party control and lack of civil liberties, as anything but democratic. As you can see, each side uses different criteria to define democracy.

How can we make any comparisons if democracy is in the eye of the beholder? One way is to go back to the origin of the word. *Democracy* comes from the Greek words *demos*, meaning "the common people," and *kratia*, meaning "power" or "rule." Based on this origin, we can define democracy at its most fundamental as a system in which political power resides with the people. The people, in turn, may exercise that power either directly or indirectly. And the exercise of power typically takes three forms: participation, through means such as voting and elections; competition, such as that between political parties; and liberty, such as freedom of speech or of assembly. **Democracy**, then, can be fully defined as political power exercised either directly or indirectly by the people through participation, competition, and liberty.

This definition is subjective; it clearly emphasizes individual freedom and is in keeping with the ideology of liberalism. Indeed, many political scientists use the more specific term **liberal democracy** to indicate they are referring to a political system that promotes participation, competition, and liberty. Liberal democracies are rooted in the ideology of liberalism, with its emphasis on individual rights and freedoms.[1] But liberal democracy is not found only where a liberal ideology and a liberal political-economic system are predominant. Many liberal democracies have social-democratic political-economic systems, which emphasize collective welfare much more than individual rights and so curtail individual freedoms in favor of greater equality. But social democracies nevertheless continue to respect the basic liberal-democratic tenets of participation, competition, and liberty. Mercantilist political economies, too, emphasize a strong role for the state, resulting in fewer personal freedoms, but this has not prevented countries such as India, Japan, Taiwan, and South Korea from developing strong liberal-democratic institutions. In each case, we find the basic rights of participation, competition, and liberty, though to different degrees. This variation in turn affects the degree of state autonomy and capacity.

Finally, it is important to remember what is not being said here about democracy. This book makes no claim that a particular kind of democracy, or even democracy itself, is the best way to organize politics. It is presenting democracy only as a particular system of institutions that have developed over time and out of liberal thought. Each person must decide whether the particular goals enshrined in liberal democracy are the most important and whether society is best served by being organized in this manner.

Origins of Democracy

We now have an understanding of the most basic elements of democracy, but this still does not explain why it has come about and where it comes from. Some elements of democratic participation can be found in many societies around the world, dating back thousands of years. But liberal-democratic institutions and practices have their roots in ancient Greece and Rome, where each country contributed to modern democracy in different ways.

Athenian and other early Greek democracies are important because they provide the foundation for the concept of public participation. Typically found in small communities, ancient Greek democracy allowed the public (excluding women, children, foreigners, and slaves) to participate directly in the affairs of government, choosing policies and making governing decisions. In this sense, the people were the state.[2] In contrast, the Roman Empire laid out the concept of **republicanism**, which emphasized the **separation of powers** within a state and the representation of the public through elected officials (as opposed to the unaccountable powers of a monarchy or the direct participation of the people). Thus, while Greece gives us the idea of popular sovereignty, it is from Rome that we derive the notion of legislative bodies like a senate. In their earliest forms, neither Greek democracy nor Roman republicanism would be defined as liberal democracies by today's standards. Both emphasized certain democratic elements but restricted them in fundamental ways. As political rights and institutions have expanded over the centuries, republicanism and democracy—Roman and Greek thought and practices—have become intertwined to produce the modern liberal-democratic regime we know today.

The discussion so far may lead us to conclude that the development of democracy was a long, unbroken line from Greece to today. But that was not the case. Roman republicanism was quite different from Greek participatory democracy, and in time both collapsed. Yet democratic institutions and practices slowly reemerged, most notably in thirteenth-century England. At that time, English nobles forced King John to sign the Magna Carta, a document that curbed the rights of the king and laid the foundation for an early form of legislature, a key element of republicanism. In addition, the Magna Carta asserted that all freemen (at the time, only male members of the aristocracy) should enjoy due process before the law; this assertion set the stage for the idea of liberty. The Magna Carta states:

> No freeman shall be taken, imprisoned, ... or in any other way destroyed ... except by the lawful judgment of his peers, or by the law of the land. To no one will we sell, to none will we deny or delay, right or justice.

Although the Magna Carta was limited in its goals and application, it presented the idea that no individual, not even the king, was above the law. This concept thrived in England over the centuries as democratic practices expanded and an ever-greater proportion of the public was given political rights. The emergence of democracy in England was thus incremental, developing across centuries.

Was there something special about England that allowed democracy to flourish there in the first place? As noted in Chapter 2, European states emerged out of centuries of conflict as rival warlords slowly concentrated their holdings and extended their power. For various reasons, in England neither the state nor the feudal elite was able to get the upper hand, leading to a relative balance of power. This balance may have been facilitated by the defensive benefits of being an island; the need to maintain a large army to unify and defend the country was much lower for isolated England than for the many other European states. Ocean trade, too, provided revenue through port duties, which meant less need for a strong state to squeeze taxes from the public. The result was a relatively clear separation of power that facilitated individual freedom. This in turn would eventually give shape to the ideology of liberalism. It is no accident that an ideology emphasizing individual freedom and private property emerged in a country where state capacity and autonomy were

IN FOCUS: Two Forms of Democracy

DIRECT DEMOCRACY	Public participates directly in governance and policy making; historically found in small communities such as ancient Athens.
INDIRECT DEMOCRACY	Public participates indirectly through its elected representatives; the prevalent form of democracy in the modern age.

not excessive. The public, able to gain the upper hand against the state early on in England's political development, could check attempts by the state to increase its power. This public power paved the way for an expansion of rights over time, culminating in modern liberal democracy.[3]

Contemporary Democratization

Historical background helps us understand the emergence of democracy, but for scholars of contemporary politics it does not provide much guidance. Why is South Africa a democracy when neighboring Zimbabwe is not? What explains the wave of democratization across Latin America in the 1980s? Competing explanations for democratization and democratic institutionalization have fallen in and out of favor over time. Some of this may be a function of improved scholarship, but it may also be that explanations that were accurate at one time lose their explanatory power as the world changes.

Modernization and Democratization

One of the most prominent theories argues that democratization is correlated with, if not caused by, modernization. As we recall from Chapter 1, the behavioral revolution in political science was strongly connected to modernization theory, which posited that as societies became more modern, they would inevitably become more democratic. Why? Modernization is associated with better education, a weakening of older traditional institutions that stressed authority and hierarchy, greater gender equality, and the rise of a middle class. To sum up, modernization theory suggests that as societies become better educated and more economically sophisticated, they need and desire greater control over the state to achieve and defend their own interests.

In the 1970s, this theory fell out of favor. Democracy was failing in many countries in Latin America, while development in Asia leapt forward alongside nondemocratic regimes. It seemed that modernization at best was irrelevant to the development of democracy and at worst could destabilize existing institutions and lead to political violence (see Chapter 7) and democratic failure. Scholars no longer make sweeping claims that modernization inevitably leads to democracy. However, some note that while democracy can emerge in a variety of circumstances, wealth and ongoing economic development are critical to the institutionalization and long-term survival of any democracy.[4]

TIMELINE

Milestones in the Rise of Democracy

18TH CENTURY B.C.E.	Babylonian ruler Hammurabi establishes the earliest-known legal code.
6TH CENTURY B.C.E.	Autocratic rule overthrown and first democracy established in Athens.
5TH CENTURY B.C.E.	Democracy collapses in Athens as it is undermined by war and economic crisis.
1ST CENTURY B.C.E.	Roman philosopher Cicero writes of *res publica*, or "affairs of the people," viewing the public as an important source of political power.
5TH–10TH CENTURIES C.E.	European Dark Ages: power in Europe is fragmented, fostering intense competition among rulers and setting the stage for the emergence of the nation-state.
1215	English Magna Carta establishes an early precedent for the rule of law.
1648	Treaty of Westphalia asserts the right of European states to choose their own religion, enforcing the notion of state sovereignty.
1689	Bill of Rights is passed in England, establishing parliamentary supremacy.
1690	English philosopher John Locke writes *Two Treatises of Government*, arguing that government's job is to protect "the right to life, liberty, and the ownership of property."
1762	Jean-Jacques Rousseau writes *The Social Contract*, arguing that if a government fails to serve its subjects the populace has the right to overthrow it.
1787	U.S. Constitution and Bill of Rights codify the separation of powers and civil rights.
1832–84	Reform Acts in the United Kingdom expand voting rights to much of the male population.
1893	New Zealand is the first country to grant women the right to vote.
1945	Defeat of the Axis powers eliminates fascism as a threat to democracy in Europe and Japan.
1948	United Nations approves the Universal Declaration of Human Rights, setting the stage for the internationalization of civil rights.
1989–91	Soviet Union disintegrates, leading to democratization in Eastern Europe.
1994	First democratic elections in South Africa, ending racial restrictions on voting.

Elites and Democratization

We noted earlier that modernization theory has risen, fallen, and risen again in prominence over time. In the past, modernization theory implied that democratization was almost automatic once a country developed a strong middle class and reached a certain standard of living. This argument, however, did not explain how the change would come about. We can also point to countries where standards of living have risen but democracy has not followed, such as the oil states of the Middle East. What explains this?

One answer may lie in the role of those in power, the political elites. For the past several decades, many scholars who had turned away from modernization theory concentrated instead on the strategic motivations of those in power, and on what would lead them to hang on to or surrender power. Much of this work tended to describe rather than explain political change, but of late these arguments have gained new life by drawing on some earlier ideas of modernization theory.

Central to modernization theory is the idea that a middle class is essential for democratization—a significant segment of the population with the economic resources necessary to advance and demand their own rights. Similarly, overall poverty can be an obstacle to democracy; where people have little, they have little to fight for. But the distribution of wealth may be more important. Where economic assets are concentrated in the hands of those in power, political change is much less likely if they believe that it would divest them of their wealth. Think, for example, of countries like Nigeria or Saudi Arabia, where those in power control significant natural resources, such as oil. Those who control these assets may be loath to give them up. But sources of wealth are not fixed; natural resources may decline, and an economy may stagnate. Those in power may no longer see much value in clinging to power, especially if they believe they can take some wealth with them in exchange for stepping aside.[5] In short, economic development is important, but the nature of the resources that fuel it can determine the likelihood that democracy will emerge. We will speak of this in much greater detail in the next chapter, on nondemocratic regimes.

Society and Democratization

A somewhat different view of democratization emphasizes not the importance of political elites but the political power of society itself. Elite-based theories can give us a sense of why leaders may be more or less willing to surrender power to the public but not why the public would demand power in the first place. Likewise, modernization theory, though it explains how societies might change in a direction more in tune with democratic institutions, does not provide a clear sense of why society would want to move in this direction.

Scholars more interested in the role of society have in the past stressed the importance of public organization or, specifically, what is called **civil society**. Basically, civil society can be defined as organized life outside the state, or what the French scholar Alexis de Tocqueville called the "art of association."[6] Civil society is a fabric of organizations, not necessarily political, created by people to help define their own interests, whatever they may be: environmental groups, churches, sports teams, fraternal organizations, and the like. Under the right circumstances, these associations serve as a vehicle for democratization by allowing people to articulate, promote, and defend what is important to them.

Where civil society has been able to take root, it is argued, democratization is more likely because it provides the ideas and the tools of political action and mobilization that allow small-scale democratic practices to spread. (See "Questions and Methods" on pp. 176–77 for a discussion of what happens as civil society decreases in established democracies.) Indeed, the term *civil society* gained currency in reference to movements in Eastern Europe in the 1970s that organized independent of communist rule.[7] Where civic association can emerge, it may create a powerful incentive for democratic change, even if that is not the original intent. Modernization may help foster civil society, and civil society in turn may pressure elites for change—and these elites may or may not acquiesce, depending on their incentives to do so. Malaysia can be viewed as an example where all these factors were in play.

International Relations and Democratization

So far, our discussion of democratization has focused on variables inside the country in question. Can international factors also play a role? We can think of extreme cases, such as the occupation of Japan and Germany after World War II, or of Iraq and Afghanistan more recently. But scholars believe that the international community also plays a role in less overt ways. Modernization resulting from foreign investment, globalization, and trade may push democratization forward. In addition, international pressure or incentives may cause elites to favor democracy; some have suggested that the institutionalization of democracy in southern and eastern Europe came about partly because democracy was a prerequisite for membership in the European Union. Civil society, too, can be strengthened by the transmission of ideas across borders by education, media, and nongovernmental organizations.

How influential the international community may be in each case probably depends on a number of factors, including how open to, and dependent on, the outside world that society is. North Korea's isolation means that little contact takes place between that society and those beyond its borders. The vast size of China's economic resources means that the international community has far fewer tools it can use to press for change within that country. (See "Institutions in Action" on pp. 170–71 for a discussion of democratization in Asia.) Pressure from the international community for democracy can also backfire, playing into the hands of those who oppose change by allowing them to frame it as part of a foreign conspiracy to weaken sovereignty.

Culture and Democratization

Our last argument is a familiar one. In Chapter 3, we spoke of the idea of political culture, which is essentially the argument that differences in societal institutions—norms and values—shape the landscape of political activity. Political culture may influence the preference for certain kinds of policies as well as the particular relationship between freedom and equality. Some scholars take this idea much further, arguing that democracy is basically a culture emerging from historical, religious, and philosophical foundations. In this view, for example, modernization does not lead to individualism and democracy; rather, Western democratic and individualist practices gave rise to modernity.

If this argument is true, then democratization is less likely to be found the farther we travel from the West, where historical developments forged strong national identities as well as a commitment to democracy in its own right. As we discussed earlier, such arguments make many scholars uncomfortable, both because they are difficult to test and because they smack of stereotyping and determinism. They also have a questionable track record. Not long ago, countries such as Spain, Portugal, Italy, and many Latin American nations, whose cultures were dominated by hierarchical Roman Catholicism, were seen as unlikely to democratize—until they did. Similar arguments have been raised regarding Asia, as we discussed in Chapter 3. However, we can certainly argue that political culture, while not necessarily determining democracy, can shape its particular character and the debates around what kinds of freedoms democracy should entail in each country.

To summarize, there are numerous ways to explain why democratization takes place in some cases and not others. While individual scholars tend to favor one of these explanations over the others, we see that most, if not all, of these factors play some role in each case of democratization. Modernization can set the stage for political activity and awareness, which can find its organizational expression in civil society. Elites may be influenced by economic conditions at home and by international inducements or sanctions. Even culture may encourage certain kinds of identities and ideas that catalyze democracy or get in its way. In the end, changing domestic and international conditions may mean that what leads to democracy now may be unrelated to how it comes about in the future. Politics is not a physical law, unchanging across time and space.

Institutions of the Democratic State

We now have an understanding of the basic definition of liberal democracy and some of the explanations for how it emerged in the past and present. Next, we should spend some time looking at how liberal democracies are constructed. As we shall see, liberal-democratic institutions vary dramatically. Legislatures differ greatly from country to country, as do executives, and the legislative-executive relationship in each country is unique. Each judiciary, too, plays a distinct role in the democratic process. There is tremendous variation in the range and number of political parties, and this in part is shaped by the myriad electoral systems used around the world. Even what we consider basic civil rights and civil liberties differ from one liberal democracy to another. There is no one way—no right way—to build a liberal democracy. Let's look at some of the major ways in which each institution differs from country to country before we consider several of their most common combinations.

Executives: Head of State and Head of Government

We begin with what is the most prominent office in any country, the **executive**—the branch that carries out the laws and policies of a state. When we think of this office, what often comes to mind is a single person in charge of leading the country and setting a national agenda as well as leading foreign policy and serving as commander in chief in times of war. But in fact, the executive comprises two distinct roles. The first is **head of state**, a role that symbolizes and represents the people, both nationally and internationally, embodying and articulating the goals of the regime. Conducting foreign policy and waging war are also sometimes considered duties of the head of state. In contrast, the **head of government** deals with the everyday tasks of running the state, such as formulating and executing domestic policy, alongside a cabinet of ministers who are charged with specific policy areas (such as education or agriculture). This distinction between direct policy management and international and symbolic functions is an old one that goes back to the days when monarchs reigned over their subjects, leaving ministers in charge of running the country.

Countries combine or separate these two roles to different degrees. Heads of government are usually referred to as prime ministers: they serve as the main executive over the other ministers in their cabinet. They may serve alongside a head of state, who may be a monarch or a president. A country may also combine the two roles, as in the United States, where the president is both head of state and head of government. The balance of power between the head of state and head of government differs from country to country, as you will learn shortly.

Legislatures: Unicameral and Bicameral

The **legislature** is typically viewed as the body in which national politics is considered and debated. It is charged with making or at least passing legislation. As with executives, legislatures vary in their political powers and construction. The major distinction is between bicameral and unicameral systems. As you might guess from their names, **bicameral systems** are legislatures that contain two houses, whereas **unicameral systems** are those with one house. Small countries are more likely to have unicameral systems, though the majority of liberal democracies are bicameral.

Bicameral systems can be traced back to predemocratic England and other European states, where two or more chambers were created to serve the interests of different economic classes. Even as feudalism gave way to liberal democracy, the idea of bicameralism remained, for two major reasons. First, in some countries an upper chamber was retained as a check over the lower house, often reflecting a fear that a popularly elected lower house, too close to the people's current mood, would make rash decisions. Thus upper houses can often amend or veto legislation originating in the lower house. We can also see this concern reflected in tenure: members of upper houses often serve for longer terms than members of lower houses.

A related element is federalism. Federal states typically rely on an upper house to represent the interests of certain geographic subunits, so that members are able to oversee legislation particularly relevant to local policies. In some cases, local legislatures may even appoint or elect the members of that upper chamber, again reflecting a desire to check a directly elected lower house. In the United States, the Senate was indirectly elected by local legislatures until 1913. However, many unitary (nonfederal) liberal-democratic systems also have bicameral legislatures. Legislatures may wield a great deal of power over the executive, serving as the prime engine of policy or legislation, or take a backseat to executive authority. Moreover, the balance of power between upper and lower houses differs from country to country and issue to issue, though upper houses generally are weaker than lower houses.

> ### IN FOCUS: Branches of Government
>
> | BRANCH | FUNCTIONS, ATTRIBUTES, AND POWERS |
> |---|---|
> | **EXECUTIVE** | Head of state/head of government
Parliamentary, presidential, and semi-presidential systems
Term length may be fixed (president) or not (prime minister) |
> | **LEGISLATIVE** | Lawmaking
Unicameral or bicameral |
> | **CONSTITUTIONAL COURT** | Determines the constitutionality of laws and acts
Judicial review (abstract and concrete) |

Judiciaries and Judicial Review

The judiciary is the third major institution central to liberal democracies. All states rely on laws to prescribe behavior and lay out the rules of the political game. At the core of this body of laws lies a constitution, which is the fundamental expression of the regime and the justification for subsequent legislation and the powers of executives, legislatures, and other political actors. In nondemocratic systems, constitutions may count for little because the state acts as it sees fit. In liberal democracies, however, constitutional power is central to maintaining what we refer to as the **rule of law**—the sovereignty of law over the people and elected officials. As a result, judicial institutions are important components in upholding law and maintaining its adherence to the constitution.

As with executives and legislatures, judiciaries vary greatly across liberal democracies—not simply in their authority but also in how laws are interpreted and reviewed. Most (but not all) liberal democracies have some form of **constitutional court** charged with ensuring that legislation is compatible with the constitution. This is a relatively new development; in 1950, only a third of liberal democracies provided for **judicial review**, whereas now nearly 90 percent do. Alongside this rise in judicial review is the growth in the sheer number of rights that are protected under constitutions. This correlation makes sense; as constitutions define more rights, there is a greater need for judiciaries to rule on them.[8]

How these judiciaries function regarding the constitution varies from country to country. In most countries, the right of judicial review is explicitly written into the constitution. However, in a few, such as the United States and Australia, this right is implicit and has become institutionalized in the absence of any specific provision in the constitution. Another variation is in the authority and division of high courts. Some countries, like the United States, Canada, Japan, and Australia, have a combined appellate and constitutional court. In other words, a single high court serves as a final court of appeals (to which lower court rulings can be appealed) and as a court of constitutional review. Because of this dual function, trials can be an important source of constitutional interpretation. Other countries, such as Brazil, have two separate high courts—a final court of appeals and a constitutional court. This structure greatly limits the influence of trials on constitutional interpretation.

Judicial systems also vary in their powers and how they can wield those powers. We might imagine that unified constitutional and appellate courts are by their nature more powerful than those whose two functions are separate. Yet other important variations can shape judicial authority as much, if not more. Judicial review can take different forms—most specifically, concrete or abstract. In **concrete review**, courts can consider the constitutionality of legislation only when a specific court case triggers this question—for example, in the case of separate appellate and constitutional courts, a case before a court of appeals may be forwarded to the constitutional court if the court of appeals believes there is a constitutional issue at stake. In **abstract review**, a constitutional court may rule on legislation without a specific court case. Such rulings are typically initiated on request by one or more elected officials, such as members of the national or local legislatures. Courts can also differ in the timing of their review. In some countries, constitutional review may occur only after a piece of legislation is passed; in others, the constitutional court may give a ruling beforehand. Finally, courts differ in the appointment and tenure of their judges; these are typically fixed terms (the lifetime tenure of U.S. Supreme Court judges is an anomaly, and appears to be increasingly a source of polarization and deadlock). The combination of these factors can radically affect the power of the courts in the democratic process.

Models of Democracy: Parliamentary, Presidential, and Semi-Presidential Systems

With our overview of state institutions in hand, let's look at the main differences in how some of these institutions can be constructed in relation to one another. This section provides a generalized portrait of these systems; in reality, there are numerous variations within these basic categories.

Parliamentary Systems

Parliamentary systems can be found in most of the democracies around the world. Parliamentary systems comprise two basic elements: first, prime ministers and their cabinets (the other ministers who make up the government) come out of the legislature; and second, the legislature is also the instrument that elects and removes the prime minister from office. In these cases, political power and roles are divided between a head of government and a head of state. The overwhelming majority of power resides with the head of government (the prime minister). In contrast, the head of state may be a president who is indirectly elected by the legislature, or a monarch who has inherited the office. The head of state's powers are typically little more than ceremonial, particularly in the case of monarchs. They may hold some reserve powers, such as the ability to reject legislation or forward it to a constitutional court if it is seen as undemocratic. Even in these cases, however, the powers of the president or monarch are rarely exercised.

The prime minister is elected from the legislature and therefore reflects the balance of power between parties in the legislature. Typically, he or she is the head of the party in the lower house that holds the largest number of seats. Indeed, in most parliamentary systems the prime minister continues to hold a seat in the lower house of the legislature, as do other members of her or his cabinet. This tight connection between the executive and the legislature means that, although these two branches of government have separate powers and responsibilities, they do not check and balance each other's power to the degree that they do in presidential systems. A party with a majority of seats in the legislature can choose its own prime minister and cabinet with little concern for other parties. However, when a party holds a plurality of seats—that is, more seats than any other party but fewer than 50 percent of them—it must commonly forge a coalition government with one or more other parties. In such a government, the prime minister will come from the largest party, while other members of the cabinet come from the coalition parties. When the largest party lacks a majority, it is also possible for a coalition of smaller parties to form a government and select the prime minister, in effect shutting out the largest party.

It is important to note that in these systems, the public does not directly elect its country's leader. That task is left to the parties. As a result, the length of time the prime minister serves in office is uncertain. Members of the legislature are voted in and out of office in direct elections, but prime ministers usually serve in office for as long as they can command the support of their party and its allies. Prime ministers sometimes remain in office for many years—in Australia, Robert Menzies served from 1949 until 1966. Yet prime ministers can often be removed relatively easily through what is known as a **vote of no confidence**. Parliaments typically retain the right to dismiss a prime minister by taking a vote of confidence. In such a vote, the absence of majority support for the prime minister will bring down the government. Depending on the constitution, this outcome may trigger a national parliamentary election or a search for a new government and prime minister from among the parties. Prime ministers also hold the right to call elections. While the constitution may specify that elections must be held within a specific time frame (such as every four or five years), prime ministers can often schedule these elections when they imagine it will serve their party best.

In parliamentary systems, legislatures and judiciaries often take a back seat to the prime minister, who along with the cabinet is the main driver of legislation and policy. Especially when the prime minister enjoys a majority in the parliament, the lower house's role may be limited to debating policy that comes down from the cabinet. The upper house, too, typically has little say in the selection or removal of the prime minister, and what powers its members may have in rejecting legislation can often be overturned by the lower house. Judicial systems are frequently much weaker under these conditions as well. In parliamentary systems, the idea of checks and balances is subordinated to a concentration of power that guarantees greater political autonomy. In addition, the fusion of the prime minister's power with that of the lower house, and the weakness of the upper house, means that fewer opportunities arise for real constitutional conflicts that would empower constitutional courts. Finally, in some cases heads of state and upper houses themselves have certain powers of constitutional review, further limiting the opportunity for independent judicial power.

Presidential Systems

Presidential systems make up a minority of democratic systems around the world. In this system, the president is directly elected by the public for a fixed term and has control over the cabinet and the legislative process. The positions of head of state and head of government are typically fused in the presidency. Here we see a significant difference between parliamentary and **presidential systems**. In parliamentary systems, prime ministers and their cabinets come from the legislature and must command a majority of support to stay in office. In presidential systems, however, the president and members of the legislature serve for fixed terms, typically between four and seven years. Election dates may not be altered easily. Nor can presidents or legislatures be removed by anything resembling a vote of no confidence. Only in the case of malfeasance can elected officials lose their seats.

This institutional relationship affects government profoundly. First, as a directly elected executive, the president is able to draw on a body of popular support in a way that no member of a legislature, or even a prime minister, can. Only a president can say that she or he has been elected by the whole of the people in a single national vote (even if the reality is more complicated than that). Second, as the head of both state and government, the president serves as an important national symbol as well as the overseer of policy. Third, the president is able to choose a cabinet, many or perhaps all of whom are not members of the legislature. Unlike prime ministers, presidents need not be concerned that their cabinets are composed of party leaders. Since the president is directly elected, minority parties lack the kind of influence over the executive that can be found in parliamentary systems, especially in coalition governments. Fourth, the president's power is not directly beholden to the legislature, and vice versa. Neither branch has the ability to easily remove the other, creating a much stronger separation of powers between executive and legislature. This separation of powers is also more likely to lead to checks and balances and divided government. Presidents and legislative majorities can be from different parties, and even when they belong to the same party, the separation of these institutions means greater independence from each other. President and legislature can easily check each other's ability to pass legislation in a way unlikely to occur in a parliamentary system. Presidentialism can in fact weaken political parties, since their leaders are concerned with winning a single national and directly elected office. To become prime minister, by contrast, an individual must come up through the ranks of the party.

Finally, the conflict between an independent legislature and president may pave the way for a more active judiciary, drawing it into disputes between the president and legislature, as has often been the case in the United States. There are relatively few presidential democracies around the world. The United States is the most typically cited example, but presidentialism is also the norm in Latin America.

Semi-Presidential Systems

Our final variant is an interesting hybrid between parliamentary and presidential systems that has become more widespread, though it remains far less common than presidential and parliamentary systems. In this model, power is divided between the head of state and the head of government—a prime minister and a directly elected president both exercise power. Presidents enjoy fixed terms, while prime ministers remain subject to the confidence of the legislature and, in some cases, the confidence of the president as well.

How power is divided between these two offices depends on the country. In some cases, the prime minister is relatively independent from the president; the president exercises important powers but has limited control over the prime minister. In other cases, the prime minister is beholden to both the legislature and the president, thus giving the president greater authority over the selection, removal, and activity of the prime minister. In both cases, the president holds power independently of the legislature yet shares powers with a prime minister. Some scholars refer to the latter scenario as "president parliamentarism" to emphasize the power of the presidency, as opposed to "premier presidentialism" to refer to those systems where the president's powers are more restricted, particularly in the ability of the president to dismiss the prime minister.

Semi-presidential systems tend to reflect the old distinction between "reign" and "rule" that existed under monarchies. Presidents will often set forth policy but expect the prime minister to translate those policy ideas into legislation and ensure that it is passed. Presidents will also take the lead in foreign policy and serve as commander in chief, representing the country in international relations. The most prominent semi-presidential systems, like the French one, place much of the power

IN FOCUS

Parliamentary, Presidential, and Semi-Presidential Systems: Basic Features

TYPE	EXECUTIVE POWERS AND RELATIONSHIPS
PARLIAMENTARY	Indirectly elected prime minister holds executive power as head of government. Directs cabinet, formulates legislation and domestic and international policies. Serves for an unfixed term and may be removed by a vote of no confidence. Head of state (president or monarch) is largely ceremonial.
PRESIDENTIAL	Directly elected president holds majority of executive power as head of state and government. Directs cabinet and formulates legislation and international and domestic policies. Serves for a fixed term and cannot be easily removed from office.
SEMI-PRESIDENTIAL	Directly elected president and indirectly elected prime minister share power. President helps set policy, while prime minister executes it. President also manages foreign policy. Which office holds more power depends on the country.

in the hands of the president while the prime minister plays a supporting role. In semi-presidential systems, the role of the judiciary varies. The independence of constitutional courts is often limited because they are appointed by the president. At the same time, however, conflicts between presidents and prime ministers, and a lack of clarity over which executive has what power, have on a few occasions created opportunities for more judicial authority. Since the collapse of communism, semi-presidentialism has spread into several former Soviet republics, most notably Russia and Ukraine, and it is also the form of government in a few countries in Asia and Africa, such as Taiwan, Sri Lanka, Rwanda, and Mali.

Parliamentary, Presidential, and Semi-Presidential Systems: Benefits and Drawbacks

Now that we have reviewed these three systems, it makes sense to ask which of them offers the best system of governance. Of course, that depends on how we define *best*; each system has certain advantages and drawbacks. Nevertheless, scholars have made some arguments about how effective, democratic, or stable these systems may be.

Advocates of parliamentary systems point out that the fusion of power between the executive and legislature promotes greater efficiency by reducing the chances of divided government and deadlock. The prime minister's office, even when beholden to several parties in a coalition government, can normally promulgate and pass legislation relatively quickly, without having to take into consideration the narrow interests of individual legislators or smaller parties. In fact, prime ministers can use the vote of no confidence to their own advantage, threatening, for example, to make a vote against an individual piece of legislation an effective vote of no confidence; should the legislature vote against the legislation, the prime minister will call for new elections. Critics assert that the efficiency made possible by parliamentary systems—the prime minister's ability to generate and quickly pass legislation—comes at the cost of a weaker separation of powers. Legislatures may have far fewer opportunities to influence the passage of legislation or effectively express the voters' specific interests, since legislation is more a top-down than a bottom-up process. The voters' distance from government decision making can apply to the executive as well, since that individual is directly accountable only to the legislature. Greater efficacy may thus mean weaker public oversight and control over elected officials.

IN FOCUS: Parliamentary, Presidential, and Semi-Presidential Systems: Benefits and Drawbacks

TYPE	BENEFITS AND DRAWBACKS
PARLIAMENTARY	Benefits: Prime minister can usually get legislation passed. Prime minister may also be more easily removed by the legislature through a vote of no confidence. Drawbacks: Public does not directly select prime minister and may feel that it has less control over the executive and the passing of legislation.
PRESIDENTIAL	Benefits: President is directly elected and can draw on a national mandate to create and enact legislation. Drawbacks: President and legislature may be controlled by different parties, leading to divided government. Office does not allow for power sharing, and president may not be easily removed from office except through elections.
SEMI-PRESIDENTIAL	Benefits: Directly elected president and indirectly elected prime minister share power and responsibilities, creating both a public mandate (presidency) and an indirectly elected office that may be supported by a coalition of parties (prime minister). Drawbacks: Conflict possible between prime minister and president over powers and responsibilities.

Presidentialism has its own problems. The chief benefit of this system is the public's ability to directly select its leader, who serves for a fixed term. But this situation can generate difficulties. Unlike prime ministers, who must keep the confidence of their party (or parties, in the case of coalition governments), presidents are not dependent on their parties in this way. Even if a president loses the public's confidence, he or she cannot be replaced except through new elections. Presidents also enjoy (or suffer from) the separation of power from the legislature, which can lead to divided government. Whether checks and balances are a benefit or a hindrance to democracy is open to debate. Several prominent scholars have asserted that presidentialism is a more unstable system since it limits power sharing and also lacks a mechanism through which legislators and executives can be easily removed from office. The result can be more polarized, and therefore unstable, politics. In times of crisis, people may gravitate toward presidentialism precisely because they seek to bypass representative institutions in favor of something that looks more like direct rule via a single strong leader. This can be a pathway to authoritarianism.

We might conclude, then, that semi-presidentialism would be the best of both worlds, but its track record is limited and mixed. Some research suggests that in cases where the presidency is strong relative to the prime minister, government effectiveness is lower than in parliamentary systems, perhaps due to the lack of a clear locus of authority.

Political Parties

James Madison, one of the Founders of the U.S. political system and the country's fourth president, once wrote that "in every political society, parties are unavoidable."[9] Observers have offered several reasons for the forming of political parties. Parties are important organizations that bring together diverse groups of people and ideas under the umbrella of an ideological mandate. These organizations serve two functions. By bringing different people and ideas together, they help establish the means by which the majority can rule. Without political parties that provide candidates and agendas for politics, the political process would be too fragmented, and it would be impossible to enact policy or get much else done. But political parties remain relatively loose, containing various factions built around differing issues. This heterogeneity helps limit a "tyranny of the majority" since parties are often diverse enough that they are unable to fully dominate politics even when they hold a majority of power. Parties in liberal democracies are thus homogeneous enough to create majority rule but too weak to facilitate a tyranny of the majority, so long as open and regular elections create the opportunity to turn the ruling party out of power.

Political parties also create the means for the electorate and fellow political elites to hold politicians accountable. By articulating an ideology and a set of goals, parties ensure that their members work toward those goals. Voters are able to evaluate politicians on the basis of their fulfillment of a party's policy platform. A party can thus serve as a political symbol, a kind of shorthand for a set of ideas and objectives, and voters can distill a complex set of beliefs and preferences into the decision of whether to vote for party A or party B.

Countries exhibit a variety of party systems, shaped by a number of factors. Some countries have seen the virtual dominance of two or even one party over a long period of time—Sweden's Social Democratic Party and Japan's Liberal Democratic Party have been able to control government for much of the postwar era. In other countries, such as Italy, power has moved back and forth among a handful

> ## IN FOCUS
> ### Competition in Democracy
>
> - Political parties encourage democratic competition by gathering diverse groups under an ideological mandate while simultaneously preventing domination by any one group. Parties also create the means to hold government accountable.
> - The separation of powers between different branches of government prevents abuses of power by any one branch.

of parties on a frequent basis, creating greater instability. In some parliamentary systems, like Italy's, coalition governments are the norm, while in others coalition governments are rare. These differences involve so many reasons, specific to each case, that it is hard to make easy generalizations. One factor that accounts for the diversity in party politics, however, is the diversity in **electoral systems**.

Electoral Systems

We have discussed why political parties form, but we must look more closely at why certain countries have more parties than others and why each party exhibits its particular ideological content. These questions might have no simple answer—the fortunes of political parties rise and fall over time. But in looking around the world, we see tremendous diversity in the ways that members of the public cast their votes, how those votes are applied, and, as a result, how many and what kinds of parties enter the legislature.

All democracies divide their populations geographically into a number of electoral districts or **constituencies**—each a geographic area that an elected official represents. These constituencies are allocated a certain number of legislative seats. The total number of constituencies varies widely from country to country: Argentina is broken up into 24 constituencies that correspond to the country's 23 provinces plus Buenos Aires, whereas in Nigeria 360 constituencies elect members of the country's lower house. How these boundaries are drawn matters, too. For example, if an ethnic or religious minority is concentrated in one constituency, it may have more political power (by winning a greater share of seats) than it would have if it were divided across a number of constituencies. Also, different districts may have very different population sizes but the same number of legislative seats, giving those in less populated districts more power. How governments draw electoral boundaries can thus have a huge impact on who gets elected, and these boundaries are often a source of great contention in new (and old) democracies.

A second distinction is how votes are cast and counted.[10] Essentially, two broad forms of electoral systems are being used in liberal democracies today. The first is made up of plurality and majority systems, often called **single-member-district (SMD)** systems, and the second consists of **proportional representation (PR)** systems. Let us consider each one in turn.

A minority of democratic countries around the world, including the United Kingdom, Canada, the United States, India, Nigeria, and several other former British colonies, rely on plurality-based SMD systems, also called **first past the post** systems. In these systems, as in all SMD systems, electoral constituencies are single-member districts, which means that each constituency has only one representative. In plurality-based SMDs, the candidate who receives the most votes—whether a majority or plurality—wins the seat. In SMD systems, the votes cast for other candidates are effectively wasted—that is, if a candidate for whom a vote is cast does not win, his or her votes do not count toward any other candidate's electoral bid. The SMD system's "winner take all" approach can amplify the political power of some parties while weakening the political power of others.

Political scientists have long argued that under SMD systems, most people are unwilling to vote for smaller parties. Since such parties are unlikely to win a plurality of the votes, voters feel that a vote cast for a small party will be wasted, so they are better off giving their vote to a stronger party that has a chance of coming in first.[11] As a result, an SMD system is much more likely to produce a legislature dominated by two parties, as in the United States, Canada, and the United Kingdom, and to marginalize or eliminate smaller parties.

To illustrate, let's look at the outcome of the 2019 elections for the House of Commons (the lower legislative house) in the United Kingdom. As Figure 5.1

IN FOCUS

Participation

- One of the most basic ways in which the public participates in politics is through voting and elections.

- Voters may also participate in political decision making through referenda and initiatives.

- The two main types of electoral systems are single-member district (SMD) and proportional representation (PR). Most of the democratic countries today use PR. Many use a mix of SMD and PR.

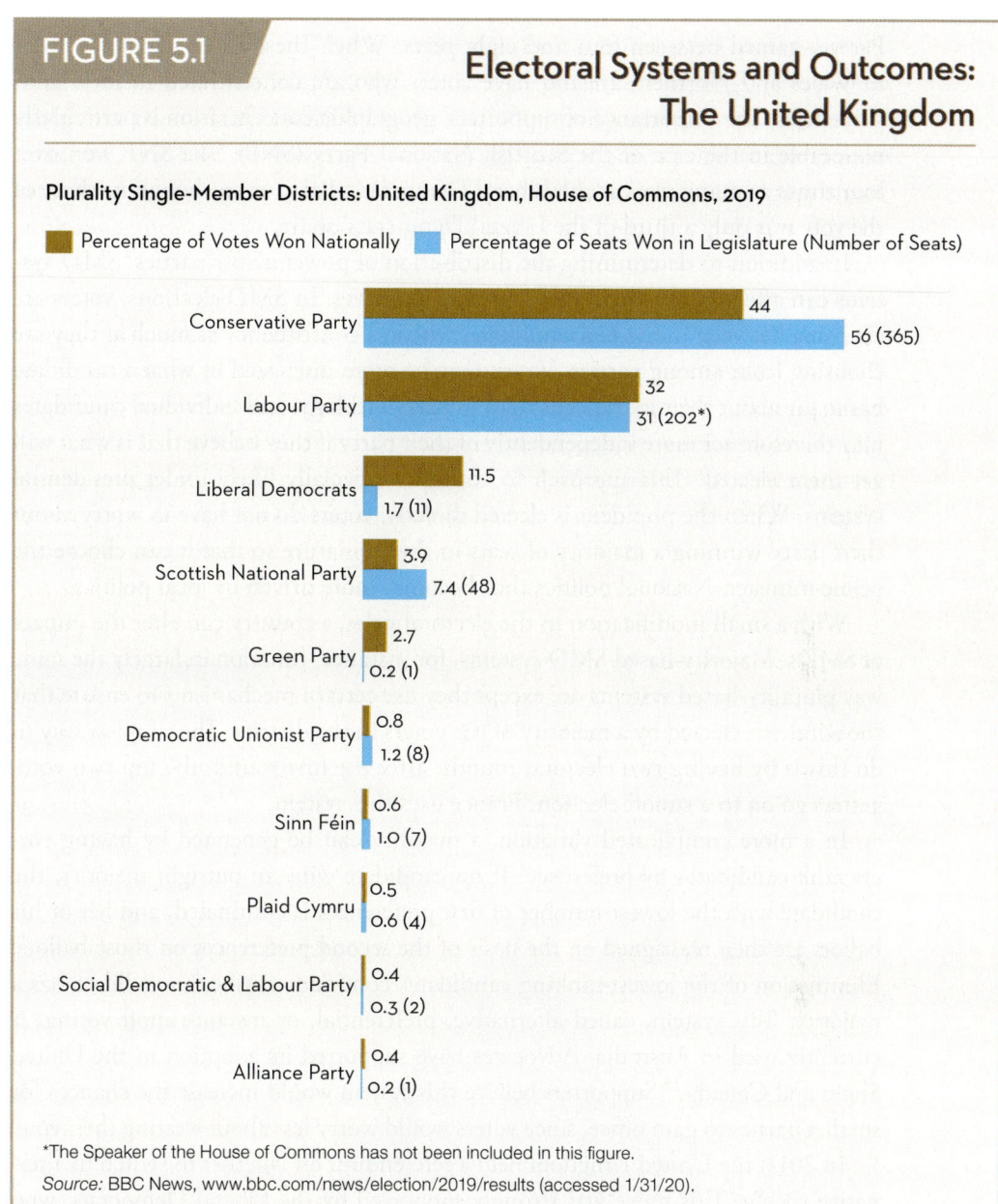

FIGURE 5.1 Electoral Systems and Outcomes: The United Kingdom

*The Speaker of the House of Commons has not been included in this figure.
Source: BBC News, www.bbc.com/news/election/2019/results (accessed 1/31/20).

shows, the Conservative Party won 44 percent of the vote and 56 percent of the seats; the Labour Party won 32 percent of the votes and 31 percent of the seats. The importance of this winner-take-all system, built around single-member districts, can also be seen in the case of smaller parties. Some parties with a small share of the vote—like Sinn Féin, Plaid Cymru, and the Democratic Unionist

Party—gained between four and eight seats. Why? These three regional parties in Wales and Northern Ireland have voters who are concentrated in local constituencies. The importance of supporters' geographic concentration is particularly noticeable in the case of the Scottish National Party (SNP). The SNP won over four times as many seats as the Liberal Democratic Party, even though its share of the vote was only a third of the Liberal Democrats' share.

In addition to determining the distribution of power across parties, SMD systems can affect power within the parties themselves. In SMD elections, voters are choosing between individual candidates within a constituency as much as they are choosing from among parties. Voters may be more interested in what a candidate has to say about their local needs than in party ideology, and individual candidates may therefore act more independently of their party if they believe that is what will get them elected. This approach to voting is especially likely under presidential systems. When the president is elected directly, voters do not have to worry about their party winning a majority of seats in the legislature so that it can choose the prime minister. National politics thus becomes more driven by local politics.

With a small modification in the electoral rules, a country can alter the impact of SMDs. Majority-based SMD systems, for instance, function in largely the same way plurality-based systems do, except they use certain mechanisms to ensure that the winner is elected by a majority of the voters in the district. The simplest way to do this is by having two electoral rounds: after the first round, the top two vote-getters go on to a runoff election. France uses this system.

In a more complicated variation, a majority can be generated by having voters rank candidates by preference. If no candidate wins an outright majority, the candidate with the lowest number of first preferences is eliminated, and her or his ballots are then reassigned on the basis of the second preferences on those ballots. Elimination of the lowest-ranking candidates continues until one candidate has a majority. This system, called alternative, preferential, or instant-runoff voting, is currently used in Australia. Advocates have supported its adoption in the United States and Canada.[12] Supporters believe this system would increase the chances for smaller parties to gain office, since voters would worry less about wasting their vote.

In 2011, the United Kingdom held a referendum on whether to switch to alternative voting. This move was strongly supported by the Liberal Democrats, who believed they would do much better under such a system. However, more than two-thirds of voters opposed the change.

Quite different from plurality- and majority-based SMD systems is proportional representation (PR), which is used in some form by a majority of democracies around the world. PR generally attempts to decrease the number of votes that are wasted, thus increasing the number of parties in the legislature. Instead of relying on SMDs, PR relies on **multimember districts (MMDs)**—in other words, more than one legislative seat is contested in each district.

In PR systems, voters cast their ballots for a party rather than for a candidate, and the percentage of votes a party receives in a district determines how many of that district's seats the party will gain. In a simple theoretical version, a party that won 17 percent of the vote in a district would receive 17 percent of that district's seats; if it won 100 percent of the vote in a district, it would receive all the seats. Votes are counted and applied in complex ways that can profoundly affect how seats are distributed among competing parties. Yet overall, in comparison with plurality and majority SMD systems, PR enables even a small percentage of the vote to win representation. The 2019 elections in South Africa, detailed in Figure 5.2, show how the number of votes under PR can correspond much more closely to the percentage of seats won in the legislature. Small parties that would not have won a single seat under plurality- or majority-based SMD systems are represented in the South African National Assembly.

Because PR is based on multimember districts, elections are not centered on competitions between individuals, as in SMD systems. Instead, political parties draw up in advance a list of their candidates for each electoral district, often proposing as many candidates as there are seats. If a district has 10 seats and a party wins 50 percent of the vote in that district, the party will send the first five candidates on its party list to the legislature. Political parties themselves decide who will be placed on their party list and at what rank, and they list the most senior members at the top. A candidate would want to be listed as high on the list as possible to gain a seat even if the party gets a small share of the district vote.

Unlike voters in plurality or majority SMD systems, who tend to support only parties with a chance of winning a large share of votes in a district, PR voters are more willing to vote for small parties since they stand a better chance of winning at least some seats in the legislature. Even if a party wins less than 10 percent of the vote, it may well gain seats, as the 2019 South African elections show. As a result, countries with PR systems are likely to have many more parties in the legislature. Israel's legislature, for example, has more than 15 parties, some of which are coalitions of several smaller parties. Some PR systems try to limit the number of small parties by establishing a minimum percentage of the vote that parties need to receive to gain seats in the legislature; in Germany and several other countries, the threshold is 5 percent; Israel established a threshold for the first time in 2015 of 3.25 percent. Of course, this also leads to wasted votes, since voters choosing parties that do not make it over the threshold will not have their votes count. Still, the number of wasted votes tends to be much smaller in PR than in SMD systems.

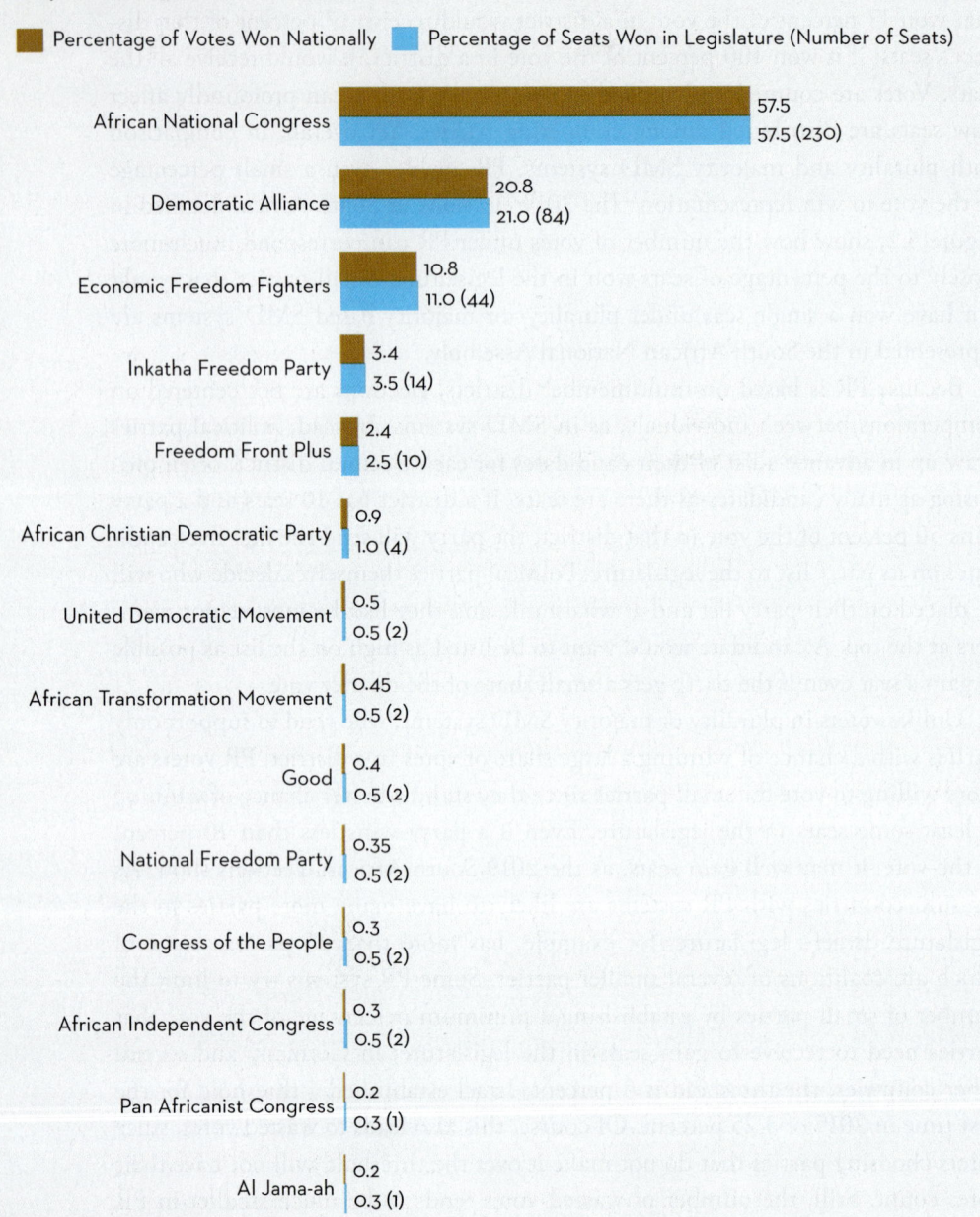

FIGURE 5.2 Electoral Systems and Outcomes: South Africa

Finally, party discipline and ideology may be more pronounced in a PR system, for two reasons. First, the diversity of parties is related to their need to carve out distinct ideological spaces. This is different from SMD systems, in which parties want to reach as many people as possible in order to win a plurality or majority. Second, PR may lead to more internally disciplined parties, since those who do not follow the party rules can be dropped from the party lists in the next election. Where PR is combined with a parliamentary system, party discipline may be even greater because it can make the difference between stable government and a vote of no confidence. Brazil makes for an interesting contrast. In addition to a strong presidency, the legislature uses an "open-list" system of PR, where voters not only choose a party but also select their preferred candidate in that party. Seats are then allocated by the percentages of votes cast for a party and for each candidate in that party. This leads to candidates competing as much against their own party members as the opposing parties, which weakens party cohesion.

Which system is more representative, SMD or PR? Supporters of PR note that it wastes fewer votes and in so doing allows for a greater range of interests to be expressed politically. These can include the interests of groups defined by existing societal distinctions such as religion and ethnicity. One way to resolve ethnic conflict, we noted in Chapter 3, is to use institutions like PR to allow ethnic or religious groups to advance their causes, especially if these groups are not geographically concentrated and would fare poorly under SMD. PR can also encourage the sharpening and expansion of different ideological views, increasing the competition of ideas and providing a way for new issues to enter the system. Environmental parties, for example, were able to form and make an impact in many PR systems as early as the 1970s, but they remain marginal forces in SMD systems. In addition, when combined with the parliamentary form of government, PR often makes it necessary for parties to form coalitions to muster a majority of votes, thus building consensus across a range of views. Finally, PR's use of party lists can also make it easier for the parties themselves to expand the representation of underrepresented groups, such as women and minorities, by placing them high on their party lists.[13]

Those who favor SMD systems emphasize the benefits of single-member districts and winner-take-all elections. Under such systems, individuals can connect with their elected representatives more easily than they can under PR. As mentioned earlier, since SMD voters express their support or rejection of particular candidates, these candidates form ties to their constituents that are as close as those to their party, if not closer. Supporters also note that an SMD system allows for the creation of large parties that are able to muster the majorities needed to govern without being held hostage by smaller, often fringe parties. The flip side of party diversity under PR, critics argue, may be fragmentation and political instability—especially if the system allows for the creation of parties with radical or reactionary political attitudes.

Given that SMD and PR systems both have advantages and disadvantages, some countries have combined the two. For example, Germany, Hungary, Japan, and Mexico use what is known as a **mixed electoral system** that combines plurality or majority SMDs with PR. Voters are given two votes—one for a candidate and the other for a party (these two votes can be divided on one ballot paper itself, or voters may participate in two separate elections, one for the PR candidates and one for the SMD candidates). Candidates in the SMDs are elected on the basis of plurality or majority, while in the PR segment of the election votes are allocated proportionally. The percentage of seats allotted for each electoral method varies from country to country. For example, in Germany, the seats in the lower house of the legislature are divided evenly between SMDs and PR, whereas in Japan, the breakdown is 60 percent SMDs and 40 percent PR. Under this system, voters not only get two votes but also have the option to split their choice, voting for a candidate from one party with their SMD vote while choosing a different party with their PR vote. For example, in Germany an individual might vote for the large, left-wing Social Democratic Party on the plurality SMD portion of the ballot (since only a large party is likely to get the plurality of votes needed to win) while reserving the PR portion of the ballot for the smaller, environmentalist Green Party.

IN FOCUS: Electoral Systems

	TYPE	VOTER CHOICE	EFFECT
SINGLE-MEMBER DISTRICTS	Votes cast for individuals	Candidate with the largest share wins seat or majority	Fewer and larger parties
PROPORTIONAL REPRESENTATION (MULTIMEMBER DISTRICTS)	Votes cast for parties	Seats divided among parties on basis of share of vote	More smaller parties
MIXED SYSTEM	Votes cast both for parties and for individuals	Some seats filled by individual races, some by party outcome	Mixed outcome

Finally, we should consider what bearing, if any, electoral systems have on legislative-executive relations. First, parliamentary systems that rely on SMDs are less likely to have coalition governments, since small parties are less likely to get into office and single parties are often able to command a majority of seats in the legislature. PR in parliamentary systems may make coalition governments more likely; this form of government can broaden the range of participation but also increase the likelihood of government instability inherent in managing so many contending interests. Second, the electoral system used for the legislature is unconnected to the form of legislative-executive relations. A presidential or parliamentary system may use PR or SMD for the legislature. A country could change its constitution so that the executive position changes from president to prime minister without changing its electoral system, or it could switch from PR to SMD (or vice versa) without having to modify its executive structure.

Referendum and Initiative

In addition to shaping how a voter's participation is counted, electoral systems can affect policy. Although voting is typically used to choose parties or candidates for office, many countries offer the public the option of voting directly on particular policy issues. Such a ballot is commonly known as a **referendum**. In contrast to the more indirect impact that elections have on politics, referenda allow the public to make direct decisions about policy.

There is no constitutional provision for national referenda in the United States and Canada (although they exist in some local and state governments in those countries), but many other democracies use them. Italy and New Zealand have used national referenda to dramatically restructure their electoral and legislative systems. In Switzerland, where the political system comes closer to the idea of direct democracy than in any other country, many of the most important national decisions are regularly made by referenda. Constitutions and constitutional reforms are often put to referenda, and some European countries use referenda to approve changes in their relationship with the European Union. Most recently, the United Kingdom put their continued membership in the European Union to a vote, narrowly deciding to leave. These referenda may be called by the government, and the formal power to do so often rests with the head of state. In some countries, the citizens themselves may collect signatures to put a question to a national vote in what is known as an **initiative**.

For many, referenda and initiatives are the purest representation of democracy, and they have become more attractive as people have grown frustrated with democratic institutions. However, scholars warn that national votes place too

INSTITUTIONS IN ACTION

What Explains Democratization in Asia?

Many scholars once regarded Asia as not amenable to democratization. Observers typically relied on cultural explanations, often referred to as the Asian Values argument. According to this view, Asian culture, strongly influenced by Confucianism, stresses deference to authority; an emphasis on community, hierarchy, and stability; and the importance of a strong leader who serves as the embodiment of the state. Democratic values with their emphasis on individual competition, participation, and liberty would run counter to this dominant culture. As we saw in Chapter 3, self-expression values are much lower in Asia than in Europe or North America. But this argument assumes that such values themselves are a barrier to democracy, rather than forces that would shape the actual practice of democracy in Asia.

In fact, over the past three decades several Asian countries have made the transition from authoritarianism to democratic regimes, while others made a partial transition to hybrid or illiberal regimes. The Philippines was one of the first to democratize in the late 1980s, followed shortly thereafter by South Korea. Taiwan began to democratize in the mid-1990s, with Indonesia following more recently. There have been setbacks, such as the 2014 military coup in Thailand, while communist regimes in China, Vietnam, and North Korea show little sign of increasing democratization. Yet overall, in the past decade Asia has made significant gains in democracy. Why?

The first and most common explanation for democratization focuses on the impact of modernization. Recall from Chapter 1 that modernization theory argues that economic growth is associated with a number of changes likely to push the public toward greater demands for democracy. Higher levels of education increase political awareness, fostering demands for greater participation in the state. Traditional forms of authority and hierarchy are also challenged. Finally, modernization means the emergence of a middle class, with an increased incentive for citizens to control the state. Such an explanation works particularly well in South Korea and Taiwan, whose democratization followed on the heels of their rapid industrialization. It is less helpful in cases like the Philippines, where gross domestic product was and remains far lower. Nor does it account for the ongoing presence of authoritarianism in Singapore, which has the distinction of being both authoritarian and one of the wealthiest countries in the world. Nevertheless, as we noted in Chapter 4, we do see rising incomes and an emerging middle class across Asia that coincide roughly with democratization.

Societal explanations of democratization in Asia overlap with modernization theory. In our discussion, we looked at the important role played by civil society, defined as a fabric of organizations created by people to help define their interests. In fact, in a number of Asian countries, civil society drove democratization. In Taiwan and Indonesia, environmental groups played an important role; in South Korea, it was labor unions and student organizations; in the Philippines, the Catholic Church.

What about the role of elites? Recall that elite explanations focus on the distribution of power in society, both economic and political, and on how this might affect the calculations of those in power. A more equal society means a political system where those in power do not monopolize wealth and therefore are less threatened by a loss of political power. South Korea and Taiwan's industrialization, for example, also created a political-economic system where inequality was relatively low and the Human Development Index relatively high. On the other side, another elite role we have overlooked is that played by pro-democracy leaders. In several Asian cases, individuals like Kim Dae Jung in South Korea and Corazon Aquino in the Philippines were critical in galvanizing and sustaining support for democracy, especially where dictators had been especially resistant to giving up power.

Finally, we should not overlook the role of international factors. Starting in the mid-1980s, the United States began putting pressure on authoritarian leaders in Asia. Democracy assistance by states and international nongovernmental organizations also expanded during the 1990s, supporting civil society in particular. We should also not underestimate the impact of demonstration effects. Once democratization began in the region, it increased expectations in neighboring states that such transitions were indeed possible. We saw similar kinds of regional waves in Latin America and eastern Europe.

This discussion raises an interesting question about the big outlier in Asia: China. By some indicators, China seems primed for democratization. Levels of development and incomes have risen. We can see the emergence of civil society, such as new religious organizations and environmental groups.

Workers at a technology manufacturing facility in Hsinchu, Taiwan, where electronics manufacturing constitutes a substantial share of exports. Some have argued that modernization pushed the public toward democracy.

At the same time, growing inequality and the increasing concentration of wealth in the hands of party elites means they have a strong incentive to stay in power, as already evidenced by the 1989 crackdown against democracy. Some observers have already asserted that China could be a democracy within the next decade.[a] Skepticism is in order. Earlier, some argued that China would democratize by 2015. But if the predictions come true, China's change in regime would represent a historic turning point: a world where the majority of people live under democratic rule.

1. What are the strongest explanations for democratization in Asia?

2. Do you think China will be more or less democratic in the future? Why?

much power in the hands of an uninformed public, and they are often called by political leaders (sometimes of marginal political parties or movements) primarily to advance their own personal agenda.[14] While they can easily mobilize people around their heated rhetoric, there is often little recourse after such votes to rethink or reconsider the implications of the vote. The United Kingdom's political paralysis following the Brexit vote, over how exactly to leave, is an excellent example of this. We'll speak more of this in Chapter 8.

Civil Rights and Civil Liberties

The last component of liberal democracy is liberty itself. To speak of liberty, we must go beyond democratic processes and consider the substance of democracy: civil rights and civil liberties. The term **civil rights** typically refers to the promotion of equality, whereas the term **civil liberties** refers to the promotion of freedom, though the two overlap. Civil rights and liberties include free speech and movement, the right to religious belief, the right of public assembly and organization, equal treatment under the law, the prevention of inhumane punishment, the right to a fair trial, the right to privacy, and the right of people to choose their own government. Rights and liberties depend on the rule of law—on legal institutions that all, rulers and ruled, are subject to and that uphold the laws supporting liberty.

Democratic constitutions around the world vary in the number of rights they articulate and the kinds of rights they emphasize. Despite these discrepancies, all can be characterized by their emphasis on one of two basic kinds of rights. In the first case, individuals are considered the primary vehicle of democratic rights, and their rights are defended from intrusion by the state and other individuals. The South African constitution goes quite far in this regard, asserting that "the state may not unfairly discriminate directly or indirectly against anyone on one or more grounds, including race, gender, sex, pregnancy, marital status, ethnic or social origin, color, sexual orientation, age, disability, religion, conscience, belief, culture, language and birth." This was the first constitution to explicitly deal with rights associated with sexual orientation. At the same time, the constitution bans "advocacy of hatred that is based on race, ethnicity, gender or religion," which some would regard as a violation of individual free speech. Similarly, Germany's constitution has strong provisions for individual rights, but it also asserts, "Parties that, by reason of their aims or the behavior of their adherents, seek to undermine or abolish the free democratic basic order . . . shall be unconstitutional."

In the second case, democratic rights are seen as institutions created and defended by the state. Thus some democratic constitutions, particularly those of social-democratic regimes, speak at length about social or economic institutions as rights, such as universal education, health care, and retirement benefits. For example, the Swedish constitution states that "the public institutions shall secure the right to employment, housing and education, and shall promote social care and social security, as well as favorable conditions for good health." The Brazilian constitution states that among its fundamental objectives are national development and the eradication of poverty, and it includes such provisions as a minimum wage, overtime, and annual vacations. Other constitutions enshrine state control over natural resources or the obligation of the state to preserve the natural environment. What are the limits of individual rights and liberties, and what is the acceptable balance between individual rights and the role of the state in meeting society's needs? The concept of liberty will continue to evolve.

In the preceding discussion, we see that liberty is not simply the absence of controls over our scope of action—a negative freedom. Rather, liberty is also something that must be created, institutionalized, and defended—a positive freedom. The state, government, and regime are thus central to fostering and furthering liberty. But it would be a mistake to conclude that liberty flows only from the state as a gift to the people. Recall our opening discussion of democratization. Domestic and international institutions, culture, civil society, modernization, committed leaders, and other factors can open the space for democratic change. The challenge becomes vesting that space with liberty—with the institutionalization of civil rights and civil liberties that fuels democratic participation and competition. Where liberty is weak or absent, the trappings of democracy may be in place, but repression will remain the norm. This will be the focus of our next chapter, as we turn to nondemocratic regimes.

In Sum: Future Challenges to Democracy

As we have seen, democracy is one way to maintain a balance between individual freedom and collective equality. It is a form of government whose origins this chapter has traced back thousands of years. In its modern, liberal form, democracy emphasizes individual freedom through participation, competition, and liberty. Participation, often through elections, helps provide the public a means of control over the state and the government; competition ensures an open arena of ideas and prevents too great a centralization of power; and liberty creates norms for human freedom and equality. When these elements are institutionalized—valued for their own sake, considered legitimate by the public—democracy is institutionalized and we can speak of the existence of the rule of law. No one can claim to stand above the democratic regime.

In the next chapter, we shall consider politics when this is not the case. In nondemocratic regimes, all those things we have taken for granted are weakly institutionalized or absent. Participation, competition, liberty, and the rule of law are circumscribed, with the preponderance of power resting in the hands of a few elites who are not accountable to the public. How do these systems come about? How do they differ from each other? Can democracy slip into authoritarian rule, and if so, how? For many years we have assumed that it was authoritarianism that was embattled and destined to defeat. Of late, however, it has seemed resilient while democracy has faltered, unable to provide clear answers to such things as growing inequality and globalization. To understand the challenges to democracy, we must turn our attention to its nondemocratic alternatives.

Key Terms

abstract review (p. 153)
bicameral system (p. 151)
civil liberties (p. 172)
civil rights (p. 172)
civil society (p. 148)
concrete review (p. 153)
constituency (p. 161)
constitutional court (p. 152)
democracy (p. 142)
electoral system (p. 161)
executive (p. 150)
first past the post (p. 162)
head of government (p. 150)
head of state (p. 150)
initiative (p. 169)
judicial review (p. 152)

legislature (p. 151)
liberal democracy (p. 142)
mixed electoral system (p. 168)
multimember district (MMD) (p. 165)
parliamentary system (p. 154)
presidential system (p. 155)
proportional representation (PR) (p. 162)
referendum (p. 169)
republicanism (p. 143)
rule of law (p. 152)
semi-presidential system (p. 157)
separation of powers (p. 143)
single-member district (SMD) (p. 162)
unicameral system (p. 151)
vote of no confidence (p. 155)

For Further Reading

Acemoglu, Daron, and James A. Robinson. *Economic Origins of Dictatorship and Democracy.* New York: Cambridge University Press, 2006.

Dalton, Russell J. *Citizen Politics: Public Opinion and Political Parties in Advanced Industrial Democracies.* 7th ed. Washington, DC: CQ Press, 2019.

de Tocqueville, Alexis. *Democracy in America.* Translated by Henry Reeve. Vol. 2. New York: J. & H. G. Langley, 1841.

Diamond, Larry, and Marc F. Plattner, eds. *Electoral Systems and Democracy.* Baltimore, MD: Johns Hopkins University Press, 2006.

Duverger, Maurice. *Political Parties: Their Organization and Activity in the Modern State.* New York: Wiley, 1954.

Macpherson, C. B. *The Life and Times of Liberal Democracy.* New York: Oxford University Press, 1977.

Nathan, Andrew J., Larry Diamond, and Mark F. Plattner, eds. *Will China Democratize?* Baltimore, MD: Johns Hopkins University Press, 2013.

Schmitter, Philippe C., and Terry Lynn Karl. "What Democracy Is . . . and Is Not." *Journal of Democracy* 2, no. 3 (Summer 1991): 75–88.

INQUIZITIVE

Earn a better grade on your test. InQuizitive personalizes your learning path to help you master the concepts from this chapter and practice applying them to examples from the text and beyond (see back cover).

QUESTIONS AND METHODS

What Is Undermining Democracy?

As we transition from a discussion of democratic to nondemocratic regimes, one issue that emerges is the way in which democracy can erode over time. Representative institutions can become inflexible and "sticky," unable to evolve in the face of changing needs and challenges. The norms of democracy can also decline, a concern that has been raised in many developed democracies over the past decade. Why would this be the case?

One facet of this discussion concerns the concept of social capital. Social capital can be defined as social networks, social trust, and the "norms of reciprocity" that bind people together. This definition in many ways seems the same as our discussion of civil society, but while that term emphasizes organized life—clubs and associations—social capital expands the idea to include wider norms of trust that bind people together. The foremost scholar of social capital, Robert Putnam, goes further to distinguish between *bridging* and *bonding* social capital. Bridging social capital creates links between different kinds of people (one example could be a large university), while bonding cements connections within groups (like a university club or fraternal organization). Both can sustain democracy by maintaining the norm that people can be trusted to do the right thing. Where social capital is high, democratic participation is higher and things like corruption tend to be lower.

For the past two decades scholars like Putnam have been raising the alarm over the decline of social capital in the United States and western Europe, which can be seen in the accompanying figure. Studies show that declining trust and lower rates of participation in social and civic organizations are associated with an increase in nondemocratic and extremist ideas and movements. But this begs the question of why this decline would be occurring in the first place. What is undermining social capital?

One frequent argument is immigration. In this view, as

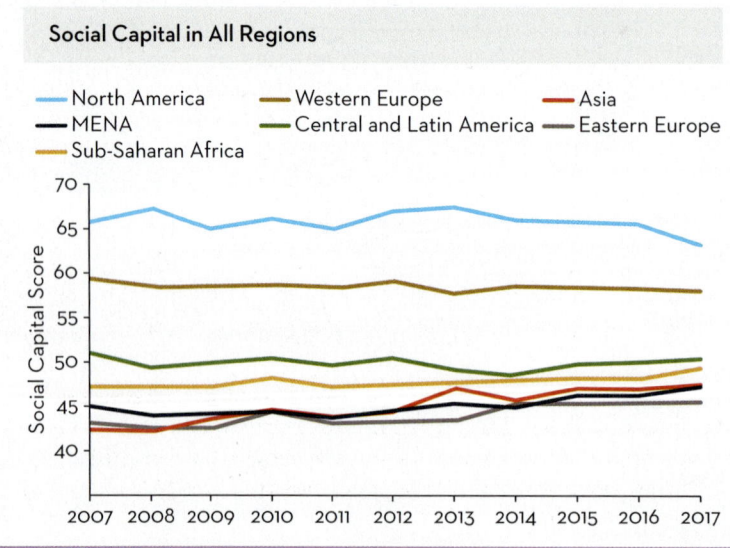

Social Capital in All Regions

176 CHAPTER FIVE ■ DEMOCRATIC REGIMES

immigration has increased in many democracies (something we will cover in Chapter 8), this has put stress on social capital. Cultural gaps between native and immigrant populations make forging networks of reciprocity difficult. Immigrants may create bonding social capital, such as houses of worship, but these fail to "link up" with existing networks. Not surprisingly, then, one response would be the rise of nationalism or ethnic chauvinism in response to immigration.

This argument seems logical, and there is historical precedent. In the United States, high levels of immigration before World War I unleashed a wave of nationalism that eventually restricted immigration for decades. But the evidence is not clear that social capital is directly affected by immigration. In fact, in the United States social capital has been declining since the 1970s, before the most recent wave of immigration. Research suggests instead that increased inequality has played a stronger role in eroding social ties. And we can see how this can connect to immigration—even if the cause of inequality is something like globalization or technological change, people may turn on immigrants as the source of their woes, further undercutting social capital.[a]

1. *Articulate the cause and effect of the hypothesis*

   Why would social capital be needed in a democracy? What is the challenge of a "low trust" society?

2. *Apply theory to consider and explore policy choices*

   Can governments promote social capital? Think about policies that could create bridging and bonding social capital in a low-trust society.

3. *Generate new questions related to the discussion*

   What is the relationship between the much broader notion of diversity and social capital? What questions might we consider about the relationship between these two concepts?

---

a. Christel Kesler and Irene Bloemraad, "Does Immigration Erode Social Capital? The Conditional Effects of Immigration-Generated Diversity on Trust, Membership, and Participation across 19 Countries, 1981–2000," *Canadian Journal of Political Science* 43, no. 2 (June 2010): 319–47. Also see "Social Capital and Prosperity," *The Legatum Prosperity Index 2017*, https://prospersitysite.s3-accelerate.amazonaws.com/3515/1187/1128/Legatum_Prosperity_Index_2017.pdf (accessed 11/13/19).

6

Zimbabwean president Emmerson Mnangagwa tours the site of Zimbabwe's new parliament building, under construction by a Chinese firm. In recent years, China's investment—and indifference to human rights violations—has helped authoritarian regimes extract valuable resources.

NONDEMOCRATIC REGIMES

Why have some countries failed to establish democracy?

Zimbabwe is one country that has experienced dramatic erosion in its state despite its great potential. As recently as the mid-1980s, Zimbabwe's gross domestic product (GDP) per capita, as well as several other development indicators, were roughly the same as those of Vietnam. But while Vietnam has enjoyed rapid economic development, Zimbabwe has experienced a long period of government mismanagement and economic decline. Vietnam's GDP has grown by more than fivefold, while Zimbabwe's GDP per capita has undergone a dramatic decline in the last decade. In perhaps the most striking example of dysfunction, Zimbabwe experienced one of the highest rates of hyperinflation in modern history. The central bank actually printed a 100-trillion-dollar bill shortly before the currency collapsed in 2008. While the country has recently returned to economic growth, this remains tenuous and far below its past level of economic development.

And yet, even though Zimbabwe faced these tremendous hardships, former president Robert Mugabe was able to remain in office from 1980 to 2017 (he died in 2019 at the age of 95), when he was finally deposed by the military. Mugabe's ruling party, the Zimbabwe African National Union-Patriotic Front (ZANU-PF), hung on to power, winning the presidency and a majority of seats in parliament in 2018 (albeit through questionable elections). In an environment of such economic stress, what explains the longevity of this authoritarian regime?

One answer lies in natural resources. Many of us are familiar with the notion of "blood" or conflict diamonds. Typically, we are thinking about civil wars and illegal mines that fund arms sales. However, conflict diamonds need not emerge only out of civil war; Zimbabwe's diamonds are also a product of conflict. Unlike in many other African countries, where diamonds have been mined for many decades or longer, Zimbabwe's Marange diamond fields began operation only in 2006, during the depths of the country's economic crisis. Shortly thereafter, the fields were nationalized, providing the potential for hundreds of millions of dollars in sales for the state.

While these resources should have been a lifeline for Zimbabwe, a large share—perhaps the majority—of revenues from diamond sales did not go into the hands of the state. Rather, the diamonds helped fund what the nongovernmental organization (NGO) Global Witness calls a parallel government. Diamond mining rights were extended to firms with clear links to those in power. Significant or majority shares are held by high-ranking members of the Zimbabwean Central Intelligence Organisation (CIO), a secret police force loyal to the party, as well as by individuals in charge of the Ministry of Defense, armed forces, and police.

The implications of this relationship are significant. First, the revenue has helped sustain ZANU-PF and the security institutions it controls. Funds from diamond sales were directed toward radio-jamming equipment to block broadcasts from stations critical of the government, fleets of vehicles to deploy supporters and attack opposition forces, and direct payments to individuals and tribal leaders to secure their support in elections. Some observers suggest that nearly $1 billion has been spent toward this end. Second, diamond wealth in the hands of ZANU-PF and the security institutions has created a new opportunity for corruption within the state and government. As we discussed in Chapter 5, when economic assets are concentrated in the hands of those in power, they create a disincentive to leave office. Zimbabwe clearly suffers from the "resource curse," where natural resources in fact weaken economic development and strengthen authoritarian rule. It is not surprising, then, that only a fraction of Zimbabwe's diamond wealth has actually wound up in the state treasury.

A final point has to do with the international community. For a number of years, various states and NGOs exerted pressure on the Zimbabwean governemnt, deploying such tools as an embargo on military supplies, limits on development aid, and a boycott on diamonds. But Zimbabwe found a new source of support in China. Unlike the United States or the European Union, China is not concerned about Zimbabwe's authoritarianism or human rights record. China has provided upward of $1 billion in loans and aid to Zimbabwe, and Chinese firms have been active in various development projects, including diamond mining. Toward the end of his presidency Mugabe canceled foreign rights over the mines, angering the Chinese (and, some say, leading them to throw their support behind those inside the state who ousted Mugabe). Since the coup, China has returned to mining in Zimbabwe, alongside a new firm that is partially owned by the Russian state. And Emmerson Mnangagwa, the current president, has a long history inside the security forces and with the Chinese government. For now, those in power retain a source of wealth and the international allies needed to sustain it.

LEARNING OBJECTIVES

- Describe the components of nondemocratic regimes and outline the explanations for their persistence.
- Explain how nondemocratic regimes maintain power.
- Distinguish between types of nondemocratic regimes.

"Man is born free, but everywhere he is in chains," wrote Jean-Jacques Rousseau in 1762. Since his time, democracy has emerged and flourished in many places throughout the world. However, according to Freedom House, an American NGO that monitors and promotes democratic institutions around the world, over 60 percent of the world's population lives in societies defined as either "partly free," where significant personal liberties and democratic rights exist in theory but are not institutionalized and are subject to restriction, or "not free," where the public has little in the way of civil liberties or opportunity for political participation.[1] In neither case can these regimes be described as democratic.

In this chapter, we will look at the internal dynamics and origins of nondemocratic regimes. After defining these regimes and their relationship to freedom and equality, we will look at their origins, addressing the puzzle of why nondemocratic regimes are the norm in some countries but not in others. Behind this puzzle lies the broader question of the origins of nondemocratic rule, which mirrors our discussion in Chapter 5 on competing explanations for democratization. What variables are associated with nondemocratic rule? This discussion of the possible sources of nondemocratic regimes will lead us into an examination of how nondemocratic rulers maintain their hold on power. Nondemocratic regimes display great diversity; nevertheless, we can identify a number of common features. Finally, we will consider the future of nondemocratic rule. At the end of the Cold

War, many assumed that liberal democracy was the wave of the future. In recent years, however, nondemocratic rule has shown an ability to adapt and thrive. The "wave of democracy" may be facing a reverse tide. Whether this is true, and what its implications would be, will be the final consideration of our chapter.

Defining Nondemocratic Rule

One challenge to studying nondemocratic regimes is that they constitute what we could call a residual category—a group of dissimilar things. Unlike democratic regimes, which can be defined and identified, nondemocratic regimes represent a wide array of systems, many of them bearing little resemblance to one another. This diversity in turn leads to a proliferation of terms that are often used interchangeably and indiscriminately: *autocracy, oligarchy, dictatorship, tyranny*. Even more confusing, in some cases nondemocratic regimes may resemble democracies more closely than they do other nondemocratic regimes. As a result, we tend to speak of nondemocratic regimes in terms of what they deny their citizens: participation, competition, and liberty (the very things that define democracy). We will often use the term **authoritarianism** to cover many of these different forms of nondemocratic rule.

If we want to speak of nondemocratic regimes as more than simply the absence of democracy, however, we need a definition to work with. Scholars define **nondemocratic regimes** as those in which a political regime is controlled by a small group of individuals who exercise power over the state without being constitutionally responsible to the public. In nondemocratic regimes, the public plays no significant role in selecting or removing leaders from office. Political leaders in nondemocratic regimes have much greater leeway to develop policies that they "dictate" to the people (hence the term *dictator*). Not surprisingly, nondemocratic regimes by their nature are built around the restriction of individual freedom. At a minimum, they eliminate people's right to choose their own leaders, and they also restrict to varying degrees other liberties, such as freedom of speech or assembly. The relationship of nondemocratic regimes to equality is less clear. Some nondemocratic regimes, such as communist ones, limit individual freedom in order to produce greater economic equality. Others, such as Zimbabwe, seek to provide neither freedom nor equality, existing only to enhance the power of those in control.[2] (See "Institutions in Action" on pp. 204–5 for a discussion of Zimbabwe's political trajectory.)

There are various kinds of nondemocratic regimes. Nondemocratic leaders do not necessarily rule in a capricious or an arbitrary manner; indeed, nondemocratic regimes can have a strong institutional underpinning of ideology. As ideologies,

> **IN FOCUS**
>
> ## Nondemocratic Regimes
>
> - A small group of individuals exercise power over the state.
> - Government is not constitutionally responsible to the public.
> - The public has little or no role in selecting leaders.
> - Individual freedom is restricted.
> - Nondemocratic regimes may be institutionalized and legitimate.

fascism and communism, for instance, explicitly reject liberal democracy as an inferior form of social organization, favoring instead a powerful state and restricted individual freedoms. This ideology provided the norms that fascist and communist nondemocratic leaders followed in places like Nazi Germany and the Soviet Union. But other nondemocratic regimes are not ideological and may even be anti-ideological, asserting that the leadership speaks for "the people."

In other cases, few, if any, substantial political ideas are evident among those in power, whose rule is predicated simply on power for power's sake and the benefits it brings. In these cases, it becomes difficult even to speak of a regime, since we are not talking about a set of institutionalized rules and norms for political activity. In describing these cases, critics often pejoratively use the term *regime*, coupled with a leader's name (such as the "Kim Jong-Un regime" in North Korea). This terminology reflects the critics' view that all decisions flow from the ruler, unfettered by political institutions of any sort. The leader, in essence, is the regime.

Totalitarianism and Nondemocratic Rule

Before continuing, we should examine *totalitarianism*, a tricky and often misused term that is applied to a range of nondemocratic regimes. Totalitarianism, which should not be confused with *authoritarianism*, connotes violence and terror, and so people often use the word in a partisan way to label a political system that they particularly dislike. This problem of definition goes back to the earlier part of the last century. Many scholars used the term *totalitarianism* to describe Nazi Germany and the Soviet Union and its satellite states. Others countered that when the term was used in a way that equated fascism and communism, it was being applied more for political reasons than for objective classification. Some called for abandoning the term altogether, claiming that it had no real scholarly utility. However, *totalitarianism* remains a valuable term, especially if used consistently and judiciously.

What, then, is the difference between totalitarianism and other forms of nondemocratic rule? **Totalitarianism** has several important elements. It is a form of nondemocratic rule with a highly centralized state whose regime has a well-defined ideology and seeks to transform and fuse the institutions of state, society, and the economy. The main objective of totalitarianism, unlike those of other nondemocratic regimes, is to use power to transform the total institutional fabric of a country to meet an ideological goal. Finally, because of the ambitious goals of totalitarianism, violence and the resulting terror often become necessary tools to destroy any obstacle to change.[3] Violence and terror not only destroy enemies of the totalitarian ideology, but also, as the political philosopher Hannah Arendt pointed out, they shatter human will, thus eliminating individuals' ability to aspire to, much less create, freedom.[4] Because they achieve these effects, terror and violence are commonly used to break down existing institutions and remake them in the leadership's own image. This is not to say that all violent regimes are totalitarian. The central issue is to what end violence is used. Totalitarianism often emerges when those who have come to power profess a radical or reactionary political attitude that rejects the status quo and sees dramatic, often revolutionary change as indispensable and violence as a necessary or even positive force toward that goal.

To sum up, nondemocratic rule is a political regime in which power is exercised by a few, unbound by public or constitutional control. The public lacks not only the right to choose its own leaders but also other personal liberties that those in power may see as a threat, such as freedom of speech or assembly. Totalitarianism is distinguished from other forms of nondemocratic rule by its totalistic ideology, which seeks the fundamental transformation of most domestic institutions and the potential use of violence toward that end.

IN FOCUS

Totalitarian Regimes...

- Seek to control and transform all aspects of the state, society, and economy.
- Use violence as a tool for remaking institutions.
- Have a strong ideological goal.
- Have arisen relatively rarely.

Origins and Sources of Nondemocratic Rule

Now that we have defined nondemocratic regimes, we might consider their emergence and perseverance. In the last chapter, we spoke about some of the competing explanations regarding why democracy comes about. In a number of these explanations, the discussion was built on the ways in which authoritarian rule can give way to democracy. Let's return to these arguments, with an emphasis on nondemocratic perseverance rather than decline. As always, there is no single or dominant explanation for nondemocratic regimes, and the explanatory power of any theory may be limited by space or time. What may be helpful in explaining authoritarianism in Latin America in the 1970s may be of little use in explaining authoritarianism across the former Soviet Union.

Modernization and Nondemocratic Rule

Recall that a central assertion of the behavioral revolution was that with modernization, societies would become more urban, educated, and politically sophisticated, creating the basic conditions that would catalyze democracy. And indeed, a strong correlation exists between societies that lack modern institutions and nondemocratic rule. Societies that are poor and poorly developed are less likely to have democracy, for a number of reasons that we noted in Chapter 5. One important explanation is the role of the middle class. According to the common political science dictum "no middle class, no democracy," modernization is necessary for the development of an urban, educated middle class with specific political, social, and economic interests that it can articulate and advance, helping to generate demands for democratic rule. The absence of a middle class is more likely to result in polarization between those few in power and a wider population that is weakly organized.

Yet modernization can sometimes lead to nondemocratic rule—even replacing existing democratic regimes. Contrary to our expectations, modernization can be a disruptive and uneven process. Urban areas may experience a sudden transformation of institutions and norms while rural areas lag behind; some people may enjoy technology like telephones and Internet access, as well as infrastructure such as roads and schools, while others lack these benefits. Disruptive shifts in economic institutions (such as from agricultural to industrial) and social institutions (such as changes in gender relations or increased secularism) can generate instability. Modernization can also trend backward, bringing increased inflation or unemployment, weakening economic development, and destabilizing the political order. Where a sufficient number of individuals feel disoriented by change, political movements and leaders may emerge with promises to restore "order" and reconcile the tensions between old institutions and new. Such movements can bring down a democratic regime if it appears unable to resolve these tensions or avoid the pitfalls of modernity. Turkey may be an example of this process. While the country has rapidly developed and urbanized over the past 20 years, it has become less democratic over time, not more so.

Nondemocratic regimes run the spectrum of levels of wealth and modernization. We may think of nondemocratic countries as necessarily poor. Yet Singapore and many Persian Gulf states are commonly cited as modern and economically advanced societies where nondemocratic regimes are highly institutionalized. (We can also think of countries, like India and South Africa, that are democracies yet relatively poor.) Regime type and poverty do not correlate neatly, though it is worth noting that most countries with a per capita GDP at purchasing power parity (PPP) of more than $20,000 are democracies.

Elites and Nondemocratic Rule

In our discussion so far, we've noted that the absence or destabilizing effects of modernization may be a factor in the emergence of authoritarianism. Much of this argument assumes that modernization is strongly correlated with wealth, as agricultural societies become more industrial and developed. However, modernization and wealth do not take into account inequality. As we saw in Chapter 4, countries can vary dramatically in their levels of financial equality, and we can imagine that in highly unequal societies those who monopolize economic power will also monopolize political power.

In particular, elites may be less willing to share power when they fear losing their economic opportunities in the process. In fact, the longevity of nondemocracy may be due precisely to the fact that rivals for power seek control specifically so that they can enrich themselves. The state under these conditions becomes a tool to siphon off resources and maintain control. Regimes that have increased inequality in this way may be particularly loath to surrender power, not only because they may be forced to give up their assets but also because they may lose their lives in retribution. The threat of revolution may make these systems particularly unlikely to provide much in the way of participation, competition, or liberty.

One variant of this argument that we referred to in the case of Zimbabwe is the theory of development known as the **resource curse**. Since natural resources, such as oil, gas, and minerals, might be a source of great wealth, the puzzle is why so many resource-rich countries are underdeveloped or nondemocratic. According to this theory, the existence of natural resources is a barrier to modernization and democracy for several reasons. Resources in the ground give leaders the wealth necessary to run the state without taxation. This means those in power need not bother themselves with the taxation-and-representation trade-off; because they do not need to tax the people, they can effectively ignore their political demands. Even worse, natural resources tend to stunt the development of a modern economy and middle class, since neither is of concern (and may in fact be a threat) to those in power. Finally, since natural resources are not portable, those in power know that should they give up power, they would not be able to take these assets with them. The result is that wealth is highly concentrated in the hands of those in power. Under these conditions, nondemocratic rule can effectively subsidize itself, so long as the resources last and have a market. Oil is the most obvious example of a resource curse, but diamonds, timber, or metals could also serve this function. The "Questions and Methods" section on pp. 208–9 provides additional examples.

Society and Nondemocratic Rule

This discussion returns us to the idea of civil society introduced in Chapter 5. Recall that we defined civil society as a fabric of organizations created by people to help define their own interests. These organizations are not necessarily political—in fact, the vast majority of them have no specific political content. Sports teams, groups of collectors and enthusiasts, and religious and other organizations all form civil society. Observers commonly argue that civil society is crucial to democratic life because it allows individuals to organize, articulate their preferences, and form networks that cross economic, social, or political divides. Civil society is thus commonly viewed as a crucible for democratic action, laying the groundwork for democratic institutions.

Conversely, many authoritarian systems are characterized by the absence of civil society. This condition can result from those in power taking steps to absorb, monitor, or destroy any form of independent action not sanctioned by the state. Civil society may also have little precedent in society or be hindered by ethnic or other societal divisions that dissuade people from forming organizations across institutional barriers. The result can be a society that views the state as the primary arena for social organization and therefore focuses more on winning control over the state than on building strong institutions outside it. Interestingly, this emphasis on the state can sometimes go hand in hand with what is known as *populism*. **Populism** is not a specific ideology and in fact draws much of its power from an anti-institutional approach. But generally, populism carries within it the view that elites and established institutions do not fully represent the will of the people and that a new movement, free from ideology and often led by a charismatic leader, can usher in a new order. While populism commonly takes on an anti-governmental, anti-institutional orientation, it often assumes that people need to "take back" the state and set it on the correct path. Populism need not lead to an antidemocratic outcome; however, we can see how it can destabilize democratic practices and provide a foundation for antidemocratic leaders to come to power.

Finally, civil society may emerge alongside a nondemocratic regime but take on nondemocratic tendencies, especially where more democratic forms of civil society have been repressed by the state. Many countries have an array of active organizations with antidemocratic tendencies, such as groups that advocate preferred rights for one ethnic or religious group over another. Anti-Muslim groups in the United States and Europe can be seen as a form of civil society, much as we might not like them. Greater civic activism can undermine democracy if many nonstate groups view the political process as legitimate only if it meets their specific needs and marginalizes others. If people participate in the game of politics but argue that unless they win the game must be "rigged," democracy is in danger.

International Relations and Nondemocratic Rule

International influences can contribute to nondemocratic rule, most obviously through occupation. After World War II, the occupation of Japan and Germany led to democratization, but in Eastern Europe, Soviet control brought an end to democratic movements and eliminated much of civil society. Western imperialism has also contributed to nondemocratic rule. Borders badly drawn by imperial powers, as we discussed in Chapter 3, have created many countries with sharp ethnic and religious divisions that make consensus building difficult and authoritarianism an effective way for one group to monopolize power over others. Imperial institutions can similarly foster authoritarianism by contributing to such things as uneven modernization and weak state autonomy and capacity. Even after the end of Western imperialism, during the Cold War both the Soviet Union and the United States backed authoritarian rulers against democratic forces in order to maintain or expand their influence. The United States played a significant role in overthrowing the democratically elected government in Iran in 1953, fearing that the prime minister was tilting toward the Soviet Union. The Soviet Union crushed revolts in Hungary in 1956 and Czechoslovakia in 1968. China and Russia have more recently become important supporters of nondemocratic regimes in Africa and the Middle East through investment and by building diplomatic support for them in the international community. Iran and Saudi Arabia, too, have sought to use their oil wealth to support like-minded regimes in the region, thereby deepening problems in countries like Iraq and Syria.

Culture and Nondemocratic Rule

Let us return to the idea of political culture, which argues that the differences in societal institutions—norms and values—shape the landscape of political activity. In previous chapters, we discussed the controversial idea that a culture of democracy or liberty may be a precondition for institutionalized democracy and that certain societies may, for whatever reason, hold these values while others do not. By extension, it could be argued that some societies hold nondemocratic political values. In challenging modernization theory, which essentially equates "Western" with "modern," some scholars argue that culture is much more fixed than modernization theory holds it to be; they believe that modernization will not necessarily cause cultures to Westernize—that is, to adopt such values as secularism, individualism, and liberal democracy. Nondemocratic rule in this view is not the absence of democracy—it is its own set of values.

One common argument in this regard is that democracy is a unique product of interconnected historical experiences in Europe, such as Christianity (particularly Protestantism), the emphasis on individualism and secularism, the development of the nation-state, modern ideologies, early industrialization, and the development of capitalism, among others. These factors, the argument goes, allowed for the creation of democracy as a type of regime built on liberal values that emphasize freedom—what we typically call Western values.

In contrast, some (both inside and outside the Muslim world) have asserted that Islam views political power and religious power as one and the same. Laws are handed down by God to be observed and defended, and democracy is essentially anathema to the will of God. Cultural arguments can also be found in the debate about Asian values, which we discussed in Chapter 5. As we recall, proponents of the Asian Values argument contend that Asia's cultural and religious traditions stress conformity, hierarchy, and obedience, which are more conducive to a political regime that limits freedom in order to defend social harmony and consensus. The philosophy of Confucianism is frequently cited in this regard, with its emphasis on obedience to hierarchy and its notion of a ruler's "mandate from heaven."

As we have noted, many scholars reject the idea that certain cultures preclude democratic rule. These societies and the peoples within them, it is argued, are far too diverse to represent one set of values. Differences in history, religion, social structure, and other institutions have led to an array of contrasting and overlapping ideas that are in a continuous process of interaction and reinterpretation. Cultural arguments may inform the content of nondemocratic or democratic institutions, but we should be wary of making sweeping arguments about culture and regime type.

There are numerous explanations for nondemocratic rule, and they are contingent on time and space—what might explain one country's regime at one time may be irrelevant at another time or for another country. The lack of modernization or its disruptive nature may reinforce nondemocratic rule. Elite strategies and the fear of sharing power can also help support nondemocratic rule, especially when natural resources are in play. A weak civil society at home and international factors can also play an important role. Finally, culture can be a factor in shaping the contours of nondemocratic institutions, but whether this can explain authoritarianism itself is a much more contentious question. The intersection of these forces can illuminate how and why nondemocratic rule comes to power. Looking at Figure 6.1, we see that authoritarianism remains strong in the Middle East and the former Soviet Union, while in places like Asia and Latin America many authoritarian regimes have given way. There is no simple answer to explain these differences.

Nondemocratic Regimes and Political Control

We have so far covered some of the main explanations for the establishment of nondemocratic regimes. In this section, we consider how these systems stay in power.

In liberal democracies, we take the system of government for granted; so long as participation, competition, and liberty are provided and defended, democracy can continue, often even in the face of significant domestic or international crises. We may assume that nondemocratic regimes are much more precarious, held in place only by fear and vulnerable to revolution at any moment. This is misleading. Nondemocratic regimes vary in their mechanisms of political control, some of which can generate legitimacy like that found in democratic systems. A consideration of the means of nondemocratic rule will give us a sense of this complexity.

Coercion and Surveillance

One feature that we initially, and perhaps primarily, associate with nondemocratic regimes and especially with totalitarianism is the use of coercion. Coercion can be defined as compelling individuals by threatening their lives or livelihoods. Compliance with regime goals is often enforced through the threat or use of force against

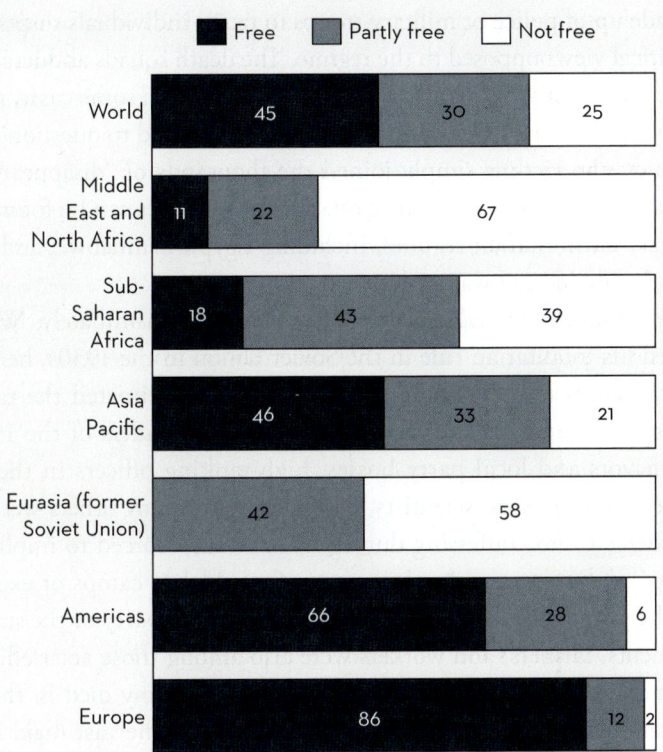

FIGURE 6.1 Political Systems, 2019

Source: Freedom House, https://freedomhouse.org/report/countries-world-freedom-2019 (accessed 12/30/2019).

the population, sending a clear signal that those who oppose the regime or government will be dealt with harshly; they may face the loss of their jobs or access to certain resources, arrest, detention without trial, torture, and death. In an extreme example, in the 1970s many nondemocratic regimes in Latin America used "death squads" made up of police or military troops to target individuals suspected of harboring political views opposed to the regime. The death squads abducted and murdered these individuals, frequently after torturing them. In some cases, their bodies were dumped in the open as a warning to others who dared to question the regime. In other cases, the victims simply joined the thousands of "disappeared"—those who were abducted and never seen again. Similar practices can be found in several contemporary authoritarian regimes, including Egypt, Zimbabwe, and Syria both before and during its civil war.

Other regimes have used violence even more indiscriminately. When Stalin consolidated his totalitarian rule in the Soviet Union in the 1930s, he carried out what are known as purges—widespread arrests that decimated the ranks of the Communist Party and the state bureaucracy. Former leaders of the 1917 revolution, city mayors and local party bosses, high-ranking officers in the army and navy, university professors, scientists, diplomats, and many others were detained, tortured, coerced into confessing during "show trials," forced to implicate others in their supposed crimes, and either sent to forced labor camps or executed. The targets of the purges were not limited to members of the party or the state; writers, artists, students, farmers, and workers were also among those accused of political sabotage and anti-Soviet views. It is not known how many died in these purges; estimates range from 5 to 20 million. Undoubtedly, in the vast majority of these cases the victims were innocent. Yet innocence was unimportant to Stalin's regime. When everyone was made to fear that they, too, could be arrested, the public could be controlled and even turned against itself since everyone feared being denounced by someone else. Arbitrary arrests, torture, disappearances, and murder continue to be common in many nondemocratic regimes.

Another important means of control is the ability to maintain a close watch over the population. Surveillance allows the government to prevent opposition from organizing and also instills uncertainty among the population—who is being watched? Surveillance may be conducted through the use of an internal security force, or "secret police," charged with monitoring public activity, spying on individuals, and interrogating members of the public suspected of political activity hostile to the regime. In some countries, surveillance has included widespread telephone tapping and the creation of a huge network of public informers, whereby nearly anyone may be the eyes and ears of those in power. With the rise of the Internet and the widespread use of mobile phones, surveillance has become more sophisticated, including the ability to monitor and control many forms of electronic communication, such as e-mail, social networking, and text messages.

Co-optation: Corporatism and Clientelism

The prevalence of coercion and surveillance in some nondemocratic regimes may give the impression that those in power must be ever vigilant against the public to prevent opposition or revolution, which might spring up at any time. But not all nondemocratic regimes need or choose to rely on punishment or surveillance as a central means of control. Another method they may use is co-optation, the process by which individuals outside an organization are brought into a beneficial relationship with it, making them dependent on the regime for certain rewards. Although co-optation is not unique to nondemocratic regimes, it tends to be much more widespread under such regimes than under democratic ones, where people are usually more suspicious of such favoritism and see it as contrary to the democratic process.

CORPORATISM

Co-optation can take many forms. The most structured form is **corporatism**, which emerged as a method by which nondemocratic regimes attempted to solidify their control over the public by creating or sanctioning a limited number of organizations to represent the interests of the public and restricting those not set up or approved by the state. These organizations are meant to replace independent organizations with a handful that alone have the right to speak for various sectors of society. For example, under a corporatist regime, churches, labor unions, agricultural associations, student groups, neighborhood committees, and the like are all approved, funded, and at least partially controlled by the state. Non-sanctioned, alternative organizations are not allowed.

Unlike the overlapping memberships, competition, and ever-changing nature of civil society and political parties in a pluralistic society, corporatism arranges society so that each organization is empowered by the state to have a monopoly of representation over a given issue or segment of society (meaning that no other organization may act in that area or speak on that issue). State, society, and the market under corporatism are viewed as a single organic body: each institution cooperates and performs its own specific and limited role and is subordinate to the state and regime.

Corporatism can be an effective form of control, for it gives the public a limited influence (or at least the pretense of influence) in the policy-making process. Farmers or students, for example, may have an official organization with elected officers and resources that are meant to serve their interests. In return, the regime is able to better control the public through these institutions, and civil society is marginalized or eliminated. For the average individual, a state-sanctioned organization is better than none at all, and many willingly participate in the hope that their needs will be met.

Many nondemocratic regimes have used variants of corporatism as a means of control. It is an integral part of totalitarianism, but it also existed in authoritarian Spain and Portugal up to the 1970s. In Spain, for example, a single political party organized most of the business and labor interests into a limited number of "syndicates" that represented both owners and workers in different sectors of the economy. Communist regimes are similarly corporatist. In Cuba, for example, all labor is organized under a single union directly controlled by the state, and independent unions are illegal. Although corporatism differs in form and degree, in all corporatist regimes a limited number of organizations represent and direct societal interests, bringing the public under organized state control.

CLIENTELISM

A less structured means of co-optation is **clientelism**, whereby the state co-opts members of the public by providing specific benefits to people in return for public support (such as voting in elections). Unlike corporatism, clientelism relies on individual patronage rather than organizations that serve a large group of people, and it is more ad hoc than corporatism. Clientelism does not require a set of sanctioned and licensed organizations but allows those in power to target and respond to individuals and groups as they see fit, trading benefits for particular forms of support.

In both corporatism and clientelism, the state has a number of perquisites it can use in co-opting individuals. Jobs within the state or in state-run sectors of the economy, business contracts or licenses, public goods such as roads and schools, and kickbacks and bribes are a few of the tools in its arsenal. Such largesse often leads to **rent seeking**, a process in which political leaders essentially use parts of the state to extract income for their supporters, giving them preferred access to public goods that would otherwise be distributed in a nonpolitical manner. For example, leaders might use a nationalized industry for rent seeking, providing supporters with jobs and the ability to siphon off resources from that branch of the state.

In general, co-optation is likely to be much more successful than coercion at maintaining nondemocratic regimes, since many in the public may actively support the regime in return for the benefits they derive from it. Political opposition is dealt with not through repression and violence but by withholding largesse or incorporating opponents into the system and making them dependent on it. Such a regime, however, faces limitations. Corporatist and clientelist regimes can run out of benefits with which to pacify the public, especially if a great deal of the economy is built around state-controlled industries whose major function is to reward the loyal with jobs or opportunities for corrupt practices. Also, in a regime that doles out economic resources for political reasons, problems may emerge as productive resources are siphoned off to secure the acquiescence of the public. At its worst, such a regime can decline into a **kleptocracy** (literally, "rule by theft"), where those in power seek only to drain the state of assets and resources. Russia and Zimbabwe are good examples of such practices. As these assets and resources dry up, co-optation can quickly unravel.

Personality Cults

Nondemocratic regimes may also reinforce their rule by emphasizing veneration of the leadership—essentially an emotional appeal to legitimize rule. The most extreme example is what is known as a personality cult. First used to describe Stalin's rule in the Soviet Union, the term *personality cult* refers to promotion of a leader not merely as a political figure but as someone who embodies the spirit of the nation, possesses far more wisdom and strength than the average individual, and is thus portrayed in a quasi-religious manner as all-wise, all-seeing, all-knowing. In other words, personality cults attempt to generate a charismatic form of authority for the political leader from the top down by convincing the public of the leader's admirable qualities.

The media and culture play a vital role in a personality cult: news reports, public rallies, art, music, films, and other means are used to spread flattering imagery of the leader. The country's successes are attributed to the power of the leader, and mistakes are blamed on the mortal flaws of the public or on external enemies. Cults of personality may also be coupled with coercion; the public may not believe the praise, but no one is willing to say so. This is especially the case where charismatic power has faded over time to become little more than a façade, held up only by force. Under these conditions, there is always the chance that the cult will crack, leading to a rapid political decompression. This situation occurred in Romania in 1989, when Nicolae Ceaușescu, the self-styled "conductor" of his country, was shown on national television reacting in a stunned and confused manner when attendees at a public rally he was addressing suddenly grew hostile. Within hours, revolution swept the country; within three days, Ceaușescu and his wife had been executed by firing squad.

Personality cults may also take a weaker but still powerful form. In Iran, the image of Supreme Leader Ayatollah Ali Khamenei adorns shops and billboards around the country, and he is portrayed as an embodiment of the 1979 revolution and the country's Shia Muslim faith. Yet in spite of his power, few Iranians

> ## IN FOCUS: Nondemocratic Means of Control
>
> - **Coercion:** public obedience is enforced through violence and surveillance.
> - **Co-optation:** members of the public are brought into a beneficial relationship with the state and government, often through corporatism or clientelism.
> - **Personality cult:** the public is encouraged to obey the leader, based on his or her extraordinary qualities and compelling ideas.

would view him as a kind of deity or believe that he has superhuman powers. Russia's Vladimir Putin has built around himself a similar kind of veneration as the embodiment of the state and regime, and some worry that China's president Xi Jinping, in defining himself as the "core leader," is in the process of doing the same.

In looking back over what we have discussed so far, we find that nondemocratic regimes come to power and stay in power in various ways. Some of these are "carrots" (rewards for compliance and support); others are "sticks" (threatened or actual punishments). A combination of such carrots and sticks may cause some people, perhaps even a majority, to view the regime as legitimate. They may agree with the regime's ideology, directly benefit from its rule, venerate its leaders, or simply fear political change. The idea of nondemocratic legitimacy may be hard for us to accept. Particularly in Western democracies, there is an assumption that in every nondemocratic regime the people are simply waiting for the chance to install democracy. Yet nondemocratic regimes can be just as institutionalized, stable, and legitimate as any democratic regime. They enjoy some, or even a great deal of, public support, especially if benefits are widespread enough, coercion limited, and political change viewed as fraught with risk. Many, for example, would suggest that the current Chinese regime enjoys widespread public support and that the public has little interest in democratization, which many citizens fear could bring political and economic instability.

Models of Nondemocratic Rule

By now, it should be clear that nondemocratic regimes emerge for different reasons and persist in various ways by using, to varying degrees, tools of coercion and co-optation. Political scientists often classify such regimes according to how they use these tools. The most important forms of nondemocratic rule are personal and monarchical, military, one-party, theocratic, and illiberal regimes. Personal and monarchical rule is based on the power of a single strong leader who typically relies on charismatic or traditional authority to maintain power. Under military rule, in contrast, the monopoly of violence that characterizes militaries tends to be the strongest means of control. One-party rule is often corporatist, creating a broad membership as a source of support and oversight. Theocracies derive their power from their claim to rule on behalf of God. Finally, in illiberal regimes the basic structures of democracy exist but are not fully institutionalized and often not respected. Across regimes, we find structures we are familiar with in liberal democracies: heads of state and government, judiciaries, legislatures, and elections. But these are not subject to the rule of law, in the absence of which they reflect the preferences of those in power.

Personal and Monarchical Rule

Personal and monarchical rule is what usually comes to mind when people think of nondemocratic rule, perhaps because long before modern politics, states, and economies came into being, people were ruled by powerful figures—kings and caesars, emperors and sultans, chiefs and caudillos. Drawing on charismatic or traditional legitimacy, personal and monarchical rule often rests on the claim that one person alone is fit to run the country, with no clear regime or roles to constrain that person's rule. Under this form of rule, the state and society are commonly taken to be possessions of the leader, to be dispensed with as he (or, occasionally, she) sees fit. The ruler is not a subject of the state; rather, the state and society are subjects of the ruler. Ideology may be weak or absent, since rulers justify their control through the logic that they alone are the embodiment of the people and therefore uniquely qualified to act on the people's behalf. This claim may be coupled with a strong personality cult or a reliance on the traditional authority of bloodlines.

In some cases, personal and monarchical rule relies less on charismatic or traditional authority than on a form of co-optation known as **patrimonialism**. Patrimonialism can be seen as a form of clientelism, since a patrimonial leader trades benefits for political support. However, under patrimonialism the benefits are not distributed in an ad hoc way among individuals in society but are instead limited to a small group of regime supporters inside the state itself. This ruling group gains direct benefits in return for enforcing the ruler's will. The state elites swear allegiance to the leadership in return for personal profit. This is a form of co-optation, although under patrimonialism only the ruler's own personal followers benefit. All others in society tend to be held in check by force.

An example of personal rule based on patrimonialism was found in Zaire (now the Democratic Republic of the Congo) under the rule of Mobutu Sese Seko from 1965 until 1997. Although he once commanded a great deal of charismatic legitimacy, over time Mobutu increasingly used patrimonialism as a way to maintain his power. In particular, Mobutu built his patrimonial regime around Zaire's abundant natural resources, such as diamonds, gold, copper, and cobalt. He used these resources not to benefit the country as a whole but to amass his personal fortune; he siphoned off the profits from these resources to enrich himself and his followers. The result was a coterie of supporters who were willing to defend Mobutu in order to maintain their economic privileges.[5] This system of dependence and economic reward helps explain how Mobutu maintained power for more than three decades while Zaire's per capita GDP dropped by two-thirds from the 1970s to the 1990s.

Although monarchies have waned, they remain powerful in parts of the Middle East, such as in Saudi Arabia and across the Persian Gulf. Even when they are not monarchies, regimes with a single ruler attempt to keep power within one family, typically transferring it from father to son. Leaders of such regimes may take on titles such as president, but in essence they function much like traditional monarchs. Personal rule remains common in Africa and is typically coupled with patrimonial regimes that are enriched through control over natural resources or trade. Russia's regime is patrimonial as well, with economic and political power held in the hands of a narrow elite around President Vladimir Putin.

Military Rule

A second form of nondemocratic regime is military rule. Once considered relatively unusual, military rule has become much more common over the past 50 years, particularly in Latin America, Africa, and parts of Asia. Where governments and states are struggling with legitimacy and stability, often as a result of modernization, and where there is a high level of public unrest or violence, the military has sometimes chosen to intervene directly in politics, seeing itself as the only organized force able to ensure stability. This view is often combined with a sense among military leaders that the current government or regime threatens the military's or the country's interests and should be removed. Military rule may even have widespread public support, especially if people believe that the strong arm of the military can bring an end to corruption or political violence, prevent revolution, and restore stability.

Military rule typically emerges through a coup d'état, in which the armed forces seize control of the state. In some cases, military actors may claim that they have seized control reluctantly, promising to return the state and government to civilian rule once stability has been restored. This was the case in Thailand in 2006 and following Egypt's revolution in 2011. Often, under military rule, political parties and most civil liberties are restricted; civilian political leaders or opponents of military rule are arrested and may be killed. The use of coercion is a common aspect of military rule, since by their nature militaries possess an overwhelming capacity for violence.

This form of government usually lacks both a specific ideology and a charismatic or traditional source of authority. Hence, if the military seeks legitimacy in the eyes of the people, it must often fall back on rational authority. One variant of military rule that reflects this logic is known as **bureaucratic authoritarianism**, a regime in which the state bureaucracy and the military share a belief that a technocratic leadership, focused on rational, objective, and technical expertise, can solve the problems of the country—unlike "emotional" or "irrational" ideologically based party politics. Public participation, in other words, is seen as an obstacle to effective and objective policy making and so is done away with. In the 1960s and 1970s, bureaucratic authoritarian regimes emerged in a number of less-developed countries as rapid modernization and industrialization generated a high degree of political conflict. State and industry, with their plans for rapid economic growth, clashed with the interests of the working class and peasantry, who sought greater political power and a larger share of the wealth. This increasing polarization in politics often led business leaders and the state bureaucracy to advocate military rule as a way to prevent the working class and the peasantry from gaining power over the government.

Over the past 30 years, many bureaucratic authoritarian regimes have transitioned to democracy. However, military rule has not disappeared, and there is no reason to think it may not return in difficult times, as it did in Egypt. Supporters of military rule believe that dispensing with democracy can help facilitate modernization and development. They point to cases like South Korea, Taiwan, and Chile as success stories. But this is a problem of selection bias (see Chapter 1), where people have looked only for cases of economic success. If we concentrate instead on instances of military rule, we can find many more cases that led to poor economic development, such as in much of Latin America.[6] Nevertheless, the lure of military rule remains, especially in times of uncertainty. Some surveys suggest that upwards of 20 percent of Americans would support military rule under certain conditions.[7]

One-Party Rule

One-party rule is a regime in which a single political party monopolizes politics and bans other parties or excludes them from power. The ruling party serves several corporatist functions. It helps incorporate the people into the political regime through

IN FOCUS: Types of Nondemocratic Rule

TYPE	DEFINITION	PRIMARY TOOLS OF CONTROL
PERSONAL AND MONARCHICAL RULE	Rule by a single leader with no clear regime or rules constraining that leadership	Patrimonialism: supporters within the state benefit directly from their alliance with the ruler (corruption)
MILITARY RULE	Rule by one or more military officials, often brought to power through a coup d'état	Control of the armed forces, sometimes also allied with business and state elites (bureaucratic authoritarianism)
ONE-PARTY RULE	Rule by one political party that bans or excludes other groups from power	Large party membership helps mobilize support and maintain public control, often in return for political or economic benefits (corporatism, clientelism)
THEOCRACY	"Rule by God"; holy texts serve as foundation for regime and politics	Religious leadership and political leadership fused into single sovereign authority
ILLIBERAL REGIMES	Rule by an elected leadership through procedures of questionable democratic legitimacy	A regime where democratic institutions that rest on the rule of law are weakly institutionalized and poorly respected

membership and participation. Typically, the party includes only a small minority of the population—in most communist countries, for instance, party membership has been less than 10 percent—but this still means that hundreds of thousands or millions of people are party members.

Through membership, the party can rely on a large segment of the public that is willing to help develop and support the policies of nondemocratic rule as well as to transmit information back to the leadership on developments in all aspects of society. Single-party regimes are often broken down into smaller units or "cells" that operate at the university, workplace, or neighborhood level. These cells report back to higher levels of the party, help to deal with local problems and concerns, and keep tabs on society as a whole. No area is untouched by the presence of the party, and this helps the party maintain control over the public.

In return for their support, members of the party are often granted privileges that are otherwise denied to the public at large. They may have access to certain resources (better health care or housing, for instance) that nonmembers do not. Positions in government and other important areas of the economy or society are also reserved for party members. One important result of such membership is that a large group of individuals in society directly benefit from the regime and are therefore willing to defend it. This pragmatic membership, however, can backfire: those who embrace party membership only for the personal benefits and not out of any ideological conviction may quickly desert the leadership in a time of crisis.

Finally, the party serves as a mechanism of mobilization. The leadership uses the party as an instrument to deliver propaganda that extols the virtues of the current regime and government; it relies on its rank-and-file members, through demonstrations and mass rallies, to give the appearance of widespread public support and enthusiasm for the leadership. If necessary, it also uses party members to control and harass those who do not support the regime. However, co-optation is the primary mechanism that ensures compliance and support.

One-party regimes are often associated with communism and fascism and have been present in all cases of totalitarianism. However, they can also be found around the world in a variety of nondemocratic regimes. Other parties may exist, but they are typically highly restricted by the government so that they cannot challenge the current regime. For many years, this was the case in Mexico, which was dominated by the Partido Revolucionario Institucional, or PRI. Cuba, North Korea, China, Vietnam, and Laos are other examples of one-party regimes, each controlled by a single communist party.

Theocracy

Theocratic rule is probably the hardest form of nondemocratic rule to describe and analyze, though it is likely one of the oldest forms of rule. *Theocracy* literally means "rule by God," and a theocratic regime can be founded on any number of faiths and variations within them. A Christian theocracy might look completely unlike a Jewish one, drawing on different beliefs, texts, and traditions. Another obstacle to describing theocracy is the paucity of current examples of such regimes. In fact, some scholars would say there are no remaining theocracies, which would make a discussion of the term in contemporary politics irrelevant. However, we can observe in several countries some elements of theocratic rule, even if such a system does not exist in pure form. In Chapter 3, we noted that one of the recent challenges to ideology has been the rise of fundamentalism, which we defined as the fusion of religion and politics into an ideology that seeks to merge religion and the state. Such a merger, where faith is the sole source of the regime's authority, would render democratic institutions subordinate or in contradiction to the perceived will of God. In the vast majority of cases, such a goal remains hypothetical. Yet we can note cases where theocratic institutions are present and powerful.

Saudi Arabia is one example of a country that combines monarchical and theocratic forms of rule. The ruling family monopolizes politics, and the king acts as the supreme religious leader. Judicial and other matters must conform to Islamic law and are enforced by the Mutawwa'in, or morality police.[8] In Saudi Arabia, conversion from Islam is punishable by death, and other religions and sects within Islam (Saudi Arabia is majority Sunni) are brought under strict control or banned outright. Afghanistan between 1996 and 2001 could also be described as a theocracy, lacking any constitution and relying instead on local clerics authorized by the Taliban to rule on judicial matters based on their interpretation of Islamic law. Theocratic movements have grown in power not just in majority-Muslim states, but also in places like Buddhist Myanmar, Hindu India, or Jewish Israel. We will speak of this in more detail in Chapter 7. However, as with fundamentalism in general, we should not confuse religiosity, or even a wish for religion to play a greater role in politics, with a desire for theocracy.

Illiberal Regimes

In recent years, we have seen the rise of a new kind of nondemocratic regime around the world. Figure 6.1 (see p. 191) includes a large group of countries, such as Colombia, Kenya, Lebanon, and Turkey, that are categorized as neither "free" nor "not free" but as "partly free," meaning they fall somewhere between democratic and nondemocratic regimes. These regimes go by a number of names, such as *hybrid*, *electoral authoritarian*, and *semi-democratic*. We will use the term **illiberal regimes**.

What do illiberal regimes have in common? These regimes feature many of the familiar aspects of democracy, though with important qualifications. As a starting point, while the rule of law may be in place, it is weak. As a result, all the democratic institutions that rest on the rule of law are weakly institutionalized and poorly respected. Executives, legislatures, and judiciaries have their respective arenas of authority; the public enjoys the right to vote; elections take place regularly; and political parties compete. But these institutions and processes are circumscribed or unpredictable in ways inconsistent with democracy. Executives typically hold an overwhelming degree of power—often concentrated in a presidency—while the country has a limited ability to remove its executive.

Moreover, presidents in illiberal systems often rely on referenda to bypass the state and confirm executive power. Legislatures in turn are less able to check the power of the executive, and judicial institutions such as constitutional courts are often packed with the supporters of those in power. In addition, while political competition may exist on paper, parties and groups are restricted or harassed. Government monopolies over print and electronic media are used to deny the opposition a public platform, while the judicial system is used to harass opponents. The military often is not subject to civilian control. Elections are manipulated through changing electoral rules, vote buying, intimidation, or barring candidates from running.

Illiberal regimes in many ways represent a gray area between nondemocratic and democratic rule. Although these regimes look much like democracies on paper, they are much less so in practice. The big question here is whether illiberal regimes are transitional, in the process of moving from nondemocratic to democratic rule (or vice versa), or are a new form of nondemocracy that uses the trappings of democracy to perpetuate control. We are increasingly seeing examples of the latter—countries where the transition from authoritarianism to democracy has stalled and government institutions are democratic in name only, so that participation, competition, and liberty are severely curtailed. Equally worrisome is the possibility of developed democracies themselves becoming illiberal over time, something we will explore in Chapter 8.[9]

In Sum: Retreat or Retrenchment for Nondemocratic Regimes?

Although nondemocratic regimes exhibit an amazing diversity and flexibility in maintaining political control, for decades the global trend has been away from this form of rule. In the early part of the last century, democratic countries were few and beleaguered, wracked by economic recession, whereas nondemocratic regimes and totalitarianism in particular, backed by communist and fascist ideologies, seemed to promise radically new ways to restructure state, economic, and societal institutions. The German philosopher Oswald Spengler summarized this view in his 1922 work *The Decline of the West*: "The era of individualism, liberalism and democracy, of humanitarianism and freedom, is nearing its end. The masses will accept with resignation the victory of the Caesars, the strong men, and will obey them. Life will descend to a level of general uniformity, a new kind of primitivism, and the world will be better for it."[10]

INSTITUTIONS IN ACTION

What Explains the Different Paths of Zimbabwe and South Africa?

In Chapters 2 and 3, we looked at the different paths India and Pakistan took after gaining independence from British rule. Like those two countries, Zimbabwe and South Africa are neighbors whose historical, economic, racial, and political institutions are similar but whose political trajectories over the past three decades could not have been more different. South Africa's democratic transition is well known and regarded as a triumph in the face of tremendous obstacles. In contrast, as we read at the opening of this chapter, Zimbabwe has undergone several decades of political and economic decline. What explains this difference?

For a century, South Africa was controlled by a small white minority that accorded itself political and economic privileges while oppressing the black majority. In response, a resistance movement, the African National Congress (ANC), formed, using peaceful and, later, violent means to bring down the regime. Its leader, Nelson Mandela, spent nearly three decades in prison, and yet in spite of this and other repressive government actions, the ANC grew in strength. Faced with international isolation and the growing power of the black majority, the government released Mandela from prison in 1990, conducted negotiations with the ANC and other political parties, and inaugurated full democratic elections in 1994. The result has since been a stable liberal democracy.

What is less well remembered is that South Africa's next-door neighbor Zimbabwe (formerly Rhodesia) confronted a similar set of conditions much earlier. Like South Africa, Rhodesia was controlled by a white minority that dominated the country's economy and politics. Its government was also challenged by a liberation movement, the Zimbabwe African National Union-Patriotic Front (ZANU-PF), which relied on politics, guerrilla warfare, and terrorism to achieve majority rule. To defuse this conflict, the Rhodesian government began negotiations for a transition to democracy in 1978, and the first elections were held in 1980. Yet unlike South Africa, Zimbabwe never became an institutionalized democracy. It functioned as an illiberal regime for 20 years, eroding over time until eventually the country slid into authoritarianism in the early part of this century.

Why did these two countries take such different paths? The answers are unclear and at times seem contradictory. For many, the answer simply lies in leadership. Nelson Mandela's leadership of the ANC, even while in prison, was exceptional. He combined charismatic authority with the organizational skills necessary to keep the movement alive in spite of his detention. His long period in jail only increased his stature at home and abroad, reinforcing the legitimacy of the struggle and helping to intensify international pressure on South Africa. In contrast, the resistance movement in Zimbabwe was led by several different and clashing figures who divided rather than unified the movement. Robert Mugabe, who came to power in 1980 and ruled Zimbabwe until 2017, was talented politically but more interested in accumulating power than engendering democracy. This argument assumes that political change is essentially a function of individual leadership.

Yet other institutional factors set the stage on which such leadership can function.

In many respects, the paths of Zimbabwe and South Africa differ in degree rather than kind. ZANU-PF was from its inception a highly authoritarian party that allowed for no internal democratic practices and suppressed external opposition. Although the ANC was similarly undemocratic internally, its members worked to include other opposition groups under a common political umbrella. Scholars have also suggested that Zimbabwe's authoritarianism stemmed from ZANU-PF's close alliance with China and the Soviet Union during the Cold War. This alliance radicalized ZANU-PF's objectives, which came to entail a revolution against colonialism and capitalism. The ANC also benefited from close ties to the Soviet Union, and its founding charter similarly called for the nationalization of industry and land; but unlike ZANU-PF, its political platform did not call for a revolution against capitalism.

An important difference between Zimbabwe's and South Africa's societies also has a bearing on the divergence of their political paths. South Africa is a highly urbanized and relatively industrialized society, especially in comparison with Zimbabwe, whose economy has been largely based on agriculture. South Africa's urbanization, combined with its ethnic, religious, and cultural diversity, contributed to a strong civil society that gave rise to the ANC and helped create and institutionalize that organization's civic and democratic commitments. ZANU-PF could not rely on such foundations, and it became instead a largely rural military movement dominated by one ethnic group.[a]

In part as a result of South Africa's civil institutions, the ANC was careful about how it used violence in its struggle. It consistently emphasized the primacy of politics over violence and the need to minimize the loss of life despite numerous deaths at the hands of the state. The ANC did not directly target white civilians (though a number were killed as a result of attacks on security forces), even though this would have been an easy way to terrorize that minority and mobilize the majority population. In Zimbabwe, by contrast, violence became the primary means toward revolution. When ZANU-PF came to power, it continued to rely on violence to suppress its opponents. As the party faced growing opposition in the 1990s, it seized agricultural land held by white Zimbabweans, arrested oppositional leaders, and killed or tortured hundreds of people. The result was economic collapse and international isolation.

A farm in Zimbabwe previously owned by a white farmer was appropriated in 2000 by veterans of the war against the previous regime.

1. Which country has experienced greater modernization? What role has that played in their differing paths?

2. How might the presence of a vibrant civil society in South Africa have given it an advantage toward democratization over Zimbabwe?

3. Why might Zimbabwe's use of coercion make its regime more vulnerable?

Yet the exact opposite has taken place. As Figure 6.2 shows, in the 1980s, only 35 percent of all countries were democratic; now nearly 45 percent of them are. Does this mean that the days of nondemocratic regimes are numbered? If we look closely at our figure, there are concerns. According to Freedom House, the last decade has seen a steady decline in political rights and civil liberties around the world, with the exception of Asia. In 2019, for the fourteenth year in a row, the number of democracies in the world declined. Freedom of expression and the rule of law have been particularly affected, not just in undemocratic and illiberal states but also in many established democracies, including the United States, and recently democratized states, such as Hungary and Poland. As we shall discuss in Chapter 8, even the wealthiest and most long-lasting democracies confront economic, social, and

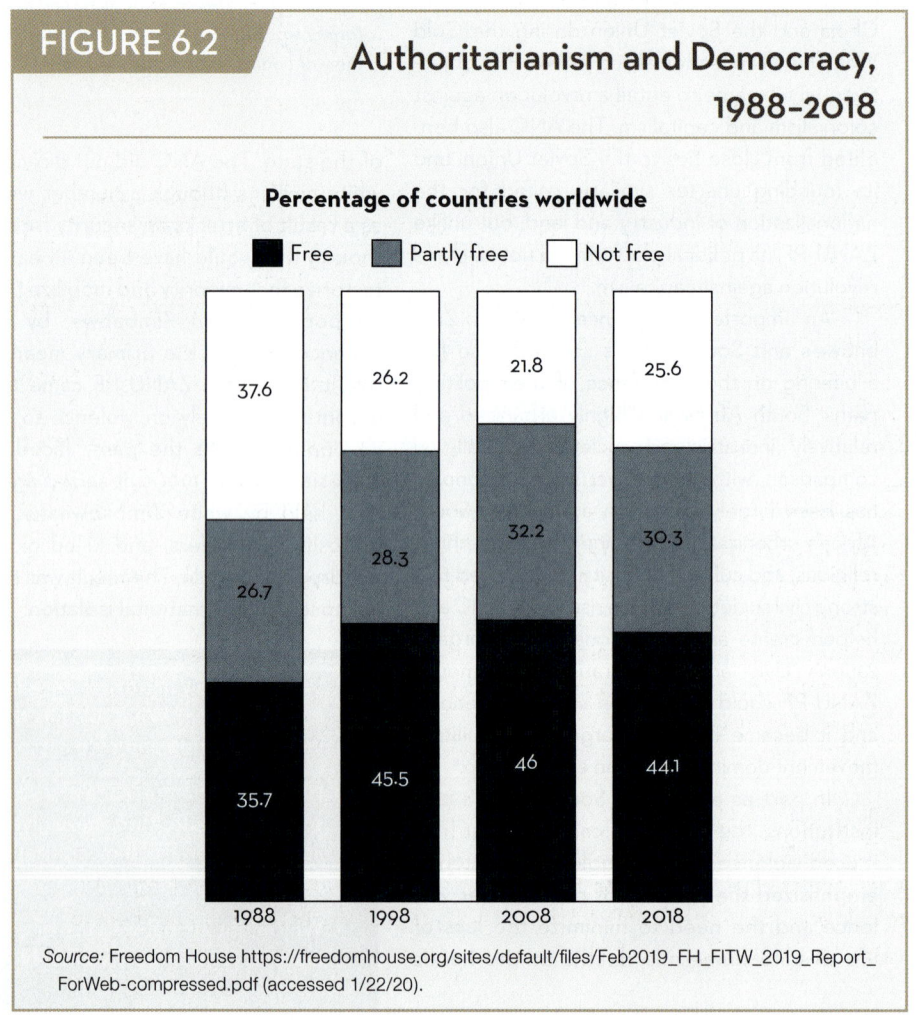

FIGURE 6.2 Authoritarianism and Democracy, 1988–2018

Percentage of countries worldwide

■ Free ▨ Partly free □ Not free

1988: 35.7 / 26.7 / 37.6
1998: 45.5 / 28.3 / 26.2
2008: 46 / 32.2 / 21.8
2018: 44.1 / 30.3 / 25.6

Source: Freedom House https://freedomhouse.org/sites/default/files/Feb2019_FH_FITW_2019_Report_ForWeb-compressed.pdf (accessed 1/22/20).

political challenges that threaten to delegitimize democratic institutions and democratic practices. This may be providing a new opportunity for authoritarianism with its promise to provide stability in exchange for personal liberty. Such threats are often associated with political violence, which we will consider in the next chapter.

Key Terms

authoritarianism (p. 182)
bureaucratic authoritarianism (p. 199)
clientelism (p. 194)
corporatism (p. 193)
illiberal regime (p. 202)
kleptocracy (p. 195)

nondemocratic regime (p. 182)
patrimonialism (p. 197)
populism (p. 187)
rent seeking (p. 189)
resource curse (p. 186)
totalitarianism (p. 184)

For Further Reading

Arendt, Hannah. *The Origins of Totalitarianism.* New York: Schocken Books, 1951.

Diamond, Larry, Marc F. Plattner, and Christopher Walker, eds. *Authoritarianism Goes Global: The Challenge to Democracy.* Baltimore, MD: Johns Hopkins University Press, 2016.

Hamid, Shadi. *Temptations of Power: Islamists and Illiberal Democracy in a New Middle East.* New York: Oxford University Press, 2014.

Levitsky, Steven, and Lucan A. Way. "The Rise of Competitive Authoritarianism." *Journal of Democracy* 13, no. 2 (April 2002): 51–65.

Linz, Juan J. *Totalitarian and Authoritarian Regimes.* Boulder, CO: Lynne Rienner, 2000.

Linz, Juan J., and Alfred Stepan. *Problems of Democratic Transition and Consolidation: Southern Europe, South America, and Post-Communist Europe.* Baltimore, MD: Johns Hopkins University Press, 1996.

Moffitt, Benjamin. *The Global Rise of Populism: Performance, Political Style, and Representation.* Stanford, CA: Stanford University Press, 2016.

Weinthal, Erika, and Pauline Jones Luong. "Combating the Resource Curse: An Alternative Solution to Managing Mineral Wealth." *Perspectives on Politics* 4, no. 1 (March 2006): 35–53.

INQUIZITIVE

Earn a better grade on your test. InQuizitive personalizes your learning path to help you master the concepts from this chapter and practice applying them to examples from the text and beyond (see back cover).

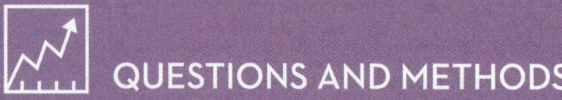

QUESTIONS AND METHODS

Are Resources Good for Democracy?

At the start of this chapter we introduced the example of Zimbabwe and noted how its long-standing authoritarian regime has stayed in power in part through its control of natural resources. From this one case it's easy to conclude that natural resources are bad for democracy and governance. But we can just as easily cherry pick other examples that challenge our hypothesis that natural resources undermine democracy. Norway, one of the largest oil and gas producers in the world, also boasts a highly robust democracy. So then how do scholars get at the puzzle of natural resources' impact on states and regimes?

One problem is that of conflicting definitions. What constitutes a natural resource? Gold or diamonds may be clear, but what about agriculture or forestry? A second prob-

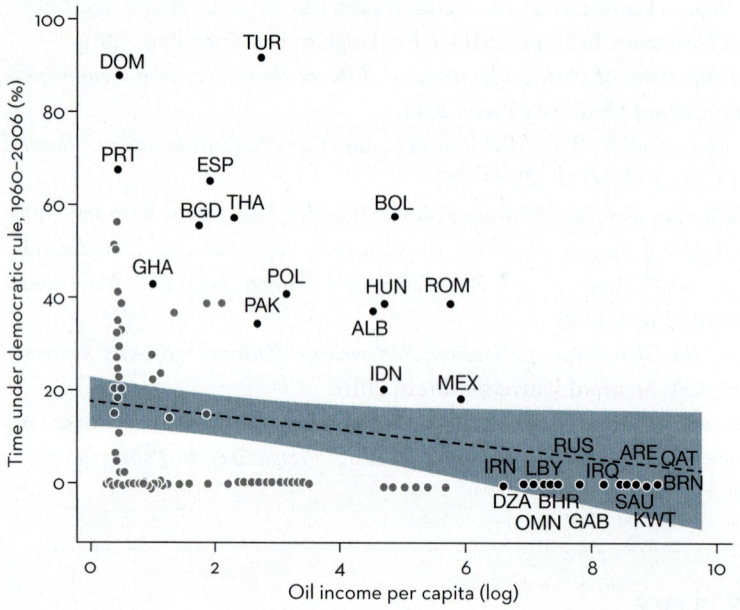

Oil and Transitions to Democracy, 1960–2006

Note: ALB, Albania; ARE, United Arab Emirates; BGD, Bangladesh; BHR, Bahrain; BOL, Bolivia; BRN, Brunei; DOM, Dominican Republic; DZA, Algeria; ESP, Spain; GAB, Gabon; GHA, Ghana; HUN, Hungary; IDN, Indonesia; IRN, Islamic Republic of Iran; IRQ, Iraq; KWT, Kuwait; LBY, Libya; MEX, Mexico; OMN, Oman; PAK, Pakistan; POL, Poland; PRT, Portugal; QAT, Qatar; ROM, Romania; RUS, Russian Federation; SAU, Saudi Arabia; THA, Thailand; TUR, Turkey.

Source: Annual Review of Political Science.

lem is one of measurement. We need to measure a resource in order to look for correlations between resource levels and possible effects. Do we measure resources by total quantity? By the value of exports? By share of government revenues? A third and final point is about the quality of data itself, which can be hard to collect and compare between countries. Between these variations in definitions, measurement, and data, it is possible to come up with any number of findings that contradict one another. Thus scholars have argued over the extent to which the resource curse is real.

Where scholars of the resource curse seem to be on firm ground is in the area of oil. Here, we have good definitions, measurements, and data, and the relationships seem relatively clear. Repeated statistical studies have shown that there is a significant relationship between oil wealth and regime type, helping to keep authoritarian regimes in place in ways similar to those we read about in Zimbabwe. As one scholar notes, no country with high levels of oil and gas has successfully transitioned to democracy since 1960.[a] This trend can be seen in the figure at left. These findings can help us make sense of why the Arab Spring did not reach the oil-rich Persian Gulf, and how Putin has managed to hold on to power in Russia. In many cases, natural resources can be the fuel of patrimonialism, where elites back the leadership in return for a cut of the resources. This leads us to a question regarding the practical policy implications of the resource curse. Let's assume a new government seeks to break the curse—what changes might work? How can they "get to Norway"? That is a whole other research project in itself.

1. ***Articulate the cause and effect of the hypothesis***

    Looking back at the case of Zimbabwe, how did resources can keep an authoritarian leader in power?

2. ***Apply theory to consider and explore policy choices***

    If you were to come to power in a country suffering from the resource curse, what changes could you make to break out of this trap? What would be the biggest challenges in making these changes?

3. ***Generate new questions related to the discussion***

    The resource curse looks at the relationship between resources and authoritarianism. What about democracy? What questions might we ask about the relationship between natural resources and existing democratic regimes?

---

a. Michael L. Ross, "What Have We Learned about the Resource Curse?" *Annual Review of Political Science* 18 (May 2015): 239–59; Zack Beauchamp, "The Oil Curse—How Black Gold Makes Countries More Authoritarian, Corrupt, and Violent," *Vox*, April 10, 2014, www.vox.com/2014/4/10/5601062/oil-curse-explained (accessed 12/16/19).

7

Syrians fleeing bombings in the southern region drive toward the Syrian-Turkish border.

POLITICAL VIOLENCE

When does political conflict turn deadly?

How did Syria end up like this? Among the many calamities of the Arab Spring, Syria has by far seen the most suffering—perhaps as many as a half million dead, and nearly 5 million are now refugees. A peaceful movement for change against the rule of President Bashar al-Assad eventually turned to calls for revolution, and this in turn fanned the flames of ethnic and religious conflict, guerrilla warfare, and terrorism. Thinking about how Syria fell apart can help frame many of the concepts and questions we will deal with in this chapter.

Since its independence after World War II, Syria has been an authoritarian regime. It has also been highly patrimonial. As described in the previous chapter, patrimonialism is a system that distributes political and economic power to a small group of regime supporters within the state while holding society in check by force. In Syria, power has been monopolized by the Assad family—first under Hafez al-Assad, who came to power in a military coup in 1970, and since his death in 2000 under his son Bashar al-Assad. The top ranks of the state and military are dominated by the Assad family's own Alawite Muslim sect, which makes up less than 15 percent of the population. Because of its patrimonialism, Syria has been more repressive than many other authoritarian regimes in the Middle East, relying more on coercion than co-optation.

The nature of patrimonialism in Syria helps us understand why the regime did not give way as regimes did in places like Tunisia and Egypt. Events in Syria began with a protest movement not unlike those occurring elsewhere in the region; it was catalyzed by the torture of several young men who were caught writing antigovernment graffiti in the city of Daraa. In response, in March 2011 protesters held a "day of dignity" protest in several Syrian cities, calling for a peaceful liberalization of the regime. Given the Assads' history of repression, it is not surprising that the regime opted to react with deadly force. In response, citizens began to take up weapons to overthrow the regime.

Within this struggle, new factors began to emerge. First, the ongoing conflict radicalized some Syrians, who rejected the original call for secular democracy in favor of a theocratic regime. They were soon joined by fighters from outside the country (including some from Europe and North America) whose objectives were less about the Assad regime and more focused on creating a new Islamic state across the region. Such groups were more willing to embrace terrorism as a means to destroy both the Syrian state and rival guerrilla groups. The most extreme of these groups has been the Islamic State of Iraq and Sham (ISIS). First organized as a branch of Al Qaeda against the United States in Iraq, following the Arab Spring it began to expand into Syria through a mixture of guerrilla warfare (attacking the state) and terrorism (attacking civilians). Where ISIS gained power, it quickly laid the groundwork for its own state, including a severe religious law. Though now shattered, ISIS was able to build many of the elements of an independent state out of the wreckage of Syria and Iraq. And even if ISIS is truly defeated, it may well live on as a source of emulation for future terrorism around the globe. The revolutions of the Arab Spring, initially viewed as a step toward democracy, have led to consequences far from what most observers imagined.[1]

LEARNING OBJECTIVES

- Explain the factors that contribute to political violence.
- Compare and contrast revolution and terrorism as forms of political violence.
- Describe the relationship between political violence and factors such as religion, regime type, and state capacity and autonomy.

In previous chapters, we identified various institutions that define states, societies, and types of economic structures and regimes. We also saw how these institutions are constructed and function in different parts of the world. Power and legitimacy rest in these institutions, to varying degrees, but what happens when they lose power altogether or when people seek to take them down by force?

This chapter will shed some light on this complex question, providing ways to think about political violence and its implications. We begin by defining our terms: What do we mean by *political violence*, and how does it relate to the political institutions we have already covered? Next, we will look at some of the motivations of political violence, examining the different (and often conflicting) explanations for why such violence occurs. We will then concentrate on two important forms of political violence: revolution and terrorism. Each form is a phenomenon that can threaten governments, regimes, and states. Each form is also a loaded political term that stirs emotional responses, complicating analysis. We will look at some of the different ways revolution and terrorism can be defined and understood. In addition, we will explore the extent to which the two are related—how terrorism is often justified as a tool to achieve revolution. Once we have these concepts and arguments before us, we will look at them in the contemporary context of political violence motivated by religion. Finally, we will conclude with a discussion of how states and societies prevent or manage political violence and what this means for freedom and equality.

What Is Political Violence?

This textbook began with a focus on the state. This institution is the cornerstone of modern politics, one that we defined in its most basic terms as the organization that maintains a monopoly of violence or force over a territory. Across human history, centralized political authority has been a part of this monopoly whereby states vanquish their domestic rivals, defend themselves from external threats, and establish order and security at home. This process has been described as the shift from "private war" to "public war," meaning that individuals lose the freedom to use violence against one another, turning that right over to the state. This right is exchanged for a greater sense of security for all.

Of course, the state's monopoly of violence is never perfect or complete. Other states always represent a potential threat, given their own capacity for violence. Even at the domestic level, violence persists in such forms as murder and armed robbery. In many countries, such problems, though persistent, are manageable and do not threaten the stability and security of the state, society, or economy. But under certain conditions, this may not be true. Public violence may grow so pervasive or destructive that the state loses its control. Governments, regimes, states, and individuals are subject to attack, and sovereignty is weakened or lost. We have already seen this in some detail in our discussion of ethnic and national conflict in Chapter 3.

Political violence, or politically motivated violence outside of state control, is the focus of this chapter. Some political scientists see much of this political violence as part of a larger category of "contentious politics," or collective political struggle. This can include such things as revolutions, civil war, riots, and strikes, but it also includes more peaceful protest movements, some of which we will consider at the end of this chapter. In the case of political violence, we are speaking of a phenomenon that operates beyond state sovereignty, neither war nor crime, and that seeks to achieve some political objective through the use of force. Such definitions are always cleaner in theory than in reality, of course. The lines between domestic and international and between war, crime, and contentious politics are often quite blurry.

Why Political Violence?

Although defining political violence presents some challenges, a more controversial issue is why political violence occurs. What leads civilians to take up arms against a state or its citizens in pursuit of a political aim? Scholars have offered diverse reasons that have changed over time, but we can group them into three basic categories: institutional, ideational (based on ideas), and individual. These three explanations overlap to some degree; where one explanation ends and the others begin is not always clear. At the same time, such explanations are often debated by scholars or policy makers who frequently tend to favor one explanation over others. We will examine each of these reasons generally before looking at how each one is used specifically in studies of revolution and terrorism. Each explanation seeks to answer the same questions: What motivates political violence, and toward what end is it perpetrated?

Institutional Explanations

Because we have covered institutions at length, what we mean by this term should be relatively clear: we are referring to self-perpetuating organizations or patterns of activity that are valued for their own sake. Institutions define and shape human activity, and institutional explanations argue that their specific qualities or combinations are essential to political violence. The emphasis can be on political institutions, such as states and regimes; economic institutions, such as capitalism; or societal institutions, such as culture and religion. Moreover, these explanations can be based on either a constraining or an enabling argument. It may be that institutions contain values or norms that implicitly or explicitly encourage political violence, or that they constrain human activity, thus provoking political violence. In

Chapter 5, on democratic institutions, we covered variations in executive structures and electoral systems; as some have argued, the variants that reduce the opportunity for power sharing—versions that produce "winner-take-all" outcomes, like presidencies—increase the likelihood of marginalization, polarization, and conflict. Under these conditions, political violence can be a logical reaction when other forms of participation are blocked. Institutional explanations can be seen as a quest for a "root source" of violence, a necessary condition for violent actions to take place, and a presumption that changes in the institutional structure would eliminate the motivation for this violence.

Ideational Explanations

If institutional explanations emphasize the impact of fixed organizations and patterns in fostering political violence, ideational explanations focus more on the rationale behind that violence. By **ideational**, we simply mean having to do with ideas. Ideas may be institutionalized—concepts rooted in some institution such as a political organization or a religion—but just as often they are not institutionalized, with no real organizational base. The argument here is that ideas play an important role in political violence in the way they set out a worldview, diagnose a set of problems, provide a resolution, and describe the means of getting there. Any or all of these elements can be bound up with a justification of violence. These ideational factors take us back to our discussion of political attitudes in Chapter 3. As we noted there, political violence is more likely to be associated with attitudes that are radical or reactionary since each attitude views the current institutional order as bankrupt and beyond reform. Hence, it is not only the content of the ideas that matters but also their relation to the domestic political status quo. Ideas seen as conservative in one context may become a source of radicalism or reaction, and perhaps violence, elsewhere.

Individual Explanations

Finally, individual explanations center on those who carry out the violence. Here, the scholarship emphasizes the personal motivations that lead people to contemplate and carry out violence toward political ends. Scholars who study individual explanations of political violence usually follow one of two paths. One emphasizes psychological factors and conditions that draw individuals toward violence. Such factors can be a function of individual experiences, or they may be shaped by broader conditions in society, such as levels of economic development or gender roles. Such an approach

> **IN FOCUS**
>
> ## Explanations for Political Violence
>
> | EXPLANATION | REASONING | EXAMPLES |
> |---|---|---|
> | **INSTITUTIONAL** | Existing institutions may encourage violence or constrain human action, creating a violent backlash. | Presidentialism |
> | **IDEATIONAL** | Ideas may justify or promote the use of violence. | Some forms of religious fundamentalism; nationalism |
> | **INDIVIDUAL** | Psychological or strategic factors may lead people to carry out violence. | Humiliation; alienation |

tends to concentrate on how people may be driven to violence as an expression of desperation, the desire for liberation, or social solidarity. For example, some scholars of religious violence emphasize the role of humiliation as a motivating force, a sense that an individual's own beliefs are actively marginalized and denigrated by society. Individuals drawn to violence may be alienated from the society around them as well. Revolutionaries or terrorists, in this view, see violence as a way to give meaning to their lives and may not be concerned with whether they are effectively achieving their goals—or even truly understand what their political goals are.

A contrary approach, however, rejects this view, seeing political violence as a rational act, carried out by those who believe it to be an effective political tool. Strategy, rather than despair, drives these actions. Political violence is in this view not an expression of deviance but a strategy that is carefully wielded by those who understand its costs and potential benefits.[2]

Comparing Explanations of Political Violence

One important element of comparison across these three explanations is how they approach free will—that is, to what extent people are the primary actors in political violence. Institutional explanations often are quite deterministic, seeing people as shaped and directed by larger structures that they do not control. An individual's recourse to violence is simply the final step in a much larger process. In contrast, individual explanations place their focus squarely on people; they are the primary makers of violence because they choose to be. Ideational explanations lie somewhere in between. Ideas are influenced by institutions but are also actively taken up and molded by individuals to justify political violence.

A second element of comparison concerns universal versus particularistic explanations. Institutional explanations tend to be more particularistic, stressing the unique combination and role of institutions in a given case that are not easily generalized and applied elsewhere. Individual explanations typically center on those personal or psychological attributes common to all humans that can lead to violence. Ideational explanations, again, lie somewhere in the middle, generalizing the importance of ideas while noting the distinct lessons that different ideas impart.

Which explanation is most convincing: institutional, ideational, or individual? These explanations are often placed in competition with one another, but they work well in conjunction. Institutional factors provide a context in which particular preconditions, problems, and conflicts may emerge. Ideational factors help describe and define those problems, ascribe blame, and provide solutions by calling for the transformation of the status quo. These ideas in turn influence and are shaped by individuals and groups that may already be prone to violent activity. Let's look at the case of the Basque nationalist group Euskadi Ta Askatasuna (ETA) in Spain, which used violence as a political tool for several decades until finally disbanding in 2018. If we examine the ETA, we can see institutional factors that include a long period of repression under authoritarian rule and its effects on the Basque region. There are ideational factors as well, such as a belief among ETA members and supporters that the Basque people faced cultural extermination at the hands of the Spanish. Finally, individual factors include the role and motivations of many Basque youth in conducting *kale borroka* (urban struggle) in their support for an independent, revolutionary Basque state. We could do a similar analysis of ISIS, taking into consideration the role of authoritarianism in Iraq and Syria, the role of political Islam and anti-Americanism following the invasion of Iraq, and the appeal to many young foreigners to join the cause of building a new revolutionary religious state. These examples help illustrate the interconnection of these three factors, and why political violence is relatively unpredictable and has emerged in a variety of contexts. We will consider these various explanations next as we look at revolution and terrorism.

Forms of Political Violence

So far, we have spoken of political violence in general terms, defining it as violence that is outside state control and politically motivated. This definition encompasses many forms of political violence: assassinations, riots, rebellions, military coups, civil war, and ethnic conflict, to name a few. We will concentrate on two forms of political violence: revolution and terrorism. Revolution is important to study because of its profound effects. Revolutions have ushered in sweeping changes in modern politics, overturning old institutions and dramatically transforming domestic and international relations. Terrorism, while less sweeping, holds our attention as a similar challenge to modern political institutions, one whose impact on domestic and international politics has spiked in recent years. Both are forces that seek dramatic change. Yet in many ways, revolution and terrorism are opposites. Revolution is an uprising of the masses, who take to the streets, seize control of the state, and depose the old regime. In contrast, terrorism is much more secret and hidden, a conspiratorial action carried out by a small group. But there are similarities in their sources and goals. As we analyze and compare the dynamics of revolution and terrorism, we will draw out some of these elements and show how these seemingly disparate forms of political violence can be linked.

Revolution

The term *revolution* has many connotations. Although we speak of revolution as a form of political violence, the word is also used much more indiscriminately. Any kind of change that is dramatic is often described as revolutionary, whether the change is political or technological, and the term has a generally positive connotation, one that evokes progress. People speak of dramatic change as positive, so *counterrevolution* is seen as an attempt to turn back the clock to a darker time. None of this should be surprising; across much of the world, significant political change has been a result of revolution, and in countries where this is the case revolution is often associated with independence, sovereignty, and development. Thus *revolution* is a loaded term, albeit with mostly positive connotations.

For our purposes, we shall speak of revolution in a more limited manner. **Revolution** can be defined as a public seizure of the state in order to overturn the existing government and regime. Several factors are at work here. First, revolutions involve some element of public participation. To be certain, revolutions typically have leaders, organizers, and instigators who play a key role. But unlike a coup d'état, in which elites overthrow the government, in a revolution the public plays an important role in seizing power. Russia is an interesting example. While we typically speak of communism's triumph in 1917 as a revolution, some scholars call it a coup because Lenin and a handful of followers seized power rather than being part of some mass action toppling the government.

Another factor in our definition of revolutions is that the people involved are working to gain control of the state. This objective distinguishes these actions from such violence as ethnic conflict, through which groups may gain local control or even seek independence but do not or cannot take over the entire state. Finally, the objective of revolution is not simply removing those in power but removing the entire regime. Protests or uprisings and other forms of contentious politics intended to pressure a leader to leave office are not necessarily revolutionary. At their core, revolutions seek to fundamentally remake the institutions of politics and often economic and societal institutions as well. As a result, scholars sometimes speak of "social revolutions" to indicate that they are referring to events that completely reshape society.

Must revolutions be violent? This is a tricky question. Given the dramatic goals of revolution, violence is often difficult to avoid. Governments will resist overthrow, and such conflict can often lead to the fragmentation of the monopoly of violence as parts of the state (such as elements of the military) often side with revolutionaries. The aftermath of revolutions can also be very bloody—the losers may be killed or carry out a counterrevolutionary struggle against the new regime.

However, not all revolutions are violent. In 1989, communist regimes in Eastern Europe collapsed in the face of public pressure, sweeping away institutions that many thought immovable. In most cases, violence was limited; only Romania experienced a violent struggle between the communist regime and revolutionaries that led to numerous deaths. Due to this absence of violence, many scholars would resist calling the collapse of communism in Eastern Europe revolutionary, preferring instead to speak of these changes as political transitions. Yet in most important ways, specifically in the overturning of governments and regimes, these events did fulfill our definition of revolution. South Africa is another case of regime change, from apartheid to multiracial democracy, that most scholars are uncomfortable calling a revolution, because it was an elite-driven, largely nonviolent, and slowly negotiated process. One of the problems here is whether we believe that violence is a necessary component to revolutionary outcomes.

What causes revolution? There is no agreement on this question, and the consensus has changed over time. Scholars group studies of revolution into three phases. In the first phase, before World War II, scholars tended to describe rather than explain revolution. When causes were assigned, explanations were often unsystematic, blaming bad government policies or leaders. In the second phase, coinciding with the behavioral revolution of the 1950s and 1960s (see Chapter 1), social scientists sought more generalized explanations. Their new research efforts took on varied forms and areas of emphasis, but they shared a common view that dramatic economic and social change or disruption, such as modernization, was central in sparking revolutionary events. These views tended to focus on the role of individuals as potential revolutionaries and sought to understand what motivated them.

Among the main arguments emerging from this work was a psychological approach known as the **relative deprivation model**. According to this model, revolutions are less a function of specific conditions than of the gap between actual conditions and public expectations. Improving economic or political conditions might even help lead to revolution if, for example, such changes cause increased public demands that go unmet and thus foster discontent. It has been suggested that the 1979 Iranian Revolution and the 2011 Egyptian Revolution are examples of relative deprivation at work. As Iran experienced rapid modernization in the decades before the revolution, its progress only increased people's expectations for greater freedom and equality, especially among young adults. This is what is meant by *relative* deprivation: it is not absolute conditions that instigate revolution but rather how the public perceives them.

By the 1970s, these studies of revolution began to lose favor. In the third phase, critics argued that theories of revolution predicated on sudden change could not explain why some countries could undergo dramatic change without revolution (as in Japan during the early twentieth century) or what levels of change would be enough to trigger revolution. In the case of the relative deprivation model, there was little evidence that rising expectations or discontent preceded many past revolutions. Similarly, in many cases both expectations and discontent rose, but revolution did not result. New studies of revolution took a more institutional approach, moving away from a focus on public reactions to a focus on the target of revolutions: the state.

Most influential in this regard has been the work of political scientist Theda Skocpol and her landmark book *States and Social Revolutions*.[3] Focusing on France, China, and Russia, Skocpol argues that social revolutions require a very specific set of conditions. The first is competition between rival states as they vie for military and economic power in the international system through such things as trade and war. Such competition is costly and often betrays the weakness of states that cannot match their rivals. Second, as a result of this competition,

IN FOCUS: Shifting Views of Revolution

PHASE	APPROACH	CRITICISMS
FIRST: PRE-WORLD WAR II	Studies of revolutionary events	Unsystematic and descriptive
SECOND: POST-WORLD WAR II BEHAVIORAL REVOLUTION	Studies of disruptive change, such as modernization, as driving revolutionary action	Not clear why change or rising discontent leads to revolution in some cases but not others
THIRD: 1970s–PRESENT	Studies of domestic and international state power as providing the opening for revolution	Too focused on institutions, to the neglect of ideas and individual actors

weaker states often seek reform to increase their autonomy and capacity, hoping that changes to domestic institutions will boost their international power. These reforms can include greater state centralization and changes in agriculture, industry, education, and taxation. Such changes, however, can threaten the status quo, undermining the power of entrenched elites, sowing discord among the public, and creating resistance. The result is discontent, political paralysis, and an opening for revolution. In this view, it is not change per se that is central to revolution, but the power and actions of the state. Other actors are of relatively little importance.

The institutional approach to revolution became the dominant view during the 1980s, paralleling a wider interest in institutions and the power of the state. Yet institutional approaches themselves are subject to questions and criticism. Some argue that an overemphasis on institutions ignores the role played by leadership, civil society, or ideology in helping to catalyze and direct revolutionary action. Skocpol herself noted that the important example of Iran's revolution was a poor fit for her model.

These criticisms were underscored by the revolutions in Eastern Europe in 1989 and again in the (often failed) revolutions of the Arab Spring in 2011. In the case of Eastern Europe, there can be no doubt that changes in the international system, specifically the Cold War and the Soviet Union's loosening of control over Eastern Europe, led to conflict and paralysis within these states. At the same time, however, public action was mobilized and shaped by opposition leaders who were strongly influenced by the ideas of liberalism, human rights, and nonviolent protest. In addition, mass protest appeared to be influenced by strategic calculation: successful public opposition in one country changed the calculations of actors elsewhere, increasing their mobilization and demands. Similar events have been at work in the Middle East (see "Institutions in Action," p. 236).

Drawing on these events, some scholars have reintegrated individual and ideational approaches. While state actions do matter, so do the motivations of opposition leaders, ruling elites, and the public as a whole; the views of all three groups regarding political change; and the resources available and used to mobilize the public. Small shifts in ideas and perceptions may have a cascading effect, bringing people into the streets when no one would have predicted it the day before—including the revolutionaries themselves.[4]

Though revolutions may be instruments of progress, it is important to note what they do not achieve. Despite the call for greater freedom and equality that is a hallmark of revolution, the result is often the reverse. Revolutionary leaders who once condemned the state quickly come to see it as a necessary tool to consolidate their victory, and they often centralize power to an even greater extent than before. This is not necessarily bad if the centralization of power can facilitate the creation of a modern state with a necessary degree of autonomy and capacity. Revolutions are often the foundation of a modern state. However, revolutionary leaders may seek a high degree of state power, rejecting democracy as incompatible with the sweeping goals of the revolution. Egypt, Cuba, China, Russia, France, and Iran are all cases in which public demands for more rights ended with yet another dictatorship that uncannily echoed the previous authoritarian order.

Another impact is the high human cost that revolutionary change can incur. Revolutions are often destructive and bloody, especially if removing those in power is a protracted affair. Moreover, in the immediate aftermath revolutionary leaders and their opponents often use violence in their struggle over the new order. The Mexican Revolution led to the deaths of 1.5 million people; the Russian Revolution and subsequent civil war may have claimed the lives of well over 5 million. This violence can become an end in itself, as in the case of the Reign of Terror that followed the French Revolution of 1789. Enemies, supporters, and bystanders alike may all be consumed by an indiscriminate use of violence. It has been suggested that revolutionary states are also more likely to engage in interstate war, whether to promote their revolutionary ideology or because other countries feel threatened or see an opportunity to strike during this period of turmoil. Given the fragmentation of state power and the loss of the monopoly of force associated with revolution, the violence that follows in its wake is not surprising. One general observation we can make is that the greater the violence involved in bringing down the old regime, the more likely it is that violence will continue under the new one.

Terrorism

The word *terrorism*, like *revolution*, is loaded with meaning and used rather indiscriminately. However, the conceptual difficulties surrounding the two terms are diametrically opposed. While *revolution*'s conceptual fuzziness comes in part from its inherently positive connotation (which can lead people to associate the term with all sorts of things), the word *terrorism* carries a stigma and is a term few willingly embrace. As a result, some confuse terrorism with a variety of other words, many of which are misleading, while others use the term indiscriminately to describe any kind of political force or policy they oppose. This situation has led some to conclude that terrorism is effectively impossible to define, and they fall back on an old cliché: "One man's terrorist is another man's freedom fighter." Such a conclusion undercuts the whole purpose of political science, which is to define our terms objectively. We should therefore seek out a definition as precise as possible and use it to distinguish terrorism from other forms of political violence. The continued rise of incidents of terrorism makes this particularly important (see Figure 7.1).

Terrorism can be defined as the use of violence by nonstate actors against civilians in order to achieve a political goal. As with revolution, several components are at work in this definition, and we should take a moment to clarify each. First, there is the question of nonstate actors. Why should the term not be applied to states as well? Do they not also terrorize people? Indeed, as we shall discuss later, the concept of terrorism originally referred to state actions, not those of nonstate actors. Over time, the term came to be associated with nonstate actors who used terrorism in part because conventional military force was not available to them. This, however, does not mean that states cannot terrorize. Rather, other terms have come to describe such acts. When states use violence against civilian populations, we speak of war crimes or human rights violations, depending on the context. Both can include such acts as genocide and torture. *Terrorism* as a term is as much about the kind of political actor as it is about their actions and intent.

Finally, there is **state-sponsored terrorism**. States do sometimes sponsor nonstate terrorist groups as a means to extend their power by proxy, using terrorism as an instrument of foreign policy. For example, India has long faced terrorist groups fighting for control over Kashmir, a state with a majority Muslim

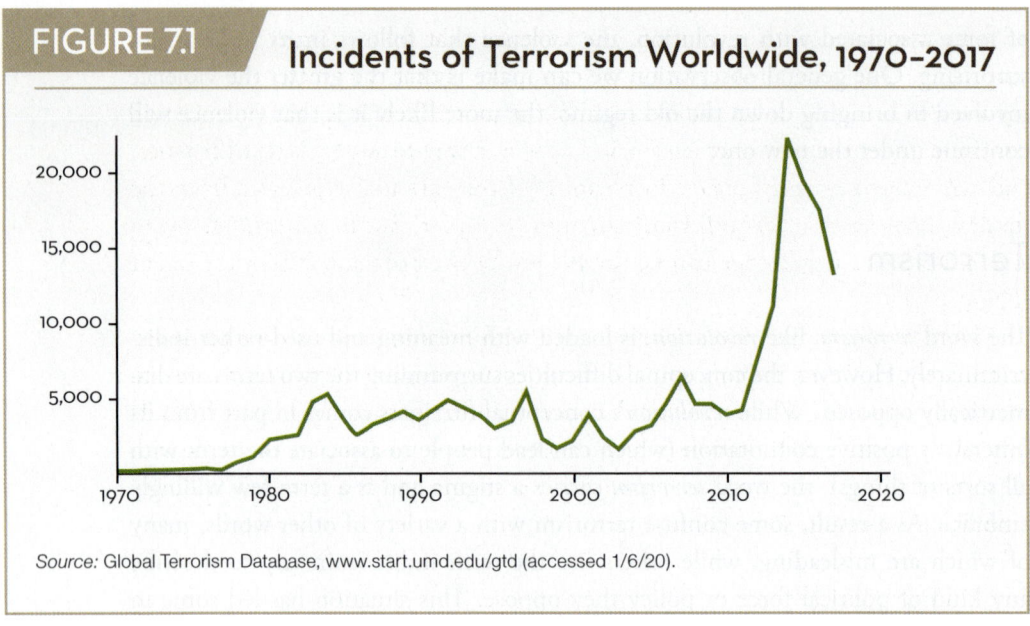

FIGURE 7.1 Incidents of Terrorism Worldwide, 1970-2017

Source: Global Terrorism Database, www.start.umd.edu/gtd (accessed 1/6/20).

population (unlike the rest of India, which is majority Hindu). These terrorists are widely believed to be trained and armed by the Pakistani military (see Chapter 2), which sees this as a way to influence Indian politics. In short, we speak of terrorism as a nonstate action not because states are somehow above such violence but rather because other terminology exists to describe forms of violence perpetrated by states.

Our definition of terrorism also emphasizes that the targets of violence are civilians. Here, the issue of intent is important. Violent conflicts often result in civilian casualties. But terrorists specifically target civilians, believing that this is a more effective way to achieve their political ends than attacking the state. This allows us to distinguish terrorism from **guerrilla war**, something that came up in Chapter 6 when we compared South Africa and Zimbabwe. In contrast to terrorism, guerrilla war involves nonstate combatants who largely accept traditional rules of war and target the state rather than civilians. In the case of South Africa, during the military struggle against the regime the African National Congress considered, and then explicitly rejected, targeting civilians. In contrast, the Zimbabwe African National Union engaged in both guerrilla warfare and terrorism to achieve power. However, the line between these two can often be blurry: Is killing a policeman or a tax collector an act of terrorism or guerrilla warfare? Still, the central distinction remains, not only to observers but also, as suggested earlier, to those carrying out the violence. We will return to this point in a moment.

A further issue in defining terrorism centers on the political goal. It is important to recognize that terrorism has some political objective; as such, it is not simply a crime or a violent act without a larger purpose. Here, too, the lines can be less than clear: terrorists may engage in crime as a way to support their activities, and criminal gangs may engage in terrorism if they are under pressure from the state. Groups can also morph from one into the other. But in general, terrorism and other forms of violence can be sorted out by the primacy of political intent (Figure 7.2).

What are the causes of terrorism? As with revolution, scholars have proposed varied and conflicting hypotheses, and these have changed over time as the nature of terrorism has shifted. In addition, because terrorism is so amorphous and shadowy, we find few of the comprehensive theories we see in studies of revolution, though we can again group the hypotheses we have in terms of institutional, ideational, and individual explanations.

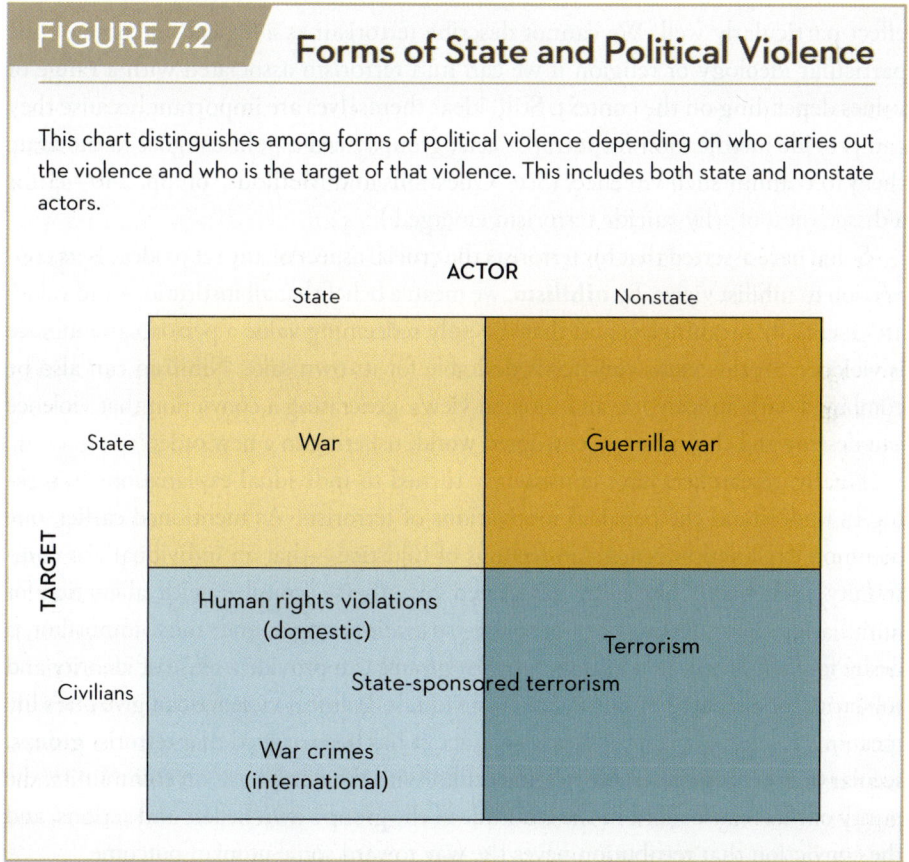

FIGURE 7.2 Forms of State and Political Violence

This chart distinguishes among forms of political violence depending on who carries out the violence and who is the target of that violence. This includes both state and nonstate actors.

	ACTOR	
TARGET	State	Nonstate
State	War	Guerrilla war
Civilians	Human rights violations (domestic) State-sponsored terrorism War crimes (international)	Terrorism

One of the most common responses to terrorism is to cast it in institutional terms, often with the assertion that economic and educational background is critical to understanding terrorists' motivations. Poverty and lack of education are commonly cited in this regard, and terrorism is viewed as a tool of desperation when avenues for personal advancement (getting a job, starting a family) are absent or blocked. However, we know that terrorists are not necessarily impoverished—Osama bin Laden, for example, came from a wealthy background, and many European terrorists active in the 1970s were well-educated members of the middle class. It may be the case, however, that economic inequality helps foster terrorism by contributing to a sense of relative deprivation.[5] This may be compounded by political institutions. Where state capacity and autonomy are weak and mechanisms for public participation poorly institutionalized, terrorists may find both the rationale and opportunity to use force.

Ideational explanations are similarly useful and problematic. Terrorism is commonly blamed on some ideology, religion, or set of values. However, given how terrorism morphs over time, these explanations often cannot account for cause and effect particularly well. We cannot describe terrorism as a logical outcome of one particular ideology or religion if we can find terrorism associated with a range of values depending on the context. Still, ideas themselves are important because they can provide justification for terrorist acts; groups need a political goal to motivate them to commit such violence. (See "Questions and Methods" on pp. 240–41 for a disscussion of why suicide terrorism emerged.)

Some have asserted that for terrorists the crucial aspect of any set of ideas is its connection to nihilist views. By **nihilism**, we mean a belief that all institutions and values are essentially meaningless and that the only redeeming value a person can embrace is violence. In this view, violence is desirable for its own sake. Nihilism can also be combined with apocalyptic and utopian views, generating a conviction that violence can destroy and thus purify a corrupted world, ushering in a new order.

Finally, researchers have consistently turned to individual explanations in seeking to understand the personal motivations of terrorists. As mentioned earlier, one common explanation centers on feelings of injustice—that an individual's or community's self-worth has been denigrated by others—coupled with alienation or humiliation. Such feelings can generate frustration, anger, and, most important, a desire for vengeance. In addition, terrorist groups can provide a sense of identity and solidarity for alienated or humiliated individuals. Political violence can give one's life meaning, a sense of greater purpose. In fact, it has been argued that terrorist groups, secular or otherwise, resemble religious cults, with their emphasis on community, the purity of their cause, faith in the rectitude of the group's own beliefs and actions, and the conviction that retribution paves the way toward some utopian outcome.

The effects of terrorism are harder to discern than the effects of revolutions. The first question to ask is whether terrorists are able to achieve their goals. In the case of revolution, the political violence is by definition successful—we study cases in which regimes have been successfully overthrown. In the case of terrorism, however, we focus on a tactic. Overall, evidence suggests that terrorism is mostly unsuccessful in achieving its goals, if we simply define success as getting states to change their policies to be more in line with what the terrorists want. The very nature of targeting civilians appears typically to signal to states that terrorists cannot be bargained with or satisfied; this stands in contrast to guerrilla fighters, who by targeting the state rather than civilians signal that they respect some fundamental political rules.[6]

However, this is not to say that terrorism has no impact. Economically, terrorism can be highly successful in depressing tourism, foreign direct investment, stock markets, and other sectors of the economy. Society can feel a similar impact, due not just to the effects of a weakened economy but also to increasing anxiety and insecurity that undermines people's sense of well-being.[7]

Terrorism can also distinctly affect politics. Countering terrorism can be a costly and frustrating process with little to show for itself, diverting national resources while failing to address public concerns. An eroded sense of confidence in the state can be the result. In the quest for greater security, governments and their citizens may favor increasing state power and curtailing civil liberties in the hope that such steps will limit terrorists' ability to act. However, this can lead to a weakening of democratic institutions and civil liberties. The result can be less trust in government and less public control over it. At an extreme, terrorism can help bring down a regime. In 1992, Alberto Fujimori, the president of Peru, dissolved the legislature and suspended the constitution, acts that he justified in part as necessary to battle two separate terrorist groups that had destabilized the country. Much of the public supported this action, seeing it as the only way to reestablish order. Terrorism in Russia by Chechen separatists similarly helped pave the way for Vladimir Putin to win the presidency in 2000, and Russia used subsequent attacks to justify removing democratic institutions and limiting civil liberties. And as we well know from Afghanistan, terrorism can also be used as a tool to provoke international conflict.

This destruction of a regime is, of course, what most terrorists seek. Terrorism uses violence against civilians to undermine the institutional fabric of state, society, and economy, calling into question all those things we take for granted, including stability, security, and predictability. By disrupting these most basic elements of modern life and instilling fear, terrorists believe they will help pave the way for revolution.

Terrorism and Revolution: Means and Ends

What do terrorists want? That question leads us to consider terrorism and revolution as related forms of political violence. While we might think of these two as quite separate, it was not always this way. In modern politics, the concepts of terrorism and revolution were initially bound together as parts of a single process, having their origins in the French Revolution. For revolutionary leaders like Maximilien de Robespierre, terror was an essential part of revolution. Robespierre argued that "terror is nothing other than justice, prompt, severe, inflexible; it is therefore an emanation of virtue" in the service of revolutionary change.[8] Thus terror was not only a positive act but also a tool in the service of the revolutionary state.

Over time, this concept of the relation between terrorism and revolution began to shift. Revolutionaries who embraced the lessons of Robespierre concluded that terror is not needed to consolidate revolution after a regime has been overthrown but can instead be used as the means toward that revolutionary end. A small group could speak for and lead the masses, instigating violence as a way to spark revolution. These revolutionaries thus openly embraced the name *terrorist* as an expression of their desire to use violence to achieve their political goals. Although the label *terrorist* has become stigmatized over time, this relationship between terrorism and revolution remains in place.

Terrorism can therefore be understood not simply in terms of who is directing political violence toward whom but also in terms of its revolutionary nature. Terrorists rarely seek limited goals, such as political or economic reform, since they see the entire political system as illegitimate. Rather, they believe that through their seemingly indiscriminate use of violence, all the dominant institutions can be shattered and remade. Consider, for example, this passage from an early manifesto of the Peruvian terrorist group the Shining Path:

> The people rise up, arm themselves and rebel, putting nooses on the necks of imperialism and reaction. The people take them by the throat, threaten their lives and will strangle them out of necessity. The reactionary meat will be trimmed of fat, they will be torn to tatters and rags, the scraps sunk into mire, and the remainders burned. The ashes will be thrown to the winds of the world so that only the sinister reminder of what must never return will remain.[9]

This link between terrorism and revolution also helps us to distinguish between terrorism and guerrilla war. We mentioned earlier that the line between these two forms of political violence is blurry but that we can distinguish between them in terms of their targets. Guerrilla war seeks to abide by traditional rules of war and avoids the targeting of civilians. This decision is driven by political goals. Guerrillas typically accept that their opponents are legitimate actors, and they themselves wish to be regarded as legitimate by their opponents and the international community. Their demands, while sometimes extensive (such as greater civil rights or independence for an ethnic group), do not deny the legitimacy of the other side, as is normally the case with terrorism. These distinctions matter, for such differences in means and ends will affect how extensively states can or will negotiate with such groups to bring an end to conflict.

For example, during the civil conflict in Algeria in the 1990s, two nonstate groups were operating: the Islamic Salvation Front (FIS) and the Armed Islamic Group (GIA). Both opposed the Algerian regime, which suppressed Islamic fundamentalist groups, but they fought it in very different ways. The FIS, which began as a nonviolent political movement, created an armed wing that targeted specific parts of the state seen as directly supporting the regime. The FIS declared that they could come to a compromise with the regime if certain demands were met, such as holding democratic elections. In contrast, the GIA rejected the entire regime and political process as un-Islamic and argued that anyone they viewed as having cooperated with the state in any manner, such as by voting, deserved to be killed. The GIA's killing was thus much more indiscriminate and widespread, directed at state, society, and the FIS. Jihad (war), they argued, was the only means to an Islamic state.[10]

In short, revolution and terrorism have close connections. Revolution is often the ultimate goal of terrorists, who believe that using violence will help set the stage for revolution. More limited use of force, as in guerrilla war, reflects a desire to participate in or work with existing institutions rather than overthrow them. The issue, then, for nonstate wielders of violence is whether they desire a seat at the political table or seek to knock the table over.

Political Violence and Religion

Now that we have considered different ways to approach political violence, particularly revolution and terrorism, let us apply these ideas to the most pressing example in contemporary domestic and international politics: religious violence. In Chapter 3, we spoke about the rise of ideology and other secular identities, such as nationalism, as a challenge to religion in the modern world. Such identities appropriated for themselves many of the same claims and values that belonged to religion in the past, forcing religion out of the public and political sphere and into private life. However, the role of religion has reemerged in the public realm. This religious resurgence is accompanied by a particular element of fundamentalism: the desire to unite faith and the state, transforming religion into the ideological foundation for a political regime. While such fundamentalism may be uncompromising (as with many ideologies), it is not necessarily violent. Many fundamentalists believe that reestablishing God's sovereignty can be accomplished through nonviolent engagement in politics or by withdrawing from politics and instead working to increase the societal power of religion. But, as in the case of secular ideologies, this form of religious fundamentalism contains a violent strain of thought.

What are the conditions under which religion becomes a source of political violence? As in our earlier discussion, they include institutional, ideational, and individual factors. First, one common factor is hostility to modernity. In this view, modern institutions such as states and nations, capitalism, and political ideology have stripped the world of greater meaning and driven people to alienation and despair. Indeed, political violence is often embraced by those who initially enjoyed modernity but at some point turned away from its "corrupt" lifestyle. This view has emerged in many different contexts but seems to be most powerful in societies where modern institutions are foreign in nature and poorly grafted onto traditional structures and values, and/or where modern institutions are under stress, often as a result of economic challenges. This can often be seen in developing countries, which we will turn to in Chapter 10. At this border between traditional and modern institutions, the tension can be the greatest, which may explain why proponents of religious violence are often urban and well-educated individuals: such persons are frequently most deeply immersed in modernity and may feel its contradictions most sharply.

A second factor is what the sociologist Mark Juergensmeyer calls "cosmic war."[11] In this view, the modern world not only actively marginalizes, humiliates, and denigrates the views of religious believers but also seeks to exterminate the believers outright. Those who hold this view see themselves as soldiers in a struggle between the righteousness of faith and its enemies (modernity), a war that transcends space and time. This perspective is often bound up in conspiracy theories that point to shadowy forces in league to exterminate the good. People holding these views can rationalize violence against civilians because they see the conflict not in terms of civilians versus combatants but in terms of the guilty versus the innocent: those who do not stand on the side of righteousness are by definition on the side of evil. Scholars note that this dehumanization of the enemy is an important component in justifying violence against civilians, since social or religious taboos against murder must be overcome.

Third, religion as a source of political violence is often connected to messianic, apocalyptic, and utopian beliefs. Although the forces of darkness (modernity) have gained the upper hand, the role of the righteous is to usher in or restore the sovereignty of God on earth. Violence is therefore not only acceptable but also a form of ritual, whether in the form of self-sacrifice (martyrdom) or the sacrifice of others. ISIS propaganda is frequently couched in these terms.

Religious groups or movements that resort to violence represent an extreme form of fundamentalism since their path to violence requires them to reinterpret their faith in a way that divorces it from its conventional foundations. These groups or movements thus tend to break away from the mainstream faith and other fundamentalists, whom they accuse of having lost their way, by presenting their radical alternatives as restorations of religious truth. Most Muslim, Christian, and other fundamentalists would thus find many of these radical views to be horrific and far removed from their views of faith.

To reiterate, it is a mistake to confuse fundamentalism with violence. Indeed, much of what we have noted—hostility toward rival institutions, dehumanization, and utopian views—can be found in modern political ideologies. We can see this in the bloody revolutions that established communism in the Soviet Union and China. Even the French Revolution of 1789 that helped usher in the modern era was described by Alexis de Tocqueville in 1856 as akin to a religious revolution directed toward "the regeneration of the human race" that "roused passions such as the most violent political revolutions had been incapable of awakening . . . able, like Islamism, to cover the earth with its soldiers, its apostles, and its martyrs."[12] Bearing this in mind, we can consider some specific examples of how religion has intersected with politics to generate political violence.

Within Al Qaeda, ISIS, and similar jihadist groups, individuals like Osama bin Laden frequently have couched their violence in terms of a long global struggle against unbelievers. Hence, when bin Laden referred to the West as "Crusaders" in his 1996 manifesto he was reaching back to the battles between the Islamic and Christian worlds in the Middle Ages. In the modern world, bin Laden argued, this crusade against Islam and its followers continues, though the West's conspiracies are often cloaked by international organizations like the United Nations.

In the September 11 attacks, we can see how the logic of cosmic war also fits into a greater narrative. Al Qaeda carried out these attacks not simply to weaken the United States but also to provoke a backlash that they believed would intensify the conflict between the Islamic and non-Islamic worlds and would in turn lead to the overthrow of "un-Islamic" regimes in the Middle East. Expanding on this idea, ISIS argued that this violence would eventually culminate in a final apocalyptic battle with the West and the subsequent restoration of an Islamic empire and golden age.

In these circumstances, even Muslim civilians are fair targets, whether in the United States, Europe, or the Middle East. This position is justified because their "collaboration" with the forces of evil means that they are not true Muslims and therefore can be killed, sacrificed to the cause. Such justifications are commonly used by ISIS, which claims for itself the right to "excommunicate" other Muslims, thus making them fair targets.

Such views have strong parallels to certain violent strains drawn from Christianity. In the United States, some racist groups assert that Western Christianity has been corrupted and weakened by a global Jewish conspiracy, and they seek to rebuild Western society on the basis of a purified white race. One particularly important proponent of this ideology was William Pierce, who died in 2002. Pierce, who held a Ph.D. in physics and was at one time a university professor, formed the National Alliance, a white supremacist organization, in 1974. Pierce departed from Christianity altogether as a faith tainted by its association with Judaism, offering instead a "cosmotheist" faith that viewed whites as belonging to a superior evolutionary track, on the road to unity with God. In his novel *The Turner Diaries*, Pierce describes the creation of a dedicated underground that would attack symbols of American authority, seize territory, and eventually launch a nuclear attack against the country itself. This apocalypse would destroy the state, allowing the revolutionaries to exterminate all non-whites and those who do not accept the new order. This genocide would eventually extend worldwide. Timothy McVeigh's bombing of the federal courthouse in Oklahoma City in 1995, which killed 168 people, was directly inspired by *The Turner Diaries* and Pierce's argument that terrorism could trigger revolution. Pierce, while dissociating himself from McVeigh's act, nevertheless stated that McVeigh was

> a soldier, and what he did was based on principle. . . . He was at war against a government that is at war against his people. . . . In this war the rule is: Whatever is good for our people is good, and whatever harms our people is evil. That is the morality of survival.[13]

The Turner Diaries has been described as "arguably the most important single work of white nationalist propaganda in the English language" and continues to inspire political violence in the United States and abroad, including the 2019 attacks in New Zealand.[14]

Violence also extends outside the monotheistic religions of the West. In Myanmar (Burma), a form of violent Buddhism has emerged, led by the monk Ashin Wirathu, which focuses its hostility on the country's small Muslim minority. Although Muslims make up less than 5 percent of the population, Wirathu and his followers articulate a worldview that emphasizes the destruction of Buddhist communities in South and Southeast Asia by Islamic armies in the twelfth century as the beginning of an ongoing existential threat. Wirathu describes Muslims as an inherently violent "race" rather than followers of a religion, and followers of his movement have targeted Muslims in a series of deadly attacks, destroying mosques and displacing entire communities. The goal is to place Buddhism at the center of the nation and state. However, one important question we should ask is whether this is better described as terrorism, ethnic conflict, or some combination of the two.[15]

In these three cases, we see important similarities. First, these groups radically reinterpreted an existing faith by arguing that it had lost its way. Osama bin Laden, William Pierce, and Ashin Wirathu each claimed the ability to recast the faith in an overtly ideological manner. Second, through this reinterpretation, they viewed the world in terms of an existential battle between good and evil, purity and corruption. Third, as the defenders of truth, they placed themselves in the role of warriors in the service of faith, able to mete out justice to all those who were seen as the enemy, whether state or society. And finally, they described this violence not as an unfortunate necessity but as a sacrifice to the cause that would bring forth or restore a higher order.

Religiously motivated political violence can parallel similar acts carried out by nonreligious groups. The failures and humiliations of modernity, the creation of a group of "true believers" who see the world in stark terms of good versus evil, and the idea of a transformation that will destroy the old order and usher in a new age can all be ascribed to many secular ideologies and similarly used to justify violence.

Countering Political Violence

Our discussion indicates that political violence is a varied and constantly shifting force in the modern world. As long as states monopolize force, there will be actors who seek to wrest this power from the state so they can use it to pursue their own political objectives. Violence can be motivated by institutional, ideational, and individual factors—most likely some combination of the three. Though religious violence is a pressing concern, we see that in many ways the distinctions between secular and religious violence are not as great as we might have supposed.

Given the amorphous nature of political violence, what can states do to manage or prevent it? This is difficult to answer, since the response depends partly on the nature of the political violence itself. Although violence differs across time and from place to place, we can nevertheless make a few tentative observations, understanding that these are not ironclad answers.

One observation is that regime type appears to make a difference; terrorism and revolution are less likely in democratic societies. Why? The simplest answer is that democracies allow for a significant degree of participation among a wide enough number of citizens to make them feel that they have a stake in the system. While democracies produce their own share of cynicism and public unrest, including political violence, they also appear to co-opt and diffuse the motivations necessary for serious organized or mass violence against the state and civilians. Again, this is not to say that democracies are impervious to political violence, as we have seen in the United States and elsewhere. The observation is merely that democracies appear to be more effective at containing and limiting such groups by providing more options for political opposition.

Of course, one of the dangers is that terrorism and revolution sparked by one kind of regime can easily spill across national borders, particularly in such an interconnected world. While democracy may be an important factor in preventing violence carried out by its own citizens, it does not offer protection against political violence carried out by groups operating outside the state. Indeed, the paradox here is that open democratic societies may limit domestic conflict but make for a much more tempting target for globalized political violence.

What about states that are already liberal democracies and yet face political violence from domestic or international actors? In this case, the classic dilemma of freedom versus security raises its head. In the face of threats, democratic states and their citizens will often favor limiting certain civil liberties and increasing state autonomy and capacity in order to bring an end to political violence. In the United States, the 2001 PATRIOT Act, which increased the government's power to conduct public surveillance, is one such counterterrorist measure. Suspects in the United Kingdom can be detained up to 14 days without charge and under certain conditions can even be stripped of their

IN FOCUS: Regime Type and Terrorism

REGIME TYPE	EFFECT ON TERRORISM	RESULT	RISK OF TERRORISM
AUTHORITARIAN	Authoritarianism may foster terrorism, but the state can repress domestic terrorists; the state is unhindered by civil liberties.	Limited terrorism, but may be redirected outside of the country toward more vulnerable targets.	Lower
DEMOCRATIC	Participatory institutions and civil liberties are likely to undercut public support for terrorism.	Domestic terrorism less likely, but country may be a target of international terrorism generated in nondemocratic regimes.	Moderate
ILLIBERAL/ TRANSITIONAL	Weak state capacity, instability, and limited democratic institutions may generate both opportunities and motivations for terrorism.	Terrorism more likely, due to domestic and/or international support.	Higher

citizenship if suspected of terrorism. In France, state of emergency laws since the 2015 Paris terrorist attacks have allowed for raids and house arrests without judicial authorization.

There are dangers here. Focusing excessively on security over freedom may be dangerous to democracy. Placing too much power in the hands of the state to observe and control the public could seriously threaten to erode individual rights and with them democracy, creating what some have called a "surveillance state."[16] Such activities can in turn contribute to further political violence, since they confirm the idea that the state is conspiring to destroy its opponents, thus justifying violent resistance. Despite these dangers, people and politicians often seek dramatic and visible solutions because they provide a sense of security, although in reality they may have limited or even counterproductive effects. The old adage often (if perhaps incorrectly) attributed to Benjamin Franklin is worth recalling: "Those who would give up essential liberty to purchase a little temporary safety deserve neither liberty nor safety."[17]

INSTITUTIONS IN ACTION

Why Did the Arab Spring of 2011 Occur?

In Chapter 1, we began this book with a puzzle: Why did the Arab Spring take place, and why did these uprisings lead to such different results in different countries? Revolutions and transitions often seem to come out of the blue. Regimes that appeared impervious to change a year earlier are swept away before our eyes. No one expected that communism would collapse in Eastern Europe in the 1980s; at best, it seemed, reforms within the Soviet Union would lead to some modest liberalization, perhaps even reinvigorating the one-party regimes in the region. Just the opposite occurred.

In the more recent case of the Arab Spring in North Africa and the Middle East, the signs were even less promising. Modernization in the region is often viewed as stunted. If we turn to the Human Development Index (see Chapter 4), we find development is especially lagging in levels of education and health care. This is true even in countries with significant natural resources, like Saudi Arabia, whose life expectancy trails that of much poorer China. Gender inequalities are also significant.

Oil, as well as foreign aid from the United States in particular, has helped support many of these states, creating systems built around a coterie of supporters who benefit directly from the state. These elite groups have relied on various means of repression—harassing, jailing, and killing opponents—to maintain their control over the state and the benefits they have drawn from it.

Civil society in much of the region is weak and fragmented, a result of state repression and low levels of development. Democratization and liberalization are ideas tainted by their association with Western colonialism and U.S. foreign policy in the region, particularly after the invasion of Iraq. There is wariness of U.S. foreign policy, which for many years has supported nondemocratic regimes in the region.

How, then, in the face of all these challenges, did the Arab Spring burst forth? Why revolutions break out when they do is beyond the understanding of social scientists, much as geologists cannot simply tell us when an earthquake is going to occur. But to make some sense of these changes, we can turn to our institutional, ideational, and individual explanations. These explanations are not comprehensive but rather point to the complexity of revolutionary change.

Institutional explanations for the Arab Spring focus on the nature of authoritarian rule. For example, while Tunisia functioned as a highly repressive one-party system that sought to co-opt or control civil society, its regime also maintained just a small military force and a limited degree of patrimonialism. Thus, when protests intensified, the military refused to fire on the population, helping pave the way for revolution and democratization. In contrast, as we mentioned at the start of this chapter, Syria's highly patrimonial regime has relied largely on armed forces directly controlled by the ruling Assad family, giving those in power both the desire and the means to use violence against their opponents. Egypt seems to fall somewhere between the two, where the military first sided with revolutionaries but also had the capacity to seize power for itself, which it eventually did. Institutions like the military cannot fully account for why revolution succeeded where it did, but they can be seen to have influenced the resources and strategies of political elites across the various cases.

Ideational explanations are similarly useful. In the case of Egypt, many point to the role young people played in shaping the message of the protests that brought down President Hosni Mubarak. Their April 6 Youth Movement studied how public protests brought down authoritarian regimes in Eastern Europe. To mobilize the public, activists relied on Facebook and YouTube, prompting the regime to cut off Internet access in a failed last-ditch effort to fend off the revolution. The role of Islam as a democratic or fundamentalist force across the region is also central to any understanding of political change. The rise to power of the Muslim Brotherhood in Egypt polarized the population, paving the way for a military coup in 2013, whereas in Tunisia the Islamist Ennahda Party supported a democratic and secular constitution, making that country the only one to successfully transition to democracy as a result of the Arab Spring.

Finally, we should not discount the role of individual action, which sparked these revolutions. Mohamed Bouazizi was a 26-year-old Tunisian man who had worked from a young age to support his family, selling produce as a street vendor. The police repeatedly harassed Bouazizi, ostensibly for lacking a business license but in reality because he failed to pay bribes. These repeated assaults took their toll; as his sister later noted, "those with no connections and no money for bribes are humiliated and insulted and not allowed to live."[a] After a final clash in December 2010, Bouazizi stood before the local governor's office, amid the traffic, where he doused himself in gasoline and set himself alight. Protests began soon thereafter and spread across the region, raising common demands: dignity and change. Large-scale,

Egyptian protesters gather at Tahrir Square, Cairo, at the start of the Egyptian Revolution in 2011.

domestic and international, and state and societal forces were critical in explaining the Arab Spring (and all revolutions), but we should not forget the role of one apparently powerless person in shaping history.

1. What institutional factors help explain why Tunisia's revolution took such a different shape from Syria's?

2. How did institutional and ideational factors combine in the case of Egypt to spur its revolution?

3. Why did revolution overturning authoritarian regimes in the Middle East seem so unlikely in the first place?

Institutions in Action

In Sum: Meeting the Challenge of Political Violence

Political violence is a complex issue for scholars, states, and societies. Often its objectives are cast in idealistic terms as part of necessary historical change. At the same time, this violence can come at a tremendous cost of human life when violence becomes an end in itself. Because political violence is a response to existing institutions, the institutional context differs across time and space, making it hard to extrapolate general properties from specific instances. Like a virus, it may suddenly emerge in unexpected places, ravaging the population before disappearing again. Or it may lie dormant for many years, only to break out when certain conditions come together.

There is clearly no one way to stop or prevent political violence. Countries have to balance prevention, such as by providing democratic institutions and opportunities for political contention, with treatment, such as military and legal methods to counter terrorism. Treatment carries its own risk, and even the most comprehensive forms of prevention cannot guarantee that political violence will never break out.

Key Terms

guerrilla war (p. 224)
ideational (p. 215)
nihilism (p. 226)
political violence (p. 214)

relative deprivation model (p. 220)
revolution (p. 218)
state-sponsored terrorism (p. 223)
terrorism (p. 223)

For Further Reading

Abrahms, Max. "The Political Effectiveness of Terrorism Revisited." *Comparative Political Studies* 45, no. 3 (March 2012): 366–93.

Boot, Max. *Invisible Armies: An Epic History of Guerrilla Warfare from Ancient Times to the Present*. New York: Norton, 2013.

Crenshaw, Martha. "The Causes of Terrorism." *Comparative Politics* 13, no. 4 (July 1981): 379–99.

Goldstone, Jack A. *Revolutions: A Very Short Introduction*. Oxford: Oxford University Press, 2014.

Juergensmeyer, Mark. *Terror in the Mind of God: The Global Rise of Religious Violence*. 3rd ed. Berkeley: University of California Press, 2003.

Kuran, Timur. "Now Out of Never: The Element of Surprise in the East European Revolution of 1989." *World Politics* 44, no. 1 (October 1991): 7–48.

Skocpol, Theda. "France, Russia, China: A Structural Analysis of Social Revolutions." *Comparative Studies in Society and History* 18, no. 2 (April 1976): 175–210.

Tilly, Charles, and Sidney Tarrow. *Contentious Politics*. Boulder, CO: Paradigm Publishers, 2007.

Walt, Stephen M. *Revolution and War*. Ithaca, NY: Cornell University Press, 1996.

INQUIZITIVE

Earn a better grade on your test. InQuizitive personalizes your learning path to help you master the concepts from this chapter and practice applying them to examples from the text and beyond (see back cover).

QUESTIONS AND METHODS

Why Has Suicide Terrorism Emerged?

One of the most important questions in political science involves the use of terrorism as a political tool. Of particular interest is suicide terrorism—an action that breaks many taboos and challenges our understanding of what we consider rational behavior for both individuals and political groups. Why has suicide terrorism emerged? If we were to understand this, would this generate effective methods for preventing it?

The most cited work on this topic, by the political scientist Robert Pape, began by trying to determine the cause of suicide terrorism by looking at all attacks between 1980 and 2003 (315 in all) to see if they shared common antecedents. In reviewing these events, he concluded that suicide terrorism is an essentially rational act directed toward a clear objective. In his words, "the specific goal sought in almost all suicide terrorist campaigns in modern history is the same: to compel a democratic state to withdraw combat forces from territory prized by the terrorists."[a]

Democratic societies, Pape argues, have a low threshold for political violence and their publics have a high degree of influence over policy. Groups with territorial claims thus resort to suicide bombings when they believe that their actions will horrify the public, who in turn will compel their democratic leaders to end their control over that territory. Religious differences are important only in how they can help terrorists demonize the other side, further justifying suicide terrorism. The argument helps us think about the ways in which the U.S. presence in places like Saudi Arabia before September 11, or Israel's presence in the West Bank and Gaza, may have encouraged groups like Al Qaeda and Hamas to take up suicide attacks.

But while intriguing, one of the greatest problems with this work is something we discussed in Chapter 1: selection bias.[b] As several scholars have pointed out, Pape's scholarship began with collecting examples of suicide terrorism and working backward to discover the

SELECTED RECENT SUICIDE ATTACKS	DISPUTE OVER TERRITORY?	DEMOCRACY?
Russia, 2017	Yes	No
Iran, 2019	Yes	No
Sri Lanka, 2019	No	Limited
Pakistan, 2019	No	Limited
Algeria, 2017	No	No
Egypt, 2019	No	No

independent variable, or cause—in his view, foreign occupation by a democracy. This approach fails to start with the independent variable, which would be the presence of troops in a disputed area that is viewed as the occupying force of a democracy. If we do sample on the independent variable, the argument begins to have problems. For example, terrorist groups in Northern Ireland sought independence from the United Kingdom, viewing the British government as the occupying force of another nation and religion. This was also true of Basque terrorists in Spain. Why then did they not turn to suicide attacks? Indeed, in both cases the terrorist groups eventually swore off violence and disbanded, short of their goals.

If one starts instead with the independent variable (which also allows us to widen the timeframe), since 1945 we can find many examples where foreign troops and conflict over a "prized territory," to use Pape's words, have not led to suicide terrorism. And in fact, since Pape's work was published we have seen (and illustrated in the table on the opposite page) numerous cases of suicide bombings where either there is no foreign military occupation or territorial dispute (Pakistan), no democracy (Russia), or both (Egypt). Dependent variables can generate interesting puzzles, but to find answers we need to start with causes, rather than effects.

1. *Articulate the cause-and-effect relationship*

   What are some of the reasons why we might fall into the trap of selecting cases on the dependent variable?

2. *Consider ways in which definitions and variables can strengthen or weaken a hypothesis*

   Suppose a critic says that our definition of a territorial dispute is too narrow, arguing that in the cases of Pakistan, Egypt, and Algeria, these were all actions by groups seeking to create a greater Islamic state. How broadly should we define "territorial dispute"? Or "foreign occupation"? Do broader definitions resolve the problem of selecting on the dependent variable? Do they create any problems of their own?

3. *Generate new questions and assertions related to the discussion*

   What would be some alternative variables you might hypothesize would lead to suicide terrorism? How would you define and measure those independent variables?

---

a. Robert A. Pape, "Suicide Terrorism and Democracy: What We've Learned Since 9/11," Cato Institute Policy Analysis no. 582, November 1, 2006, www.cato.org/publications/policy-analysis/suicide-terrorism-democracy-what-weve-learned-911 (accessed 9/18/19).
b. Scott Ashworth, Joshua D. Clinton, Adam Meirowitz, and Kristopher W. Ramsay, "Design, Inference, and the Strategic Logic of Suicide Terrorism," *American Political Science Review* 102, no. 2 (May 2008): 269–73.

8

Anti-Brexit demonstrators protest in Ireland ahead of Prime Minister Boris Johnson's first official negotiations visit in July 2019. The United Kingdom's exit from the EU has the potential to reignite tensions over the border between Northern Ireland, which exited the EU with the rest of the United Kingdom, and the Republic of Ireland, which remains in the EU.

DEVELOPED DEMOCRACIES

Is democracy the key to peace and prosperity?

Ever since the European Union (EU) was founded in 1951, some have been skeptical about its objectives and suspicious of its powers. The United Kingdom did not apply to join until 10 years later, and even then it was blocked by the French until 1973. Norway declined to join, as did Switzerland. Countries have also balked at new treaties that expanded the EU's powers, including adoption of the euro as a single currency in 2000. But in general, Euroskepticism has existed on the margins of the EU as it continued to expand in members and powers. By the mid-2000s, some even imagined—and wrote entire books about—how the European Union was on the road to becoming a "United States of Europe" and a superpower that would end American dominance.[1]

What a difference a decade makes. Even as pundits were lauding the emergence of this imagined superpower, hostility toward the EU among its citizens was growing. Rather than generating a common European identity, as its founders imagined, the EU began to generate a backlash across a number of nation-states. Economic recession led many to criticize the EU for being too bureaucratic, too economically liberal (or not liberal enough), and undemocratic. These concerns merged with fears of immigration and its impact on jobs, national identity, and political culture. Rising Euroskepticism began to shape domestic politics in a number of important states.

The rise and impact of the United Kingdom Independence Party (UKIP) is the best example of Euroskepticism. Founded in 1993, for years it was largely on the fringe of British politics. Yet in recent years, the UKIP began to attract more supporters through its blunt party platform to leave the European Union. In the 2014 direct elections to the EU's European Parliament (EP), the UKIP came in first place, winning 28 percent of the vote and 24 of the United Kingdom's 73 seats. As the UKIP leader, Nigel Farage, put it, European integration, once seemingly inevitable, was no longer so. Hoping to stem this rising Euroskepticism, the United Kingdom's ruling Conservative Party offered a referendum on continued membership in the European Union. The UKIP and other backers of a British exit, or "Brexit," argued that only by leaving the EU could the country control its borders, trade, and foreign policy and retain British identity in the face of global challenges. Such populist arguments appealed to individuals across the political spectrum, but by and large they tended to appeal to older individuals and those with less education, who believed that they had been hurt the most by globalization. While prediction markets (see Chapter 1) expected that the referendum would fail, on June 23, 2016, 52 percent of British voters chose Brexit. The UKIP would quickly fade away after the success of the referendum, but its impact has been profound and lasting.

Since the 2016 referendum, the United Kingdom has struggled with how exactly to exit the European Union while maintaining some of the existing relationships. The most problematic issue has been the border between the Republic of Ireland and Northern Ireland, the latter being part of the United Kingdom. An open border was an essential part of the 1998 Good Friday Agreement, which brought an end to the violent conflict between Protestants and Catholics in Northern Ireland over the future of the region. As the United Kingdom leaves the EU, its sovereignty over its borders will be restored, potentially affecting the movement of people and goods between Northern Ireland and the Republic of Ireland. This runs the risk of reigniting the conflict in Northern Ireland by once again separating the region from the Republic of Ireland.

Britain is not the only country where Euroskeptic parties have gained in power. France, traditionally an engine for European integration alongside Germany, similarly has seen the rise of the National Rally (once known as the National Front). The National Rally has long tapped into a current of French nationalism that views the EU as a threat to national values, and Europe's economic recession provided a new opportunity for the party to make its case. Unlike the UKIP, whose liberal orientation led its members to portray the EU as a regulatory monster that stifled British enterprise, the National Rally has taken the opposite position by asserting that European integration was destroying the French economy through economic liberalization. Both parties, however, shared in common a view that immigration from within and without the EU is a threat to jobs and national identity. In the 2019 European Parliament elections, the National Rally secured 23 percent of France's seats—the largest share of any French party. Euroskeptics now control around a quarter of all the seats in the European Parliament from across a wide range of EU member states.

An optimistic interpretation could be that Euroskepticism will open the doors for important reforms inside the EU and deepen relationships between EU members. This may be more likely if Britain's economy declines as a result of Brexit, weakening other Euroskeptic groups. A less sanguine view is that Euroskepticism, fueled by fears of immigration and globalization, will expand across the European Union, weakening it. Rather than a United States of Europe, a divided EU will be unable to meet the needs of its citizens or play an important role in the global community. Growing numbers of individuals across the developed democracies are now questioning economic and political integration to a degree not seen since before World War II. What we had considered to be a relatively fixed set of institutions and values that represented developed democracies is now openly challenged.

LEARNING OBJECTIVES

- Describe the characteristics of developed democracies.
- Explain the challenges to sovereignty faced by developed democracies.
- Summarize the rise of, and challenges posed by, postmodern values in developed democracies.

Now that we are familiar with various concepts that help us compare a range of political institutions, we can investigate how these institutions manifest themselves in the world. Instead of grouping countries by geographic location, we will look at countries whose political institutions resemble one another. Our first group of countries is commonly known as the **developed democracies**. This term is problematic since it is both value laden and teleological—that is, *developed democracies* connotes some "end stage" that other countries are heading toward. In recalling the hubris and disappointment of the behavioral movement and modernization theory, we should emphasize that the term can cover a diverse set of countries that may become only more diverse in the future. We use the term here to refer to countries that have institutionalized democracy and a high level of economic development and prosperity.

In this chapter, we look at the basic institutions and dynamics that characterize developed democracies, applying the concepts we have studied so far. What do developed democracies have in common with one another? What differences exist between them? This comparison will lead us to a discussion of the roles of individual freedom and collective equality in the developed democracies. How do these countries reconcile the two? Once we have a grasp of these ideas, we will move on to consider the challenges their institutions face in contemporary politics. The forces of integration and devolution—the transfer of power to international institutions or down to local ones—may challenge the notion of state sovereignty that has been at the core of modern politics. In economics, too, the emergence of postindustrial societies is transforming the very nature of wealth and labor. Similar changes can be seen in societal institutions as old and new social values come into conflict. All of these issues are compounded by demographic challenges as the populations of the developed democracies become older and more diverse.

Are the developed democracies on the brink of transformation, or are they approaching stagnation and decline? And what are the implications of either for comparative and international politics? This chapter lays out evidence that will allow us to consider possible scenarios.

Defining Developed Democracy

What, exactly, are developed democracies? In the past, scholars typically spoke of economically developed countries as belonging to the "First World." They were contrasted with the countries of the "Second World," or communist states, and those of the "Third World," the vast body of less developed and often politically nonaligned countries. Dividing countries into these three "worlds" was always somewhat problematic, since even within each category there was a great deal of institutional diversity. With the end of the Cold War and the collapse of communism, the three-worlds approach became even less useful.

Instead of using this problematic three-worlds approach, this book refers to "developed democracies," "communist and postcommunist countries," and "developing countries." These categories, too, have their limitations, and critics might say they differ from past approaches only in name. Indeed, in 2016 the World

TABLE 8.1 — Developed Democracies, 2020

NORTH AND SOUTH AMERICA		EUROPE	
Antigua and Barbuda	Dominica	Andorra*	Latvia
Argentina	Grenada	Austria	Luxembourg
Bahamas	Mexico†	Belgium	Malta
Barbados	Panama	Bulgaria	Netherlands
Bermuda	Suriname	Croatia	Poland
Brazil	Trinidad and Tobago	Cyprus	Portugal
Canada	United States	Czech Republic	Romania
Chile	Uruguay	Denmark	Slovakia
Costa Rica		Estonia	Slovenia
		Finland	Spain
		France	Sweden
ASIA AND AUSTRALIA		Germany	United Kingdom*
Australia	Palau	Greece	
Japan	South Korea	Hungary†	Iceland*
New Zealand	Taiwan	Ireland	Norway*
		Italy	Switzerland*
MIDDLE EAST AND AFRICA			
Botswana			
Israel			
Mauritius			

* Non-EU members.
†Freedom House recognizes Hungary and Mexico as partly free.

Bank began to phase out its classifications of developed and developing countries, referring instead only to differences in terms of income.[2] However, being able to make comparisons requires some control over variables, and as we discussed in Chapter 1, grouping countries by institutional similarities is a useful way to study politics. In Table 8.1, we list what we can consider developed democracies. At the same time, some of these countries will also appear in the subsequent chapters on postcommunist and developing countries, especially those that lie in an area of transition from one category to another.

How do we determine which countries are developed democracies? In the area of democracy, we can rely on the factors discussed in Chapter 5, looking at the degree and institutionalization of participation, competition, and liberty in each. In the area of economic development and prosperity, we can consider the issues raised in Chapter 4: the presence of private property, open markets, and the level of gross domestic product (GDP) at purchasing power parity (PPP). We might also consider the kind of economic output that countries produce. Developed democracies tend to derive a relatively small portion of their GDP from agriculture and industrial production. During and after the Industrial Revolution, industry displaced agriculture in many of today's developed democracies; today, industry itself is increasingly being displaced by the service sector, which includes jobs in retail sales, information technology, and education. Finally, we should also consider the output of wealth by looking at the overall well-being of society as measured by the Human Development Index (HDI). Table 8.2 provides measurements of some of these factors for several developed democracies as well as for a few that are not developed democracies. The countries listed as developed democracies in Tables 8.1 and 8.2 have high levels of economic development (GDP per capita at PPP of over $15,000) and small agricultural sectors. They are also democratic regimes and are among the top third of countries on the HDI, classified by the United Nations as having very high or high levels of human development. As we noted earlier, within this category are several recently democratized and postcommunist countries that also exhibit the hallmarks of economic development and democracy. They contrast with countries that are poorer, have low HDI rankings, and lack a strong industrial and service sector and/or institutionalized liberal democracy.

Given our definition of developed democracies, the countries that we place in this category are diverse—and they have grown markedly more diverse over the past decade. Postcommunist Poland now has much more in common economically and politically with countries like Germany and France than it does with neighboring countries that also were once part of the communist world; South Korea has more in common with Japan and the United States than it does with other, less-developed countries in Asia.

This group is not meant to be exhaustive or definitive—no doubt many readers would add or remove some countries on the basis of other criteria. There are also some countries, such as Hungary and Mexico, whose level of democracy is open to question and perhaps should not be on this list. In fact, a number of these countries will be discussed again in the chapters on postcommunist countries and developing countries. The central point for us to consider is that, due to recent global economic and political changes, the camp of developed democracies has expanded well beyond its traditional provinces of western Europe and North America.

TABLE 8.2 — Developed Democracies in Comparative Perspective

COUNTRY	PERCENTAGE OF GDP CONTRIBUTED BY: AGRICULTURE	INDUSTRY	SERVICES	GDP PER CAPITA (PPP IN US $)	DEMOCRACY?	HDI RANK
United States	1	19	80	62,600	Y	13
Saudi Arabia	2	43	55	56,000	N	39
Sweden	2	34	64	52,900	Y	7
Germany	1	30	69	52,600	Y	5
Canada	2	28	70	46,600	Y	12
France	2	19	79	45,800	Y	24
Japan	1	28	71	44,200	Y	19
South Korea	2	38	60	41,400	Y	22
Poland	3	40	57	32,000	Y	33
Mexico	4	33	63	20,600	Y*	74
Iran	9	40	51	19,600	N	60
China	8	41	51	18,100	N	86
Brazil	6	22	72	16,200	Y	79
South Africa	2	29	69	13,700	Y	113
India	15	23	62	7,900	Y	130
Nigeria	21	19	60	6,000	Y*	157

*Freedom House categorizes Mexico and Nigeria as partly free.
Note: Countries in italics are *not* developed democracies.
Sources: CIA World Factbook, World Bank, United Nations Development Programme.

Freedom and Equality in Developed Democracies

How do developed democracies achieve a balance between freedom and equality? All such countries share an institutionalized liberal democracy, private property, free markets, and a high level of economic development based on industry and services. However, developed democracies reconcile freedom and equality differently, particularly in the area of political economy. Countries with liberal political-economic systems are focused more on individual freedoms than on collective equality and, thus, limit the role of the state in regulating the market and providing public goods, whereas social-democratic political-economic systems normally do the opposite. Mercantilist systems, meanwhile, tend to focus more on development than either freedom or equality. Despite this wide variation, however, these countries are united by common democratic regimes and political-economic institutions.

First, consider the role of freedom: all developed democracies are institutionalized liberal democracies, sharing a belief in participation, competition, and liberty. Yet they define these terms differently. For example, civil rights or liberties may be expanded or restricted without calling into question the democratic nature of a country. Take the case of abortion. Some developed democracies, such as Sweden, Greece, and Canada, allow abortions during a pregnancy's first trimester with relatively few restrictions. In other countries, such as South Korea and Argentina, abortions have significant limitations. And some developed democracies ban abortions altogether or allow them only under exceptional circumstances (Chile, Mexico, Brazil, and Poland, for example). We can find similar discrepancies in the regulation of same-sex marriage, prostitution, and hate speech or in the degree to which privacy is protected from state or economic actors. The judicial systems of developed democracies interpret and defend their citizens' rights in various ways. Some of these countries rely on vigorous constitutional courts whose wide array of powers allows them to overturn legislation; other courts play a more conservative role, circumscribed by the existing forms of abstract and concrete review (see Chapter 5).

The public's level of political participation also varies among developed democracies. One or more of the electoral systems discussed in Chapter 5 can be found in all these countries. Their use of referenda and initiatives also differs greatly. Most developed democracies use them to some degree, although in a few countries (like the United States and Germany) such votes take place only at the local level, and in some others (like Japan) not at all. Nor is electoral competition uniform across the developed democracies. Its variations include the ways in which political parties and campaigns are funded: some countries limit the amount of money that private actors can contribute to any political party or candidate and require the disclosure of the source of private political contributions.

Politics is also shaped by the electoral systems in use. The majority of developed democracies rely on some form of proportional representation to elect their legislatures, but some developed democracies (the United States, France, the United Kingdom, Australia, and Canada) rely on some form of single-member district plurality or majority. Another group (including Mexico, Hungary, Italy, and Japan) uses mixed electoral systems that combine proportional representation and single-member districts. The role of the executive, too, differs. As we read in Chapter 5, prime ministers tend to be the dominant executive in most developed democracies, though we find purely presidential systems in the United States, Chile, Brazil, and Mexico and semi-presidential systems in France and South Korea. Some of these states have federal systems and others are unitary; their legislatures may be bicameral or unicameral. All these institutions manage liberal democracy in different ways.

In short, developed democracies are politically diverse. They all guarantee participation, competition, and liberty, but they differ in where the boundaries of these elements are drawn and how they are exercised. Freedom is a basic guarantee of the state to its citizens, but the form and content of freedom vary from case to case.

In addition to a commitment to freedom, developed democracies share a similar approach to equality that emphasizes capitalism—that is, private property and free markets. This approach appears to have generated a great deal of economic prosperity—basic standards of living are higher across the developed democracies than in other countries, and life expectancy is over 70 years (over 80 in some countries). But this prosperity coexists with varying degrees of inequality, and the wealth is sometimes concentrated disproportionately among certain ethnic groups. Recall from Chapter 4 that the Gini index, a measurement of inequality around the world, finds a surprising amount of difference even among countries whose levels of economic development are roughly the same. For example, Germany, Canada, and the United States have comparable levels of economic development as measured by GDP but very different levels of inequality as measured by the Gini index.

This difference in equality is in part a function of the role of the state. Across the developed democracies, the economic functions of the state, including its role in the distribution of wealth, differ greatly. States may play a relatively small role in providing public goods, especially in liberal political-economic systems. In contrast, in social-democratic systems, such as those in much of Europe, taxation is often higher and the resulting revenues are used for income redistribution through an extensive system of social expenditures. Here, too, social-democratic systems are

> ### IN FOCUS: Political Diversity in Developed Democracies
>
> **PARTICIPATION**
> - Referenda and initiatives are used in varying degrees.
>
> **COMPETITION**
> - Different methods and levels of funding are used for political parties and campaigns.
> - Separation of powers varies greatly and is based primarily on the relative strength of different branches of government.
>
> **LIBERTIES**
> - Distinctions exist in the regulation, allowance, or prohibition of activities such as abortion, prostitution, and hate speech.
> - Different degrees of individual privacy are protected from state and corporate intrusion.

not uniform; some have more job protection or high levels of unemployment insurance. All of these variations do not change the fact that in each developed democracy, private property and free markets are fundamental institutions (Table 8.3).

In sum, the developed democracies share a basic set of institutions through which they reconcile freedom and equality. These institutions include liberal democracy, with its emphasis on participation, competition, and liberty; and capitalism, with its emphasis on free markets and private property. Yet each of the developed democracies has constructed these institutions in a different way, resulting in quite significant variations among them.

Contemporary Challenges for Developed Democracies

The institutions that the developed democracies share are part of what makes these countries **modern**—that is, secular, rational, materialistic, technological, bureaucratic, and concerned more with individual freedom than with collective equality. But like any other group of countries, developed democracies are not only diverse but also dynamic; their institutions are subject to change under the influence of domestic and international forces. Indeed, for a number of years some scholars have argued that developed democracies are undergoing a significant shift away from modern social, political, and economic institutions. Those writing on this

TABLE 8.3   Income Redistribution in Developed Democracies

COUNTRY	POLITICAL-ECONOMIC SYSTEM	TAXES AS A PERCENTAGE OF GDP, 2017	GINI INDEX
Sweden	Social democratic	43	29
Germany	Social democratic	36	32
France	Social democratic	45	33
Canada	Liberal	31	34
United Kingdom	Liberal	33	33
Japan	Mercantilist	30	38
United States	Liberal	26	42

Sources: CIA World Factbook, World Bank, Heritage Foundation.

topic lack a proper word to describe this change, using instead the awkward term **postmodern**. Clearly, this word says more about what isn't than what is.

We'll spend the remainder of this chapter considering the challenges to modernity in the developed democracies and whether these challenges are indicators of dramatic change. If so, are the developed democracies making a transition to postmodernity, and what would that mean? Or is change overstated or perhaps not in the direction we imagine? These are big questions that lie in the realm of speculation and rely on fragmentary evidence. We will look at them in the context of the categories that have defined our discussion up to this point: political, societal, and economic institutions.

Political Institutions: Sovereignty Transformed?

In Chapter 2, we discussed a number of ways to analyze and compare states. In particular, we spoke about state sovereignty and noted that state power can be viewed in terms of autonomy and capacity. Yet in recent decades, we have seen a movement toward greater integration between countries and greater devolution within countries.

Integration is a process by which states pool their sovereignty, surrendering some individual powers in exchange for political, economic, or societal benefits. Integration blurs the line between countries by forging tight connections, common policies, and shared rules that bind them together. In contrast, devolution is a process of devolving, or "sending down," political power to lower levels of government. This process is intended to increase local participation, efficiency, and flexibility by having local authorities manage tasks once handled at the national level. Although both integration and devolution can be found to varying degrees around the world, such processes have most profoundly changed the developed democracies.

Many have expected these twin processes of integration and devolution to effectively transform the modern state and sovereignty as we know it. However, countervailing processes may limit, or even end, these movements, as we already saw in our opening discussion.

The European Union: Integration, Expansion, and Resistance

The best-known example of integration, and one that we spoke of at the start of the chapter, is the European Union (EU). While the idea of a unified Europe may seem unexceptional today, it came on the heels of a devastating war between European countries that left millions dead.

In the aftermath of World War II, a number of European leaders argued that the repeated conflicts in the region were caused by a lack of interconnection between countries, which fostered insecurity, inequality, and nationalism. These leaders believed that if their countries could be bound together through economic, societal, and political institutions, they would reject war against one another as irrational. Moreover, they argued, a common political agenda would give European states greater international authority in a postwar environment that had become dominated by the Soviet Union and the United States. Some wanted integration to lead to a federal Europe; others had more limited expectations. With these motivations, a core of Western European countries began the process of integration in the early 1950s. This was a radical step away from sovereignty and not an easy one for any state or society to take. As a result, integration moved forward slowly and in piecemeal fashion.[3]

As the timeline on page 257 shows, the EU developed incrementally. It began among a handful of countries as a small agreement that dealt primarily with the production of steel and coal. The EU then expanded over time to become a body that included many more members and held vastly greater responsibilities. Out of this expansion, a basic set of institutions developed that gave the EU increasingly sovereign power in many areas over the member states.

The European Council is charged with setting the "general political direction and priorities" of the EU and with helping member states resolve the complex or sensitive issues that arise between them.[4] The council comprises the heads of state or government of every EU member; the EU's own president is elected for 2.5-year terms by the council to help manage its affairs. The president is not directly elected by the EU public, nor does the office hold the kind of executive power that its title suggests.

The European Commission, in contrast, is a body made up of 27 members (one per member state), each responsible for some specific policy area, such as transport, environment, and energy. The commission, confusingly, has its own president, who is first chosen by the European Council but then must be approved by the European Parliament. He or she serves a 5-year term. The commission's president manages the work of the commission, which is to set policy objectives, propose legislation, as well as manage the EU budget.

A third body is the European Parliament. Unlike the council and commission, which are staffed, directed, or chosen by EU member governments, the European Parliament is a legislature whose 705 members are directly elected by the EU member states for 5-year terms. The parliament passes legislation proposed by the commission. It also passes the budget for the EU and approves members of the commission (and can call for their resignation). Each country's number of representatives is roughly proportional to the size of its population.

Finally, the EU Court of Justice, made up of one judge for each country, rules on EU laws and conflicts between EU laws and the laws of member states. Member countries, EU bodies, companies, and individuals all may appeal to the Court of Justice. EU laws supersede national laws.

As these statelike institutions gained power over time, many people no longer saw the EU as an **intergovernmental system** like the United Nations, whose member countries cooperate on issues but may not be bound by the organization's resolutions. Instead, the EU looked more like a **supranational system**, where sovereignty is shared between the member states. In other words, the EU looked more like "an ever closer union," as the EU itself put it, on the road to becoming a federal state. However, state sovereignty would not so easily give way, eventually coming to threaten integration and unity.

One important point to make about European integration is that this was in many ways a technical project led by elites. Of course, most political projects are shaped by elites, who are able to provide the leadership and authority necessary to create institutions. However, successful institutions are not simply technical in nature; remember our discussion in Chapter 1, where we examined how institutions become valued for their own sake and take on a life of their own. For states and regimes, it is necessary to mobilize the public through ideas and identities, such as ideology, ethnicity, citizenship, and nationalism. Yet after World War II, these were seen as precisely the identities that had gotten Europe into trouble in the first place. Creating a European union was not simply a question of trying to forge a common European identity, or gaining the cooperation of leaders who had been at war only a few years before. It was also a question of whether Europe could transcend traditional political identities altogether—a postmodern view. As a result, European integration was conducted as a primarily technical project, and public participation was limited. The European Parliament became a directly elected body only in 1979, and even now it does not take on the important work of creating legislation. More fundamentally, it can be argued that the European Union lacks a democratic regime. While the EU is made up only of developed democracies and enjoys a democratically elected institution like the Parliament, for many Europeans the EU itself is not seen as a source of democratic values. Indeed, over time many came to see the EU as running counter to democracy, driven by bureaucrats who were unaccountable to their citizens. An attempt to counter this lack of legitimacy with a formal constitution in 2001 resulted in a document nearly 500 pages long. While this agreement was rejected by referenda in the Netherlands and France, a more limited treaty was eventually enacted in 2009.

The EU's inability to overcome its "democratic deficit," as some called it, was compounded by one of its achievements: monetary union. On January 1, 1999, the majority of EU member states linked their currencies to the euro, a single currency, under control of the European Central Bank. The logic of monetary union was that a single currency would allow for one measure of prices and values across the EU, increasing competition by stimulating trade and cross-border investment within the EU. Moreover, a single currency backed by some of the world's wealthiest countries would increase the EU's power in the international system by creating what could become a "reserve currency" for other countries—that is, a currency with global legitimacy that central banks would use as part of their monetary holdings. Finally, it was hoped that the euro could provide a shared sense of identity among EU citizens and their elected leaders.[5] Not all countries chose to adopt the euro: the United Kingdom, Denmark, and Sweden all opted out. However, all future members of the EU are expected to join the currency union in the future (as of 2020, six former communist countries had not yet adopted the euro).

TIMELINE: European Integration

1951	European Coal and Steel Community (ECSC) founded by Belgium, France, Germany, Italy, Luxembourg, and the Netherlands.
1957	European Economic Community (EEC) created from ECSC.
1967	European Community (EC) created from EEC.
1973	Denmark, Ireland, and the United Kingdom join EC.
1979	Direct elections to the European Parliament.
1981	Greece joins EC.
1986	Spain and Portugal join EC.
1993	European Union (EU) created from EC.
1995	Sweden, Finland, and Austria join EU.
1999	Monetary union created among most EU member states.
2002	Euro currency enters circulation; most EU national currencies eliminated.
2004	EU accepts 10 new members, most former communist countries.
2007	Bulgaria and Romania join EU.
2009	Lisbon Treaty becomes new constitution of EU.
2013	Croatia joins EU.
2016	Referendum passes in the United Kingdom to leave EU.
2020	United Kingdom leaves EU.

Why did monetary union harm the EU? As a federal project, a single currency makes sense, as it does for the United States. However, creating a single currency across many different states, each with its own central bank, is much more problematic. Each euro area member state now shared the same interest rate and exchange rate (see Chapter 4), in spite of significant economic differences. For poorer countries, interest rates under the euro dropped, encouraging rising private and government debt. This was particularly severe in Greece, where the government ran significant deficits and racked up debt as a result. When the global economic downturn occurred in 2008, the Greek state simply ran out of money and was no longer able to borrow enough to meet its public needs or cover what it already owed. Fearing economic collapse, other EU members were forced to loan money to Greece to keep it afloat. This action exposed key fears within the EU—not only that problems affecting one member of the EU would ripple across the whole institution but also that, to ensure stability, member states would need to take financial responsibility for one another. Needless to say, significant tensions have emerged among the EU countries over managing their levels of debt and determining whether some EU members must bail out other members in financial crisis. (See "Institutions in Action" on pp. 270–71 for a discussion of the resulting crisis.)

A second achievement that has proved a source of conflict has been the ongoing expansion of the EU (Figure 8.1). From 1951 to 2004, the EU grew from six member states to 15, and with the collapse of communism in Eastern Europe a new wave of mostly postcommunist countries sought membership. Thirteen new countries were accepted between 2004 and 2013, adding over 100 million people to the EU. This brought the total population of the EU to a half billion (the U.S. population, by contrast, is approximately 330 million) and made the EU's total GDP close to that of the United States.

As with monetary union, the EU's enlargement has fueled Euroskepticism. Many former communist member states are poorer, and many Eastern Europeans have migrated westward looking for work, while many Western European firms have relocated to Eastern Europe to take advantage of lower wages. Both dynamics have raised tensions over immigration and jobs. Indeed, in the case of Britain's 2016 referendum to leave the European Union, a central concern was about immigrants from countries within the European Union, such as Poland, who are seen by some as competing for jobs. Free movement within the EU for its own citizens (millions of citizens of the European Union now live in a different state than the one in which they were born) has become entangled with discussions of non-European refugees and concerns about globalization. Far from the idea of a United States of Europe, it now seems unlikely that the European Union will undergo any significant enlargement in the near future.

As we have noted, in some ways the EU has been a victim of its own success. One can make a strong argument that integration not only prevented conflict in Europe but also laid the foundation for economic development and prosperity across the continent and institutionalized democracy in countries that had never experienced it. And yet in spite of these results, the perception among many is that the cost has been an unacceptable loss of sovereignty and weakening of national identity. The lessons here are not confined to Europe. Many have assumed that the European Union

FIGURE 8.1 European Union Membership, 2020

Note: Numbers in parentheses indicate population size, in millions. The United Kingdom left the European Union on January 31, 2020.

Source: Eurostat, http://ec.europa.eu/eurostat (accessed 1/21/20).

would serve as a template for other arrangements that would increase integration around the world, such as the North American Free Trade Agreement between the United States, Mexico, and Canada. But even when integration provides tangible benefits, they are not spread evenly, and many see the trade-offs as unacceptable. We will turn more to this dilemma in our final chapter, on globalization.

Devolution and Democracy

As the struggle over integration continues, a related force—devolution—is also shaping how developed democracies manage their sovereignty. As noted here and in Chapter 3, devolution is the process of transferring powers and resources away from central state institutions and vesting them at a lower level. In many ways, devolution reverses the historical development of the state, which is noteworthy for its centralization of power over time. Typically, power over institutions such as social welfare has increasingly moved from the local to the national level. Yet across the developed democracies, moves have been made to redirect power to the local level.

Why this apparent reversal? As we discussed with regard to Euroskepticism, there is widespread concern regarding growing public mistrust of the state, viewing it as too large, too distant, and too inflexible. Devolution is seen as a way to counteract this distrust by bringing government closer to the public, thereby increasing local control and participation. Devolution can also help give voice to marginal communities, such as ethnic minorities, by giving them greater control over their local affairs. Proponents of devolution believe that democracy can be reinvigorated by increasing the public's voice and capacity to shape politics.[6]

How does devolution take shape in reality? One way is through the transfer of responsibility and funds to local authorities, giving them a greater say in how policies are crafted and executed. When local institutions have more control and responsibility, they can craft policy to meet their own particular conditions. One example of such devolution occurred in the United States in the 1990s, when welfare reform created bulk transfers of funds to the states, which could then use this money to design and implement their own particular social welfare policies. States have also been central in driving regional and even national policy, sometimes contrary to the wishes of the central government (the role of California in setting environmental standards is a good example). And even the EU has encouraged devolution through its Committee of the Regions, which focuses on bringing local communities into the EU decision-making process.

Another way to effect devolution is by creating wholly new political institutions to provide a greater level of public participation. An example of such innovation was seen in 1999, when Canada created a new territory, Nunavut, out of a portion of the Northwest Territories. By creating this new territory, the government intended to give the native Inuit people self-government and control over the natural resources in the region where they lived. Similarly, in 1999 the United Kingdom created new, directly elected assemblies for the regions of Scotland, Wales, and Northern Ireland.

We have noted that of late there has been growing resistance to integration. Is this true of devolution as well? First, we should note that devolution and integration are not necessarily zero sum, where one gains only at the other's expense. As we see in the case of the EU, integration and devolution have been viewed

> ## IN FOCUS: Means of Devolution
>
> - Transfer of policy-making responsibility to lower levels of government
> - Creation of new political institutions at lower levels of government
> - Transfer of funds and taxation powers to lower levels of government, affording them more control over how resources are distributed

as complementary projects, where greater powers at the EU level would require stronger connections to subnational institutions like regions and cities. Similarly, a new localism focus on cities can be an attempt to link urban areas more directly to international opportunities provided by globalization. But it is also true that devolution can emerge out of hostility to the state and integration, fueled by a populist demand for more local autonomy. This can weaken state capacity and autonomy. As we discussed in Chapter 3, when it is a response to ethnic conflict devolution may either help resolve the problem or only increase demands for sovereignty, depending on how the institutional reforms are structured. In the United Kingdom, devolution has gone a long way toward bringing religious conflict between Catholics and Protestants in Northern Ireland to an end, though Brexit has many worried that conflict may reemerge. Devolution in Spain similarly did not prevent the recent rise of a Catalan independence movement that sought independence against the wishes of the central government.

Finally, in the face of ongoing terrorist attacks across developed democracies a number of countries have moved away from devolution in important ways, centralizing and increasing capacity and autonomy as a way to fight the threat of terrorism and manage legal and illegal immigration. As with integration, devolution's pace and strength can be influenced by external and internal conditions. Not long ago, observers saw integration and devolution as inexorable processes that states and citizens could not stop. That no longer seems to be the case.

Societal Institutions: New Identities in Formation?

Just as advanced democratic states are facing a number of political challenges and changes in the new millennium, societies, too, are confronting change and are seemingly being pulled in two directions at once. Some political scientists point to a new set of shared norms and values emerging across the developed democracies that are not bound to traditional identities of nation and state; others emphasize the strengthening of local identities that are turning these same societies inward. These processes are strongly connected to the struggle over integration and devolution. The debate among political scientists is whether these social forces are complementary or contradictory and whether such developments are a sign of greater cooperation or conflict.

Postmodern Values and Organization

A number of political scientists track the emergence and development of what they see as postmodern values in the developed democracies.[7] In premodern societies, people were more focused on traditional forms of authority and on basic survival; this focus often led to authoritarian systems with clear standards of obedience and collectivism. Starting in the eighteenth century, the countries that would become the developed democracies began to embrace the notions of rationality and science, individualism and autonomy. The modern state, society, and economy promised a world of progress, development, and limitless possibilities, and they did enable unprecedented economic growth, material abundance, and improved standards of living for hundreds of millions of people.

Yet by the 1960s, modern values came under attack, just as they themselves had challenged premodern values more than two centuries earlier. These challenges took several forms. Questions were raised about the environmental cost of economic development. Modern values stressed the environment's utility for achieving material goals, but critics now argued that the environment should be valued for its own sake—a public good to be shared by all. Science, too, was viewed with greater skepticism. It was pointed out that technological innovation did not lead to unmitigated benefits but rather carried with it risks and uncertainty. Fears over nuclear power or pollution led many to believe that "progress" was a questionable goal. In politics, too, nationalism and patriotism were challenged, and authority, hierarchy, and deference to the state were questioned. In general, these criticisms indicated the possible emergence of a new set of social norms and values.

Political scientists identify several key differences between modern and postmodern values. As already indicated, postmodern values are much less focused on the idea of progress as embodied by material goods, technological change, or scientific innovation. Instead, they center on what have been called "quality of life" or "postmaterialist" issues, which primarily involve concerns other than material gain, including the environment, health, and leisure as well as personal equality, identity, and diversity. Recall our discussion of the World Values Survey in Chapter 3, where we noted the shift from values focused on traditional survival to those based on self-expression and rationality. In many ways, these values, with their concern for tolerance among different kinds of people and their skepticism of centralized power, reflect both integrationist and devolutionary tendencies.

We must be careful not to overstate these findings, however. The central assumption among scholars has been that all developed democracies are converging toward a shared set of postmodern values, such as the recognition of same-sex marriage. Moreover, as the camp of developed democracies expands, its new members are also expected to trend in a postmodern direction. However, there are two important caveats. First, as we noted in our earlier discussion of political culture, research indicates that a society's religious heritage continues to shape societal values irrespective of the level of development. This may limit convergence in some important ways. Second, postmodernization suggests an inexorable progress tied to economic development. But as scholars of modernization themselves note, if economic development stagnates or is spread unequally, values may not change; they may even move back toward more traditional beliefs. These factors are in turn connected to questions about diversity and identity in developed democracies.

Diversity, Identity, and the Challenge to Postmodern Values

The twenty-first century has been marked by a wave of immigration to developed democracies unseen for a century. In 1960, around 4 percent of the population of the United States was foreign born; today, that number is 14 percent. In Canada, the figure is 19 percent, while in Australia over a quarter of the population is foreign born. In many larger countries of the EU (Germany, Spain, and France), over 10 percent of the population was born in other countries. This rapid increase in immigration is changing the ethnic, religious, and racial compositions of these countries. For example, forecasters have concluded that by 2044, whites of European origin will comprise less than half of the U.S. population (down from 90 percent in 1960), and that by 2060, 20 percent of the population will be foreign born.[8]

Moreover, the makeup of the immigrant population is quite different across the advanced democratic countries. In the United States, the largest proportion of immigrants comes from Latin America; in Canada, Australia, and New Zealand, the largest group comes from Asia; and in Europe, the largest group comes from North Africa and the Middle East. Thus, while many developed democracies are experiencing immigration, the nature of that immigration and the challenges or opportunities it brings are very different.

In many countries, growing numbers of immigrants have led to increased xenophobia—fear of foreigners—in the existing population. This xenophobia has economic, societal, and political dimensions. The economic dimension is perhaps most familiar to us. Although supporters of immigration note the benefits of new sources of labor and skills that can come from immigrants, critics view immigrants as a threat to existing workers, saying they compete for scarce jobs and depress wages. Debates in Europe over the expansion and powers of the EU have turned in large part on fears of immigration. Immigration has been a similar sticking point in U.S.-Mexico relations, and Australians express concern over an influx of immigrants and refugees from Asia and beyond. Some countries, like Japan, have avoided this issue by strictly limiting immigration, though this tactic has its own problems, as we shall discuss shortly.

A more complicated issue is that of societal institutions. As more diverse groups of immigrants enter the developed democracies, they raise questions about what it means to be American, Canadian, French, or European. Developed democracies struggle with questions of assimilation and multiculturalism. How much leeway should new groups be given in deciding whether to participate in national institutions and take on national identities? At one end of the spectrum, arguments for multiculturalism assert that societies should help support these new groups, preserving what is distinct about them as a positive contribution to a diverse society. At the other end, arguments for assimilation hold that immigration implies an agreement to accept and adapt to the existing culture, values, and norms of a given society. For countries like the United States, Canada, and Australia, multiculturalism may be somewhat easier to embrace because a large number of citizens have come from somewhere else within the last two or three generations, so that the norm is for each person to bring a new contribution to society that can be incorporated into it. Yet even in these countries, people exhibit strong tendencies toward assimilation and fears that the sheer number of immigrants makes assimilation, even if desired, impossible. Openly xenophobic and racist arguments have grown in American political discourse, questioning how institutionalized postmodern values really are.

If multiculturalism is a source of controversy in traditionally immigrant countries, it is an explosive subject in countries where ethnic and national identities are much more tightly fused, as in much of Europe. There the influx of non-Europeans, especially Muslims from North Africa and the Middle East, has raised even greater fears. Racially, religiously, and ethnically homogeneous populations now confront people whose cultural, religious, and historical traditions are quite different. The paradox that has emerged is uniquely postmodern. In the past, many

European states prided themselves on their high degree of secularism and tolerance for different lifestyles. But how do they tolerate immigrant groups that may be much more religiously and socially conservative? These are the kinds of concerns that have helped give rise to nationalist and far-right parties that have drawn on more traditional values like family and nation to build support. The rise of such political parties suggests that postmodern values may be more contingent than we imagine. Under periods of material stress, postmaterialist views are also likely to come under duress, and xenophobia, nationalism, and illiberal political values can reemerge. (See "Questions and Methods" on pp. 274–75 for a discussion of authoritarian views in developed democracies.)

Finally, the new wave of immigrants may affect relations between the developed democracies. Although most of these countries, as we noted, face similar questions regarding immigration and its effects, the source of migration differs from country to country or from region to region. This growing difference between the developed democracies may pull them apart by shaping different cultural values and external orientations. In North America, migration from Latin America and East Asia may reorient these countries south and east, away from Europe. In Europe, larger Muslim communities and EU expansion may draw these countries closer to the Middle East and South Asia. Faith may also come into play. As Hispanic immigrants moving into the United States are bringing with them Roman Catholic, Evangelical, or Pentecostal religious values, Islam is growing more central to European life. The developed democracies may see less and less of themselves in one another. This transformation need not be a source of conflict; democratic values and a commitment to prosperity link very different countries together as part of the community of developed democracies. But some speculate that a growing divergence of the developed democracies may eventually mean an end to the idea of a single set of secular, postmodern values that would define developed democracies.

Economic Institutions: A New Market?

Our discussion so far has asked to what extent postmodernity is changing state and societal institutions. Our last area of interest, economic development, is perhaps the most obvious. Dramatic changes have taken place in the economic structures of developed democracies over the past generation. Specifically, their reliance on traditional industries, such as manufacturing, has shifted to such an extent that it is no longer logical to refer to them as "industrial" at all. At the same time, long-standing assumptions about the role of the state in such areas as the redistribution of income and social expenditures have come into question, challenging the traditional functions of the welfare state. This situation may lead to an overturning of existing ideas and policies regarding the proper balance of freedom and equality in developed democracies.

Postindustrialism

So far, we have considered how postmodernity has affected advanced democratic states and societies. In both of these arenas, what is going on is open to interpretation. But in the economic realm, the data are clearer: developed democracies have experienced a dramatic shift during the last half-century from economies based primarily on industry and manufacturing to postindustrial economies.

In postindustrial countries, the bulk of profits are made and most of the people are employed in the service sector—work that involves not the creation of tangible goods, such as cars or computers, but industries such as finance, insurance, real estate, education, retail sales, transportation, communication, high technology, utilities, health care, and business and legal services. This shift has been occurring across developed democracies over the past several decades; on average, around three-quarters of the working population are now employed in the service sector (see Table 8.2, on p. 249). This shift has occurred for a number of reasons. Much industrial production has migrated outside developed democracies in search of lower labor and other costs. Globalization is accelerating this trend. Furthermore, technological innovation is changing the requirements for labor. Employees are expected to have higher levels of education than in the past; in the United States and Canada, over 40 percent of those between ages 25 and 34 have a college degree.[9] Automation is also reducing the need for much unskilled and even skilled labor.

Postindustrialism in some ways reflects and may reinforce the political and social trends discussed earlier. The emergence of an information-based economy, for example, may contribute to a greater devolution of power within the economy as firms become less hierarchical and more decentralized, less physical and more "virtual," less national and more international, and as they grant their employees greater autonomy and flexibility. However, for those who do not have specialized training and education—and even for many of those who do—postindustrialism may mean less freedom and equality. Technological changes may well marginalize many workers, creating an underclass whose prospects for upward mobility are limited. We can recall from Chapter 4 that inequality in the United States has risen over time. In 1979 the Gini index measurement for the United States was below 35; by 2016, it was 42. Increases in inequality have taken place across almost all developed democracies.[10]

Slow economic growth in most developed democracies over the past decade has raised significant questions about the long-term prospects of many postindustrial economies. Some have called for greater domestic and international economic regulation; a rethinking of how to invest public funds in education, infrastructure, and technology to meet the needs of the rapidly changing economic environment; and redesigned social safety nets that can protect the many individuals now on the margins of economic life. Others believe that the answer lies in rolling back globalization, limiting trade and immigration in favor of a more mercantilist political-economic system. These ideas share in common a major concern that the economic changes and disruptions of the last two decades will lead to an increasing concentration of opportunities and wealth into fewer and fewer hands, pushing even the well educated into lower-paying jobs with fewer opportunities for advancement. This will in turn put pressure on the state to change how it approaches its social expenditures, which we will turn to next.

Maintaining the Welfare State

As our final aspect of economic transformation in the developed democracies, we will consider the future of the welfare state. As we discussed in Chapter 4, for the past half-century a defining element of developed democracies has been the development of social expenditures as a way to reduce inequality and provide public goods through such programs as national pension plans, public health care, education, and unemployment benefits. There can be no doubt that the welfare state has provided a wide array of benefits among developed democracies: extreme poverty has been reduced; infant mortality has declined, and life expectancy has increased; and literacy and education have improved dramatically. Social expenditures have played an important role in socializing risk—that is, making the uncertainties that come with work, health, and age a public rather than a private concern.

However, the welfare state has brought with it costs and controversies that have only been exacerbated by recent economic difficulties. First, although social expenditures have been lauded as an essential part of a humane society, they are increasingly expensive. During the early part of the twentieth century, social expenditures typically amounted to around 10 to 15 percent of developed democracies' GDPs. Currently, however, in most of these countries social expenditures (not including education) consume between a quarter and a third of GDP. This increased spending has required a choice. The first is to raise taxes, which among developed democracies consume nearly 35 percent of GDP (over 40 percent in several social democracies). Of course, if the public is willing to pay higher taxes in return for benefits this is not necessarily a problem, though the ideology of liberalism would assert that such large state expenditures reduce private income and profit and thus hinder growth. The second option is to borrow from the public or other states to cover budget deficits. Japan, whose public debt is now over 200 percent of its GDP, is the most extreme example, but the debts of many developed democracies, including the United States, Canada, the United Kingdom, and France, are between 80 and 100 percent of their GDP. As with individuals, paying interest on high levels of debt means fewer resources to spend elsewhere and less financial flexibility.

These trends will be magnified by important demographic changes within developed democracies. In 1900, residents of these countries had an average life expectancy of around 40 to 50 years; most now can expect to live more than 80 years. As life expectancies have risen, birthrates have declined. In most of the developed democracies, the birthrate is below the replacement level—more people die than are being born.[11] This is true even in some poorer democracies like Brazil. There are two results from these demographic changes. First, the populations of many developed democracies may eventually begin to shrink. Second, all developed democracies will see a growing elderly population. According to some estimates, by 2050 a third of the population in the developed democracies will be over 65 years old, compared with around 15 percent in 2000. As an ever-larger proportion of the population, this older segment of society will seek more welfare benefits, such as health care, but declining birthrates mean fewer working-age individuals are available to fill needed jobs and pay into these systems.

The solutions are not easy. Increased immigration is one obvious solution, especially given that the world population, most notably in Africa, will continue to grow. However, we've already noted the problems that accompany immigrants who are seen as competing for jobs. This dynamic becomes even more contentious when it involves social expenditures. Young immigrants may in fact be necessary to expand the labor force, but many instead view immigrants as the ones burdening the welfare system.[12] A second course is to cut back on benefits. However, politicians face well-organized opposition to welfare reform, and in many countries benefits have continued to increase even as revenues have shrunk, leading to deficits and debt. A third solution would be to reform the labor market. This could be done by raising the retirement age and making job markets more flexible, thus encouraging more part-time work among parents and younger or older workers. Although there is resistance, many European countries are now raising their retirement ages, which have typically been below 65. Some combination of increased immigration, reduced benefits, and later retirement will be necessary. Otherwise, developed democracies will borrow even more against the young and their future, cutting long-term investments in such areas as education and infrastructure in order to protect benefits directed toward older citizens. This high debt and lack of investment could result in further economic troubles down the road.

Japan provides an extreme example of the complexities involved in these demographic changes and policy responses. The population of Japan, around 127 million, has already peaked and is beginning to decline. By 2050, it is expected to have dropped to 100 million. Moreover, a third or more of the population will be over age 65. To prevent population decline, the country would need to accept several hundred thousand immigrants every year, which would dramatically transform the composition of a country that is ethnically very homogeneous. As can be imagined, people in Japan have little desire to follow such a course; in fact, during the recent economic downturns immigrants have been encouraged to leave, making it one of the few developed democracies where immigration has decreased over the last decade. The alternative is for the country to shrink significantly in population and wealth. If solutions are not found for Japan and the other developed democracies, many will find themselves unable to sustain some of the most basic elements of social security constructed over the past century, and they will face societal conflict that pits young against old and immigrant against native.

In Sum: Developed Democracies in Transition

Developed democracies—their institutions and the challenges they face—are unlike other countries in many ways. Although there is variation among them, these countries are all characterized by liberal democracy and high levels of economic development. They represent what we consider modern social, economic, and political life. Yet their institutions are being directly challenged. State sovereignty is confronted by the twin dynamics of devolution and integration. Social norms are similarly in flux, as postmodern values challenge the status quo and are challenged in turn. Modern industrial structures have given way to a new, information-based economy that empowers some and dislocates others, and demographic changes will affect how countries provide public goods to their people. All these factors can affect general prosperity and shape the existing balance between freedom and equality.

In the coming chapters, we will turn to these same issues as they exist outside the developed democracies. Communist, postcommunist, and developing countries all confront issues of state sovereignty, social values, industrialization, and social welfare. The next two chapters will focus on the unique challenges these

INSTITUTIONS IN ACTION

What Explains the Greek Economic Crisis?

In 2008, a number of developed democracies underwent a profound economic crisis that by many measures was the worst since the Great Depression. These countries saw a sharp decline in housing prices and stocks, high unemployment, and negative or minimal growth. While many developed democracies have since slowly emerged from this crisis, profound effects remain, such as increased inequality. Of all the countries affected by the recession, the worst hit was a seemingly unlikely one—Greece. After 15 years of steady growth, between 2008 and 2012 Greece's GDP fell by an astounding 27 percent, which is roughly the same amount as in the United States during the Great Depression. Why did Greece fall so far?

Greece was a latecomer to both industrialization and liberal democracy. After World War II, the country experienced a devastating civil war that pitted communists against the monarchist government. During that war, both sides received support from their respective Cold War allies. The defeat of the communists and the end of the civil war did not create stability, however. Battles between leftist and rightist parties eventually resulted in a military coup and a dictatorship that lasted from 1967 to 1974. Following the end of military rule, the political parties that came to dominate politics—particularly the Panhellenic Socialist Movement, which ruled for much of the next 30 years—used clientelism to institutionalize their support. This strategy was reinforced by the relatively underdeveloped economy. In the absence of private economic opportunities, political parties could offer state benefits, such as jobs, to their backers.[a]

The result was a system that benefited those connected to the political parties but raised significant barriers to others. The Greek civil service grew large and offered some of the highest levels of compensation. The state created many regulatory barriers, making economic development difficult. Regulations emerged that limited such things as the number of pharmacies, lawyers, and long-haul truckers that were allowed to operate. These regulations have contributed to discrepancies in unemployment; the unemployment rate stood at 17 percent in 2019 (over double the rate across the European Union as a whole), and for those under 25 it was over 30 percent.

Finally, the deep connections created by clientelism between the state, economy, and political parties have led to widespread corruption. According to Transparency International, on its scale of corruption Greece ranks 67th out of 180 countries. That is a big improvement due to recent reforms, but it remains one of the worst in Europe. Many businesses function in a "gray" or informal sector (see Chapter 10) where they are unlicensed and can therefore avoid state regulations and tax obligations. By some estimates, this group comprises over a quarter of the economy, functioning outside the law. Individuals and formal businesses similarly evade taxes, often by bribing tax officials or simply counting on the fact that an overburdened tax-collection system cannot catch them. This corruption points to a broader failure of state autonomy, capacity, and overall legitimacy; as we have noted earlier, tax compliance can be a function less of enforcement than of the public's general sense that taxation is acceptable and that most people are participating. In Greece, the *fakelaki*—a small envelope of cash, necessary to secure public services ranging from health care to building permits—has essentially replaced the tax system.

The combination of these institutional factors explains the Greek crisis. In Greece, the weakness of the private economy combined with the state's corruption and outlays through clientelism has meant that the government has consistently faced a large budget deficit. Greece adopted the euro in 2001 on the condition that it would reduce its budget deficit. Instead, it fudged its books and continued to run high deficits, which as an EU member, it easily covered by borrowing money. As deficits continued to grow, so did debt.

What finally triggered the Greek crisis was the recession in the United States. Once the U.S. housing bubble popped, investors grew nervous about investments elsewhere in the world—including Greece, whose debt and deficits were becoming clearer. Investors were no longer confident that Greece could sustain its economic situation or that the EU could or would bail the country out. Short of funds, the Greek government was forced into dramatic austerity measures: tax increases, a later retirement age, limits on pension benefits, and massive cuts to defense, health care, and education. Total household income dropped by a third. Not surprisingly, the economic crisis has led to political instability and polarization, which saw the rise of parties on the far left and far right. Greece's economic situation has improved, but it still is burdened by the highest unemployment rate in the EU—six times higher than that of Germany. Not surprisingly, Greece also confronts a brain drain as young people leave the country in search of jobs. This hampers economic recovery, as those leaving tend to be university graduates and other highly skilled individuals—precisely those needed to sustain economic recovery.

A woman walks past the Bank of Greece headquarters with a wall covered with graffiti: "Rob to Get Money," as well as "Bank of Berlin." This reflects the widespread view that the European Union, dominated by Germany, has forced unbearable economic cuts on the Greek state.

1. In what ways did the Greek government's use of clientelism hinder economic development?

2. What role did Greece's membership in the EU play in advancing its economic crisis? What concerns does this raise about the EU in general?

3. How has Greece's political and economic corruption affected the state's capacity and legitimacy?

groups of countries face in these areas. Will these countries eventually join the ranks of the developed democracies in a convergence of political, economic, and social institutions around the globe? Will they face the same kinds of challenges on the paths to prosperity and democracy? These questions will follow us through our remaining discussion.

Key Terms

developed democracy (p. 245)
intergovernmental system (p. 255)
modern (p. 252)

postmodern (p. 253)
supranational system (p. 255)

For Further Reading

Brym, Robert. "After Postmaterialism: An Essay on China, Russia and the United States." *Canadian Journal of Sociology* 41, no. 2 (2016): 195–212.

Crepaz, Markus M. L. *Trust beyond Borders: Immigration, the Welfare State, and Identity in Modern Societies.* Ann Arbor: University of Michigan Press, 2008.

Dinan, Desmond. *Europe Recast: A History of European Union.* 2nd ed. Boulder, CO: Lynne Rienner Publishers, 2014.

Hemerijck, Anton. *Changing Welfare States.* Oxford: Oxford University Press, 2013.

Howard, Marc Morjé. *The Politics of Citizenship in Europe.* New York: Cambridge University Press, 2009.

Inglehart, Ronald F. "After Postmaterialism: An Essay on China, Russia and the United States: A Comment." *Canadian Journal of Sociology* 41, no. 2 (2016): 213–22.

Mudde, Cas, and Cristóbal Rovira Kaltwasser, eds. *Populism in Europe and the Americas: Threat or Corrective for Democracy?* Cambridge: Cambridge University Press, 2012.

Putnam, Robert D. "*E Pluribus Unum*: Diversity and Community in the Twenty-First Century. The 2006 Johan Skytte Prize Lecture." *Scandinavian Political Studies* 30, no. 2 (2007): 137–74.

Steinmo, Sven. *The Evolution of Modern States: Sweden, Japan, and the United States.* Cambridge: Cambridge University Press, 2010.

INQUIZITIVE

Earn a better grade on your test. InQuizitive personalizes your learning path to help you master the concepts from this chapter and practice applying them to examples from the text and beyond (see back cover).

QUESTIONS AND METHODS

What Explains Authoritarian Views in Developed Democracies?

We've spoken in this chapter about the idea that developed democracies have over time moved from modern values to postmodern ones, emphasizing among other things personal identity and equality. With the rise of far-right groups in many developed democracies, the durability of postmodern values even in those countries seems open to question. Is this a temporary phase, or a harbinger of something more powerful?

Political scientists who have been studying these questions have turned their attention to the study of latent authoritarian values in democratic societies. The scholars Karen Stenner and Jonathan Haidt, in their analysis of the European Union and the United States, found that nearly a third of white respondents were inclined toward authoritarian views—notably, significant constraints on individuals' moral, political, and racial freedoms.[a] Such

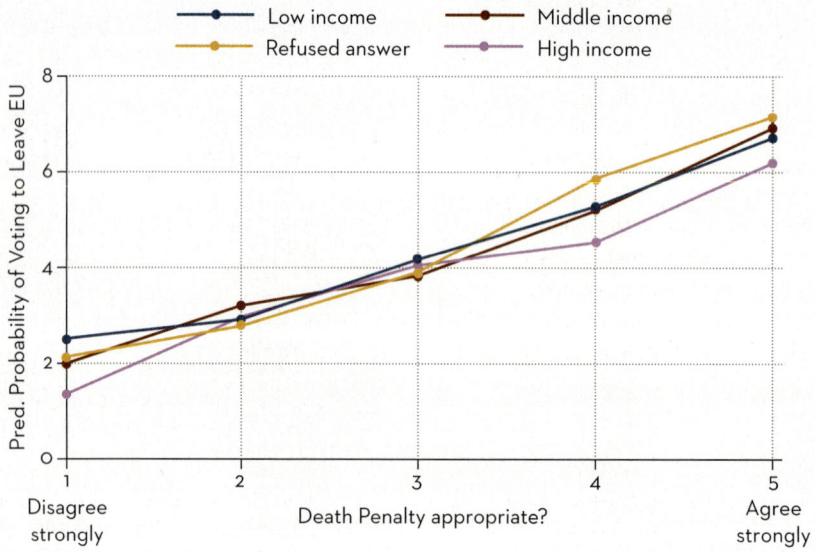

The Correlation between Support for Brexit and Support for the Death Penalty

Source: Eric Kaufman, "It's NOT the Economy, Stupid: Brexit as a Story of Personal Values," London School of Economics, July 7, 2016, https://blogs.lse.ac.uk/politicsandpolicy/personal-values-brexit-vote (accessed 2/11/20).

views, they argue, are a common and consistent human predisposition across all societies. This is radically different from common explanations for authoritarian viewpoints such as economic factors, which the authors argue is not well supported by evidence. Indeed, one study in the United Kingdom found that one of the strongest predictors of support for Brexit was support for the death penalty (which, incidentally, the United Kingdom abolished in 1969).[b] In short, an authoritarian predisposition for order and similarity is always present among every population, irrespective of the regime type.

But if authoritarianism is a consistent human mindset, what explains why authoritarian viewpoints and organizations are rising in power now? The answer is straightforward: the rise of diversity. Rather, an influx of people who look different, speak different languages, and have unfamiliar customs and forms of worship is perceived as a threat to the common public identity, a destruction of old institutions that provided certainty and order.

How, then, should democracies respond to a rise in authoritarian politics? Stenner and Haidt argue that one common prescription—to double down on diversity and multiculturalism—is only likely to deepen authoritarian responses. Instead they suggest that a reemphasis on shared values and civic institutions may be a more fruitful path, alongside difficult discussions about the goals of immigration policy.

1. *Examine assumptions about cause-and-effect relationships*

    Why might we be more likely to turn to an economic, rather than psychological, explanation for authoritarianism, and what policy conclusions might we draw from that belief?

2. *Consider related scholarship to draw broader conclusions*

    A related study found that when subjects with an authoritarian predisposition were told that alien life positively exists, their racial intolerance decreased by half. What would be the explanation?

3. *Generate new ideas related to the discussion*

    What kinds of shared values and civic institutions might be created or revitalized in order to counter concerns about diversity and multiculturalism?

---

a. Karen Stenner and Jonathan Haidt, "Authoritarianism Is Not a Momentary Madness, But an Eternal Dynamic within Liberal Democracies," in *Can It Happen Here? Authoritarianism in America*, ed. Cass R. Sunstein (New York: HarperCollins, 2018), 175–219.
b. Eric Kaufmann, "It's NOT the economy, stupid: Brexit as a story of personal values," London School of Economics, July 7, 2016, https://blogs.lse.ac.uk/politicsandpolicy/personal-values-brexit-vote (accessed 1/21/20).

9

In Hungary in 2018, opposition to Syrian migration is displayed on a government billboard as part of the campaign of the ruling Fidesz Party. In the background, a second billboard reads "For Us, Hungary is First!"

COMMUNISM AND POSTCOMMUNISM

Why did communism fail, and what are its legacies?

When we think about the end of communism in Eastern Europe and the Soviet Union, one of the clearest images that comes to mind is the fall of the Berlin Wall. But the images of people dancing on the wall in November 1989 obscure a process that had already been underway elsewhere for some time. Most notably, a year earlier the Hungarian Communist Party had been moving toward political liberalization that might move Hungary out of Soviet control and closer to the European Union (EU). One step was the decision to remove the electrified barbed wire fence between that country and Austria in May. By August, hundreds of East Germans had traveled to Hungary to escape across the border and head to West Germany. It was in Hungary where, as a former German prime minister put it, "the first stone was removed from the Berlin Wall," in turn emboldening protests in East Germany and across the region.[1]

Consistent with its role in leading the trend toward ending communism, after 1989 Hungary underwent a rapid transition to liberal democracy and capitalism. This in turn paved the way to membership in the European Union, ostensibly completing the institutionalization of democracy. Yet over the past decade many of Hungary's democratic institutions have weakened. Power has been increasingly concentrated into the hands of the prime minister, Viktor Orbán, and his ruling party, Fidesz. Since 2010 Fidesz has revised the constitution and related laws in ways that have limited the power of independent media, restricted nongovernmental organizations, and weakened the constitutional court. Worryingly, Orbán has openly spoken of "illiberal democracy" as his ideal for the country, and professed his admiration for Russia and President Vladimir Putin, in spite of the long history of Soviet rule over Hungary. Thirty years ago, no scholar of Hungarian politics would have ever imagined such a situation. Why has Hungary seemed to turn away from democratic institutions and many of the values it embraced in 1989?

Three related explanations can help answer this puzzle: the institutional legacies of postcommunism, the regional dynamics of EU politics, and the implications of a globalized identity politics. As for the first, the relatively smooth transition from communism to liberal democracy in 1989—peaceful negotiations followed by free elections—did not so much resolve old differences as exacerbate them. The Communist Party, rather than collapsing, refounded itself as a social-democratic party, returning to power in 1994 and 2002. The old communist-era constitution, while modified, also remained in place. For many, this was evidence that a true political transition had never really occurred, and Fidesz capitalized on this view that they would carry out the belated and "true" transition from communism that had never really happened.

Second, this tension within Hungarian politics over the past and future of the country was in fact exacerbated by membership in the European Union. We have already read about the rise of Euroskepticism in our previous chapter, and similar factors were at work in Hungary as well. EU membership had provided benefits in areas like investment and mobility, but at the same time many people experienced economic stagnation or insecurity as communist-era industries collapsed in the face of free trade and foreign competition. Expectations that Hungarians would quickly become as rich as Western Europeans were quickly dispelled, especially for the older generation and those less well educated. Following the 2008 financial crisis, which hit Hungary hard, Fidesz came to power on a campaign that framed the European Union as unaccountable, seeking to dictate Hungarian politics just as the Soviet Union had done under communism. Orbán's ability to stay in power for a decade has depended in part on his claim that Fidesz is the only party that can stand up for the welfare of the people against, as he called it, "an empire directed from Brussels."

Finally, this rhetoric was further shaped by the migration crisis of 2015. That year more than a million individuals crossed into the European Union, with over 100,000 into Hungary itself. While few hoped to stay, seeking instead to continue to Germany or elsewhere in the European Union, the Hungarian government portrayed the migration crisis as an existential threat to the nation. The government argued that migration was part of an EU plan, supported by other global elites, to force multicultural and non-Christian values onto Europe and destroy national identity. For many Hungarians, used to living in a country with relatively low levels of diversity and few foreign-born residents, this was an unnerving prospect—consistent with our earlier discussion of authoritarian viewpoints in Chapter 6. Thus, we see an evolution of Fidesz's rhetoric from that of anticommunism and economic security to the defense of national values in the face of disorienting global changes. For now Orbán's strategy continues to work, and the party again dominated elections in 2018.

Is Hungary now effectively an "electoral authoritarian" regime, where a combination of rhetoric and illiberal tactics keeps the opposition from gaining power? Many believe so, and numerous observers have already written the epitaph of Hungarian democracy. Yet as we saw in the case of Malaysia (Chapter 5), even seemingly invulnerable parties can lose their legitimacy, no matter the array of tools they can deploy in the pursuit of power.

LEARNING OBJECTIVES

- Explain the foundations and spread of communist ideology.
- Describe the political, economic, and social structures of the communist state.
- Summarize how postcommunist states have and have not transformed since the end of communism.

The advanced democracies we studied in the last chapter have become the wealthiest and most powerful countries in the world. Yet these wealthy countries continue to struggle with problems of poverty and inequality. Can poverty and inequality be solved? This concern goes to the heart of communist theory and practice, for communism has sought to create a system that limits individual freedoms in order to divide wealth in an equitable manner. This vision of a world without economic distinctions drove the formation of communist regimes, eventually bringing hundreds of millions of people under their banners.

Yet despite the lofty ideals of communist thought, and despite the dramatic emergence of communism as a political regime in the early part of the twentieth century, within less than a century most of the world's communist regimes began to unravel. Why? In this chapter, we look at how communism attempted to reconcile freedom and equality and why communist systems have largely failed at that endeavor. We will begin by looking at the original theories of modern communism, particularly the ideas of Karl Marx. From there, we will investigate how communism progressed from theory into practice as communist regimes were built around the world, most notably in the Soviet Union, Eastern Europe, and China (Table 9.1). How did these systems seek to create equality and bring Marx's ideas to life?

After examining the dynamics of communism in practice, we will study its demise. What were its shortcomings, and why could these limitations not be overcome? Our look at the downfall of communism will take us to our final questions: What comes after communism, and is communism dead? In addressing each of these questions, we will uncover the enormous scope and vision of communist thought, the tremendous challenges of putting it into practice, the serious flaws

TABLE 9.1 Communist Regimes in the 1980s

EUROPE	ASIA	AFRICA AND THE MIDDLE EAST	LATIN AMERICA
Albania	Afghanistan	Angola	*Cuba*
Bulgaria	Cambodia	Benin	
Czechoslovakia	*China*	Ethiopia	
East Germany	*Laos*	Mozambique	
Hungary	Mongolia	South Yemen	
Poland	*North Korea*		
Romania	*Vietnam*		
Soviet Union			
Yugoslavia			

Note: Countries still controlled by a communist party as of 2020 are shown in italics.

and limitations that this implementation encountered, and the daunting work of building new political, social, and economic institutions from the rubble of communism's demise.

Communism, Equality, and the Nature of Human Relations

Communism is a set of ideas that view political, social, and economic institutions in a manner that is fundamentally different from most political thought, challenging much of what we have studied so far. At its most basic level, it is an ideology that seeks to create human equality by eliminating private property and market forces.

Communism as a political theory and ideology can be traced primarily to the German philosopher Karl Marx (1818–83).[2] Marx began with a rather straightforward observation: human beings impart value to the objects they create by investing their own time and labor in them. This value can be greater than the cost of creating the object—for example, a chair maker may spend $50 on materials to build a chair that would sell for $60. The extra $10 reflects the added value of the maker's time and energy. This "surplus value of labor" stays with the object and makes it useful to anyone, not just the maker. This ability to create objects with their own innate value sets humans apart from other animals, but it also inevitably leads to economic injustice, Marx concluded. He argued that as human beings develop their knowledge and technological skills, an opportunity is created for those with political power to extract the surplus value from others, enriching themselves while impoverishing other people. In other words, once human beings learned how to produce things of value, others found that they could gain these things at little cost to themselves simply by using coercion to acquire them. Using the previous example, if the chair maker were employed by a "capitalist," then this employer would benefit from the surplus value of labor and get to keep the extra $10.

For Marx, then, the world was properly understood in economic terms; all human action flowed from the relations between the haves and the have-nots. Marx believed that structures, rather than people or ideas, made history. Specifically, Marx spoke of human history and human relations as functions of what he termed the base and the superstructure. The **base** is the system of economic production, including the level of technology (what he called the "means of production") and the kind of class relations that exist as a result (the "relations of production"). Resting on the base is the **superstructure**, which represents all human

IN FOCUS: Terms in Marxist Theory

Base The economic system of a society, made up of technology (the means of production) and class relations between people (the relations of production).

Bourgeoisie The property-owning class.

Communism According to Marxists, the final stage of history once capitalism is overthrown and the dictatorship of the proletariat destroys its remaining vestiges. In communism, state and politics would disappear, and society and the economy would be based on equality and cooperation.

Dialectical materialism Process of historical change that is not evolutionary but revolutionary. The existing base and superstructure (thesis) would come into conflict with new technological innovations, generating growing opposition to the existing order (antithesis). This would culminate in revolution, overthrowing the old base and superstructure (synthesis).

Dictatorship of the proletariat Temporary period after capitalism has been overthrown during which vestiges of the old base and superstructure are eradicated.

False consciousness Failure to understand the nature of one's exploitation; essentially amounts to "buying into" the superstructure.

Proletariat The working class.

Superstructure All noneconomic institutions in a society (for example, religion, culture, national identity). These ideas and values derive from the base and serve to legitimize the current system of exploitation.

Surplus value of labor The value invested in any human-made good that can be used by another individual. Exploitation results when one person or group extracts the surplus value from another.

Vanguard of the proletariat Lenin's argument that because of false consciousness, an elite communist party would have to carry out revolution; otherwise, historical conditions would not automatically lead to capitalism's demise.

---

institutions—politics and the state, national identity and culture, religion and gender, and so on. Marx viewed this superstructure as a system of institutions created essentially to justify and perpetuate the existing order. People consequently suffer from "false consciousness," meaning that they believe they understand the true nature of the world around them, but in reality they are deluded by the superstructure imposed by capitalism. Thus Marx and most other communists rejected liberal democracy as a system created to delude the exploited into thinking they have a say in their political destiny when in fact those with wealth actually control politics.

Revolution and the "Triumph" of Communism

Having dissected what he saw as the nature of politics, economics, and society, Marx used this framework to understand historical development and to anticipate the future of capitalism. Marx concluded that human history developed in phases, each driven by a particular kind of exploitation. In each phase, he argued, the form of exploitation was built around the existing level of technology. In early agrarian societies, for example, feudalism was the dominant political and economic order; the rudimentary technology available tied individuals to the land so that their labor could be exploited by the aristocracy. Although such relations may appear stable, technology itself is always dynamic. Marx recognized this and asserted that the inevitable changes in technology would increase tensions between rulers and ruled as these changes empowered new groups who clashed with the base and the superstructure. In the case of feudalism, emerging technology empowered an early capitalist, property-owning middle class, or **bourgeoisie**, whose members sought to gain political power and to remake the economic and social order in a way that better fit capitalist ambitions.

Eventually, the tensions resulting from technological advances would lead to revolution; those in power would be overthrown, and a new ruling class would come to power. In each case, change would be sudden and violent and would pave the way for a new economic base and superstructure. Marx called this entire process **dialectical materialism**. *Dialectic* is the term he used to describe history as a struggle between the existing order (the thesis) and the challenge to that order (the antithesis), resulting in historical change (the synthesis). *Materialism* simply refers to the fact that this tension is over material factors, specifically economic ones. Marx believed that revolutions inevitably result from this dialectic process.

On the basis of these ideas, Marx concluded that capitalist democracy, which had displaced feudalism, would itself be overthrown by its own internal flaws. As capitalism developed, competition between firms would intensify. The working class, or **proletariat**, would find itself on the losing end of this process as firms introduced more and greater technology to reduce the number of workers and as unprofitable businesses began to go bankrupt in the face of intense competition. The bourgeoisie would grow smaller and smaller as the wealth of society became concentrated in fewer and fewer hands, and large monopolies would come to dominate the economy. The oversupply of labor created by these factors would drive down the wages of the working class and swell the ranks of the unemployed.

Alienated and driven to desperation by these conditions, the proletariat would "gain consciousness" by realizing the true source of their poverty and rise up in rebellion. They would carry out a revolution, seizing control of the state and the economy. Marx saw this process not simply as a national phenomenon but also as an international one. When the conditions were right, he hypothesized, revolution would spread among all the capitalist countries, sweeping away this unjust order.

Once world revolution had taken place, Marx foresaw, there would be a temporary "dictatorship of the proletariat," during which the last vestiges of capitalism, particularly the old remnants of the superstructure, would be swept away. After the institutions of capitalism had been decisively eliminated, the institutions of the state itself would begin to "wither away." There would be no more need for laws or police, because all people would share equally in the fruits of labor. No longer would there be a need for armies or flags, because people would be united in equality rather than blinded by the false consciousness of nationalism. People would live in a stateless world, and history, which in Marx's view had been driven by exploitation and class struggle, would essentially come to an end. Only then could a person actually speak of "communism"—which is why communist parties would usually describe their own countries as "socialist," since they were still controlled by the state. To further this confusion, in the advanced democracies people often use the word *socialism* interchangeably with *social democracy*. However, most contemporary social democrats view socialism as an end stage, where the state

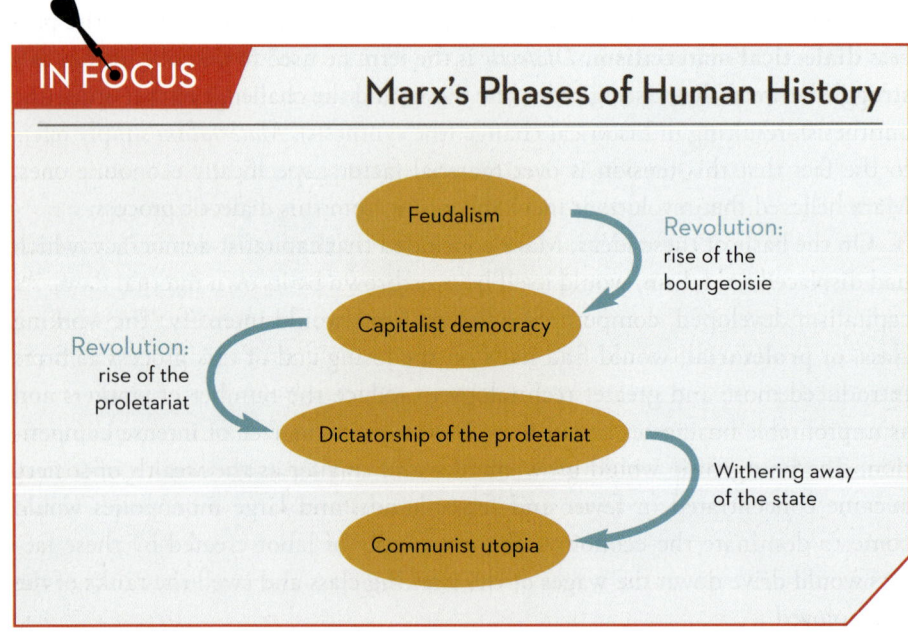

IN FOCUS

Marx's Phases of Human History

Feudalism

Revolution: rise of the bourgeoisie

Capitalist democracy

Revolution: rise of the proletariat

Dictatorship of the proletariat

Withering away of the state

Communist utopia

exercises significant but not total control over the economy. For communists, however, socialism is a transitional phase toward a time when private property and the state no longer exist.

Putting Communism into Practice

Communism thus provides an entire worldview, explaining the course of human history and the inevitable ascent into utopia as the products of economic interaction. As we know, such a sweeping theory has proved compelling for many people, especially those who sought to put Marx's ideas into practice.

Two of the most notable followers of Marx's ideas were Vladimir Ilyich Ulyanov, more commonly known as Lenin, and Mao Zedong. Lenin and Mao came to lead communist revolutions in Russia (1917) and China (1949), respectively. Yet although both were inspired by Marx, they departed from his ideas by seeking to carry out revolution in two countries that were weakly industrialized and far from being capitalist. Marx had argued that revolution would occur only where and when capitalism was most advanced and thus most prone to collapse; however, at the end of his life he did hold out the possibility that revolution could occur in less developed Russia, in contradiction to his own theories.[3] Lenin in particular believed that revolution could be carried out in less advanced countries if leaders constructed a **vanguard of the proletariat**—his term for a small revolutionary movement that could seize power on behalf of the people, who may lack the consciousness necessary to rise up.[4] This approach meant that in reality, communism spread where the level of economic development was relatively low—exactly the opposite of what Marx had originally theorized.

Yet even as the number of communist regimes grew, they faced a common quandary: how exactly to go about building communism. Marx had left no blueprint for what to do once the revolution had succeeded. In many ways, communists assumed that the revolution was the difficult part and that what should occur afterward would unfold as a matter of course. In part because Marx provided no specific outline for how communism should be built, the institutions that were created varied widely. Most were based on forms first built in the Soviet Union after 1917. Because they desired to fundamentally reshape human relations, communist states accrued a high level of autonomy and capacity; their regimes have at times become totalitarian in their drive to transform virtually all basic human institutions.

The task of this transformation was entrusted to the communist elite who came to direct and staff the state.[5] At its apex, political power rested within the

Communist Party, a relatively small "vanguard" organization (typically comprising less than 10 percent of the population) whose leading role in the country was typically written directly into the constitution—meaning that there was no constitutional way to remove the party from power. Because the Communist Party embodied what it saw as the "correct" view of human history and future relations, alternative organizations and ideologies making up civil society were seen as hostile to communism and were repressed.

Still, as we discussed in Chapter 6 on nondemocratic regimes, no system of rule can survive through the threat of force alone. Communist parties maintained control over society not only through repression but also by carefully allocating power throughout the country's various political, social, and economic institutions—a thorough form of co-optation. This strategy can be seen clearly in the **nomenklatura**, politically sensitive or influential jobs in the state, society, or economy that were staffed by people chosen or approved by the Communist Party. The nomenklatura encompassed a wide range of important positions: the head of a university, the editor of a newspaper, a military officer, a film director. Not surprisingly, party approval often required party membership, making joining the party the easiest way to prove one's loyalty and rise up the career ladder. Party membership could also bring other benefits: better housing, the ability to travel abroad, or access to scarce consumer goods. As a result, party membership was often driven more by opportunism than by idealism; many joined so that they could pursue certain careers or simply gain the benefits that party membership could buy.[6]

The dominant role played by the Communist Party and the nomenklatura created a power relationship different from those in democratic and many other nondemocratic systems. Rather than being centered within the state and government, power rested within the party. For example, when observers referred to the "leader" of a communist country, they were usually referring not to a government official but to the general secretary of the Communist Party. Indeed, top party leaders often did not hold any important formal position within the state. Though the political systems in communist countries by and large resembled those we see elsewhere in the world, typically with a prime minister or president, a parliament, a judiciary, and local government, all these positions were part of the nomenklatura and thus staffed by party members appointed by the party leaders. Although the trappings of democracy, such as parliamentary elections, typically existed, electoral candidates were almost exclusively Communist Party members with no real competition. Moreover, parliaments and other organs of power were little more than rubber-stamp institutions, approving decisions sent down the party hierarchy.

IN FOCUS: Important Figures in Communism

Karl Marx (1818-83) First philosopher to systematically construct a theory explaining why capitalism would fail and be replaced by communism; father of modern communist thought.

Lenin (Vladimir Ilyich Ulyanov) (1870-1924) Applied Marxist thought to Russia, leading a successful revolution in 1917; modified Marxist ideas by arguing that revolution would occur not in most-developed societies but rather in struggling countries such as Russia.

Joseph Stalin (Josef Vissarionovich Dzhugashvili) (1878-1953) Succeeded Lenin as leader of the Soviet Union; embarked on rapid industrialization of the country, modifying Marxism to argue that socialism could be built within just a single country; extended communism to Eastern Europe after World War II; denounced by Nikita Khrushchev in 1956 for his use of a personality cult and terror.

Mao Zedong (1893-1976) Led the Chinese Communist Party and fought against Chinese rivals and Japanese occupiers during World War II; modified communism to focus on the peasantry instead of the working class, given the primarily agrarian nature of China; unleashed the Cultural Revolution in 1966 to weaken the party and increase his own power.

Deng Xiaoping (1904-97) Fought with Mao Zedong against Chinese nationalists and Japanese occupiers during World War II; named general secretary of the Chinese Communist Party in 1956; stripped of all posts during the Cultural Revolution, but emerged as the country's leader after Mao's death; pursued economic liberalization in the 1980s and supported repression of the Tiananmen Square protests.

Fidel Castro (1926-2016) Led the Cuban Revolution in 1959 and defended the communist system against anticommunist forces and U.S. opposition; continued to defend Cuban socialism despite the collapse of the Soviet Union and other communist regimes in Eastern Europe.

Mikhail Gorbachev (1931-) Made general secretary of the Communist Party of the Soviet Union in 1985; initiated the twin policies of perestroika (economic restructuring) and glasnost (political liberalization), which eventually led to increasing discord within the country and a failed coup attempt by hard-line communists who opposed further reform; the resulting dissolution of the Soviet Union left Gorbachev without a country to lead.

As for the party itself, in many ways it intentionally mirrored the state. A general secretary served as chief executive, and a **Politburo** (short for "Political Bureau") and **Central Committee** acted as a kind of cabinet and legislature, respectively, shaping national policy and confirming the decisions of the party leadership. Below the Central Committee, various other bodies extended all the way down to individual places of work or residence, where party members were assigned to basic party organizations called *cells*. These cells were ostensibly intended to represent the interests of the people, but they were primarily mechanisms used by the party to closely monitor the population. Traditionally, the party held a congress every few years. At these meetings, delegates sent from the cells elected the party leadership, but these elections were little more than confirmations of those already in power. Outside the party and state, a limited number of organizations, such as unions, were allowed to function; these were in turn linked to the state and party, completing this highly corporatist structure that included sanctioned organizations for all facets of society.

While the party and its nomenklatura controlled key organizations, communist ideology shaped policy and sought to legitimize authoritarian control. Based fundamentally on the theories of Marx as adapted by Lenin and Mao, communist ideology focused on eliminating inequality and promoting economic development. Because of the expansive nature of communist ideology and its promise of a future utopia, it was, perhaps more than the other ideologies we discussed in Chapter 3, a secular "religion." It required unquestioning faith in a set of beliefs and sacrifice for a future reward and boasted its own collection of holy texts, shrines, saints, martyrs, and devils. Adherents venerated charismatic leaders who served as prophets of communism, such as Lenin, Mao, Joseph Stalin, and Fidel Castro. Many charismatic communist leaders reinforced their position through elaborate personality cults, as we discussed earlier.

The quest for and exercise of this monopoly on power, as expressed through the nomenklatura and through the party's deep penetration of the state and society down to the most basic level of home and work, proved to be dangerous and even lethal. In the first decades of communist rule in the Soviet Union, China, and Eastern Europe, the party used terror to eliminate opposition and maintain control. Tens of millions perished, especially in the Soviet Union under Stalin and in China under Mao.

Under Stalin's rule, many people were purged from the Soviet Communist Party and executed for imaginary crimes. These were not cases of mistaken punishment: Stalin used terror and victimized symbolic "criminals" as a way to intimidate the Communist Party and the population as a whole.[7] Similarly, in China, Mao unleashed the Cultural Revolution in the late 1960s, encouraging the public (students, in particular) to attack any institution or individual that was either a remnant of precommunist China or lacked revolutionary zeal. Mao's targets included the **party-state**, which he believed had grown conservative over time and was restricting his power—indeed, his notable slogan was "Bombard the party headquarters." During the next decade, countless Chinese died, books were burned, art was destroyed, and cultural relics were demolished—all for the crime of being "reactionary."[8]

Communist Political Economy

If the Communist Party's singular quest for power led, in the cases of Stalin and Mao, to its gross abuse, the centralization of economic power similarly created problems that Marxist theory did not anticipate. Communist political-economic systems shared a set of institutions fundamentally different from liberal, mercantilist, or social-democratic alternatives, for the state had essentially absorbed both markets and property.[9]

Because the state held the means of production, many of the typical aspects of capitalism that we take for granted—individual profit, unemployment, competition between firms, bankruptcy—were eliminated. Individuals lost their right to control property, including their own labor; the party-state made the decisions about how these resources should be used. Communist leaders redirected national wealth toward the goal of collective equality through such mechanisms as industrialization and social expenditures. Several million died in the Soviet Union in the 1930s during the forced collectivization of agriculture. An attempt at rapid industrialization and the collectivization of agriculture during the Great Leap Forward in China (1958–60) led to some 45 million famine deaths. As Mao himself put it, "When there is not enough to eat people starve to death. It is better to let half of the people die so that the other half can eat their fill."[10]

IN FOCUS: Communist Political Economy

- Markets and property are wholly absorbed by the state.
- Central planning replaces the market mechanism.
- Individual property rights, individual profit, unemployment, competition between firms, and bankruptcy are all virtually eliminated.
- Most of the nation's means of production are nationalized.
- The economy functions in essence as a single large firm whose sole employees are the public.
- The state provides extensive public goods and social services, including universal systems of public education, health care, and retirement.
- Inequality and poverty are reduced but not eliminated.

Along with private property, communist systems also eliminated the market forces of supply and demand, believing that these factors were incapable of equitably distributing wealth. Communist countries largely chose to replace the market with the state bureaucracy, which explicitly allocated resources by planning what should be produced and in what amounts, setting the final prices of these goods, and deciding where they should be sold. This system is known as **central planning**.

As might be imagined, planning an entire economy is an extremely difficult task. And communist planners found the task of matching up all the inputs and outputs necessary for producing goods overwhelming. There are simply too many things to plan—in the Soviet Union, for instance, the materials included some 40,000 to 50,000 kinds of physical items—and there are too many unforeseen outcomes, such as a factory failing to deliver its full output or needing to adjust to a change in demand. Because most entities in an economy are interdependent, small problems can have a huge effect on the entire plan. A miscalculation resulting in the underproduction of steel, for example, would have disastrous effects on all those goods dependent on steel, some of which would themselves be components in other finished goods. Central planning, with its emphasis on industrialization, also focused less on consumer goods, leaving things like televisions and cars in short supply.

Another problem encountered in centrally planned economies was the lack of worker incentives. Factories and farms were unconcerned about the quality of their goods, since central planners simply indicated a numerical quota they had to fulfill. Workers did not have to fear losing their jobs or factories going out of business thanks to shoddy work, because under communism employment was guaranteed and firms, being owned by the state, could not go bankrupt. This structure explains in part why all communist countries eventually fell behind economically. In the absence of competition and incentives, innovation and efficiency disappeared, leaving these systems to stagnate.

As we consider these changes, a final question is whether communist institutions eliminated poverty and inequality as they claimed. Under communism the Gini index for the Soviet Union and other European communist states was under 30—extremely low, even in comparison with social democracies. Moreover, widespread social expenditures, from roads and electricity to health care and pensions, lifted millions out of severe poverty. At the same time, these benefits were unevenly distributed. Rural areas and regions with ethnic minorities often were far less developed, and poverty never truly disappeared. In addition, members of the nomenklatura were able to use their political power to gain access to scarce goods, like better apartments, cars, or foreign travel. The absence of private property did not eliminate corruption. So while communism did create a more equal system, it did so at a high price, and significant elements of inequality remained.

Societal Institutions under Communism

In addition to reengineering politics and economics to eliminate the inequality and exploitation associated with capitalist systems, communist parties also sought to reorder human relations, hoping to sweep away the old superstructure held responsible for generating false consciousness. One aspect of this superstructure viewed with particular hostility was religion.

Marx is known for his oft-cited statement that "religion is the opiate of the masses." Like a drug, religion numbs its practitioners to their pain, in this case by promising them they will be rewarded in the afterlife for enduring their present suffering, thus legitimizing the inequality and poverty perpetuated by the superstructure. As a result, in most communist countries religion was strongly suppressed. In the Soviet Union, most places of worship were closed, converted to other uses, or torn down. In China during the Cultural Revolution, temples and other religious shrines were destroyed. Even where religion was tolerated to a greater extent, it was directly controlled or its practitioners were harassed by the Communist Party.

Marxists also viewed traditional gender relations as a function of capitalism—specifically, as a microcosm of class relations. Men exploit women through the family structure, just as the bourgeoisie exploit the proletariat, and sexual morality serves as a means to perpetuate this gender inequality. Communism envisioned complete economic, social, and political equality between men and women. Even the repressive institution of marriage, like the state, would fade away, replaced by what Marx called "an openly legalized community of free love."[11]

In spite of Marxist ideals, gender relations only partially changed under communist rule. In most communist countries, women were given many more opportunities than they had experienced previously. To promote industrialization, communist parties encouraged women to enter the workforce and to increase their education. Most countries also enacted liberal divorce and abortion laws and provided social benefits such as state-run child care. Despite these changes, however, women's traditional roles as housekeepers and mothers did not change. The "new socialist woman" was not complemented by a "new socialist man." Traditional patterns of sexism persisted, and women found themselves burdened by the double duty of work inside and outside the home. In addition, while many women worked in important occupations, few rose to positions of any significant political or economic power. Men continued to dominate the top ranks of the party membership, the state, and the economy.[12]

A final aspect of society that communist countries sought to change was national and ethnic identity. As part of the superstructure, nationalism and ethnicity were seen as mechanisms by which the ruling elite pitted the working classes of different countries against one another to divide and rule them. With the advent of the world communist revolution, such divisions were expected to disappear, to be replaced by equality and harmony among all peoples. As a result, communist parties tended to reject any overt expressions of nationalism and ethnicity, though national and ethnic identities often lurked beneath the surface. For example, encompassed within the vast Soviet Union were many ethnic groups, although the Communist Party tended to be dominated by Russians, who made up the single largest ethnic group. Many non-Russians resented this Russian domination. Many Eastern Europeans also viewed communist rule as little more than Russian

IN FOCUS

Societal Institutions under Communism

INSTITUTION	IDEAL	REALITY
RELIGION	Religion, "the opiate of the masses," will disappear.	Religion was suppressed but not eliminated.
GENDER ROLES	Men and women will be economically, socially, and politically equal.	Opportunities for women increased, but women were still expected to fulfill traditional duties in the home.
SEXUALITY	Repressive institutions such as marriage will be replaced by "an openly legalized system of free love."	Many communist countries remained very sexually conservative.
NATIONALISM	Nationalism, exposed as part of the elite's "divide and conquer" strategy, will be eliminated.	Though discouraged from doing so, people clung to old national and ethnic identities.

imperialism; their national identities were therefore sharpened, not erased. This simmering nationalism played an important role in the fall of communism in Eastern Europe and the Soviet Union as well as in the politics thereafter.

The Collapse of Communism

In retrospect, it may seem obvious that communism was bound to fail. And yet on the eve of its collapse in Europe, few expected that it would happen anytime soon. Two factors played an important role in bringing about communism's sudden decline.

The first was the reemergence of Cold War struggles between the Soviet Union and the United States. After the tense decades of the 1950s and 1960s, which were marked by international competition, arms races, and harrowing events such as the Cuban missile crisis, the United States and the Soviet Union settled into a period of détente, in which peaceful coexistence became the main goal. But détente lasted less than a decade. The Soviet Union's invasion of Afghanistan in 1979 to prop up the failing communist regime there and the election of Ronald Reagan as president of the United States in 1980 soured relations between the two countries. Reagan, who viewed the Soviet Union as an "evil empire," embarked on a new policy of military buildup. Growing economic stagnation made it difficult for the Soviet Union to meet this expensive challenge.

At the same time that the United States and the Soviet Union entered a new and costly stage of the Cold War, a new generation of political leaders rose to power in the Soviet Union. Among them was Mikhail Gorbachev, who was chosen as general secretary of the Communist Party in 1985. Unlike his predecessors, Gorbachev recognized the stagnation of the Soviet system and understood the cost of a new arms race. He thus proposed reforming international relations and domestic politics and thereby revitalizing both the Soviet Union and communist thought.

At the domestic level, Gorbachev initiated the twin policies of glasnost (openness) and perestroika (restructuring), with the intention of liberalizing and reforming communism. **Glasnost** encouraged public debate with the hope that a frank discussion of the system's shortcomings would help foster change and increase the legitimacy of the regime. **Perestroika**, or actual institutional reforms in the economy and political system, would flow from this critique. These reforms were expected to include some limited forms of democratic participation and market-based incentives in the economy. Moderate reform, not wholesale transformation, was Gorbachev's goal.

In the international arena, Gorbachev similarly proposed widespread, if moderate, changes. To reduce the Soviet Union's military burdens and improve relations with Western countries, he began to loosen his country's control over Eastern Europe, which had been under the thumb of the Soviet Union since the end of World War II. Gorbachev hoped that some limited liberalization in the region would ease tensions with Europe and the United States, enabling expanded trade and other economic ties.

Nevertheless, as Alexis de Tocqueville famously wrote about the French monarchy, the most dangerous moment for a bad government is usually when it begins to reform itself. Glasnost encouraged public debate, but rather than simply criticize corruption among the nomenklatura or the quality or absence of consumer goods, as Gorbachev expected, people began to challenge the very nature of the political system. Ethnic groups within the Soviet Union and citizens of Eastern European states also used glasnost to agitate for greater freedom from Russian domination.

Perestroika had similarly unexpected effects. By seeking political and economic reform, Gorbachev threatened those within the party who had long benefited from the status quo. Political leaders, administrators, factory bosses, and many other nomenklatura members resisted reform, taking a stance that led to infighting and instability. This problem was compounded by the uncertainty over how far Gorbachev's reforms would go. Confusion deepened within the party, the state, and society about where communism and the Soviet Union were heading.

Meanwhile, among the Soviet Union's satellite states change was proceeding faster than anyone expected. In 1989, civil society rapidly reasserted itself across Eastern Europe as people used Gorbachev's new hands-off policy to oppose their countries' communist regimes, demanding open elections and an end to one-party rule. Eastern European Communist Party leaders, realizing that the Soviet Union would no longer intervene militarily to support them, had little choice but to acquiesce. As a result, by 1990 communists had been swept from their monopolies on power across the region. In most cases, this regime change was largely peaceful.

The Soviet Union would not be far behind. By 1991, the country was in deep turmoil: limited reforms had increased the public's appetite for greater change, the end of communism in Eastern Europe further emboldened opposition within the Soviet Union, and ethnic conflict and nationalism were on the rise as various groups sought political power.[13] Communist hard-liners eventually tried to stop the reform process through a coup d'état intended to seize power and detain Gorbachev. However, these leaders lacked the support of important actors, such as the military, and public demonstrations helped bring the poorly planned coup to an end.[14]

TIMELINE

Communist History

1848	Karl Marx and Friedrich Engels write *The Communist Manifesto*, a central document in communist thought.
1917	Vladimir Lenin leads the Russian Revolution, creating the Soviet Union as the world's first communist country.
1930s	Joseph Stalin begins to arrest and execute Soviet Communist Party members and others to consolidate power.
1945	The Soviet Army occupies Eastern Europe, imposing communist regimes; tensions between the United States and the Soviet Union lead to the Cold War.
1949	The Chinese Communist Party, led by Mao Zedong, gains control over mainland China.
1953	Stalin dies.
1956	Nikita Khrushchev denounces Stalin's use of terror and allows limited open debate; protests in Hungary lead to open revolution against communism; Hungarian revolution put down by the Soviet Army.
1966–76	Mao unleashes the Cultural Revolution in China; the student "Red Guard" attacks symbols of precommunism and party leaders accused of having grown too conservative.
1976	Mao Zedong dies; China and the United States begin to improve relations; Deng Xiaoping rises to power and starts to enact widespread economic reforms.
1985	Mikhail Gorbachev becomes general secretary of the Soviet Communist Party and begins economic and political reforms.
1989	Student protests for political reform in China's Tiananmen Square are crushed by the military.
1989–90	Eastern Europeans seize on reforms in the Soviet Union to press for dramatic political change; largely peaceful political protests lead to free elections and the elimination of communist rule in Eastern Europe.
1991	Increasing turmoil in the Soviet Union leads communist conservatives to oust Gorbachev and seize power; the coup fails because of weak military support and public demonstrations; the Soviet Union breaks into 15 separate states.

Following the failed coup, the individual republics that formed the Soviet Union broke apart. Some of this was the logical result of nationalist, secessionist movements. In addition, Communist Party elites in many republics saw this as a chance to hang on to power as the leaders of new, sovereign states. Fifteen new independent countries were created, of which Russia is but one. But communism did not collapse everywhere. Although 1989 marked liberalization and the first moves toward democracy in Eastern Europe and the Soviet Union, similar protests in China that year, led by students and encouraged by Gorbachev's example, were met with deadly military force in Tiananmen Square, Beijing. Communist leaders in China did not heed public demands for reform and political liberalization and showed themselves both willing and able to use the army to violently quell peaceful protests. Why did the Soviet Union and China go down such different paths? We will turn to this question at the end of the chapter (see "Institutions in Action," p. 310).

The Transformation of Political Institutions

So far, we have discussed the communist theory regarding the origins of and solutions to inequality, the difficulties in translating theory into reality, and how institutions controlled by the state unraveled across most of the communist world. Yet although the downfall of communism was dramatic, what followed was no less awesome. Postcommunist countries faced, and continue to face, the challenge of building new political, economic, and social institutions to strike a new balance between freedom and equality. Simultaneous transformation of all three areas is unprecedented, and this task has met with varying degrees of success.

Reorganizing the State and Constructing a Democratic Regime

An underlying task in the transition from communism has been to reorganize the state in terms of its autonomy and capacity. Under communism, the party-state was able to dominate virtually all aspects of human relations without any effective check. But with the collapse of communism, the party was ejected from its leading role in political life. This left many formerly communist countries with a sprawling, if not always powerful or particularly legitimate, postcommunist state that did not embody the rule of law.

Postcommunist countries have also faced the prospect of building democratic regimes where authoritarianism has long been the norm. This project requires numerous tasks: creating a separation of powers between branches of government, choosing between different kinds of executive and legislative institutions, establishing electoral laws and regulating political parties, and doing all of this in a way that generates support among most of the actors in society.

Civil rights and civil liberties have been a final area of concern. As we discussed in Chapter 5, *civil rights* refers to the promotion of equality, whereas *civil liberties* refers to the promotion of freedom, though the two overlap. Civil rights and liberties include such things as free speech and equal treatment under the law. Under communism, constitutions typically established an elaborate set of civil liberties, though in reality they were largely ignored by those in power. With the collapse of communism, the challenge has been to expand and protect these once-hollow rights and liberties. This has meant not only strengthening the rule of law so that those rights could be enforced but also deciding what kinds of rights and liberties should be enshrined in the constitution and who should be the final arbiter of disputes over them. The role of constitutional courts has been an important issue in countries where traditionally the judiciary had been neither powerful nor independent.

Evaluating Political Transitions

Nearly three decades have passed since communism collapsed in Eastern Europe and the former Soviet Union. How have the postcommunist countries' political transitions fared? The picture is mixed. In Chapter 6, we looked at the data from Freedom House, which ranks countries on a 0-to-100 freedom scale, scoring the most-free countries as 100 and the least free as 0. This ranking is based on such considerations as electoral competition, freedoms of speech and assembly, rule of law, levels of corruption, and protection of human and economic rights.

A number of postcommunist countries have made dramatic strides toward democracy and the rule of law, to such an extent that Freedom House now considers them consolidated democracies—meaning that their democratic regimes have been ranked highly on the Freedom House scale for a decade or so and are therefore stable and largely institutionalized. Most of these democracies can be found in Central Europe (including Poland, the Czech Republic, Slovakia, and Slovenia) and the Baltics (Estonia, Latvia, and Lithuania), areas that share a precommunist history of greater economic development, civil society, democratic institutions, and experience with the rule of law. They also enjoyed more contact with Western Europe and a shorter period of communist rule. All of these factors may help explain why democratic transition in these regions has been more successful and culminated in EU membership. Interestingly, this move to democracy also indicates the power of precommunist institutions despite the best efforts of communist regimes to eradicate them. In contrast, the Balkan countries of Southern Europe (such as Romania, Bulgaria, Croatia, and Serbia) have lagged further behind in the quality of their democratic institutions.

Table 9.2 provides an evaluation of postcommunist countries on political rights and civil liberties, where a rating of 1 represents the most democratic and 7 the least. As noted above, democracy has tended to be stronger in the Central European countries and Baltic countries than in the Balkans. Nevertheless, a critical variable remains the kinds of choices made by elites during the transition process and afterward. Thus the Balkans, after two decades of civil conflict and the persistence of communist elites, lately have seen marked improvement in their democratic practices. Why? One important explanation is the European Union's expansion into this region: Romania and Bulgaria joined in 2007, Croatia joined in 2013, and Montenegro and North Macedonia are currently negotiating membership. This "EU anchor," as it has been termed, has played an important role in institutionalizing democratic norms as a condition for membership. But we should not overstate the power of the European Union in this regard. As we noted, democracy scores have steadily eroded in Hungary, an EU member since 2004 and once considered a leader in postcommunist democratization. Given the recent turmoil in the European Union (see Chapter 8), the extent to which this organization will continue to shape or reinforce democratic norms among and beyond its members is an open question.

As we move eastward from the European Union the situation is less promising. In many of the former Soviet states, including Russia, democracy is illiberal and weakly institutionalized or completely absent. These countries tend to be poorer, and they have little historical experience of democracy because of a long period of imperial Russian and Soviet control. In many of them, authoritarian leaders, often from the communist nomenklatura, have consolidated power in strong presidencies, limiting the possibility for power sharing and democratic accountability. Democratic rights and freedoms are restricted, civil society is weak, and those in power have enriched themselves through corrupt practices. Support for democracy across the former Soviet Union is often very weak, as we can see from the examples in Table 9.3. Most worrisome, in Central Europe, the Balkans, and the former Soviet Union, average democracy scores have declined each year since 2004.[15]

TABLE 9.2 — Democratic Progress in Selected Communist and Postcommunist Systems, 2019

1 = MOST DEMOCRATIC; 7 = LEAST DEMOCRATIC

COUNTRY	POLITICAL RIGHTS	CIVIL LIBERTIES	COUNTRY	POLITICAL RIGHTS	CIVIL LIBERTIES
Czech Republic	1	1	North Macedonia	4	3
Estonia	1	1	Kosovo	3	4
Lithuania	1	1	Moldova	3	4
Slovenia	1	1	Ukraine	3	4
Croatia	1	2	Armenia	4	4
Slovakia	1	2	Bosnia-Herzegovina	4	4
Bulgaria	2	2	Kyrgyzstan	5	4
Latvia	2	2	Kazakhstan	7	5
Poland	2	2	Azerbaijan	7	6
Romania	2	2	Belarus	7	6
Albania	3	3	Russia	7	6
Georgia	3	3	Tajikistan	7	6
Hungary	3	3	Turkmenistan	7	7
Serbia	3	3	Uzbekistan	7	6
Montenegro	4	3			

Source: Freedom House, *Freedom in the World 2019*, https://freedomhouse.org/report/countries-world-freedom-2019 (accessed 2/9/20).

TABLE 9.3 Support for Authoritarianism, 2010–2014

**HAVING A STRONG LEADER WHO DOES NOT HAVE TO BOTHER WITH PARLIAMENT AND ELECTIONS IS...
(PERCENTAGE ANSWERING)**

COUNTRY	VERY/FAIRLY GOOD	BAD/VERY BAD
Poland	22%	78%
Azerbaijan	23	77
Estonia	32	68
Slovenia	32	68
China	42	58
Belarus	47	53
Ukraine	71	29
Romania	75	25
Russia	76	24
Kyrgyzstan	82	18

Source: World Values Survey, 2014.

Outside Eastern Europe and the former Soviet Union, democracy has been even slower to spread, and communist regimes in China, Laos, Vietnam, North Korea, and Cuba continue to hold on to power. In some cases, like North Korea and Cuba, opposition to liberalization has helped maintain the status quo, though at the cost of a severely stunted economy. China and Vietnam (and to a lesser extent Laos) have opted instead for economic reform without political change as a way to maintain the Communist Party's hold on power.

Elsewhere in Asia and in Africa, communist regimes have given way, but such events have often resulted in state collapse and civil war. The most notable of these is Afghanistan. On the Soviet Union's withdrawal from that country in 1989, civil war raged until 1996, when the Taliban gained power over most of the country, paving the way for the eventual establishment of Al Qaeda. The legacies of communism and the Cold War in these regions are significant.

The Transformation of Economic Institutions

In addition to transforming the state and the regime, transitions from communism have confronted the task of reestablishing some separation between the state and the economy. This work involves two processes: privatization, or the transfer of state-held property into private hands, and marketization, or the re-creation of market forces of supply and demand. In both cases, decisions about how to carry out these changes and to what end were influenced by different political-economic alternatives. Let's consider the ways of approaching privatization and marketization before we investigate the different paths postcommunist countries have taken in each area.

Privatization and Marketization

The transition from communism to capitalism requires a redefinition of property. To generate economic growth and limit the power of the state, the state must reentrust economic resources to the public, placing them back into private hands. But the task of privatization is neither easy nor clear. In fact, before 1989 no country had ever gone from a communist economy to a capitalist one, so no model existed.

Among the many questions and concerns facing the postcommunist countries was how to place prices on the various elements of the economy—factories, shops,

IN FOCUS: Reestablishing Separation of State and Economy

- Privatization: the transfer of state-held property into private hands.
- Marketization: the re-creation of the market forces of supply and demand.

land, apartments. To privatize these assets, the state first must determine their value, something difficult in a system where no market has existed. And who should get these assets? Should they be given away? Sold to the highest bidder? Made available to foreign investors? Each option has its own advantages in developing a thriving economy but also risks increasing inequality and generating public resentment.

Privatization was carried out in several different ways, depending on the country and its economic assets. Small businesses, like restaurants or retail shops, were often sold directly to their employees, and some countries also sold many large businesses, like automobile manufacturers, to the highest bidders—often foreign investors. Other countries essentially distributed shares in firms to the public as a whole. Scholars debated the benefits of each model; but in the end each form, whether alone or in combination, was shown to work well in some circumstances and badly in others.

No matter what the privatization process, ultimately postcommunist countries included many firms that were overstaffed, outdated, and unable to turn a profit in a market economy. Most problematic were very large industrial firms, such as coal mines and steel plants built in the early years of industrialization; these antiquated behemoths could not compete in the international market. Such firms often needed to be sold or radically downsized, leading to unemployment in a society where employment had previously been guaranteed. Such firms sometimes employed thousands of people and represented the main source of work in a city or region. As a result, in some countries privatization proceeded slowly and unevenly for fear of widespread unemployment and resulting social unrest.

Along with re-creating private property, states needed to re-create a market in which property, labor, goods, and services could all function in a competitive environment that would determine their value. On the surface, marketization appears easier than privatization—a simple matter of eliminating central planning and allowing the market to resurface naturally. But marketization, too, is complicated. One issue of debate concerned how rapidly marketization should take place. Some argued that given the profound nature of the economic transformation in postcommunist states, changes should be gradual to minimize any social disruptions that might undermine these fledgling economies and democracies. In particular, supporters of this "gradualism" feared that sudden marketization would lead to a wild jump in prices as sellers became able to charge whatever they wanted for their goods. Inflation and even hyperinflation could result, undermining confidence in the transition process and generating widespread poverty. Others rejected these arguments, advocating rapid market reforms that would free prices and bring an end to central planning and state subsidies for businesses virtually overnight—a policy known as **shock therapy**. Such changes would be painful and might initially trigger high rates of inflation, but the pain would end sooner than that accompanying gradualism.

In choosing particular forms of privatization and marketization, postcommunist countries adopted new political-economic models—some gravitating toward the social-democratic models of Western Europe, others to the liberalism of the United States and the United Kingdom, and still others to more mercantilist policies.

Evaluating Economic Transitions

How successful have all of these reforms been? The answer again depends on what country we are evaluating. Table 9.4 shows some of the results of over 30 years of transition. A number of countries are now as wealthy as some poorer noncommunist European states, such as Greece and Portugal. In contrast, many of the former Soviet republics have not done nearly as well. Why this variation? The countries that have done particularly well have benefited from many of the factors we discussed earlier: shorter periods of Soviet control; more precommunist experience with industrialization, markets, and private property; closer ties with Western Europe; and strong support from the European Union, including membership. Stronger democratic institutions have also led to better judicial structures that can stem corruption and protect property rights.

The countries that have done less well experienced just the opposite. In these countries, freeing up markets often led to uncontrollable inflation and a rapid decline in the standard of living. These problems were compounded by the way privatization was carried out. Many of the most valuable assets fell into the hands of the old nomenklatura or a few private individuals, typically supported by corrupt political leaders. Some countries that have done well, such as Russia and Azerbaijan, owe their economic success to natural resources (oil and gas) rather than to the development of a private sector, reflecting the problem of the resource curse we spoke of in Chapter 6. A theme running through all these cases is the correlation between economic growth and the rule of law. Where the rule of law is weak, economic transition is much less successful because entrepreneurs (both domestic and international) lack a predictable environment in which to invest, while political leaders and state officials use their positions to siphon off resources for themselves. All of the resource-rich post-Soviet states suffer levels of corruption similar to what we see in the poorer parts of Africa.

Overall, postcommunist countries have seen an increase in inequality, poverty, and unemployment, which is to be expected as markets and private property become central economic forces. Where this process has been balanced by economic prosperity for most of the population, support for change has been stronger.

TABLE 9.4 — Economic Indicators in Selected Communist and Postcommunist Countries, 2019

COUNTRY	PER CAPITA GDP, 2019 (PPP US $)	PER CAPITA GDP, 1989–90 (PPP US $)	TRANSPARENCY INTERNATIONAL CORRUPTION RANK (1 = LEAST CORRUPT)
Slovenia	38,000	10,400	35
Portugal*	33,400	11,800	30
Poland	33,300	6,000	41
Hungary	31,100	8,500	70
Latvia	30,300	7,800	44
Greece*	29,600	13,200	60
Romania	28,200	5,200	70
Russia	27,100	8,000	137
China	18,300	1,000	80
Azerbaijan	18,000	5,500	126
Albania	13,400	2,700	106
Georgia	12,000	5,200	44
Ukraine	9,200	6,700	126
Moldova	7,300	4,200	120

*Greece and Portugal, non-postcommunist countries, are included for comparison.

Source: World Bank, https://data.worldbank.org/indicator/NY.GDP.PCAP.PP.CD (accessed 2/9/20); Transparency International, https://transparency.org/country (accessed 2/9/20).

Where a significant part of the population has felt worse off, as in parts of the former Soviet Union, economic change has bred resentment, nostalgia for the old order, and obstacles to democratization. A notable example is Russia, where during the last decade many large industries and natural resources have been renationalized and mercantilist economic policies have been adopted. This nostalgia also ties into Russia's resurgent nationalism and its military involvement in Ukraine.

In general, most postcommunist countries will struggle to maintain the high level of growth necessary to close the gap between themselves and the developed democracies. The rapid growth experienced during the last decade has declined due in part to global economic difficulties, and this has increased skepticism of economic and political reform. It has also increased the appeal of populist and nationalist leaders, thereby undercutting democracy.

Outside of Eastern Europe and the former Soviet Union, the success rate of economic transition has been equally varied. Much attention has focused on China, which is still controlled by a communist party but in many ways can be thought of as "postcommunist" in its economic system. Since the 1970s, China's reforms have included a dramatic expansion of private business and agriculture, all with the support of the Chinese Communist Party. The slogan of this set of economic reforms—"to get rich is glorious"—sounds anything but Marxist, and it is rooted in the practical realization that earlier drives for rapid economic growth led to disaster. Some observers argue that these reforms have succeeded where those in many other communist and postcommunist countries have failed because the Chinese introduced economic transition while restricting political change so as to better manage the course of reform. Indeed, since 1989 the Chinese economy has grown by leaps and bounds, lifting hundreds of millions out of poverty and dramatically transforming the country, not to mention world trade. As we will discuss in Chapter 11, in many ways the very idea of globalization is strongly tied to China's integration into the world market.

Yet the Chinese model has its own problems. Alongside economic growth and the development of a free market and private property, problems such as inflation, corruption, unemployment, and growing inequality have also surfaced, often exacerbated by the still-powerful presence of the state in the Chinese economy. The weakness of the rule of law only compounds these problems. China's rapid development has been profound; now the question is how strong the country will become. Some see in China a growing economic superpower that will eclipse the economies of much of Asia and perhaps the world. This development is fostering a middle class and civil society that many believe will pave the way for the democratization of one-fifth of the world's population. Indeed, levels of economic development in China now are not much different from those of South Korea and Taiwan when they transitioned to democracy. Others caution, however, that the Chinese "miracle" covers up serious problems like environmental damage. Economic development in China has also slowed, and the country must provide new economic opportunities for an increasingly well-educated population.[16] Domestic and international challenges mean that economic development in China is perhaps more uncertain now than at any time since reforms began in the 1980s.

The Transformation of Societal Institutions

Like political systems and economies, societies, too, have been fundamentally transformed in postcommunist countries. Where once communist control asserted a single unquestionable understanding of human relations and development, people now face a world much more uncertain and unclear. Individuals in postcommunist societies have the freedom to act more independently, but this potential carries with it greater risk. The elimination of an all-encompassing ideology from people's lives has created a social vacuum that must be filled. In all of these countries, the transition from communism has been a wrenching process as people adjust to new realities and seek new individual and collective identities.

Changing Identities

This transformation of society has manifested itself in various ways. Religion, once suppressed by communist parties, has reappeared in many countries. Public-opinion research conducted by the World Values Survey (see our discussion of political culture in Chapter 3) indicates that since 1989 religion has increased in prominence in many communist and postcommunist countries. A 1989–93 survey found that nearly 80 percent of Chinese said God was not at all important in their lives; as of 2010–14, that number had dropped to less than a third. Similar shifts can be seen in Russia and many other postcommunist countries. In postcommunist Europe, Christianity has resurfaced as an important force, often as part of nationalism rather than a private profession of faith. Islam has also reemerged in countries with traditionally large Muslim populations, much to the chagrin of leaders who are holdovers from the anti-religious Soviet era. In China, too, new and old religious movements are growing. Various Christian movements have gained ground, and Islam has regained its potency among Turkic peoples in far western China. The Communist Party itself has sought to increase its legitimacy by promoting Confucian ideals and practices that were once attacked as symbols of feudal oppression. The re-creation of religious institutions can provide social support during periods of political and economic disruption. It can also increase sectarianism and fundamentalism.

Like religion, ethnic and national identities have also reemerged as potent forms of identification. Levels of national pride have risen across many of those same states surveyed over the same time period. In many postcommunist countries, both leaders and publics have sought to instill national pride and resurrect the values, symbols, and ideas that bind people together. The scope of this task varies among the postcommunist countries. In much of Eastern Europe, a clear sense of ethnic and national identity has existed for many generations. Despite communist rule, many of these social structures not only remained intact but also were reinforced as a form of resistance to communism. In contrast, across the diverse ethnic groups of the former Soviet Union, national identity has historically been weaker or divided. Many of these peoples have more limited historical institutions to draw on, and their identities often rely on institutionalizing new symbols and myths. All such identities can be a double-edged sword, of course. (See "Questions and Methods" on pp. 316–17 for a discussion of how these concepts account for differences in transitions from communism.) Although they can help mobilize the public and provide stability in times of great transition, religious, ethnic, and national identities can also generate division and conflict. This is particularly true when several identities coexist in one country or spill across borders. Conflict between ethnic Chinese and the Muslim Turkic Uighur minority in western China is one such example.

The changes underway in social identities cannot help but affect gender relations as well. Recall our earlier discussion of how communist theory advanced the radical notion of gender equality. Although equality was not realized in practice, women were incorporated into the workforce and provided with social benefits that generated new opportunities for them. With the end of communism, however, many of these policies and institutions have been weakened or challenged. Critics have attacked many communist-era practices such as easy access to abortions, while economic reforms have cut back much of the elaborate social safety net that once benefited women and families. The reemergence of religion has also challenged women's roles in society in some cases. Authoritarianism may also be patriarchal, asserting that women's primary role in society is to be the mothers of the nation.

Finally, there is the question of gender identity and sexual orientation. Under communism, lesbian, gay, bisexual, and transgender (LGBT) identities were viewed as either psychological disorders or a result of capitalism's focus on hedonism and individualism. The decline of communism, however, allowed for these identities to enter the public sphere. This change has been met with varying degrees of resistance from some religious institutions and nationalists who view the LGBT community as a danger to their countries' moral health and sovereign values.

Evaluating Societal Transitions

Societal transformation among the postcommunist countries has been as varied as political and economic change. An initial, pessimistic take would be that the resurgence of national and religious identities has been a source of destabilization in these countries. There is certainly much evidence to justify this view. In Eastern Europe, the dissolution of Yugoslavia in the 1990s pitted ethnic and religious groups against one another, claiming more than 200,000 lives. Tajikistan, Uzbekistan, Moldova, Azerbaijan, and Armenia as well as the Russian region of Chechnya also saw violent religious and ethnic conflicts as the Soviet Union collapsed, again leading to several hundred thousand dead.

Another related factor is the way in which postcommunist identities have shaped international terrorism. In 1979, the Soviet Union invaded Afghanistan in order to prop up a communist regime on the verge of collapse; this led to a guerrilla movement that drew in support and recruits from around the world, including the Saudi Osama bin Laden, who would found Al Qaeda. Afghanistan would become a crucible for Islamic fundamentalist views that would spread around the world. And just as Afghanistan became magnets for Middle Eastern fighters in the 1980s, Syria and Iraq have become magnets for fighters from Russia and postcommunist Central Asia. Some of the strongest supporters of the Islamic State of Iraq and Sham (ISIS) have been young Muslims from countries of the former Soviet Union, radicalized by economic difficulties and religious and ethnic marginalization.

Finally, at the state level we see attempts to promote nationalism as a means to legitimize authoritarian rule, especially as ideological legitimacy has waned. In both Russia and China, political leaders stress the unique nature of their societies, which are under threat by outside forces, be they countries or values. This can contribute to ethnic and national conflict both within these countries and between them and their neighbors.

In spite of this, we should not go so far as to say that the legacy of communism is conflict. Ethnic and nationalist violence, while significant after 1989, has largely waned. Moreover, even as surveys document the importance of religion and nationalism, this does not necessarily result in a greater propensity for conflict. Indeed, the World Values Survey shows that publics are less likely to say they are willing to fight for their country now than they were 25 years ago. This is even true in countries like China and Russia, where nationalist values have been a strong component of regime legitimacy. In 1989–93, over 90 percent of Chinese said they were willing to fight for their country; in 2010–14, that number was below 75 percent. In Russia during that same period, willingness to fight declined from 68 percent to 53 percent. This is consistent with responses across the developed democracies, suggesting deeper societal changes in communist and postcommunist countries.

Gender relations in postcommunist countries are equally interesting. The World Economic Forum's Global Gender Gap Index (Table 9.5) measures inequality between women and men in four key areas: economic participation and

TABLE 9.5 — Global Gender Gap Index Rankings, 2020

COUNTRY	RANK	COUNTRY	RANK
Germany	10	Croatia	60
Latvia	11	Slovakia	63
Slovenia	12	Kazakhstan	72
France	15	Czech Republic	78
South Africa	17	Russia	81
Canada	19	Vietnam	87
United Kingdom	21	*Brazil*	92
Moldova	23	Hungary	105
Mexico	25	*China*	106
Cuba	31	*India*	112
Poland	40	*Japan*	121
Bulgaria	49	Tajikistan	137
United States	53	*Iran*	148
Ukraine	59		

Note: The Global Gender Gap Index is a composite measure reflecting economic participation and opportunity, educational attainment, health and survival, and political empowerment. Countries are ranked from 1 to 153; non-postcommunist countries in italics are included for comparison.

Source: World Economic Forum, "Mind the 100 Year Gap," www.weforum.org/reports/gender-gap-2020-report-100-years-pay-equality (accessed 1/30/20).

opportunity, educational attainment, health and survival, and political empowerment. When we look at the data, we see that many postcommunist countries perform well relative to their level of economic development, ranking higher on the index than the United States or the United Kingdom. This is in part a function of social institutions created under communism, such as mass education and health

INSTITUTIONS IN ACTION

Why Did Reform Fail in the Soviet Union but Succeed in China?

One of the greatest puzzles regarding the collapse of communism has to do with a revolution that did not happen. In 1989, as communism was coming to an end in Eastern Europe and the Soviet Union was on the verge of breaking up, China, too, was experiencing a wave of political protests that threatened to bring down the communist regime. Most notably, student protesters occupied Tiananmen Square in Beijing, the political center of China, calling for liberalization and political reform. At their peak, these protesters numbered in the tens of thousands in Beijing alone, and they spread to other cities throughout the country. Many observers believed that China, like the Soviet Union and Eastern Europe, was at a turning point. The movement expanded from students to professionals and the working class, and the protests were amplified by the widespread presence of the international media, which in turn influenced the actions of the movement.

However, the revolution never occurred. The Chinese leadership declared martial law. Although there were massive public protests to block the approach of the military, army units violently forced their way into Tiananmen Square and dispersed the protesters. Estimates are that several hundred died and thousands were arrested. This outcome is puzzling in comparison with what happened in the Soviet Union and Eastern Europe, where most regimes were overwhelmed by largely nonviolent protests like those in China. What led to such different outcomes?

In Eastern Europe and the Soviet Union, modernization under communism had generated a well-educated class of professionals who were able to articulate their desires for greater political and economic independence. This nascent civil society reacted to a centrally planned economy that was increasingly unable to deliver economic growth or even maintain existing standards of living. Elites in power lost legitimacy—not just in the eyes of society at large but also among themselves. Gorbachev initiated reforms precisely because he faced this crisis of legitimacy and realized that even the ranks of the party no longer had faith in the viability of communism.

As these reforms began to accelerate faster and go further than elites anticipated, international factors amplified this process. Civil society in Eastern Europe looked to the rest of Europe and the European Union as a model to emulate. Moreover, Gorbachev's desire to end the Cold War led him to release the Soviet Union's military control over Eastern Europe, emboldening opposition forces there into challenging and toppling those in power. Cultural forces also played a role, for many Eastern European societies viewed their protests as part of a quest to "return to Europe," from which they felt they had been separated while under Soviet rule. At the same time, rival nationalisms within the Soviet Union led to violent clashes, even outright war, between different ethnic groups that helped bring down the country as a whole.

Meanwhile, China in 1989 could not have been more different. Modernization was far behind the levels of the Soviet Union or Eastern Europe. The country remained overwhelmingly agricultural, and while the student protests did contain the seed of civil society, it was small relative to the size of the Chinese public as a whole. Further, while economic reforms in the Soviet Union in the 1980s were a late and limited response to the stagnation of a centrally planned industrial economy, China's reforms had begun earlier and had led to the doubling of its economy over the course of that same decade. Given the chaos and economic disasters that accompanied the Great Leap Forward and the Cultural Revolution, many Chinese could look on the country in 1989 as finally moving in the right direction. This view in turn bolstered the government's legitimacy both within and outside the regime. Public support for the Communist Party remained strong, and party members and leaders retained a firm conviction that the Tiananmen Square protests would only undermine the country's progress.

With regard to international factors, it is true that the foreign media widely covered the student protests. Still, the Chinese leadership did not need to worry that the use of force would jeopardize the country's future in the same way that Gorbachev believed that the use of force would prevent any integration with Europe or an end to the Cold War. Gorbachev and others argued that communist reforms would mean that Russia and Eastern Europe could "return to Europe" or "rejoin the West." There was no similar sentiment in China, which, if anything, sought recognition as a power unto itself.

This kind of comparative analysis of these differing institutional trends and state trajectories helps make sense of this puzzle, but we should be careful not to assume we can fully explain the outcomes in either of these cases. Chinese liberalization akin to that in the Soviet Union was perhaps closer to occurring than it seems. Documents leaked from the Chinese government suggest that party leader Deng Xiaoping had to push the government and military toward the use of force. In his absence, might Tiananmen Square have become the starting point for political change? If so, what kind of regime and government would we see in China today?

The National Congress of the Communist Party of China convenes every five years in Beijing to make leadership changes within the party.

1. How did the level of modernization in the Soviet Union versus that in China contribute to differences in civil society?

2. How might economic performance explain the difference in the public's view of party elites between the Soviet Union and China?

3. In what way was the "return to Europe" sentiment an international factor in the Soviet Union's path to reform?

Institutions in Action

TABLE 9.6 — LGBT Global Acceptance Index

COUNTRY	SCORE (10 = MOST ACCEPTING)	COUNTRY	SCORE
Iceland	7.4	Bulgaria	3.8
Germany	5.6	Slovakia	3.8
United Kingdom	5.6	Croatia	3.7
Canada	5.4	Latvia	3.4
United States	4.9	China	3.2
Brazil	4.8	Ukraine	3.1
Czech Republic	4.7	*India*	3.0
Mexico	4.6	Russia	2.9
Japan	4.5	Kazakhstan	2.7
Slovenia	4.4	Moldova	2.6
Vietnam	4.1	Armenia	2.0
Poland	4.0	Georgia	2.0
South Africa	4.0	*Iran*	1.8
Hungary	3.9	Azerbaijan	1.0

Note: Non-postcommunist countries in italics are included for comparison.
Source: Williams Institute, University of California, Los Angeles, School of Law, https://williamsinstitute.law.ucla.edu/uncategorized/lgbt-acceptance-around-the-world (accessed 2/9/20).

care. But the variation is also significant between postcommunist countries, and this gap has grown as some countries make greater commitments to gender equality while others neglect or downplay its importance.

Progress is much more limited in the area of LGBT rights. Several Central European states allow for same-sex partnerships, though neither China nor virtually any of the states from the former Soviet Union do so. In many of these countries there is a constitutional prohibition on same-sex marriage. Outright discrimination has also grown in a number of places, most notably Russia and Central Asia. There we find increased propaganda that attacks the LGBT community as pedophiles and agents of the West—a view little different from that promoted during the Soviet era. As shown in Table 9.6, public-opinion surveys indicate a higher degree of homophobia among European postcommunist countries in comparison with countries that did not experience communism, and this is true even for most postcommunist states that are now EU members. Yet while homophobia remains high, it has steadily declined in Russia, China, and most other postcommunist states surveyed.[17]

In Sum: The Legacy of Communism

According to Marxist thought, capitalism would inevitably lead to great industrialization but also to great injustice, a contradiction that would result in its downfall. On the ruins of capitalism, communism would build a society of total equality. But constructing communism proved to be a daunting task. People in communist systems found little incentive for hard work and innovation and had little freedom to express themselves individually.

For the Soviet Union and Eastern Europe, attempts to solve these problems led to outright collapse. An apt analogy might be the attempts to renovate a dilapidated house that reveal the whole structure to be unsound and that only make the situation worse. At that point, the choice is either to demolish the whole structure or be demolished by it. In 1989, people in a number of Eastern European countries chose to demolish the institutions of communism. Communist structures in the Soviet Union eventually collapsed on the Communist Party and Soviet society. China seems to be in a process of endless (and perhaps precarious) remodeling, while other communist countries, such as North Korea, have yet to carry out any major reforms.

It is not clear what the coming decades will bring to the postcommunist world. All of the world's societies are attempting to grapple again with the challenge of balancing freedom and equality. New political, economic, and social institutions are needed, but in many cases they must be forged out of the rubble of the old order, a situation that is creating unique difficulties and contradictions. Over the past decade, both individual freedom and collective inequality have grown in many countries. Increased civil liberties have arisen alongside poverty, and society has been reborn alongside conflict and hostility.

The results of this diverse process have been dramatically different across the communist and postcommunist world. In some countries, we see the institutionalization of democracy and capitalism; in others, authoritarianism and state-dominated economies remain in place. Moreover, it is apparent that over time these countries will grow increasingly dissimilar. Most Eastern European states have joined the European Union and enjoyed economic growth and democracy, though not without challenges. Within parts of the former Soviet Union, however, economic difficulties, political instability, and nondemocratic rule are more common; those countries more closely resemble developing countries. China and Russia remain question marks. Everywhere, the legacies of communism are likely to last for many generations.

Key Terms

base (p. 281)
bourgeoisie (p. 283)
Central Committee (p. 287)
central planning (p. 290)
communism (p. 281)
dialectical materialism (p. 283)
glasnost (p. 293)
nomenklatura (p. 286)

party-state (p. 288)
perestroika (p. 293)
Politburo (p. 287)
proletariat (p. 283)
shock therapy (p. 302)
superstructure (p. 281)
vanguard of the proletariat (p. 285)

For Further Reading

Bunce, Valerie, and Sharon Wolchik. *Defeating Authoritarian Leaders in Postcommunist Countries.* New York: Cambridge University Press, 2011.

Darden, Keith, and Anna Grzymala-Busse. "The Great Divide: Literacy, Nationalism, and the Communist Collapse." *World Politics* 59, no. 1 (October 2006): 83–115.

Krastev, Ivan. "Paradoxes of the New Authoritarianism." *Journal of Democracy* 22, no. 2 (April 2011): 5–16.

Lampton, David M. *Following the Leader: Ruling China, from Deng Xiaoping to Xi Jinping.* Berkeley, CA: University of California Press, 2014.

Marx, Karl, and Friedrich Engels. "Manifesto of the Communist Party." In *Selected Works in Three Volumes*, vol. 1. Moscow: Progress Publishers, 1969.

McAuley, Mary. *Soviet Politics 1917–1991.* New York: Oxford University Press, 1992.

Shambaugh, David. *China's Future.* Malden, MA: Polity Press, 2016.

Zimmerman, William. *Ruling Russia: Authoritarianism from the Revolution to Putin.* Princeton, NJ: Princeton University Press, 2014.

INQUIZITIVE

Earn a better grade on your test. InQuizitive personalizes your learning path to help you master the concepts from this chapter and practice applying them to examples from the text and beyond (see back cover).

QUESTIONS AND METHODS

What Explains Variations in the Exit from Communism?

In Chapter 8 we discussed the ongoing persistence of authoritarian views, seeking to understand the rise of such values in developed democracies. A similar question concerns differences in the transition from communism since 1989. In a number of countries, communist parties and their elites were effectively routed from power, leading to an array of parties across the ideological spectrum. In other countries communist elites have been able to hold on for a much longer period of time. What explains this variation?

The scholars Keith Darden and Anna Maria Grzymala-Busse have suggested that the levels of literacy prior to communism may be an important factor in understanding the "half-life" of communism. Why would literacy *before* communism make any difference in the kind of regime that might emerge afterward? Their view is consistent with our understanding of the rise of nationalism and its impact on the creation of nation-states. As the authors argue, countries that experienced early mass schooling also experienced stronger common

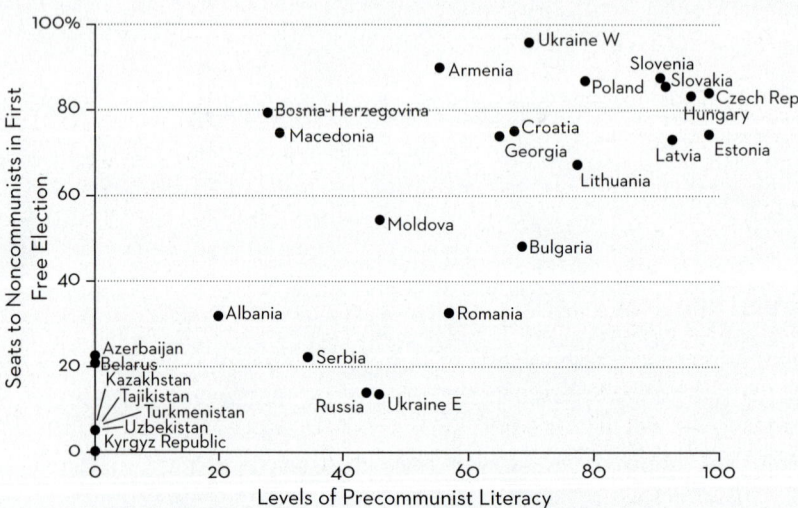

Precommunist Schooling and Share of Seats to Noncommunist Parties in the First Free Postcommunist Elections

Source: Keith Darden and Anna Grzymala-Busse, "The Great Divide: Literacy, Nationalism, and the Communist Collapse," *World Politics* 59, no. 1 (October 2006): 91.

ethnic identities, as education fostered the creation of shared institutions and values—common languages, history, mythologies, and rituals. This in turn helped set the stage for nationalist ideas, which asserted that "the people" deserved sovereign control over their own political destiny. For those areas that had experienced early literacy and the subsequent emergence of national identity, a communist regime was viewed as an inferior imposition. In contrast, areas with low levels of literacy, such as Central Asia, only saw the benefits of mass education once they came under communism. Education also did not serve to establish a national identity, but to connect individuals to the broader ideology of communism. As a result, when communism began to wane in the Soviet Union, successful opposition groups were able to capitalize on precommunist institutions, returning to histories, cultures, and other institutions to promise a "restoration" of the past. Where such legacies did not exist, opposition movements had much less to build upon.

What does this mean for countries that remain strongly under the control of communist parties, like China? If Darden and Grzymala-Busse are correct, we should not expect an end to communism there akin to what we saw in Eastern Europe. Levels of literacy in China before the communist revolution in 1949 were below 25 percent. If anything, a more likely outcome might be more akin to postcommunist Central Asia or Russia—a formal end to communism, but one where former communist elites retain power for decades afterward. Where there is no strong precommunist national identity, opposition forces lack an important tool with which to mobilize the public.[a]

1. ***Articulate critiques of a specific ideology and regime type***

   Given what we have learned about communist ideology, how could opposition forces have used nationalism as a critique of communism?

2. ***Consider challenges to existing political science theories***

   We have often spoken about modernization theory, which has argued in part that developments like literacy would lead to democracy. But could high early literacy and nationalism lead to a political transition that simply replaces one authoritarian regime and its elites with another?

3. ***Generate new research ideas***

   In recent years there have been large protests for greater democracy in Hong Kong, which came under Chinese control after a century of British rule. If we were to speculate that Darden and Grzymala-Busse's theory helps explain these protests, what kind of evidence would we want to look for?

---

a. Keith Darden and Anna Grzymala-Busse, "The Great Divide: Literacy, Nationalism, and the Communist Collapse," *World Politics* 59, no. 1 (October 2006): 83–115.

10

White coffee beans dry in the sun at a Fair Trade coffee farm in Jimma, Ethiopia. The attempt to promote "fair trade" between richer and poorer countries is an example of the complexities facing political-economic development in the developing world.

DEVELOPING COUNTRIES

What are the causes of poverty and wealth?

Up to this point, we have repeatedly considered the role of economic and political institutions in helping (or hindering) development and democracy. These institutions are of particular concern among the poorer or developing countries, where for many a basic standard of living remains far out of reach. How to promote development? And where should those changes begin?

One example that many of us have direct experience with is Fair Trade. At some point, probably everyone reading this has purchased something labeled "Fair Trade" that was produced in the developing world. Most likely it was a cup of coffee with beans originally harvested in Latin America or Africa, but Fair Trade–certified goods run the gamut from coffee and tea to seafood and sugar, from flowers to basketballs. Fair Trade seems like a clear opportunity for producers and consumers to overcome economic and political barriers and create a more beneficial relationship to promote development. Is this the case?

Before we can consider that question, we should understand exactly what Fair Trade means. The idea goes back as far as the 1960s, but a labeling organization was not developed until the late 1980s. The Fair Trade mark is meant to certify that goods meet certain standards in several areas. Laborers are to be guaranteed basic working conditions, such as minimum wages and a ban on child labor. Farmers are also organized as cooperatives to pool resources and distribute the premium earned from

Fair Trade goods. Environmental standards deal with such practices as the use of pesticides. In return, Fair Trade buyers provide long-term contracts and financing to producers and agree to a fixed higher price. In 2018, $9 billion in Fair Trade coffee and other foods was sold worldwide, and over a million and a half individuals in 75 countries were involved in the production of Fair Trade goods.

As Fair Trade consumption has grown in the developed democracies, so has scrutiny of the system. One argument is that premiums paid through Fair Trade keep inefficient farmers in operation although they would be better off working in some other part of the economy. Others suggest that premiums do not trickle down to the producers but are eaten up by the overhead costs of administering a cooperative. Unfortunately, much of this debate has been driven by ideological preferences or anecdotes.

More recently, a deeper study of Fair Trade raised some significant questions about the impact of the certification system. Researchers at the University of London conducted a four-year study of Fair Trade production of coffee, tea, and flowers in Ethiopia and Uganda. Some of their findings were disturbing. Contrary to assumptions, many of those involved in producing Fair Trade goods were not farm owners but hired workers, including children. These wage laborers often made less than those at typically larger non–Fair Trade farms. Moreover, premiums tended to be gained by a minority of larger farms, meaning the poorest farmers and laborers got far less from the arrangement. Schools, clinics, and other benefits built by cooperatives were often denied to wage laborers.

Do the Ethiopian and Ugandan cases undermine the Fair Trade model? Beyond Africa, Fair Trade has been used extensively in Latin America, where it first began. Studies there do show positive benefits for many farmers, though, as in Africa, wage laborers do not enjoy similar benefits, and cooperatives often suffer from the same kinds of inequality that cooperatives in Uganda and Ethiopia do. In short, evidence suggests that Fair Trade does provide benefits, but it is not an easy answer to problems of development.

Interestingly, both the African and Latin American cases suggest that profits and other benefits are more equitably distributed when Fair Trade production takes place at a larger scale. This idea may go against our beliefs that large businesses are by nature unjust while small-scale production is more fair and equal. But research suggests that larger firms have greater resources at their disposal, can provide a wider array of benefits, and can be held accountable via unionization and regulation. The image of a family harvesting coffee may have a strong visual and emotional appeal when we buy our latte. But it may distract us from the role of strong institutions as a foundation for large-scale development.[1]

LEARNING OBJECTIVES

- Describe the key characteristics and future prospects of developing countries.
- Explain how imperialism and colonialism have affected developing countries.
- Examine the difficulties and successes of post-imperial countries.

So far, we have investigated two major kinds of countries: the developed democracies and communist and postcommunist countries. But these two categories leave out much of Latin America, Asia, and Africa. Many of the countries in these regions have had neither liberal-democratic nor communist regimes. Of these countries, the vast majority have levels of economic industrialization far below those in the developed democracies or the communist and postcommunist world. The traditional labeling of these countries as belonging to a "Third World" unhelpfully grouped together a diverse range of people and political systems according to what they were not, rather than what they were—what we call a residual category. The more recent term "the Global South" is vaguely geographic but no more helpful.

How, then, should we understand these countries? Whereas the developed democracies are notable for their early modernization and capitalist development and the communist states for their later, rapid, state-directed modernization and industrialization, the countries discussed in this chapter are characterized by hybrid forms of economic, societal, and political institutions, both foreign-imposed and indigenous.

In this chapter, we develop some ideas and categories to investigate and understand these countries. We will begin by distinguishing among developing countries and examining the relationship between freedom and equality across them. From there, we will look at some of the fundamental experiences and institutions shared by these countries, particularly those associated with imperialism and colonialism. Although imperialism had different effects in different parts of the world, we can generalize about its legacies. Next, we will consider what challenges and obstacles these countries have faced after gaining independence. How does a country reconcile freedom and equality when the conditions may favor neither? And how have some countries managed to enjoy economic and political development while others have stagnated or declined? These topics will lead us into a final discussion of the prospects for political, economic, and societal development in developing countries. What policies might help generate greater democracy, political stability, and economic prosperity in these countries? The difficulties they face are great and the tasks daunting. But out of such challenges can emerge new ideas and innovations with the potential to bring about positive change.

Freedom and Equality in the Developing World

The developing world has often been divided into two groups that indicate important differences in their levels of development. Over the past 60 years, some of these countries, particularly in Asia and parts of Latin America, have experienced dramatic rates of economic growth and democratization, to the point that they now resemble the developed democracies in many ways. These are known as **middle income countries**. In other cases, economic and political structures have remained weak or even grown weaker over the past decades. Some of these countries have slid into greater poverty, violence, and civil conflict. They are often referred to as **lower income countries**, sometimes also known as less-developed countries (LDCs). The World Bank defines lower income countries as those below $4,000 per capita gross domestic product (GDP) at purchasing power parity (PPP), and middle income countries as those between $4,000 and $13,000. We will speak of these lower and middle income countries together as **developing countries** (Table 10.1).

As mentioned in Chapter 8, developing countries, like postcommunist countries, have grown increasingly dissimilar, making organizations like the World Bank even abandon the term of late. However, comparisons can help us understand variations among these countries. Why have some broken out of the trap of underdevelopment and others have not? Does it have to do with how states are constructed? Their regimes or political-economic systems? The absence or presence of democracy? Their ethnic, national, or religious institutions? Their culture? Their relationship to developed democracies or other, more powerful states? Can we draw lessons from some developing countries and apply these lessons to others?

Before addressing present problems, we should turn to history. Despite differences in their current conditions, developing countries share a legacy of colonialism and imperialism and the experience of belonging to large empires, being possessions of more powerful states. Imperial rule, which lasted for decades or even centuries, dramatically and often rapidly transformed economic, political,

TABLE 10.1 — Developing Countries, 2020

LATIN AMERICA AND CARIBBEAN	ASIA AND OCEANIA	NORTH AFRICA AND MIDDLE EAST	AFRICA (CONTINUED)
Belize	Afghanistan	Algeria	Equatorial Guinea
Bolivia	Bangladesh	Bahrain	Gabon
Brazil	Bhutan	Egypt	Gambia
Colombia	Brunei	Eritrea	Ghana
Costa Rica	Burma (Myanmar)	Ethiopia	Guinea
Dominica	Cambodia	Iran	Guinea-Bissau
Dominican Republic	Cyprus	Iraq	Côte d'Ivoire
Ecuador	Fiji	Jordan	Kenya
El Salvador	India	Lebanon	Lesotho
Guatemala	Indonesia	Libya	Liberia
Guyana	Kiribati	Morocco	Madagascar
Haiti	Kuwait	Oman	Malawi
Honduras	Laos	Qatar	Mali
Jamaica	Malaysia	Saudi Arabia	Mauritania
Nicaragua	Maldives	Syria	Mauritius
Panama	Marshall Islands	United Arab Emirates	Mozambique
Paraguay	Micronesia	Yemen	Namibia
Peru	Nauru		Niger
Saint Kitts and Nevis	Nepal	**AFRICA**	Nigeria
Saint Lucia	Pakistan		Rwanda
Saint Vincent and the Grenadines	Palau	Angola	São Tomé and Príncipe
Venezuela	Papua New Guinea	Benin	Senegal
	Philippines	Burkina Faso	Seychelles
EUROPE	Samoa	Burundi	Sierra Leone
	Solomon Islands	Cameroon	Somalia
Turkey	Sri Lanka	Cape Verde	South Africa
	Thailand	Central African Republic	South Sudan
	Tonga	Chad	Sudan
	Tuvalu	Comoros	Swaziland
	Vanuatu	Congo (Democratic Republic of)	Tanzania
	Vietnam	Congo (Republic of)	Togo
		Djibouti	Tunisia
			Uganda
			Zambia
			Zimbabwe

and societal institutions in the colonized countries. Although resistance eventually brought down imperial rule, the changes this system wrought could not be easily unmade. To better understand these institutional legacies, it is worth looking at them in some detail, though we should also keep in mind that history is not destiny—imperialism matters, but it is only one factor in explaining the problems of the post-imperial world.

Imperialism and Colonialism

In the first three chapters of this book, we saw that over the past millennium Europe, the Middle East, and Asia embarked on a series of dramatic societal, economic, and political changes that formed the outlines of what are now recognized as the hallmarks of modern society: ethnic and national identity, technological innovation, and political centralization. Modern societies soon projected their growing power outward to conquer and incorporate new lands and peoples that could contribute to their rapid development. The result was the emergence of **empires**—single political authorities that have under their sovereignty a large number of external regions or territories and different peoples. Although this definition might lead a person to conclude that any large, diverse country is an empire, central to the definition is the idea that lands and peoples that are not seen as an integral part of the country itself are nonetheless under its direct control. The term **imperialism** describes the system whereby a state extends its power to directly control territory, resources, and people beyond its borders. People often use *imperialism* interchangeably with *colonialism*, though these terms are different. **Colonialism** indicates the physical occupation of a foreign territory through military force, businesses, or settlers. Colonialism, then, is often the means for consolidating an empire.

Although imperialist practices began many thousands of years ago, modern imperialism can be dated from the fifteenth century, when technological development in Europe, the Middle East, and Asia—advanced seafaring and military technology in particular—had advanced to such an extent that these countries were able to project their military might far overseas. In Asia, the powerful Chinese Empire turned away from this path. Having consolidated power hundreds of years before the states of Europe did, the Chinese state grew conservative and inflexible, interested more in maintaining the status quo than in striking out to acquire new lands. Indeed, at the same time that Europeans were setting out for the Americas, the Chinese were actually retreating from overseas voyages; by 1500, it had become illegal for Chinese subjects to build oceangoing vessels. Similarly, although the powerful Ottoman Empire in the Middle East expanded its power over much of the Arab world and into Asia, North Africa, and parts of Europe, nearly conquering Vienna in 1683, it failed to expand its power beyond the Islamic world. Whatever the reasons for this shift in China and the Ottoman Empire, in both cases there existed early state building and imperialism that predated and rivaled that of Europe. It is thus important to recognize that the peoples who became subject to modern imperialism were not a blank slate, without any of their own institutions. Many of the regions that came under imperial rule already possessed highly developed economic, political, and societal institutions.

Thus, in the 1500s, Europe began a process of imperial expansion that would continue for nearly five centuries. Driven by economic and strategic motives as well as a belief that Christianity and Western culture needed to be brought to the rest of the world, European empires stretched their power around the globe. First, Spain and Portugal gained control over South America, Central America, and large parts of North America. By the seventeenth century, British, French, and other settlers began to arrive in North America, displacing the local populations. In the eighteenth century, Europeans started to assert control over parts of North Africa and the Middle East, shocking Ottoman elites who had long viewed Europeans as technologically and culturally backward. Their shock was shared by the Chinese in the nineteenth and early twentieth centuries as European imperialism rapidly expanded into Asia. Nearly all of Africa, too, was eventually divided up by the European states. This European imperialist expansion was joined briefly by Japan, which in the early twentieth century established its own empire across parts of Asia. In each of these cases, imperial powers possessed well-organized political systems and military structures, technological advances, and economic resources; these advantages were combined with a belief that imperial control was not only possible but also necessary, just, and willed by God.[2]

IN FOCUS

Imperialism...

- Is a system in which a state extends its power beyond its borders to control other territories, resources, and peoples.
- Was propagated by European powers from the sixteenth to the twenty-first centuries.
- Is driven by economic, strategic, and religious motives.
- Often led to colonialism, the physical occupation of foreign territories.

TIMELINE — Modern Imperialism

1494	Following European discovery, Spain and Portugal partition the Americas between their two empires.
1519–36	Indigenous groups (Aztecs, Incas) are defeated by imperial powers in Central and South America.
1602–52	The Dutch begin to establish control over parts of the Indonesian archipelago and southern Africa. English settlement begins in North America.
1810–25	Wars of independence in Latin America; Spanish and Portuguese rule is brought to an end.
1839–58	United Kingdom expands control into Asia, notably Hong Kong and India.
1884	The Berlin Conference; Africa is rapidly divided among European powers, notably France, Portugal, and Belgium.
1939–45	World War II catalyzes the eventual decolonization of Asia and Africa.
1947	Independence of India; first major decolonization of the twentieth century.
1956–68	Independence of most British, French, and Belgian colonies in Africa after local rebellions against imperial rule.
1975	Independence of most former Portuguese colonies in Africa and Asia.
1997–99	Hong Kong (United Kingdom) and Macau (Portugal) returned to China.

Institutions of Imperialism

The effect of imperialism on the societies that came under foreign rule differed across time and place, but some common elements resulted from the imposition of modern political, societal, and economic systems onto non-Western societies. As we shall see, this imposition had a dramatic (and often traumatic) effect that continues to the present.[3]

Exporting the State

One of the first major effects of imperialism was the transfer of the state to the rest of the world. Recall from Chapter 2 how the modern state that we take for granted today emerged as a result of a long historical process in Europe; before that time, political units tended to have much weaker control over land and their subjects, and territorial sovereignty and the rule of law were tenuous. States, however, eventually succeeded in consolidating power over other forms of political organization, eliminating their rivals, clearly delineating their borders, and establishing sovereignty.

When European empires began to expand around the world, they incorporated new territories into these state structures. Rival states carved up territories in the quest for economic resources and strategic advantages. The borders drawn by imperial states therefore often reflected the shape of their colonial ambitions rather than existing geographic, religious, or linguistic realities. The borders of 80 percent of African states are drawn according to longitude and latitude, not local geography or population groups. Many of these externally imposed and arbitrary boundaries became the demarcations for independent countries once imperial rule ended. Even countries that were able to resist direct imperial rule, such as Iran, Thailand, and Ethiopia, found themselves under the continuous influence and pressure of these empires.

Having conquered these territories, imperial powers went about establishing state power and authority. In many empires, this meant creating bureaucratic structures similar to those found in the home country in an attempt to "civilize"— to modernize and Westernize—the local population. These institutions commonly included a national language (typically that of the imperial power), police and a military, taxation and legal systems, and basic public goods such as roads, schools, and hospitals. How new institutions were established and new laws enforced differed. Some empires relied on local leaders to enforce their will, whereas others bypassed indigenous elites in favor of their own centralized forms of authority. These differences tended to reflect the degree of state capacity and autonomy found in the imperial country itself. In both cases, few, if any, democratic practices were introduced, even if they were the norm in the home country. Individuals under colonial rule were considered subjects, not citizens, and thus had few political rights.

This imposition of the state had mixed effects. Many subject peoples experienced increased education and the benefits of basic communication and transportation infrastructure. Life expectancies often rose and infant mortality rates declined, although when those trends were combined with traditional family practices, they produced a population explosion that in many poor countries continues today. Traditional institutions such as local religions and customs were eroded and replaced by or fused with Western practices and institutions. This transition was incomplete and uneven. Imperial territories remained economically and politically underdeveloped, placing many subject peoples in a kind of institutional limbo, with a hybrid of Western and traditional institutions. The frustration that grew out of this conflicted identity helped fan the flames of anti-imperialism: the desire for freedom from foreign control.

Social Identities

The imposition of organizational forms from outside included various new identities that often displaced or were incorporated into existing social institutions. Among these were ethnic and national identities. In much of the world that came under imperial control, people often identified themselves by tribe, religion, economic position, or vocation rather than primarily by some ethnic or national identity (institutions that were particularly strong in the West). But just as empires brought their own political institutions with them, they also introduced the concepts of ethnicity and nation. Imperial elites, themselves shaped and defined by national and ethnic identities, took great interest in identifying and classifying different ethnic groups in the regions they came to occupy and structuring their political and economic control around these classifications. Ironically, even as groups were subject to Western classification, they were often divided across imperial borders that had been drawn with little regard for their tribal, religious, or any other identities.

Suddenly, people who had not specifically defined themselves by ethnicity found their basic rights being tied to how they were ethnically defined by the empire. In some cases, this ethnic classification was determined by early pseudoscientific notions of race, which held that certain ethnic groups were naturally superior to others. The European and Japanese empires were influenced by the assumption that the colonizing race was superior to the colonized and thus destined to rule them. Different peoples within the empire, too, were subject to hierarchical classification. Certain ethnic groups were promoted to positions of power and economic advantage, while other groups were marginalized. Colonialism often exacerbated these hierarchies as nonindigenous peoples migrated to colonies. Sometimes these migrants were settlers from the home country; in other cases, they were peoples from other parts of the empire or beyond (for example, Indians migrating to Africa or African slaves being brought to Brazil). These foreign presences further sharpened ethnic and racial divisions, especially when such groups were accorded specific economic or political privileges. In short, inequality became tightly interconnected with ethnicity or race.

In addition to ethnicity, imperial powers also introduced the idea of national identity. During the late nineteenth and early twentieth centuries, in particular, national identity grew to be a powerful force in the industrializing world, helping drive competition between the industrial powers and in turn advancing the imperialist cause. But the peoples brought under imperial control had little or no sense of a strong national identity, little notion of any right to a sovereign state. This combination of nationalism and imperialism proved to be unstable. Empires viewed the peoples living in their overseas possessions as inferior subjects and gave them only limited ability to improve their standing within the empire. Yet the imperial powers' own concept of nationalism provided these subject peoples with the very means to challenge foreign rule. If nationalism meant the right for a people—any people—to live under their own sovereign state, did this not mean that subject peoples had a right to rule themselves? Empires thus provided the ideological ammunition that their subjects would eventually use to overturn imperialism.

Colonialism also affected gender roles in the colonies. It is hard to make generalizations in this area, since in each region existing gender roles differed greatly and each imperial power viewed gender somewhat differently. Some scholars argue that imperialism brought a number of benefits to women, increasing their freedom and equality by improving their access to health care and education. Others reject this argument, asserting that in many cases colonialism restricted women's roles in society. In many non-Western societies, gender roles may have been much less fixed than those found in the imperial home country, allowing women particular areas of individual freedom, equality, and autonomy. Imperial powers brought with them their own assumptions regarding the status of women, views that were

IN FOCUS

Political and Social Institutions of Imperialism

- The state, as a form of political organization, was imposed on much of the world outside of Europe.
- Ethnic and national identities were created where none had existed before colonization.
- Gender roles from the imperial country were often imposed on colonies.

shaped in part by their religious values. These views were imposed through such institutions as education and the legal system. The economic systems imposed by the colonizers often marginalized women.

One example can be found in research on agriculture and gender equality. Some studies suggest that in societies where farming was done through "shifting cultivation" (performed with hoes and hand-weeding rather than plows, which require greater upper body strength), women more actively participated in the agricultural economy as equals with men. These norms of equal participation extended outward into other areas, such as politics. However, with the advent of imperialism, such practices were transformed by agricultural modernization and industrial development, shifting participatory power away from women and toward men.[4] Even so, given the wide range of imperial practices and non-Western institutions, it is too simplistic to say that imperialism made women's lives worse in all respects. Imperial rule also created new economic opportunities that challenged traditional roles of women within patriarchal family and tribal orders. Women who could get an education, be freed from traditional codes of family and tribal honor, and hold a job outside of the home saw their lives transformed.

Dependent Development

Just as imperialism transformed political and social institutions in colonial areas, creating an amalgam of local and Western forms, economic change occurred in a similarly dramatic and uneven way. The first important change in many imperial possessions was the replacement of a traditional agricultural economy with one driven by the needs of the industrializing capitalist home country. Systems that were based largely on subsistence agriculture and barter were transformed into cash economies in which money was used to pay for goods and labor.

Alongside a cash-based economy came the transformation of economic production. Using a mercantilist political-economic system (see Chapter 4), empires sought to extract revenue from their colonies while at the same time using these territories and their people as captive markets for finished goods from the home country. Free trade thus did not exist for the colonies, which were obliged to sell and buy goods within the confines of the empire. Moreover, colonial production was organized to provide goods that were not easily available in the home country. Rather than finished goods, local economies were rebuilt around primary products such as cotton, cocoa, coffee, tea, wood, rubber, and other valuable commodities that could be extracted from the natural environment.

Large businesses were established to oversee these so-called extractive economies, which were often dominated by a single monopoly. For example, in Indonesia the United East India Company, a Dutch firm, gained control over lucrative spice exports while monopolizing the local market for finished goods from Europe, thereby destroying indigenous trade networks that had existed in the region for centuries. Similarly, during the nineteenth century the British East India Company functioned virtually as a state of its own, controlling a large portion of the Indian economy and much of its foreign trade. Export-oriented imperialism also led to the creation of large plantations that could produce vast quantities of rubber, coffee, or tobacco.

This form of economic organization was quite different from that of the home countries and in many respects was ill suited to domestic development. Infrastructure was frequently developed primarily to facilitate effective extraction and export rather than to improve communication or movement for the subject peoples. Jobs were created in the extractive sector, but local industrialization and entrepreneurialism were more limited. The development of agriculture for export instead of for subsistence damaged the ability of these peoples to feed themselves, and large-scale agricultural production drove many small farmers off the land. Many colonies saw a resulting boom in urbanization, typically in the colonial capital or other cities central to imperial politics and trade. By the late 1500s, for example, the Spanish had established more than 200 cities in Latin America, which to this day remain the central urban areas in the region. Urbanization brought specific benefits, such as improved infrastructure along with new economic opportunities, but it also exacted clear costs. For example, greater population densities meant greater public health problems, such as disease (which the developed countries themselves had experienced earlier).

IN FOCUS: Economic Institutions of Imperialism

- Traditional agricultural economies were transformed to suit the needs of the imperialist power.
- Economic organization under imperialism impeded domestic development in the colonies.
- Free trade was often suppressed, as colonies were forced to supply goods only to the imperial country, creating extractive economies in the colonies.

Let us take a moment to summarize what we have considered so far. By virtue of their organizational strengths, modern states expanded their power around the globe, establishing new political, economic, and social institutions and displacing existing ones. In some cases, these institutions were reflections of the home country; in others, they were designed specifically to consolidate imperial rule. The result was an uneasy mixture of indigenous and foreign structures. New political institutions and new societal identities were introduced or imposed while participation and citizenship were restricted; economic development was encouraged but in a form that would serve the markets of the home country. Imperialism thus generated new identities and conflict by classifying people and distinguishing between them—between rulers and ruled and between subject peoples themselves. At the same time, the contradictions inherent in this inequality and restriction of freedom became increasingly clear to subject peoples as they began to assimilate and develop their own ideas and values. By the early twentieth century, the growing awareness of this system and its inherent contradictions helped foster public resistance to imperialism and paved the way for eventual independence.

The Challenges of Post-Imperialism

Despite the power of empires to extend their control over much of the world, their time eventually came to an end. In Latin America, where European imperialism first emerged, Napoleon's invasion of Spain and Portugal in 1807–08 led to turmoil in the colonies and a series of wars for independence, which freed most of the region by 1826. In Africa and Asia, where imperialism reached its zenith only in the nineteenth century, decolonization came after World War II. Numerous independence movements emerged within the Asian and African colonies, catalyzed by the weakened positions of the imperial powers and promoted by a Western-educated indigenous leadership able to articulate nationalist goals and organize resistance. Some imperial powers resisted bitterly. France fought a brutal war to retain Algeria in the 1960s. Portugal did not fully withdraw from Africa until 1975. Hong Kong was returned to China by the United Kingdom in 1997. For the most part, colonies in Africa and Asia gained independence by the 1960s.

The elimination of imperialism, however, did not bring a sudden end to the problems of the developing world. These countries have continued to struggle with political, social, and economic challenges to development and stability, freedom and equality. In many cases, these problems are a legacy of imperial rule, although in other cases they stem from particular domestic and international factors that have developed in the years since independence. But herein lies an important puzzle. If we consider the development of successful economic, social, and political institutions over the past 60 years, Asia has fared the best, Africa the worst, and the picture in Latin America is mixed. Even in these regions there is significant variation. What accounts for these differences? Let's first consider some of the more common problems faced across post-imperial countries and then return to this question to see if the answer can provide some strategies for development and democracy.

Building State Capacity and Autonomy

One central problem that many developing countries have faced in the years after imperialism has been the difficulty in creating effective political institutions. In Chapter 2, we distinguished between weak states and strong states and noted that many scholars look at state power as consisting of state capacity and state autonomy. *Capacity* refers to a state's ability to fulfill basic policy tasks, and *autonomy* refers to its ability to act independently of the public and foreign actors. Both are necessary to carry out policy, and both have been difficult for post-imperial countries to achieve.

In terms of capacity, developing countries are frequently unable to perform many of the basic tasks expected by the public, such as creating infrastructure, providing education and health care, or delivering other public goods. This lack of capacity stretches back to the absence of a professional bureaucracy; the foreigners who ran the imperial bureaucracies in the colonies typically left as soon as the colonies gained independence, precluding an effective transition to a local bureaucracy. These initial problems of capacity were exacerbated by the politicization of the state; in many cases, the bureaucracy has become an important source of jobs, resources, and benefits that political leaders dole out as a way to solidify control. Recall our discussion in Chapter 6 regarding clientelism and rent seeking. Under clientelism, the state co-opts members of the public by providing specific benefits to a person or group in return for public support, like voting in elections. One facet of clientelism, rent seeking, uses parts of the state to extract income for supporters, giving them preferred access to public goods (like jobs) that would otherwise be distributed in a nonpolitical manner. In many developing countries, limited economic development and relatively weak states have fostered a high degree of clientelism and rent seeking, which political leaders have used to gain and hold on to power.[5] Politics thus becomes a question of buying support and understanding how to bypass formal institutions with informal relationships. As we well know, this is not unique to the developing world, but it is most acute among these states.

Autonomy has been equally problematic in the post-imperialist world. On the surface, many of these countries appear to be highly autonomous, able to function without having to respond to public pressure. The prevalence of nondemocratic regimes in much of the developing world seems only to reinforce this impression. However, these states are largely captured by patrimonial systems along the lines of what we see in Zimbabwe (see Chapter 6). The state is not a highly independent actor but is instead penetrated by groups that see it as a resource to be exploited rather than as a tool for achieving national policy. The result of weak capacity and autonomy is high levels of corruption. For example, during military rule in Nigeria in the 1990s, officials stole more than $1 billion from the state treasury. In 2016, the U.S. government seized $1 billion in assets believed to be stolen by individuals close to the Malaysian prime minister (see Chapter 5). Studies of corruption indicate that the most corrupt countries in the world are developing and postcommunist countries, and there is a clear correlation between the level of development and the degree of corruption (see Table 10.2).

In addition to compromised capacity and autonomy, states of the developing world are often constrained by international factors. Developing countries are subject to pressure from other, more powerful states and international actors such as the United Nations, the World Bank, multinational corporations, and nongovernmental organizations like Amnesty International and the Red Cross. Frequently wielding much greater economic and political power than the states themselves, these actors can significantly influence the policies of these countries, shaping their military and diplomatic alliances, trade relations, local economies, and domestic laws. Sovereignty is thus compromised.

IN FOCUS: Challenges to Building State Autonomy and Capacity in Developing Countries

- Absence of professional bureaucracy (following departure of foreign imperial bureaucrats)
- Clientelism, rent seeking, and corruption in the handling of state jobs and revenue
- Sovereignty often compromised by external actors (other states, international organizations)

TABLE 10.2 — Corruption Index, 2019

COUNTRY	RANK (1 = LEAST CORRUPT)	COUNTRY	RANK (1 = LEAST CORRUPT)
Denmark	1	China	80
Canada	12	Indonesia	85
United Kingdom	12	Brazil	106
Japan	20	Pakistan	120
France	23	Mexico	130
United States	23	Russia	137
Taiwan	28	Iran	146
Botswana	34	Nigeria	146
South Korea	39	Zimbabwe	158
South Africa	70	Venezuela	173
India	80	Somalia	180

Note: The corruption index is based on national surveys regarding the overall extent of corruption (size and frequency of bribes) in the public and political sectors. Rankings: 1–180; some countries share rankings.

Source: Transparency International, www.transparency.org/cpi2019 (accessed 3/2/20).

These constraints on state capacity and autonomy have clear implications for freedom and equality. A state with weak capacity and autonomy is unlikely to be able to establish the rule of law. Laws will not be respected by the public if the state itself is unwilling or unable to enforce and abide by them. Freedom is threatened by conflict and unpredictability, which in turn hinder economic development. A volatile environment and the absence of basic public goods such as roads or education will dissuade long-term investment. Wealth flows primarily into the hands of those who control the state, generating a high degree of inequality. There is no clear regime, and no rules or norms for how politics is to be played.

Unfortunately, where instability is so high, often only one institution has a great deal of capacity and autonomy: the military. Where states are weak, military forces often step in and take control of the government themselves, either to stave off disorder or simply to get a turn at draining the state. Military rule has been common in developing countries, and we have seen the military reemerge as an important political force in the Middle East, where political change has been disruptive.

Even where military rule has ended, the military often remains a powerful actor with its own political and economic interests, as we saw in the case of Pakistan in Chapter 2.

Creating Nations and Citizens

In the aftermath of colonialism, many developing countries have struggled with the challenge of forging a single nation out of highly diverse societies. Where centralized political authority did not exist before imperialism, identities tended to be quite heterogeneous. This diversity became problematic when imperial powers began categorizing societal groups and establishing political boundaries and economic and social hierarchies. Migration within empires further complicated relations among these groups. When colonies gained independence, several problems rose to the surface.

First, group divisions often have economic implications, just as they did under colonial rule. Some ethnic or religious groups favored under colonialism continue to monopolize wealth in the post-independence society. For example, in Malaysia and Indonesia, ethnic Chinese hold a disproportionate share of national wealth, generating resentment. Similarly, in some African countries, Indian immigrants—often brought in by the British as indentured labor—came to control a large portion of the business sector. At the other end of the spectrum, many indigenous populations, such as those in Latin America, are among the poorest in the world, a situation that has sparked ethnically based political movements in several of these countries. Many civil conflicts in developing countries are driven largely by economic concerns that intersect with ethnic or religious differences.

Second, ethnic and religious divisions can similarly complicate politics. In countries where populations are heterogeneous, the battle for political power often falls along ethnic or religious lines as each group seeks to gain control over the state in order to serve its own particular ends (see Chapter 3). Each ethnic or religious group competes for its share of public goods or other benefits from the state. This struggle is central to clientelism and patrimonialism, as each group competes to gain access to resources controlled by the state. At an extreme, this can contribute to authoritarian rule if groups fear losing access to resources if they lose elections.

As a result, where ethnic or religious divisions are strong we often see a form of patrimonialism in which one group dominates the state while effectively freezing other groups out of the political process.[6] In some countries, a majority or plurality may dominate politics, as people of European origin do in Mexico, where the minority indigenous population has little political power. In other cases, a minority may dominate a much larger majority. For example, in Iraq, though most members of the population belong to the Shia sect of Islam, those in power have traditionally been members of the minority Sunni sect. With the overthrow of Saddam Hussein in 2003, conflict emerged between Sunnis and Shias over the future control of the country. A similar dynamic is at work in the Syrian civil war, where individuals from the Alawite sect of Islam have monopolized political power and have been unwilling to relinquish it (see Chapter 7). Economic and political interests thus become entangled with different social identities.

Economic and political difficulties that arise from such social divisions make the creation of a single national identity difficult and weaken the notion of citizenship—that all individuals have a common political relationship to the state. Amid such ethnic and religious diversity, many populations are much less inclined to see the postcolonial state as a true representation of their group's wishes, and states themselves have little beyond the initial struggle for independence on which to build a shared political identity. When ethnic and religious conflicts are extreme, disaffected groups may seek to secede and create their own independent countries. The most recent example of this was the creation in 2011 of South Sudan, which separated from Sudan following a long civil war that pitted a black African south against an Arab north. Under the British Empire, they had been administered as two separate political entities. In advance of Britain's withdrawal in 1956, it oversaw the unification of these two areas despite southern Sudanese opposition. South Sudanese independence in turn led to a civil war within the new state between leaders from two different ethnic groups.

Gender and family is another important area shaped by the legacies of imperialism. As we noted, gender and family identities and roles have been affected by rapid urbanization and the commercialization of agriculture, which often favored male

IN FOCUS

Challenges to Building a Unified Nation-State

- Ethnic and religious divisions among different groups in heterogeneous societies (often exacerbated by economic inequality)
- Arbitrary political boundaries imposed by imperial powers

labor and property rights (such as titles to land). This structure can give women much less leverage in family decisions, such as family size. It also may lead families to view girls as a burden, since they must be married off (often with a dowry) and cannot be expected to take care of their parents in their old age. Thus families may be less willing to invest in their daughters, especially if family sizes are shrinking, placing more pressure on families to have male children. At its most extreme, this favoritism can be deadly, taking the form of female neglect or infanticide. There are estimates that in India and China tens of millions of girls are "missing" from the expected demographic, having been aborted or having died shortly after birth. Vietnam, Pakistan, and other countries have faced similar issues, either through sex-selective abortions or through neglect of girl babies. Some scholars have already noted that violent conflict and crime, including human trafficking, in part results from a large number of unmarried young men. In the coming years, the security of women may be a key variable in predicting the security of states.[7]

Generating Economic Growth

Economic growth attracts the most focus among those who study developing countries. Indeed, when we think of development, typically economic progress first comes to mind. Because of imperialism, instead of undergoing economic modernization on their own terms, these countries experienced rapid changes directed by the imperial powers to serve their own needs. As a result, on gaining independence many of these countries found themselves in a continued state of economic dependency on their former empire. But such dependent relationships did not bode well for long-term development, since they often stressed the production of agricultural and other basic commodities in return for finished products. For many developing countries, this unequal relationship was simply a new, indirect form of imperialism, or what some scholars call **neocolonialism**. Breaking this cycle of dependent development was thus the greatest concern for the developing countries following independence.

The former colonies' need to break this cycle resulted in two distinct mercantilist economic policies that were applied throughout the developing world.[8] The first is known as **import substitution**. Under import substitution, countries restrict imports, raising tariff or nontariff barriers to spur demand for local alternatives. To fill this demand, new businesses are built with state funds by creating subsidized or parastatal (partially state-owned) industries. Patents and intellectual property rights are weakly enforced to tap into foreign innovations. Eventually, the hope goes, these firms will develop the productive capacity to compete domestically and internationally. Following World War II, import substitution was commonly used across Latin America and was also taken up in Africa and parts of Asia.

How successful was import substitution? Most observers have concluded that it did not produce the benefits expected, creating instead a kind of "hothouse economy." Insulated from the global economy, the state-supported firms could dominate the local market, but, lacking competition, they were much less innovative or efficient than their international competitors. The idea that these economies would eventually be opened up to the outside world became hard to envision; the harsh climate of the international market, it was thought, would quickly kill off these less competitive firms.

Import substitution thus resulted in economies with large industries reliant on the state for economic support and unable to compete in the international market. Such firms became a drain on state treasuries and a tempting resource for clientelism and rent seeking. This compounded the problem of international debt in these countries, for states had to borrow from other countries to build and subsidize their industries. Uncompetitiveness and debt led to economic stagnation. By and large, these countries also seem to have suffered from what is known as the **middle income trap**. A middle income trap is a situation where countries experience economic growth but are unable to develop at the speed necessary to catch up with developed countries. Thus for every South Korea, there is a Brazil or a South Africa experiencing initially rapid growth that slows down before the country reaches high income status. (We will speak more of this in the "Questions and Methods" section on pp. 352–53.)

Not all postcolonial countries pursued import substitution, however. Several Asian countries eventually discarded import substitution in favor of **export-oriented industrialization**. Countries that pursued an export-oriented strategy sought out technologies and developed industries that focused specifically on exports, capitalizing on what is known as the *product life cycle*. Initially, the innovator of a good produces it for the domestic market and then exports it to the rest of the world. As this product spreads, other countries find ways to make the same good more cheaply or more efficiently and eventually export their own version back to the country that originated the product. Thus, in South Korea, initial exports focused on basic technologies such as textiles and shoes but eventually moved into more complex areas, including automobiles and computers. This policy also had its problems: countries that pursued export-oriented industrialization also relied on high levels of government subsidies and tariff barriers. Yet overall, this strategy has led to levels of economic development much higher than those achieved through import substitution. Some Asian export-oriented countries originally had per capita GDPs far below those of many Latin American and even some African countries. The question of why Latin America pursued a path of import substitution while much of Asia focused on export-oriented industrialization is an interesting puzzle, and one that we will turn to at the end of this chapter (see "Institutions in Action," pp. 348–49).

By the 1980s, many developing countries—whether focused on import substitution or still largely focused on agricultural exports, as in Africa—faced deep economic problems, including high levels of government debt. Support from organizations like the World Bank or International Monetary Fund (IMF; see Chapter 11) was conditioned on economic liberalization (see Chapter 4). These policies of liberalization, often known as **neoliberalism**, **structural-adjustment programs**, or the **Washington Consensus**—since they reflect the policy preferences of institutions based in Washington, D.C., such as the World Bank and IMF—typically required countries to privatize state-run firms, end subsidies, reduce tariff barriers, shrink the size of the state, and welcome foreign investment. These reforms have been controversial and their benefits have been mixed. We will discuss this situation in greater detail shortly, when we consider future directions for economic prosperity in the poorer countries.

IN FOCUS: Three Paths to Economic Growth

IMPORT SUBSTITUTION	Based on mercantilism. State plays a strong role in the economy. Tariffs or nontariff barriers are used to restrict imports. State actively promotes domestic production, sometimes creating state-owned businesses in developing industries. Criticized for creating "hothouse economies," with large industries reliant on the state for support and unable to compete in the international market.
EXPORT-ORIENTED INDUSTRIALIZATION	Based on mercantilism. State plays a strong role in the economy. Tariff barriers are used to protect domestic industries. Economic production is focused on industries that have a niche in the international market. Seeks to integrate directly into the global economy. Has generally led to a higher level of economic development than import substitution.
STRUCTURAL ADJUSTMENT	Based on liberalism. State involvement is reduced as the economy is opened up. Foreign investment is encouraged. Often follows import substitution. Criticized as a tool of neocolonialism and for its failure in many cases to bring substantial economic development.

Puzzles and Prospects for Democracy and Development

We have covered some of the common challenges faced by developing countries in building institutions that will generate economic development and political stability. Our discussion may suggest that much of the developing world faces insurmountable challenges. This is incorrect. Despite ongoing difficulties, much of the developing world has seen dramatic improvements since independence. In 1960, the average life expectancy in India was age 43, and in Brazil, 54; as of 2019, these averages had increased to ages 70 and 76, respectively. As recently as 1990, the infant mortality rate in Indonesia was 84 per 1,000; in 2019, that rate had dropped to 21.

Of course, we can measure development in many different ways, and different parts of the world have had very different experiences. In general, Asia has done the best. Rapid growth is taking place in many of these countries alongside a trend toward effective states and democratization. Several countries in Latin America have also made great strides, particularly in the last decade, albeit with slower economic growth and high (though shrinking) levels of inequality. Africa remains one of the greatest challenges; it has the lowest rankings on the Human Development Index (HDI) and high levels of civil conflict and corruption. Yet even here, there is progress. For example, between 2000 and 2018 the GDP in sub-Saharan Africa increased fourfold, from $400 billion to $1.7 trillion.

What explains variations in development, either between countries or between regions? Scholars increasingly agree on some of the major factors at work, though their assessments of how to solve the problems differ widely. One important factor we have discussed is the interplay between ethnic divisions and borders (see Chapter 3). Deep ethnic divisions appear to correlate with greater economic and political instability. As we noted earlier, it may be much more difficult to forge a sense of national identity or national welfare when economic and political institutions are viewed as a means for one group to dominate others rather than as instruments to share power and wealth. This difficulty in forging national identities can be compounded by borders, which may exacerbate conflict by dividing ethnic or religious groups across international boundaries. Such conditions are particularly difficult in Africa.[9]

A second factor is resources. In Chapter 6, we spoke about the resource curse theory of development, which argues that countries with natural resources are hindered from political and economic development because the state or political actors can rely on these resources and effectively ignore public demands or needs. This strategy can further polarize politics when combined with ethnic divisions, since each group will seek to control those assets at the expense of others. Again, while many natural resources are relatively scarce in Asia, they are a central part of African economies, where such things as timber, oil, and diamonds not only lead to conflict but also fuel it, generating revenue for private militias and civil war.

Third, there is the question of governance. This is the hardest factor of the three to get a handle on, though it is perhaps the most important. It is evident to scholars that the obstacles discussed previously, among others, cannot be addressed unless there is an effective state. The state must be able to establish sovereignty and develop public goods and property rights while resisting corruption and allowing for the transfer of power between governments over time. But what is cause and what is effect? Are states weak because of ethnic division and the resource curse, or do weak states facilitate these outcomes? This confusion has generated a great deal of controversy in the policy realm. Should reforms be driven by the international community? Centered within developing states? Concentrated at the grassroots societal level? The remainder of this chapter will look at some possible solutions and the debates surrounding them.

Making a More Effective State

The view of the state as an aid or obstacle to development in the postcolonial world has shifted over time. In the immediate postwar era, modernization theory focused on the importance of the state in economic and political development, seeing it as the source of industrialization and modern political identities. Aid agencies and developed countries relied on states to be conduits for aid focused on large-scale, top-down development projects like dams or health care. Since 1960, overseas development aid from developed to developing countries has amounted to more than $3 trillion. However, many states failed to live up to expectations because corruption siphoned off resources and many development goals went unrealized. Large but inefficient states, often abetted by foreign funds, were common. As a result, by the 1980s the Washington Consensus took a different tack, encouraging (or pressuring) many developing countries to roll back state power, promote private industry, and limit regulation in the belief that market forces could succeed where states had failed. But while the Washington Consensus viewed states as too big and interventionist, others asserted that the power of these states needed to be redirected rather than reduced. Smaller would not be better if basic public needs still could not be met.[10] Of late, there has been a return to focusing on the state as a vital actor in such areas as delivering public goods. Reducing corruption, improving health care, increasing economic growth, and other basic state responsibilities require greater and more effective state capacity. The question is how we achieve this.

One important place to begin is to remember that there is no one-size-fits-all model, just as there is no homogeneous "developing world." There is tremendous variation in the developing world in terms of pre-imperial, imperial, and post-imperial history, natural resources, ethnic diversity, and other elements. This means that it is difficult to create a common sequence of actions that will improve institutions and create more effective and accountable states. How states can be made more effective depends on the existing institutions one must work with. We will consider some different approaches, understanding that none of these is necessarily the "right" response.

For developing countries that already have a reasonable degree of capacity and autonomy, improving governance may benefit from an emphasis on the rule of law. In Chapter 5, we spoke about this concept, where all individuals and groups are subject to the law irrespective of their power or authority. Much emphasis has been placed on the importance of the rule of law, especially in transitional countries that are moving from nondemocratic to democratic systems. Elected government may increase public participation, but in the absence of the rule of law democratic practices are less likely to become institutionalized. Elections may instead function as a contest to gain control over spoils rather than a system of democratic representation to serve the citizenry as a whole. The puzzle, though, is how to build the rule of law in the first place. Historical models, such as those of the developed democracies where the rule of law emerged over a century or longer, are of limited help. International donors, think tanks, and aid agencies typically argue that building the rule of law requires judicial reform, including stronger constitutional courts (as we discussed in Chapter 5), police, and civil service reform with tougher measures against corruption. The goal is a state that is more predictable and fairer in how it treats its citizens.

However, critics of such reforms argue that policy makers confuse cause and effect. It is not that institutional reforms will create norms regarding the rule of law; rather, norms must first emerge to generate pressure for institutional change. For example, political elites must demonstrate a commitment to institutional reform. This means not just new rules of the game but also a commitment from political players that they will follow the rules and abide by the outcomes. If individuals with political power are not committed to changes when they work against their immediate interests, rule of law cannot be institutionalized.[11] Equally important is the role of social actors to transmit and promote those values. The Progressive era in the United States in the late nineteenth century is a good example, where a host of movements and organizations sprang up to fight for such things as labor rights, women's rights, improved health and safety standards, and anticorruption measures. During this era, many powerful civic institutions, such as the League of Women Voters and the American Red Cross, were founded. Similar kinds of groups have emerged in many developing countries. Fostering social movements and nongovernmental organizations that embody and advance ideas such as the impartiality and universal application of rights may need to go hand in hand with changes in political elites and the institutions they control.

Developing Political Engagement

We saw earlier that making developing states more effective is connected to institutionalizing the rule of law. Political elites are important in that they must get on board with such changes, and society is central in helping articulate new norms and holding leaders accountable. But this leads us to another puzzle—how do societies get organized in the first place? Recall our discussion in Chapter 5 of civil society, which we defined as organized life outside the state. Civil society can accomplish several important things: it binds people together, creating a web of interests that cuts across class, religion, ethnicity, and other divisions; through activism and organization, it can hold political elites accountable and forms a bulwark against the abuse of state power; and it can inculcate a sense of democratic politics based on interaction, negotiation, consensus, and compromise. But how one builds this is unclear. Discussions of civil society often assume that when a society develops economically people necessarily cultivate a more diverse array of interests, and these inevitably lead to civil society. Even if this is true, it does not provide much guidance for how to consciously build civil society in countries that are less developed.

The lack of clarity around fostering organized political engagement is compounded by the fact that, for many development experts, this has not been an area of focus, a legacy of the attention paid instead to the state. For example, the World Bank (a major international development organization we will discuss in the next chapter) has only recently begun to think explicitly about how people mobilize and to what end. Even this discussion, they note, has tended to emphasize how to "get around" politics rather than improve how politics functions.[12] For example, recall our discussion of Pakistan's electricity problem in Chapter 2. Dealing with electricity theft can be seen as a technical problem to be solved with regulations, meters, and fines. But this ignores the bigger question of how to use civil society as a way to manage a public good and hold citizens, political leaders, and the state accountable to each other. Institutions that work well in developed countries cannot be simply imported into developing countries and expected to work unless the public believes in, trusts, and is part of the process. History is littered with examples of development projects that failed for lack of public legitimacy.

What encourages political engagement and strengthens civil society? Research suggests that accountability, that is, monitoring how political leaders and the state are delivering public goods and disseminating information, is key. While there has been a good deal of interest in promoting civil society in developing countries, such advocacy groups have often not been focused on institutional reform. Instead, civil society is promoted as a way to manage local issues that have been neglected by the state. This emphasis on the role of local politics is very much consistent with our discussions of devolution in Chapter 8, so it is not surprising that experts from developed democracies would promote the kinds of changes that are under way in their own countries. But to be effective, local engagement needs to hold individuals and institutions accountable all the way up to the national level, influencing parties and national policy. This may seem like a tall order; however, the widespread penetration of mass media and electronic communication (TV, radio, cell phones) across developing countries can allow for effective engagement, increasing the public's political efficacy.[13]

One final caveat: we have discussed civil society as an essential component of democratic participation and state efficacy. These go hand in hand. A state is unlikely to reform without both leadership and pressure from a politically organized and engaged society. But political engagement does not automatically mean better politics. One major challenge is that organized groups are a tempting target for clientelist politics, where political leaders can buy off local groups in return for political support. Civil society can overwhelm a state if it lacks the capacity to meet public demands. Interwar Germany has been cited as an example of a country with a vibrant civil society alongside a weak state, and the Soviet Union can be viewed as another example where growing civil society did not simply bring down the regime but fractured the state as well. Thus, just as we should not look to the state as the sole instrument of development, we should not conclude that development strategies can be carried out by society alone.

Promoting Economic Prosperity

Our discussion of states and societies in developing countries has emphasized the critical interaction between organized political engagement and institutional reform. But we have so far not discussed economic development itself, which many people would put front and center. Recall, however, our argument that a primarily economics-based approach, which has dominated development strategies for decades, has in many cases been ineffective because of a failure to focus on political institutions.

One important aspect of this problem lies in the nature of markets and property. Earlier in this chapter, we discussed import substitution versus export-oriented industrialization as methods of industrialization chosen by many developing countries. But these strategies do not account for the majority of workers, who otherwise work in local service, agriculture, or manufacturing. Moreover, these individuals often are part of what is known as the **informal economy**. The term *informal sector* refers to a segment of the economy that is not regulated, protected, or taxed by the state. Typically, the informal economy is dominated by the self-employed or by small enterprises, such as an individual street vendor or a family that makes or repairs goods out of its home. In some cases, the informal economy may represent over half of a country's GDP, and women play a large role. According to some studies, in many developing countries a majority of women working outside the agricultural sector are part of the informal economy. The informal economy can be very flexible, creating opportunities for work where it might otherwise not be available. However, it raises the question of why informal economic activities are so much stronger in developing countries than in more developed ones.

Informal economies are often associated with weak states that are unable to effectively regulate the economy or prevent corruption. Under these conditions, the state may be highly bureaucratic but unable to provide the oversight of property or markets that would be found where the rule of law is strong. In this environment, state and government officials often capitalize on their authority by demanding bribes from business owners to ease their way through regulations. An informal economy is also much more difficult to tax, making it a challenge for states to generate revenue. Finally, because of state weakness in managing markets and property, it is much harder for businesses to scale up into larger firms.

These economic circumstances take us back to the fundamental question of where development efforts should be focused, and they can be clearly seen in the debate over one popular development tool, known as *microcredit* or *microfinance*. Though these terms are often used interchangeably, there is a difference. **Microcredit** refers to a system where small loans (often of less than $1,000) are made available to small-scale businesses that otherwise lack access to capital. Microfinance covers a much broader spectrum, including credit, savings, insurance, and financial transfers. Microcredit is often funded through nonprofit organizations, and in some cases the borrower is also held accountable to other borrowers in a local association, in that a failure of one individual to repay limits further loans that can be taken out by the members in that association. This system increases the desire for members to vet loans and oversee their use within the association.

With globalization, microcredit has expanded; now organizations like the United States–based Kiva allow individuals around the world to make loans to people in need. As of 2019, nearly 2 million lenders had loaned over $1 billion to over 3 million individuals.[14] Kiva is modeled after Bangladesh's Grameen Bank, whose founder, Muhammad Yunus, won a Nobel Peace Prize in 2006.

While attractive in theory, critics of microcredit and microfinance note that there is scant evidence as to its effectiveness. Studies in India, for example, showed that poor communities that had access to microcredit did not show a drop in poverty or an improvement in outcomes like education, health care, or women's empowerment (the latter of which is a frequent claim made by advocates). There is also no evidence that they are a means for firms to grow and take on employees—a critical step in development and the creation of a middle class. Recalling our discussion of Fair Trade coffee, while the idea of a small business may sound appealing, historically, successful development has been dependent on a transition to larger firms and an economy where most of the workers are employees rather than entrepreneurs.[15]

If microlevel solutions are not the means to generate economic development, others suggest that focusing on larger-scale projects is what is required. The Millennium Villages created in sub-Saharan Africa are the best known—and, like microcredit, controversial—examples. Linked to the United Nations' Millennium Development Goals to improve living standards in the developing world, the Villages' 14 small communities were given targeted interventions to improve the residents' lives, ranging from changes in crop production and improved education to the distribution of bed nets to reduce malaria. The idea was that successes could then be tweaked and expanded to new communities. Overall, about $120 million was spent on the project—not a small sum, but far below the trillions that have been spent on global development aid over the past decades.

How did the Millennium Villages fare? The program concluded in 2016, and the findings are mixed and a source of great debate. One surprising problem goes back to the comparative method that we spoke of in Chapter 1. While scholars could track changes in many of the Millennium Villages, these villages needed to be compared with similar communities that lacked such intervention. For example, one report noted the rapid rise of mobile phone use in the Millennium Villages without noting that this had occurred at the same rate across sub-Saharan Africa as a whole.[16] The absence of reliable data across Millennium and non-Millennium villages meant that researchers had no way to control variables and thus make effective comparisons. As a result, many conclude that it is nearly impossible to evaluate how effective the Millennium Villages have been to date relative to their surrounding communities.

INSTITUTIONS IN ACTION

Why Did Asia Industrialize Faster than Latin America?

The rise of Asia over the past four decades as a global exporter, producing increasingly sophisticated goods over that time, presents an interesting puzzle, especially when we compare the region's economic development with that of Latin America. In 1970, Brazil's and Argentina's per capita GDP at PPP were between $2,500 and $3,500, higher than South Korea's or Taiwan's. By 2019, while these Latin American countries had GDPs between $16,000 and $21,000, the GDPs of South Korea and Taiwan had soared to between $40,000 and $55,000. How did these Asian countries come from behind and grow so much wealthier than many of their Latin American counterparts? A simple explanation—such as a correlation between democracy and speed of economic growth—does not work, since all of these states were authoritarian during most of the last 50 years. What, then, might be the explanation?

There are several theories regarding Asia's faster growth. According to one argument, which we can describe as geostrategic, the major difference between Latin America and Asia lies in their relationships to the United States and how their political-economic institutions were shaped by these relationships. Latin America's experience of U.S. influence during much of the nineteenth and early twentieth centuries has been described as neocolonial. In this interpretation, the subordinate relationship of Latin America to the United States effectively prevented the development of industries that could reach an export capacity and be competitive in world markets. Instead, economic development was dominated by foreign (U.S. and European) goods and foreign investments that concentrated on the production of consumer goods for the small upper and middle classes rather than on broader industrialization.

In contrast, following China's 1949 revolution, the United States viewed Asia as under direct threat from communism and as a result supported industrialization policies—through preferential trade agreements—that limited foreign direct investment and promoted export-oriented growth. Whereas Latin American markets were influenced (if not dominated) by Western investments, Asia's drive toward industrialization and export-led growth was fueled by state investments. While this argument can help explain why the regions' economies developed so differently, it doesn't account for a country like Mexico. There, for much of the early twentieth century, foreign investment was limited by the state, and rapid industrial development resembled that of Asia later in the century.

A second argument concentrates on domestic politics and institutions within these regions. One area that has attracted a great deal of attention is land ownership and land reform. In many countries, agriculture is a powerful economic and political force. This is especially the case where agriculture takes the form of large landholdings, which concentrate power in relatively few hands, so that much of the population works land they do not own. Where such landowners are powerful, states may find it difficult to raise funds and build capacity and autonomy. Urbanization and industrialization are held back by the interests of landed elites (who often oppose the rise of both).

In the case of Latin America, economies dominated by large landholders and estates, known as latifundia (*haciendas*, in Spanish), developed as part of Spanish and Portuguese colonialism to produce commodities such as sugar and coffee on a large scale for export. Independence from imperialism did not destroy this agricultural system, however, and latifundia economies remained in Latin America as landed elites continued to dominate economic and political institutions. Latin America's economy developed more slowly, therefore, not because it lacked integration with the global economy or exported fewer goods but because the nature of its exports—agriculture and natural resources—did not provide a strong foundation for industrial development.

In Asia as in Latin America, much of the agricultural land was originally concentrated in a small number of estates. However, in places like South Korea and Taiwan, one of the first steps the state took after gaining independence was to enact widespread agricultural reform to break the landed elites' monopoly and empower the peasantry. A central motivating factor was the desire to stave off peasant-backed communist revolutions like the ones that happened in China and North Korea, where land reform was a key promise of the Communist Party. This argument in many ways takes us back to the geostrategic issue, though the critical issue here is the role of political elites in Asian countries in bringing the old feudal order to an end. As in the case of our first possible explanation, however, this argument has flaws. The emphasis on the overwhelming power of the latifundia needs to be balanced by a consideration of the fact that Latin America has become an overwhelmingly urban region—over 80 percent of its population now lives in cities. Moreover, as mentioned earlier, many Latin American

Workers collect sugar cane on a plantation in the Dominican Republic. A cane cutter earns approximately four U.S. dollars per ton.

countries did develop a significant industrial base, even in the absence of land reform.

What, then, is the solution to our puzzle? We cannot draw clear conclusions, though certain factors seem significant. The institutional legacies of imperialism do appear to be stronger in Latin America than in Asia, although the economic policies in the two regions have been influenced differently by postwar international politics. This intersection of institutions and policies may explain what moved Asia and Latin America down different paths of development that will continue to influence their future.[a]

1. What role did foreign direct investment in Latin America versus state investment in Asia play in the regions' differing paths?

2. How did the legacy of colonialism and its institutions affect Latin America's industrial development?

3. How did concerns about communism influence both the Asian countries' relationship with the United States and their own approach to land reform?

Institutions in Action   349

This brings us to a dilemma, one that plagues governments, international actors, and citizens alike. States are necessary to support and protect economic development, but in many developing countries they lack capacity and are one of the biggest obstacles to progress. A common response to this challenge is to effectively bypass the state, whether through grassroots microfunding or attempts to improve conditions village by village. Neither of these approaches fully addresses how to capitalize on any successes they might achieve.

It is easy to draw pessimistic conclusions from our discussions so far. Various attempts to improve institutions in developing countries have produced mixed responses, leaving many to wonder what, if any, progress has been made. However, we can point to steps in the right direction, focused more on methodology than specific policies. As was already mentioned regarding Fair Trade, microcredit, and the Millennium Villages, one major concern has been that hardly any comparative research has been done in attempting to control variables and look for causal relationships. This may be surprising, but states and international agencies alike have done relatively little comparative research to assess what kinds of policies can work and under what conditions. Now scholars are attempting to more carefully study development strategies before, during, and after they are implemented, comparing these with similar cases where such actions are absent. Only with such comparisons will we be able to draw conclusions about what kinds of development policies actually work.[17]

In Sum: The Challenges of Development

Although they are at different levels of development, almost all developing countries share the legacies of imperial rule. The fusion of local institutions with those of imperial powers created challenges as these countries sought to chart their own independent courses. Weak states; conflicts over ethnicity, nation, religion, and gender; and incomplete and distorted forms of industrialization all contributed to instability, authoritarianism, economic difficulties, and overall low levels of freedom and equality. Some countries have overcome many of these obstacles, but it is unclear whether their strategies and experiences provide lessons that can be easily applied elsewhere in the world.

There is no consensus on how to tackle the most pressing problems of the developing world. Some have advocated ambitious top-down goals and a recommitment of foreign aid toward these outcomes. Others are skeptical that aid interventions are effective. More generally, we have little hard evidence about what does and does not work. This situation suggests that a better bet may be to focus instead on those policies where we can control our variables in order to evaluate what works. Whichever path we choose, globalization, which we will turn to in the next chapter, will shape future development. Will it provide new solutions or create new barriers to progress?

Key Terms

colonialism (p. 324)
developing countries (p. 322)
empire (p. 324)
export-oriented industrialization (p. 339)
imperialism (p. 324)
import substitution (p. 338)
informal economy (p. 346)
lower income countries (p. 322)

microcredit (p. 346)
middle income countries (p. 322)
middle income trap (p. 339)
neocolonialism (p. 338)
neoliberalism/structural-adjustment
    programs/Washington Consensus
    (p. 340)

For Further Reading

Banerjee, Abhijit V., and Esther Duflo. *Poor Economics: A Radical Rethinking of the Way to Fight Global Poverty.* New York: PublicAffairs, 2011.

Collier, Paul, and Jan Willem Gunning. "Why Has Africa Grown Slowly?" *Journal of Economic Perspectives* 13, no. 3 (Summer 1999): 3–22.

Deaton, Angus. *The Great Escape: Health, Wealth, and the Origins of Inequality.* Princeton, NJ: Princeton University Press, 2013.

Easterly, William. *The Tyranny of Experts: Economists, Dictators, and the Forgotten Rights of the Poor.* New York: Basic Books, 2013.

Fukuyama, Francis. *State-Building: Governance and World Order in the 21st Century.* Ithaca, NY: Cornell University Press, 2004.

Gann, L. H., and Peter Duignan, eds. *Colonialism in Africa, 1870–1960.* 5 vols. Cambridge: Cambridge University Press, 1969–74.

Haggard, Stephan. *Pathways from the Periphery: The Politics of Growth in the Newly Industrializing Countries.* Ithaca, NY: Cornell University Press, 1990.

Kohli, Atul. *State-Directed Development: Political Power and Industrialization in the Global Periphery.* New York: Cambridge University Press, 2004.

INQUIZITIVE

Earn a better grade on your test. InQuizitive personalizes your learning path to help you master the concepts from this chapter and practice applying them to examples from the text and beyond (see back cover).

QUESTIONS AND METHODS

How Can Countries Avoid the Middle Income Trap?

There has been a great deal of discussion in recent years regarding the idea of the middle income trap, which we mentioned earlier. The concept is relatively straightforward, and in some ways it can be connected to the discussion of different paths of industrialization that we have already considered in the chapter. As seen in the figure below, developing countries, after a period of rapid growth, remain stuck at a middle income level (under $15,000 per capita GDP at PPP), unable to sustain a rate of growth that would lead them to become a high income economy. These countries find themselves squeezed between those economies that are able to rely on cheap labor and those that have become high-tech innovators. A more extreme version of the middle income trap concerns not the relative distance between wealthier and poorer countries—both are growing but the poorer countries can't catch up—but the fact that some middle income countries may eventually confront minimal or even negative economic growth.

In short, the idea of a middle income trap suggests that while it may be easy for poor countries to boost their economies, it is much harder for them to sustain growth to bring them to a high income level. The evidence for the middle income trap seems strong: a World Bank study found that of 101 middle income economies in the 1960s, only 13 had become high income by 2008.[a] South Korea, which in 1950 had a GDP per capita at PPP under $1,500, is thus an economic anomaly. This suggests that while sound economic policies may be able to cut absolute poverty, it is much more difficult to narrow the

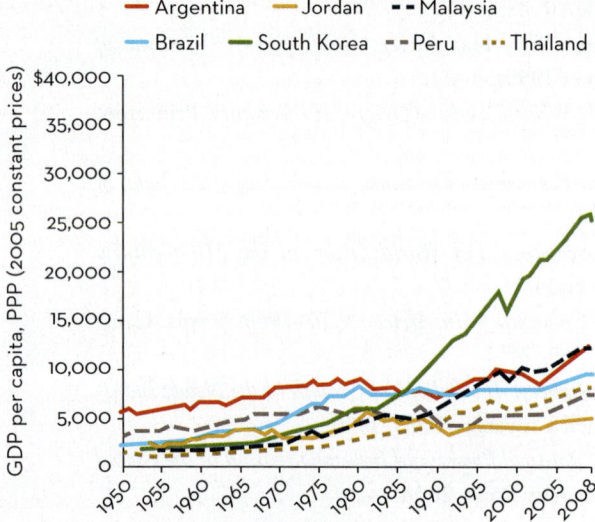

Developing Countries Stuck in the Middle Income Trap

Source: World Bank and Development Research Center of the State Council, the People's Republic of China, *China 2030: Building a Modern, Harmonious, and Creative Society* (Washington, DC: World Bank, 2013), p. 12.

inequality gap between countries in the long run. It also suggests that countries like China may find it much harder to grow wealthy past their initial phase of development, something we will touch on in the next chapter on globalization.

How can countries avoid the middle income trap? There may be several factors. One possible area is a commitment to higher education. Strong higher education institutions seem to correlate strongly with greater economic development—70 percent of South Koreans between 24 and 35 have college degrees, compared with 40 percent in Argentina and only 20 percent in Brazil, helping facilitate the transition from a labor- to knowledge-intensive economy. Another factor is one we have spoken of at length—the rule of law. Countries with stronger protection of individual and property rights and lower levels of corruption also create an environment more conducive to innovation and investment. In short, establishing "inclusive" institutions that benefit a wide range of society (as opposed to more clientelist or patrimonial ones) may be the key to economic transitions, as opposed to traps.

1. ***Connect related arguments***

   Can we draw any connections between the idea of the middle income trap and our earlier discussion about import substitution and export-led growth?

2. ***Consider the policy implications***

   If solutions to the middle income trap include an improved rule of law, what steps could policy makers take in order to improve in this area? Think carefully of what policy improvements would strengthen the rule of law and why.

3. ***Generate new questions and assertions***

   What would be some alternative variables you might hypothesize would help overcome the middle income trap? How would you define and measure those independent variables?

---

a. World Bank and Development Research Center of the State Council, the People's Republic of China, *China 2030: Building a Modern, Harmonious, and Creative Society* (Washington, DC: World Bank, 2013).

11

Crowds of people queue up in front of a new Apple Store in Chongqing, China. China is Apple's largest market, ahead of the United States and Europe.

GLOBALIZATION AND THE FUTURE OF COMPARATIVE POLITICS

How do global forces shape local communities?

In the past decade, China overtook the United States as the world's largest economy when calculated at purchasing power parity (PPP). By this measure, America's domination of the global economy, which emerged in the mid-nineteenth century by surpassing the United Kingdom, has come to an end. China's economy is expected to continue growing faster than the U.S. economy, further increasing the gap between them. By 2029, China could surpass the U.S. gross domestic product (GDP) in total market terms, not just in PPP.

Several questions prompted by these circumstances have been the source of heated debate around the globe, and they inevitably revolve around globalization. The first is one of cause and effect. Did globalization lead to the rise of China, or did China lead to the rise of globalization? Most observers assume the former, that the rise of globalization—the spread of new forms of communication like the Internet, the end of the Cold War, and the expansion of liberal economic ideas over communism—meant that China, long isolated from the rest of the world, could finally partake in and benefit from a global order. In this view, globalization has been an inexorable force that has drawn in China just as it has other countries and parts of the world. Others, however, make a convincing case that it is China that has driven globalization. Domestic economic reforms in China starting in the 1980s focused on export-driven growth. This in turn transformed economies around the world. Local industries have disappeared worldwide in the face of Chinese competition, while commodities like copper and oil are exported to feed China's development. Even the decline of global poverty that we discussed in Chapter 10 has been driven largely by China's economic growth.

These developments lead to a second set of questions. What will the rise of China mean to political globalization—the spread and deepening of shared political ideologies and values? We tend to see two diametrically opposed views.[1] The first posits that China's deepening international ties are transforming the country's domestic politics. This is essentially a liberal view, asserting that globalization leads to the global spread of democratic ideas alongside the emergence of a middle class. Combined, these changes will eventually sweep the Communist Party away. No authoritarian system can block this process.

Others are more skeptical. In their view, China is the country driving global political change, not the one being changed by it. Reforms in domestic economic institutions have allowed China to capitalize on and expand globalization, but these reforms serve only to reinforce authoritarian legitimacy at home by promising prosperity in exchange for acquiescence. Moreover, growing economic power means that China increasingly has the ability to reshape the global order to its liking. This power includes pressuring its Asian neighbors to accede to Chinese demands as well as expanding its influence via trade and investment from Latin America to Africa (recall our discussion of Zimbabwe in Chapter 6). All of these changes are undercutting the West's promotion of liberal values. The world may continue to globalize, as this argument goes, but it will be on China's authoritarian terms.

We are thus presented with two fairly stark alternatives, each based on a very different view of the causes and effects of globalization. Is globalization changing and transforming China in a way that will bring it to democracy? Or is China the engine of globalization, shaping the international system in a way that serves its authoritarian regime? Interestingly, despite their very different conclusions, these arguments share an emphasis on globalization that diminishes the role of domestic institutions, which have been central to this book. Both arguments rest on the assumption that China is inexorably rising to the position of a dominant world actor and tend to ignore domestic factors within China.

As comparativists, we should scrutinize these arguments more closely. For example, although China's GDP has leaped forward, in per capita terms it is still far behind most developed democracies. And the belief that it will soon catch up to the developed democracies is not so certain, either. China may face the kind of middle income trap that we spoke of in the last chapter. Slowing economic growth, an aging population, extensive environmental damage, increased corruption, deepening inequality, and growing public protests are all domestic factors that may limit China's rise to prominence and even undermine globalization itself. Who knows?

A generation ago, scholars and pundits spoke of "Japan as Number One," as one famous book was titled.[2] Perhaps China, like globalization itself, will not change the world in ways we expect.

LEARNING OBJECTIVES

- Define globalization and the types of organizations that have facilitated it.
- Describe political, economic, and social globalization and the arguments for and against each.
- Evaluate the depth and novelty of globalization in the modern era.

The central theme of this textbook has been the struggle to balance freedom and equality. When societies clash over how to reconcile these two values, states must confront the resulting problems by using their capacity to generate and enforce policy. Democratic institutions presume that freedom and equality are best reconciled through public participation, whereas nondemocratic regimes significantly restrict such rights. The variety of institutional tools available has led to a diverse political world, where freedom and equality are combined and balanced in many different ways.

Over the past two decades or more, this dynamic has become more international in scope. Of course, domestic politics has always been shaped by international forces, such as war and trade, empires and colonies, migration and the spread of ideas. But to some observers, linkages between states, societies, and economies appear to be intensifying, and at an increasingly rapid pace they are challenging long-standing institutions, assumptions, and norms. This process is commonly known as **globalization**, a term that fills some with a sense of optimism and others with dread. Although the extent of globalization and its long-term impact remain unclear, behind it lies the sense that the battle over freedom and equality is an international one, no longer a concern to be solved by each country in its own way.

What does this mean for comparative politics? At the end of Chapter 1, we discussed how comparative politics (and political science) remains hindered by problems of data and theory that are often unable to predict, much less explain, human behavior. Comparative politics has suffered in the past from scholars understanding too few cases, thus making comparisons difficult. But if globalization is transforming domestic politics, the very idea of comparative politics could be open to question. To play devil's advocate, wouldn't studying Brazil's energy-export sector be more valuable than investigating the internal workings of its legislature? Wouldn't a study of Internet traffic in the European Union yield better puzzles and answers than a study of German political culture? Wouldn't comparativists learn more from studying transnational crime networks than judicial politics in South Africa?

Of course, we can argue that "globalized" questions need not come at the expense of comparative politics, but the question remains whether scholars of political science are missing the big questions that lie in the space between comparative politics (the study of politics within countries) and international relations (the study of politics between them). The questions just listed present a false dilemma, because we needn't choose between these areas of research. However, such questions help us consider the issue that comparative politics as it is structured now may not be focused on important global puzzles and institutions. In summary, is there even such a thing as domestic politics any longer? Is everything that we've read in this book up to this point becoming obsolete or irrelevant? And if so, how are we to study politics in a globalized world?

In this chapter, we look at the concept of globalization and its potential impact on both comparative politics and the ongoing struggle over the balance of freedom and equality. We will begin by defining globalization and determining how we might measure it. Next, we will consider some possible effects of globalization, including how it may change political, economic, and societal institutions at the domestic level. We will also ask some questions about the progress of globalization—whether it is in fact something fundamentally new, profound, and inevitable. We will then conclude with a discussion of how the old dilemma of balancing freedom and equality may change in a globalized world.

What Is Globalization?

We could argue that we have lived in a globalized world for millennia. Even as early humans dispersed around the world tens of thousands of years ago, they maintained and developed long-distance connections with one another through migration and trade. Such contacts helped spur development through the dissemination of knowledge and innovations. For example, it is speculated that the technology of written language was created independently only three or four times in human history: in the Americas, in Asia, and in the Middle East. All other written languages were essentially modeled after these innovations as the idea of writing things down spread to other communities.[3] Thousands of years ago, empires stretched from Asia to Europe and people moved between these areas, exchanging goods, ideas, and illnesses. Trade routes forged even more far-flung connections between people who were only dimly aware of each other's existence. For example, in the first century C.E. the Romans treasured silk imported from distant China, although they did not fully understand how it was made or where it came from. Were these, then, "globalized" societies?

When we speak about globalization, we don't simply mean international contacts and interaction, which have existed for tens of thousands of years. According to the political scientists Robert O. Keohane and Joseph S. Nye Jr., one important distinction between globalization and these earlier ties is that many of these past relationships were relatively "thin," involving a small number of people. Although such connections may have been extensive across a vast region, these connections did not directly affect large numbers of individuals. In contrast, globalization can be viewed as a process by which global connections grow increasingly "thick," creating an extensive and intensive web of relationships between many people across vast distances. In the twenty-first century, people are not distantly connected by overland routes plied by traders, diplomats, and missionaries; they are directly participating in a vast and complex international network through travel, communication, business, and education. Globalization is a system in which human beings are no longer part of isolated communities that are linked through narrow channels of diplomatic relations or trade. Entire societies are now directly connected to global affairs. Thus globalization represents a change in human organization and interconnection.[4]

Globalization has a number of potential implications for comparative politics. First, because of the thickening of connections between people across countries, globalization breaks down the distinction between international relations and domestic politics, making many aspects of domestic politics subject to global forces. Debates over environmental policy become linked to climate change; struggles over inequality are framed by concerns about trade, offshore outsourcing, and immigration; health care is influenced by the threat of pandemics. As a result, political isolation becomes difficult or even impossible. (See "Institutions in Action" on pp. 378–79 for a discussion of the relationship between globalization and climate change.)

Second, globalization can also work in the other direction, essentially "internationalizing" domestic issues and events. Given that globalization deepens and widens international connections, local events, even small ones, can have ripple effects throughout the world. These interconnections across space are further amplified by the speed of today's world. Whereas technological change once took years or centuries to spread from region to region, today a new piece of software or video can be downloaded or viewed at the same time everywhere. The

Internet allows the rapid dissemination of news and information from every corner of the globe, no matter how remote. The world seems to live increasingly in the same moment—what happens to someone in one place immediately affects others around the world.

In short, globalization is a process that creates intensive and extensive international connections, changing traditional relationships of time and space. Is globalization overturning or transforming the very foundations of politics? Would such a change make the world a better place—more prosperous, stable, and democratic—or just the opposite? And finally, is any of this inevitable? These are big questions of profound significance that have found little consensus. Let us first consider how we can think about the nature of institutions in a globalizing world.

Institutions and Globalization

We have spoken of globalization as a process, one that creates more extensive and intensive connections across the globe. These changes can, in turn, change the institutions of economics, politics, and society. At the start of this textbook, we spoke of institutions as being a key reference point for modern life. Institutions are organizations or patterns of activity that are self-perpetuating and valued for their own sake. The modern world is codified by them. Institutions such as states, culture, property, and markets establish borders, set boundaries for activity and behavior, and allocate authority, norms, rights, and responsibilities. Moreover, by doing so they establish local identity and control—a particular state, religion, or set of cultural values holds sway over the land and people here but not there. Space and time are thus understood and measured through institutions.

The question we now ask is whether this will still be true in the future. It may be that before long, domestic institutions will not be the most important actors in people's lives. Long-standing institutions like states, cultures, national identities, and political-economic systems now face a range of international forces and organizations that transform, challenge, or threaten their traditional roles. Let's look at some of the reasons this might be the case.

To begin, globalization is associated with the growing power of a host of nonstate or supra-state entities. Most can be grouped into three categories that we touched on in previous chapters: **multinational corporations (MNCs), nongovernmental organizations (NGOs), and intergovernmental organizations (IGOs)**. All three organizational forms are decades, if not centuries, old, but their role and impact are rapidly expanding as they benefit from and contribute to globalization. MNCs are firms that produce, distribute, and market goods and services in more than one country. They wield assets and profits far larger than the GDPs of most countries in the world and are able to influence politics, economic developments, and social relations through the goods and services they produce and the wealth at their disposal. NGOs are national and international groups that are independent of any state and pursue policy objectives and foster public participation. Some, such as Greenpeace and Amnesty International, can shape domestic and international politics by mobilizing public support across the globe. IGOs, groups created by states to serve particular policy ends, include the United Nations, the World Trade Organization (WTO), the European Union, and the Organization of American States.

In some cases, these forms of organizations are part of a broader **international regime**. The use of this term in the study of international relations is similar to our use of *regime* in comparative politics. Recall from Chapter 2 that in comparative politics, regimes are defined as the fundamental rules and norms of politics, a set of institutions that empower and constrain states and governments. International regimes function in the same way, but they link states together through rules and norms that shape their relationships to one another, usually regarding some specific issue (such as greenhouse gases or trade).

In addition to MNCs, NGOs, and IGOs, technology-driven forms of organization also play a role in globalization. This is not new. All earlier waves of human interconnection were dependent on technological changes, such as the domestication of plants and animals, the invention of writing, advances in seafaring, and the invention of the telegraph. Technology is not inherently globalizing or globalized, though in many cases technology and globalization can reinforce each other.

In the last 40 years, one of the most important examples of such reinforcement has been the development of the Internet. Originally created by the U.S. government as a way to decentralize communications in the event of a nuclear war, the Internet has grown far beyond this initial limited objective to become a means for people to exchange goods and information, much of it beyond the control of any one state or regulatory authority. As bandwidth has increased and more information has been digitized, the Internet has been transformed from a tool into an entity in its own right, holding a tremendous amount of content. Unlike MNCs, NGOs, or IGOs, the Internet has no single "location" to speak of—indeed, we hardly even speak of "the Internet" any longer, so ubiquitous is its presence. The Internet is also unlike a typical regime: it has technical standards, but it does not have norms that link states together to address a specific issue or meet a specific goal; it is not the means toward any one end. Discussions of authority, sovereignty, and control become problematic. But as technological change facilitates the

> ## IN FOCUS: Nonstate Organizations and Globalization
>
> | ORGANIZATION | DEFINITION | EXAMPLE |
> |---|---|---|
> | **MULTINATIONAL CORPORATIONS (MNCs)** | Firms that produce, distribute, and market their goods or services in more than one country | Apple, General Electric |
> | **NONGOVERNMENTAL ORGANIZATIONS (NGOs)** | National and international groups, independent of any state, that pursue policy objectives and foster public participation | Greenpeace, Red Cross |
> | **INTERGOVERNMENTAL ORGANIZATIONS (IGOs)** | Groups created by states to serve particular policy ends | United Nations, European Union |

growing reach of nonstate or supra-state actors, these actors in turn tend to foster further technological change.

Are these organizations, whether the United Nations or the Internet, indeed institutions? This is an important question, for as we have noted, institutionalization carries with it authority and legitimacy. Many MNCs, IGOs, and NGOs are legitimate and highly valued—seemingly indispensable parts of the global system. The same could be said of the Internet or other forms of technology, such as satellite television or the global positioning system (GPS). As institutions, then, they can call on a degree of influence and power. This influence may augment and improve the workings of domestic institutions; it may also conflict with or undermine them. Let us consider this idea further through the familiar categories of states, economies, and societies.

Political Globalization

In Chapter 2, we noted that in historical terms the state is relatively new, a form of political organization that emerged only in the past few centuries. Because of their unique organization, states were able to spread quickly across the globe, supplanting all other forms of political organization. Yet we also noted that if states have not always been present, there may come a time when they will no longer be the dominant political actor on the face of the earth. States may at some time cease to exist. Some see globalization as the force that will bring about this dramatic political change, but whether such a change is to be welcomed or feared is uncertain.

At the core of this debate is the fact that globalization and globalized institutions complicate the ability of states to maintain sovereignty. In some cases, states may give up sovereignty intentionally—giving authority to IGOs, for instance, to gain some benefit or alleviate some existing problem. The European Union is an excellent example of this—though, as we have seen, even under these conditions sovereignty is often given up reluctantly or rejected outright. The United Kingdom's decision to leave the European Union reminds us how sovereignty and integration can clash and that the former does not easily give way to the latter. In other cases, the loss of sovereignty may be unintentional. The growth of the Internet, for example, has had important implications for states regarding legal authority in many traditional areas, since it does not readily conform to international boundaries or rules. It can circumvent legal restrictions on certain forms of speech in a way that traditional newspapers or television cannot, through e-mail, websites, and social networks. Developments such as electronic currency may further erode the powers of states by undercutting their ability to print money, levy taxes, or regulate financial transactions—all critical elements of sovereignty.

What do these changes mean for state autonomy and capacity? One possible scenario is that states will become bound to numerous international institutions that will take on many of the tasks that states normally conduct. In this scenario, a web of organizations, public and private, domestic and international, would shape politics and policy, set standards, and enforce rules on a wide range of issues where states lack effective authority. The rule of law would become a preserve less of individual states than of a set of global institutions created for and enforced by a variety of actors.

With this diffusion of responsibility, sovereignty would decline. States would be "hollowed out," constrained by their reliance on the globalized world. This would affect their use of force. People cannot arrest computer viruses or enact sanctions against global warming, and despite the United States' call for a "war on drugs" and a "war on terror," we cannot declare war on such threats in the conventional sense. For globalized states, then, war may become largely ineffective and too risky, for it may undermine vital international connections. This narrowing of state sovereignty as a result of globalization is what the *New York Times* columnist Thomas Friedman famously referred to as a "golden straitjacket."[5] In this view, political globalization may bring about a more peaceful world order, constraining states' tendencies toward violent conflict by dispersing sovereignty among numerous actors and diminishing the capacity and autonomy of states.

In addition, it has been argued that globalization will change not only the utility of force but also the nature of public participation and democracy. The increasing interconnection between domestic and international institutions makes it more difficult for sovereign actors to function without oversight from other organizations and to hide their actions from others. An example here is the development of the International Criminal Court, which has been charged with holding state leaders accountable for human rights violations in Libya, Sudan, and the former Yugoslavia. NGOs, such as Human Rights Watch or Transparency International (an anticorruption NGO), can play a similarly powerful watchdog role. Globalization will thus make politics less opaque and more open to scrutiny by domestic and international communities.

In contrast to these optimistic views, others see political globalization not as a pathway to peace and participation but as a source of dangerous fragmentation and weakened democracy. First, in their view, violence will not lose its utility in the international system as optimists hope; it will simply change form, much as it did when states themselves first appeared. According to this argument, globalization can empower violent international actors and movements that in many ways are the exact opposite of the modern state. These groups are decentralized and flexible, hold no territory, exercise no sovereignty, and are able to draw financial and other support from across the globe. In many ways, then, they are like other nonstate actors. Yet unlike NGOs and MNCs, these groups seek to achieve their objectives by acquiring and using force, applying it in ways that may be difficult for states or other international actors to counter.

Globalized criminal organizations and terrorist groups are perfect examples of this new threat. These are decentralized groups empowered by globalized technology, such as cell phones, encrypted e-mail, websites, social media, and satellite television, which allows them to communicate, disseminate propaganda, access money, and recruit new members. Indeed, many argue that such groups look more like a social network than any formal nonstate actor.[6] Although states may at times be able to use conventional force against such groups where they have a physical presence, there is often no central location to attack or any easy way to keep individuals and information from simply dispersing and regrouping elsewhere. States, whose military capacity is geared toward fighting other states, may be ill-equipped to battle small groups and "dark networks" that can take advantage of globalization to attack and undermine existing institutions.

Second, many question how a more globalized political system can be more democratic. Although deeper international connections may increase transparency, this does not necessarily lay out a mechanism that enables individuals to act on available information. As we noted in Chapter 5, modern liberal democracy is based on republicanism, the ability of people to choose their representatives through a competitive process. But who votes for international organizations? These bodies may be indirectly elected or appointed by the member states—or they may not be directly accountable to anyone at all. Thus, while a person may laud the work of Greenpeace or the World Wildlife Fund, it is instructive to note that these organizations are neither subject to popular democratic control nor necessarily more transparent than states themselves. A "democratic deficit" becomes a concern, an idea first raised with regard to the European Union. If power moves to global institutions, representation and democratic control may grow weaker since citizens lack the ability to control these bodies, which then grow distant from the citizenry and their preferences. At an extreme, this process could lead to a new form of global illiberalism such as we discussed in Chapter 6, whereby representative institutions exist but have been hollowed out by the loss of sovereignty and by the power of global technocratic institutions and elites.[7]

These are two starkly different visions of politics in a globalized world, and they reflect our opening discussion of China. In both scenarios, states and state functions become more diffused as power shifts to the global level. For optimists, international cooperation follows; these developments undermine the logic of war and increase transparency. For pessimists, deepening international connections facilitate new violent organizations and weaken democratic ties between the people and their representatives. Some combination of both scenarios is also possible.

Economic Globalization

Politics is not the only realm in which globalization is taking place. In fact, when many people think about globalization economics comes to mind, and this is the area that tends to generate the most controversy and debate. Economic globalization entails several distinct but interrelated elements that we should take into consideration. While the development of political globalization may be thought of as piecemeal or incremental, scholars tend to point to a set of specific institutions and regimes as vital components of economic globalization.

The **Bretton Woods system** is a global economic regime created in 1944 to manage international economic relations, the instability of which was commonly cited as a driving force behind the Great Depression and World War II. Three important institutions emerged from the Bretton Woods system: the International Monetary Fund (IMF), the World Bank, and the General Agreement on Tariffs and Trade (GATT), later replaced by the WTO. The objectives of these three institutions were to expand and manage economic relations between countries. The IMF helps manage exchange rates between countries and provides loans to states in financial difficulty (recall our discussion of Greece in Chapter 8, which had to turn to the IMF for loans when it faced economic crisis). The World Bank provides loans and technical assistance to advance development in developing countries, something we discussed in the previous chapter. The WTO oversees trade agreements between the member states to lower tariffs and remove other, nontariff barriers. For the past 75 years, these organizations have been at the center of a global liberal economic regime. The Bretton Woods system also helped facilitate the policies of the Washington Consensus, which we mentioned in our discussion of structural adjustment in Chapter 10. The Washington Consensus emphasized rolling back the state's control over the market through privatization, deregulation, trade, and financial liberalization. Many assert that the deepening of economic globalization over the past two decades was enabled by the Bretton Woods system and catalyzed by the policies of the Washington Consensus.

Observers point to several important facets of economic globalization that are directly or partially related to the emergence of the Bretton Woods system and the Washington Consensus. First, and perhaps most obvious, is the globalization of international trade. National economies have grown deeply integrated as the production and marketing of goods has become more mobile—goods can be made by workers, and sold to consumers, in many more places around the world. Some of this is due to technological changes, but much can be traced back to the creation of a global liberal economic regime that has encouraged trade between countries. Alongside trade globalization is the integration of capital and financial markets—markets for money—around the world. Banking and credit, stocks, and investments abroad all fall under this category. Money, too, is more mobile—investments and loans can be made from, and to, many more places around the world. Globalization deepens the connections between workers, goods, and wealth.

Some examples can offer perspective on the growth of economic globalization. In 1992, world exports in merchandise came to approximately $3 trillion; by 2019, the total was over $19 trillion. **Foreign direct investment (FDI)** (the purchase of assets in a country by a foreign firm) was under $200 billion in 1992; by 2007, it had reached approximately $2 trillion (though it had fallen back to just over $1.39 trillion in 2019—see Figure 11.1).[8] As mentioned earlier, economic globalization is also associated with the emergence of a number of MNCs that dominate global markets. Assisted by more-open markets and reduced transportation costs, large firms can make profits that rival the GDPs of many countries. For example,

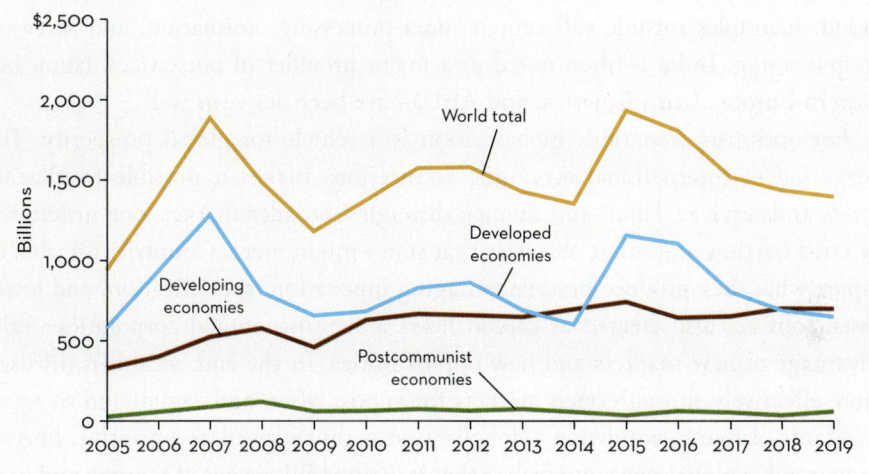

FIGURE 11.1 Foreign Direct Investment, 2005–2019

This graph shows fluctuations in foreign direct investment over the last fifteen years. While developing countries have seen a modest increase in investment in recent years, investment in postcommunist countries and developed countries has stayed relatively flat overall in comparison.

Source: UNCTAD Global Investment Trends Monitor, https://unctad.org/en/PublicationsLibrary/diaeiainf2021d1_en.pdf (accessed 3/17/20).

Apple's gross profit in 2019 was around $100 billion, close to Costa Rica's GDP at PPP. Another commonly noted example of financial globalization is through financing; around one-third of the United States' $23 trillion in state debt is held internationally, with the biggest owners being China and Japan.

These economic developments are amplified by expanding global communication, which we spoke of earlier, which has transformed the way that markets, firms, and individuals interact. Technological innovations, alongside economic liberalization, have reduced many traditional economic barriers. People are able to buy goods and services from around the world using fewer or no intermediaries. As a result, markets are more open and firms and workers face greater competition. In the area of investment, too, changes have allowed firms, states, and individuals to move their money internationally and rapidly, jumping in and out of markets as they see fit. Many people liken these changes to the creation of railroads and the telegraph in the nineteenth century, which helped transform the way economies were networked.

Perhaps the best-known example of this intersection among globalized labor, technology, and markets is **offshore outsourcing**. Outsourcing has long existed: it is simply one process a firm uses to move some of its work to a secondary business that can do the work more efficiently or cheaply. However, in the past much of this outsourcing was done inside domestic or regional economies. The rise of a postindustrial and information-based economy, however, has meant that many jobs can now be moved a great distance away to wherever a cost advantage can be found. Examples include call centers, data processing, animation, and software programming. India is often noted as a major provider of outsourced labor, but Eastern Europe, Latin America, and Africa have been active as well.

For optimists, economic globalization is a vehicle for global prosperity. The expansion of international economic connections makes it possible to allocate goods and services, labor, and finance through a broader market, one unfettered by tariff barriers and other obstacles that states might erect. Countries are able to export what they produce best, encouraging innovation, specialization, and lower costs. Jobs are also created as capital flows and transnational corporations take advantage of new markets and new opportunities. In the end, wealth is diffused more effectively through open markets for goods, labor, and capital and so raises standards of living worldwide. Globalization is thus viewed as a positive, liberalizing trend, a global division of labor that is lifting billions out of poverty and generating greater prosperity by allowing more people to be a part of an international marketplace for goods and labor. And in fact, globalization is associated with the decline in extreme poverty, especially in export-oriented countries in Asia.

Others view economic globalization with more suspicion. To return to our discussion of political economy in Chapter 4, while optimists emphasize how globalization has increased overall wealth, critics would instead point to rising inequality. While it is true that increased wealth has reduced inequality between many developing and developed countries, inequality within many countries has at the same time grown dramatically. More globalized trade has lowered prices and increased the variety and quality of goods. It has also contributed to the loss of jobs when firms have been able to move overseas to take advantage of cheaper labor or lower levels of regulation. More generally, critics say that the globalization of firms, markets, and labor means that businesses are able to avoid government taxation, oversight, and public accountability. In this view, as economic globalization weakens state capacity and autonomy, it is replaced not with a global rule of law but rather a global economy that lacks any sovereign control. Freedom and equality are thus compromised.

Societal Globalization

Whether globalization and the political and economic transformations it brings become instruments of greater cooperation and prosperity or sources of conflict and hardship may depend on how societies themselves are transformed by globalization.

We have explored how political globalization may challenge state sovereignty and power and how economic globalization changes markets for goods, labor, and capital. The idea of societal globalization views a similar process, in which traditional societal institutions are weakened, possibly creating new identities that do not belong to any one community or nation. As we know from previous chapters, in the premodern world people's identities were rather limited and narrow, focused on such things as family, tribe, village, and religion. Only with the rise of the state did national identities begin to emerge. Individuals began to see themselves tied to a much larger community of thousands, or millions, of strangers bound together by complex myths and symbols including flags, legends, and anthems. This transformation coincided with the development of sovereignty, whereby borders and citizenship reinforced the notion of national identity—one people, one state.

Some argue that as globalization proceeds, these central aspects of individual and collective identity are giving way. Just as the state and domestic economic institutions are being challenged, so, too, are traditional identities. One factor is demographic—specifically, the increasing mobility of humans, many of whom are fleeing conflict but also seeking better economic opportunities elsewhere in the world. In 2019, over a quarter of a billion people moved across international borders. These are figures that have not been seen for a century.[9] As we spoke of in Chapter 8, migration flows have the potential to change the cultural and political landscapes of many countries as they deal with questions of integration, multiculturalism, and citizenship.

As increasing numbers of people move around the globe, technological innovations like the Internet and cell phones also expand the capacity of individuals to become interconnected. Cell phone penetration is now high even among developing countries, and broadband is rapidly expanding across the globe (Figure 11.2). As electronic communications continue to grow, people find ways to link up with one another across time and space, building and deepening connections. Text messaging, websites, and social networks are all examples of virtual interconnections that have become integral to, or perhaps have even displaced, physical spaces and relationships.

How might this process shape societal institutions and identities? We can point to two possible trajectories. The first is that societal globalization will engender

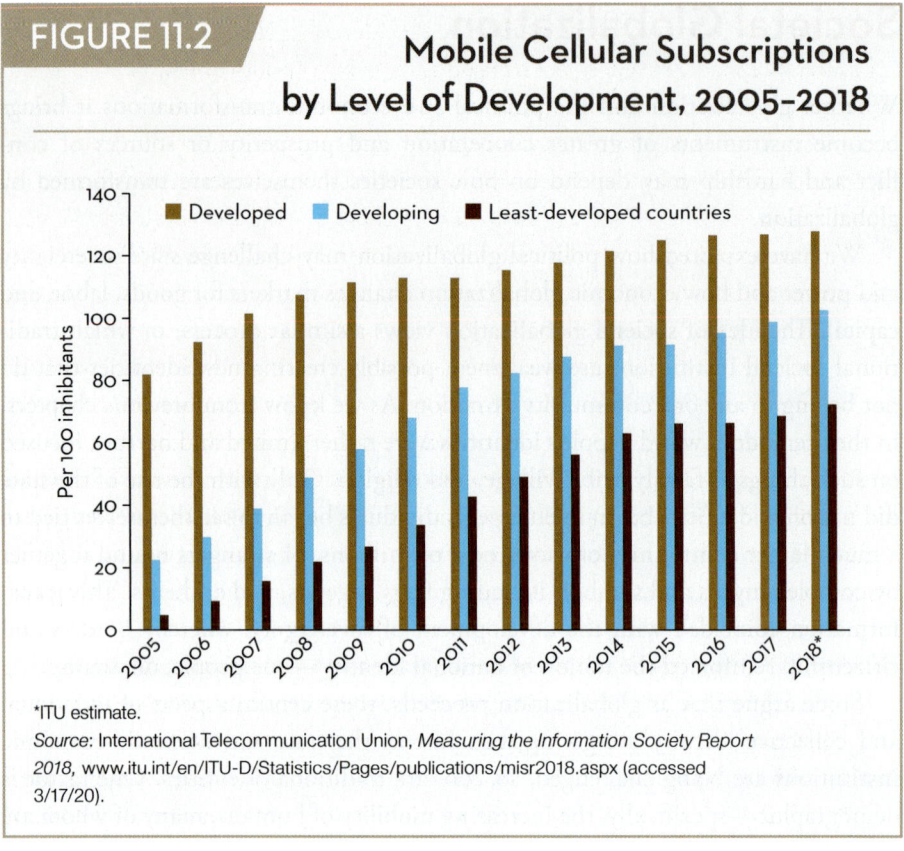

FIGURE 11.2 Mobile Cellular Subscriptions by Level of Development, 2005–2018

*ITU estimate.
Source: International Telecommunication Union, *Measuring the Information Society Report 2018*, www.itu.int/en/ITU-D/Statistics/Pages/publications/misr2018.aspx (accessed 3/17/20).

global multiculturalism. Different cultures will link and combine to a greater extent thanks to connections that are not bound by traditional barriers of time and space. This means not only that a globalized society will draw from many sources but also that the interconnection of domestic institutions at the global level will create new values, identities, and culture—a process of "creative destruction" or "hybridity" that will enrich all cultures.[10] One result of this outcome could be a global cosmopolitanism—a term that comes from the Greek *kosmos*, or "universe," and polis, or "state." Cosmopolitanism is thus a universal, global, or "worldly" political order that draws its identity and values from everywhere. Historically, the cosmopolis was the physical space where disparate ideas usually came together—notably, the city. A globalized world, however, holds the potential for an international cosmopolitanism that binds people together irrespective of where they are. (See "Questions and Methods" on pp. 382–83 for a discussion on globalization and growing mistrust among young people.)

Parallel to global cosmopolitanism is the idea of globalized democracy. We have already spoken of how globalization might shape political institutions at the domestic and international levels, though we focused largely on the development of nonstate and supra-state organizations as rivals to the state. When we focus on societal globalization and its effects on democracy, however, we return to our notion of civil society. The argument here is that growing international connections at the societal level would generate not only a form of cosmopolitanism but also a civic identity that stretches beyond traditional barriers and borders. This global civil society—organized life stretching beyond and above the state—can take shape in formal organizations like NGOs as well as in such informal manifestations as social movements or more basic grassroots connections between people drawn together by shared interests and values. This global civil society could in turn shape politics by creating new opportunities for concerted public action and new ways of thinking about politics and participation at the domestic and international levels.[11] Finally, this development of global cosmopolitanism and civil society could help facilitate democratic change across countries by informing and amplifying local political action.

As you might expect, there are critics of such views, skeptical of the notion that increased globalization will benefit social progress. Their criticisms are twofold. First, some contend that globalization overwhelms people with innumerable choices, values, ideas, and sources of information that they are unable to understand, evaluate, or escape—especially people who are not part of the globalized elite. Confusion, alienation, and public backlash can emerge as people seek to hold on to their identities in the face of these changes. Nationalism and fundamentalism can be viewed as reactions to a globalized society that people find alien and hostile to their own way of life. A possible result of societal globalization is thus atomization or a retreat into old identities, rather than the creation of some kind of widespread global cosmopolitanism or civil society. Of course, much of this argument assumes that national identities are inherently problematic. An alternative view asserts that national identities are worth preserving and such things as mass immigration should be limited to preserve these institutions.

Along those lines, a second criticism emphasizes not the reaction to societal globalization but rather its eventual outcome. Even in the absence of a backlash against globalization, the critics contend, societal globalization will not generate a richer global culture and cosmopolitanism. Rather, it will trigger cultural and intellectual decline. Societies will trade their own cultures, institutions, and ideas for a common global society shaped not by values or worldliness but by speed and consumption. The things that make each society unique—languages, food, music, history, customs, values, and norms—will be absorbed, rationalized, and packaged for mass consumption everywhere. Such critics would note that it is no accident that after the U.S. and Chinese militaries, the third- and fourth-largest employers in the world (and the largest private employers) are Walmart and McDonald's. This view of globalization sees a process whereby what is unique in each society is repackaged and sold to the rest of the planet, while those things that lack mass appeal are thrown away or driven out, replaced by what satisfies the widest public and the lowest common denominator. This process can be thought of as a disenchantment of the world, what one scholar calls "the globalization of nothing."[12]

Taking Stock of Globalization

Globalization, like many processes of change, conjures up utopian and dystopian visions of the future. Perhaps a better way to look at globalization is to think about it as a set of choices that involve difficult trade-offs. The economist Dani Rodrik has spoken of globalization creating a "trilemma" involving global economic integration, the nation-state, and democracy. For Rodrik, these three elements are difficult to reconcile; it is possible to have any two of the three, but not all three at once. Whatever framework we use, any discussion of globalization rests on the assumption that it is an unprecedented and inevitable turning point in history. But what is the evidence for this? Our task now is to match evidence against argument and consider what impact globalization has had on the world to date and whether, as is often assumed, this is truly something new that lacks historical analogy.

Is Globalization New?

We can begin by questioning the assumption that globalization is a fundamentally new development in human history. As we noted earlier, for thousands of years humanity was linked across great distances, spreading people, goods, and ideas around the world. Scholars, however, have noted that such connections were often extensive but not intensive. But we should not underestimate how deep many of these connections were for their time. Medieval Europe was tightly interconnected through political, economic, and societal institutions, while 1,000 years earlier the Persian Empire bound together people from Europe to North Africa and as far as India, shaping cultural values and human development. In many of these cases, war was an important component, disrupting old institutions and propelling change.

Let us look at a more recent phenomenon: the development of modern imperialism. The spread of European power into Latin America, Africa, the Middle East, and Asia profoundly reshaped domestic and international relations as Western political, economic, and social systems were transplanted into these parts of the world. Imperialism and the declining costs of transportation also helped facilitate the migration of millions of Europeans to these regions. By comparison, the current world of passports, visas, and immigration in some ways constrains human mobility far more than other factors did just a century ago.

The late nineteenth century saw the rise of the first NGOs and IGOs, such as the Red Cross, founded in 1863, and the International Telegraph Union (ITU) in 1865. And those who marvel at the advent of Internet communication forget that the first transatlantic cable connected Europe and North America by telegraph in 1866, spurring a global system of rapid communication and trade. In his famous work *The Economic Consequences of the Peace*, the economist John Maynard Keynes wrote of the dramatic impact of such changes:

> The inhabitant of London could order by telephone, sipping his morning tea in bed, the various products of the whole earth, in such quantity as he might see fit, and reasonably expect their early delivery upon his doorstep; he could at the same moment and by the same means adventure his wealth in the natural resources and new enterprises of any quarter of the world, and share, without exertion or even trouble, in their prospective fruits and advantages; or he could decide to couple the security of his fortunes with the good faith of the townspeople of any substantial municipality in any continent that fancy or information might recommend.[13]

This may sound like the current global economy, but Keynes was actually writing about the period before World War I. Indeed, the rise of electronic commerce, often heralded as a central piece of globalization, would not be possible without the previous establishment of such institutions as the telephone, national postal services, passable roads, ports, and commercial shipping—all things that far predate globalization.

At that time, many observers believed that globalization would lead to the abolition of war and the spread of international law and world government. For others, however, these rapid changes also brought with them concerns and dangers not unlike those discussed today. The 1918 pandemic swept the world, killing 50 million and leading to widespread economic and societal disruption. Migration and trade triggered not only fears of cultural destruction but also violent resistance, including nationalism and fascism. Marxist and anarchist ideas also attracted followers around the world, some of whom sought revolution and engaged in terrorism. In these confusing and often violent developments, some predicted the decline and collapse of Western society, not unlike some of the gloomier prognostications we hear today.

These examples suggest that it may be shortsighted of us to think that today's global interconnections are more dramatic than any that came before or that they portend changes that are beyond our power to control. History may help us better understand the present; we should not assume that what is occurring now is unique and that the past has nothing to teach us.

Is Globalization Exaggerated?

Earlier in this chapter, we considered globalization's impact on political, economic, and societal institutions and whether globalization is making the world better or worse. Is its impact as great as many of its supporters or critics assert? In light of the recent global recession, it may seem obvious that globalization is real and can be dangerous. But given the different ways we can think about globalization, the situation is more complicated.

As is often the case, the data present a mixed picture. Let us begin with political globalization. Some have suggested it would lead to greater transparency and global democratic institutions, while others have worried that the result would be an important loss of democratic participation and the rise of rival nonstate and nondemocratic actors. In both of these cases, the assumption is essentially that globalization means the eclipse of the state, yet there is still not a great deal of evidence showing that either scenario is taking place. At the most basic level, even as globalization has spread, the number of states has increased; sovereignty has remained a critical demand of people around the world, from Kurdistan to South Sudan. While observers of globalization have long pointed to the European Union as evidence that globalization is reducing state sovereignty, no other part of the world has shown a desire or ability to replicate this model. The European Union itself faces unprecedented difficulties as states reassert their sovereignty, and it showed little ability to manage the novel coronavirus pandemic in 2020 on behalf of its member states. In fact, member states quickly reestablished border controls against one another, something few could have imagined.

Indeed, over the past decade sovereign authority has reasserted itself in many areas. For instance, while many have assumed that the stateless, almost anarchic nature of the Internet and electronic communications would virtually displace the state, governments have found ways to regulate content and limit access. Chinese censorship of websites and social media like Facebook and the European Internet privacy laws are good examples. There is little comprehensive evidence that states are becoming more transparent or hollowed out under globalization; rather, it seems that the nature of their capacity and autonomy is changing to meet new challenges. At the same time, the idea that stateless actors such as terrorists are beyond the reach of states seems exaggerated, as new technologies can weaken or empower states and nonstate actors alike. Terrorist groups may have a global reach, but often they are—or aspire to be—more centralized than globalization suggests. The very name of the Islamic State fighting in Syria and Iraq showed its aspirations—not to function as a borderless political community, but to form a military, conquer land, and build a modern empire. For now, at least, states and the aspiration to statehood still matter.

If the picture of states and globalization is not clear, it may seem that in the area of economic globalization, our evidence could be more comprehensive. Although people may not agree on the effects of economic globalization, even the limited data we have regarding trade and foreign direct investment do indicate a profound change over the last two decades.

But here, too, caveats are in order. In spite of globalization, business continues to be heavily driven by such factors as physical proximity and cultural connections. In fact, while a decade ago some scholars asserted that as many as a quarter of U.S. jobs were at risk of being offshored, recent studies suggest that little of that has in fact occurred. Instead, firms have often opted to move to remote work within national borders. Cultural barriers and time zone differences have proven to be more powerful obstacles to offshoring than once imagined. The "home bias" in economic activity continues to be strong, much more so than initially expected.[14] Like states, distance itself still matters.

What about prosperity and poverty? Has globalization made a difference? In Chapter 4, we noted that since the 1980s the number of people in extreme poverty has fallen dramatically as a percentage of the world population. Much of this change has been driven by domestic reforms in one very large country—China—and China's subsequent integration into the global market. In other words, what we see as a uniform and inexorable process of globalization may be more effectively viewed through the lens of traditional comparative politics.

Finally, we should note that many of the economic changes that have occurred during the period of globalization don't have anything to do specifically with international relations. Economies have been transformed less by the Internet than by the expansion of computer technology and robotics that have replaced unskilled and some skilled labor. The applications of these innovations, both at home and abroad, are critical to explaining rising inequality.[15]

Is Globalization Inevitable?

For the sake of argument let us reject all of the qualifiers just raised and assume that globalization is a fundamentally new phenomenon whose effects are profound, whether for good or ill. For those who make this assumption, it often follows that globalization is a juggernaut that people, groups, societies, and states cannot stop. Is this true? To illustrate this point, let us return to history, and to Keynes. After noting the profound economic changes that occurred before World War I, he remarked that, above all, the average individual regarded these changes as "normal, certain, and permanent, except in the direction of further improvement, and any deviation from it as aberrant, scandalous, and avoidable."[16]

Yet this state of affairs was not permanent. International trade was disrupted by the onset of World War I, the effects of which were further compounded by a subsequent world depression. Keynes himself came to play a role in the Bretton Woods system precisely because he noted that global economic development was fragile and required the active role of states. History suggests, then, that globalization is not unstoppable; deglobalization can occur as well, as it has in the past.

Globalization can be limited or reversed in a number of ways. One is through economic crisis. The heady period of economic development 100 years ago was finally undermined by financial collapse in the 1930s. In its immediate aftermath, trade, investment, and immigration across the globe declined, often as a result of new national barriers that reflected increased isolationism, protectionism, and nationalism. To take one example, between 1901 and 1910 the United States accepted nearly 1 million immigrants a year; it would not reach even half that level again until the 1970s. Ongoing global economic difficulties could continue to work against globalization, reducing economic ties, migration, or other forms of globalization. The novel coronavirus pandemic is a tragic example of this.

Indeed, recent global economic challenges have pointed to this very possibility. As we noted in previous chapters, much of what has developed in comparative politics over the past decade has taken place in the context of rapid global economic growth. The rise of China as a major exporting power, Russia and Brazil as suppliers of energy and other natural commodities, and India as a hub for outsourcing, as well as the integration of global markets for investment, have all had important political implications. Even before the pandemic, a good portion of this development was challenged by significant economic difficulties and political resistance to globalization.

Ongoing difficulties may also increase public opposition to globalization. Many people's concerns about how globalization might affect such things as the environment, labor standards, immigration, and democratic practices are being translated into antiglobalization activism. Opposition to more liberalized global trade already emerged in the late 1990s. The proposed **Trans-Pacific Partnership (TPP)**, which sought to liberalize trade across a number of Asian and Latin American countries, has been abandoned by the United States, and tensions have arisen surrounding the **North American Free Trade Agreement (NAFTA)**, an agreement between Canada, Mexico, and the United States that has liberalized trade between the three countries. In 2020, NAFTA was renegotiated and replaced by the United States-Mexico-Canada Agreement (USMCA). We find such opposition to increased integration and globalization across the political spectrum and around the world, though it is particularly pronounced in the developed democracies. Recent surveys show that in countries such as the United States, Japan, Germany, and Mexico, less than half of the public believes that trade creates jobs, and this has become a central focus of political campaigns in many countries.[17] In the face of such opposition countries may choose to resolve the "trilemma" of economic integration, democracy, and the nation-state by choosing the latter two over the former.

Whatever the outcome, it seems premature to declare that either a world of states or an age of globalization has come to an end. Certainly, it is more provocative to claim that a new era is upon us, whether it is a utopia of prosperity and peace or a dystopia of inequality and conflict. As we saw in Chapter 1, politics is one arena where new activities emerge, are institutionalized, and come to define our lives. But the resulting institutions can become ossified and break down, leading to turmoil. New institutions emerge to take their place—some of which produce more human happiness, and some less. Wherever we find ourselves now, it is not certain that we face major changes in our political institutions. And even if we do, it is not clear whether such changes will be a pathway to progress or a setback for humanity. So long as domestic political institutions matter, the study of comparative politics remains a critical endeavor. And you, too, are now a participant in that important work.

INSTITUTIONS IN ACTION

Is Globalization Causing Climate Change?

Any discussion about the future of the globe and the people who live on it would be incomplete without a discussion of climate change. According to some estimates, since the advent of industrialization global temperatures have risen approximately 1°C (1.8°F), and they continue to rise unchecked. The impact of a warming earth is already evident. For example, in some countries temperature change has led to a shift in rainfall patterns that intensifies aridity in regions that are already dry. Globally, changes in rain patterns also appear to be making the Southern Hemisphere drier while the Northern Hemisphere becomes wetter. As can be expected, these changes can have a dramatic impact on such things as agricultural production, access to drinkable water, and the health of local ecosystems. A related concern is the emergence of possible "tipping points"—dramatic changes that can trigger a series of interconnected climate changes. For example, the melting of Greenland's ice sheet could rapidly alter ocean currents in a way that would push warmer waters southward. This could accelerate thawing in Antarctica and also increase ocean acidity, with a resulting rise in sea levels and a decline in marine life. Both of those changes would have disastrous effects on humans and other living creatures that live in or depend on the sea.

So climate change is clearly a "global" problem. But can we also call it a problem of globalization? If at its most basic globalization can be defined as the broadening and deepening of international connections, then globalization can be a useful concept through which to consider climate change. Let's look at one specific area in which climate change, globalization, and comparative politics come together: the Amazon rainforest. According to some, the Amazon represents one of those possible tipping points in global climate change. Covering much of Brazil and extending into several neighboring countries, this rainforest is almost twice as large as India. It acts as a repository for between 150 and 200 billion tons of carbon, absorbing it from the atmosphere and thus retarding global warming.

But the role of the Amazon as a carbon sink is changing. In 2018 the Amazon experienced the worst deforestation in 10 years. This was a loss of about 3,000 square miles, or 10 times the size of New York City. What has led to this increased deforestation? An important part of the answer lies in our opening discussion in the chapter: the rise of China. As China has become wealthier, its food demands and preferences have increased and changed. Specifically, China's consumption of beef has doubled in the past 20 years, and nearly half of Brazil's meat exports now go to China. Brazil has also seen a huge jump in soybean production, and nearly 80 percent of that production is also exported to China, where much of it is used as animal feed. China's economic development and the expansion of its global agricultural trade have created a great deal of pressure to convert more of the Amazon to farmland, especially as these exports become a key part of Brazil's economy.

It is not just Chinese economic development that is playing a part in the globalization of the Amazon, but Brazilian domestic politics as well, coinciding with a dramatic shift in Brazilian politics away from environmental conservation. In 2019 Brazil elected a new president, Jair Bolsonaro, who came to power on a conservative platform that, among other things, promised to roll back environmental regulations. Bolsonaro announced that his election represented the country's "liberation from socialism, inverted values, the bloated state and political correctness."[a] Within hours of his swearing into office, he signed an executive order giving the Ministry of Agriculture greater authority over Amazonian land and placed the former head of Brazil's agricultural lobby in charge, while weakening the powers of the Ministry of the Environment. Brazil's new foreign minister, meanwhile, asserted that the idea of climate change itself was a "Marxist plot." Illegal deforestation is widely expected to rise.

An aerial view of severe deforestation in Brazil's Amazon rainforest.

As the size of the Amazon rainforest continues to decline, so does its ability to capture and store global pollution. At the national and regional levels, too, a shrinking canopy affects the local climate, and the region has seen both record-breaking droughts and floods over the past 10 years. Thus, the feedback loops of climate change are not simply shifts in the forces of nature, but they also contain the choices made by individuals, countries, and their political leaders. In a world in which such complex relationships can have a cascading effect on the entire globe, what kinds of political tools can be wielded for the benefit of the planet? For example, could an active global civil society create new norms that would push humans away from resource-intensive food—especially since agricultural production accounts for a quarter of greenhouse gasses? Can global regimes, IGOs, or NGOs find a way to gain and exercise power in a way that regulates activities, like deforestation or energy production, that contribute to climate change? So far the jury is out. In the meantime, President Trump indicated that the United States will withdraw from the Paris Agreement on climate change in 2020. States and sovereignty remain a powerful force, even as globalized challenges limit the ability of any one state to isolate itself from global change.

1. How is climate change both a global problem as well as a problem of globalization?

2. How does China and Brazil's association demonstrate the complicated relationship between economic development and the environment?

3. What type of political tools do you think would be most effective in fighting climate change?

In Sum: The Future of Freedom and Equality

Our world may now be undergoing a profound change in institutions, though this idea is subject to debate. One result of this transformation could be an evolution of the struggle over freedom and equality. Both values can be measured not just within states but also between them. Does one country's freedom or equality come at the expense of another's? How can freedom or equality be balanced globally in the absence of any single sovereign power or dominant regime? The very meanings of freedom and equality may evolve as new ways of thinking about individual choice and collective aspirations emerge. These changes could lead to greater stability, peace, and prosperity for humanity or to greater conflict and misery. Whatever the path, states and nations, regimes, ideologies, and culture continue to play the dominant role in driving domestic politics, and domestic politics in driving world affairs. Comparative politics gives us the power to analyze the present, glimpse the future, and play a role in shaping the course of human progress.

Key Terms

Bretton Woods system (p. 365)
foreign direct investment (FDI) (p. 366)
globalization (p. 357)
intergovernmental organization (IGO) (p. 360)
international regime (p. 361)
multinational corporation (MNC) (p. 360)
nongovernmental organization (NGO) (p. 360)
North American Free Trade Agreement (NAFTA) (p. 377)
offshore outsourcing (p. 368)
Trans-Pacific Partnership (TPP) (p. 377)

For Further Reading

Bhagwati, Jagdish. *In Defense of Globalization.* Oxford: Oxford University Press, 2007.

Collier, Paul. *Exodus: How Migration Is Changing Our World.* Oxford: Oxford University Press, 2013.

Dryzek, John S. "Global Civil Society: The Progress of Post-Westphalian Politics." *Annual Review of Political Science* 15 (June 2012): 101–19.

Findlay, Ronald, and Kevin H. O'Rourke. *Power and Plenty: Trade, War, and the World Economy in the Second Millennium.* Princeton, NJ: Princeton University Press, 2007.

Ford, Martin. *Rise of the Robots: Technology and the Threat of a Jobless Future.* New York: Basic Books, 2015.

Keynes, John Maynard. *The Economic Consequences of the Peace.* New York: Harcourt, Brace and Howe, 1920.

Pieterse, Jan Nederveen. *Globalization and Culture: Global Mélange.* New York: Rowman & Littlefield, 2015.

Rodrik, Dani. *The Globalization Paradox: Democracy and the Future of the World Economy.* New York: W. W. Norton, 2011.

INQUIZITIVE

Earn a better grade on your test. InQuizitive personalizes your learning path to help you master the concepts from this chapter and practice applying them to examples from the text and beyond (see back cover).

QUESTIONS AND METHODS

Does Globalization Create Mistrust?

From the outset of this text we have grappled with the question of development and political change. For decades there has been a long-standing assumption that as societies progress economically, they move through a series of social changes, like greater individualism, that can pave the way for democratization. Globalization adds another factor into the mix, as it suggests not only change within countries but the emergence of a shared set of values—the idea of a global cosmopolitanism that we spoke about earlier. In the most recent rounds of the World Values Survey, surveyors began to ask people whether they saw themselves as world citizens. Among the countries surveyed, respondents agreed strongly with this proposition, with the most positive responses among those under age 29. This figure increased slightly between the survey period of 2005-09 and those surveys taken in the period 2010-14. This increase would seem to be consistent with increasing societal globalization.

Youth, Globalization, and Trust

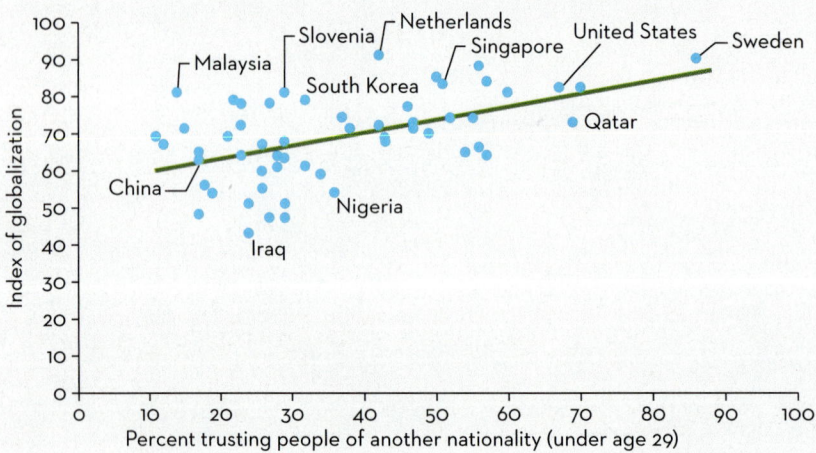

Source: Ronald Englehart et al., eds., *World Values Survey: Round Six, Country-Pooled Datafile Version* (Madrid: Jo Systems Institute, 2014), www.worldvaluessurvey.org/WVSDocumentationWV6.jsp (accessed 3/17/20).

Yet when we look at other related questions, we get a different view. When those same respondents are asked whether they trust individuals of another nationality, the response is quite negative. Even more interesting is that these levels of mistrust are higher among young people than among older generations.

In the 2010 survey, over 65 percent of young people said they did not trust people of another nationality, compared with 60 percent for those over age 50. Nor does the level of mistrust correlate easily with levels of globalization in a given country. Let's compare our findings with the Index of Globalization developed by the Swiss Federal Institute of Technology, which includes economic, social, and political forms of globalization, such as foreign direct investment, trade in cultural goods, and international treaties.

We can see countries with a high level of youth trust that are also highly globalized, such as Sweden, supporting our hypothesis regarding globalization and cosmopolitanism. But we also find a number of highly globalized countries like Malaysia, South Korea, and Slovenia that exhibit high levels of mistrust. The world's most globalized country in the Index of Globalization, the Netherlands, shows high youth mistrust, and those levels are nearly 15 percent higher for people under 29 than citizens over 50. Sweden, the United States, Australia, and Germany also show higher levels of mistrust among the youth than older generations. Rather than younger and presumably more globalized generations feeling a greater sense of trust of other nationalities, they in fact feel more mistrustful. This raises the possibility that as countries become more globalized, younger generations come to feel themselves more globally connected, but also wary of those connections.

1. *Generate new research ideas related to the discussion*

   What might be some possible explanations for why mistrust of other nationalities is higher among young people? How could we test these hypotheses?

2. *Unpack different variables and consider their relative effects*

   The Index of Globalization weights equally economic, social, and political forms of globalization. In your view, might one of these generate more trust between national groups than others? If you sought to increase trust, which of these three would you emphasize, and why?

3. *Consider the future ramifications of an existing dynamic*

   In your view, if globalization creates mistrust, is that a temporary price that comes with greater interaction and diversity, or a barrier that will only increase if globalization deepens?

NOTES

CHAPTER 1: INTRODUCTION

1. Gary King, Robert O. Keohane, and Sidney Verba, *Designing Social Inquiry: Scientific Inference in Qualitative Research* (Princeton, NJ: Princeton University Press, 1994).

2. Gerardo L. Munck and Richard Snyder, "Debating the Direction of Comparative Politics: An Analysis of Leading Journals," *Comparative Political Studies* 40, no. 1 (January 2007): 5–31. See also Jason P. Abbott and Kevin Fahey, "The State and Direction of Asian Comparative Politics: Who, What, Where, How?" *Journal of East Asian Studies* 14, no. 1 (April 2014): 109–34.

3. Adam Przeworski, "Is the Science of Comparative Politics Possible?" and Robert J. Franzese Jr., "Multicausality, Context-Conditionality, and Endogeneity," in *The Oxford Handbook of Comparative Politics*, ed. Carles Boix and Susan C. Stokes (Oxford: Oxford University Press, 2009).

4. Aristotle, *The Politics*, trans. T. A. Sinclair (New York: Penguin, 1981).

5. Niccolò Machiavelli, *The Prince*, trans. W. K. Marriott (New York: Knopf, 1992).

6. For more on the behavioral revolution, see Robert A. Dahl, "The Behavioral Approach in Political Science: Epitaph for a Monument to a Successful Protest," *American Political Science Review* 55, no. 4 (December 1961): 763–72.

7. James D. Fearon and David D. Laitin, "Integrating Qualitative and Quantitative Methods," in *The Oxford Handbook of Political Methodology*, ed. Janet M. Box-Steffensmeier, Henry E. Brady, and David Collier (Oxford: Oxford University Press, 2008); Amel Ahmed and Rudra Sil, "When Multi-Method Research Subverts Methodological Pluralism—or, Why We Still Need Single-Method Research," *Perspectives on Politics* 10, no. 4 (December 2012): 935–53.

8. Brian Resnick, "The 'marshmallow test' said patience was a key to success. A new replication tells us s'more," *Vox*, June 6, 2018, www.vox.com/science-and-health/2018/6/6/17413000/marshmallow-test-replication-mischel-psychology (accessed 9/18/19).

9. Nicholas Kristof, "Professors, We Need You!" *New York Times*, February 15, 2014.

10. Veronica Herrera and Alison E. Post, "The Case for Public Policy Expertise in Political Science," *PS: Political Science and Politics* 52, no. 3 (July 2019): 476–80.

INSTITUTIONS IN ACTION

a. Daniel Kahneman, *Thinking, Fast and Slow* (New York: Farrar, Straus and Giroux, 2011).

b. Philip E. Tetlock and Dan Gardner, *Superforecasting: The Art and Science of Prediction* (New York: Crown Publishing, 2015).

CHAPTER 2: STATES

1. U.S. history explains why *state* has different connotations for Americans. During the period of revolutionary struggle and the creation of a federal system, the former British colonies in America viewed themselves as independent political units—that is, as states. With the creation of a federal system of government, however, their individual powers were subordinated to a central authority. The United States of America, in other words, eventually became a system of national government, and the term *state* was left as a remnant of the brief period when these units acted largely as independent entities.

2. Max Weber, "Politics as a Vocation," in *From Max Weber: Essays in Sociology*, ed. and trans. H. H. Gerth and C. Wright Mills (New York: Oxford University Press, 1946), 77–128.

3. This idea has been developed by Charles Tilly, "War Making and State Making as Organized Crime," in *Bringing the State Back In*, ed. Peter B. Evans, Dietrich Rueschemeyer, and Theda Skocpol (New York: Cambridge University Press, 1985), 169–91.

4. Azar Gat, *War in Human Civilization* (New York: Oxford University Press, 2006); Lawrence H. Keeley, *War before Civilization: The Myth of the Peaceful Savage* (New York: Oxford University Press, 1996).

5. Angus Maddison, *Contours of the World Economy, 1–2030 AD: Essays in Macro-Economic History* (New York: Oxford University Press, 2007).

6. Charles Tilly, *Coercion, Capital, and European States, AD 990–1990* (Oxford: Blackwell, 1990).

7. Francis Fukuyama, *The Origins of Political Order: From Prehuman Times to the French Revolution* (New York: Farrar, Straus and Giroux, 2011).

8. Mancur Olson, "Dictatorship, Democracy, and Development," *American Political Science Review* 87, no. 3 (September 1993): 567–76; Margaret Levi, "The State of the Study of the State," in *Political Science: State of the Discipline*, ed. Ira Katznelson and Helen V. Milner (New York: W. W. Norton, 2002), 40–43.

9. For the cultural explanation, see David S. Landes, *The Wealth and Poverty of Nations: Why Some Are So Rich and Some So Poor* (New York: W. W. Norton, 1999), as well as Fukuyama, *The Origins of Political Order*, and Ricardo Duchesne, *The Uniqueness of*

Western Civilization, vol. 28 of *Studies in Critical Social Sciences*, ed. David Fasenfest (Leiden and Boston: Brill, 2011).

10. Stephen D. Krasner, "Building Democracy after Conflict: The Case for Shared Sovereignty," *Journal of Democracy* 16, no. 1 (January 2005): 69–83.

11. Bruce Gilley, *The Right to Rule: How States Win and Lose Legitimacy* (New York: Columbia University Press, 2009), 4.

12. Weber, "Politics as a Vocation."

13. Robert I. Rotberg, ed., *When States Fail: Causes and Consequences* (Princeton, NJ: Princeton University Press, 2004).

14. Graham Denyer Willis, *The Killing Consensus: Police, Organized Crime, and the Regulation of Life and Death in Urban Brazil* (Berkeley: University of California Press, 2015).

INSTITUTIONS IN ACTION

a. Christophe Jaffrelot, "India and Pakistan: Interpreting the Divergence of Two Political Trajectories," *Cambridge Review of International Affairs* 15, no. 2 (July 2002): 251–67; Philip Oldenburg, *India, Pakistan, and Democracy: Solving the Puzzle of Divergent Paths* (New York: Routledge, 2010).

CHAPTER 3: NATIONS AND SOCIETY

1. Alfred Stepan, Juan J. Linz, and Yogendra Yadav, *Crafting State-Nations: India and Other Multinational Democracies* (Baltimore, MD: Johns Hopkins University Press, 2011).

2. See, for example, J. Philippe Rushton, "Ethnic Nationalism, Evolutionary Psychology and Genetic Similarity Theory," *Nations and Nationalism* 11, no. 4 (October 2005): 489–507.

3. Edward L. Glaeser, "Inequality," KSG Working Paper no. RWP05-056 (October 2005), http://ssrn.com/abstract=832653 (accessed 1/14/20); see also Marc Hooghe, Tim Reeskens, Dietlind Stolle, and Ann Trappers, "Ethnic Diversity and Generalized Trust in Europe: A Cross-National Multilevel Study," *Comparative Political Studies* 42, no. 2 (February 2009): 198–223.

4. Évolution du Climat Politique au Québec, 11 au 15 Février, 2016, Politique Provinciale et Fédérale, https://sondage.crop.ca/survey/start/cawi/Rapport%20politique%20-%20F%C3%A9v%202016.pdf, also "Quebec Election Analysis," Angus Reid Institute, October 4, 2018, http://angusreid.org/quebec-election-2018-analysis (accessed 10/23/19).

5. Charles Tilly, ed., *The Formation of National States in Western Europe* (Princeton, NJ: Princeton University Press, 1975); see also Reinhard Bendix, *Nation-Building and Citizenship: Studies of Our Changing Social Order* (Berkeley: University of California Press, 1977); Douglass C. North and Robert Paul Thomas, *The Rise of the Western World: A New Economic History* (New York: Cambridge University Press, 1973).

6. Stathis N. Kalyvas, "Civil Wars," in *The Oxford Handbook of Comparative Politics*, ed. Carles Boix and Susan C. Stokes (New York: Oxford University Press, 2009); James D. Fearon and David D. Laitin, "Ethnicity, Insurgency, and Civil War," *American Political Science Review* 97, no. 1 (February 2003): 75–90.

7. Stefan Wolff, "Building Democratic States after Conflict: Institutional Design Revisited," *International Studies Review* 12, no. 1 (March 2010): 128–41.

8. Max Rollwage, Raymond J. Dolan, and Stephen M. Fleming, "Metacognitive Failure as a Feature of Those Holding Radical Beliefs," *Current Biology* 28, no. 24 (December 2018): 4014–21.

9. Antoine Louis Claude Destutt de Tracy, *A Treatise on Political Economy* (1817; New York: Augustus M. Kelley, 1970).

10. Thomas Jefferson, "Notes on the State of Virginia: Query XVII: Religion," https://teachingamericanhistory.org/library/document/notes-on-the-state-of-virginia-query-xvii-religion (accessed 10/23/19).

11. Roger Burrows, "Urban Futures and *The Dark Enlightenment*," in Keith Jacobs and Jeff Malpas, eds., *Philosophy and the City: Interdisciplinary and Transcultural Perspectives* (New York: Rowman & Littlefield, 2019), 245–58.

12. Quoted in George Plechanoff, *Anarchism and Socialism* (Chicago: Kerr, 1909), 80.

13. Bruce B. Lawrence, *Defenders of God: The Fundamentalist Revolt against the Modern Age* (New York: Harper & Row, 1989), 78.

14. For an excellent discussion of fundamentalism in Christianity, Islam, and Judaism, see Karen Armstrong, *The Battle for God* (New York: Ballantine, 2000).

15. Gilles Kepel, *The Revenge of God: The Resurgence of Islam, Christianity and Judaism in the Modern World*, trans. Alan Brayley (Cambridge: Polity Press, 1994); see also Daniel Philpott, "Has the Study of Global Politics Found Religion?" *Annual Review of Political Science* 12 (2009): 183–202.

16. Samuel P. Huntington, *The Clash of Civilizations and the Remaking of World Order* (New York: Simon & Schuster, 1996).

17. Ronald Inglehart and Christian Welzel, "How Development Leads to Democracy: What We Know about Modernization," *Foreign Affairs* 88, no. 2 (March/April 2009): 33–48.

CHAPTER 4: POLITICAL ECONOMY

1. For a discussion of the difficulties inherent in providing public goods, see Mancur Olson, *The Logic of Collective Action: Public Goods and the Theory of Groups* (Cambridge, MA: Harvard University Press, 1965).

2. On deflation, see Nouriel Roubini and Stephen Mihm, *Crisis Economics: A Crash Course in the Future of Finance* (New York: Penguin, 2010).

3. Clyde Edward Dankert, ed., *Adam Smith: Man of Letters and Economist* (Hicksville, NY: Exposition Press, 1974), 218.

4. Eduard Bernstein, *Evolutionary Socialism: A Criticism and Affirmation* (1899; New York: Schocken, 1961).

5. OECD Tax Database, available at www.oecd.org/tax/tax-policy/tax-database (accessed 10/21/19).

6. For more on the variation within social-democratic systems, see Gøsta Esping-Andersen, *The Three Worlds of Welfare Capitalism* (Princeton, NJ: Princeton University Press, 1990).

7. For a discussion of communist political economies, see Robert W. Campbell, *The Socialist Economies in Transition: A Primer on Semi-Reformed Systems* (Bloomington, IN: Indiana University Press, 1991).

8. The classic work on mercantilism is Friedrich List, *The National System of Political Economy* (1841; New York: Kelley, 1966).

9. For a defense of mercantilism, see Ha-Joon Chang, *Bad Samaritans: The Myth of Free Trade and the Secret History of Capitalism* (New York: Bloomsbury, 2008); on Trump, see Binyamin Appelbaum, "On Trade, Donald Trump Breaks with 200 Years of Economic Orthodoxy," *New York Times*, March 10, 2016.

10. Charles I. Jones and Peter J. Klenow, "Beyond GDP? Welfare across Countries and Time," NBER Working Paper no. 16352 (September 2010), https://ssrn.com/abstract-1674796 (accessed 1/14/20).

11. For calculation of global Gini index, see Branko Milanovic, *The Haves and the Have-Nots: A Brief and Idiosyncratic History of Global Inequality* (New York: Basic Books, 2011); on poverty, see Maxim Pinkovskiy and Xavier Sala-i-Martin, "Parametric Estimations of the World Distribution of Income," NBER Working Paper no. 15433 (October 2009), https://ssrn.com/abstract-1493045 (accessed 1/14/20).

12. The United Nations Human Development Indicators are available at http://hdr.undp.org (accessed 10/30/19).

13. Richard A. Easterlin, *Happiness, Growth, and the Life Cycle* (New York: Oxford University Press, 2010).

14. John F. Helliwell, Richard Layard, and Jeffrey D. Sachs, *World Happiness Report 2019* (New York: Sustainable Development Solutions Network).

15. Fraser Institute, *Economic Freedom of the World: 2019 Annual Report*, www.fraserinstitute.org/studies/economic-freedom-of-the-world-2019-annual-report (accessed 11/19/19).

INSTITUTIONS IN ACTION

a. Economic Commission for Latin America and the Caribbean (ECLAC), *Social Panorama of Latin America 2018* (Santiago, Chile: ECLAC, 2019); see also World Bank, *A Slowdown in Social Gains* (Washington, DC: World Bank Group, 2016), http://documents.worldbank.org/curated/en/2016/04/26211205/slowdown-social-gains (accessed 10/30/19).

CHAPTER 5: DEMOCRATIC REGIMES

1. C. B. Macpherson, *The Life and Times of Liberal Democracy* (New York: Oxford University Press, 1977).

2. Christopher W. Blackwell, ed., *Dēmos: Classical Athenian Democracy* (A. Mahoney and R. Scaife, eds., *The Stoa: A Consortium for Scholarly Publications in the Humanities*), www.stoa.org/demos (accessed 11/24/19).

3. For details, see Charles Tilly, "War Making and State Making as Organized Crime," in *Bringing the State Back In*, ed. Peter B. Evans, Dietrich Rueschemeyer, and Theda Skocpol (New York: Cambridge University Press, 1985), pp. 169–91; see also Francis Fukuyama, *The Origins of Political Order: From Prehuman Times to the French Revolution* (New York: Farrar, Straus and Giroux, 2011).

4. Adam Przeworski and Fernando Limongi, "Modernization: Theories and Facts," *World Politics* 49, no. 2 (January 1997): 155–83.

5. Daron Acemoglu and James A. Robinson, *Economic Origins of Dictatorship and Democracy* (New York: Cambridge University Press, 2006).

6. Alexis de Tocqueville, *Democracy in America*, trans. Henry Reeve, vol. 2 (New York: J. & H. G. Langley, 1841), p. 116, http://books.google.com/books?ID-BZETAAAAYAA

7. Vladimir Tismaneanu, ed., *In Search of Civil Society: Independent Peace Movements in the Soviet Bloc* (New York: Routledge, 1990).

8. David S. Law and Mila Versteeg, "The Evolution and Ideology of Global Constitutionalism," *California Law Review* 99 (2011): 1163.

9. Philip B. Kurland and Ralph Lerner, eds., *The Founders' Constitution* (Chicago: University of Chicago Press, 1987), http://press-pubs.uchicago.edu/founders/documents/v1ch15s50.html (accessed 11/25/19).

10. An exhaustive discussion of the different forms of electoral systems and other facets of voting and elections can be found at the ACE Electoral Knowledge Network website, www.aceproject.org (accessed 11/25/19).

11. Maurice Duverger, *Political Parties: Their Organization and Activity in the Modern State* (New York: Wiley, 1954).

12. Advocates for majority SMDs in the United States can be found at the FairVote website, www.fairvote.org (accessed 11/25/19).

13. For more on this debate, see the ACE Electoral Knowledge Network website, www.aceproject.org (accessed 11/26/19), as well as Andrew Reynolds, Ben Reilly, and Andrew Ellis, *Electoral System Design: The New International IDEA Handbook* (Stockholm: International Institute for Democracy and Electoral Assistance, 2005).

14. Liubomir Topaloff, "The Rise of Referendums: Elite Strategy or Populist Weapon?" *Journal of Democracy* 28, no. 3 (July 2017): 127–40.

INSTITUTIONS IN ACTION

a. Minxin Pei, "5 Ways China Could Become a Democracy," *Diplomat*, February 13, 2013, https://thediplomat.com/2013/02/5-ways-china-could-become-a-democracy (accessed 1/22/20).

CHAPTER 6: NONDEMOCRATIC REGIMES

1. See the Freedom House website, www.freedomhouse.org (accessed 12/16/19).

2. For an excellent discussion of the bewildering varieties of nondemocratic rule, see Juan J. Linz, *Totalitarian and Authoritarian Regimes* (Boulder, CO: Lynne Rienner, 2000).

3. Linz, *Totalitarian and Authoritarian Regimes*.

4. Hannah Arendt, *The Origins of Totalitarianism* (New York: Schocken Books, 1951).

5. Michael Bratton and Nicolas Van de Walle provide details of Mobutu's rule in "Neopatrimonial Regimes and Political Transitions in Africa," *World Politics* 46, no. 4 (July 1994): 453–89.

6. See Guillermo A. O'Donnell, *Modernization and Bureaucratic-Authoritarianism: Studies in South American Politics* (Berkeley, CA: Institute of International Studies, 1973); see also Hristos Doucouliagos and Mehmet Ali Ulubaşoğlu, "Democracy and Economic Growth: A Meta-Analysis," *American Journal of Political Science* 52, no. 1 (January 2008): 61–83.

7. German Feierherd, Noam Lupu, and Susan Stokes, "A Significant Minority of Americans Say They Could Support a Military Takeover of the U.S. Government," *Washington Post*, February 16, 2018, www.washingtonpost.com/news/monkey-cage/wp/2018/02/16/a-significant-minority-of-americans-say-they-would-support-a-military-takeover-of-the-u-s-in-the-right-circumstances (accessed 12/16/19).

8. Muhammad Al-Atawneh, "Is Saudi Arabia a Theocracy? Religion and Governance in Contemporary Saudi Arabia," *Middle Eastern Studies* 45, no. 5 (2009): 721–37.

9. Martin R. Rupiya, ed. *Zimbabwe's Military: Examining Its Veto Power in the Transition to Democracy, 2008–2013* (Pretoria: African Public Policy and Research Institute, 2013).

10. Oswald Spengler, *The Decline of the West*, vol. 2 (New York: Knopf, 1928), p. 347.

INSTITUTIONS IN ACTION

a. Jan-Werner Müller, "Defending Democracy within the EU," *Journal of Democracy* 24, no. 2 (2013): 138–49.

CHAPTER 7: POLITICAL VIOLENCE

1. William McCants, *The ISIS Apocalypse: The History, Strategy, and Doomsday Vision of the Islamic State* (New York: St. Martin's Press, 2015).

2. For the opposing views, see Max Abrahms, "What Terrorists Really Want: Terrorist Motives and Counterterrorism Strategy," *International Security* 32, no. 4 (Spring 2008): 78–105; and Robert A. Pape, *Dying to Win: The Strategic Logic of Suicide Terrorism* (New York: Random House, 2005).

3. Theda Skocpol, *States and Social Revolutions: A Comparative Analysis of France, Russia, and China* (Cambridge: Cambridge University Press, 1979).

4. Timur Kuran, "Now Out of Never: The Element of Surprise in the East European Revolution of 1989," *World Politics* 44, no. 1 (October 1991): 7–48. See also Bruce Bueno de Mesquita and Alastair Smith, "Political Succession: A Model of Coups, Revolution, Purges, and Everyday Politics," *Journal of Conflict Resolution* 61, no. 4 (April 2017): 707–43.

5. Tim Krieger and Daniel Meierrieks, "Does Income Inequality Lead to Terrorism?" CESifo Working Paper Series no. 5821, April 21, 2016, https://papers.ssrn.com/sol3/papers.cfm?abstract_id=2766910 (accessed 1/2/20).

6. Max Abrahms, "The Political Effectiveness of Terrorism Revisited," *Comparative Political Studies* 45, no. 3 (March 2012): 366–93.

7. Subhayu Bandyopadhyay, Todd Sandler, and Javed Younas, "The Toll of Terrorism," *Finance and Development* 52, no. 2 (June 2015): 26–28.

8. Paul Halsall, "Modern History Sourcebook: Maximilien Robespierre: Justification of the Use of Terror," Internet History Sourcebooks Project, https://sourcebooks.fordham.edu/mod/robespierre-terror.asp (accessed 1/2/20).

9. Orin Starn, "Maoism in the Andes: The Communist Party of Peru—Shining Path and the Refusal of History," *Journal of Latin American Studies* 27, no. 2 (May 1995): 399–421.

10. Mohammed M. Hafez, "Armed Islamist Movements and Political Violence in Algeria," *Middle East Journal* 54, no. 4 (Autumn 2000): 572–91.

11. Mark Juergensmeyer, *Terror in the Mind of God: The Global Rise of Religious Violence*, 3rd ed. (Berkeley, CA: University of California Press, 2003). See also David Livingstone Smith, *Less than Human: Why We Demean, Enslave, and Exterminate Others* (New York: St. Martin's Press, 2011).

12. Alexis de Tocqueville, *The Old Regime and the Revolution* (New York: Harper and Brothers, 1856), p. 27.

13. William Pierce, "The Morality of Survival," *National Vanguard*, May 2001, https://nationalvanguard.org/2018/12/the-morality-of-survival/ (accessed 1/6/20). See also Brad Whitsel, "*The Turner Diaries* and Cosmotheism: William Pierce's Theology," *Nova Religio* 1, no. 2 (April 1998): 183–97.

14. J. M. Berger, "The Turner Legacy: The Storied Origins and Enduring Impact of White Nationalism's Deadly Bible," International Centre for Counter-Terrorism, September 2016, https://icct.nl/wp-content/uploads/2016/09/ICCT-Berger-The-Turner-Legacy-September2016-2.pdf (accessed 1/2/20).

15. Matthew J. Walton and Susan Hayward, "Contesting Buddhist Narratives: Democratization, Nationalism, and Communal Violence in Myanmar," *Policy Studies* 71 (2014): 1–81.

16. Shane Harris, *The Watchers: The Rise of America's Surveillance State* (New York: Penguin, 2010).

17. Anonymous, *An Historical Review of the Constitution and Government of Pennsylvania* (London, 1759), p. 289.

INSTITUTIONS IN ACTION

a. Lin Noueihed, "Peddler's Martyrdom Launched Tunisia's Revolution," Reuters, January 11, 2011, https://uk.reuters.com/article/uk-tunisia-protests-bouazizi/peddlers-martyrdom-launched-tunisias-revolution-idUKTRE70I7TV20110119 (accessed 1/6/20).

CHAPTER 8: DEVELOPED DEMOCRACIES

1. T. R. Reid, *The United States of Europe: The New Superpower and the End of American Supremacy* (New York: Penguin, 2005).

2. See the discussion of the 2016 edition of World Development Indicators at http://blogs.worldbank.org/opendata/2016-edition-world-development-indicators-out-three-features-you-won-t-want-miss (accessed 1/21/20).

3. Desmond Dinan, *Europe Recast: A History of European Union*, 2nd ed. (Boulder, CO: Lynne Rienner Publishers, 2014).

4. See the website of the EU at https://europa.eu/european-union/about-eu_en (accessed 1/21/20).

5. Martin Feldstein, "The Failure of the Euro: The Little Currency That Couldn't," *Foreign Affairs* 91, no. 1 (January/February 2012): 105–16.

6. Jean-Paul Faguet, "Decentralization and Governance," *World Development* 53, no. 1 (January 2014): 2–13.

7. Ronald Inglehart, "Globalization and Postmodern Values," *Washington Quarterly* 23, no. 1 (Winter 2000): 215–28.

8. U.S. Census Bureau, "Projections of the Size and Composition of the U.S. Population: 2014 to 2060 Population Estimates and Projections," March 2015, www.census.gov/content/dam/Census/library/publications/2015/demo/p25-1143.pdf (accessed 1/21/20).

9. Organisation for Economic Co-operation and Development (OECD), "Education at a Glance 2019: OECD Indicators," 2019, www.oecd-ilibrary.org/education/education-at-a-glance-2019_f8d7880d-en (accessed 1/21/20).

10. OECD, "An Overview of Growing Income Inequalities in OECD Countries: Main Findings," 2011, www.oecd.org/els/soc/49499779.pdf (accessed 1/21/20).

11. Kenneth M. Johnson, Layton M. Field, and Dudley L. Poston Jr., "More Deaths Than Births: Subnational Natural Decrease in Europe and the United States," *Population and Development Review* 41, no. 4 (December 2015): 651–80.

12. Johnson, Field, and Poston Jr., "More Deaths Than Births."

INSTITUTIONS IN ACTION

a. Aris Trantidis, *Clientelism and Economic Policy: Greece and the Crisis* (New York: Routledge, 2016).

CHAPTER 9: COMMUNISM AND POSTCOMMUNISM

1. Walter Mayr, "Hungary's Peaceful Revolution: Cutting the Fence and Changing History," *Spiegel International*, May 29, 2009, www.spiegel.de/international/europe/hungary-s-peaceful-revolution-cutting-the-fence-and-changing-history-a-627632.html (accessed 2/9/20).

2. For a good overview of communist theory, see Alfred G. Meyer, *Communism* (New York: Random House, 1984).

3. See Marx's 1882 preface to the Russian translation of the *Communist Manifesto*, www.marxists.org (accessed 2/9/20).

4. See V. I. Lenin, *What Is to Be Done? Burning Questions of Our Movement*, trans. Joe Fineberg and George Hanna (New York: International Publishers, 1969).

5. For a comparative discussion of different communist systems, see Stephen White, John Gardner, George Schöpflin, and Tony Saich, *Communist and Postcommunist Political Systems: An Introduction*, 3rd ed. (New York: St. Martin's Press, 1990).

6. See Michael Voslensky, *Nomenklatura: Anatomy of the Soviet Ruling Class* (Garden City, NY: Doubleday, 1984).

7. See Robert Conquest, *The Great Terror: A Reassessment* (New York: Oxford University Press, 1990).

8. See Lowell Dittmer, *China's Continuous Revolution: The Post-Liberation Epoch, 1949–1981* (Berkeley, CA: University of California Press, 1987).

9. Robert W. Campbell, *The Socialist Economies in Transition: A Primer on Semi-Reformed Systems* (Bloomington, IN: Indiana University Press, 1991).

10. Quoted in Frank Dikötter, *Mao's Great Famine: The History of China's Most Devastating Catastrophe, 1958–62* (New York: Bloomsbury, 2010), p. 88.

11. Karl Marx and Friedrich Engels, *Manifesto of the Communist Party*, www.marxists.org/archive/marx/works/1848/communist-manifesto (accessed 2/9/20).

12. Joni Lovenduski and Jean Woodall, *Politics and Society in Eastern Europe* (Bloomington, IN: Indiana University Press, 1987), p. 158.

13. The best retrospective studies of the collapse of communism in Eastern Europe and its effects in the Soviet Union can be found in Mark Kramer, "The Collapse of East European Communism and the Repercussions within the Soviet Union," parts 1–3, *Journal of Cold War Studies* (5, no. 4 [Fall 2003], 6, no. 4 [Fall 2004], and 7, no. 1 [Spring 2005]).

14. On the collapse of communism in Eastern Europe, see Timothy Garton Ash, *The Magic Lantern: The Revolution of '89 Witnessed in Warsaw, Budapest, Berlin and Prague* (New York: Random House, 1990); on the collapse of communism in the Soviet Union, see David Remnick, *Lenin's Tomb: The Last Days of the Soviet Empire* (New York: Random House, 1993).

15. Freedom House, *Nations in Transit 2018* (Washington, DC: Freedom House, 2018), https://freedomhouse.org/sites/default/files/NIT2017_booklet_FINAL_0.pdf (accessed 2/10/20).

16. Robert J. Barro, "Economic Growth and Convergence, Applied Especially to China" (National Bureau of Economic Research [NBER] Working Paper 21872, January 2016) www.nber.org/papers/w21872 (accessed 2/10/20). See also David Shambaugh, *China's Future* (Malden, MA: Polity Press, 2016).

17. Global Acceptance Index, Williams Institute, University of Southern California Los Angeles School of Law, https://williamsinstitute.law.ucla.edu/uncategorized/lgbt-acceptance-around-the-world (accessed 2/9/20).

CHAPTER 10: DEVELOPING COUNTRIES

1. Christopher Cramer, Deborah Johnston, Bernd Mueller, Carlos Oya, and John Sender, "Fairtrade and Labour Markets in Ethiopia and Uganda," *Journal of Development Studies* 53, no. 6 (2017): 841–56. Raluca Dragusanu, Daniele Giovannucci, and Nathan Nunn, "The Economics of Fair Trade," *Journal of Economic Perspectives* 28, no. 3 (Summer 2014): 217–36.

2. For two excellent studies of imperialism in practice, see L. H. Gann and Peter Duignan, eds., *Colonialism in Africa, 1870–1960*, 5 vols. (Cambridge: Cambridge University Press, 1969–74); and Nicholas Tarling, ed., *The Cambridge History of Southeast Asia*, 2 vols. (Cambridge: Cambridge University Press, 1992).

3. A general discussion of the impact of imperialism can be found in Philip D. Curtin, *The World and the West: The European Challenge and the Overseas Response in the Age of Empire* (Cambridge: Cambridge University Press, 2000).

4. Alberto F. Alesina, Paola Giuliano, and Nathan Nunn, "On the Origins of Gender Roles: Women and the Plough," *Quarterly Journal of Economics* 128, no. 2 (May 2013): 469–530; Elizabeth Schmidt, *Peasants, Traders, and Wives: Shona Women in the History of Zimbabwe, 1870–1939* (New York: Heinemann, 1992).

5. See Joel S. Migdal, *Strong Societies and Weak States: State-Society Relations and State Capabilities in the Third World* (Princeton, NJ: Princeton University Press, 1988).

6. For a discussion of these issues, see Stuti Khemani et al., *Making Politics Work for Development: Harnessing Transparency and Citizen Engagement*, Policy Research Report (Washington, DC: World Bank, 2016).

7. Valerie M. Hudson, Mary Caprioli, Bonnie Ballif-Spanvill, Rose McDermott, and Chad F. Emmett, "The Heart of the Matter: The Security of Women and the Security of States," *International Security* 33, no. 3 (Winter 2008/09): 7–45; John Bongaarts and Christophe Z. Guilmoto, "How Many More Missing Women? Excess Female Mortality and Prenatal Sex Selection, 1970–2050," *Population and Development Review* 41, no. 2 (June 2015): 241–69.

8. For a discussion of different paths of industrialization, see Stephan Haggard, *Pathways from the Periphery: The Politics of Growth in the Newly Industrializing Countries* (Ithaca, NY: Cornell University Press, 1990).

9. Raphaël Franck and Ilia Rainer, "Does the Leader's Ethnicity Matter? Ethnic Favoritism, Education, and Health in Sub-Saharan Africa," *American Political Science Review* 106, no. 2 (May 2012): 294–325.

10. Francis Fukuyama, *State-Building: Governance and World Order in the 21st Century* (Ithaca, NY: Cornell University Press, 2004).

11. Anna Persson, Bo Rothstein, and Jan Teorell, "Why Anticorruption Reforms Fail—Systemic Corruption as a Collective Action Problem," *Governance* 26, no. 3 (July 2013): 449–71.

12. Khemani et al., *Making Politics Work for Development*, p. 213.

13. Claudio Ferraz and Frederico Finan, "Exposing Corrupt Politicians: The Effects of Brazil's Publicly Released Audits on Electoral Outcomes," *Quarterly Journal of Economics* 123, no. 2 (May 2008): 703–45.

14. See www.kiva.org (accessed 2/24/20).

15. Esther Duflo, Abhijit Banerjee, Rachel Glennerster, and Cynthia G. Kinnan, "The Miracle of Microfinance? Evidence from a Randomized Evaluation," MIT Department of Economics Working Paper no. 13-09, https://papers.ssrn.com/sol3/papers.cfm?abstract_id=2250500 (accessed 2/24/20); see also Daniel Altman, "Please Do Not Teach This Woman to Fish," *Foreign Policy*, June 10, 2014, https://foreignpolicy.com/2014/06/10/please-do-not-teach-this-woman-to-fish (accessed 2/24/20).

16. Michael Clemens and Gabriel Demombynes, "The New Transparency in Development Economics: Lessons from the Millennium Villages Controversy," Center for Global Development Working Paper no. 342, September 2013.

17. Abhijit V. Banerjee and Esther Duflo, *Poor Economics: A Radical Rethinking of the Way to Fight Global Poverty* (New York: PublicAffairs, 2011.

INSTITUTIONS IN ACTION

a. Atul Kohli, *State-Directed Development: Political Power and Industrialization in the Global Periphery* (New York: Cambridge University Press, 2004).

CHAPTER 11: GLOBALIZATION AND THE FUTURE OF COMPARATIVE POLITICS

1. Jeffrey Wasserstrom, "China & Globalization," *Daedalus* 143, no. 2 (2014): 157–69.

2. Ezra F. Vogel, *Japan as Number One: Lessons for America* (Cambridge, MA: Harvard University Press, 1979).

3. Jared Diamond, *Guns, Germs, and Steel: The Fates of Human Societies* (New York: W. W. Norton, 1997).

4. See Robert O. Keohane and Joseph S. Nye Jr., "Introduction," in *Governance in a Globalizing World*, ed. Joseph S. Nye Jr. and John D. Donahue (Washington, DC: Brookings Institution Press, 2000), pp. 1–41.

5. Thomas L. Friedman, *The Lexus and the Olive Tree: Understanding Globalization* (New York: Farrar, Straus and Giroux, 2000).

6. Daniel Cunningham, Sean Everton, and Philip Murphy, *Understanding Dark Networks: A Strategic Framework for the Use of Social Network Analysis* (New York: Rowman & Littlefield, 2016).

7. Charles A. Kupchan, "The Democratic Malaise: Globalization and the Threat to the West," *Foreign Affairs* 91, no. 1 (January/February 2012): 62–67.

8. United Nations, *World Investment Report 2019*, www.unctad.org/en/Publications Library/wir2019_en.pdf (accessed 3/17/20).

9. See the United Nations Department of Economic and Social Affairs Population Division, *International Migrant Stock 2019*, www.un.org/en/development/desa /population/migration/data/estimates2/estimates19.asp (accessed 3/17/20).

10. Tyler Cowen, *Creative Destruction: How Globalization Is Changing the World's Cultures* (Princeton, NJ: Princeton University Press, 2002); Jan Nederveen Pieterse, *Globalization and Culture: Global Mélange* (New York: Rowman & Littlefield, 2015).

11. John S. Dryzek, "Global Civil Society: The Progress of Post-Westphalian Politics," *Annual Review of Political Science* 15 (June 2012): 101–19.

12. George Ritzer, *The Globalization of Nothing*, 2nd ed. (Thousand Oaks, CA: Pine Forge Press, 2007), and *Enchanting a Disenchanted World: Continuity and Change in the Cathedrals of Consumption*, 3rd ed. (Thousand Oaks, CA: Pine Forge Press, 2010).

13. John Maynard Keynes, *The Economic Consequences of the Peace* (New York: Harcourt, Brace, and Howe, 1920), pp. 11–12.

14. Ben Casselman, "The White-Collar Job Apocalypse That Didn't Happen," *New York Times,* September 27, 2019, www.nytimes.com/2019/09/27/business/economy/jobs -offshoring.html (accessed 3/17/20).

15. Martin Ford, *Rise of the Robots: Technology and the Threat of a Jobless Future* (New York: Basic Books, 2015).

16. Keynes, *The Economic Consequences of the Peace*, p. 12.

17. Pew Research Center, "Faith and Skepticism about Trade, Foreign Investment," September 16, 2014, www.pewresearch.org/global/2014/09/16/faith-and-skepticism -about-trade-foreign-investment/ (accessed 3/17/20).

INSTITUTIONS IN ACTION

a. Anthony Boadle, "Bolsonaro Takes Office in Brazil, Says Nation 'Liberated from Socialism'," *Reuters*, December 31, 2018, www.reuters.com/article/US-brazil-politics /bolsonaro-takes-office-in-brazil-says-nation-liberated-from-socialism-idUSK CN10V1AU (accessed 4/17/20).

GLOSSARY

ABSTRACT REVIEW Judicial review that allows the constitutional court to rule on questions that do not arise from actual legal disputes

ANARCHISM A political ideology that stresses the elimination of the state and private property as a way to achieve both freedom and equality for all

AREA STUDIES A regional focus when studying political science, rather than studying parts of the world where similar variables are clustered

ASYMMETRIC FEDERALISM A system in which power is divided unevenly among regional bodies—for example, some regions are given greater power over taxation or language rights than others, a more likely outcome in a country with significant ethnic divisions

AUTHORITARIANISM A political system in which a small group of individuals exercises power over the state without being constitutionally responsible to the public

AUTONOMY The ability of the state to wield its power independently of the public or international actors

BASE The economic system of a society, made up of technology (the means of production) and class relations between people (the relations of production)

BEHAVIORAL REVOLUTION A movement within political science during the 1950s and 1960s to develop general theories about individual political behavior that could be applied across all countries

BICAMERAL SYSTEM A political system in which the legislature comprises two houses

BOURGEOISIE The property-owning class

BRETTON WOODS SYSTEM An economic regime that manages international economic relations; this includes the International Monetary Fund (IMF), the World Bank, and the World Trade Organization (WTO)

BUREAUCRATIC AUTHORITARIANISM A system in which the state bureaucracy and the military share a belief that a technocratic leadership, focused on rational, objective, and technical expertise, can solve the problems of the country without public participation

CAPACITY The ability of the state to wield power to carry out basic tasks, such as defending territory, making and enforcing rules, collecting taxes, and managing the economy

CAPITALISM A system of production based on private property and free markets

CAUSAL RELATIONSHIP Cause and effect; when a change in one variable causes a change in another variable

CENTRAL BANK The state institution that controls how much money is flowing through the economy as well as how much it costs to borrow money in that economy

CENTRAL COMMITTEE The legislature-like body of a communist party

CENTRAL PLANNING A communist economic system in which the state explicitly allocates resources by planning what should be produced and in what amounts, the final prices of goods, and where they should be sold

CHARISMATIC LEGITIMACY Legitimacy built on the force of ideas embodied by an individual leader

CITIZENSHIP An individual's relationship to the state, wherein citizens swear allegiance to that state and the state in return is obligated to provide rights to those citizens

CIVIL LIBERTIES Individual rights regarding freedom that are created by the constitution and the political regime

CIVIL RIGHTS Individual rights regarding equality that are created by the constitution and the political regime

CIVIL SOCIETY Organizations outside of the state that help people define and advance their own interests

CLIENTELISM A process whereby the state co-opts members of the public by providing specific benefits or favors to a single person or a small group in return for public support

COLONIALISM An imperialist system in which a foreign territory is physically occupied, using military force, businesses, or settlers

COMMUNISM (1) A political-economic system in which all wealth and property are shared so as to eliminate exploitation, oppression, and, ultimately, the need for political institutions such as the state; (2) a political ideology that advocates such a system

COMPARATIVE ADVANTAGE The ability of one country to produce a particular good or service more efficiently relative to other countries' efficiency in producing the same good or service

COMPARATIVE METHOD The means by which social scientists make comparisons across cases

COMPARATIVE POLITICS The study and comparison of domestic politics across countries

CONCRETE REVIEW Judicial review that allows the constitutional court to rule on the basis of actual legal disputes brought before it

CONSERVATIVES Those with a political attitude that is skeptical of change and supports the current order

CONSTITUENCY A geographical area that an elected official represents

CONSTITUTIONAL COURT The highest judicial body in a political system that decides whether laws and policies violate the constitution

CORPORATISM A method of co-optation whereby authoritarian systems create or sanction a limited number of organizations to represent the interests of the public and restrict those not set up or approved by the state

CORRELATION An apparent relationship between two or more variables

COUNTRY A state, government, and regime, and the people who live within that political system

CULTURE Basic institutions that define a society

DEDUCTIVE REASONING Research that works from a hypothesis that is then tested against data

DEFLATION A period of falling prices and values for goods, services, investments, and wages

DEMOCRACY A political system in which political power is exercised either directly or indirectly by the people

DEPENDENT VARIABLE A variable whose value changes based on that of another

DEVELOPED DEMOCRACY A country with institutionalized democracy and a high level of economic development

DEVELOPING COUNTRIES Lower and middle income countries

DEVOLUTION A process in which political power is "sent down" to lower levels of state and government

DIALECTICAL MATERIALISM Process of historical change that is not evolutionary but revolutionary; the existing base and superstructure (thesis) would come into conflict with new technological innovations, generating growing opposition to the existing order (antithesis)—this would culminate in revolution, overthrowing the old base and superstructure (synthesis)

ECONOMIC LIBERALIZATION Changes consistent with liberalism that aim to limit the power of the state and increase the power of the market and private property in an economy

ELECTORAL SYSTEM A set of rules that govern how votes are cast, counted, and translated into seats in a legislature

EMPIRE A single political authority that has under its sovereignty a large number of external regions or territories and different peoples

ENDOGENEITY The issue that cause and effect are not often clear, in that variables may be both cause and effect in relationship to one another

EQUALITY A material standard of living shared by individuals within a community, society, or country

ETHNIC CONFLICT A conflict in which different ethnic groups struggle to achieve certain political or economic goals at each other's expense

ETHNIC IDENTITY/ETHNICITY Specific attributes and societal institutions that make one group of people culturally different from others

EXECUTIVE The branch of government that carries out the laws and policies of a state

EXPORT-ORIENTED INDUSTRIALIZATION A mercantilist strategy for economic growth in which a country seeks out technologies and develops industries focused specifically on the export market

FAILED STATE A state so weak that its political structures collapse, leading to anarchy and violence

FASCISM A political ideology that asserts the superiority and inferiority of different groups of people and stresses a low degree of both freedom and equality in order to achieve a powerful state

FEDERALISM A system in which significant state powers, such as taxation, lawmaking, and security, are devolved to regional or local bodies

FIRST PAST THE POST An electoral system in which individual candidates compete in single-member districts; voters choose between candidates, and the candidate with the largest share of the vote wins the seat

FOREIGN DIRECT INVESTMENT (FDI) The purchase of assets in a country by a foreign firm

FORMAL INSTITUTIONS Institutions usually based on officially sanctioned rules that are relatively clear

FREEDOM The ability of an individual to act independently, without fear of restriction or punishment by the state or other individuals or groups in society

FUNDAMENTALISM A view of religion as absolute and inerrant and that it should be legally enforced by making faith the sovereign authority

GAME THEORY An approach that emphasizes how actors or organizations behave in their goal to influence others; built upon assumptions of rational choice

GINI INDEX A statistical formula that measures the amount of inequality in a society; its scale ranges from zero to 100, where zero corresponds to perfect equality and 100 to perfect inequality

GLASNOST Literally, openness; the policy of political liberalization implemented in the Soviet Union in the late 1980s

GLOBALIZATION The process of expanding and intensifying linkages between states, societies, and economies

GOVERNMENT The leadership or elite in charge of running the state

GROSS DOMESTIC PRODUCT (GDP) The total market value of all goods and services produced by a country over a period of one year

GUERRILLA WAR A conflict whereby nonstate combatants, who largely abide by the rules of war, target the state

HEAD OF GOVERNMENT The executive role that deals with the everyday tasks of running the state, such as formulating and executing policy

HEAD OF STATE The executive role that symbolizes and represents the people both nationally and internationally

HUMAN DEVELOPMENT INDEX (HDI) A statistical tool that attempts to evaluate the overall wealth, health, and knowledge of a country's people

HYPERINFLATION Inflation of more than 50 percent a month for more than two months in a row

IDEATIONAL Having to do with ideas

ILLIBERAL REGIME A regime where democratic institutions that rest on the rule of law are weakly institutionalized and poorly respected

IMPERIALISM A system in which a state extends its power to directly control territory, resources, and people beyond its borders

IMPORT SUBSTITUTION A mercantilist strategy for economic growth in which a country restricts imports in order to spur demand for locally produced goods

INDEPENDENT VARIABLE A variable whose value does not depend on that of another

INDUCTIVE REASONING Research that works from case studies in order to generate hypotheses

INFLATION An outstripping of supply by demand, resulting in an increase in the general price level of goods and services and a consequent loss of value in a country's currency

INFORMAL ECONOMY A segment of the economy that is not regulated, protected, or taxed by the state

INFORMAL INSTITUTIONS Institutions with unwritten and unofficial rules

INITIATIVE A national vote called by members of the public to address a specific proposal

INSTITUTION An organization or activity that is self perpetuating and valued for its own sake

INTERGOVERNMENTAL ORGANIZATION (IGO) Group created by states to serve particular policy ends

INTERGOVERNMENTAL SYSTEM A system in which two or more countries cooperate on issues

INTERNATIONAL REGIME The fundamental rules and norms that link states together and shape their relationships to one another, usually regarding some specific issues (such as greenhouse gases or trade)

INTERNATIONAL RELATIONS A field in political science that concentrates on relations between countries, such as foreign policy, war, trade, and foreign aid

JUDICIAL REVIEW The mechanism by which courts can review the actions of government and overturn those that violate the constitution

KLEPTOCRACY "Rule by theft," where those in power seek only to drain the state of assets and resources

LAISSEZ-FAIRE The principle that the economy should be "allowed to do" what it wishes; a liberal system of minimal state interference in the economy

LEGISLATURE The branch of government charged with making laws

LEGITIMACY A value whereby an institution is accepted by the public as right and proper, thus giving it authority and power

LIBERAL DEMOCRACY A political system that promotes participation, competition, and liberty and emphasizes individual freedom and civil rights

LIBERALISM (1) A political attitude that favors evolutionary transformation; (2) an ideology and political system that favors a limited state role in society and the economy and places a high priority on individual political and economic freedom

LIBERALS Those with a political attitude that favors evolutionary change and who believe that existing institutions can be instruments of positive change

LOWER INCOME COUNTRIES Countries that lack significant economic development or political institutionalization or both; also known as less-developed countries (LDCs)

MARKET The interaction between the forces of supply and demand that allocates resources

MERCANTILISM A political-economic system in which national economic power is paramount and the domestic economy is viewed as an instrument that exists primarily to serve the needs of the state

MICROCREDIT A system in which small loans are channeled to the poor through borrowing groups whose members jointly take responsibility for repayment

MIDDLE INCOME COUNTRIES Historically less-developed countries that have experienced significant economic growth and democratization

MIDDLE INCOME TRAP A situation where countries experience economic growth but are unable to develop at the speed necessary to catch up with developed countries

MIXED ELECTORAL SYSTEM An electoral system that uses a combination of single-member districts and proportional representation

MODERN Characterized as secular, rational, materialistic, technological, and bureaucratic, and placing a greater emphasis on individual freedom than in the past

MODERNIZATION THEORY A theory asserting that as societies developed, they would take on a set of common characteristics, including democracy and capitalism

MONOPOLY A single producer that is able to dominate the market for a good or service without effective competition

MULTICAUSALITY When variables are interconnected and interact to produce particular outcomes

MULTIMEMBER DISTRICT (MMD) An electoral district with more than one seat

MULTINATIONAL CORPORATION (MNC) Firm that produces, distributes, and markets its goods or services in more than one country

NATION A group that desires self-government through an independent state

NATION-STATE A state encompassing one dominant nation that it claims to embody and represent

NATIONAL CONFLICT A conflict in which one or more groups within a country develop clear aspirations for political independence, clashing with others as a result

NATIONAL IDENTITY A sense of belonging to a nation and a belief in its political aspirations

NATIONALISM Pride in one's people and the belief that they have a unique political destiny

NEOCOLONIALISM An indirect form of imperialism in which powerful countries overly influence the economies of less-developed countries

NEOLIBERALISM/STRUCTURAL-ADJUSTMENT PROGRAMS/WASHINGTON CONSENSUS A policy of economic liberalization adopted in exchange for financial support from liberal international organizations; typically includes privatizing state-run firms, ending subsidies, reducing tariff barriers, shrinking the size of the state, and welcoming foreign investment

NIHILISM A belief that all institutions and values are essentially meaningless and that the only redeeming value is violence

NOMENKLATURA Politically sensitive or influential jobs in the state, society, or economy that were staffed by people chosen or approved by the Communist Party

NONDEMOCRATIC REGIME A political regime that is controlled by a small group of individuals who exercise power over the state without being constitutionally responsible to the public

NONGOVERNMENTAL ORGANIZATION (NGO) A national or international group, independent of any state, that pursues policy objectives and fosters public participation

NONTARIFF REGULATORY BARRIERS Policies and regulations used to limit imports through methods other than taxation

NORTH AMERICAN FREE TRADE AGREEMENT (NAFTA) An agreement between Canada, Mexico, and the United States that liberalizes trade between the three countries, renegotiated in 2020 and replaced with the United States-Mexico-Canada Agreement (USMCA)

OFFSHORE OUTSOURCING A process by which a firm moves some of its work to a secondary business, outside the home country, that can do the work more efficiently or cheaply

PARASTATAL Industry partially owned by the state

PARLIAMENTARY SYSTEM A political system in which the roles of head of state and head of government are assigned to separate executive offices

PARTY-STATE A political system in which power flows directly from the ruling political party (usually a communist party) to the state, bypassing government structures

PATRIMONIALISM An arrangement whereby a ruler depends on a collection of supporters within the state who gain direct benefits in return for enforcing the ruler's will

PATRIOTISM Pride in one's state

PERESTROIKA Literally, restructuring; the policy of political and economic liberalization implemented in the Soviet Union in the late 1980s

POLITBURO The top policy-making and executive body of a communist party

POLITICAL ATTITUDE Description of one's views regarding the speed and methods with which political changes should take place in a given society

POLITICAL CULTURE The basic norms for political activity in a society

POLITICAL ECONOMY The study of the interaction between states and markets

POLITICAL IDEOLOGY The basic values held by an individual about the fundamental goals of politics or the ideal balance of freedom and equality

POLITICAL VIOLENCE Violence outside of state control that is politically motivated

POLITICAL-ECONOMIC SYSTEM The relationship between political and economic institutions in a particular country and the policies and outcomes they create

POLITICS The struggle in any group for power that will give one or more persons the ability to make decisions for the larger group

POPULISM A political view that does not have a consistent ideological foundation, but that emphasizes hostility toward elites and established state and economic institutions and favors greater power in the hands of the public

POSTMODERN Characterized by a set of values that center on "quality of life" considerations and give less attention to material gain

POWER The ability to influence others or impose one's will on them

PRESIDENTIAL SYSTEM A political system in which the roles of head of state and head of government are combined in one executive office

PROLETARIAT The working class

PROPERTY Goods or services that are owned by an individual or a group, privately or publicly

PROPORTIONAL REPRESENTATION (PR) An electoral system in which political parties compete in multimember districts; voters choose between parties, and the seats in the district are awarded proportionally according to the results of the vote

PUBLIC GOODS Goods, provided or secured by the state, available to society, and which no private person or organization can own

PURCHASING POWER PARITY (PPP) A statistical tool that attempts to estimate the buying power of income across different countries by using prices in the United States as a benchmark

QUALITATIVE METHOD Study through an in-depth investigation of a limited number of cases

QUANTITATIVE METHOD Study through statistical data from many cases

QUOTA A nontariff barrier that limits the quantity of a good that may be imported into a country

RADICALS Those with a political attitude that favors dramatic, often revolutionary change

RATIONAL CHOICE Approach that assumes that individuals weigh the costs and benefits and make choices to maximize their benefits

RATIONAL-LEGAL LEGITIMACY Legitimacy based on a system of laws and procedures that are highly institutionalized

REACTIONARIES Those who seek to restore the institutions of a real or an imagined earlier order

REFERENDUM A national vote called by a government to address a specific proposal, often a change to the constitution

REGIME The fundamental rules and norms of politics, embodying long-term goals regarding individual freedom and collective equality, where power should reside, and how it should be used

REGULATION A rule or an order that sets the boundaries of a given procedure

RELATIVE DEPRIVATION MODEL Model that predicts revolution when public expectations outpace the rate of domestic change

RENT SEEKING A process in which political leaders essentially rent out parts of the state to their patrons, who as a result control public goods that would otherwise be distributed in a nonpolitical manner

REPUBLICANISM Indirect democracy that emphasizes the separation of powers within a state and the representation of the public through elected officials

RESOURCE CURSE Theory of development in which the existence of natural resources in a given state is a barrier to modernization and democracy

REVOLUTION Public seizure of the state in order to overturn the existing government and regime

RULE OF LAW A system in which all individuals and groups, including those in government, are subject to the law, irrespective of their power or authority

SELECTION BIAS A focus on effects rather than causes, which can lead to inaccurate conclusions about correlation or causation

SEMI-PRESIDENTIAL SYSTEM An executive system that divides power between two strong executives, a president and a prime minister

SEPARATION OF POWERS The clear division of power among different branches of government and the provision that specific branches may check the power of other branches

SHOCK THERAPY A process of rapid marketization

SINGLE-MEMBER DISTRICT (SMD) An electoral district with one seat

SOCIAL DEMOCRACY/SOCIALISM (1) A political-economic system in which freedom and equality are balanced through the state's management of the economy and the provision of social expenditures; (2) a political ideology that advocates such a system

SOCIAL EXPENDITURES State provision of public benefits, such as education, health care, and transportation

SOCIETY Complex human organization; a collection of people bound by shared institutions that define how human relations should be conducted

SOVEREIGNTY The ability of a state to carry out actions and policies within a territory independently of external actors and internal rivals

STATE (1) The organization that maintains a monopoly of force over a given territory; (2) a set of political institutions that generates and executes policy regarding freedom and equality

STATE-SPONSORED TERRORISM Terrorism supported directly by a state as an instrument of foreign policy

STRONG STATE A state that is able to fulfill basic tasks, such as defending territory, making and enforcing rules, collecting taxes, and managing the economy

SUPERSTRUCTURE All noneconomic institutions in a society (for example, religion, culture, national identity); these ideas and values derive from the base and serve to legitimize the current system of exploitation

SUPRANATIONAL SYSTEM An intergovernmental system with its own sovereign powers over member states

TARIFF A tax on imported goods

TERRORISM The use of violence by nonstate actors against civilians in order to achieve a political goal

THEORY An integrated set of hypotheses, assumptions, and facts

TOTALITARIANISM A nondemocratic regime that is highly centralized, possessing some form of strong ideology that seeks to transform and absorb fundamental aspects of state, society, and the economy, using a wide array of institutions

TRADITIONAL LEGITIMACY Legitimacy that accepts aspects of politics because they have been institutionalized over a long period of time

TRANS-PACIFIC PARTNERSHIP (TPP) Proposed agreement among 12 countries to liberalize trade though reduced tariffs and common regulations; abandoned by the United States in 2017

UNICAMERAL SYSTEM A political system in which the legislature comprises one house

UNITARY STATE A state in which most political power exists at the national level, with limited local authority

VANGUARD OF THE PROLETARIAT Lenin's argument that an elite communist party would have to carry out revolution, because as a result of false consciousness, historical conditions would not automatically lead to capitalism's demise

VOTE OF NO CONFIDENCE Vote taken by a legislature as to whether its members continue to support the current prime minister; depending on the country, a vote of no confidence can force the resignation of the prime minister and/or lead to new parliamentary elections

WEAK STATE A state that has difficulty fulfilling basic tasks, such as defending territory, making and enforcing rules, collecting taxes, and managing the economy

CREDITS

TEXT:

p. 90, Figure 3.4: Ronald Inglehart and Christian Welzel, Cultural Map–World Values Survey Wave 6 (2010–2014), http://www.worldvaluessurvey.org/images/Culture_Map_2017_conclusive.png. Reprinted with permission.

p. 136: Sawyer, Bradley and Cynthia Cox, "How does health spending in the U.S. compare to other countries?" Peterson-KFF Health System Tracker, December 7, 2018.

p. 176: "Source: 2017 Legatum Prosperity Index™ (www.prosperity.com)".

p. 208: Republished with permission of Annual Reviews, from "What Have We Learned about the Resource Curse?," Michael L. Ross, *Annual Review of Political Science*, vol. 18: 239–259 © 2015; permission conveyed through Copyright Clearance Center, Inc.

p. 274: Kaufmann, Eric. Graph: "Income, Capital Punishment and Brexit, Whites Only" from *It's NOT the Economy, Stupid: Brexit as a Story of Personal Values; British Election Study 2015 Internet Panel, waves 1–3*. Used by permission of Eric Kaufmann.

p. 316: Darden, Keith, and Anna Grzymala-Busse. Figure: Precommunist Schooling and Share of Seats to Noncommunist Parties in the First Free Postcommunist Elections from "The Great Divide: Literacy, Nationalism, and the Communist Collapse." *World Politics*, vol. 59, no. 1, 2006, pp. 83–115.

p. 352: World Bank & P.R.C. Development Research Center of the State Council, 2012. "China 2030: Building a Modern, Harmonious, and Creative High-Income Society [prepublication version]," World Bank Publications, The World Bank, number 6057.

PHOTOS:

CHAPTER 1
p. 2: Yassine Gaidi/Anadolu Agency/Getty Images; **p. 25:** AP Photo

CHAPTER 2
p. 28: Arif Ali/AFP/Getty Images; **p. 55:** Pacific Press Agency/Alamy Stock Photo

CHAPTER 3
p. 60: AP Photo/Mahesh Kumar A.; **p. 93:** Manish Paudel/AFP via Getty Images

CHAPTER 4
p. 98: Edilzon Gamez/Getty Images; **p. 133:** Vanderlei Almeida/AFP via Getty Images

CHAPTER 5
p. 138: Adli Ghazali/Anadolu Agency/Getty Images; **p. 171:** Maurice Tsai/Bloomberg via Getty Images

CHAPTER 6
p. 178: Xinhua News Agency/Newscom; **p. 205:** Odd Andersen/AFP/Getty Images

CHAPTER 7
p. 210: Aaref Watad/AFP via Getty Images; **p. 237:** Miguel Medina/AFP/Getty Images

CHAPTER 8
p. 242: Charles McQuillan/Getty Images; **p. 271:** Louisa Gouliamaki/AFP/Getty Images

CHAPTER 9
p. 276: Michal Fludra/NurPhoto via Getty Images; **p. 311:** Carlos Barria/Reuters/Newscom

CHAPTER 10
p. 318: Eric Lafforgue/Art in All of Us/Corbis via Getty Images; **p. 349:** Erika Santelices/AFP via Getty Images

CHAPTER 11
p. 354: Visual China Group via Getty Images; **p. 379:** Marcelo Sayao/EPA-EFE/Shutterstock

INDEX

Page numbers in **boldface** refer to in-text glossary definitions. Page numbers in *italics* refer to figures and tables.

abortion, 250, 291
   sex-selective, 338
abstract review, **153,** 250
accountability, and political engagement in developing countries, 345
Afghanistan, 148
   communist regime in, *280*
   ethnic conflicts in, 73
   as fragile state, 49, *50–51*
   Islam in, 308
   and Pakistan, 54, 55
   and Soviet Union, 293, 300–301, 308
   terrorism in, 54, 227
   theocracy in, 202
Africa. *See also specific countries.*
   developed democracies in, *247*
   developing countries in, 321, *323,* 332, 333, 336, 339–340, 341, 342, 347
   ethnic conflicts in, 73–75, 341
   ethnolinguistic diversity in, *74*
   Fair Trade with countries in, *318,* 319, 320
   Human Development Index in, 341
   imperialism and colonialism in, 41, 325, 327, 332, 373
   import substitution in, 339
   Indian immigrants in, 336
   microcredit in, 347
   military rule in, 198
   Millennium Villages in, 347, 350
   natural resources in, 342
   nondemocratic regimes in, 188
   origin of human population in, 36
   origin of political organization in, 38
   outsourcing to, 368
   personal rule in, 198
   political systems in, *191*
   political transitions in,
      postcommunist, 300
   post-imperialism in, 332, 333, 336, 339–340
   social capital in, *176*
African Christian Democratic Party, *166*
African Independent Congress, *166*
African National Congress, *166,* 204, 205, 224
African Transformation Movement, *166*
aging population in developed democracies, 268
agriculture
   in Brazil, 378, 379
   in China, 305
   climate change affecting, 378
   collectivization of, 289
   deforestation of Amazon rainforest for, 378
   in developed democracies, 248, *249*
   in developing countries, 337–338, 340, 346, 347, 348–349
   Fair Trade in products of, *318,* 319–320, 347
   gender roles in, 330
   in imperialism and colonialism, 330, 331, 338, 349
   land ownership and land reform in, 348–349
   modernization theory on, 186
   and origins of political organization, 36, 38
   in post-imperialism, 337–338, 340, 349
   and rise of modern states, 40

agriculture (*continued*)
    in Soviet Union, 289
    subsistence, 40
    in Zimbabwe, 205
Alawite Muslim sect, 211, 337
Albania, *280, 299, 304*
Algeria, 229, 240, 332
Al Jama-ah party, *166*
Alliance of Hope, 139, 140
Alliance Party, *163*
Al Qaeda, *55,* 212, 231, 232, 240, 301, 308
alternative runoff voting, 164
Amazon rainforest, in globalization and climate change, 378–379
American Red Cross, 344
American Revolution, 73
Amnesty International, 334, 361
anarchism, **83,** *84,* 85, 112, 374
Angola, *280*
Antarctica, 378
Anwar Ibrahim, *138,* 139, 140
apartheid, 47, 69, 204, 219
Apple Inc., *354, 367*
April 6 Youth Movement, 237
Aquino, Corazon, 171
Arab Spring, 2, 3–4, *25,* 209, 236–237
    Bouazizi as inspiration for, *2,* 3, 24, 237
    macro-level approach to, 24
    political violence in, 211–212, 236–237
    as revolution, 221, 222, 236, 237
    surprise of, 25
    in Syria, 4, 211–212, 236
area studies, **9**–10
Arendt, Hannah, 184
Argentina
    as developed democracy, 250
    electoral system in, 161
    gross domestic product of, 348
    middle income trap in, *352,* 353
Aristotle (384–322 b.c.e.), 12, 13
Armed Islamic Group (GIA), 229
Armenia, *299,* 308, *312*
ascription of ethnic identity, 65
Asia. *See also specific countries.*
    area studies of, 9–10
    cultural values in, 170, 189
    democratization in, 3, 149, 170–171, 341
    developed democracies in, *247*
    developing countries in, 321, 322, *323,* 332, 333, 339–340, 341, 342
    economic growth in, 4, 17, 122, 130, 170, 341, 348–349, 368
    export-oriented industrialization in, 339–340, 348
    gross domestic product of, 348
    immigration from, 263, 264, 265
    imperialism and colonialism in, 41, 324, 325, 332, 349, 373
    import substitution in, 339
    and Latin America compared, 348–349
    mercantilism in, 119
    middle class in, 130, 170
    military rule in, 198
    natural resources in, 342
    Ottoman Empire in, 325
    political systems in, *191*
    political transitions in, postcommunist, 300
    post-imperialism in, 332, 333, 339–340, 349
    religious violence in, 233
    semi-presidential systems in, 158
    social capital in, *176*
    and United States relations, 348
Asian Values, 170, 189
al-Assad, Bashar, 4, 211, 212, 236
al-Assad, Hafez, 211
assimilation, 264
asymmetric federalism, **48,** 62
Athens, 42, 70, 146
attitudes, political. *See* political attitudes
Australia
    as developed democracy, *247,* 251, 263, 264
    electoral system in, 164, 251
    ethnic and national identity in, 68
    gross domestic product of, *123, 136*
    health expenditures in, *136*
    immigrant population in, 263, 264
    judiciary in, 152–153
    liberalism in, 114
    parliamentary system in, 154
    societal globalization and trust in, 383
    wealth measures in, 122, *123*
Austria, *136,* 277

authoritarianism, 3, **182,** 190
    and Arab Spring, 236
    bureaucratic, 199
    in China, *300,* 308, 356
    civil society in, 187
    corporatism in, 194
    and developed democracies, 265, 274–275
    in developing countries, 336
    emergence of, 186
    illiberal regime in, 202
    international relations in, 188
    in Latin America, 185
    and nationalism, 7
    political control in, 192, 194
    postcommunist, *300,* 308, 314, 316
    in premodern societies, 262
    rise in, 275
    in Soviet Union, 185, 190
    in Syria, 211, 217
    terrorism risk in, *235*
    totalitarianism compared to, 183
    trends in, *206*
    in Zimbabwe, *178,* 180, 204, 205, 208, 209
autocracy, 182
autonomy of states, 31, **49**–53, 56, 58
    in democracy, 142, 144
    in developed democracies, 253, 261
    in developing countries, 327, 333–336, 343, 348
    and ethnic and national conflicts, 72, 73
    in globalization, 363, 368, 375
    in imperialism, 188, 327
    in India, 63
    in nondemocratic regimes, 188
    in political-economic systems, 113, 115, 117, 118, 119
    political ideologies on, 81, 82, 83
    in postcommunism, 296
    in post-imperialism, 333–336
    of strong and weak states, 52–53
    in terrorism concerns, 234
Azerbaijan
    economic transitions in, 303, *304*
    LGBT acceptance in, *312*
    political transitions in, *299, 300*
    societal transitions in, 308

Bahrain, 114
Bakunin, Mikhail (1814–76), 83
Balkan states, 298
Baltic states, 297–298
Bangladesh, 347
banks, central, **108**–109, 110
    in European Union, 256, 257
    in Zimbabwe, 179
barbarians, 70
base, Marxist theory on, **281**
Basques, 217, 241
behavioralism, 15, 17, 21
behavioral revolution, **15,** 21, 145, 185, 220
Belarus, *299, 300*
Belgium, *136*
Benin, *280*
Berlin Wall, fall of, 277
Bernstein, Eduard (1850–1932), 114, 117
Bharatiya Janata Party (BJP), 62
bias, 10, 25
    selection, **10,** 11, 199, 240
bicameral systems, **151**
bin Laden, Osama, 54, 226, 231–232, 233, 308
biological studies of politics, 24
birthrate in developed democracies, 268
Bolivarian socialism in Venezuela, 99–100
Bolsa Família program in Brazil, 53, *133*
Bolsonaro, Jair, 379
bonding social capital, 176, 177
Bosnia, 65
Bosnia-Herzegovina, *299*
Botswana, *335*
Bouazizi, Mohamed, *2,* 3, 24, 237
bourgeois democracy, 82
bourgeoisie, Marxist theory on, 282, **283,** 291
Brazil
    Amazon rainforest in, 378–379
    Bolsa Família program in, 53, *133*
    Bolsonaro as president of, 379
    civil rights and liberties in, 173, 250
    conditional cash transfers in, 133, *133*
    corruption in, *335*
    as developed democracy, *249,* 250, 251
    economic liberalization in, *129*
    electoral system in, 167

Index   A-29

Brazil (*continued*)
    gender equality in, *125, 309*
    in global economy, 377
    gross domestic product of, *123, 125, 249,*
        348
    happiness in, *127*
    judiciary in, 153
    LGBT acceptance in, *312*
    life expectancy in, 268, 341
    mercantilism in, 119
    middle income trap in, 339, *352,* 353
    slaves in, 328
    state capacity and autonomy in, 53
    trade with China, 378
    wealth measures in, *123, 125*
Bretton Woods system, **365**–366, 376
Brexit, *242,* 243–245
    and Euroskepticism, 243–245
    immigration issue in, 258
    predictions on, 25, 244
    referendum on, 25, 169, 172, 244
    sovereignty issue in, 261, 363
    support of, and death penalty support,
        274, 275
bridging social capital, 176
British East India Company, 331
British Empire, 325
    in future United States, 73
    in India, 46–47, 54, 55, 61, 331, 336
    mercantilism in, 119
    in Sudan, 337
Buddhism, 92, 202, 233
Bulgaria
    communist regime in, *280*
    democratic progress in, 298, *299*
    as developed democracy, *247*
    in European Union, 298
    gender equality in, *309*
    happiness in, *127*
    LGBT acceptance in, *312*
bureaucracy
    in communist political economy, 290
    in developing countries, 327,
        333, 346
    in imperialism, 327, 333
    in post-imperialism, 333
bureaucratic authoritarianism, **199**
Burundi, *50*–51

cabinet, 151
    in parliamentary systems, 154, 155
    in presidential systems, 155, 156
Cambodia, *280*
Cameroon, *50–51*
campaign funding, 251
Canada
    corruption in, *335*
    democratic regime in, 33
    as developed democracy, *249,* 250, 251,
        253, 259, 260
    devolution in, 96, 260
    economic liberalization in, *129*
    electoral system in, 162, 164, 169, 251
    ethnic and national identity in, 67, 69–70
    federalism in, 48, 53, 96
    gender equality in, 126, *309*
    gross domestic product of, *107, 123, 125,*
        136, 249, 251, 268
    health care in, 105, *136*
    immigrant population in, 263, 264
    institutions in, 19
    judiciary in, 153
    LGBT acceptance in, *312*
    liberalism in, 114, 122, *253*
    in NAFTA, 377
    patriotism in, 69
    political attitudes in, 79
    political parties in, 162
    postindustrialism in, 266
    public debt in, 268
    public goods in, 105
    referenda and initiatives in, 169
    secular-rational values in, 91
    state capacity and autonomy in, 53
    taxation in, *107, 253*
    trade regulations in, 111, 259, 377
    in USMCA, 377
    wealth measures in, *122, 123,* 124, *125*
capacity of states, 31, **49**–53, 56, 58
    in democracy, 142, 144
    in developed democracies, 253, 261
    in developing countries, 327, 333–336,
        343, 348
    and ethnic and national conflicts, 73
    in globalization, 363, 368, 375
    in imperialism, 188, 327
    in India, 63

in Latin America, 133
measurement of, 58
in nondemocratic regimes, 188
in political-economic systems, 113, 115, 117, 118, 119, 136
political ideologies on, 81, 82, 83
in postcommunism, 296
in post-imperialism, 333–336
of strong and weak states, 52–53, 333
in terrorism concerns, 234
capitalism, **113**, 128
in developed democracies, 251, 252
in imperialism, 330
in Latin America, 132
in liberalism, 113
in Marxism, 116, 282, 283, 284, 285, 313
in mercantilism, 119
in modernization theory, 14, 15
in postcommunism, 301, 314
in social democracy, 114, 115
capital punishment, support for, and Brexit support, *274, 275*
captured states, 52, 53, 75, 334
case studies
challenges in, 7–11
in qualitative and quantitative methods, 16
cash-based economy in imperialism, 330
caste system, 61, 92, 93
Castro, Fidel (1926–2016), *287,* 288
Catalan independence movement, 261
Catholic Church, 88
and democratization, 149, 170
in Northern Ireland, 244, 261
and rise of modern state, 40, 41
causal relationship (cause-and-effect relationship), **7**, 8, 10–11, 91
in behavioralism, 21
in institutions, 21–22
multicausality in, 8, 91
in suicide terrorism, 241
variables in, 10, 11
Ceausescu, Nicolae, 195
cell phones
and societal globalization, 369, *370*
in sub-Saharan Africa, 347
cells in one-party rule, 200, 287–288
censorship, 375

Central African Republic, *50–51*
Central America, 325
central banks, **108**–109, 110
in European Union, 256, 257
in Zimbabwe, 179
Central Committee, **287**
centralization, 47–48, 53
in communism, 116, 117
and origins of political organization, 36
in revolutions, 222
in totalitarianism, 184
central planning, **290**, 302, 310, 311
Chad, *50–51*
change, political attitudes on, 75, 76–80
charismatic legitimacy, **45**, 46–47, 56
of Mandela, 204
in personal and monarchial rule, 45, 197, 198
in personality cults, 46, 195
Chávez, Hugo, 99–100, 132
Chechnya, 227, 308
checks and balances
in parliamentary systems, 154, 155
in presidential systems, 156, 159
child labor, and Fair Trade, 319, 320
Chile
as developed democracy, 250, 251
economic liberalism in, 114, *129,* 133
happiness in, 127
military rule in, 199
taxation and GDP in, *107*
China
area studies on, 9
authoritarianism in, *300,* 308, 356
ban on overseas travel in, 324
censorship in, 375
centralization of power in, 48
challenges in studies of, 9
civil society in, 311
communism in, 34–35, 82, 170, 280, *280,* 285, 288, 300, 305, 311, 313, 314
corruption in, 53, *304,* 305, *335*
Cultural Revolution in (1966), *287,* 288, 291, 311
democracy in, 142, 171
economic growth in, 353, 355, 356, 375, 378

China (*continued*)
  economic transitions in, 128, *129, 304,*
    305, 311, 356
  gender equality in, *125,* 126, *309*
  gender imbalance in population of, 338
  and globalization, 305, *354,* 355–357,
    365, 367, 375, 377, *382*
  Great Leap Forward in, 289, 311
  gross domestic product of, *123, 125, 249,*
    304, 355, 356
  happiness in, *127*
  and Hong Kong, 332
  imperialism of, 324, 325
  independence movements in, 66
  international relations of, 149, 188
  land reform in, 349
  LGBT acceptance in, 312, *312,* 313
  literacy in, 317
  Mao Zedong in, 92, 285, *287,* 288, 289
  mercantilism in, 120
  modernization in, 310–311
  nationalism in, 308
  nondemocratic regime in, 33
  one-party rule in, 201
  origins of political organization in, 38
  personality cult in, 196
  political attitudes in, 79–80
  political economy in, 289
  political reforms in, 34
  purchasing power parity in, 355
  religion in, 291, 306, 307
  revolution in, 222, 231, 285, 317, 348
  rise of modern state in, 39–40
  societal globalization and trust in, *382*
  societal transitions in, 308
  and Soviet Union compared, 296,
    310–311
  state capacity and autonomy in, 52, 53
  Tiananmen Square protests (1989) in, 79,
    296, 310, 311
  trade with Brazil, 378
  as unitary state, 48
  wealth measures in, 121, 122, *123, 125*
  and Zimbabwe, *178,* 180–181, 205, 356
Chinese Empire, 40, 324
Christianity
  Catholic Church in. *See* Catholic Church
  and imperialism, 325
  in India, 61
  in Northern Ireland, 244, 261
  in postcommunist countries, 306
  Protestantism in. *See* Protestantism
  and religious violence, 232
  and rise of modern state, 40
Cicero, 146
citizenship, 63, **68**–69, 91
  in developing countries, 337
  in globalization, 369, 382
  in India, 62
  origins and persistence of, 70–75
  and patriotism, 69–70
city-states, Greek, 12, 38
civilian targets of violence
  in religious violence, 230–231
  in terrorism, 224, *225,* 227
civil rights and liberties, 170, **172**–173, 174
  in communist countries, 297, *299*
  in definition of democracy, 141, 142
  in developed democracies, 250, 251, 252
  in imperialism and colonialism, 327,
    328–329
  in liberal democracy, 150
  in nondemocratic regimes, 182, 184, 186,
    190
  political ideologies on, 81, 82
  in postcommunist countries, 297–298,
    299, 313
  in terrorism concerns, 234–235
  trends in, 206
  in Zimbabwe, *178,* 180
civil society, **148**
  and Arab Spring, 236
  in China, 311
  in communist countries, 286, 288, 294,
    310
  and democratization, 147–148, 170, 171
  in developing countries, 344–345
  in Eastern Europe, 148, 294, 310
  in globalization, 371, 379
  and nondemocratic rule, 187–188, 190,
    193–194
  in postcommunist countries, 298, 305
  in Soviet Union, 294, 345
civil wars, 214, 218
The Clash of Civilizations and the Remaking of
    World Order (Huntington), 89

class
    Marx on, 283, 284
    middle class. *See* middle class
clientelism, **194**–195
    in developing countries, 333, 336, 339, 345
    in Greece, 270, 271
    and patrimonialism, 197
climate change, and globalization, 359, 378–379
coalition governments in parliamentary systems, 154, 158, 161, 169
coercion
    in military rule, 199
    in nondemocratic regimes, 190–192, 193, 194, 195, 196, 199
    in origins of political organization, 36–37
    in weakly institutionalized states, 47
coffee
    in export-oriented imperialism, 331
    Fair Trade in, *318,* 319–320, 347
cognitive factors in micro-level research, 24–25
Cold War, 14, 17, 181–182, 188
    and cultural influences on international relations, 89
    and Eastern Europe, 221, 310
    end of, 89, 246
    and Greece, 270
    reemergence of, 293
    and Zimbabwe, 205
collectivization of agriculture, 289
Colombia, 202
colonialism, 322, **324**
    dependent development in, 330–332, 338
    ethnic and national identity in, 328
    extractive economy in, 330–331
    gender roles in, 329–330
    imperialism compared to, 324
    in Latin America, 132, 331, 332, 349, 373
    and neocolonialism, 338, 348
    political rights in, 327
communism, 277–314, 321
    anarchism compared to, 83
    in China, 34–35, 82, 170, 280, *280,* 285, 288, 300, 305, 311, 313, 314
    collapse of, 246, 280, 293–296
        in Eastern Europe, 3, 219, 221–222, 236, 258, 277, 296, 297, 310, 313
    comparative method in study of, 7
    corporatism in, 194
    definition of, **281**
    democracy in, 286
    freedom and equality in, 116, 117–118, 182, 279, 280, 281–282, 284, 289, 291, 297, *299,* 313
    history of, *287, 295*
    legacy of, 308, 313–314
    literacy levels prior to, *316,* 316–317
    and Marxist theory, 116, 281–285
    in Nepal, 92–93
    nomenklatura in, 286, 288, 290, 294, 298, 303
    one-party rule in, 200, 201, 286–289, 294
    political attitudes in, 79
    political economy in, 112, 116–118, 128, 289–291
    political ideology in, 82, 83, *84,* 85, 183, 281
    and postcommunism. *See* postcommunism
    in practice, 285–288
    radical, 78, 92
    regimes in 1980s, *280*
    revolution and triumph of, 283–285
    societal institutions under, 291–293, *292*
    totalitarianism in, 183, 203
    and transition to liberal democracy, 278
Communist Party, 286–289, 313
    in China, 34–35, 305, 311
    in Eastern Europe, 294, 296
    in Hungary, 277, 278
    religion in, 306
    in Soviet Union, 192
comparative advantage, **111**
comparative method, **7**–11
comparative politics, **5**–27
    analytical concepts in, 5
    challenges of research in, 7–11
    comparative method in, 7–11
    compared to international relations, 5, 358

comparative politics (*continued*)
    concept of institutions in, 5–6, 18–22
    in globalization, 357–358, 359, 376–377, 380
    historical studies on, 12–16
    ideals of freedom and equality in, 6, 22–23
    methods in study of, 5
    qualitative and quantitative research in, 16
    regimes in, 361
    relevance of, 18
    science of, 11–18, 24–25
    trends in, 15
competition
    in democracy, 141, 142, 161, 165, 167, 170, 173, 174, 190
    in developed democracies, 250, 251, 252
    in nondemocratic regimes, lack of, 182, 186
concrete review, **153,** 250
conditional cash transfers, 133
conflict diamonds, 180
conflicts, ethnic. *See* ethnic conflicts
Confucianism, 170, 189, 306
Congo, Democratic Republic of, *50–51*
    ethnic conflicts in, 74
    happiness in, *127*
    patrimonialism in, 198
Congress of the People (South Africa), *166*
Congress Party (India), 47
consensus
    and legitimacy of state, 44
    in origin of political organization, 36–37
Conservative Party (United Kingdom), 163, *163,* 244
conservatives, **77,** 79, 80, 85
    in continuum of political attitudes, 78, *78*
    religious, 87
constituencies, **161,** 162, 164
constitution
    of Hungary, 278
    of Nepal, 93
    of postcommunist countries, 297
    of United States, 13, 35, 47
constitutional courts, **152**–153
    in developed democracies, 250
    in illiberal regimes, 203
    in parliamentary systems, 155
    in postcommunist countries, 297

    in semi-presidential systems, 158
control in nondemocratic regimes, 190–196, 197, 200
    in military rule, 199, 200
    in one-party rule, 200, 201
    in patrimonialism, 197
    in Syria, 192, 211
co-optation, 193–195, 196
    in developing countries, 333
    in one-party rule, 201
    in patrimonialism, 197
coronavirus pandemic (2020), 374–375, 376
corporatism in nondemocratic regimes, **193**–194, 195, 197, 199
correlation, **7,** 8
corruption
    Arab Spring as protest against, *2,* 3
    autonomy and capacity of state in, 53
    in communist countries, 291, 294, *304*
    in developing countries, 334, 341, 342, 343, 346, 353
    in Greece, 270–271
    index ranking countries by, *335*
    in mercantilism, 120
    in nondemocratic regimes, 195
    nongovernmental organizations concerned with, 364
    in Pakistan, 54, *335*
    in postcommunist countries, 303, *304,* 305, 334
    in post-imperialism, 334
    social capital affecting, 176
    in Zimbabwe, 180, *335*
cosmic war, 230
cosmopolitanism, global, 370, 371, 382, 383
Costa Rica, 127, 367
cost of living, 121
counterrevolution, 218, 219
country, **35**
coup d'état, 219
    and military rule, 198
    in Soviet Union, 294, 296
Court of Justice in European Union, 255
court systems, 152–153. *See also* judiciary
Croatia, 298, *299, 309, 312*
Cuba
    area studies on, 9
    communism in, *280,* 300

corporatism in, 194
gender equality in, *309*
missile crisis in, 293
nondemocratic regime in, 33
one-party rule in, 201
public goods in, 105
revolution in, 132, 222, *287*
cults of personality, 46, 195–196, 197
Cultural Revolution (China), *287,* 288, 291, 311
culture, **88**
    and democracy, 91, 149–150, 170, 189
    and ethnic identity, 65, 66, 70, 71
    and nondemocratic rule, 189–190
    norms on freedom and equality in, 53
    and personality cults, 195
    political, 88. *See also* political culture
    religion in, 88–89
    and rise of modern state, 41, 71
    and societal globalization, 369–372
currency, 107–110
    digital, 83, 363
    in European Union, 243, 256–258, 271
    exchange rate in, 121, 257
    in Zimbabwe, 179
Czechoslovakia, 96, 188, *280*
Czech Republic, 297, *299*
    gender equality in, *309*
    LGBT acceptance in, *312*
    taxation and GDP in, *107*

Darden, Keith, 316–317
death penalty, support for, and Brexit support, *274,* 275
death squads, 192
decentralization, 47–48, 53
    of markets, 103
    and political globalization, 364
The Decline of the West (Spengler), 203
deductive reasoning, **7,** 10, 17
    in quantitative research, 16
deflation, **110**
deforestation of Amazon rainforest, 378–379
democracy, 4–5, 6, 139–177
    in Asia, 3, 149, 170–171, 341
    balance of power in, 151
    causal relationships in, 11
    civil rights and liberties in, 150, 172–173

    and civil society, 147–148, 170, 171
    in communism, 286
    comparative method in study of, 7
    and contemporary democratization, 145–150
    and culture, 91, 149–150, 170, 189
    decline of, 176–177
    definition of, 141–143, **142**
    developed democracies, 243–275. *See also* developed democracies
    in developing countries, 322, 341–350
    direct, 144
    electoral systems in, 161–169
    and elites, 142, 144, 147, 149–150, 171
    freedom and equality in, 142, 144, 172–173, 234–235, 357
    future challenges to, 173–174
    in globalization, 356, 364, 365, 371, 372, 374, 377, 382
    indirect, 144
    as institution, 19, 20
    institutions of, 20–21, 150–153, 172–173
    and international relations, 148–149, 171
    liberal. *See* liberal democracy
    Marx on, 283
    milestones in rise of, 146
    models of, 153–160
    in modernization theory, 14, 15, 145, 147, 148, 149, 170, 185, 186, 189, 382
    in Nepal, 92–93
    origins of, 88, 143–145
    parliamentary systems in, 154–155, 158, 159
    political parties in, 160–161
    political violence in, 234–235, *235,* 240–241
    in postcommunist countries, 296–300, 314
    presidential systems in, 155–156, 159–160
    referenda and initiatives in, 169, 172
    semi-presidential systems in, 156–158, 159, 160
    social. *See* social democracy
    social capital in, 176–177
    taxation in, 20–21
    trends in, 206, *206*

Democratic Alliance (South Africa), *166*
democratic deficit in European Union, 256, 365
democratic regimes, 33, 34, 35, 139–177
Democratic Unionist Party (United Kingdom), *163,* 163–164
Deng Xiaoping (1904–97), *287,* 311
Denmark, *107,* 256, *335*
dependent development, 330–332, 338
dependent variables, **10,** 97
    in suicide terrorism, 241
détente in Soviet and U.S. relations, 293
developed democracies, 243–275, 321
    authoritarian views in, 265, 274–275
    contemporary challenges for, 252–253
    definition of, **245,** 246–248
    devolution in, 254, 259–261, 266, 269
    and economic crisis in Greece, 270–271
    economic institutions in, 250, 252, 265–269
    in European Union, 254–259
    freedom and equality in, 250–252, 266
    gross domestic product of, 248, *249,* 251, *253,* 267–268
    immigration in, 245, 258, 263–265, 268, 269, 275
    income redistribution in, 251, *253*
    list of, 247, *247, 249*
    political diversity in, 251, 252
    political institutions in, 253–261
    postindustrialism in, 266–267
    postmodern values in, 262–265
    social expenditures and welfare in, 106, 260, 267–269
    societal institutions in, 261–265
    in transition, 269, 272
developing countries, 246, 247, 318–353
    cell phone use in, *370*
    corruption in, 334, 341, 342, 343, 346, 353
    creating nations and citizens in, 336–338
    definition of, **322**
    democracy and development in, 322, 341–350
    dependent development in, 330–332, 338
    diversity of, 343
    economic development in, 322, 330–332, 335, 338–342, 345–350

economic inequality in, 352–353
extractive economy in, 330–331
Fair Trade with, *318,* 319–320
foreign aid to, 342, 350
freedom and equality in, 321, 322–324, 327, 328–329, 332, 335, 350
imperialism and colonialism in, 322, 324–332
informal economy in, 346
land ownership and land reform in, 348–349
list of, *323*
mercantilism in, 119–120
middle income trap in, 339, 352–353
nondemocratic regimes in, 334
political engagement in, 344–345
post-imperialism in, 332–340
religious violence in, 230
social identity in, 328–330, 332
state capacity and autonomy in, 327, 333–336, 343, 348
devolution, 48, 75
    compared to integration, 260–261
    definition of, **48,** 260
    in developed democracies, 254, 259–261, 266, 269
    in developing countries, 345
    in ethnic conflicts, 96–97, 261
    in India, 62, 63, 96
dialectical materialism, 282, **283**
diamond mining in Zimbabwe, 180
dictatorship, 182
    of proletariat, Marxist theory on, 282, 284
digital currency, 83, 363
direct democracy, 144
districts, electoral, 161–169
    boundaries of, 161–162
    multimember, 165
    proportional representation of, 165, 167
    single member. *See* single-member districts
Dominican Republic, *349*
Dutch colonizers, 331
Dzhugashvili, Josef Vissarionovich (Stalin), 192, 195, *287,* 288

Easterlin, Richard A., 126
Easterlin paradox, 126, 127
Eastern Europe

civil society in, 148, 294, 310
communism in, 280, 288, 292–293
    collapse of, 3, 219, 221–222, 236, 258, 277, 296, 297, 310, 313
democratization in, 148, 171
ethnic and national identity in, 292–293, 294, 307, 308
in European Union, 314
nondemocratic rule in, 188
outsourcing to, 368
"return to Europe" view in, 310, 311
revolutions in, 219, 221–222
social capital in, *176*
and Soviet Union, 221–222, 236, 292–293, 294

East Germany, 277, *280*

The Economic Consequences of the Peace (Keynes), 373

Economic Freedom Fighters (South Africa), *166*

economic globalization, 355–356, 360, 365–368, 369, 383
history of, 358–359, 366, 367–368, 374
impact of, 375–376
inequality in, *130,* 130–131, 368, 375–376
Latin America in, 132, 368
microcredit in, 347
opposition to, 377

economic growth, 108–110
in Asia, 4, 17, 122, 130, 170, 341, 348–349, 368
in China, 353, 355, 356, 375, 378
democratization in, 170
in developed democracies, 266–267
in developing countries, 322, 338–340, 341–342, 345–350
Gini index in, 122, 266
in global economy, *130,* 130–131
and happiness, 126
inequality in, 122
interest rates affecting, 108, 112
in Latin America, 132, 348–349
in liberalism, 113
microcredit and microfinance in, 346–347
middle income trap in, 339, 352–353
in postcommunist countries, 303, 305
in social democracy, 114
trade affecting, 112, 338–340

economic inequality, 23
in communism, 116, 279, 290–291
in developed democracies, 251–252, 266
in developing countries, 352–353
Gini index on. *See* Gini index
in global economy, *130,* 130–131, 368, 375–376
and happiness, 126–127
in Latin America, 132–133
in liberalism, 136
in middle income trap, 352–353
political ideologies on, 81, 82
in postcommunist countries, 122, 303–304, 305, 313
in postindustrialism, 266
redistribution of wealth in, 23
and social capital, 177
in social democracy, 115, 136
social expenditures in, 105–106
and terrorism, 226
in Venezuela, 99

economic institutions, 101
in communism, 116, 289–291
in developed democracies, 250, 252, 265–269
in developing countries, 319, 341
in globalization, 360, 365–368
in imperialism and colonialism, 330–332
in liberalism, 131
modernization affecting, 185
in political-economic systems, 112, 137
and political violence, 214
in postcommunism, 301–305
in social democracy, 173

economic liberalization, **128,** *129,* 340
and economic globalization, 366, 367
in France, *129,* 244
in Latin America, 132, 133

economic recession (2008), 258
Greece in, 270, 271
Hungary in, 278

economy
balance of freedom and equality in, 23, 101–102
cash-based, in imperialism, 330
central planning of, 290, 302, 310, 311
and democratization, 147

economy (*continued*)
    in developed democracies, 246–248, *249,* 250, 251–252, 265–269, 270–271
    in developing countries, 322, 330–332, 335, 338–342, 345–350
    and ethnic and national conflicts, 73
    extractive, 330–331
    globalization of. *See* economic globalization
    of Greece, 257–258, 270–271, 303, *304,* 366
    gross domestic product of, 106. *See also* gross domestic product
    growth of. *See* economic growth
    inequality in. *See* economic inequality
    informal, 270, 346
    information-based, 266, 269, 368
    institutions in. *See* economic institutions
    middle income trap in, 339, 352–353, 356
    money supply in, 107–110
    and origins of political organization, 36
    political. *See* political economy
    political attitudes toward, 79
    political ideologies on, 81, 82
    postindustrial, 266–267
    regulation of, 110–112
    in rise of modern state, 40, 41
    of Venezuela, *98,* 99–101, 109, *129,* 132, 133
    of Zimbabwe, *178,* 179–181
education
    in communist countries, 291, 317
    conditional cash transfers for, 133
    in developing countries, 333, 335, 353
    and economic development, 353
    and Human Development Index, 124, 125, *125,* 236
    in imperialism and colonialism, 327, 329, 330
    in modernization theory, 145, 170
    in postcommunist countries, 309
    in post-imperialism, 333, 335
    in postindustrialism, 266
    and precommunist literacy levels, *316,* 316–317
    as public good, 105, 113, 114, 115
    social expenditures on, 106, 117, 121
    as universal right, 173
Egypt
    Arab Spring in, 3, 4, *25,* 211, 236–237
    dictatorship in, 4
    military rule in, 199
    nondemocratic regime in, 192, 199
    political control in, 192
    revolution in (2011), 199, 220, 222
    suicide terrorism in, 240, 241
elections
    campaign funding in, 251
    in communism, 286, 288
    in democracy, 142
    in developed democracies, 250–251
    in developing countries, 343
    electoral systems in, 161–169, 250–251
    in European Union, 255, 256
    in illiberal regimes, 202, 203
    as institution, 21
    in Malaysia, *138,* 139–140
    in Nepal, 93, 139
    in Nigeria, 73, 161, 162
    in Pakistan, 29
    in parliamentary systems, 154, 155
    political parties in, 160, 161–169
    in presidential systems, 155, 156, 159
    rational-legal legitimacy of, 46
    referenda and initiatives in, 169, 172, 250
    in semi-presidential systems, 156
    in South Africa, 204
    in United Kingdom, 162–164, *163*
    in United States, 140, 162
    in Venezuela, 99
    winner-take-all, 162, 167, 215
    in Zimbabwe, 179, 180, 204
electoral systems, **161,** 161–169
    in developed democracies, 250–251
    mixed type, 168
    political parties in. *See* political parties
    proportional representation in, 162, 164–169, 251
    single-member districts in. *See* single-member districts
electricity shortages in Pakistan, *28,* 29–30, 44, 54, 344

elites
- in communism, 285–286, 292, 296, 310, 316
- in coup d'état, 219
- and democratization, 142, 144, 147, 149–150, 171
- in developing countries, 344, 349
- in imperialism, 328
- and nondemocratic rule, 186–187, 190, 197, 209
- and political parties, 160

El Salvador, 100
empires, **324,** 329, 330, 332, 338
endogeneity, **11,** 91
energy problems in Pakistan, *28,* 29–30, 44, 54, 344
England, 143–145, 151. *See also* United Kingdom
Ennahda Party (Tunisia), 237
entrepreneurialism, 113, 116
environmental issues
- in China, 305
- in globalization and climate change, 359, 378–379
- political parties concerned about, 167, 168
- postmodern values on, 262

equality
- definition of, **22**
- economic. *See* economic inequality
- and freedom. *See* freedom and equality
- gender. *See* gender equality

Eritrea, 50–51
Estonia, 297, *299, 300*
Ethiopia, 96, *280*
- Fair Trade with, *318,* 320
- imperialism in, 327

ethnic conflicts, 5, 64, **72**–75
- in developing countries, 336, 341
- devolution in, 96–97, 261
- federalism in, 96–97
- in India, 61, 62
- in Nepal, 92–93
- in postcommunist countries, 308
- prevention of, 75
- proportional representation in, 167
- in Soviet Union, 73, 294, 310
- views of, 73
- violence in, 72

ethnic identity, 63, **64**–66, 70, 91
- and citizenship, 69, 72
- in communism, 292
- conflicts related to. *See* ethnic conflicts
- in developed democracies, 264–265
- in developing countries, 328–329, 336–337, 341
- education affecting, 317
- immigration affecting, 264–265
- in imperialism, 328–329, 336
- in India, 61, 62, 65
- institutions in, 71
- and national identity, 67–68, 71, 72, 96
- in Nepal, 92–93
- origins and persistence of, 70–75
- and patriotism, 69, 70
- in postcommunist countries, 306–308
- in post-imperialism, 336–337
- and rise of modern state, 41

ethnolinguistic diversity in Africa, *74*
Eurasia, political systems in, *191*
euro currency, 243, 256–258
- in Greece, 257–258, 271

Europe. *See also specific countries.*
- civil society in, 188
- democracy in, 88, 142, 144, 148, 151, 189
- developed democracies in, *247,* 248
- developing countries in, *323*
- electricity use in, 29
- ethnic and national identity in, 70, 71
- imperialism of, 72, 324, 325, 327, 328, 332, 373
- inflation in, 109
- institutions in, 19
- Internet privacy laws in, 375
- and Latin America relations, 132
- Medieval, interconnections in, 372
- nationalism in, 71
- nation-states in, 71–72
- Ottoman Empire in, 325
- political attitudes in, 78, 79, 80
- political culture in, 88, 89, 189
- political ideologies in, 82, 83
- political systems in, *191*
- referenda and initiatives in, 169
- research focus on, 9–10
- retirement age in, 268

Europe (*continued*)
    and "return to Europe" view in Eastern Europe, 310, 311
    rise of modern state in, 38–43, 56, 327
    social capital in, 176
    social democracy in, 82, 115, 251
    social expenditures and taxation in, 106
European Central Bank, 256
European Commission, 255
European Council, 255
European Parliament, 244–245, 255, 256
European Union, 254–259
    authoritarian views in, 274
    British exit from. *See* Brexit
    Committee of the Regions in, 260
    coronavirus pandemic in (2020), 374–375
    creation of, 243
    currency of, 243, 256–258, 271
    democratic deficit in, 256, 365
    devolution in, 260–261
    Eastern European countries in, 314
    Euroskepticism of, 243–245, 258, 260, 278
    expansion of, 258, *259*
    and globalization, 245, 361, 363, 365, 374–375
    Greece in, 257–258, 271
    gross domestic product of, 258
    and Hungary, 277, 278, 298
    immigration in, 245, 258, 263, 264, 265, 278–279
    as intergovernmental organization, 255, 361, 363
    map of, *259*
    Parliament of, 244–245, 255, 256
    population of, 258
    postcommunist countries in, 258, 298
    as supranational system, 255
    timeline on development of, 254–255, 257
Euroskepticism, 243–245, 258, 260, 278
Euskadi Ta Askatasuna (Spain), 217
Evolutionary Socialism (Bernstein), 114, 117
exchange rate, 121
    in European Union, 257
executive branch, **150**–151, 152
    in developed democracies, 251
    in illiberal regimes, 202–203
    in parliamentary system, 154–155, 157, 158
    in presidential system, 155–156, 157, 159–160
    in semi-presidential system, 156–158, 160
export-oriented imperialism, 331
export-oriented industrialization, **339**–340, 346, 348
extractive economy, 330–331
Facebook, 237, 375
failed states, **49,** 58
Fair Trade, *318,* 319–320, 347, 350
false consciousness, Marxist theory on, 282, 291
family
    organization by, 36, 37
    in post-imperialism, 337–338
    traditional legitimacy of, 47
Farage, Nigel, 244
fascism, **82,** 86
    in globalization, 374
    one-party rule in, 201
    political-economic system in, 112, 120, 128
    political ideology in, 82–83, *84,* 85, 183
    reactionary, 78
    totalitarianism in, 183, 203
federalism, **48,** 75
    asymmetric, 48, 62
    in developed democracies, 251
    in ethnic conflicts, 96–97
    legislatures in, 151
    measuring success of, 75
    in Nepal, 63, 92, 93
    state capacity and autonomy in, 53
Federal Reserve (United States), 108
feudalism, 151, 283
Fidesz Party (Hungary), *276,* 277–279
financial crisis (2008), 258
    Greece in, 270, 271
    Hungary in, 278
first past the post systems, **162**
First World, 246
foreign direct investment (FDI), 348, **366,** *367,* 375, 383
formal institutions, **20**
fragile states, 49, *50–51*
France
    corruption in, *335*
    counterterrorism measures in, 235

as developed democracy, 248, *249,* 251, 263, 264
economic liberalization in, *129,* 244
electoral system in, 164
electricity use in, 29
in European Union, 243, 244–245, 256, 263
gender equality in, *125, 309*
gross domestic product of, *107, 123, 125, 136, 249,* 268
health expenditures in, *136*
Human Development Index in, 125, *125*
immigrant population in, 263
imperialism and colonialism of, 41, 325, 332
nationalism in, 71
public debt in, 268
regimes in, 33
Reign of Terror in, 222
revolution in, 80, 222, 228, 231
scope and strength of state, 58
semi-presidential system in, 157–158, 251
social democracy in, 115, *253*
taxation in, *107, 253*
as unitary state, 48
wealth measures in, *123, 125*
Franklin, Benjamin, 235
freedom, definition of, **22**
freedom and equality, 6, 22–23, 26
    capacity and autonomy of state affecting, 52–53, 335
    in centralization and decentralization, 47
    in communism, 116, 117–118, 182, 279, 280, 281–282, 284, 289, 291, 297, *299,* 313
    cultural norms on, 53
    in democracy, 142, 144, 172–173, 234–235, 357
    in developed democracies, 250–252, 266
    in developing countries, 321, 322–324, 327, 328–329, 332, 335, 350
    in economy, 23, 101–102
    in fundamentalism, 87–88
    future of, 56–57
    in globalization, 357, 358, 368, 380
    government ideas on, 34, 36
    greater good in, 23
    in imperialism and colonialism, 327, 328–329, 332
    and legitimacy of state, 44
    in national identity, 66
    in nondemocratic regimes, 181, 182, 183, 186, 357
    and origins of political organization, 36, 37
    political attitudes on, 64, 76, 79
    in political-economic systems, 112–120, 128, 131, 136, 142
    political ideologies on, 76, 80–85, *84*
    in postcommunist countries, 297–298, *299*
    in post-imperialism, 332, 335
    in postindustrialism, 266
    in regimes, 33, 34, 56
    in revolutions, 10, 222
    role of state in management of, 31
    trends in, 206
freedom and security in terrorism concerns, 234–235
Freedom Front Plus (South Africa), *166*
Freedom House, 181, 206, 297
free will, and political violence, 216
French Revolution, 80, 222, 228, 231
Friedman, Thomas, 363
Fujimori, Alberto, 227
Fukuyama, Francis, 58–59
fundamentalism, 85–88, 91, 230
    definition of, **87**
    in globalization, 371
    reactionary, 87, 92
    and theocracy, 201–202
    violence in, 87, 230, 231

Gaddhafi, Mu'ammar, 3
game theory, **17**
Gandhi, Indira, 47, 62
Gandhi, Mohandas K., 46–47
Gandhi, Rahul, 47
Gandhi, Rajiv, 47
Gandhi, Sonia, 47
gender equality, 11, 91
    in communism, 291–292
    and Human Development Index, 125–126

gender equality (*continued*)
   in imperialism and colonialism, 329–330, 337
   in modernization theory, 145
   in postcommunist countries, 307, 308–309, *309*, 312
   in post-imperialism, 337–338
Gender Gap Index, 308, *309*
General Agreements on Tariffs and Trade (GATT), 365–366
genetics
   in biological studies of politics, 24
   in origin of human population, 36
genocide, 223
Georgia (country), *299, 304, 312*
Germany
   civil rights and liberties in, 172
   civil society in, 345
   democratization in, 148, 188
   as developed democracy, 248, *249,* 250, 251, *253,* 263
   economic liberalization in, *129*
   electoral system in, 165, 168, 250
   electricity use in, 29
   ethnic and national identity in, 65, 67
   in European Union, 244, 263
   federalism in, 48
   gender equality in, *125, 309*
   in globalization, 377
   government employment in, 137
   gross domestic product of, *107,* 115, *123, 125, 136, 249,* 251
   happiness in, *127*
   health expenditures in, *136*
   immigrant population in, 263
   LGBT acceptance in, *312*
   Nazi regime in, 83, 183
   political-economic system in, *253*
   proportional representation in, 165
   social democracy in, *253*
   societal globalization and trust in, 383
   taxation in, *107,* 115, *253*
   wealth measures in, 121, *123, 125*
gerrymandering, 140
Gini index, **122,** 124, 137
   in communist countries, 290
   in developed democracies, 251, *253*
   and gross domestic product in different countries, *123*
   in Latin America, 132
glasnost, **293,** 294
Global Gender Gap Index, 308, *309*
globalization, 4, 5, 355–383
   causes and effects of, 356
   China in, 305, *354,* 355–357, 365, 367, 375, 377, *382*
   and climate change, 359, 378–379
   and comparative politics, 357–358, 359, 376–377, 380
   definition of, **357,** 358–360
   democracy in, 356, 364, 365, 371, 372, 374, 377, 382
   economic. See economic globalization
   European Union in, 245, 361, 363, 365, 374–375
   freedom and equality in, 357, 358, 368, 380
   history of, 358–359, 367–368, 372–374, 376
   and immigration, 369–370, 371, 373, 374, 376, 377
   impact of, 374–376
   inevitability of, 376–377
   institutions in, 360–362, 363, 364, 365, 369, 377
   Latin America in, 132, 368
   liberalism in, 130–131, 365, 368
   and localism, 261
   microcredit in, 347
   mistrust in, 370, 382–383
   political, 356, 360, 362–365, 369, 374–375, 383
   postindustrialism in, 266
   societal, 359, 360, 369–372, 382, 383
   United States in, 355, 367, 377
Global South, 321
Global Witness, 180
Good Friday Agreement (1998), 244
Good Judgment Project, 25
Good Party (South Africa), *166*
goods
   market for, 102, 103
   price of. See price of goods and services
   private ownership of, 104, 105
   public, 104–105. See also public goods

Gorbachev, Mikhail (1931–), 34, *287,* 293–294, 310, 311
government, **34**
    balance of power in, 151, 154, 156
    compared to regime and state, 34–35, *35,* 36, 56
    executive branch of, 150, 152. *See also* executive branch
    head of, 150, 151, 154, 155, 156
    judicial branch of, 152–153. *See also* judiciary
    legislatures in, 151, 152. *See also* legislatures
    as weakly institutionalized, 35
Grameen Bank, 347
Great Britain. *See also* United Kingdom
    in future United States, 73
    imperialism and colonialism of, 41
    independence of India from, 46–47, 54, 55, 61
    mercantilism of, 119
Great Depression, 270, 365
Great Leap Forward in China (1958–60), 289, 311
Greece
    citizenship in, 70
    city-states in, 12, 38
    as developed democracy, 250, 257–258, 270–271
    economy of, 257–258, 270–271, 303, *304,* 366
    in European Union, 257–258, 271
    gross domestic product of, 270, *304*
    origins of democracy in, 143
Greenland, 378
Green Party (Germany), 168
Green Party (United Kingdom), *163*
Greenpeace, 361, 365
gross domestic product, **106,** 186
    of China, *123, 125, 249, 304, 355,* 356
    of developed democracies, 248, *249,* 251, *253,* 267–268
    of developing countries, 322, 339, 341, 346, 348, 352
    of European Union, 258
    of Greece, 270, *304*
    and happiness, 126, 127
    and health expenditures, *136*
    and Human Development Index, 124
    informal sector in, 346
    as measure of wealth, 121, 122, *123,* 124
    of postcommunist countries, *304*
    and social expenditures, 267–268
    and taxation, 106–107, *107,* 115, *253,* 267–268
    of United States, *107, 123, 125, 136, 249,* 251, 268, 355
    of Venezuela, 132
    of Zaire, 198
Grzymala-Busse, Anna Maria, 316–317
Guaidó, Juan, 101
Guatemala, happiness in, 127
guerrilla war, **224**
    actors and targets in, *225,* 229
    in Syria, 211, 212
    terrorism compared to, 224, 227, 228–229
    in Zimbabwe, 212, 224
Guinea, *50–51*
Guinea-Bissau, *50–51*
gun ownership laws, 8

haciendas, 349
Haidt, Jonathan, 274, 275
Haiti, *50–51*
Hamas, 240
happiness, 126–127, *127*
head of government, **150,** 151
    in parliamentary systems, 154
    in presidential systems, 155, 156
    in semi-presidential systems, 156
head of state, **150,** 151
    in parliamentary systems, 154, 155
    in presidential systems, 155, 156
    in semi-presidential systems, 156
health care
    as global concern, 359
    and gross domestic product, *136*
    and Human Development Index, 124, 236
    in imperialism and colonialism, 329
    in liberal political-economic systems, 137
    in postcommunist countries, 309, 312
    in post-imperialism, 333
    as public good, 105, 106, 115
    in social democracy, 137

health care (*continued*)
    social expenditures on, 105, 106, 117, 121
    as universal right, 173
Hinduism
    in India, 54, 61, 62, 92, 202, 224
    in Nepal, 92, 93
Hitler, Adolf, 45
Hobbes, Thomas (1588–1679), 12–13, 37
homophobia, 313
Honduras, 100
Hong Kong, 332
House of Commons (United Kingdom), 162–164
housing
    and economic recession (2008), 271
    social expenditures on, 106
Human Development Index (HDI), **124**–126, 171
    and Arab Spring, 236
    in developed democracies, 248, *249*
    in developing countries, 341
    and happiness, 127
human rights violations, *225*, 364
Human Rights Watch, 364
human trafficking, 338
Hungary, 277–279
    communist regime in, *280*
    democracy in, 206, 277–278
    as developed democracy, 248, 251
    economic transitions in, postcommunist, *304*
    electoral system in, 168, 251
    and European Union, 277, 278, 298
    gender equality in, *309*
    immigration to, *276,* 278–279
    LGBT acceptance in, *312*
    political transitions in, postcommunist, 277–279, *299*
    and Soviet Union relations, 188, 278
Huntington, Samuel P., 89
Hussein, Saddam, 337
Hutu ethnic group, 65, 66
hybrid or illiberal regimes, 202
hyperinflation, **109**
    in postcommunist countries, 302
    in Venezuela, *98,* 109
    in Zimbabwe, 179
hypothesis, 7, 10, 12

Iceland, *312*
ideational factors in political violence, 214, **215,** 216, 217
    in Arab Spring, 236, 237
    counter-measures in, 234
    in religious violence, 230
    in revolutions, 222
    in terrorism, 226
identity, 63–94
    citizenship in, 68–69
    in developed democracies, 261–265
    ethnic. *See* ethnic identity
    in globalization, 369–370, 371
    in imperialism, 328–330
    national. *See* national identity
    political attitudes and ideology in, 75–85
    religion in, 85–88
    in rise of modern state, 41
ideology
    in fundamentalism, 85–88
    political. *See* political ideologies
    on political economy, 102
illiberal regimes, 197, 200, **202**–203
    in globalization, 365
    terrorism risk in, *235*
immigration
    assimilation in, 264
    in colonialism, 328
    in developed democracies, 245, 258, 263–265, 268, 269, 275
    in European Union, 245, 258, 263, 264, 265, 278–279
    and globalization, 369–370, 371, 373, 374, 376, 377
    to Hungary, *276,* 278–279
    multiculturalism in, 264, 275
    and social capital, 176–177
    social expenditures in, 105, 268
    to United States, 263, 264, 376
    xenophobia in, 264, 265
imperialism, 322, **324**–332
    colonialism compared to, 324
    dependent development in, 330–332, 338
    economic development in, 338
    and globalization, 373
    historical timeline on, *326*
    institutions of, 326–332
    legacy of, 349, 350

and nondemocratic rule, 188
social identity in, 328–330
state authority and power in, 327–328
import substitution, **338**–339, 340, 346
income
in global economy, *130*
and happiness, 126
and purchasing power parity, 121
redistribution of, 251, *253*
in social democracy, 115, 251
in wealth measures, 121, 122, 124, *125*
independent variables, **10,** 97
in suicide terrorism, 241
Index of Globalization, 383
India, 10, 61–63
charismatic leaders in, 46–47
corruption in, *335*
democracy in, 92, 142, 186, *249*
devolution in, 62, 63, 96
economic liberalization in, *129*
electoral system in, 162
ethnic identity in, 61, 62, 65
federalism in, 48, 62, 93, 96
gender equality in, *125, 309*
gender imbalance in population of, 338
and globalization, 368, 377
gross domestic product of, *123, 125, 249*
happiness in, *127*
immigrants from, in Africa, 336
imperialism and colonialism in, 331, 336
independence of, 46–47, 54, 55, 61
LGBT acceptance in, *312*
life expectancy in, 341
microcredit and microfinance in, 347
national identity in, 62, 69–70
outsourcing to, 368, 377
Pakistan compared to, 54, 55, 61, 62
patriotism in, 69
religion in, 54, 61–62, 92, 202, 223–224
secession of Pakistan from, 54–55, 66
Telangana state in, *60,* 62
terrorism in, 54, 223–224
traditional legitimacy in, 47
wealth measures in, 121, 122, *123, 125*
indigenous populations
and devolution in Canada, 260
in imperialism and colonialism, 327
in post-imperialism, 336, 337

indirect democracy, 144
individual factors in political violence, 214, 215–216, 217
in Arab Spring, 236, 237
counter-measures in, 234
in religious violence, 216, 230
in revolutions, 216, 220, 222
in terrorism, 216, 226
universal, 217
individualism, 189, 203
primordial, 37
Indonesia
corruption in, *335*
democracy in, 170
imperialism and colonialism in, 331
infant mortality rate in, 341
post-imperialism in, 336
inductive reasoning, **7,** 9, 15, 17
Industrial Revolution, 88, 248
industry
in Asia and Latin America compared, 348–349
and climate change, 378
in communism, 289, 290
in developed democracies, 248, *249,* 250, 265
in developing countries, 339–340, 346, 348–349
in export-oriented industrialization, 339–340, 346, 348
in import substitution, 338–339
in mercantilism, 119, 120
in postcommunism, 302
in post-imperialism, 338, 339–340
and postindustrialism, 266–267
state-owned, 338, 339
infanticide, 338
infant mortality rate, 341
inflation, **109**–110
and deflation, 110
and hyperinflation, *98,* 109, 179, 302
in postcommunist countries, 302, 303, 305
in Venezuela, *98,* 100
in Zimbabwe, 179
informal economy, **346**
in Greece, 270
informal institutions, **20**

information-based economy, 266, 269
    offshore outsourcing in, 368
Inglehart, Ronald, 89, 90, 91
Inglehart World Values Survey, 89–90, *90*
initiatives, **169**
    in developed democracies, 250
Inkatha Freedom Party (South Africa), *166*
instant-runoff voting, 164
institutional factors in political violence, 214–215, 216–217
    in Arab Spring, 236
    counter-measures in, 234
    in religious violence, 230
    in revolutions, 220–221
    in terrorism, 226
institutions, 5–6, 18–22
    balance of freedom and equality in, 26, 31
    cause and effect relationship in, 21–22
    change in, 20, 21, 77
    civil rights and liberties as, 172–173
    definition of, **5,** 214
    in democracy, 20–21, 150–153, 172–173
    in developed democracies, 253–269
    in developing countries, 319, 329, 333, 341, 343, 350
    economic. *See* economic institutions
    in ethnic identity, 65, 66
    formal and informal, 20
    in globalization, 360–362, 363, 364, 365, 369, 377
    in illiberal regimes, 202
    in imperialism, 326–332, 349
    legitimacy of, 30, 32, 44–47, 362
    in nondemocratic regimes, 184, 185, 186, 202
    and origins of political organization, 36–38
    political. *See* political institutions
    political attitudes on, 77, 79
    political ideologies on, 80
    and political violence, 214–215
    societal. *See* societal institutions
    of state, 30, 31, 32–33
integration process, 254, 269
    and devolution, 260–261
    in Europe, 254–259
    in North America, 259
intellectual property, 104, 338

interest rates, 108, 112
    in European Union, 257
intergovernmental organizations (IGOs), 255, **360**–361, 362, 363, 373
intergovernmental systems, **255**
International Criminal Court, 364
International Monetary Fund, 340, 365–366
international regimes, **361**
international relations, **5**
    compared to comparative politics, 5, 358
    and democratization, 148–149, 171
    in globalization, 358, 359
    and international regimes, 361
    and nondemocratic rule, 188–189
    in semi-presidential systems, 157
International Telegraph Union (ITU), 373
Internet
    and Arab Spring, 237
    in globalization, 131, 355, 360, 361, 362, 363, 364, 369, 373, 375
    intellectual property on, 104
    in modernization, 185
    surveillance on, 192
Inter-Services Intelligence (Pakistan), *55*
Inuit, 260
Iran, 188–189
    corruption in, *335*
    economic liberalization in, *129*
    gender equality in, *125, 309*
    gross domestic product of, *123, 125, 249*
    happiness in, *127*
    imperialism in, *327*
    LGBT acceptance in, *312*
    personality cult in, 195–196
    revolution in (1979), 195, 220, 221, 222
    suicide terrorism in, 240
    and United States relations, 188
    wealth measures in, *123, 125*
Iraq, 148, 189, 308
    authoritarianism in, 217
    devolution in, 48
    as fragile state, *50–51*
    invasion of, 236
    Islam in, 217, 337, 375
    political violence in, 5, 212, 217
    societal globalization and trust in, *382*
Ireland, Republic of, *242, 244*
irrational states, 54

ISIS (Islamic State of Iraq and Sham), 212
 and globalization, 375
 motivations for violence in, 217, 231–232
 and postcommunist societal transitions, 308
Islam
 in Afghanistan, 308
 in Algeria, 229
 and anti-Muslim groups in civil society, 188
 in Arab Spring, 237
 in China, 306, 307
 culture of, 89, 91, 189
 fundamentalist, 308
 and globalization, 375
 immigrant values of, 264, 265
 in India, 61, 62, 223–224
 in Iran, 195
 in Iraq, 217, 337, 375
 in Nepal, 92
 nondemocratic nature of, 3, 189
 in Pakistan, 54, 55, 61
 in postcommunist countries, 306, 307, 308
 and religious violence, 89, 212, 217, 231–232, 233, 375
 in Saudia Arabia, 202
 Shia and Sunni sects of, 195, 202, 337
 in Syria, 211, 212, 217, 337, 375
 and theocracy, 202
Islamic Salvation Front, 229
Islamic State of Iraq and Sham (ISIS), 212
 and globalization, 375
 motivations for violence in, 217, 231–232
 and postcommunist societal transitions, 308
Israel, 20, 69, 202
 electoral system in, 165
 proportional representation in, 165
 in West Bank and Gaza, 240
Italy
 culture and democratization in, 149
 as developed democracy, 251
 political parties in, 160–161
 referenda and initiatives in, 169

Jammu, 61
Japan
 corruption in, *335*
 deflation in, 110
 democracy in, 142, 148, 188
 demographic changes in, 269
 as developed democracy, 248, *249,* 250, 251, *253,* 269
 dramatic change without revolution in, 220
 economic liberalization in, *129*
 electoral system in, 168, 250, 251
 ethnic and national identity in, 67
 gender equality in, *125,* 309
 in globalization, 367, 377
 gross domestic product of, *107, 123, 125, 249, 268*
 happiness in, 127, *127*
 immigrant population in, 264, 269
 imperialism of, 325, 328
 judiciary in, 153
 LGBT acceptance in, *312*
 mercantilism in, 119, 120, *253*
 political parties in, 160
 public debt in, 268
 state capacity and autonomy in, 53
 taxation in, *107, 253*
 traditional legitimacy in, 47
 as unitary state, 48
 wealth measures in, *123, 125*
Jefferson, Thomas, 81
Jerusalem, 20
Jews, 232
jihad, 229, 231
John, King of England, 143
Johnson, Boris, *242*
Jordan, middle income trap in, *352*
Judaism, 232
judicial review, **152**–153
judiciary, 150, 152–153
 in developed democracies, 250
 in illiberal regimes, 203
 in parliamentary systems, 155
 in presidential systems, 156
 in semi-presidential systems, 158
Juergensmeyer, Mark, 230
justice, freedom and equality in, 23

Kashmir, 61, 63, 223–224
Kazakhstan, *299, 309, 312*
Kenya, 74, 202

Keohane, Robert O., 359
Keynes, John Maynard, 373, 376
Khamenei, Ayatollah Ali, 195
Khan, Imran, 29, 30
Kim Dae Jung, 171
Kim Jong-Il, 46
Kim Jong-Un, 46, 183
Kiva, microcredit from, 347
kleptocracy, **195**
Kosovo, 66, *299*
Kyrgyzstan, *299, 300*

labor
    civil rights in, 173
    in communism, 116–117, 281, 283, 289, 290
        and work of women, 291, 292
    in Fair Trade products, 319, 320
    in globalization, 368, 375, 377
    Marx on, 281, 283
    offshore outsourcing of, 368, 375, 377
    in social democracy, 115
    surplus value of, 281
    and unemployment. *See* unemployment
    wages in, 103, 109, 116, 173
Labour Party (United Kingdom), 163, *163*
laissez-faire, **113**
land ownership and land reform, 348–349
language
    in Africa, *74*
    in ethnic and national identity, 65, 67, 70
    in federalism, 48
    in globalization, 358, 371
    in imperialism, 327
    in India, 61, 62
    as research challenge, 9, 10
    in rise of modern state, 41, 43, 71
Laos, 201, *280,* 300
latifundia, 349
Latin America. *See also specific countries.*
    area studies on, 9
    and Asia compared, 348–349
    authoritarianism in, 185
    decline of poverty and inequality in, 132–133
    democracy in, 3, 145, 149, 171
    developing countries in, 321, 322, *323,* 333, 336, 339–340, 341
    economy in, 100, 132–133, 341, 348–349
    Fair Trade with countries in, 319, 320
    in globalization, 132, 368
    gross domestic product of, 348
    immigration from, 263, 265
    imperialism and colonialism in, 132, 331, 332, 349, 373
    import substitution in, 339, 340
    land ownership and land reform in, 349
    military rule in, 198, 199
    nondemocratic regimes in, 192, 198, 199
    outsourcing to, 368
    post-imperialism in, 333, 336, 339–340, 349
    presidential system in, 156
    social capital in, *176*
    and United States relations, 132, 348
Latvia, 297, *299, 304, 309, 312*
law
    and rational-legal legitimacy, 45–46, 47
    rule of. *See* rule of law
Lawrence, Bruce, 86
League of Women Voters, 344
Lebanon, 202
Legatum Institute, 29
legislatures, 150, **151,** 152
    in bicameral systems, 151
    in developed democracies, 251
    elections to, 161–169
    in European Union, 255
    in illiberal regimes, 203
    as institution, 20
    multimember districts in, 165
    origin of, 143
    in parliamentary systems, 154–155, 158
    in presidential systems, 155–156, 159
    proportional representation in, 162, 164–169
    in semi-presidential systems, 156, 157
    single-member districts in, 140, 162–169. *See also* single-member districts
    in unicameral systems, 151
legitimacy, 31, 32, **44**–47, 56
    charismatic, 45. *See also* charismatic legitimacy
    of institutions, 30, 32, 44–47, 362
    and national identity, 71

in nondemocratic regimes, 196
in postcommunist countries, 296
rational-legal, 45–46, 47, 56
traditional, 44–45, 46, 47, 56, 197
Lenin (Vladimir Ilyich Ulyanov)
(1870–1924), 219, 285, *287*, 288
lesbian, gay, bisexual, and transgender
(LGBT) issues
global acceptance index on, *312*
in postcommunist countries, 307,
312–313
same-sex partnerships and marriage in, 91,
250, 263, 312
less-developed countries, 322. *See also* developing countries
LGBT issues
global acceptance index on, *312*
in postcommunist countries, 307,
312–313
same-sex partnerships and marriage in, 91,
250, 263, 312
liberal democracy, **81,** 82, **142,** 173
civil rights and liberties in, 150
in developed democracies, 250, 251, 252
electoral systems in, 161–169
freedom and equality in, 250
in globalization, 365
institutions of, 150–153
legislatures in, 151
Marxist theory on, 282
origins of, 143, 144
political parties in, 160
political violence in, 234–235
rule of law in, 152
transition from communism to, 278
unitary (nonfederal), 151
Liberal Democratic Party (Japan), 160
Liberal Democratic Party (United Kingdom),
163, 164
liberalism, **77,** 112, 113–114
challenges to, 128–131
change in, 77
communism compared to, 82, 118
definitions of, 77, 81
and democracy, 81, 142
in developed democracies, 250, 251
and economic liberalization, 128, *129*
Gini index in, 122, *253*

in globalization, 130–131, 365, 368
ideology in, 81, 83, 84, *84,* 85, 86, 113, 142
mercantilism compared to, 118
political attitude in, 77, 78, *78,* 79, 81, 85
in postcommunist countries, 303
Smith on economics in, 113, 117
social democracy compared to, 82, 114,
116, 118, 136–137, 142
social expenditures in, 268
liberalization, economic, **128,** *129,* 340
and economic globalization, 366, 367
in France, *129,* 244
in Latin America, 132, 133
libertarianism, 83
liberties, civil, **172**–173. *See also* civil rights
and liberties
Libya, 3, 4, 364
life expectancy, *125*
in developed democracies, 251, 268
in developing countries, 341
and Human Development Index, 124,
125, *125*
in imperialism and colonialism, 327
List, Friedrich, 117
literacy, 11
precommunist, *316,* 316–317
Lithuania, 297, *299*
local government in developing countries, 345
localism, 261
Locke, John (1632–1704), 13, 146
Louis XIV, King of France, 33
lower income countries, **322.** *See also*
developing countries

Machiavelli, Niccolò (1469–1527), 12, 13
macro-level studies, 24
Madhesi population in Nepal, 92, 93
Madison, James, 160
Maduro, Nicolás, 100–101
Magna Carta, 143–144
Mahathir Mohamed, *138,* 139, 140
majority-based single-member districts, 164,
165, 167, 251
malapportionment, 140
malaria, 347
Malaysia, 148, 279
corruption in, 334
elections in (2018), *138,* 139–140

Malaysia (*continued*)
  middle income trap in, *352*
  post-imperialism in, 334, 336
  societal globalization and trust in, *382, 383*
Mali, semi-presidential system in, 158
Mandela, Nelson, 47, 204
Mao Zedong (1893–1976), 92, 285, *287,* 288, 289
maps
  of ethnolinguistic diversity in Africa, *74*
  of European Union, *259*
  of World Values Survey, *90*
marketization in postcommunist countries, 301–303
markets, **102**–104, 112
  in communism, 116, 117, 118, 290
  in developing countries, 346
  in globalization, 366, 367, 368
  in liberalism, 113, 114, 118
  in mercantilism, 118, 119
  monopoly in, 110
  in postcommunist countries, 301–303, 305
  in social democracy, 114, 118
  state regulation of, 103, 110
  supply and demand in, 102–103, 109
  Washington Consensus on, 342, 366
Marx, Karl (1818–83), 13, 117, 280, 281–285, *287*
  on capitalism, 116, 282, 283, 284, 285, 313
  on gender relations, 291
  on phases of human history, 283–284, *284*
  on religion, 291
  on revolution, 114, 116, 283, 284, 285
  terms in theory of, 282
Marxism, 132, 281–285, 374
materialism, 283
  dialectical, 282, 283
McDonald's, 372
McVeigh, Timothy, 232
means of production, 281, 289
media
  censorship of, 375
  and democratization, 148
  in developing countries, 345

  in globalization, 364, 375
  in Hungary, 277
  in illiberal regimes, 203
  international, present in China, 310, 311
  and personality cults, 195
Menzies, Robert, 154
mercantilism, **118,** 128
  export-oriented industrialization in, 339–340
  Gini index in, 122, *253*
  Human Development Index in, 124
  in imperialism and colonialism, 330
  import substitution in, 338–339
  political-economic system in, 112, 118–120, 131, 132, 142, 250, *253*
Mexican Revolution, 222
Mexico
  colonial rule of, 43
  conditional cash transfers in, 133
  corruption in, *335*
  as developed democracy, 248, *249,* 250, 251, 259
  economic liberalization in, *129*
  electoral system in, 168, 251
  gender equality in, *125, 309*
  in globalization, 377
  gross domestic product of, *107, 123, 125, 249*
  happiness in, 127, *127*
  immigration from, 264
  industrial development in, 348
  LGBT acceptance in, *312*
  in NAFTA, 377
  one-party rule in, 201
  patrimonialism in, 336–337
  revolution in, 222
  taxation in, *107*
  trade of, 259, 377
  in USMCA, 377
  wealth measures in, *123, 125*
microcredit, **346**–347, 350
microfinance, 346–347
micro-level research, 24–25
Middle Ages, 40
middle class
  in Asia, 130, 170
  and democratization, 147, 170
  and globalization, 130–131, 356

and liberalism, 130
Marx on, 283
and nondemocratic rule, 185
in resource curse, 187
social expenditures on, 106
Middle East. *See also specific countries.*
    Arab Spring in. *See* Arab Spring
    authoritarianism in, 3, 190
    developed democracies in, *247*
    developing countries in, *323*
    immigration from, 263, 264, 265
    imperialism and colonialism in, 324–325, 373
    macro-level research on, 24
    military rule in, 335–336
    monarchies in, 4, 198
    nondemocratic regimes in, 188, 198, 211–212
    oil reserves in, 209
    origins of political organization in, 36, 38
    political systems in, *191*
    political violence in, *210,* 211–212
    revolutions in, 221, 222
    theocracy in, 202
middle income countries, **322,** 352. *See also* developing countries
middle income trap, **339,** 352–353, 356
migration
    in developed democracies, 265
    in European Union, 278–279
    and globalization, 357, 358, 369, 373, 374, 376
    in imperialism, 336, 373
    of Syrians, 4, *276*
military
    in developing countries, 335–336
    in imperialism and colonialism, 324, 327
    as institution, 20
    and nationalism, 71
    in Pakistan, 54, 55, 336
    in post-imperialism, 335–336
    in power of state, 32
    in rise of modern state, 40, 41
    rule by officials in, 197, 198–199, 200
    in Soviet Union, 293, 294, 310
    in United States, 293
military rule, 197, 198–199, 200
Millennium Villages, 347, 350

minimum wage, 103, 173
mixed electoral system, **168**
Mnangagwa, Emmerson, *178,* 181
mobile phones
    and societal globalization, 369, *370*
    in sub-Saharan Africa, 347
Mobutu Sese Seko, 198
modern countries, **252**
modernization in Soviet Union and China compared, 310–311
modernization theory, **14**–15, 91, 342
    capitalism in, 14, 15
    civil society in, 148
    compared to behavioralism, 15
    culture in, 88–89
    democracy in, 14, 15, 145, 147, 148, 149, 170, 185, 186, 189, 382
    nondemocratic rule in, 185–186, 189, 190
    political violence in, 230
    religion in, 17, 86, 88–89, 230
    resource curse in, 187
    revolution in, 220
modern state
    rational-legal foundation of, 46
    religion in, 86, 87
    revolutions as foundation of, 222
    rise of, 38–43, 56, 70–71, 262, 327, 332
    secularism in, 86
Moldova, *299, 304,* 308
    gender equality in, *309*
    LGBT acceptance in, *312*
monarchy, 197–198, 200
    charismatic legitimacy in, 45, 197, 198
    in Nepal, 92, 93
    parliamentary system in, 154
    in Persian Gulf, 4
    traditional legitimacy in, 44–45, 47
money, 107–110
    in central banks, 108–109
    digital, 83, 363
    in European Union, 243, 256–258, 271
    exchange rate for, 121, 257
    and wealth, 108, 121
    in Zimbabwe, 179
Mongolia, *280*
monopoly, **110**

Montenegro, 298, *299*
Montesquieu, Charles-Louis de Secondat, Baron de (1689–1755), 13
morality police, 202
Mozambique, *280*
Mubarak, Hosni, 3, *25,* 237
Mugabe, Robert, 179, 180–181, 204
multicausality, **8,** 91
multiculturalism, 264, 275, 279
    in societal globalization, 369–370
multimember districts, **165**
multinational corporations (MNCs), **360**–361, 362, 364, 366–367
Muslim Brotherhood, 237
Muslim League, 55
Muslims. *See* Islam
Mutawwa'in (morality police), 202
Myanmar, 202, 233

Najib Razak, 140
Napoleon, 332
nation, **66**
National Alliance, 232
National Assembly (South Africa), 165, *166*
national conflicts, 64, **72**–75, 92
    federalism adopted after, 75, 97
    in India, 62
    political violence in, 213
    in postcommunist countries, 308
    prevention of, 62, 75
    views of, 73
National Freedom Party (South Africa), *166*
National Front (France), 244
National Front (Malaysia), 140
national identity, 63–64, **66**–68, 91, 94
    and citizenship, 69, 72
    in communism, 292–293
    conflicts related to. *See* national conflicts
    and democratization, 149
    in developed democracies, 264–265
    in developing countries, 328, 329, 336–337, 341
    education and literacy affecting, 317
    and ethnic identity, 67–68, 71, 72, 96
    in European Union, 244
    globalization affecting, 369, 371
    immigration affecting, 264–265, 279
    in imperialism, 328, 329

    in India, 62, 69–70
    institutions in, 19
    and nationalism, 67
    origins and persistence of, 70–75
    in Pakistan, 55
    and patriotism, 69, 70
    in postcommunist countries, 306–308
    and rise of modern state, 41
    in Soviet Union, 310
nationalism, **67,** 70, 71, 94
    and authoritarianism, 7
    in communism, 284, *292,* 292–293
    education and literacy affecting, 317
    and ethnic identity, 67–68
    in globalization, 371, 374
    immigration affecting, 177
    and imperialism, 329
    in India, 62
    and patriotism, 64, 69
    in postcommunist countries, 306–308
    in rise of modern state, 41
nationalization in Venezuela, 100
National Rally (France), 244–245
nation-state, **71–72**
natural resources, 208–209
    and democratization, 147, *208,* 208–209
    in developing countries, 330–331, 341–342, 349
    elites in control of, 147, 180
    and ethnic conflicts, 74
    in extractive economy, 330–331
    of Latin America, 132
    oil as. *See* oil reserves
    and patrimonialism, 198, 209
    of postcommunist countries, 303, 304
    and resource curse, 180, 186–187, 209, 341–342
    of Venezuela, *98,* 99, 100, 109
    of Zaire, 198
    of Zimbabwe, *178,* 180–181, 186, 208, 209
Nazi regime in Germany, 83, 183
neocolonialism, **338,** 348
neoliberal economic policies, 114, **340**
neo-Maoists, 79
neo-reaction philosophy, 83
Nepal, 48, 92–93
    elections in, 93, 139
    federalism in, 63, 92, 93

Netherlands, 256, *382,* 383
New Zealand
　economic liberalization in, *129*
　liberalism in, 114
　political violence in, 233
　referenda and initiatives in, 169
Niger, *50–51,* 124
Nigeria
　colonial rule of, 43
　corruption in, 334, *335*
　as developed democracy, *249*
　economic liberalization in, *129*
　elections in, 73, 161, 162
　electoral system in, 161, 162
　ethnic conflicts in, 73, 74
　federalism in, 96
　as fragile state, *50–51*
　gross domestic product of, *123, 125, 249*
　happiness in, *127*
　natural resources in, 147
　societal globalization and trust in, *382*
　wealth measures in, *123, 125*
nihilism, **226**
Nobel Peace Prize, 347
nomenklatura, **286,** 288, 290, 294, 298, 303
nondemocratic regimes, 33, 34, 35, 179–209
　and civil society, 187–188, 190, 193–194
　and culture, 189–190
　definition of, **182**–183
　in developing countries, 334
　diversity of, 182, 203
　and elites, 186–187, 190, 197, 209
　fascist, 83
　freedom and equality in, 181, 182, 183, 186, 357
　illiberal, 197, 200, 202–203
　and international relations, 188–189
　military rule in, 197, 198–199, 200
　models of, 196–203
　and modernization, 185–186, 189, 190
　one-party rule in, 197, 199–201
　origins and sources of, 181, 185–190
　personal and monarchical rule in, 197–198, 200
　political attitudes in, 79
　political control in, 190–196, 197, 200
　political-economic systems in, 114, 120
　theocratic rule in, 197, 200, 201–202
　totalitarianism in, 183–184
　trends in number of, 203, 206, *206*
　United States support of, 236
　in Zimbabwe, *178,* 179–181, 182, 186, 192, 204
nongovernmental organizations (NGOs), **360**–361, 362, 364, 371, 373
　in developing countries, 334, 344
nontariff regulatory barriers, **111**
　in economic globalization, 366
　in mercantilism, 119
norms
　in developed democracies, 262, 269
　in ethnic groups, 65
　on freedom and equality, 53
　in political culture, 189
　in political institutions, 19, 21
　and political violence, 214
　postmodern, 262
　in regimes, 33–34
　in social capital, 176
North Africa
　Arab Spring in, 236
　developing countries in, *323*
　immigration from, 263, 264
　imperialism and colonialism in, 325
　Ottoman Empire in, 325
　political systems in, *191*
North America. *See also specific countries.*
　developed democracies in, *247,* 248
　imperialism and colonialism in, 325
North American Free Trade Agreement (NAFTA), 259, **377**
Northern Ireland, 164, 241, 260, 261
　and European Union, *242,* 244
　and Republic of Ireland, *242,* 244
North Korea, 6
　area studies on, 9
　charismatic leadership in, 46
　communism in, 7, 170, *280,* 300, 313
　international relations of, 149
　land reform in, 349
　nondemocratic regime in, 183
　one-party rule in, 201
North Macedonia, 298, *299*
Norway
　democracy in, 208
　and European Union, 243

Norway
    Human Development Index on, 124
    natural resources in, 208
    social democracy in, 115
nuclear technology in Pakistan, 44, 54, 55
Nunavut, 260
Nye, Joseph S., Jr., 359

Oceania, developing countries in, *323*
offshore outsourcing, **368,** 375, 377
oil reserves, 236
    and Arab Spring, 236
    and democratization, 147, *208*
    elites in control of, 147
    as resource curse, 187, 209
    of Venezuela, *98,* 99, 100, 109
Oklahoma City federal courthouse bombing, 232
oligarchy, 182
one-party rule, 197, 199–201, 236
    in communism, 200, 201, 286–289, 294
Orbán, Viktor, 277–278, 279
Organization of American States, 361
Ottoman Empire, 324–325
outsourcing, **368,** 375, 377

Pakatan Harapan (Alliance of Hope), 139, 140
Pakistan, 54–55
    civil society in, 344
    corruption in, 54, *335*
    elections in (2018), 29
    energy problems in, *28,* 29–30, 44, 54, 344
    as failing state, 54–55, 61
    gender imbalance in population of, 338
    happiness in, 127, *127*
    India compared to, 54, 55, 61, 62
    Inter-Services Intelligence agency in, *55*
    military rule in, 55
    nuclear weapons of, 44, 54, *55*
    scope and strength of state, 58
    secession from India, 54–55, 66
    state capacity and autonomy in, 54
    and state-sponsored terrorism, 54, 224
    and suicide terrorism, 240, 241
Palestinians, 20, 69, *127*
Pan Africanist Congress (South Africa), *166*
pandemics, 359, 374, 377
    coronavirus (2020), 374–375, 376

Panhellenic Socialist Movement, 270
Pape, Robert, 240–241
parastatals, **119**
Paris Agreement on climate change, 379
parliamentary systems, **154–155**
    basic features of, 157
    benefits and drawbacks of, 158, 159
    compared to presidential systems, 155, 156
    political parties in, 154, 155, 158, 161, 167
    proportional representation in, 167, 169
    single-member districts in, 169
    vote of no confidence in, 155, 158, 167
participation, 162
    as core characteristic of democracy, 141, 142
    and democratization in Asia, 170
    in developed democracies, 250, 251, 252
    in direct and indirect democracy, 144
    globalization affecting, 364, 374
    in liberal democracy, 142, 173, 190
    in nondemocratic regimes, lack of, 174, 182, 186
    in origin of democracy, 143
    political violence in lack of, 215, 234
    in proportional representation, 162, 169
    in revolutions, 218–219
    and social capital, 176
    in social democracy, 142
    in voting and elections, 142, 162, 169, 173
particularistic and universal factors in political violence, 217
Partido Nacional Revolucionario (Mexico), 201
partition of Pakistan and India, 54–55, 66
party-state, **288**
    in communism, 289, 296
path dependence, 21
patrimonialism, **197**–198, 236, 330, 334, 336
    in Syria, 211, 236
    in Zimbabwe, 334
PATRIOT Act (2001), 234
patriotism, 64, **69**–70
Pentagon, terrorist attack on, 20
perestroika, **293,** 294
Persian Empire, 372–373

Persian Gulf countries
    Arab Spring in, 209
    monarchies in, 4, 198
    nondemocratic regimes in, 186, 198
personality cults, 46, 195–196, 197
personal rule, 197–198, 200
Peru, 67, 227, 228, *352*
Philippines, democratization of, 170, 171
philosophy in study of politics, 12, 26, 37
Pierce, William, 232, 233
Plaid Cymru, 163, *163*
plurality-based single-member districts, 162,
    164, 165, 167, 251
Poland
    communist regime in, *280*
    democracy in, 206
    as developed democracy, 248, *249*, 250,
        258
    economic transitions in, postcommunist,
        304
    in European Union, 258
    gender equality in, *309*
    gross domestic product of, *249*
    LGBT acceptance in, *312*
    political transitions in, postcommunist, *300*
police
    in imperialism, 327
    as institution, 20
    in power of state, 32
Politburo, **287**
political attitudes, 64, 75–80, 94
    context of, 79–80
    continuum of, 77–78, *78*
    in fundamentalism, 87
    and ideologies, 64, 75, 79, 85
    origin of, 75–76
    on political violence, 76, 77, 78, 215
    in totalitarianism, 184
political control in nondemocratic regimes,
    190–196, 197, 200
    in military rule, 199, 200
    in one-party rule, 200, 201
    in patrimonialism, 197
    in Syria, 192, 211
political culture, **88**–91, 94
    and democratization, 149
    and nondemocratic rule, 189–190
    religion affecting, 88–89, 263

political-economic systems, **112**–131
    in Bolivarian socialism, 99–100
    in communism, 112, 116–118, 128,
        289–291
    comparison of, 118, 120–127
    in developed democracies, 251–252
    happiness in, 126–127
    Human Development Index on, 124–126,
        171
    income redistribution in, *253*
    inequality and poverty in, 122–123
    in liberalism, 113–114. *See also* liberalism
    in mercantilism, 112, 118–120, 131, 132,
        142, 250, *253*
    in social democracy, 114–116. *See also*
        social democracy
    wealth in, 121–126
political economy, 99–137
    in communism, 112, 116–118, 128,
        289–291
    components of, 102–112
    definition of, **101**
    in developed democracies, 250
    in imperialism and colonialism,
        330–332
    markets and property in, 102–104
    money, inflation, and economic growth
        in, 107–110
    in postcommunism, 301–305
    public goods in, 104–105
    regulation of, 110
    social expenditures in, 105–106
    taxation in, 106–107
    trade in, 111–112
    of Venezuela, *98*, 99–101, 109, 132, 133
political engagement in developing countries,
    344–345
political globalization, 356, 360, 362–365,
    369, 383
    impact of, 374–375
political ideologies, 64, 75–76, 80–85, 94
    and attitudes, 64, 75, 79, 85
    in communism, 82, 83, *84*, 85, 183, 281
    in globalization, 356
    in nondemocratic regimes, 182–183, 184
    origin of, 75–76
political institutions, **5–6**, 18–22, 26, 32–33
    in developed democracies, 253–261

political institutions (*continued*)
   in developing countries, 319, 329, 333, 341
   in globalization, 360
   in imperialism, 329, 332
   legitimacy of, 30
   origins of, 36–38
   and political violence, 214–215
   postcommunist, 296–301
   in post-imperialism, 333
   in rise of modern state, 39
political organization, 56
   in globalization, 362–363
   origins of, 36–38
   rise of modern states in, 38–43, 327
   timeline of, 42
political parties, 160–169
   in communism, 200, 201, 286–289
   in developed democracies, 243–244, 250–251
   discipline in, 167
   in Greece, 270
   in illiberal regimes, 202
   in mixed electoral system, 168
   in one-party rule, 199–201
   in parliamentary systems, 154, 155, 158, 161, 167
   in presidential systems, 156, 159, 164
   in proportional representation, 164–169
   referenda and initiatives of, 172
   in single-member districts, 162–164, 165, 167–168, 169
political science, 5, 24–25
   comparative politics as subfield of, 6
   in globalization, 357, 358
   historical studies of, 12–16
   macro-level and micro-level approaches to, 24–25
   research challenges in, 7–11
   theory of, 11–12
political violence, 5, 211–241
   actors and targets in, *225*
   in Arab Spring, 211–212, 236–237
   counter-measures in, 233–235, 238
   definition of, 213–**214**, 218
   in ethnic and national conflicts, 72
   forms of, 218–227, *225*
   in fundamentalism, 87, 230, 231
   in globalization, 364, 374
   ideational factors in. *See* ideational factors in political violence
   individual factors in. *See* individual factors in political violence
   institutional factors in. *See* institutional factors in political violence
   in military rule, 199
   motivations for, 214–217, 234
   in nondemocratic regimes, 192, 197, 199, 205
   in Pakistan, 54
   political attitudes on, 76, 77, 78, 215
   in pre-state societies, 37–38
   regime type affecting, 234
   religion as motivation in, 5, 62, 63, 89, 212, 213, 216, 226, 229–233, 234, 240
   in revolutions, 213, 214, 218–223, 228–229
   in South Africa, 205
   in Syria, 5, *210*, 211–212, 217
   in terrorism, 213, 218, 223–229
   in totalitarianism, 183, 184
   universal and particularistic factors in, 217
   in Zimbabwe, 205, 212, 224
politics, **6**
   philosophical approach to study of, 12, 26
   power in, 6, 26
   science of. *See* political science
   values on fundamental goals of, 80
Popper, Karl, 24
populism, **187**–188
   devolution in, 261
   in postcommunist countries, 305
Portugal
   corporatism in, 194
   culture and democratization in, 149
   economic indicators in, 303, *304*
   imperialism and colonialism of, 41, 132, 325, 332, 349
   invasion by Napoleon, 332
postcommunism, 246, 248, 278, 296–314
   corruption in, 303, *304,* 305, 334
   economic institutions in, 301–305
   European Union in, 258, 298
   Gini index in, 122
   political institutions in, 296–301

precommunist literacy levels affecting, *316*, 316–317
societal institutions in, 306–313
variations in, 316–317
post-imperialism, 332–340
creating nations and citizens in, 336–338
economic growth in, 338–340, 349
state capacity and autonomy in, 333–336
postindustrialism, 266–267
offshore outsourcing in, 368
post-materialism, 91, 262, 265
postmodernity, **253**
values in, 262–265, 269, 274
poverty, 122
in communism, 279, 284, 290
conditional cash transfers in, 133
in economic globalization, 130, 368, 375
happiness in, 126, 127
in Latin America, 132–133
in lower income countries, 322
as obstacle to democracy, 147
in postcommunist countries, 303, 305, 313
and regime type, 186
in Venezuela, 99, 100, 101
power, **6,** 26, 31–32, 43–56, 58–59
and autonomy of states, 49–53, 58
and balance between freedom and equality, 23
and capacity of states, 49–53, 58
centralization or decentralization of, 47–48
in democracy, 142, 144, 145
in imperialism, 327–328
and legitimacy of states, 44–47
in nondemocratic regimes, 182, 183, 184, 186
of political elites, 147, 171
in regimes, 33, 34
in rise of modern state, 39, 40, 41
of strong and weak states, 48–49
predictions, political, 25, 26
preferential runoff voting, 164
premier presidentialism, 157
premodern societies
authoritarianism in, 262
identity in, 369
religion in, 86, 87, 89

president
in European Union, 255
in illiberal regimes, 202–203
in parliamentary system, 154
in presidential systems, 155–156
in semi-presidential systems, 156–158, 160
presidential systems, **155**–156
basic features of, 157
benefits and drawbacks of, 159–160
in developed democracies, 251
electoral system in, 164
president parliamentarism, 157
price of goods and services
in communism, 116
deflation affecting, 110
inflation affecting, 109–110
and purchasing power parity, 121
regulation of, 110
supply and demand affecting, 103, 109
prime minister, 151
in parliamentary systems, 154–155, 156, 158
in semi-presidential systems, 156–158
vote of no confidence in, 155, 158
privatization
of goods, 105
in postcommunism, 301–303
of religion, 86
Washington Consensus on, 340, 342, 366
production
in developing countries, 330, 338–339, 348
in imperialism, 330
means of, 281, 289
in post-imperialism, 338–339
relations of, 281
product life cycle in export-oriented industrialization, 339
Progressive era (United States), 343–344
proletariat, 282, **283,** 284, 291
dictatorship of, 282, 284
vanguard of, 282, 285
property, 40, **104,** 112
and agricultural land, 348–349
in anarchism, 83
and balance between freedom and equality, 23, 250, 251, 252

Index A-57

property (*continued*)
    in capitalism, 113, 116, 251
    in communism, 83, 116, 117, 281, 285, 289, 290, 291
    in developed democracies, 248, 250, 252
    in developing countries, 338, 346
    in economic liberalization, 128
    intellectual, 104, 338
    in liberalism, 113, 136, 144
    in libertarianism, 83
    in mercantilism, 119, 120
    in political culture, 88
    in postcommunism, 301–302, 303, 305
    in rise of modern state, 40
    in social democracy, 114
    in Soviet Union, 59
    and wealth, 108
property rights, 104
    in communism, 117
    in developing countries, 353
    in economic liberalization, 128
    in liberalism, 113
    in post-imperialism, 338
    in rise of modern state, 40
proportional representation, **162**, 164–169
    in developed democracies, 251
    in ethnic conflicts, 167
    in mixed electoral system, 168
prostitution, 250
Protestantism, 41
    fundamentalism in, 86
    in Northern Ireland, 244, 261
    values in, 88, 91
Protestant Reformation, 71
protest movements, 214
    in Arab Spring. *See* Arab Spring
    in Tiananmen Square (1989), 79, 296, 310, 311
psychological factors
    in macro-level research, 24
    in political violence, 215–216, 217, 220
public goods, 104–**105**
    in communism, 116
    in developing countries, 333, 335, 336, 342
    in Latin America, 132–133
    in liberalism, 113, 114
    in post-imperialism, 333, 335, 336
    in social democracy, 115, 136

    social expenditures on, 105–106
    taxation for, 106
purchasing power parity (PPP), **121**, 124, 186
    in China, 355
    in developed democracies, 248, *249*
    in developing countries, 322, 348, 352
    and happiness, 127
    in United States, 121, 355
    in Venezuela, 132
purges of Stalin, 192, 288
puritanism, fundamentalism compared to, 87
Putin, Vladimir, 196, 198, 209, 227, 278
Putnam, Robert, 176

Qatar, societal globalization and trust in, *382*
qualitative research, **16**
    compared to quantitative research, 16, 17
    in mixed-method approach, 18
quality of life
    and happiness measures, 126–127
    postmodern values on, 262
    and wealth measures, 121
quantitative research, **16**
    compared to qualitative research, 16, 17
    in mixed-method approach, 18
    rational choice theory in, 17
Québec, 67
quotas in trade, **111**

race, and social identity in imperialism, 328–329
racist groups in United States, 232
radicals, **76,** 77–78, 79, 80, 85
    attitude toward political violence, 76, 78, 215
    on continuum of political attitudes, 77–78, *78*
    fundamentalist, 87
    in totalitarianism, 184
rainforest loss in Amazon, 378–379
rational choice theory, **17,** 18
    in mixed-method approach, 18
rational-legal legitimacy, **45**–46, 47, 56
rational states, 54
reactionaries, **77,** 78, 79, 80, 85
    attitude toward political violence, 77, 78, 215
    in China, 288

on continuum of political attitudes, 78, *78*
fundamentalist, 87, 92
in totalitarianism, 184
Reagan, Ronald, 293
reasoning
    deductive, 7, 10, 16, 17
    inductive, 7, 9, 15, 17
Red Cross, 334, 344, 373
referendum, **169**
    on British exit from European Union, 25, 169, 172, 244
    in developed democracies, 250
refugees
    in European Union, 258
    Syrian, 4, *210,* 211, *276*
regimes, 31, **33**–34, 35, 36, 56
    communist, 279–280, *280*
    compared to states, 33, 35, 56
    democratic, 33, 35, 139–177
    historical research on, 12
    international, 361
    nondemocratic, 33, 179–209
regulations, **110**–112
    in economic liberalization, 128
    in liberalism, 113
    on trade, 111–112
    Washington Consensus on, 342, 366
Reign of Terror (France), 222
relations of production, 281
relative deprivation model, **220**
    on terrorism, 226
religion, 94. *See also specific religions.*
    charismatic legitimacy in, 45
    in China, 291, 306, 307
    in communist countries, 288, 291, *292*, 306
    in developing countries, 336–337, 341
    and ethnic identity, 65
    fundamentalism in, 85–88, 230, 231
    of immigrant population, 264, 265
    in imperialism, 325, 328, 330, 336
    in India, 54, 61–62, 92, 202, 223–224
    in Pakistan, 54–55
    and political culture, 88–89, 263
    and political violence, 5, 17, 62, 63, 89, 212, 213, 216, 226, 229–233, 234, 240
    in postcommunist countries, 306, 307, 308
    in post-imperialism, 336–337
    privatization of, 86
    reemergence in politics, 17
    and rise of modern state, 40, 41
    in theocracy, 197, 200, 201–202
Renaissance, 12
rent seeking, **194,** 333, 339
replication crisis, 18
republicanism, **143,** 365
research
    area studies in, 9–10
    on cause and effect, 7, 8, 10–11
    challenges in, 7–11
    comparative method in, 7–11
    historical studies in, 12–16
    inductive and deductive reasoning in, 7
    macro-level and micro-level approaches to, 24–25
    mixed-method approach to, 18
    qualitative and quantitative, 16
    replication crisis in, 18
    selection bias in, 10
    variables in, 8, 10, 11
resource curse, 180, **186**–187, 209
    in developing countries, 341–342
resources, natural. *See* natural resources
retirement age, 268, 271
retirement benefits, 82, 114, 117, 137, 173
revolutions, 213, 214, 218–223
    Arab Spring as, 221, 222, 236, 237
    causes of, 10, 219–220
    and counterrevolution, 218, 219
    definition of, **218**–219
    ideational factors in, 222
    individual explanations for, 216, 220, 222
    institutional factors in, 220–221
    Lenin on, 285
    macro-level research on, 24
    Marx on, 114, 116, 283, 284, 285
    radical attitude toward, 76
    regime type affecting, 234
    relative deprivation model of, 220
    shifting views of, 220–222
    social, 219, 220
    terrorism compared to, 218, 223, 228–229

revolutions (*continued*)
   variables in study of, 10
   violence in, 219
Rhodesia, 204. *See also* Zimbabwe
rights
   civil. *See* civil rights and liberties
   property. *See* property rights
Robespierre, Maximilien de, 228
Rodrik, Dani, 372
Roman Empire, 12, 359
   citizenship in, 70
   republicanism in, 143
   and rise of modern state, 38–39
Romania
   communist regime in, *280*
   economic transitions in, postcommunist, 304
   in European Union, 298
   personality cult in, 195
   political transitions in, postcommunist, 298, *299,* 300
   political violence in, 219
Rousseau, Jean-Jacques (1712–78), 13, 37, 181
rule of law, **152,** 173, 197
   civil rights and liberties in, 172
   in developing countries, 335, 343, 344, 346, 353
   in globalization, 363, 368
   in illiberal regimes, 202
   in postcommunist countries, 296, 297, 303, 305
   trends in, 206
rural areas, origins of nondemocratic rule in, 185
Russia
   area studies on, 9
   autonomy and capacity of state in, 53
   challenges in studies of, 9
   corruption in, *335*
   economic liberalization in, *129*
   economic transitions in, postcommunist, 303, 304, *304*
   ethnic and national identity in, 292–293
   federalism in, 48
   foreign relations of, 188
   gender equality in, *125, 309*
   in global economy, 377
   gross domestic product of, *123, 125*
   happiness in, 127, *127*
   kleptocracy in, 195
   Lenin in, 219, 285, *287,* 288
   LGBT acceptance in, *312,* 313
   nationalism in, 308
   natural resources in, 209, 304
   patrimonialism in, 198
   personality cult in, 196
   political transitions in, postcommunist, 298, *299,* 300
   Putin presidency in, 196, 198, 209, 227, 278
   Revolution of 1917 in, 83, 192, 219, 222, 231, 285
   scope and strength of state, 58, 59
   semi-presidential system in, 158
   societal transitions in, postcommunist, 306, 308
   terrorism in, 227, 240, 241
   and Ukraine, 158, 304
   wealth measures in, *123, 125*
Russian Revolution (1917), 83, 192, 219, 222, 231, 285
Rwanda, 65, 66, 74, 158

same-sex partnerships and marriage, 91, 250, 263, 312
Saudi Arabia, 188–189, 236, *249*
   monarchy in, 47, 198, 202
   natural resources in, 147, 236
   theocracy in, 202
   traditional legitimacy in, 47
   and United States relations, 240
Scandinavian countries, 91, 115
science of politics. *See* political science
scope and strength of states, 58–59, 136–137
Scotland, 260
Scottish National Party, *163,* 164
Second World, 246
secularism, 86, 87, 89, 91, 189
secular-rational values, *90,* 90–91
security, 32
   and historical development of state, 37–38
   in terrorism concerns, 234–235
selection bias, **10,** 11, 199, 240
self-expression values, *90,* 90–91, 170, 263
semi-democratic regimes, 202

semi-presidential systems, 156–158
    basic features of, 157
    benefits and drawbacks of, 159, 160
    in developed democracies, 251
Senate (United States), 151
separation of powers, **143**
    in postcommunist countries, 297
September 11, 2001, terrorist attacks, 20, 232
Serbia, 66, 298, *299*
service sector in developed democracies, 248, *249,* 250, 266
sex-selective abortions, 338
sexual morality in communism, 291, *292*
sexual orientation
    civil rights associated with, 172
    and LGBT issues. *See* LGBT issues
Shia Muslims, 195, 337
Shining Path, 228
shock therapy in postcommunist economic transitions, **302**–303
Sikh religion, 61–62
Singapore
    authoritarianism in, 170
    ethnic groups in, 65
    liberal political-economic system in, 114
    nondemocratic regime in, 186
    societal globalization and trust in, *382*
single-member districts, **162**–169
    in developed democracies, 251
    majority-based, 164, 165, 167, 251
    in Malaysia, 140
    in mixed electoral system, 168
    plurality-based, 162, 164, 165, 167, 251
    in United Kingdom, 162–164, *163,* 251
Sinn Féin, 163, *163*
Skocpol, Theda, 220–221
slave trade, 328
Slovakia, 297, *299, 309, 312*
Slovenia
    economic transitions in, postcommunist, 304
    gender equality in, *309*
    LGBT acceptance in, *312*
    political transitions in, postcommunist, 297, *299,* 300
    societal globalization and trust in, *382,* 383
Smith, Adam, 113, 117

social capital, 176–177
social contract, 37, 72
social democracy, **82,** 112, 114–116, 128, 131
    Bernstein on, 114, 117
    challenges to, 86
    civil rights and liberties in, 173
    conditional cash transfers in, 133
    in developed democracies, 250, 251–252, *253*
    economic liberalization in, 128
    fascism compared to, 82
    freedom and equality in, 82, 83, *84,* 85, 115, 118
    future of, 84
    gender equality in, 126
    Gini index in, 122, *253*
    health care in, 137
    Human Development Index in, 124, 126
    income redistribution in, 251
    as liberal democracy, 142
    liberalism compared to, 82, 114, 116, 118, 136–137, 142
    mercantilism compared to, 118, 119
    in postcommunist countries, 303
    purchasing power parity in, 121
    role of state in, 81, 82, 85, 114–115, 118
    and socialism, 82, 284–285
    taxation in, 115, 136, 251, 267
    tenets of, 85, 115, 118
    in United States, 91
    wealth measures in, 121
Social Democratic Party (Germany), 168
Social Democratic Party (Sweden), 160
Social Democratic Party (United Kingdom), *163*
social expenditures, **105**–106
    in communist countries, 117, 290, 291
    in developed democracies, 106, 260, 267–269
    in immigration, 105, 268
    in liberalism, 113, 114, 131
    in mercantilism, 119
    in social democracy, 115, 251
    taxation for, 106, 267–268
    in Venezuela, 100
social identity, 64
    ethnic. *See* ethnic identity
    in globalization, 369–370, 371

social identity (*continued*)
   in imperialism, 328–330
   national. *See* national identity
socialism, **82**
   Bolivarian, in Venezuela, 99–100
   and social democracy, 82, 284–285
social media in globalization, 375
social revolutions, 219, 220
societal institutions, 71, 214
   in communism, 291–293
   in developed democracies, 261–265
   in imperialism and colonialism, 328–330, 332
society, 61–97
   citizenship in, 68–69, 70
   civil. *See* civil society
   in communism, 291–293
   in corporatism, 193–194
   definition of, **63**
   and democratization, 147–148
   in developed democracies, 261–265
   in developing countries, 326, 328–330, 332, 336–338, 344
   ethnic identity in, 64–66. *See also* ethnic identity
   fundamentalism in, 85–88
   globalization of, 359, 360, 369–372, 382, 383
   in imperialism, 326, 328–330, 332
   national identity in, 66–68. *See also* national identity
   and nondemocratic rule, 185, 187–188, 193–194
   patriotism in, 69–70
   political attitudes in, 64, 75–80, 85
   political culture in, 88–91
   political ideologies in, 64, 75–76, 80–85
   in postcommunist countries, 306–313
   in post-imperialism, 336–338
   postmodern values in, 262–265
   premodern, 262
   pre-state, 37–38
Somalia, *50–51, 335*
South Africa
   apartheid in, 47, 69, 204, 219
   charismatic leaders in, 47
   citizenship in, 69
   civil rights and liberties in, 172
   corruption in, *335*
   democracy in, 145, 186, 204, 219, *249*
   economic liberalization in, *129*
   electoral system in, 165, *166,* 204
   ethnic and national identity in, 67
   federalism in, 96
   gender equality in, *125, 309*
   gross domestic product of, *123, 125, 249*
   LGBT acceptance in, *312*
   middle income trap in, 339
   political parties in, 165, *166*
   political violence in, 219, 224
   revolution in, 219
   wealth measures in, 122, *123, 125*
   and Zimbabwe compared, 204–205, 224
South America. *See also specific countries.*
   developed democracies in, *247*
   imperialism in, 325
   origins of political organization in, 38
South Korea, 6
   agriculture in, 349
   area studies on, 9
   corruption in, *335*
   democracy in, 6, 142, 170, 171
   as developed democracy, 248, *249,* 250, 251
   economic liberalization in, *129*
   economic transitions in, 305
   export-oriented industrialization in, 339
   gross domestic product of, *107, 123, 125, 249,* 348, 352
   happiness in, 127
   mercantilism in, 119, 120
   middle income trap in, *352,* 353
   military rule in, 199
   societal globalization and trust in, *382, 383*
   taxation in, *107*
   wealth measures in, *123, 125*
South Sudan, *50–51,* 337
South Yemen, *280*
sovereignty, **31**
   and autonomy, 49
   in developed democracies, 253–261, 269
   in developing countries, 329
   in globalization, 363, 364, 365, 369, 374–375
   in imperialism and colonialism, 329

    in mercantilism, 119
    and national conflicts, 72
    and national identity, 66, 70, 96
    of nation-states, 72
    origins of idea of, 143

Soviet Union
    and Afghanistan, 293, 300–301, 308
    authoritarianism in, 185, 190
    and China compared, 296, 310–311
    civil society in, 294, 345
    in Cold War, 14, 293, 310
    collapse and breakup of, 277, 293–296, 313
    collectivization of agriculture in, 289
    communism in, 3, 82, 192, 280, *280*, 285–314
    and Eastern Europe, 221–222, 236, 292–293, 294
    economic power of state in, 23
    ethnic and national identity in, 73, 292–293, 294, 307, 310
    federalism in, 96
    Gini index on, 290
    and Hungary, 188, 278
    international relations of, 188, 205, 293, 294
    modernization in, 310–311
    nomenklatura in, 286, 288, 290, 294, 298, 303
    nondemocratic regime in, 183, 188
    political control in, 192
    political economy in, 112, 289–291
    political ideology in, 183
    precommunist education and literacy in, 317
    regime reform in, 34
    religion in, 291
    scope and strength of state, 58, 59
    society in, 291–293
    terror used in, 288
    and Ukraine, 158
    and United States, 293, 294
    and Zimbabwe, 205

Spain
    anarchism in, 83
    authoritarianism in, 217
    corporatism in, 194
    culture and democratization in, 149
    devolution in, 261
    ethnic and national identity in, 96
    immigrant population in, 263
    imperialism and colonialism of, 41, 132, 325, 331, 349
    invasion by Napoleon, 332
    political violence in, 217, 241

Spanish Civil War (1936–39), 83

Spengler, Oswald, 203

Sri Lanka, 158, 240

Stalin, Josef (1878–1953), *287*
    as charismatic leader, 288
    personality cult of, 195
    purges of, 192, 288

state, 29–59
    autonomy of, 49. *See also* autonomy of states
    capacity of, 49. *See also* capacity of states
    captured, 52, 53, 75, 334
    centralization of, 47–48. *See also* centralization
    citizenship in, 68–69, 72
    definition of, **31**–35, 56
    in developing countries, 327–328, 342–344, 350
    failed, 49, 58
    fragile, 49, *50–51*
    in fundamentalism, 88
    in globalization, 362–363, 364, 368, 374–375
    and government, 31, 34–35, 36, 56
    head of, 150, 151, 154, 155, 156
    in imperialism, 188, 327–328
    institutions in, 30, 31, 32–33, 56
    legitimacy of, 30, 31, 32, 44–47, 56, 71
    in market regulation, 103
    modern. *See* modern state
    origins of political organization in, 36–38
    and patriotism, 69, 70
    in political economy, 99–137
    political ideologies on role of, 80–85
    in post-imperialism, 333–336
    power of, 31, 43–56, 58–59
    in property rights, 104
    public goods provided by, 105
    as rational or irrational, 54
    and regime, 31, 33–34, 35, 36, 56
    responsibilities of, 32

state (*continued*)
   revolution in, 218–223
   social expenditures of, 105–106
   sovereignty of, 31
   strength and scope of, 58–59, 136–137
   strong, 48–49, 52–53, 56
   taxation by, 106–107
   unitary, 48, 97, 151
   and violence, 213
   weak, 48. *See also* weak states
state capitalism, 119
States and Social Revolutions (Skocpol), 220
state-sponsored terrorism, 54, **223**–224
statistical data in quantitative research, 16, 17
Stenner, Karen, 274, 275
strength of states
   and scope, 58–59, 136–137
   of strong states, 48–49, 52–53, 56
   of weak states, 48. *See also* weak states
strong states, **48**–49, 56
   capacity and autonomy of, 52–53
structural-adjustment programs, **340**, 366
sub-Saharan Africa, *191,* 341, 347
Sudan
   ethnic conflicts in, 74, 337
   as fragile state, *50–51*
   human rights violations in, 364
   separation of South Sudan from, 337
suicide terrorism, 226, 240–241
Sunni Muslims, 202, 337
superforecasters, political predictions of, 25
superstructure in communism, **281**–282, 283, 284, 291, 292
supply and demand, 102–103, 109
Supreme Court (United States), 153
surplus value of labor, 281
surveillance, 192–193
   in terrorism concerns, 234–235
survival values, 90, *90*
Sweden, 10
   civil rights and liberties in, 173, 250
   as developed democracy, *249, 250, 253*
   economic liberalization in, *129*
   in European Union, 256
   gross domestic product of, *107, 123, 125, 249*
   political parties in, 160
   social democracy in, *253*

   societal globalization and trust in, *382, 383*
   taxation in, *107, 253*
   wealth measures in, 121, *123,* 124, *125*
Switzerland, *136,* 169, 243
Syria, 189, 308
   Arab Spring in, 4, 211–212, 236
   authoritarianism in, 211, 217
   civil war in, 4, 337
   as fragile state, *50–51*
   Islam in, 211, 212, 217, 337, 375
   nondemocratic regime in, 33, 192, 211
   patrimonialism in, 211, 236
   political control in, 192, 211
   political violence in, 5, *210,* 211–212, 217
   refugees from, 4, *210,* 211, *276*
   and terrorism, 4, 212

Taiwan
   agricultural reform in, 349
   corruption in, *335*
   democracy in, 142, 170, 171
   economic transitions in, 305
   gross domestic product of, 348
   military rule in, 199
   semi-presidential system in, 158
Tajikistan, *299,* 308, *309*
Taliban, 54, 55, 202, 301
Tanzania, happiness in, *127*
tariffs, **111**
   in export-oriented industrialization, 339
   in globalization, 366, 368
   in import substitution, 338
   in India, 63
   in mercantilism, 119
taxation, 106–107, 108, 112
   in communism, 116
   in developed democracies, 251, *253,* 267–268
   in economic liberalization, 128
   in Greece, 270–271
   and gross domestic product, 106–107, *107,* 115, *253,* 267–268
   in imperialism and colonialism, 327
   in informal economy, 346
   as institution, 20–21
   in liberalism, 113, 137
   in mercantilism, 119

in resource curse, 187
in rise of modern state, 39, 40
in social democracy, 115, 136, 251, 267
for social expenditures, 106, 267–268
tea, Fair Trade in, 319, 320
technological innovations, 14
   in export-oriented industrialization, 339
   and globalization, 355, 359–360,
      361–362, 364, 366, 367, 369,
      373, 376
   and imperialism, 324
   intellectual property in, 104, 338
   Internet in. *See* Internet
   job loss in, 131
   Marx on, 283
   origins of political organization in, 36, 38
   and postindustrialism, 266
   postmodern values on, 262
   and rise of modern state, 40–41
   and surveillance in nondemocratic
      regimes, 192–193
Telangana state of India, *60,* 62
terrorism, 213, 218, **223**–229
   causes of, 225–226
   civilian targets of, 224, *225,* 227
   counter-measures in, 227, 234–235, 261
   effects of, 227
   emotional response to term, 86, 213
   in globalization, 364, 374, 375
   goals of, 216, 225, 227, 228
   guerrilla war compared to, 224, 227,
      228–229
   individual explanations for, 216, 226
   in nihilism, 226
   nonstate actors in, 223, *225*
   regime type affecting, 234, *235*
   religion as factor in, 17
   revolution compared to, 218, 223,
      228–229
   in September 11, 2001, attacks, 20, 232
   and societal transitions in postcommunist
      countries, 308
   state-sponsored, 54, 223–224, *225*
   suicide, 226, 240–241
   in Syria, 4, 212
   worldwide incidents of, *224*
Tetlock, Philip, 25, 26
Thailand, 170, 199, 327, *352*

theocracy, 87, 197, 200, 201–202, 212
theory, **11–12**, 16–18, 26
   behavioral, 15
Third World, 246, 321
Thirty Years' War (1618–48), 41
Tiananmen Square protests (1989), 79, 296,
      310, 311
Tibet, 66
Tilly, Charles, 39
Tocqueville, Alexis de, 148, 231, 294
Togo, happiness in, *127*
torture, 192, 223
totalitarianism, 183–**184,** 203
   corporatism in, 194
   one-party rule in, 201
trade, 111–112
   of Asia and Latin America compared, 348
   in communism, 117
   comparative advantage in, 111
   in economic liberalization, 128
   in export-oriented imperialism, 331
   in export-oriented industrialization,
      339–340, 346, 348
   in extractive economies, 331
   in Fair Trade, *318,* 319–320, 347, 350
   globalization of. *See* economic globaliza-
      tion
   in imperialism and colonialism, 330, 331,
      349
   in import substitution, 338–339, 340,
      346
   in India, 63
   in liberalism, 131
   in mercantilism, 119, 338
   NAFTA on, 259, 377
   nontariff regulatory barriers to, 111, 119,
      366
   in post-imperialism, 338–340
   in rise of modern state, 40, 41, 70–71
   in social democracy, 115
   tariffs in, 111. *See also* tariffs
   Trans-Pacific Partnership in, 377
   Washington Consensus on, 350, 366
traditional legitimacy, **44**–45, 46, 47, 56
   in personal and monarchial rule, 197
traditional values, 90, *90*
Trans-Pacific Partnership (TPP), **377**
Transparency International, 270, 364

transportation systems as public goods, 104–105, 106
Treaty of Westphalia, 41
tribes, organization by, 36, 37, 328, 330
Trump, Donald, 25, 120, 379
trust
    of other nationalities, societal globalization affecting, 370, 382–383
    and social capital, 176
Tunisia, 3, 24, 211, 236, 237
    Arab Spring in, *2, 3, 4,* 24, 211, 236, 237
    democracy in, 4
Turkey, *107,* 202
Turkic people in China, 306, 307
Turkmenistan, *299*
The Turner Diaries (Pierce), 232–233
Tutsi ethnic group, 65, 66
tyranny, 182
    of majority, 160

Uganda, *50–51,* 320
Ukraine
    cultural divides and violence in, 89
    economic transitions in, postcommunist, *304*
    gender equality in, *309*
    LGBT acceptance in, *312*
    political transitions in, postcommunist, *299, 300*
    and Russia, 158, 304
    semi-presidential system in, 158
    societal transitions in, postcommunist, *309*
Ulyanov, Vladimir Ilyich (Lenin), 219, 285, *287,* 288
unemployment
    in Greece, 270, 271
    in liberalism, 113, 114
    in postcommunist countries, 302, 303, 305
    in social democracy, 115
    and social expenditures, 105, 106
unicameral systems, **151**
unitary states, **48,** 97, 151
United Arab Emirates, 114
United Democratic Movement (South Africa), *166*
United East India Company, 331

United Kingdom
    Brexit vote in. *See* Brexit
    corruption in, *335*
    counterterrorism measures in, 234–235
    currency in, 256
    death penalty support in, *274, 275*
    as developed democracy, 251, *253*
    devolution in, 260, 261
    economic liberalization in, *129*
    electoral system in, 162–164, 251
    ethnic and national identity in, 67
    gender equality in, *125,* 126, 309, *309*
    gross domestic product of, *107,* 115, *123, 125, 136,* 268
    happiness in, *127*
    health expenditures in, *136*
    and Hong Kong, 332
    joining European Union, 243
    LGBT acceptance in, *312*
    liberalism in, 113–114, 128, *253*
    political parties in, 162–164, *163,* 243–244
    political violence in, 241
    public debt in, 268
    referenda and initiatives in, 169, 172, 244, 258
    scope and strength of state, 58, 59
    taxation in, *107,* 115, *253*
    traditional legitimacy in, 47
    wealth measures in, *123, 125*
United Kingdom Independence Party (UKIP), 243–244
United Malays National Organisation (UMNO), 139–140
United Nations, 334
    in developing countries, 347
    Development Program, 124, 132
    Human Development Index of, 124. *See also* Human Development Index
    as intergovernmental organization, 255, 361
United States
    and Asia relations, 348
    authoritarian views in, 274
    central bank in, 108
    civil society in, 188
    in Cold War, 293

Constitution of, 13, 35, 47
corruption in, *335*
counterterrorism measures in, 234
democracy in, 33, 142, 176–177, 206
as developed democracy, 248, *249, 253*
devolution in, 260
economic inequality in, 23, 266
economic liberalization in, *129*
economic recession in (2008), 271
electoral system in, 140, 162, 164, 169, 250
ethnic and national identity in, 67–68, 69–70
executive branch in, 151
federalism in, 48, 53
gender equality in, *125,* 126, 309, *309*
Gini index in, 251, 266
in globalization, 355, 367, 377
government employment in, 137
gross domestic product of, *107, 123, 125, 136, 249,* 251, 268, 355
gun ownership laws in, 8
happiness in, *127*
health care in, 105, *136,* 137
Human Development Index in, 124, *125,* 126
immigration to, 263, 264, 376
institutions in, 19, 20
interest rates in, 108
international relations of, 171, 188, 236, 259
judiciary in, 152–153
and Latin America relations, 132, 348
legislative branch in, 151, 251
LGBT acceptance in, *312*
liberalism in, 113, 122, *253*
mercantilism in, 120
and modernization theory, 14, 16
in NAFTA, 377
national debt in, 268, 367
nondemocratic regimes supported by, 236
patriotism in, 69–70
political attitudes in, 79, 80
political culture in, 91
political ideologies in, 83
political parties in, 160, 162
political violence in, 232–233, 234
postindustrialism in, 266
presidential system in, 156, 251
Progressive era in, 343–344
purchasing power parity in, 121, 355
rational-legal legitimacy in, 47
referenda and initiatives in, 169
secular-rational values in, 91
social capital in, 176–177
societal globalization and trust in, *382,* 383
and Soviet Union relations, 293, 294
state capacity and autonomy in, 53
taxation in, *107, 253*
trade regulations in, 111, 120, 259, 377
traditional legitimacy in, 47
in USMCA, 377
and Venezuela relations, *98,* 100
wealth measures in, 121, 122, *123,* 124, *125*
United States-Mexico-Canada Agreement (USMCA), 377
universal factors in political violence, 217
urban areas
    in developing countries, 331, 348, 349
    in imperialism and colonialism, 331
    and nondemocratic rule, 185, 186
    origins of political organization in, 36, 38
Uzbekistan, *299,* 308

values
    Asian, 170, 189
    in developed democracies, 262–265
    in political ideology, 75, 80
    in political institutions, 19, 21
    in political violence, 214
    postmodern, 262–265, 274
    premodern, 262
    secular-rational, *90,* 90–91
    traditional, 90, *90*
    Western, 189
    World Values Survey of, 89–90, *90,* 263
vanguard of the proletariat, 282, **285**
variables in political science, 8
    in causal relationships, 10, 11
    dependent and independent, 10, 97
    in qualitative and quantitative methods, 16
Venezuela
    corruption in, *335*
    economic liberalization in, *129*
    elections in, 99
    hyperinflation in, *98,* 109

Index A-67

Venezuela (*continued*)
    oil reserves of, *98,* 99, 100, 109
    political economy of, *98,* 99–101, 109, 132, 133
Vietnam
    communism in, 170, *280,* 300
    economic development in, 179
    gender equality in, *309*
    gender imbalance in population of, 338
    gross domestic product of, 179
    LGBT acceptance in, *312*
    one-party rule in, 201
violence, 5, 211–241. *See also* political violence
vote of no confidence, **155,** 158, 167

wages
    in communism, 116
    in inflation, 109
    minimum, 103, 173
Wales, 164, 260
Walmart, 372
warfare
    cosmic, 230
    in globalization, 363, 373
    guerrilla. *See* guerrilla war
    political organization in, 38
    rise of modern state in, 39, 40, 41, 213
    state actors and targets of, *225*
Washington Consensus, **340,** 342, 366
weak states, 30, **48**–49, 56, 58
    capacity and autonomy in, 53, 333
    informal economy in, 346
    in liberalism, 113, 136
    patriotism in, 70
wealth
    and happiness, 126–127
    measurement of, 121–126
    in modernization, 186
    money compared to, 108, 121
    in nondemocratic countries, 186
    unequal distribution of, 23. *See also* economic inequality
Weber, Max (1864–1920), 13
    on definition of state, 31
    on political legitimacy, 44
    on Protestant work ethic, 88
    on religion, 86

welfare, 105, 267–269. *See also* social expenditures
Welzel, Christian, 91
West Germany, 277
Westphalia, Treaty of, 41
white supremacist organizations, 232
winner-take-all elections, 162, 167, 215
Wirathu, Ashin, 233
women
    in communist countries, 291–292
    in developing countries, 329–330, 337–338, 346, 347
    and gender equality. *See* gender equality
    in imperialism and colonialism, 329–330, 337
    in informal economy, 346
    microcredit programs for, 347
    in postcommunist countries, 308–309
    in post-imperialism, 337–338
World Bank, 246–247, 365–366
    in developing countries, 334, 340, 344
    on lower income countries, 322
    on middle income trap, 352
    poverty measures of, 122
World Economic Forum, 308
World Trade Center, 20
World Trade Organization (WTO), 361, 366
World Values Survey, 89–90, *90,* 263, 382
    in postcommunist countries, 306, 308
World War I, 14, 376
World War II, 14, 365
    democratization after, 148, 188
    European Union after, 254, 256
    import substitution policies after, 339
    Japan after, 119
    nondemocratic rule after, 188
    reactionary attitudes after, 78
World Wildlife Fund, 365
xenophobia, 78, 264, 265

Xi Jinping, 196
Xinjiang, 66

Yemen, *50–51*
YouTube, 237
Yugoslavia, 73, 96
    communist regime in, *280*

human rights violations in, 364
societal transitions in, 308
Yunus, Muhammad, 347

Zaire, 198
Zimbabwe
- authoritarianism in, *178*, 180, 204, 205, 208, 209
- and China, *178*, 180–181, 205, 356
- corruption in, 180, *335*
- elections in, 179, 180, 204
- as fragile state, *50–51*
- gross domestic product of, 179
- guerrilla war in, 212, 224
- kleptocracy in, 195
- natural resources in, *178*, 180–181, 186, 208, 209
- nondemocratic regime in, *178*, 179–181, 182, 186, 192, 204
- political control in, 192
- political violence in, 205, 212, 224
- and South Africa compared, 204–205, 224
- state capacity and autonomy in, 334

Zimbabwe African National Union-Patriotic Front (ZANU-PF), 179, 180, 204, 205, 224